Texts in Theoretical Computer Science
An EATCS Series

Springer-Verlag Berlin Heidelberg GmbH

Klaas Sikkel

Parsing Schemata

A Framework for Specification and Analysis of Parsing Algorithms

With 110 Figures

 Springer

Author

Dr. Klaas Sikkel
German National Research Center for Information Technology
Institute for Applied Information Technology, GMD-FIT
D-53754 Sankt Augustin, Germany

Series Editors

Prof. Dr. Wilfried Brauer
Institut für Informatik, Technische Universität München
Arcisstrasse 21, D-80333 München, Germany

Prof. Dr. Grzegorz Rozenberg
Institute of Applied Mathematics and Computer Science
University of Leiden, Niels-Bohr-Weg 1, P.O. Box 9512
2300 RA Leiden, The Netherlands

Prof. Dr. Arto Salomaa
The Academy of Finland
Department of Mathematics, University of Turku
FIN-20 500 Turku, Finland

CR Subject Classification Numbers: F.4.2-3, F.2.m, D.3.1, D.3.4, I.2.7

Library of Congress Cataloging-in-Publication Data

Sikkel, Klaas, 1954-
    Parsing schemata : a framework for specification and analysis of
parsing algorithms / Klaas Sikkel.
        p.   cm.
    Includes bibliographical references and index.
    ISBN 978-3-642-64451-1   ISBN 978-3-642-60541-3 (eBook)
    DOI 10.1007/978-3-642-60541-3

    1. Computer algorithms. 2. Parsing (Computer grammar)
3. Computational linguistics.   I. Title.   96-45082
QA76.9.A43S53 1997   CIP
005.4'5--dc21

© Springer-Verlag Berlin Heidelberg 1997
Softcover reprint of the hardcover 1st edition 1997

The use of registered names, trademarks, etc. in this publication does not imply, even in the absence of a specific statement, that such names are exempt from the relevant protective laws and therefore free for general use.

Typeseting: Camera ready by author
Cover Design: *design & production* GmbH, Heidelberg
SPIN: 10538584   45/3142-5 4 3 2 1 0 - Printed on acid-free paper.

Foreword

Introduction

In computer science, grammars are human-constructed formalisms that are meant to define languages, in particular programming languages or (in theoretical computer science) formal languages. This description is often partial, it is not unusual to see a formal description of the syntactic structure of a language, while the semantic part remains ill-defined. Finding the syntactic structure of a program (a sentence in the language) is part of the compilation process of a program. The construction of this structure is called parsing and the result of the parsing process is a hierarchical account of the elements that make up the program. This account makes it possible to assign semantics to a program.

Formal syntactic descriptions of languages were first given by the linguist Noam Chomsky. Because the descriptions were formal, the languages were also formal: sequences of symbols that satisfied descriptions based on finite state automata or regular grammars, context-free grammars, or context sensitive grammars. In Chomsky's view, these descriptions were the starting point for descriptions of the syntactic part of natural, human spoken, languages. Moreover, these descriptions would allow the assignment of meaning to sentences. Interestingly, at about the same time Chomsky introduced different classes of grammars and languages, a committee defining a programming language (ALGOL) introduced a programming language description called Backus-Naur-Form (BNF) which turned out to be equivalent to one of Chomsky's grammar classes, the so-called context-free grammars. We are talking about the period 1959-1961.

In Chomsky's view, human language grammars were not human-constructed formalisms. The rules of the formalism, or, more generally, the principles that determine the rules, are supposed to be innate. This view led to a distinction between competence and performance in human language use. Each language user has a language competence that allows him to construct all kinds of sentences using the rules of a grammar. Constructing sentences can be compared with using rules to compute a multiplication or a division in arithmetics. Language users can construct sentences using rules of syntax.

Due to environmental circumstances in normal man-to-man communication, these rules are not always obeyed. Performance differs from competence.

It is much easier, however, to formalize self-chosen rules of sentence construction and analysis than to formalize actual language behaviour. For this obvious reason, grammar formalisms and their parsing methods have drawn so much attention by computational linguists. But it should be admitted, on the other hand, that nowadays powerful language processing systems can be built that are based on these formalisms. Whether or not the used formalisms meet certain linguistic principles in some way or other, or even some principles of human language innateness, is not the main concern of those doing research and development in this area.

Parsing Methods

Parsing methods have been defined for all kinds of language descriptions. Formal descriptions define formal languages. After the introduction of the well-known Chomsky hierarchy in the late 1950s and early 1960s we see a common interest of computer scientists and computational linguists in parsing methods for context-free languages. The quest for efficient parsing methods led to polynomial-time algorithms for general context-free grammars in the middle and late 1960s. In computer science, however, these formalisms were thought to be unnecessarily general for describing the syntactic properties of programming languages, and therefore to be unnecessarily inefficient. LL and LR grammars and parsing methods were introduced. These required only linear time and were sufficiently general for dealing with the syntactic backbone of programming languages. Interest in general context-free methods diminished, or was left to theoretical computer scientists. In computational linguistics there were other reasons to become critical of the context-free grammar formalism. Its descriptional adequacy, that is, its ability to cover linguistic generalities in a natural way, was considered to be too weak. It was also doubted whether it provides sufficient generative capacity. The LL and LR approaches favoured in computer science were clearly much less suitable, because these do not allow representation of syntactic ambiguities.

It is remarkable that in the late 1970s and early 1980s we see a growing interest of LR-like methods and context-free grammars in computational linguistics and a growing interest in general context-free grammar descriptions in computer science. How can this be explained?

In computational linguistics, first of all, the so-called 'determinism hypothesis' attracted a lot of attention. The idea is that in general people do not 'backtrack' while analysing a sentence. Backtracking becomes necessary only when a started analysis cannot be continued at some point in the sentence. Mitch Marcus introduced an LR-like 'wait and see' stack formalism in order to parse sentences 'deterministically'. Reviewing the literature from that period, one sees lots of misconceptions and confusion among researchers.

Apparently these are partly due to lack of knowledge about formal parsing methods such as, for example, Earley's method and how issues like 'back-tracking', 'determinism', and 'efficiency' relate to these algorithms. Since then, however, maybe due to changes in university curricula and the rise of a new generation of computational linguists, knowledge of formal methods has become more widespread. This can also be illustrated with the intro-duction of formalisms like Lexical Functional Grammar (LFG), Generalized Phrase Structure Grammar (GPSG), Head-Driven Phrase Structure Gram-mar (HPSG), Unification Formalisms, Definite Clause Grammars and Tree Adjoining Grammars (TAGs) in the early 1980s. It led to a new discussion on the question whether the generative capacity of context-free formalisms would suffice to describe the syntax of natural languages and it led to a sys-tematic comparison of grammar formalisms, yielding weakly context-sensitive languages as a recently discovered class for which adequate generative capac-ity is claimed.

The formalisms mentioned above are certainly much more general than a pure context-free formalism. However, their backbone is context-free or the way the formalisms are defined and used bear very much resemblance to the context-free paradigm. These approaches should be contrasted with more traditional approaches in computational linguistics using so-called aug-mented transition networks or chart parsing methods. It would be interesting to investigate how the availability of the Prolog implementation mechanism has influenced the direction of research in computational linguistics.

Shift of Attention

We have not yet mentioned one of the main influences that caused researchers in computational linguistics and natural language processing to shift their at-tention to existing formal parsing methods and possible extensions of these methods. That influence was the increasing demand of society, military and funding organisations to produce research results that could be used to build tools and systems for practical natural language processing applications. Ap-plications like speech understanding systems, natural language interfaces to information systems, machine translation of texts, information retrieval, help systems for complex software and machinery, knowledge extraction from doc-uments, text image processing, and so on. The availability of a comprehensive cognitive and linguistic theory does not seem to be a precondition for appli-cations in the area of natural language understanding. Many applications do not require this comprehensive theory. Moreover, many applications can be built using research results that are not influenced in any way by cognitive, psycho-linguistic or linguistic principles. Generalized LR parsing, introduced in the mid-1980s by Masaru Tomita, is such a method that was introduced as a simple, straightforward and efficient parsing method for general context-free languages and grammars. Due to its straightforwardness, like the deterministic LR method, it has attracted a lot of attention and it has been used in many natural language applications.

In computer science, it was stated above, more and more attention has been devoted to general context-free parsing methods. The just mentioned generalized LR method, for example, has been used in grammar, parser and compiler development environments. In general, software engineering environments may offer their users syntax-dependent tools. The compiler construction level is only one level, and a rather low one, where descriptions based on formal grammar play a role. Furthermore, computer science is a growing science in the sense that borders between so-called 'pure' computer science and several application areas are disappearing. Grammars and parsing methods play a role in pattern recognition, they have been used to describe and analyse command and action languages (human interaction with a computer system through key presses, cursor movements, etc.), to describe screen layouts, etc. Human factors have become important in computer science. Increasing the accessibility of computer systems through the use of speech and natural language in the man-machine interface is an aim worth pursuing. It is obvious that computer scientists and computational linguists will meet each other here and that they can learn from each other's methods to deal with languages.

Finally, we would like to mention another influence that caused computer scientists to go back to general context-free parsing methods. Parallelism is the keyword here. The introduction of new types of machine architectures and the possibility to implement algorithms on single chips have led to new research on existing parsing algorithms. Some research has been purely theoretical, in the sense that all kinds of efficiency limits were explored. Some research has been practical, in the sense that all kinds of extensions and variations of existing parsing algorithms have been investigated in order to make them suitable for parallel implementations and that these implementations have been realized, analysed and evaluated.

About this Book

Now that we have presented views on the development of parsing theory, it is useful and necessary to review the contribution of the research reported on in this book to the future development of parsing theory. It is an important contribution. Properties of existing parsing algorithms are unraveled in detail in the first two parts, 'Exposition' and 'Foundation'. The results are used to shed new light on these algorithms and to compose new algorithms. Parsing schemata, refinement and filtering are introduced as tools and used by the author, as a surgeon using his blade, to tackle the subject. The insight obtained in the first two parts is used in the third part, 'Application', to study the parsing problem for unification grammars (while at the same time an exceptionally clear exposition of unification methods is given), to study and introduce new versions of left-corner, head-corner and generalized LR parsing algorithms, and to clarify Rytter's efficient parallel parsing algorithm for the design of Boolean circuit parsers. Throughout the book the approach taken allows observations on parallelization and parallel implementations of the discussed algorithms.

Computer scientists, computational linguists and language engineers can profit from the knowledge that is to be found in this unique book. As such it can be considered as a milestone of the 1990s in the field of parsing theory and its applications.

Anton Nijholt

Professor of Computer Science
University of Twente,
Enschede, The Netherlands

Acknowledgements

This book is based on four years of research at the University of Twente at Enschede, the Netherlands. The PARLEVINK group at the Computer Science department provided a very stimulating environment; cooperation with and feedback from colleagues has greatly contributed to the contents and quality of this work.

I am indebted to Anton Nijholt for guiding me into computational linguistics and encouraging me to do the Ph.D. research that led to this book.

I have enjoyed cooperating with Rieks op den Akker, not only in the work on Head-Corner parsing that led to Chapters 10 and 11, but also in teaching classes on formal analysis of natural language.

Some brainstorming sessions with Wil Janssen, Job Zwiers and Mannes Poel resulted in the "primordial soup" metaphor, leading to a joint paper and very suitable for the introductory Chapter 2 in this book.

Marc Lankhorst did his M.Sc. on the Parallel Bottum-up Tomita parser of which I had given but a rather sketchy first design. The resulting publications, on which Chapter 13 is based, were a joint effort, but the real work has been done by Marc. Margiet Verlinden designed and implemented a Head-Corner parser for unification grammars that is presented in Section 11.8.

Valuable technical comments and suggestions for improvements at various stages have been given by Peter Asveld, Maarten Fokkinga, Dale Gerdemann, Frank Morawietz, Mark-Jan Nederhof, Gertjan van Noord, and Giorgio Satta. Furthermore, some anonymous referees of papers have given useful comments. Interesting discussions with Rens Bod, René Leermakers, Jan Rekers, and Hans de Vreught have had a positive influence on this work. Andy Ross from Springer-Verlag has been helpful in improving language and layout.

With Toine Andernach, Marc Drossaers, and Jan Schaake I shared the joys and problems of doing Ph.D. research within the PARLEVINK project – and a lot of coffee. They have supported me in many ways.

There was also a life outside the university. I'd like to thank the following people for providing a rich social environment during my stay in Enschede: Marjo Bos, Hetty Grunefeld, Wil Janssen, Margriet Offereins, Paul Oude Luttighuis, Gert Veldhuijzen van Zanten, and Marc and Jan, for weekly meals and other events; Adri Breukink and Anton Nijholt for hosting PARLEVINK people on many occasions and providing excellent food and drink; Ruurdjan Bakker, Gerard Heijs, Rob Kemmeren, Gerrit Klaassen, John Schiffel, Joke Vonk, Theo Zeegers, and Hilde and Willem-Jaap Zwart for shared activities and good company in the local group of the cyclists' union **enfb**.

Last but not least I would like to thank Heidrun Wiedenmann, for making sure that I did take some time off, for bearing with me under the continuing pressure during the last year of my Ph.D. work, and for all other support.

Klaas Sikkel

Table of Contents

Part I

EXPOSITION

1. Introduction

Syntax describes the structure of language. A well-formed sentence can be broken down into constituents, according to syntactic rules. A constituent that covers more than a single word can be broken down into smaller constituents, and so on. In this way one can obtain a complete, hierarchical description of the syntactic structure of a sentence. A computer program that attributes such structures to sentences is called a *parser*. This book is about parsers, and our[1] particular concern is how such parsers can be described in an abstract, schematic way.

This is not the first book about parsing (nor will it be the last). In 1.3 we discuss our specific contribution to the theory of parsing. But before zooming in on the research questions that will be addressed, it is appropriate to make a few general remarks.

In the analysis of language we make a distinction between form and meaning. The relation between form and meaning is an interesting and not entirely unproblematic one. There are sentences that are grammatically correct, but do not convey any sensible meaning, and ill-formed sentences with a perfectly clear meaning. But we are not concerned with meaning of language and restrict our attention to form.

The form of a language is described by the grammar. Grammatical analysis can be further divided into *morphology*, describing the word forms, and *syntax*, describing sentence structures. In computer science, the words "grammar" and "syntax" have the same meaning, because computer programming languages do not have any morphology. In linguistics, despite the fact that these words are not equivalent, "syntax" is also known as "phrase structure grammar" which – sloppily but conveniently – is often abbreviated to "grammar". But we are not concerned with morphology either, and throughout

---

[1] It is common practice in scientific texts written by a single author to use the plural first person forms "we" and "our" to mean "I" and "my". This is to be understood as *pluralis modestiae*; scientific research is a group activity and not one's individual merit. I will conform to this custom and mostly use the plural form. I will use the singular form for personal comments and also for particularly strong claims, where I want it to be clear that none of my tutors and colleagues share any part of the blame, might I be proven wrong.

this book the word "grammar" refers to phrase structure grammar, unless explicitly stated otherwise.

We will not discuss the grammar of any existing language in any detail. So, with some overstatement, one could say that this book is not about language at all. The objects of study are *formalisms* that are used to describe the syntax of languages, and the parsing of arbitrary grammars that can be described in such formalisms. This is a useful scientific abstraction. Rather than making a parser for a particular grammar for a particular language, one constructs a parser that works on a suitable *class* of grammars. For any grammar within that class, a program can be instantiated that is a parser for that particular grammar.

Natural language is informal. Language is *living*, continuously evolving. The most rapidly changing part of a language is the lexicon. New words are added all the time and old words obtain new meanings and connotations; no lexicon is ever complete. The most elusive aspect of language is meaning. We live in an informal world, and any formal theory of meaning is at best an approximation of "real" meaning. The grammar (comprising syntax and morphology) is a rather more stable part of language. Grammars do change over time, but these changes are slow and few. If we are to construct computer systems that handle natural language in some way or other, it is a small and acceptable simplification to say that the grammar of a language is fixed.

Despite the fundamental differences between natural languages and programming languages, there is some overlap in parsing theory of both fields. Grammar formalisms that are used in both fields share the notion of *context-free grammars* (CFGs). For a complete description of the structure of a language, CFGs have too many limitations and one needs more powerful formalisms. But for the purpose of constructing parsing techniques, it makes sense to break up the complex task of parsing into different levels. Hence is it useful to distinguish between a *context-free backbone* that describes the "core" of the grammar and augmentations to the context-free formalism that describe additional characteristics of the language.[2] We are primarily interested in parsing of natural languages, but many issues have some relevance for programming language parsing as well. Only in Chapters 7, 8, and 9 we concentrate on *unification grammars*, a modern formalism (or, to be precise, a group of formalisms) that is specifically designed to describe natural language grammars.

The fact that this book is in the interface between computer science and computational linguistics has advantages and disadvantages. On the positive

---

[2] This does not necessarily mean that a parser should first construct a context-free parse and afterwards augment this with other features. A parser that integrates these aspects into a single process can still be thought of as consisting of different (but interacting) modules for context-free phrase structure analysis and for evaluation of other features.

side, the purpose and contents of the discussed subjects must be explained to a heterogeneous audience. This means that one cannot – as many theoretical computer scientists, by virtue of their specialty, are inclined to do – engage in increasingly technical and formal reasoning and along the way forget about the motivation behind the theory that is being developed. One has to make clear what is being done and why it makes sense to do it that way; not all the readers will be familiar with the culture of one's own sub-field in which such considerations are part of common knowledge and, if the subject is well-established, might never be questioned. A disadvantage, perhaps, is the increased length of the text. Many subjects could be discussed rather more concisely for a small group of fellow specialists. But this has a positive side as well: at least some chapters and sections should be easy reading. The more mathematically inclined reader with some knowledge of the field may skip large pieces of introductory text and trivial examples and move straight to definitions, theorems, and proofs. The less mathematically inclined reader, on the other hand, may skip much of the technical stuff if he[3] is prepared to take for granted that the claimed results can be formally established. To the reader who might be put off by the size of this volume it is perhaps a comforting thought that many parts can be read independently and hardly anybody is expected to read everything.

In Section 1.1 we will devote a few words to the history of syntax as a field of study. Phrase structure grammars and parsing are introduced in 1.2, the general idea of parsing schemata is presented in 1.3. Section 1.4, finally, gives an overview of the following chapters.

1.1 The structure of language

Modern linguistics starts in the 1950s with the work of Noam Chomsky. He was the first (in the Western world[4]) to develop a formal theory of syntax. Native speakers of a language have an intuitive understanding of the syntax. One is able to understand a sentence as syntactically correct, even though it does not convey a sensible meaning. An example, given by Chomsky, is the sentence "Colorless green ideas sleep furiously." Even though it is nonsense,

---

[3] In contexts where the gender of a third person is of no importance, I will sometimes write "he" and sometimes "she".

[4] A formal grammar of Sanskrit (as it was spoken 1000 years earlier but preserved in ritual Vedic texts) was produced between 350 B.C. and 250 B.C. by the Indian scholar Pāṇini. This was unknown to the European school of general linguistics (with its roots in the Greek and Roman tradition) until the 19th century. Pāṇini used rewrite rules, both context-free and context-sensitive. His grammar was more concerned with morphology than syntax, as word order in Sanskrit is rather free (Cf. [Staal, 1969], [Bharati et al., 1995]).

the syntax is correct, in contrast to a string of words "Furiously sleep ideas green colorless". This shows that syntax is *autonomous*, one does not need to know the meaning of a sentence in order to decide whether the sentence is well-formed or ill-formed. People with the same native language, despite great differences in learning and linguistic felicity, share this intuition of what is syntactically correct. It is this human faculty of syntax that Chomsky set out to investigate.

A syntactic theory, like any scientific theory, is *inductive*. A theory can never be derived from a given set of facts, however large. The design of a theory is speculative. But when a theory has been postulated, one can investigate how well it matches the facts. A good theory of syntax will describe as well-formed those sentences that are recognized as evidently well-formed by native speakers and describe as ill-formed those sentences that are evidently ill-formed. In between these, there is a group of sentences of which the correctness is doubted, even by grammarians. One should not worry about these fringe cases and let the theory decide. Chomsky set forth to develop such a theory by introducing a grammar formalism and describing the syntax of English by means of that formalism. In order to obtain a universal theory of syntax, it should be possible to describe the syntax of all human languages in similar fashion.

But before we discuss any detail of modern linguistics and computational linguistics, let us consider the question why everything Chomsky did was so new. What was wrong with pre-Chomskian linguistics, and why do we know so little about it?

Science makes abstractions of the world. A coherent set of abstractions is called a *paradigm*. Science (or at least good science) is objective within a paradigm, but the question whether a given set of abstractions is better than a set of different abstractions cannot be answered scientifically. Thomas Kuhn [1970] has shown that scientific knowledge is not necessarily accumulative. In a scientific revolution an old, established paradigm is rejected in favour of a new one; our understanding of the world is reconstructed in terms of the new paradigm. Chomsky initiated such a paradigm shift.

Many aspects of syntactic theory as we see it now were in fact known in pre-Chomskian times. But they were seen in a different light. Linguistic research concentrated on other issues. Linguistics described the languages that occur in the world, and their development. An important sub-field was that of comparative linguistics: how are languages related to one another, and how do languages develop over time? A major achievement is the reconstruction of the development of Indo-European languages from a common ancestor.

Comparative linguistics must be based on facts, and these facts are provided by descriptive linguistics. The description of existing languages did include the syntax. Syntax was a collection of constructs that could be used to form sentences. But the interesting point about syntax was in which way it differs from and corresponds to the syntax of other languages. When Pāṇini's grammar of 3000 year old Sanskrit became known to Western scholars, this gave a great impulse to comparative linguistics, not so much to general theories of language.

Wilhelm von Humboldt [1836] was the first in Europe to note that only a finite number of rules is needed to construct a language with an infinite variety of sentences. But theories of language in the Western tradition had since antiquity been troubled by a mixture of facts and philosophical preconceptions. They discussed "the place of language in the universe" [Bloomfield, 1927] rather than the structure of language. It took another century to disentangle these issues, get rid of all metaphysical speculation and simply take the facts for the facts. Leonard Bloomfield [1933] is generally seen as the person who established general linguistics as a science.

In this view, distinguishing "correct" sentences and forms from "incorrect" ones was a non-issue. Or even worse, it was a hobby of schoolmasters and people of some learning but with no clue about contemporary linguistics. Linguistics as a science is *descriptive*, not prescriptive.

Many elements of modern syntactic theory are given already by Bloomfield, but (as we have pointed out abundantly) from a different perspective. Constituents could be decomposed into smaller constituents, hence, as we see it now, syntax trees are implicitly defined as well. There was a distinction between recursive (*endocentric*) and non-recursive (*exocentric*) constituent formation. It was stipulated that every language has only a small number of exocentric constructs.

It was Chomsky [1957] who put the notion of competence grammar on the linguistic agenda, and started to develop a formal theory of syntax. He introduces transformational grammar (TG) and compares it with two other formalisms that could serve as a basis for such a linguistic theory. These two formalisms are nowadays (but not then) known as finite state automata and context-free grammars. The first is shown to be insufficient (because it cannot handle arbitrary levels of recursion). The second is also rejected. A transformational grammar is much smaller and more elegant than a context-free grammar for the same language. Moreover, a transformational grammar provides more insight as it shows the relation between different, but related sentences. A small set of kernel sentences is produced by a a set of rewrite rules (that constitute a context-free grammar). All other sentences can be produced from these kernel sentences by applying transformations. In this way a much smaller number of rules is needed than in a context-free grammar of English – if one exists.[5]

---

[5] Whether English can be described by a context-free grammar was posed as an open question by Chomsky [1957]. The issue has attracted a lot of discussion. Pullum and Gazdar [1982], in a review of the debate, inspected all the arguments opposing context-freeness and refuted all of these as either empirically or formally incorrect. Huybregts [1984], Shieber [1985b], and Manaster-Ramer [1987] have

Chomskian linguistics has developed considerably over the last three decades. The initial notion of a kernel set of sentences has been replaced by the notion of a *deep structure*, that is produced by the rewrite rules of the grammar. Sentences occurring in the language have a *surface structure* that is obtained from the deep structure by means of transformations. A much more elaborate version of TG, also including semantics, is known as the *standard theory* [Chomsky, 1965]. Continuing research led to an *extended standard theory* in the 1970s. But transformational grammar was eventually abandonded in favour of *Government and Binding* (GB) theory [Chomsky, 1981].

A context-free phrase structure grammar of a language has many more rules than a transformational grammar, but from the perspective of *computational* linguistics, context-free grammars are much simpler. Parsing a sentence according to a transformational grammar is, in general, not computationally tractable (and the same holds for GB), whereas parsing of context-free grammars can be done efficiently. General-purpose context-free grammars have been constructed that have an adequate coverage of English phrase structure (see, e.g., Sager [1981]).

As has been stated in the introduction of this chapter, there are various ways in which other grammatical information (as subject-verb agreement) and semantic information can be added to a context-free phrase structure. The trend in computational linguistics is towards so-called unification grammars, in which this distinction is blurred. Nevertheless, for the purpose of constructing efficient parsers, it is useful to keep making a distinction between phrase structure and other syntactic and semantic features. The first six chapters deal exclusively with (context-free) phrase structure and we postpone an introduction of unification grammars to Chapter 7.

The development of "high-level", third generation programming languages started in the 1950s as well. Before such languages were available, one had to instruct computers in languages that are much more closely related to the hardware capabilities of such a machine. Move a number from this location to that location; if the contents of a specific memory location is zero, then jump to some other position in the computer program; and so on. High-level languages offered the possibility of "automatic programming". Rather than writing machine instructions (at the level of second generation languages), one could concentrate on what a program is supposed to *do*. Such a program could be translated into "real" computer language by means of another program, called a *compiler*.

In the definition of the programming language ALGOL 60 the structure of the grammar was described by a formalism that later became known as

-----
established beyond doubt that Swiss-German and Dutch are not context-free languages.

Backus-Naur Form (BNF). It was only *after* the publication of the ALGOL definition [Naur, 1960] that computer scientists realized similarities in BNF and phrase structure grammars that were studied by linguists. Ginsburg and Rice [1962] proved that BNF is equivalent to context-free grammars. This insight sparked off a of body of research in formal languages, which is now part of the foundations of computer science as well as formal linguistics. Hence is it not a coincidence that, despite the radical differences in structure and complexity, there is considerable overlap in the underlying theory of syntax of natural languages and programming languages.

1.2 Parsing

We will define the parsing problem for context-free (backbones of) grammars and discuss briefly why this is still a relevant area for research. We do not dwell upon the historical development of various parsing techniques. This cannot be properly done in a few paragraphs without getting involved in some technical detail. The interested reader is referred to Nijholt [1988] for a good and easy to read overview.

A parse tree is a complete, hierarchical description of the phrase structure of a sentence. The *parsing problem*, for a given grammar and sentence, is to deliver all parse trees that the grammar allows for that sentence. Stated in this very general way, the parsing problem is actually underspecified: we do not prescribe a formalism in which these parse trees are to be denoted. There are techniques to specify such a forest of trees in a compact way, without listing all the trees individually (cf. Chapter 12). The savings can be considerable. Because we look at syntactic structure only and do not rule out parse trees that yield an absurd interpretation, most sentences have a lot of different parse trees.

Related to the parsing problem is the *recognition problem*. For a given grammar and sentence it is to be determined whether the sentence is well-formed (i.e., at least one parse tree exists). This is a fully specified problem. There are only two possible answers and how these are denoted ("true" or "false", or "1" or "0") is not relevant.

An *algorithm* is a prescription how to solve some problem in a systematic way. Algorithms can be encoded in programming languages, so that a computer can solve the problem. A *parsing algorithm*, or *parser*[6] for short, is an algorithm that solves the parsing problem. A *recognizing algorithm*, or *recognizer* for short, is an algorithm that solves the recognition problem.

There is an intermediate form between parsers and recognizers. Such algorithms provide an answer to the question whether the sentence is well-formed

---

[6] Usually a parser is understood to be a computer program, rather than an algorithm encoded in the program, but this distinction is irrelevant here.

and, additionally, deliver a structured set of intermediate results that have been computed in order to obtain the answer. These intermediate results encode various details about the sentence structure and are of great help to actually construct parse trees. Such algorithms could be called "enhanced recognizers", but in the literature these are usually called parsers as well, despite the fact that no parse trees are produced. With the exception of Chapters 2 and 3 we will mostly be concerned with parsers in this improper sense.

In different sub-fields there are some variants of the parsing problem. In the field of stochastic grammars, the task is to find the *most likely* parse tree according to some probability distribution. In parsing of programming languages one is interested in a single, uniquely determined parse tree. In case of ambiguities there must be additional criteria that specify which is the right parse tree – otherwise a program may have an ambiguous interpretation, which is highly undesirable.

Programming language grammars are much simpler than natural languages, but the sentences (programs) are much longer. Hence the specialized techniques to construct efficient parsers are different, but there is some crossover. Mostly this is the adaptation of computer science parsing techniques to parsing of natural languages. Occasionally, however, it also happens that the compiler construction community adapts techniques that were developed in computational linguistics.

The theory of parsing is some 30 years old now, and one may wonder whether there is anything of general interest that has not yet been uncovered in this field. There are always enough open questions (and more answers lead to even more open questions) and a field is never finished. But as the body of knowledge grows, the frontier of research is pushed to more and more specialized issues in remote corners of knowledge that perhaps nobody except a small bunch of fellow scientists is even aware of. There are two reasons, however, that make parsing theory an interesting field up to this day.

Firstly, there is the issue of *parallel* parsing. A variety of parallel parsing algorithms has been proposed in the last decade, in particular in the field of Computational Linguistics [Hahn and Adriaens, 1994]. There are great differences, not only in the type of parsing algorithm employed, but also in the kind of parallel hardware (or abstract machine) that such algorithms should run on. In order to compare the relative merits of different parallel parsing algorithms, one should start to describe these in a uniform way. Parsing schemata have originally been conceived as a framework for comparing different parallel parsers on a theoretical level. In order to find such a common description, one has to abstract from a great many details. As it turned out, the framework is also useful for a high-level description of traditional, sequential parsing algorithms; it is stated nowhere that an implementation of a parsing schema must be parallel.

Secondly, the formalisms in which natural language grammars are described have changed over the last decade. This has some consequences for parsing natural language grammars. *Logic* has gained an important role in the interface between grammarians and computers. On the one hand, there are programming languages as PROLOG or, more recently, *Constraint Logic Programming* (CLP), [Jaffar and Lassez, 1987], [Cohen, 1990], that allow programs to be written as a set of logic formulae. On the other hand, grammars can also be written as a set of logic formulae. A parse, then, corresponds to a proof. The sentence is postulated as a hypothesis, and the sentence is correct (and a parse is produced) if a formula can be proven that can be interpreted as "this is a sentence (and its structure is so-and-so)". Such a proof can be carried out by a PROLOG or CLP interpreter, i.e., a computer program. So we have another level of "automatic programming", where one only needs to specify the grammar and there is no more need to construct a parser. There is a catch, however. Such specifications in logic can (under certain restrictions) be interpreted directly by machines, but that does not necessarily mean that a machine will do so in an efficient manner. From a computational point of view it is more appropriate to see such a grammar as an *executable specification*, not as the most suitable implementation of a parser. Computer science, therefore, can make valuable contributions to the construction of efficient parsers for these grammar formalisms.

A nice example of this last point is the following. The context-free backbone is no longer particularly relevant for the specification of a grammar. Hence, as things go in evolution, context-free backbones tend to dwindle away. A modern grammar specification with "degenerated" context-free backbone, typically has a much larger context-free backbone hidden inside the grammar. It has recently been shown by Nagata [1992] and Maxwell and Kaplan [1993] that retrieving and using a more elaborate context-free backbone can substantially increase the efficiency of a parser.

1.3 Parsing schemata

There are many different ways to design a parser. One can build trees branch by branch, adding grammar productions one at the time. Or one can collect various bits of tree and combine small trees to larger trees in various ways. The important thing is that it is a *constructive* process. Parsing schemata can be use to describe any parser that works in a constructive way.

There are non-constructive parsers as well. An entirely new brand of computation is embodied in *neural networks*. We will briefly discuss these in Chapter 14. But almost all parsers that run on von Neumann machines (i.e.

computers as we know them) are constructive.[7] A constructive parser computes a series of intermediate results and these (or, to be precise, most of these) are used for the computation of next, more advanced intermediate results, until the final result is established.

A parsing schema focuses on these intermediate results, called *items* in parsing terminology. The essential traits of a parser can be described as follows.

- for any given sentence, an *initial* set of items is constructed,
- for any given grammar there is a set of *rules* that describe how new (larger) items can be computed from known items.

All that remains to be done, then, is apply all the rules to all the items over and over again until all items that can be computed from the initial set have been computed. We see the *final set of items* as the result delivered by a parser. Some special items indicate that a parse tree exists. Hence the sentence is well-formed if and only if at least one of these special items is computed.

A parsing schema is not an algorithm. An algorithm has a number of aspects that are absent in a parsing schema:

- *data structures* in which computed items can be stored and efficiently searched for;
- *control structures*, making sure that all relevant steps are taken, in some appropriate order;
- (only for parallel algorithms) *communication structures*, ensuring that relevant items are exchanged between different cooperating processors.

Each of these structures can be designed in a variety of ways, leading to a variety of different parsing algorithms with a single underlying parsing schema. It is by abstracting from these structures that the essential traits of very different parsing algorithms can be described in a uniform way and compared.

A number of different questions come to mind. Firstly, there are some technical concerns. How general is the framework? The fact that all parsers compute intermediate results does not give any guarantee that the kinds of intermediate results computed by different algorithms are compatible. Secondly, what is the relation between this framework and other parsing frameworks that have been published in the past? Thirdly, is there any purpose

---

[7] An example of a *non*constructive parser (that is in fact an enhanced recognizer) is the the $LE(p,q)$ algorithm of Oude Luttighuis [1991], that parses a restricted class of grammars in logarithmic time. It makes essential use of a nonconstructive parallel bracket matching algorithm [Gibbons and Rytter, 1988]. The question whether a string of brackets is well-formed is answered in logarithmic time, but without giving a clue as to which opening bracket matches which closing bracket.

in writing down parsing schemata, other than an exercise in manipulation of formal systems? We will briefly address each of these questions.

Different parsers produce different kinds of intermediate results. There are a lot of different "item-based" parsers that use a lot of different kinds of items. In Chapter 4 a theory of items is developed, that provides a general understanding of what an item *is*. All the various items that are used by different parsers can be seen as special cases of these general items. It is merely the *notation* of items that differs among parsers (and for good reason: in the description of a parser it makes sense to use an item notation that is most convenient for that particular parser).

Not all parsers are "item-based", however. So what about those that use radically different kinds of intermediate results? We will argue that *every* constructive parser is, in principle, item-based. This principle might be hidden from the surface and not show up in the parsing algorithm. A typical example is a so-called *LR* parser, which is based on a state transition function and a stack of states as the guiding structures. In this particular parser, the items do not appear run-time, while parsing a given sentence, but have been employed *compile-time*, in the construction of the table that encodes the state transition function. It is possible to partly "uncompile" an LR parser and show run-time at each step which items are in fact recognized. Any constructive parser, in similar fashion, has an underlying item-based parser and hence can be described by a parsing schema.

Parsing schemata are a generalization of the *chart parsing* framework [Kay, 1980], [Winograd, 1983]. For every chart parser it is rather trivial to write down an underlying parsing schema, but a schema can be implemented by a great many algorithms that need not even remotely resemble chart parsers (in which case the relation between algorithm and schema will not be entirely trivial). One could say that the canonical implementation of a parsing schema is a chart parser.

Parsing schemata are useful devices in several respects. This research was started with the purpose of bringing some order into the field of parallel parsing. A great variety of parallel parsers have been published in the last decade (cf. Alblas et al. [1994]). Although our work has shifted to a more general nature, quite a few of these algorithms are incorporated in the framework presented here.

An interesting kind of application is *cross-fertilization* of different parsing algorithms with related underlying schemata. When the relation between algorithms is understood, most improvements and optimizations of one algorithm can easily be ported to related algorithms. An good example of cross-fertilization is the Parallel Bottom-up Tomita algorithm described in Chapter 13. A parallel version of Tomita's algorithm is obtained in which the division of tasks over processors is organized radically different from the parallel Tomita parsers that have been formulated before. The inspiration to look at the problem from a different angle came from a comparison with Earley's algorithm where bottom-up parallelization is simply the natural thing to do.

On a more fundamental level, one can see parsing schemata as a *separate, well-defined level of abstraction* in between grammars and parsing algorithms. A grammar specifies implicitly what the parse trees of a sentence are. A parsing algorithm specifies explicitly how these parse trees can be computed. A parsing schema specifies which steps could be taken that guarantee the construction of all parse trees, without considering data structures, control structures and communication structures. Such a well-defined intermediate level is a valuable aid because it allows a problem to be split into two smaller and easier problems. This is true for practical applications (the design of programs) as well as theoretical applications (the construction of proofs). It is rather more easy to prove the correctness of a parsing schema than that of a parser, simply because there is much less to prove. The correctness of a parser, then, can be established by proving that it is a correct implementation of schema that is known to be correct.

It is very hard to come up with the "right", useful abstractions and once you have found them, the result sometimes looks trivial. But this is usually a sign of being on the right track; if a complicated issue can be cast into terms that make it less complicated, something valuable has been gained. Parsing schema specifications are concise and formal, but nevertheless relatively easy to understand.

That this framework is not merely a theoretical nicety but a useful abstraction indeed is shown, I hope, by the many nontrivial applications of parsing schemata that are worked out in this book.

1.4 Overview

A scientific text is tree-structured. Sections can be divided into subsections; these into sub-subsections, and so on *ad libitum*. I have tried not to give in to this temptation and use the chapter as the main structuring element, following the adage

> *if a subject is worth spending 50 pages on, it deserves more than a single chapter.*

A broad outline of the contents is given by the division into three parts:

Part I, Exposition (Chapters 1–2) introduces the topics that will be treated in the remaining parts.

Part II, Foundation (Chapters 3–6) defines a formal theory of parsing schemata.

Part III, Application (Chapters 7–14) shows that parsing schemata can be employed for a series of different purposes.

In more detail:

Chapter 2 is a more detailed but informal introduction to parsing and parsing schemata.
The basic idea underlying our work is cast into the metaphor of the "primordial soup" algorithm. Rather than worrying about data structures, control structures and communication structures we throw a large enough supply of elementary trees into a big pot, let these float around, meet, interact and form larger trees, until after a very long (perhaps infinite) time all potential parse trees will have been formed. Schemata for sensible parsing algorithms can be derived by imposing various kinds of restrictions on this very general, but equally impractical approach to parsing.

Chapters 3–6 give a theory of parsing schemata for context-free grammars.
Most of what is done informally in Chapter 2 is done more thoroughly in Chapter 3. A notion of parsing schemata is developed in which partial parse trees constitute the intermediate results delivered by a parser.
In Chapter 4, trees are replaced by items. An item can be seen as a collection of trees that share certain properties. We give two different definitions of items, one of a more theoretical and the other of a more practical nature. It is in fact very convenient to use some items that are inconsistent with the underlying theory, but it can be shown that this has no consequences for the correctness of parsing schemata. After having dealt with these rather fundamental issues, some examples of realistic parsing schemata are presented in 4.6.
Chapters 5 and 6 discuss relations between parsing schemata. Chapter 5 concentrates on *refinement* (making smaller steps and producing more intermediate results) and *generalization* (extending a parsing schema to a larger class of grammars). Chapter 6 deals with *filtering*, that is, making a parsing schema more efficient by discarding irrelevant parts. Both chapters are illustrated with lots of examples, many of them schemata of parsing algorithms known from the literature. In Section 6.5 a taxonomy of Earley-like parsing schemata is presented.
Chapters 3–6 can be read on two levels. First and foremost, they constitute a formal theory of parsing schemata. But somebody who is familiar with some of the parsing algorithms that are discussed can get a fairly good picture of what is going on by browsing through the many examples.

Chapters 7–9 extend parsing schemata to unification grammars.
Chapter 7 is a short and easy to read introduction to unification grammars for computer scientists who have never had any involvement with computational linguistics.

Chapter 8 extends the formal theory of parsing schemata from context-free grammars to (PATR-style) unification grammars. We use a formalization of feature structures that is somewhat different from the formal-logical approach, but amounts to the same thing for all practical purposes. In order to be able to specify *transfer* of features explicitly, we introduce a notion of *multi-rooted* feature structures that describe the interrelations between features of arbitrary sets of objects. Thus we obtain a neat formalism for specifying parsers for unification grammars.

For context-free grammar parsing it is pretty clear how a simple, adequate (but perhaps not the most efficient) algorithm can be obtained from a parsing schema. This is not the case for unification grammar parsing schemata. In Chapter 9 we discuss some essential nuts and bolts of unification grammar parsing: unification of feature structures, avoiding infinite sets of predicted items, and, last but not least, *two-pass* parsers that use some essential features in a first pass and add all other features in a second pass.

For reading Chapters 7–9 one needs to have a basic understanding of the parsing schemata notation, but no detailed knowledge of the material covered in Chapters 3–6.

Chapters 10–11 are about Left-Corner (LC) and Head-Corner (HC) chart parsers. These two chapters can be read as a single paper.

An HC parser does not process a sentence from left to right; it starts with the most important words and fills in the gaps later. Because of the non-sequential way in which the HC parser hops through a sentence, its description is not easy, its correctness proof much less so. LC parsers are interesting in their own right (and the question whether LC or HC parsing is more efficient is still open for debate). But the main point we have to make about LC parsing – that it can be cast into a chart parser – has in fact been made already in Section 4.6. The reason to include Chapter 10 here is that, once it is understood how an LC parser can be defined and proven correct, we can understand the rather more complicated HC case as a pretty straightforward generalization of the LC case.

Chapters 10 and 11 exemplify that parsing schemata can be used to get a formal grip on highly complicated algorithms. This is the first ever HC parser that has been proven correct.

Chapters 12–13 place Generalized LR parsing within our framework. These two chapters can be read as a single paper.

In Chapter 12, as an example of how non-item-based parsers fit into our framework, we discuss Tomita's Generalized LR parser and uncover the underlying parsing schema. Ignoring a few trivial details, one can say that this is identical to the parsing schema of an Earley parser.

In Chapter 13, this last insight is used to cross-breed Tomita's parser with a *parallel* version of Earley's parser. Test results of this so-called Parallel Bottom-up Tomita parser show a moderate speed-up compared to the original Tomita parser.

Chapter 14 discusses parsing by boolean circuits.

This chapter gives another, very different application of parsing schemata. A maximally parallel implementation of a parsing schema can be obtained by executing, at every step, all applicable computations at the same time. The control structure of such an algorithm is not dependent on the particular sentence, hence (if we assume a maximum sentence length) the algorithm can be coded entirely into *hardware*. Any parsing schema for any grammar can be coded into a boolean circuit in this way.

As a nontrivial example, we apply this to Rytter's logarithmic-time parallel parsing algorithm. This leads to a simplification in the algorithm (and the proof of its correctness), while the complexity bounds of the boolean circuit conform to those known for other parallel machine models.

Chapter 15, finally, gives some conclusions and prospects for future research.

2. The primordial soup framework

The "primordial soup algorithm" [Janssen et al., 1992] is a metaphor for the more abstract notion of a parsing schema. One specifies which trees can be constructed during parsing and how these can be constructed; one does not specify how these trees are to be searched for and stored.

We give a very informal introduction, meant only to convey some intuition for what is going to be formalized in the next chapters. The reader who prefers formal definitions to less precise prose may skip this chapter.

The general idea of the primordial soup approach is worked out in 2.1. Some primordial soup variants that resemble well-known parsing algorithms are introduced in 2.2; extensions and related approaches are mentioned in 2.3. Section 2.4, finally, gives a brief sketch of the limitations of the primordial soup framework and introduces the generalization to parsing schemata.

2.1 Primordial soup

A simple example of a parse tree is displayed in Figure 2.1. This tree gives a complete context-free phrase structure analysis of the sentence "the cat catches a mouse." A sentence can be broken down into a *noun phrase* and a *verb phrase*; a verb phrase can be broken down into a *verb* and a noun phrase; a noun phrase can be broken down into a *determiner* and a *noun*. The word in the sentence have lexical categories determiner, noun, and verb, as indicated in the figure.

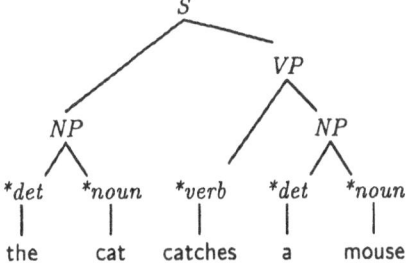

Fig. 2.1. A simple parse tree

The parse tree is well-formed according to the following very simple grammar:

$$
\begin{aligned}
S &\rightarrow NP\ VP, \\
NP &\rightarrow\ \textit{*det *noun}, \\
VP &\rightarrow\ \textit{*verb } NP.
\end{aligned}
$$

This grammar, which we call G_1 for further reference, consists of three *productions* or *rewrite rules*. The left-hand side of a production can be rewritten into the right-hand side (and a sentence decomposed accordingly). Grammar G_1 has the property that it is *binary branching*: the right-hand side of every production consist of 2 symbols. This is not necessarily the case; grammars may also have productions with 0, 1, 3, or more right-hand side symbols. But there are some very simple and elegant parsing algorithms that work only for binary branching grammars.

Grammar G_1 is extraordinarily small; a reasonable context-free phrase structure grammar for English contains a few hundred rules.[1]

A slightly larger grammar G_2, that will be used in many examples, is given by the following series of productions:

$$
\begin{aligned}
S &\rightarrow\ NP\ VP \\
S &\rightarrow\ S\ PP \\
NP &\rightarrow\ \textit{*det *noun} \\
NP &\rightarrow\ NP\ PP \\
PP &\rightarrow\ \textit{*prep } NP \\
VP &\rightarrow\ \textit{*verb } NP.
\end{aligned}
$$

In addition to noun phrases and verb phrases, it contains *prepositional phrases*. Parsing "the cat catches a mouse" according to G_2 yield the parse tree that was already shown in Figure 2.1. The canonical example sentence that can be parsed with this grammar is "the boy saw a man with a telescope." The sentence has two parse trees, reflecting the different interpretations that can be given to it.

It will be obvious that grammar G_2 is also far too small to be of any practical use. Just as G_1 its only purpose is to allow small, clear examples to illustrate various types of parsers.

From the first example it should be clear how a parse tree can be constructed for some sentence, given the productions of the grammar and the lexical categories of the words in the sentence. A formal definition will be given in Section 3.1.

We want to design a computer system that constructs all parse trees for some grammar and an arbitrary string of words.[2]

---

[1] See, for example, the context-free grammars for English as given by Sager [1981] and Tomita [1985].

[2] A string of words is called a *sentence* only if it is well-formed according to the grammar. If no parse trees are found, then the string is not a sentence.

We start with a very simple recipe, based upon the idea that large trees can be *composed* from smaller trees. A larger tree can be constructed by grafting the root of some tree onto a leaf of another tree. This can only be done, however, if both nodes carry the same label. We begin with an abundant supply of *elementary* trees. These come in two kinds:

- elementary trees representing the words with their lexical categories,
- elementary trees representing the productions of the grammar.

As time proceeds, trees float around, meet and interact, forming larger and larger trees. If the sentence is well-formed, parse trees will emerge in the primordial soup after a long, but finite amount of time.

Let us consider the sentence "the cat catches a mouse" again, and grammar G_1 as on page 20. The trees that are present in the initial primordial soup are shown in Figure 2.2 (each different tree is shown only once, but one should imagine a sufficiently large number of copies of each tree). The words are annotated with their position in the string, so as to remember the word order. These trees float around and bump into other trees. Upon such a collision, two trees may stick together. If the root of a tree carries the same label as the leaf of the other tree, the first tree can be grafted onto the second one. The root and leaf node with the same label are merged into a single node. An example of tree composition is given in Figure 2.3.

We have stated that the primordial soup contains an abundant number of elementary trees. Hence, as many copies of larger trees can be made as needed. A rather more efficient way to simulate this in a computer system is to keep single copies of each tree and make combinations of trees *nondestructively*. That is, the new tree is added to the current set of trees, but the trees from which it is constructed also remain present. Thus, in a computer simulation of the primordial soup, we start with an initial set of trees that contains only a single copy of every different kind of tree. For all possible combinations of trees in the set it is tried whether new trees can be produced. These new trees are added to the set (while the trees from which they are constructed also remain present). For each new tree, subsequently, all possible combinations with other trees are tried, and so on. This process stops if a situation is reached where all trees that can be produced are contained in the set already.

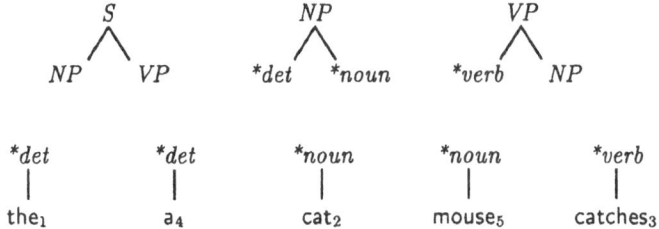

Fig. 2.2. The initial primordial soup for "the cat catches a mouse"

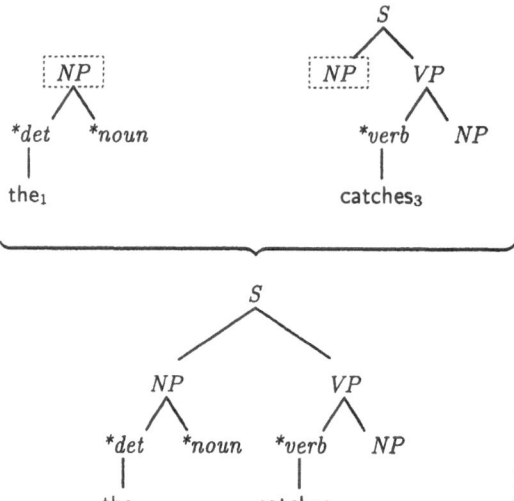

Fig. 2.3. A root is unified with a leaf of another tree

There is no guarantee, in general, that this process ever halts, it might well be the case that an infinite number of trees can be created nondestructively from the elementary trees we started with. But we will not be bothered by that problem right now; for grammar G_1 it is clear that the primordial soup will halt.

Whether the search for new trees is done systematically or at random, sequential or parallel, is not of great concern to us. As the primordial soup framework is primarily meant to model parallel parsing, the simplest interpretation is that at each step all combinations of all trees present in the soup are tried for a match.[3] In this way, the number of steps that is needed until no more new trees can be added is the *minimum* number of steps in a parallel implementation with unlimited resources. Such details will be discussed in Chapter 14, and for the next half a dozen chapters we will not be concerned with any implementation. The more interesting matter here (that will occupy us up to Chapter 6) is what the *final* contents of the primordial soup looks like, once every possible tree has been constructed. Which particular search strategy and storage structure is used to compute this final contents is irrelevant, as long as every tree that can be constructed eventually will be found.

In the remainder of this chapter we will use a simple, linear notation for trees. If we have a tree with root labelled A and *yield* (i.e., the sequence of labels of leaves, from left to right) α, we may denote such a tree by the formula $\langle A \rightsquigarrow \alpha \rangle$. The trees in Figure 2.3, for example, can be denoted by

---

[3] This resembles the "Unity" approach of Chandy and Misra [1988] for initial specification of parallel systems.

$\langle NP \leadsto \text{the}_1 \text{ *}noun \rangle$,

$\langle S \leadsto NP \text{ catches}_3 \text{ } NP \rangle$,

$\langle S \leadsto \text{the}_1 \text{ *}noun \text{ catches}_3 \text{ } NP \rangle$.

In this notation we abstract from the internal structure of the trees. Tree composition (here) only involves roots and leaves, hence a notation where all internal nodes and edges are simply replaced by the symbol $\leadsto$ is adequate and simple – and saves a lot of paper. Only for elementary trees we write $\rightarrow$, rather than $\leadsto$, indicating that the yield is produced directly by the root and that there are no internal nodes;[4] e.g.

$\langle NP \rightarrow \text{*}det \text{ *}noun \rangle$.

Next, we introduce an operator $\vartriangleleft$ that denotes tree composition. In Figure 2.3, the construction of the large tree is licensed by the equality

$$\langle S \leadsto NP \text{ catches}_3 \text{ } NP \rangle \quad \vartriangleleft \quad \langle NP \leadsto \text{the}_1 \text{ *}noun \rangle$$
$$= \quad \langle S \leadsto \text{the}_1 \text{ *}noun \text{ catches}_3 \text{ } NP \rangle.$$

A composed tree $\sigma \vartriangleleft \tau$ is defined only if some leaf of tree σ and the root of tree τ are labelled with the same symbol.

If more than one leaf of σ corresponds to the root of τ, then the notation $\sigma \vartriangleleft \tau$ is ambiguous. Formally, the ambiguity of $\vartriangleleft$ can be eliminated by writing $\vartriangleleft_1$ for tree composition with the first matching leaf, $\vartriangleleft_2$ for tree composition with the second matching leaf, and so on. A tree composition $\sigma \vartriangleleft_i \tau$ is defined only if $yield(\sigma)$ contains at least i occurrences of $root(\tau)$. In most cases it is clear what is meant and we do not bother to write the index i.

Note that for the first two trees in Figure 2.3 it holds that

$$\langle S \leadsto NP \text{ catches}_3 \text{ } NP \rangle \quad \vartriangleleft_2 \quad \langle NP \leadsto \text{the}_1 \text{ *}noun \rangle$$
$$= \quad \langle S \leadsto NP \text{ catches}_3 \text{ the}_1 \text{ *}noun \rangle.$$

There is a problem, however, with the tree $\langle S \leadsto NP \text{ catches}_3 \text{ the}_1 \text{ *}noun \rangle$. The construction of this tree is perfectly legal according to the rule of tree composition. But this tree can never be of any use for the construction of a parse tree, because the word order is violated. If we allow such trees to occur in the primordial soup, then not only the parse trees for the given string will emerge, but also the parse trees of all other strings that can be formed from the same words. Hence we introduce a special constraint, making sure that only the requested string is parsed and no other string.

Word order constraint: *the position numbers that occur as markings of leaves of a tree must be increasing from left to right.*

---

[4] This convention has no particular relevance here, but anticipates a more sophisticated linear tree notation that will be introduced in Chapter 3.

Hence a tree $\langle S \rightsquigarrow \text{the}_1 \; ^*noun \; \text{catches}_3 \; NP \rangle$ is allowed by the word order constraint, but a tree $\langle S \rightsquigarrow NP \; \text{catches}_3 \; \text{the}_1 \; ^*noun \rangle$ is discarded and should not enter into the primordial soup. As a consequence, the only full parse tree that eventually will appear is

$\langle S \rightsquigarrow \text{the}_1 \; \text{cat}_2 \; \text{catches}_3 \; \text{a}_4 \; \text{mouse}_5 \rangle$.

Let us now reconsider grammar G_2 (cf. page 20) which includes prepositional phrases as well. "The cat catches a mouse" can be parsed with grammar G_2 as well (it contains all productions of G_1), but we are faced with a problem. An infinite number of trees can be constructed, hence (a simulation of) the primordial soup does not finish. Among others, the following series of trees will emerge:

$\langle NP \to NP \; PP \rangle$
$\langle NP \rightsquigarrow NP \; ^*prep \; NP \rangle$
$\langle NP \rightsquigarrow NP \; ^*prep \; NP \; PP \rangle$
$\langle NP \rightsquigarrow NP \; ^*prep \; NP \; ^*prep \; NP \rangle$
$\langle NP \rightsquigarrow NP \; ^*prep \; NP \; ^*prep \; NP \; PP \rangle$
etc.

The word order constraint only affects leaves that are marked with position numbers, i.e., words from the string. But we can continue creating larger and larger trees without ever adding a single word. For grammar G_2 we guarantee that the primordial soup process will halt by imposing a second constraint.

Width constraint: *the yield of a tree may not be larger than a given fixed size.*

Which particular size is chosen is not important, the most natural choice is the length of the sentence.[5] For any *acyclic*[6] grammar and any string, the width constraint guarantees that only a finite number of different trees will emerge. For cyclic grammars, the depth of a tree is not bounded by the width, hence an infinite number of trees will be created. One could argue that this is right, because a cyclic grammar, in general, yields an infinite number of parse trees for a sentence. When all parse trees have to be delivered (and we do not use any sophisticated techniques to represent an infinite set of trees by a finite data structure) any parsing algorithm will run forever.

Let us now define the primordial soup parser as (an abstraction of) a parsing algorithm without data structures and control structures. That is, we define

---

[5] For grammars with empty productions (the right-hand side has 0 symbols) a certain oversize could be allowed; the length of the yield may shrink by adding an empty production to a nonterminal leaf.

[6] A grammar is *cyclic* if a symbol A can be rewritten to A by applying one or more productions; otherwise a grammar is acyclic.

- which kind of trees may occur in the primordial soup;
- an initial set of trees;
- a composition rule that allows adding new trees to a given set of trees.

Before we give the definition, a last bit of notation is needed. As shown in Figure 2.2, the string is represented by words annotated with their position and lexical category. As a general notation for this kind of initial trees we write $\langle a {\rightarrow} \underline{a}_i \rangle$, where $\underline{a}_i$ denotes the i-th word of string. The underlining is to distinguish the words proper from their lexical categories.[7] If $\underline{a}_i$ is lexically ambiguous, there will be several initial trees; one may also find $\langle b {\rightarrow} \underline{a}_i \rangle$, $\langle c {\rightarrow} \underline{a}_i \rangle$.

Definition 2.1. (*Primordial soup – simple version*)
For the sake of simplicity we assume that the grammar G is acyclic and contains no empty productions (i.e. productions with zero right-hand side symbols). We set the maximum width of a tree to the length of the string that is to be parsed.
The primordial soup for a grammar G and an arbitrary string of words is defined as follows.

- The domain of the primordial soup comprises are well-formed trees according to the grammar G that obey both the word order constraint and the width constraint.
- The initial set of trees contains a tree $\langle A {\rightarrow} \alpha \rangle$ for every production $A {\rightarrow} \alpha$ in grammar G and $\langle a {\rightarrow} \underline{a}_i \rangle$ for every lexical category of the i-th word.
- If trees σ and τ are present in the current set of trees and the tree $\sigma \lhd \tau$ exists within the domain specified above, then then $\sigma \lhd \tau$ may be added to the set of trees.

A formal definition of well-formed trees is given later (cf. Definition 3.5). Here it should be clear from the examples what is meant.   □

Implicitly defined by the primordial soup specification is the *final* set of trees. This final set, in a way, gives an account of all the intermediate results that are created by a parser in order to find the parse trees. How this set is computed (sequentially or parallel? systematically or at random?) we do not know at this level of abstraction. This is the central idea.

More restricted versions of the primordial soup – in which the final set contains only those intermediate results that are computed by a sensible parsing algorithm – can be defined by

---

[7] For a natural language parser, it is much more convenient to start parsing from the lexical categories of the words, rather than the words themselves. So, in most descriptions of parsing algorithms, the symbol a_i denotes a lexical category, rather than a "real" word.

- restricting the domain of trees that is allowed to occur in the primordial soup
- adding restrictions to tree composition operators.

These two kinds of restrictions are usually interchangeable. In the above version of the primordial soup, for example, the domain excludes trees that violate the word order constraint or width constraint. We could have given an alternative definition in which the domain of the primordial soup simply consists of all well-formed trees but the tree composition rule is defined only for those cases where none of the constraints if violated. The definition is different but the final set of trees that is implied by the definition is the same.

2.2 Restricted versions of the primordial soup

Above we have defined the most general but also most inefficient variant of the primordial soup. Even for small grammars and small sentences, the final set of trees will be huge. We will now give a few examples of more efficient variants of the primordial soup. The reader who is familiar with parsing theory will recognize that these more sensible versions are related to the algorithms of of Cocke-Younger-Kasami (CYK) and Earley. We also give a version of Rytter's algorithm, which is rather hard to comprehend in its original form, and rather more easy to understand in the primordial soup format.

Before we define further variants of the primordial soup we have to be more specific about the terminology.

We write $a, b, \ldots$, for lexical categories;
we write $A, B, \ldots$, for nonterminals (i.e., other syntactic categories),
we write $X, Y, \ldots$, for symbols for which it does not matter whether they refer to a nonterminal or to a lexical category;
we write $\underline{a}_i$ for the i-th word of the sentence; $\underline{a}_i$ is called a *marked terminal*;
we write $\alpha, \beta, \ldots$, for strings of nonterminals, lexical categories and/or marked terminals;
we write ε for the empty string.

Furthermore, we define the following species of trees.

- A *complete tree* is a tree of the form $\langle A \rightsquigarrow \underline{a}_i \ldots \underline{a}_j \rangle$.
- A *production tree* is a tree $\langle A \rightarrow \alpha \rangle$ with $A \rightarrow \alpha$ a production of the grammar.

Schematic drawings of a complete tree and a production tree for a binary production are shown in figure 2.4. A special subspecies of complete trees is worth mentioning.

- A *terminal tree* is a tree of the form $\langle a \rightarrow \underline{a}_i \rangle$.

Fig. 2.4. A complete tree and a (binary branching) production tree

In the CYK version of the primordial soup, only complete trees are constructed. The initial set contains production trees and terminal trees (but terminal trees are a subspecies of complete trees). Hence we limit the domain to production trees and complete trees. We will assume here that the grammar G is binary branching, i.e., every production has two symbols at its right-hand side. Both grammars G_1 and G_2 as defined in Section 2.1 are binary branching.

Suppose that we have a production tree $\langle A{\rightarrow}BC \rangle$ and that we have complete trees $\langle B \rightsquigarrow \underline{a}_{i+1} \ldots \underline{a}_j \rangle$ and $\langle C \rightsquigarrow \underline{a}_{j+1} \ldots \underline{a}_k \rangle$. From these we can construct a larger tree $\langle A \rightsquigarrow \underline{a}_{i+1} \ldots \underline{a}_k \rangle$. But, since we have restricted the allowed types of trees to production trees and complete trees, putting these 3 trees together must be done in a single operation. If the construction is done in two steps, the intermediate product belongs to a species that is not allowed within the domain. Hence we replace the binary composition operator by a *ternary composition operator* denoted $\overset{3}{\lhd}$, as follows:

$\pi \overset{3}{\lhd} \sigma, \tau$ is defined for binary production trees π and complete trees σ, τ if $yield(\pi) = root(\sigma)root(\tau)$.

$\pi \overset{3}{\lhd} \sigma, \tau$ denotes the tree that is constructed by grafting σ onto the first (left) leaf and τ onto the second (right) leaf of π.

Example 2.2. (*Primordial soup – CYK version*)
Let G be a binary branching grammar. The CYK version of the primordial soup for G and an arbitrary string of words is defined as follows.

- The species of trees in the domain are restricted to production trees and complete trees.
- The initial set of trees contains a tree $\langle A{\rightarrow}XY \rangle$ for every production $A{\rightarrow}XY$ in grammar G and $\langle a{\rightarrow}\underline{a}_i \rangle$ for every lexical category a of the i-th word.
- If trees π, σ, τ are in the current set and $\pi \overset{3}{\lhd} \sigma, \tau$ is defined, then $\pi \overset{3}{\lhd} \sigma, \tau$ may be added to the set.

The final set for "the cat catches a mouse", according to grammar G_2, is shown in Figure 2.5.   □

As a second example, we will make a minor variation to the CYK version of the primordial soup. This allows us to define (an abstraction of) of Rytter's algorithm [Rytter, 1985], [Gibbons and Rytter, 1988], which, in its original

production trees: $\langle S \rightarrow NP\ VP \rangle$
$\langle S \rightarrow S\ PP \rangle$
$\langle NP \rightarrow {}^{*}det\ {}^{*}noun \rangle$
$\langle NP \rightarrow NP\ PP \rangle$
$\langle VP \rightarrow {}^{*}verb\ NP \rangle$
$\langle PP \rightarrow {}^{*}prep\ NP \rangle$

terminal trees: $\langle {}^{*}det \rightarrow \text{the}_1 \rangle$
$\langle {}^{*}noun \rightarrow \text{cat}_2 \rangle$
$\langle {}^{*}verb \rightarrow \text{catches}_3 \rangle$
$\langle {}^{*}det \rightarrow \text{a}_4 \rangle$
$\langle {}^{*}noun \rightarrow \text{mouse}_5 \rangle$

other complete trees: $\langle NP \rightsquigarrow \text{the}_1\ \text{cat}_2 \rangle$
$\langle NP \rightsquigarrow \text{a}_4\ \text{mouse}_5 \rangle$
$\langle VP \rightsquigarrow \text{catches}_3\ \text{a}_4\ \text{mouse}_5 \rangle$
$\langle S \rightsquigarrow \text{the}_1\ \text{cat}_2\ \text{catches}_3\ \text{a}_4\ \text{mouse}_5 \rangle$

Fig. 2.5. The final set of trees in a CYK primordial soup

form, is much more difficult to understand than CYK. We define an additional species of trees:

An *almost-complete tree* is a tree of one of the following forms:

$$\langle A \rightsquigarrow X \rangle,$$
$$\langle A \rightsquigarrow X \underline{a}_{i+1} \cdots \underline{a}_j \rangle,$$
$$\langle A \rightsquigarrow \underline{a}_{i+1} \cdots \underline{a}_j X \rangle,$$
$$\langle A \rightsquigarrow \underline{a}_{i+1} \cdots \underline{a}_j X \underline{a}_{k+1} \cdots \underline{a}_\ell \rangle$$

with $i < j < k < l$, where applicable.

An almost-complete tree contains exactly one leaf that is not a marked terminal. If the grammar is binary branching, trees of the form $\langle A \rightsquigarrow X \rangle$ do not exist.

When we extend the domain with almost-complete trees, the tree construction operator of CYK can be simplified. Suppose, again, that we have a production tree $\pi = \langle A \rightarrow BC \rangle$ and complete trees $\sigma = \langle B \rightsquigarrow \underline{a}_{i+1} \cdots \underline{a}_j \rangle$ and $\tau = \langle C \rightsquigarrow \underline{a}_{j+1} \cdots \underline{a}_k \rangle$. Then it clearly holds that

$$\pi \overset{3}{\triangleleft} \sigma, \tau \;=\; (\pi \triangleleft \sigma) \triangleleft \tau \;=\; (\pi \triangleleft \tau) \triangleleft \sigma.$$

Both intermediate results

$$(\pi \triangleleft \sigma) \;=\; \langle A \rightsquigarrow \underline{a}_{i+1} \cdots \underline{a}_j C \rangle,$$
$$(\pi \triangleleft \tau) \;=\; \langle A \rightsquigarrow B \underline{a}_{j+1} \cdots \underline{a}_k \rangle$$

are almost-complete.

By allowing almost-complete trees and binary tree composition we have created another possibility to obtain new trees. If the set of trees contains, for example

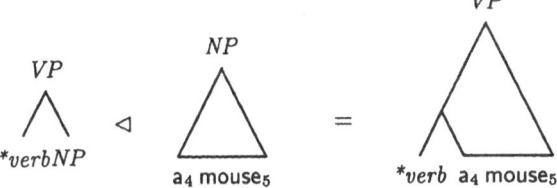

(*i*) a production tree and a complete tree yield an almost-complete tree

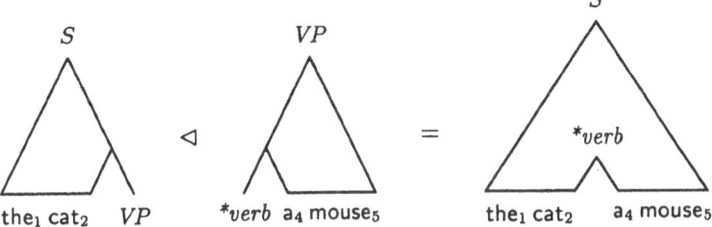

(*ii*) two almost-complete trees yield an almost-complete tree

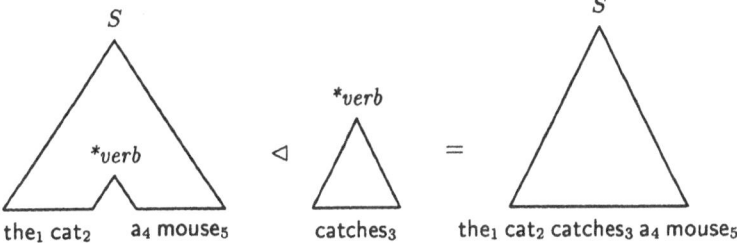

(*iii*) an almost-complete and a complete tree yield a complete tree

Fig. 2.6. Some tree compositions according to Rytter

$$\langle A \rightsquigarrow \underline{a}_{h+1} \cdots \underline{a}_i B \underline{a}_{\ell+1} \cdots \underline{a}_m \rangle,$$

$$\langle B \rightsquigarrow \underline{a}_{i+1} \cdots \underline{a}_j C \underline{a}_{k+1} \cdots \underline{a}_\ell \rangle$$

then these can be combined into a third almost-complete tree

$$\langle A \rightsquigarrow \underline{a}_{h+1} \cdots \underline{a}_j C \underline{a}_{k+1} \cdots \underline{a}_m \rangle.$$

Hence three types of tree construction can take place, which can be classified according to the species of trees involved, as follows:

- a production tree and a complete tree are merged into an almost-complete tree, for example (cf. Figure 2.6(*i*)):

$$\langle VP \rightarrow {}^*verb\ NP \rangle \lhd \langle NP \rightsquigarrow \mathsf{a}_4\ \mathsf{mouse}_5 \rangle = \langle VP \rightsquigarrow {}^*verb\ \mathsf{a}_4\ \mathsf{mouse}_5 \rangle$$

- an almost-complete tree and an almost-complete tree are merged into an almost-complete tree, for example (cf. Figure 2.6(ii)):

$$\langle S \rightsquigarrow \text{the}_1 \text{ cat}_2 \text{ } VP \rangle \lhd \langle VP \rightsquigarrow \text{*}verb \text{ a}_4 \text{ mouse}_5 \rangle$$
$$= \langle S \rightsquigarrow \text{the}_1 \text{ cat}_2 \text{ *}verb \text{ a}_4 \text{ mouse}_5 \rangle$$

- an almost-complete tree and a complete tree are merged into a complete tree, for example (cf. Figure 2.6(iii)):

$$\langle S \rightsquigarrow \text{the}_1 \text{ cat}_2 \text{ *}verb \text{ a}_4 \text{ mouse}_5 \rangle \lhd \langle \text{*}verb {\rightarrow} \text{catches}_3 \rangle$$
$$= \langle S \rightsquigarrow \text{the}_1 \text{ cat}_2 \text{ catches}_3 \text{ a}_4 \text{ mouse}_5 \rangle$$

A description of Rytter's algorithm typically defines three operators that correspond to the three cases of tree combination outlined here. In the primordial soup version, these three operators need not be defined explicitly; they are a *consequence* of the domain definition and the general composition rule based on $\lhd$.

Example 2.3. (*Primordial soup – Rytter version*)
Let G be a binary branching grammar. The Rytter version of the primordial soup for G and an arbitrary string of words is defined as follows.

- The species of trees in the domain are restricted to
  - production trees,
  - complete trees,
  - almost-complete trees.
- The initial set of trees contains a tree $\langle A {\rightarrow} XY \rangle$ for every production $A {\rightarrow} XY$ in grammar G and $\langle a {\rightarrow} \underline{a}_i \rangle$ for every lexical category a of the i-th word.
- If σ, τ are in the current set and $\sigma \lhd \tau$ is defined within the domain then $\sigma \lhd \tau$ may be added to the set.

The final set of trees for our simple example sentence and grammar G_2 is shown in Figure 2.7. □

Rytter's algorithm can compute all parses very fast, at the expense of rather large number of resources.[8] In Chapter 14 we will show how this algorithm can be implemented as a boolean circuit.

Next we turn to Earley's algorithm.[9] The grammar does not have to be binary branching and can be any context-free grammar. But the primordial soup stabilizes into a final state only if the grammar is acyclic. For cyclic

---

[8] For a sentence of length n, the final set of trees is computed in $O(\log n)$ steps, using $O(n^6)$ processors on a parallel random access machine.

[9] Note, however, that this is the bottom-up version of Earley, in which the *predict* operator is absent. Parsing can be started at any position in the string, independently of the left context. In Chapter 4 we will define a parsing schema for the conventional Earley algorithm, proceeding left-to-right and making use of top-down prediction.

production trees:	as in Figure 2.5
terminal trees:	as in Figure 2.5
almost-complete trees:	$\langle NP \leadsto \text{the}_1 \; {}^*noun\rangle$
	$\langle NP \leadsto {}^*det \; \text{cat}_2\rangle$
	$\langle NP \leadsto \text{the}_1 \; \text{cat}_2 \; PP\rangle$
	$\langle NP \leadsto \text{a}_4 \; {}^*noun\rangle$
	$\langle NP \leadsto {}^*det \; \text{mouse}_5\rangle$
	$\langle NP \leadsto \text{a}_4 \; \text{mouse}_5 \; PP\rangle$
	$\langle VP \leadsto \text{catches}_3 \; NP\rangle$
	$\langle VP \leadsto \text{catches}_3 \; \text{a}_4 \; {}^*noun\rangle$
	$\langle VP \leadsto \text{catches}_3 \; {}^*det \; \text{mouse}_5\rangle$
	$\langle VP \leadsto {}^*verb \; \text{a}_4 \; \text{mouse}_5\rangle$
	$\langle S \leadsto \text{the}_1 \; \text{cat}_2 \; VP\rangle$
	$\langle S \leadsto \text{the}_1 \; \text{cat}_2 \; \text{catches}_3 \; NP\rangle$
	$\langle S \leadsto \text{the}_1 \; \text{cat}_2 \; \text{catches}_3 \; \text{a}_4 \; {}^*noun\rangle$
	$\langle S \leadsto \text{the}_1 \; \text{cat}_2 \; \text{catches}_3 \; {}^*det \; \text{mouse}_5\rangle$
	$\langle S \leadsto \text{the}_1 \; \text{cat}_2 \; {}^*verb \; \text{a}_4 \; \text{mouse}_5\rangle$
	$\langle S \leadsto NP \; \text{catches}_3 \; \text{a}_4 \; \text{mouse}_5\rangle$
	$\langle S \leadsto \text{the}_1 \; {}^*noun \; \text{catches}_3 \; \text{a}_4 \; \text{mouse}_5\rangle$
	$\langle S \leadsto {}^*det \; \text{cat}_2 \; \text{catches}_3 \; \text{a}_4 \; \text{mouse}_5\rangle$
	$\langle S \leadsto \text{the}_1 \; \text{cat}_2 \; \text{catches}_3 \; \text{a}_4 \; \text{mouse}_5 \; PP\rangle$
(non-terminal) complete trees:	$\langle NP \leadsto \text{the}_1 \; \text{cat}_2\rangle$
	$\langle NP \leadsto \text{a}_4 \; \text{mouse}_5\rangle$
	$\langle VP \leadsto \text{catches}_3 \; \text{a}_4 \; \text{mouse}_5\rangle$
	$\langle S \leadsto \text{the}_1 \; \text{cat}_2 \; \text{catches}_3 \; \text{a}_4 \; \text{mouse}_5\rangle$

Fig. 2.7. The final set of trees in a Rytter primordial soup

grammars, there is no final state and an infinite number of trees will be created, including the (generally) infinite number of parse trees for a sentence. For the Earley version of the primordial soup we define another species of trees.

An *Earley tree* is a tree $\langle A \leadsto \underline{a}_{i+1} \ldots \underline{a}_j \beta\rangle$ having subtrees $\tau_1, \ldots, \tau_k$ such that $A \to root(\tau_1) \ldots root(\tau_k)\beta$ is a production of the grammar, and $yield(\tau_1) \ldots yield(\tau_k) = \underline{a}_{i+1} \ldots \underline{a}_j$.

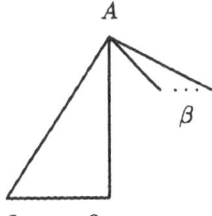

Fig. 2.8. An Earley tree

production trees:	as in Figure 2.5
terminal trees:	as in Figure 2.5
Earley trees:	$\langle NP \rightsquigarrow \text{the}_1 \ *noun\rangle$
(excluding production trees	$\langle NP \rightsquigarrow \text{the}_1 \ \text{cat}_2 \ PP\rangle$
and complete trees)	$\langle NP \rightsquigarrow \text{a}_4 \ *noun\rangle$
	$\langle NP \rightsquigarrow \text{a}_4 \ \text{mouse}_5 \ PP\rangle$
	$\langle VP \rightsquigarrow \text{catches}_3 \ NP\rangle$
	$\langle S \rightsquigarrow \text{the}_1 \ \text{cat}_2 \ VP\rangle$
	$\langle S \rightsquigarrow \text{the}_1 \ \text{cat}_2 \ \text{catches}_3 \ \text{a}_4 \ \text{mouse}_5 \ PP\rangle$
(non-terminal) complete trees:	$\langle NP \rightsquigarrow \text{the}_1 \ \text{cat}_2\rangle$
	$\langle NP \rightsquigarrow \text{a}_4 \ \text{mouse}_5\rangle$
	$\langle VP \rightsquigarrow \text{catches}_3 \ \text{a}_4 \ \text{mouse}_5\rangle$
	$\langle S \rightsquigarrow \text{the}_1 \ \text{cat}_2 \ \text{catches}_3 \ \text{a}_4 \ \text{mouse}_5\rangle$

Fig. 2.9. The final set of trees in an Earley primordial soup

A general sketch of an Earley tree is shown in Figure 2.8. The Earley tree has two important subspecies that have been defined already:

a production tree is an Earley tree with $k = 0$;
a complete tree is an Earley tree with $\beta = \varepsilon$.

If both σ and $\sigma \lhd \tau$ are Earley trees then τ must belong to the subspecies of completed trees. Thus, if a new tree $\sigma \lhd \tau$ is added to the set of trees, we can distinguish two cases:

$$\langle A \rightsquigarrow \underline{a}_{i+1} \cdots \underline{a}_j a\beta\rangle \quad \lhd \quad \langle a \rightarrow \underline{a}_{j+1}\rangle \quad = \quad \langle A \rightsquigarrow \underline{a}_{i+1} \cdots \underline{a}_{j+1}\beta\rangle$$

which is called *scan* by Earley, and

$$\langle A \rightsquigarrow \underline{a}_{i+1} \cdots \underline{a}_j B\beta\rangle \quad \lhd \quad \langle B \rightsquigarrow \underline{a}_{j+1} \cdots \underline{a}_k\rangle \quad = \quad \langle A \rightsquigarrow \underline{a}_{i+1} \cdots \underline{a}_k\beta\rangle$$

which is called *complete*.

As with Rytter, the division into operators involving different types of trees need not be specified explicitly. It is a consequence of the restriction on the domain.

Example 2.4. (*Primordial soup – Earley version*)
Let G be an arbitrary context-free grammar. The Earley version of the primordial soup for G and an arbitrary string of words is defined as follows.

- The domain is restricted to Earley trees.
- The initial set of trees contains a tree $\langle A \rightarrow \alpha\rangle$ for every production $A \rightarrow \alpha$ in grammar G and $\langle a \rightarrow \underline{a}_i\rangle$ for every lexical category a of the i-th word.
- If σ, τ are in the current set and $\sigma \lhd \tau$ is an Earley tree then $\sigma \lhd \tau$ may be added to the set.

The final set of trees of our example sentence and grammar G_2 is shown in Figure 2.9.   □

2.3 Extensions and related formalisms

The only way in which trees can be merged, so far, is by unifying a leaf
of one tree with the root of another. More complicated merges could be
allowed as well. In Figure 2.10 an example of a merge is shown in which
larger overlapping parts, rather than single nodes, are combined so as to
create a larger tree.

For most algorithms such merges are not necessary (and hence, for the
sake of efficiency, should better not be considered). If a tree can be created
by a complicated merge, the same tree can be created by simple leaf-to-root
merges from the same elementary material that was present in the initial
primordial soup. Janssen et al. [1991] give an example of a primordial soup
variant that makes essential use of other than leaf-to-root merges. This variant describes the parsing algorithm of De Vreught and Honig [1989]. The
basic idea is the following:

Suppose there is a production tree $\langle A \rightarrow \alpha\beta_1\beta_2\gamma \rangle$. A tree may emerge with β_1
fully expanded; say

$$\langle A \rightsquigarrow \alpha\underline{a}_{i+1} \cdots \underline{a}_j\beta_2\gamma \rangle.$$

If, at some moment in time, the primordial soup also contains a tree

$$\langle A \rightsquigarrow \alpha\beta_1\underline{a}_{j+1} \cdots \underline{a}_k\gamma \rangle$$

in which β_2 has been fully expanded, these trees can be merged into a single
tree

$$\langle A \rightsquigarrow \alpha\underline{a}_{i+1} \cdots \underline{a}_k\gamma \rangle.$$

The algorithm of de Vreught and Honig will be treated extensively in Chapter 6, hence we don't go into more detail here.

An operation on trees that fits very well to the primordial soup metaphor
is *tree adjoining*. A special kind of tree, called an *adjunct*, is inserted in
the middle of another tree. This is illustrated in Figure 2.11. A tree is "un-
merged" into two trees by splitting a node into a leaf of the outer tree and
the root of the inner tree. Then the root of the adjunct is unified with the
cut leaf of the outer tree and the root of the inner tree is unified with a leaf
of the adjunct. An adjunct can be any tree that has a leaf carrying the same
label as its root. This leaf is called the *foot* of the adjunct.

Tree adjoining grammars (TAGs), defined by Joshi et al. [1975, 1991],
are perhaps most easily described in the primordial soup framework. For the
construction of a parse trees in a TAG two kinds of operations can be used:
composition, which is identical to our leaf-to-root merging and *tree adjoining*
as explained above. Furthermore, the nodes in the initial trees may carry
labels that describe whether adjoining over that node is forbidden, mandatory
or optional. In a *Lexicalized* TAG [Schabes and Joshi, 1991], moreover, it is
demanded that every elementary tree contains at least one terminal. If there

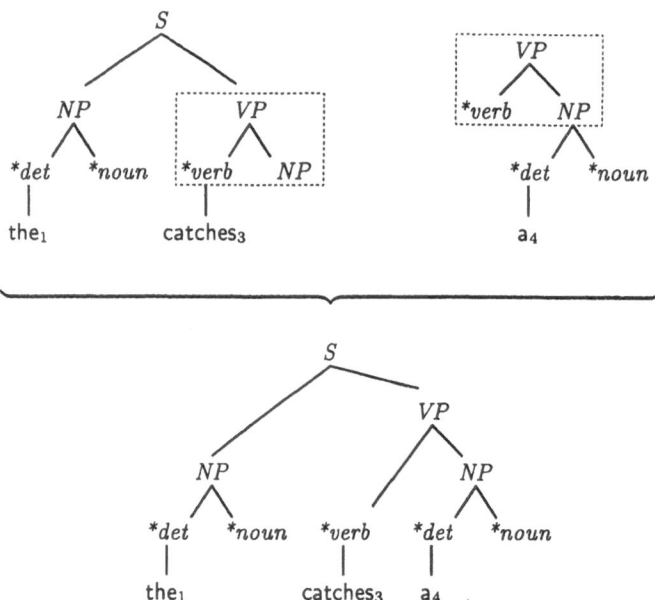

Fig. 2.10. A merge over corresponding subtrees

is a lexicon that provides elementary trees for every word, then this implies that the entire grammar is contained in the lexicon.

The primordial soup is not the first chemical metaphor for computation, or, more specifically, parsing. A "Chemical Abstract Machine" is defined by Berry and Boudol [1990] as an abstract model of asynchronous concurrent computation (a better name would have been an "Abstract Chemical Machine"). There are two kinds of chemical reactions to create compounds: the first one is reversible, compounds may spontaneously decompose again. Composition is irreversible when two *ions* with different valencies meet.
A chemical metaphor in parsing is the "test-tube model" used by Kempen and Vosse [1990]. The purpose here is to create a single parse tree (the most likely one) for a given sentence. It is essential that composition is destructive, i.e., a molecule that is initially present can be used only in one compound at the time. Compounds that do not find other material to react with will decompose after some time.
Willems [1992] uses chemical composition as a metaphor for the semantics of natural language described by means of knowledge graphs.

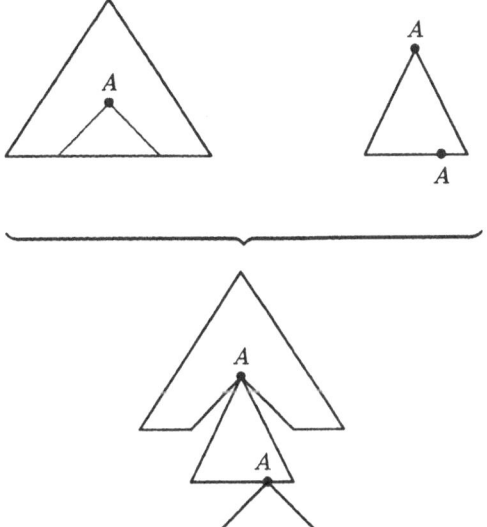

Fig. 2.11. Tree adjoining

2.4 From primordial soup to parsing schemata

We have introduced the primordial soup as a metaphor for parsing schemata. In Chapters 3 and 4, parsing schemata are introduced in an abstract and rather more formal manner. Some of the technical details differ, but the general idea is identical. One specifies

- a set of objects that constitute a domain
- an initial set of objects
- rules that allow a set of objects to be extended with new objects.

Implicitly specified by such a schema is a set of *valid* objects; the subset of the domain that can be derived from the initial set following the rules. This set of valid objects may be finite or infinite. How such a set can be computed and stored is not relevant at this level of abstraction.

The primordial soup metaphor strongly suggests that derivation of trees is *compositional*; a new tree is created by merging separately existing trees into a single structure. It violates the laws of chemistry when a tree can be derived from existing trees with which it has nothing in common. Similarly, the metaphor does not allow that trees are created spontaneously out of nothing. Yet it is rather easy and sometimes convenient to introduce a *unary* composition operator $\overset{1}{\triangleleft}$ which states that τ can be added to soup – irrespective of its current contents – if $\overset{1}{\triangleleft} \tau$ holds. Such constructs are at odds with the intuition presented here, but turn out to be useful for the specification of parsing schemata.

An example of a rule that does not quite fit the primordial soup metaphor (and which we have carefully circumvented above) is the *predict* operation in

Earley's algorithm. In Chapter 4 this will be treated properly. Hence, like any metaphor, the primordial soup metaphor is very useful to convey a superficial intuition but does not fit quite so well when one digs deeper into the theory.

Nevertheless, the general idea of parsing schemata as an intermediate level of abstraction between grammars and algorithms has been clarified sufficiently by the examples given above. All that is left is to work out the formal and practical details.

Part II

FOUNDATION

3. Tree-based parsing schemata

The primordial soup algorithms of Chapter 2 served to provide some intuition of what parsing schemata do. We specify a domain of trees, an initial set of trees and deduction steps that allow to add new trees to a current set of trees. Control structures and data structures must be added to turn these specifications into sensible algorithms (and, for parallel algorithms, communication structures as well). We will now develop a formal theory of what we have been doing informally. Furthermore (as we have argued in Section 2.4), the primordial soup metaphor carries some connotations that should not restrict the kind of parsing schemata that we intend to define.

A full-fledged parsing schema has a set of *items*, rather than trees, as its domain. But in order to develop a general theory of item-based parsing schemata one must first have a notion of what an item is. We will tackle one problem at the time. In this chapter we give a formal treatment of parsing schemata based on trees. In Chapter 4, subsequently, we will investigate the notion of an item and add that to the formalism. Having defined a general formalism for parsing schemata, we will study in Chapters 5 and 6 how different parsing schemata are related and how schemata can be transformed into other schemata.

In Section 3.1 we recall the notion of a context-free grammar and related standard definitions in parsing theory. The reader who is familiar with this theory should still glance through it; notations differ a lot in the literature, and here we introduce notational conventions that are used throughout the remainder of this book. Furthermore, a practical linear notation for trees is introduced (this is an extension of the notation already employed in Chapter 2).

A tiny extension to the standard theory of context-free grammars is made in 3.2. If one constructs a parse, this involves two different kinds of operations: constructing trees and verifying that leaves of these trees match words in the sentence. In a parsing schema we want to do *everything* in terms of trees; hence matching that a predicted word does indeed occur in the string will be defined as a tree operation as well. This extension is needed for a formal theory of parsing schemata but, as we will see in subsequent chapters, hardly relevant for the description of schemata of practical algorithms.

In 3.3 we define logical deduction systems. A *parsing system* for a given grammar and a given string is just such a deduction system. A parsing schema, then, is a more abstract object that can be instantiated to a parsing system by providing it with a grammar and a string. Parsing schemata are introduced in Section 3.5.

An interesting property of parsing schemata is *correctness*. One should be able to investigate whether a given parsing schema deduces the right parse trees (and only those). To that end, we define *enhanced* deduction systems in 3.4, for which an appropriate notion of syntactic correctness can be expressed. Parsing systems in 3.5 are defined as enhanced deduction systems.

The use of a logical system as an abstract notation for a chart parser (cf. Chapter 10) is due to Pereira and Warren [1980, 1983]. Parsing schemata have some deep relation with their work, but the emphasis is rather different. While the "Parsing as Deduction" approach is primarily interested in connecting the parsing logic with unification-based grammar formalisms, parsing schemata use deduction merely as a convenient notation in which we can describe context-free parsing algorithms.[1] Based on this notation, we can formally define and investigate *relationships* between parsing algorithms.

3.1 Context-free grammars

We recall some standard notions of formal language theory (see, e.g., [Harrison, 1978], [Sippu and Soisalon-Soininen, 1988]) that will be used throughout the remainder of this book. In addition, we introduce a convenient linear notation for trees that is somewhat more powerful than the notation used in Chapter 2.

Definition 3.1. (*strings*)
Let X be an arbitrary set. We write X^+ for the set of non-empty strings $x_1 \ldots x_k$, $(k \geq 1)$ over X.
We write X^* for the set of strings $x_1 \ldots x_k$, $(k \geq 0)$ over X. For $j = i - 1$, the sequence $x_i \ldots x_j$ denotes the empty string. For $j < i - 1$, the notation $x_i \ldots x_j$ is undefined.   □

Definition 3.2. (*context-free grammar*)
A *context-free grammar* (CFG) is a 4-tuple $G = (N, \Sigma, P, S)$ satisfying

(*i*)   the set of *nonterminals* N and the set of *terminals* Σ are alphabets taken from some universal class of symbols *Sym*, $N \cap \Sigma = \emptyset$;

---

[1] In Chapter 8 we also study unification grammar parsing, but note that we are interested in arbitrary parsing algorithms for a simple (PATR-based) unification grammar formalism, whereas, e.g., Shieber [1992] describes a single (Earley) parsing algorithm for arbitrary unification grammars.

(*ii*) the set of *productions* P consists of a finite number of pairs (A, α) with
$A \in N$, $\alpha \in (N \cup \Sigma)^*$;

(*iii*) the *start symbol* S is a nonterminal symbol from N.

We write $\mathcal{CFG}$ for the class of context-free grammars.   □

Definition 3.3. (*notations*)

(*i*)   We write V for $N \cup \Sigma$.

(*ii*)   Productions (A, α) are written as $A \to \alpha$.

(*iii*) We write
$A, B, C, \ldots$ for variables ranging over N;
$X, Y, \ldots$ for variables ranging over V;
$a, b, \ldots$ for variables ranging over Σ;
$v, w, x, \ldots$ for variables ranging over Σ^*;
$\alpha, \beta, \gamma, \delta, \ldots$ for variables ranging over V^*;
the empty string is denoted by ε.
A string that is to be parsed is usually denoted $a_1 \ldots a_n$.

(*iv*) The relation $\Rightarrow$ on $V^* \times V^*$ is defined by
$\alpha \Rightarrow \beta$ if there are α_1, α_2, A, γ such that
$\alpha = \alpha_1 A \alpha_2$, $\beta = \alpha_1 \gamma \alpha_2$ and $A \to \gamma \in P$.   □

Using the notational conventions introduced in (*iii*), we need not state from
which set an element is taken when we talk about some (arbitrary) a, A, α,
..., making the notation a little less burdensome. This practice has already
been adopted in (*iv*).

The relation $\Rightarrow$ is used mainly in combination with the transitive or the
transitive and reflective closure, denoted $\Rightarrow^+$, resp. $\Rightarrow^*$.

Definition 3.4. (*subclasses of CFG*)
We can define several useful subclasses of $\mathcal{CFG}$, the class of context-free
languages. Often used subclasses are *acyclic* CFGs and *ε-free* CFGs. In part
II we only use one subclass: grammars in Chomsky Normal Form.

• A context-free grammar G is in *Chomsky Normal Form* (CNF) if P contains productions of the form $A \to BC$ and $A \to a$ only.
We write $\mathcal{CNF}$ for the class of grammars in Chomsky Normal Form.   □

Definition 3.5. (*trees*)
Let $\mathcal{U}$ be the class of finitely branching finite trees in which children of a
node have a left-to-right ordering, and every node is labelled with a symbol
from $\mathcal{Sym}$. For $G = (N, \Sigma, P, S) \in \mathcal{CFG}$, the set $\mathcal{Trees}(G) \subset \mathcal{U}$ is the set of
trees with labels in $N \cup \Sigma \cup \{\varepsilon\}$, in which every node u satisfies one of the
following conditions:

• u is a leaf;
• u is labelled A, the children of u are labelled $X_1, \ldots, X_n$ and there is a
production $A \to X_1 \cdots X_n \in P$;

- u is labelled A, u has one child labelled ε and there is a production $A{\to}\varepsilon \in P$.

We write $\tau, \sigma, \ldots$ for tree variables. □

Definition 3.6. (*root, yield*)
For $G \in \mathcal{CFG}$ and $\tau \in \mathcal{Trees}(G)$ we define

$root(\tau)$ is the label of the root of τ;
$yield(\tau)$ is the string that is obtained by concatenating the labels of all leaves of τ in left-to-right order. □

The leaves of τ are labelled with symbols from $V \cup \{\varepsilon\}$. The yield is a string in V^*, as the empty string symbol ε disappears in concatenation. Only if all leaves are labelled ε then $yield(\tau)$ is the empty string.

Definition 3.7. (*parse tree*)
A tree $\tau \in \mathcal{Trees}(G)$ is called a *parse tree* or a *parse* for a string $a_1 \ldots a_n$ if $root(\tau) = S$ and $yield(\tau) = a_1 \ldots a_n$.
A string in Σ^* is called *valid* with respect to G if it has a parse tree. A valid string is also called a *sentence*. □

We introduce a convenient, linear notation for trees that will be used throughout the remainder of this book.

Definition 3.8. (*linear tree notation*)
An arbitrary tree with root $A \in N$ and yield $\alpha \in V^*$ is denoted $\langle A \rightsquigarrow \alpha \rangle$; see Figure 3.1(a). Note that, in general, there are many trees satisfying these conditions (if we want to be more specific about the structure of the tree, we can use nested expression as introduced below). As a special case, we write $\langle A{\to}\alpha \rangle$ for a tree that has a root and a sequence of leaves, but no intermediate nodes. Thus a tree $\langle A{\to}\alpha \rangle$ corresponds to a single production $A{\to}\alpha \in P$, see Figure 3.1(b).
We also use nested expressions for trees. The expression

$$\langle A \rightsquigarrow \alpha \langle B \rightsquigarrow \beta \rangle \gamma \rangle$$

denotes a tree $\langle A \rightsquigarrow \alpha\beta\gamma \rangle$ that can be constructed by replacing the leaf B in a tree $\langle A \rightsquigarrow \alpha B\beta \rangle$ by a subtree $\langle B \rightsquigarrow \beta \rangle$. See Figure 3.1(c). As a convenient shorthand, a tree

$$\langle A \rightsquigarrow \alpha \langle B_1 \rightsquigarrow \beta_1 \rangle \cdots \langle B_n \rightsquigarrow \beta_n \rangle \gamma \rangle,$$

as shown in Figure 3.1(d), will be denoted by

$$\langle A \rightsquigarrow \alpha \langle B_1 \cdots B_n \rightsquigarrow \beta_1 \cdots \beta_n \rangle \gamma \rangle.$$

We write $\langle A \rightsquigarrow \alpha \langle \beta \rightsquigarrow \gamma \rangle \delta \rangle$ if there is a series of n subtrees $\tau_1, \ldots, \tau_n$ such that $\beta = root(\tau_1) \cdots root(\tau_n)$ and $\gamma = yield(\tau_1) \cdots yield(\tau_n)$. Occasionally it will be convenient to use this notation for $n = 0$. It evidently holds that $\langle A \rightsquigarrow \alpha \langle \varepsilon \rightsquigarrow \varepsilon \rangle \beta \rangle = \langle A \rightsquigarrow \alpha\beta \rangle$. □

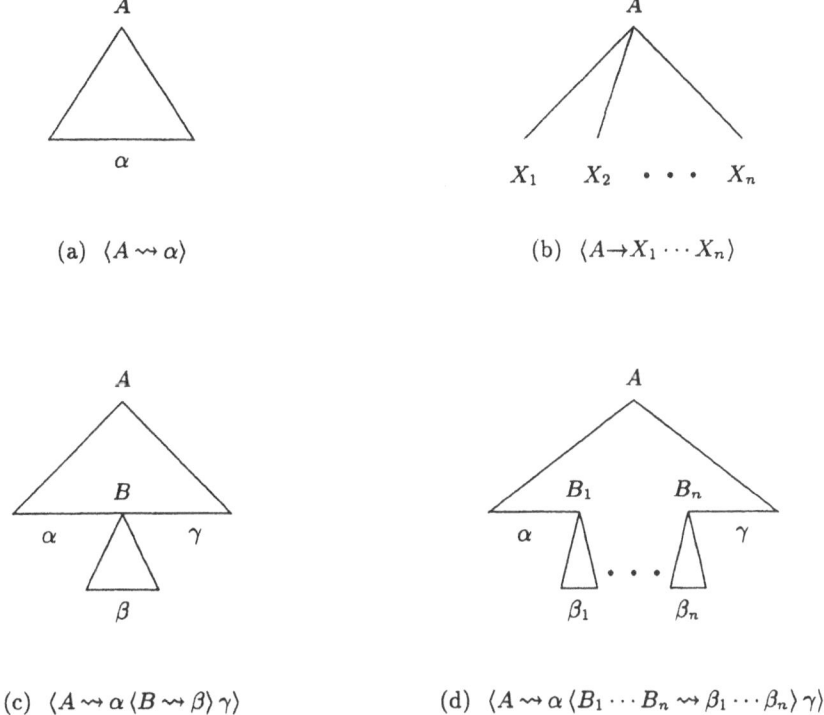

(a) $\langle A \rightsquigarrow \alpha \rangle$ (b) $\langle A \rightarrow X_1 \cdots X_n \rangle$

(c) $\langle A \rightsquigarrow \alpha \langle B \rightsquigarrow \beta \rangle \gamma \rangle$ (d) $\langle A \rightsquigarrow \alpha \langle B_1 \cdots B_n \rightsquigarrow \beta_1 \cdots \beta_n \rangle \gamma \rangle$

Fig. 3.1. Some kinds of trees and their linear denotation

3.2 Some small extensions to context-free grammars

We introduce a small nonstandard extension to context-free grammars. This is needed for the formal definition of tree-based parsing schemata in 3.5 but hardly relevant for the following chapters.

At the end of this section we have a closer look at the status of *pre-terminals* in natural language parsing.

The work that has to be done in parsing a sentence is mainly, but not exclusively, concerned with constructing (parts of) parse trees. We also have to verify that the constructed (partial) trees do indeed derive (part of) the sentence we want to have parsed.

Consider the following hypothetical example. We have a sentence *abcde*, and the grammar contains a production $A \rightarrow abc$. From reading the first a we may conclude that the production $A \rightarrow abc$ *could* apply here, so we add $\langle A \rightarrow abc \rangle$ to the set of partial trees that could contribute to the construction of a parse for *abcde*. The next two steps then would be to *verify* that indeed b is the second and c is the third word of the sentence. Only after having done so, we may conclude that $\langle A{\rightarrow}abc \rangle$ is in fact a parse tree for the subsentence abc. If we parse another sentence $abd\ldots$, we will also conjecture that $\langle A{\rightarrow}abc \rangle$ is a partial parse, but this time it will be disqualified when we read the third word of the sentence.

From this example it is clear that it makes sense to introduce some notation indicating which leaves of a tree are truly part of the sentence and which leaves are only conjectured and have to be verified still. A standard solution is to make a difference between *expanded* and *unexpanded* leaves of a tree. If we indicate expansion of leaves by underlining, the fact that $A{\rightarrow}abc$ is a partial parse for the first part of the sentence would be established by deriving a sequence of trees

$$\langle A{\rightarrow}\underline{a}bc \rangle, \ \langle A{\rightarrow}\underline{ab}c \rangle, \ \langle A{\rightarrow}\underline{abc} \rangle.$$

We will use a slightly more subtle scheme, however, in which nodes are not simply expanded but expanded *to a particular position in the sentence*. This rules out any ambiguity, for example when expanded leaves labelled with terminals are separated by an unexpanded leaf labelled with a nonterminal. Furthermore, we can denote the notion "a occurs at position j in the sentence" by a particular kind of tree (it is this tree with which a terminal leaf is expanded). Hence the entire parsing process can be described in terms of tree manipulation. This is precisely what we have done informally in the Primordial Soup approach in Chapter 2.

At the same time we introduce a notational convention that is used by many parsing algorithms: the end of the sentence can be indicated by an *end-of-sentence marker*, usually denoted $, which is added to a string $a_1 \ldots a_n$ as the $(n+1)$-st symbol. Similarly, we may sometimes use a *beginning-of-sentence marker*, denoted #, with is added to a string as the 0th symbol. It is assumed that $\#, \$ \notin V$.

Definition 3.9. (*marked terminal*)
For every $G \in \mathcal{CFG}$ a marked terminal is a pair $(a, j) \in (\Sigma \cup \{\#, \$\}) \times \mathbb{N}$. We usually write $\underline{a}_j$ rather than (a, j). We also write $\underline{\Sigma}$ for $(\Sigma \cup \{\#, \$\}) \times \mathbb{N}$.
$\square$

The natural number j is used to indicate the position of a word. For each word in the sentence a_j we will create a special tree $\langle a{\rightarrow}\underline{a}_j \rangle$. The sentence can now be represented as a *set* of trees, rather than a *string* of symbols. The initial set of trees for $a_1 \ldots a_n$ thus is

$$\{a{\rightarrow}\underline{a}_j \mid a \text{ is the } j\text{-th word of the sentence}\}$$

The beginning of the sentence in the above example is now parsed as follows. From $\langle A{\rightarrow}abc \rangle$ and $\langle a{\rightarrow}\underline{a}_1 \rangle$ we obtain $\langle A \rightsquigarrow \underline{a}_1 bc \rangle$. With $\langle b{\rightarrow}\underline{b}_2 \rangle$ this combines to $\langle A \rightsquigarrow \underline{a}_1 \underline{b}_2 c \rangle$, and so on. In this way we have replaced the concept of expanding a terminal by combining trees.

If needed, the end-of-sentence symbol may be represented by a tree $\langle \$ \rightarrow \underline{\$}_{n+1} \rangle$ and the beginning-of-sentence symbol by a tree $\langle \# \rightarrow \underline{\#}_0 \rangle$. In Section 3.5 we will argue that the end-of-sentence marker is a necessary extension, needed to infer that there is *no* word beyond position n, while the beginning-of-sentence marker is merely a notational convenience. The sentence, by definition, starts with word number 1.

In order to get things formally right, we have to extend some definitions.

Definition 3.10. (*extension of Definitions 3.2, 3.3, 3.5, and 3.7*)

(*i*)   A *pseudo-production* is a pair $(a, (a, j))$ with (a, j) a marked terminal. We usually write $a \rightarrow \underline{a}_j$ rather than $(a, (a, j))$. We write $\underline{P}$ for the set of pseudo-productions for a particular grammar.

(*ii*) The variables $\alpha, \beta, \gamma, \delta, \ldots$ may range over $N \cup \Sigma \cup \underline{\Sigma}$.

(*iii*) The class of trees $Trees(G)$ is extended to cover pseudo-productions as well. That is,
  - nodes carry labels from $N \cup \Sigma \cup \underline{\Sigma} \cup \{\varepsilon\}$,
  - in addition to the three alternatives in Definition 3.5, a node u may be labelled with a terminal a and have a single child labelled $\underline{a}_j$ for some j.

(*iv*) A tree $\tau \in Trees(G)$ is called a *marked parse tree* or *marked parse* for a sentence $a_1 \ldots a_n$ if $root(\tau) = S$ and $yield(\tau) = \underline{a}_1 \ldots \underline{a}_n$. $\square$

Definition 3.11. (*set of marked parse trees*)
The set of marked parse trees $\mathcal{P}_G^{(n)}$ for a given context-free grammar G and all strings of length n is defined by

$$\mathcal{P}_G^{(n)} = \{\tau \in Trees(G) \mid \exists a_1 \ldots a_n \in \Sigma^* : \\ root(\tau) = S \wedge yield(\tau) = \underline{a}_1 \ldots \underline{a}_n\}.$$

The set of marked parse trees $\mathcal{P}_G(a_1 \ldots a_n)$ for a given context-free grammar G and a particular string $a_1 \ldots a_n$ is defined by

$$\mathcal{P}_G(a_1 \ldots a_n) = \{\tau \in Trees(G) \mid root(\tau) = S \wedge yield(\tau) = \underline{a}_1 \ldots \underline{a}_n\}. \quad \square$$

A variety of parallel parsing algorithms can be formally expressed in terms of trees and operations on trees only. In order to cover the familiar *sequential* algorithms as well, we have to make another slight extension. One needs to express the fact that a tree with no marked terminals should expand downwards only to a particular position in the sentence.

Definition 3.12. (*left- and right-marked trees*)
A *left-marked tree* is a pair $(i, \tau) \in \mathbb{N} \times Trees(G)$. We usually write $i : \tau$ rather than (i, τ).
A *right-marked tree* is a pair $(\tau, i) \in Trees(G) \times \mathbb{N}$. We usually write $\tau : i$ rather than (τ, i). $\square$

Note that it is conceivable that trees could have a marking at some other position in the yield, rather than leftmost or rightmost. We will not formally define these; they will not be used in this book.

In formal language theory we distinguish between two kinds of symbols: terminals and nonterminals. In the analysis of natural language it is more convenient to distinguish three kinds of symbols: nonterminal categories, *lexical* (also called *pre-terminal*) categories, and words. From a formal point of view, it is clear that the words are terminals and that the pre-terminals are a subset of the nonterminals. In parsing algorithms, however, it is much more convenient to consider the lexical categories as terminals, and simply forget about the words. This has the advantage that the size of the grammar is reduced dramatically. A natural language grammar typically has not more than a few dozen lexical categories, while a dictionary may contain many thousands of words. A minor disadvantage is that a word may fall into different lexical categories, hence the (pre-)terminals in the string to be parsed are not uniquely defined. But for our theory of parsing schemata this is not a problem at all. The lexical categories of the words will be represented as hypotheses, and there is no objection to having different hypotheses about a single word. Moreover, if we regard lexical categories as terminals, than a marked terminal, as introduced above, can be seen as a lexical category annotated with a word at some position in the sentence.

Lifting terminals from real words to lexical categories causes an anomaly for grammars in Chomsky Normal Form. Consider again grammar G_2:[2]

$S \rightarrow NP\ VP$,
$S \rightarrow S\ PP$,
$NP \rightarrow *det\ *n$,
$NP \rightarrow NP\ PP$,
$VP \rightarrow *v\ NP$,
$PP \rightarrow *prep\ NP$.

If we regard $*n$, $*v$, $*det$ and $*prep$ as pre-terminal nonterminals this grammar is in $\mathcal{CNF}$. If we regard the lexical categories as terminals, on the other hand, the definition of Chomsky Normal Form must be adapted. In Chapter 2 we have avoided the issue by calling such grammars binary branching. In Chapters 3–6, where we develop a formal theory of parsing schemata, we will stick to the formal definition of Chomsky Normal Form as presented in Definition 3.4.

In sum, whether lexical categories are treated by a parser as terminals or as preterminal nonterminals is not relevant for the theory of parsing schemata.

---

[2] Following standard convention, we abreviate $*noun$ and $*verb$ to $*n$ and $*v$. Sometimes, when there are space restrictions (in many figures) we also abbreviate $*det$ and $*prep$ to $*d$ and $*p$.

3.3 Deduction systems

The general concept of a deduction system, as we will present it here, conforms to deduction systems as they are known in mathematical logic. The details of our definition are somewhat idiosyncratic, however. Here we present deduction systems in a way that facilitates easy definitions of derived concepts in subsequent sections and chapters.

A deduction system contains an arbitrary set of objects, called *entities*. The purpose of a deduction system, in a narrow sense, is that it allows to establish which entities are *valid*. From an initial set of *hypotheses*, by means of a set of *deduction steps*, the validity of entities can be deduced.

The word "entity" is not supposed to mean anything, other than an identifiable object. When we come to parsing systems and parsing schemata, these entities will be trees (in this chapter) or items (in the next chapters) that are employed by some chart parser. Note that the term "item" is, in general, equally void of meaning. We will give it a precise meaning in the context of parsing schemata in Sections 4.3 and 4.4.

The initially valid entities in a logical deduction system are usually called *axiomata*. We use the word "hypothesis" on purpose, because it suggests truth of a much more volatile nature than an axiom. In a deduction system that is (an abstraction of) a parser for a particular grammar, the entities and deduction steps are fixed; the hypotheses vary according to the string that is to be parsed.

Finally, where a deduction system conventionally has a *set of inference rules*, each rule having its own arity, we lump these together into a single set of inferences, called deduction steps.

Definition 3.13. (*deduction step, antecedent, consequent*)
Let X be a set of entities, H a set of hypotheses. A deduction step is a pair (Y, x) with $Y \subseteq H \cup X$ a finite set and $x \in X$.
We write $\wp(Z)$ for the power set (i.e. the set of subsets) of any Z. We write $\wp_{fin}(Z)$ for the set of all finite subsets of Z. Hence a deduction step (Y, x) is an element of the set $\wp_{fin}(H \cup X) \times X$.
In a deduction step $(\{y_1, \ldots, y_k\}, x)$, the entities $y_1, \ldots, y_k$ are called the *antecedents* and x is called the *consequent* of the deduction step.   □

Definition 3.14. (*deduction system*)
A deduction system $\mathbb{D}$ is a triple $\langle X, H, D \rangle$, with

X a set of entities, called the *domain* of $\mathbb{D}$;
H a set of hypotheses;
$D \subseteq \wp_{fin}(H \cup X) \times X$ a set of deduction steps.   □

The astute reader will be astonished, perhaps, that H is not necessarily a subset of X. It seems rather more natural to assume $H \subseteq X$, and $D \subseteq$

$\wp_{fin}(X) \times X$. The reason for this idiosyncratic definition is pragmatic. It does not do any harm to the theory when some (or all) hypotheses are outside the domain of the deduction system. A minor nuisance is that we have to write $H \cup X$ rather than X. The specification of realistic parsing schemata is simplified, in fact, by assuming the hypotheses to be outside the domain. In the Examples 3.19 and 3.20 that will follow shortly, hypotheses are contained in the domain as one would normally assume.

It should be noted that a deduction step may have zero antecedents. If $(\emptyset, x) \in D$ then x can always be deduced, regardless of the set of hypotheses.

If we know that x can be inferred from y_1 and y_2, using a deduction step $(\{y_1, y_2\}, x)$, then it should also be possible to infer x from a *superset* of the antecedents, e.g., y_1, y_2, and y_3. There is no guarantee, however, that if $(\{y_1, y_2\}, x) \in D$ then also $(\{y_1, y_2, y_3\}, x) \in D$. To this end we define an inference relation $\vdash$, that is the closure of D under addition of antecedents to an inference.

Definition 3.15. (*inference relation* $\vdash$)
Let $\mathbb{D} = \langle X, H, D \rangle$, be a deduction system. The relation $\vdash \subseteq \wp(H \cup X) \times X$ is defined by

$$Y \vdash x \text{ if } (Y', x) \in D \text{ for some } Y' \subseteq Y. \qquad \square$$

It has some practical advantages to allow an infinite set of antecedents of $\vdash$. If, for example, some x can be directly inferred from some hypotheses, we may write $H \vdash x$, even though H can be an infinite set.

When an entity can be deduced from a given set of entities by a *series* of inferences, we will use the notation $\vdash^*$ (to be introduced in Definition 3.17). The symbol $\vdash$ is reserved for a single-step inference.

Each deduction step is a valid inference, by definition it holds that $D \subseteq \vdash$. We will use the inference symbol $\vdash$ also to define (sets of) deduction steps. When we write $Y \vdash x$ it is usually not relevant whether $Y \vdash x$ is an element of D or $Y \vdash x$ is obtained from some $(Y', x) \in D$ with $Y' \subset Y$. The set D can be considered as a *defining subset* of $\vdash$. We make the difference between D and $\vdash$ only because it is much easier for the *specification* of a deduction system to define the "essential" subset D rather than the full set of inferences $\vdash$. In the rare cases where it is essential for some argument that a deduction step is in D, and not any derived inference, we will denote the deduction step by (Y, x) rather than the the informal notation $Y \vdash x$.

As a second, informal simplification of the notation, we write $y_1, \ldots, y_k \vdash x$, rather than $\{y_1, \ldots, y_k\} \vdash x$ to indicate that the consequent x can be deduced from the antecedents $y_1, \ldots, y_k$. In most deduction systems there is a clear distinction between entities and sets of entities and no confusion can arise when the curly brackets are deleted. Only if a set of entities can be an entity by itself, e.g., $y = \{y_1, \ldots, y_k\}$, the informal notation $y \vdash x$ is ambiguous and cannot be used. In any such case where confusion could arise, it will be stated explicitly that we switch to the formal notation where set brackets cannot be deleted.

Definition 3.16. (*deduction sequences*)
We write X^+ for the set of non-empty, finite sequences $x_1, \ldots, x_j$, with $j \geq 1$ and $x_i \in X$ $(1 \leq i \leq j)$. Let $\mathbb{D} = \langle X, H, D \rangle$, be a deduction system.
An *inference sequence* or a *deduction sequence* in $\mathbb{D}$ is a pair $(Y; x_1, \ldots, x_j) \in (H \cup X) \times X^+$, such that

$$Y \cup \{x_1, \ldots, x_{i-1}\} \vdash x_i \quad \text{for } 1 \leq i \leq j.$$

As a practical informal notation we write

$$Y \vdash x_1 \vdash \ldots \vdash x_j$$

for a deduction sequence $(Y; x_1, \ldots, x_j)$.
The *set of deduction sequences* $\Delta(\mathbb{D}) \subseteq \wp(H \cup X) \times X^+$ for $\mathbb{D}$ is defined by

$$\Delta(\mathbb{D}) = \{(Y; x_1, \ldots, x_j) \in \wp(H \cup X) \times X^+ \mid Y \vdash x_1 \vdash \ldots \vdash x_j\}.$$

When it is clear from the context which deduction system is meant, we write Δ rather than $\Delta(\mathbb{D})$. $\qquad\square$

Definition 3.17. (*transitive and reflexive inference relation* $\vdash^*$)
Let $\mathbb{D} = \langle X, H, D \rangle$ be a deduction system.
We define the relations $\vdash^0$, $\vdash^+$ and $\vdash^*$ on $\wp(H \cup X) \times X$ as follows.

$$Y \vdash^0 x \quad \text{if } x \in Y,$$
$$Y \vdash^+ x \quad \text{if } Y \vdash \ldots \vdash x,$$
$$Y \vdash^* x \quad \text{if } Y \vdash^0 x \text{ or } Y \vdash^+ x. \qquad\square$$

We do not make a distinction between semantic validity (usually denoted $\models x$) and syntactic provability (i.e. $H \vdash^* x$). We are only concerned with syntactic structure here, the concept of semantic validity simply doesn't exist in this context. A notion of correctness of a deduction system for a given specific purpose will be introduced in Section 3.4.

Definition 3.18. (*validity*)
Let $\mathbb{D} = \langle X, H, D \rangle$, be a deduction system.
The set of *valid entities*, denoted $\mathcal{V}(\mathbb{D})$, is defined by

$$\mathcal{V}(\mathbb{D}) = \{x \in X \mid H \vdash^* x\}.$$

We usually write $\mathcal{V}$, rather than $\mathcal{V}(\mathbb{D})$, if it is clear from the context which deduction system is meant. $\qquad\square$

Example 3.19. (*propositional logic*)
A logical deduction system is a deduction system $\langle \mathit{Wff}, \mathit{Ax}, D \rangle$ in which Wff is a set of well-formed formulae, $\mathit{Ax} \subset \mathit{Wff}$ is a set of axioms, and D a set that contains all instantiations of all proof rules. Standard propositional logic (see, e.g., Mendelsohn [1964]) is cast into a deduction system as follows.

Wff is the smallest set satisfying

- some given set of proposition symbols is a subset of *Wff*;
- if $\phi \in Wff$ then also $\neg\phi \in Wff$;
- if $\phi, \psi \in Wff$ then also $(\phi\rightarrow\psi) \in Wff$.

A set of axioms for propositional logic is:

$$Ax_1 = \{\phi\rightarrow(\psi\rightarrow\phi) \mid \phi, \psi \in Wff\},$$

$$Ax_2 = \{(\phi\rightarrow(\psi\rightarrow\chi))\rightarrow((\phi\rightarrow\psi)\rightarrow(\phi\rightarrow\chi)) \mid \phi, \psi, \chi \in Wff\},$$

$$Ax_3 = \{(\neg\psi\rightarrow\neg\phi)\rightarrow((\neg\phi\rightarrow\psi)\rightarrow\phi) \mid \phi, \psi \in Wff\},$$

$$Ax = Ax_1 \cup Ax_2 \cup Ax_3.$$

The set of deduction steps, finally, is given by

$$D = \{\phi, (\phi\rightarrow\psi) \vdash \psi \mid \phi, \psi \in Wff\}.$$

The set of deduction steps D is a relation over $Wff^2 \times Wff$, and is known as the inference rule *modus ponens*. □

Example 3.20. (*CYK*)
The CYK algorithm, named after Cocke, Younger and Kasami [Younger, 1967], [Kasami, 1965], is defined for grammars in Chomsky Normal Form(cf. Definition 3.4). For a given grammar (N, Σ, P, S) in $\mathcal{CNF}$ and string $a_1 \ldots a_n$ a deduction system $\langle \mathcal{I}, H, D \rangle$ for the CYK algorithm is given by

$$\mathcal{I} = \{[A, i, j] \mid 0 \leq i < j \wedge A \in N\};$$

$$H = \{[A, j-1, j] \mid A\rightarrow a_j \in P \wedge 1 \leq j \leq n\};$$

$$D = \{[B, i, j], [C, j, k] \vdash [A, i, k] \mid A\rightarrow BC \in P \wedge 0 \leq i < k < j\}.$$

Note that the set of CYK items and the set of deduction steps are infinite, as they are not bounded by the length of the string. This has been done on purpose, in the sequel we will take care to define deduction systems in such a way that only the hypotheses depend on the particular string, while the sets of entities and deduction steps are fixed for a given grammar, hence $\mathcal{I}$ and D have to be able to cope with strings of arbitrary length. The fact that there is an infinite number of entities and deduction steps does not cause any practical problems; for parsing any given string, only a finite subset needs to be used.
The set of derivable CYK-items is characterized by

$$\mathcal{V}(\mathbb{D}) = \{[A, i, j] \mid A\Rightarrow^* a_{i+1} \ldots a_j\},$$

this is easily verified by induction on the length of a derivation sequence $\Rightarrow^*$.
□

3.4 Enhanced deduction systems

In Section 3.5 and Chapter 4 we will describe (abstractions of) parsing and recognition algorithms by means of deduction systems. An important property of algorithms is *correctness*. For a deduction system, similarly, we need to be able to state that it is correct for a specific given purpose. In order to formally capture this property we introduce *enhanced* deduction systems.

We have no semantic interpretation of deduction systems, hence we must establish a purely syntactic criterion for correctness. To this end we postulate the existence of a set of *final* entities, which is a subset of $\mathcal{I}$. These final entities are divided into *correct* and *incorrect* final entities. Which ones are correct is known by definition. (When a deduction system is used for some particular purpose, there will be some motivation behind the definition of correct final items, but from a formal point of view the definition is arbitrary.) A deduction system is correct if it all correct final items are valid and all incorrect final items are invalid.

When entities are trees, for example, we can take as final entities those trees that constitute a parse for some sentence. The correct final items, then, should be all the parse trees for a given particular sentence. Incorrect final items are all those trees that are valid parse trees, but for other sentences than the one that is to be parsed.

This is formalized as follows.

Definition 3.21. (*enhanced deduction systems*)
A enhanced deduction system $\mathbb{E}$ is a quintuple $\langle X, H, F, C, D \rangle$, with

X a set of entities,
H a finite set of hypotheses,
$F \subseteq X$ a set of *final* entities,
$C \subseteq F$ a set of *correct* final entities,
$D \subseteq \wp_{fin}(H \cup X) \times X$ a set of derivation steps. $\qquad\square$

The set F represents the entities that we are really interested in; the other entities in $X \setminus (H \cup F)$ are "intermediate" entities that may help to derive the validity of the correct final entities. It is not demanded that F, or even C be finite. (In a cyclic grammar, for example, most sentences have an infinite number of parse trees. An algorithm that enumerates all parses is correct, in a sense, even though it doesn't finish.)

The relations $\vdash$ and $\vdash^*$ are as in Definition 3.15, the sets of valid entities $\mathcal{V}(\mathbb{E})$ as in Definition 3.18.

Definition 3.22. (*correctness*)
Let $\mathbb{E} = \langle X, H, F, C, D \rangle$ be an enhanced deduction system.

$\mathbb{E}$ is *sound* if all valid final entities are correct, i.e., $F \cap \mathcal{V}(\mathbb{E}) \subseteq C$,
$\mathbb{E}$ is *complete* if all correct final entities are valid, i.e., $C \subseteq F \cap \mathcal{V}(\mathbb{E})$,
$\mathbb{E}$ is *correct* if $\mathbb{E}$ is sound and complete, i.e., $C = F \cap \mathcal{V}(\mathbb{E})$. $\qquad\square$

Example 3.23. (*yes/no system*)
A yes/no system focuses on the question whether a particular single entity is correct or not. A yes/no system is an enhanced derivation system of the form

$$\langle X, H, \{y\}, C, D \rangle$$

where $y \in X$ is the entity of which the validity is to be decided upon.   □

Example 3.24.
Any deduction system $\mathbb{D} = \langle X, H, D \rangle$ can be extended to a correct enhanced deduction system

$$\langle X, H, X, \mathcal{V}(\mathbb{D}), D \rangle.$$ □

Example 3.25. (*CYK, continued*)
Consider, again, the CYK deduction system $\langle \mathcal{I}, H, D \rangle$ as in Example 3.20. How should we define the enhanced system? That depends on what we see as the result that should be computed by the CYK algorithm. If we see CYK as a recognizer *sec*, then we only want a yes/no answer to be delivered. Hence we can define

$$F = \{[S, 0, n]\},$$

and in order to prove the correctness of the system we have to show that $C = F$ if $a_1 \ldots a_n$ is a valid sentence and $C = \emptyset$ otherwise.
On the other hand, if we see the CYK algorithm as a parsing algorithm (of the kind that does not deliver parse trees but a useful set of partial results), we are interested in the entire set of valid items. From this point of view the proper way to enhance the deduction system of Example 3.20 is to define

$$F = \mathcal{I},$$

$$C = \{[A, i, j] \mid A \Rightarrow^* a_{i+1} \ldots a_j\}.$$

In order to prove the correctness of CYK, according to this definition, we have to establish that $\mathcal{V} = C$.   □

The main point in defining enhanced deduction systems is that we need a formal notion of correctness, that allows us to formally define what constitutes a correct parsing schema. From Example 3.25 it is clear that this can be done in different ways. From a formal point of view, the first approach is the right one. CYK is, strictly speaking, a recognition algorithm. Such an algorithm is correct, by definition, if it yields a single yes/no answer indicating whether the string is correct or not. From a more practical perspective, however, we see CYK as a parser and adopt the second point of view. On top of a yes/no answer whether a string is a sentence, a set of valid items is recognized from which the parse trees can be constructed. It is this set $\mathcal{V}$ we are interested in, as the "output" of CYK, hence the second enhancement is the appropriate one.

The same considerations apply to any chart parsing algorithm. It is the final chart, the set $\mathcal{V}$ in our terminology, that we are interested in. The problem is that one cannot give a *general* definition of $\mathcal{V}$. Which items are on the final chart of a parser depends, of course, on the way in which the parser tries to construct a parse tree.

Hence we cannot *formalize* the second notion of correctness. As we are constructing a formal theory here, we will adopt the first notion and regard a chart parser as a recognition algorithm. When we come to describe parsing system reflecting *real* algorithms (that is, algorithms described in the literature as parsers, not as simple examples), however, we won't even define the enhanced system but concentrate on the properties of the set $\mathcal{V}(\mathbb{D})$ instead.

3.5 Tree-based parsing schemata

A parsing system is a deduction system for a given grammar and string. A parsing schema is a more abstract object that defines a parsing system for arbitrary grammars and strings.

First, we will consider a deduction system for a given grammar $G = (N, \Sigma, P, S)$ and a given string $a_1 \ldots a_n$. The domain of such a deduction system is a subset of $\mathcal{T}rees(G)$ (including the extensions with pseudo-productions, cf. Definition 3.10.(iii)). The set of deduction steps D encodes how new trees can be obtained from trees that have been derived already. The initial set of trees is given by the set of hypotheses H.

A system is complete if all marked parse trees for the string are deduced. A system is sound if no marked parse tree for a different string *of the same length* can be deduced. It is conceivable, however, that a marked parse tree for a string of *shorter* length is deduced by a sound tree-based parsing system. Consider, for example, the case that $S \Rightarrow^* a_1 \ldots a_k$ and $S \Rightarrow^* Sa_{k+1} \ldots a_n$. Then a marked parse tree $\langle S \rightsquigarrow \underline{a}_1 \ldots \underline{a}_k \rangle$ could be found while parsing $a_1 \ldots a_n$.

Definition 3.26. ((*instantiated*) *tree-based parsing system*)
Let G be a context-free grammar and $a_1 \ldots a_n \in \Sigma^*$ and arbitrary string. A deduction system $\langle \mathcal{T}, H, D \rangle$ is called an *instantiated tree-based parsing system* for G and $a_1 \ldots a_n$ when the following conditions are satisfied:[3]

(i) $\mathcal{T} \subseteq \mathcal{T}rees(G)$,
(ii) $\mathcal{P}_G^{(n)} \subset \mathcal{T}$,
(iii) $\langle a \rightarrow \underline{a}_i \rangle \in H$ for each a_1, $1 \leq i \leq n$ □

Usually we will drop the adjective "instantiated" and talk about a *tree-based parsing system* for G and $a_1 \ldots a_n$.

---

[3] (Cf. Definition 3.11 for $\mathcal{P}_G^{(n)}$).

Definition 3.27. (*correct tree-based parsing system*)
An instantiated tree-based parsing system $\langle \mathcal{T}, H, D \rangle$ for a grammar G and a
string $a_1 \ldots a_n$ is *correct* if the enhanced deduction system

$$\langle \mathcal{T}, H, \mathcal{P}_G^{(n)}, \mathcal{P}_G(a_1 \ldots a_n), D \rangle$$

is correct. □

   The set of hypotheses H will be different for different input strings, obviously. It provides the initial trees from which everything else is derived. It
would make sense (but it is not implied by the above definition) that the set
of deduction steps D is not dependent on a particular input string. This will
be a consequence of the next definition, in which we consider parsing systems
for arbitrary strings. The fact that the domain of a parsing system should be
independent of the string that is to be parsed has been anticipated in Def-
initions 3.26 and 3.27. It would suffice to demand that $\mathcal{P}_G(a_1 \ldots a_n) \subset \mathcal{T}$,
rather than $\mathcal{P}_G^{(n)} \subset \mathcal{T}$, so as to make sure that $\langle \mathcal{T}, H, D \rangle$ is a valid parsing
system for $a_1 \ldots a_n$. (The set of final entities would then be $\mathcal{P}_G^{(n)} \cap \mathcal{T}$, which
does not necessarily equal $\mathcal{P}_G^{(n)}$). Marked parse trees of strings that are *not*
to be parsed need not necessarily be contained in the domain of the system.
But, obviously, all marked parses of any string must be in $\mathcal{T}$ if it is to serve
as a domain of a parsing system for arbitrary strings.

Definition 3.28. (*uninstantiated tree-based parsing system*)
Let G be a context-free grammar. An *uninstantiated tree-based parsing system*
for G is a triple $\langle \mathcal{T}, \mathcal{K}, D \rangle$ with with $\mathcal{K} : \Sigma^* \to \wp(\mathit{Trees}(G))$ a function such
that $\langle \mathcal{T}, \mathcal{K}(a_1 \ldots a_n), D \rangle$ is a tree-based parsing system for each $a_1 \ldots a_n \in$
Σ^*. An uninstantiated tree-based parsing system $\langle \mathcal{T}, \mathcal{K}, D \rangle$ is *correct* if $\langle \mathcal{T},$
$\mathcal{K}(a_1 \ldots a_n), D \rangle$ is correct for each $a_1 \ldots a_n \in \Sigma^*$. □

We will blur the distinction between instantiated and uninstantiated systems
somewhat; as a practical notation we write $\mathbb{T}(a_1 \ldots a_n)$ or simply $\mathbb{T}$ to denote
both. In an instantiated system, $a_1 \ldots a_n$ denotes a particular string and in
an uninstantiated system $a_1 \ldots a_n$ denotes a formal parameter for a string.
This won't cause any confusion.

Definition 3.29. (*tree-based parsing schema*)
A a tree-based parsing schema $\mathbf{T}$ for a class of grammars $\mathcal{CG}$ is a function
that assigns an uninstantiated tree-based parsing system to every grammar
$G \in \mathcal{CG}$.
$\mathbf{T}$ is *correct* if, for each $G \in \mathcal{CG}$, the uninstantiated tree-based parsing system
$\mathbf{T}(G)$ is correct. □

Definition 3.30. (*the function $\mathcal{K}$*)
In all examples of tree-based parsing systems and schemata we will use the
the same function $\mathcal{K}$, defined by

$$\mathcal{K}(a_1 \ldots a_n) = \{\langle a \to \underline{a}_i \rangle \mid a = a_i\} \cup \{\langle \# \to \underline{\#}_0 \rangle, \langle \$ \to \underline{\$}_{n+1} \rangle\}.$$ □

The end-of-sentence marker \$ and beginning-of-sentence marker # are added for convenience. In some parsing schemata it is rather more easy to define $D(G)$ when every word in the sentence has a left and right neighbour, also the first and the last word. We will not use these sentence markers until Chapter 6, however. Only when we discuss filtering we will see practical examples of their use.

It is always possible to convert a parsing system using the beginning-of-sentence marker into a system without it. One simply has to adapt the deduction steps for the special case that one of its arguments would extend to the left of position 0. The situation at the end of the sentence is different, however. It might be essential to know that a tree of a certain kind (c.q. the next word of the string) does *not* exist. As negative information can't be handled in our formalism, the *non*existence of a $(n+1)$-st word is stated in a positive way by the end-of-sentence marker.

As we always use the same function $\mathcal{K}$, a parsing schema **T** is fully specified by a defining a pair $\langle \mathcal{T}(G), D(G) \rangle$ for an arbitrary grammar $G \in \mathcal{CG}$. For each grammar $G \in \mathcal{CG}$ and string $a_1 \ldots a_n \in \Sigma^*$ the schema materializes to a deduction system

$$\mathbf{T}(G)(a_1 \ldots a_n) = \langle \mathcal{T}(G), \mathcal{K}(a_1 \ldots a_n), D(G) \rangle.$$

It is possible, although somewhat cumbersome, to give a characterization of a universal class of parsing schemata. Let $(X \rightarrow Y)$ denote the class of functions from X to Y. Let $\mathcal{CG}$ be a class of context-free grammars, Sym be a universal set of symbols from which N, Σ, and $\underline{\Sigma}$ are drawn, $\mathcal{U}$ the universal set of labelled trees. Then $\mathcal{T} \subset \mathcal{U}$, or $\mathcal{T} \in \wp(\mathcal{U})$. Furthermore, $\mathcal{K} \in (Sym^* \rightarrow \wp(\mathcal{U}))$ and $D \in \wp(\wp_{fin}(\mathcal{U}) \times \mathcal{U})$. Hence the universal class of parse schemata is a subclass of

$$(\mathcal{CG} \rightarrow (\wp(\mathcal{U}) \times (Sym^* \rightarrow \wp(\mathcal{U})) \times \wp(\wp_{fin}(\mathcal{U}) \times \mathcal{U})))$$

One could add constraints to this huge class of objects such that that only "meaningful" elements remain, but that is not very interesting. The more important fact is that we have a formally defined a "universe of parsing schemata", in which we can reason about schemata, define relations between them and invent substitutions that transform a parsing schema into a different parsing schema.

Example 3.31. (**PS**, *a schema for the Primordial Soup algorithm*)
A Primordial Soup parsing schema **PS** is defined as follows. For an arbitrary $G \in \mathcal{CFG}$ and $a_1 \ldots a_n \in \Sigma^*$ we define a tree-based parsing system $\mathbb{T}_{PS} = \langle \mathcal{T}, \mathcal{K}(a_1 \ldots a_n), D \rangle$ with $\mathcal{K}(a_1 \ldots a_n)$ as in Definition 3.30. We make use of a predicate *allowed* that is true for a tree if both the word order constraint and the width constraint are obeyed. Different definitions for these constraints are possible; which one is chosen doesn't matter for the general idea of the Primordial Soup schema (cf. Definition 2.1):

$$\mathcal{T} \;=\; \{\tau \in \mathit{Trees}(G) \mid \mathit{allowed}(\tau)\};$$

$$D^{(1)} \;=\; \{\vdash \langle A\!\rightarrow\!\alpha\rangle \mid A\!\rightarrow\!\alpha \in P\},$$

$$D^{(2)} \;=\; \{\sigma,\tau \vdash \sigma \lhd \tau \mid \sigma \lhd \tau \in \mathcal{T}\},$$

$$D \;=\; D^{(1)} \cup D^{(2)}.$$

Unlike the intuitive version of the Primordial Soup algorithm in Chapter 2, we make a distinction here between elementary trees that constitute marked terminals (the hypotheses) and elementary trees that represent the productions of the grammar. These last ones are included in the deduction steps, but do not need an antecedent. Productions are always valid, irrespective of the sentence. The second set of deduction steps denotes all possible instances of valid composition.

The description of production trees as (antecedentless) derivation steps, rather than hypotheses, is a consequence of the general principle that the sentence is coded by $\mathcal{K}$, while the grammar is covered by D.   □

Example 3.32. (TCYK, *a tree-based parsing schema for CYK*)
A tree-based parsing schema **TCYK** can be given for $\mathcal{CNF}$, the class of grammars in Chomsky Normal Form. For an arbitrary grammar $G \in \mathcal{CNF}$ we define $\mathbb{T}_{CYK} = \langle \mathcal{T}, \mathcal{K}(a_1 \ldots a_n), D\rangle$ by

$$\mathcal{T} \;=\; \{\tau \in \mathit{Trees}(G) \mid \mathit{yield}(\tau) \in \underline{\Sigma}^*\};$$

$$D^{(1)} \;=\; \{\langle a\!\rightarrow\!\underline{a}_i\rangle \vdash \langle A\!\rightarrow\!\langle a\!\rightarrow\!\underline{a}_i\rangle\rangle \mid A\!\rightarrow\!a \in P\}$$

$$D^{(2)} \;=\; \{\langle B \rightsquigarrow \underline{a}_{i+1}\cdots\underline{a}_j\rangle, \langle C \rightsquigarrow \underline{a}_{j+1}\cdots\underline{a}_k\rangle$$
$$\vdash \langle A \rightsquigarrow \underline{a}_{i+1}\cdots\underline{a}_k\rangle \mid A\!\rightarrow\!BC \in P\}.$$

$$D \;=\; D^{(1)} \cup D^{(2)}$$

The first set of deduction steps is to derive the nonterminals we usually start with, because for the sake of standardization the hypotheses cover the terminals in the sentence.   □

3.6 Conclusion

We have given a formal definition of tree-based parsing schemata. A deduction system is defined for a particular grammar and string. The hypotheses, i.e., the initial set of valid objects, are determined by the string. The grammar is encoded in the deduction steps of the system. Hence an uninstantiated parsing system for some grammar can be instantiated to a deduction system by providing the hypotheses for that string. A parsing schema specifies an uninstantiated parsing system for some class of grammars.

Parsing schemata are concise, because many practical details are abstracted from. Moreover, the description is *static*. We have objects and rules, but no behaviour of any kind. This will prove to be an asset in reasoning about systems in the next chapters. Static objects are much easier to capture formally than dynamic behaviour.

Practical parsers compute items, rather then trees, as partial results. In the next chapter we will generalize the notion of tree-based parsing schemata to item-based schemata. One could interpret tree-based schemata as a special kind of item-based schemata, where every item comprises a single tree.

4. Item-based parsing schemata

Many parsing algorithms, like CYK and Earley, are in fact recognition algorithms. Such an algorithm does not construct parse trees by glueing together partial parse trees as in a tree-based parsing system. Only the *existence* of a parse tree is derived, based on items that denote the *existence* of partial parse trees. In the CYK algorithm, as described in Example 3.20, an item $[A, i, j]$ is valid iff $A \Rightarrow^* a_{i+1} \ldots a_j$. That is, in the notation of Section 3.1, *some* tree $\langle A \rightsquigarrow \underline{a}_{i+1} \ldots \underline{a}_j \rangle$ exists, but we don't care about the structure of the particular tree. It might be the case that several different trees exist with root A and yield $\underline{a}_{i+1} \ldots \underline{a}_j$.

Taking a more abstract view, we can see an item $[A, i, j]$ as the *equivalence class* of all trees with root A and yield $\underline{a}_{i+1} \ldots \underline{a}_j$. In a more general, formal approach we will define items as equivalence classes of trees.

From a set of recognized items a parse can be constructed in several ways. In the CYK case, for example, once the item $[S, 0, n]$ has been recognized one could start to build a parse tree in "top-down" fashion, retracing the recognition steps in reverse order. For each computed $[A, i, k]$ with $k - i > 1$ it is guaranteed that some production $A \rightarrow BC$ and position j can be found such that $[B, i, j]$ and $[C, j, k]$ have been computed also.

Alternatively, one could annotate the items computed by the recognition algorithm with information *how* they were obtained. That is, when a derivation step $[B, i, j], [C, j, k] \vdash [A, i, k]$ is successfully applied, we add to the item $[A, i, k]$ the information that it is obtained from symbols B, C and position j. Thus all information that is needed to construct all parses is captured in the set of computed items in a distributed way.

Finally, if we do not limit parsing to a context-free backbone but add semantic expressions to constituents, we might not need a parse tree anyway. The desired result in such a grammar is the semantic expression (or the set of different semantic expressions) that is added to the item $[S, 0, n]$. In such an approach, the structure of the parse tree(s) is irrelevant.

From now on we will focus on parsing algorithms that do not really construct parse trees. It suffices that a parser produces a set of valid items.

We have argued that an item can be seen as an equivalence class of trees. But trees are grouped together into an item not just randomly, but because they share some relevant properties. Sets of items are *congruence classes* rather than equivalence classes. An item-based parsing schema can be seen as a *quotient system* of a tree-based parsing schema and a congruence relation.

The notions quotient and congruence are introduced for arbitrary deduction systems in 4.1. In 4.2 we apply this to enhanced deduction systems, incorporating a notion of validity. Quotient-based parsing schemata are defined in Section 4.3.

This rather algebraic approach will provide us with an understanding of what an item *is*. Such a fundamental understanding is necessary, because many different algorithms employ many different kinds of items. In this theoretical setting we can see these many different kinds of items as convenient notations for particular subtypes of items from a more universal type.

Having dealt with the underlying algebra, we will simplify matters a lot. In 4.4 we define parsing schemata based on items in much the same way as tree-based parsing schemata were introduced in Section 3.5. Items can be interpreted as partial specifications of trees, rather than congruence classes of trees. This more liberal view makes it possible to include *inconsistent* items, i.e., partial specifications that are not matched by any well-formed tree. In Section 4.5 we will clarify the relation between the two definitions of parsing schemata and argue that inconsistent items, although incompatible with the theory, do not do any harm in practice.

In 4.6, finally, we will give some nontrivial examples of parsing schemata for well-known parsing algorithms: the Earley algorithm (with and without top-down prediction) and the Left-Corner algorithm.

A remark on notation: in this chapter equivalence classes are sometimes regarded as sets and other times regarded as entities. In order to avoid any possible confusion, we will use the informal notation $y_1, \ldots, y_k \vdash x$ only in cases where it is abundantly clear that $y_1, \ldots, y_k$ are entities rather than sets of entities, viz., in examples of parsing schemata for well-known algorithms. When we discuss parsing systems on a more abstract level, we only use the formally unambiguous notation $\{y_1, \ldots, y_k\} \vdash x$ or $Y \vdash x$.

4.1 Quotient deduction systems

In this section we are concerned with equivalence relations on an arbitrary deduction system $\mathbb{D}$. We will start to establish some desirable properties of equivalence relations. Next, we introduce the notion of a *congruence* relation (denoted $\simeq$) and show that congruence relations satisfy these properties. In Section 4.2, subsequently, we will investigate properties of congruence relations on an enhanced deduction system $\mathbb{E}$.

An equivalence relation is transitive, reflexive and antisymmetric. Furthermore, an equivalence relation partitions a set into equivalence classes. We assume that the reader is familiar with these basic facts from algebra.

Let $\sim$ be an equivalence relation on a set X. We write $[x]_\sim$ or simply $[x]$ for the equivalence class of x, i.e., the subset of X containing all x' such that $x' \sim x$. A quotient deduction system is the result of contracting equivalence classes to single entities.

Definition 4.1. (*quotient deduction system*)
Let $\mathbb{D} = \langle X, H, D \rangle$ be a deduction system, $\sim$ an equivalence relation on X. Then we define the quotient system $\mathbb{D}/\sim = \langle X/\sim, H/\sim, D/\sim \rangle$ by

$$X/\sim \ = \{[x] \mid x \in X\}, \quad \text{with } [x] = \{x' \in X \mid x' \sim x\} \text{ for any } x \in X,$$

$$H/\sim \ = \{[h] \mid h \in H\}, \quad \text{with } [h] = \{h\} \text{ for } h \in H\backslash X,$$

$$D/\sim \ = \{((\{[y_1], \ldots, [y_k]\}, [x]) \mid (\{y_1, \ldots, y_k\}, x) \in D\}.$$

It is left to the reader to verify that $\mathbb{D}/\sim$ is indeed a deduction system. We also call $\sim$ an equivalence relation on $\mathbb{D}$, rather than an equivalence relation on X. □

An inference relation $\vdash^\sim$ on a quotient system is defined as the closure of the set of deduction steps $D/\sim$ under addition of antecedents (cf. Definition 3.15). The *transitive quotient inference relation* $\vdash^{\sim*}$ is derived from $\vdash^\sim$ by Definition 3.17.

On the other hand, we have a transitive inference relation $\vdash^*$ in the deduction system $\mathbb{D}$, and when $\mathbb{D}$ is contracted to $\mathbb{D}/\sim$, we obtain a *quotient transitive inference relation* $\vdash^{*\sim}$, defined by

$$\{[y_1], \ldots, [y_k]\} \vdash^{*\sim} [x] \text{ if } \{y_1, \ldots, y_k\} \vdash^* x\}.$$

What, then, is the relation between the quotient transitive inference relation $\vdash^{*\sim}$ and the transitive quotient inference relation $\vdash^{\sim*}$ on $\wp(H \cup X)/\sim \times X/\sim$? It follows from Definition 4.1 that[1]

$$\vdash^{*\sim} \ \subseteq \ \vdash^{\sim*}, \tag{4.1}$$

but the reverse is not necessarily true.

In similar fashion we can compare the equivalence classes of valid entities with the valid equivalence classes in the quotient system. It trivially holds that

$$\mathcal{V}(\mathbb{D})/\sim \ \subseteq \mathcal{V}(\mathbb{D}/\sim). \tag{4.2}$$

For deduction sequences, similarly, we find

$$\Delta(\mathbb{D})/\sim \ \subseteq \Delta(\mathbb{D}/\sim). \tag{4.3}$$

---

[1] Let $\{y_1, \ldots, y_k\} \vdash z_1 \vdash \ldots \vdash z_j \vdash x$. Then, with induction on this deduction sequence, $\{[y_1], \ldots, [y_k]\} \vdash [z_1] \vdash \ldots \vdash [z_j] \vdash [x]$.

In Theorem 4.6 we will establish sufficient conditions that guarantee equality, rather than set inclusion, in (4.1)–(4.3). But in order to discuss these matters, we will first introduce some terminology.

Definition 4.2. (*conservation properties*)
An equivalence relation $\sim$ on a deduction system $\mathbb{D}$ is called *validity conserving* if

$$\mathcal{V}(\mathbb{D})/\sim \ = \ \mathcal{V}(\mathbb{D}/\sim).$$

An equivalence relation $\sim$ on a deduction system $\mathbb{D}$ is called *inference conserving* if

$$\vdash^{*\sim} \ = \ \vdash^{\sim*} .$$

An equivalence relation $\sim$ on a deduction system $\mathbb{D}$ is called *deduction sequence conserving* if

$$\Delta(\mathbb{D})/\sim \ = \ \Delta(\mathbb{D}/\sim). \qquad \square$$

Corollary 4.3.
Let $\sim$ be an equivalence relation on some deduction system.
If $\sim$ is inference conserving then $\sim$ is validity conserving.
If $\sim$ is deduction sequence conserving, then $\sim$ is inference conserving. $\qquad \square$

Why are we interested in all these properties? The main issue, of course, is validity conservation. When we discuss quotients of enhanced deduction systems in Section 4.2, we will establish conditions on equivalence relations that guarantee that a quotient system of a correct system is correct. The stronger notion of deduction sequence conservation is needed for a technical result in Chapter 5.[2] The intermediate property of inference conservation is merely useful to simplify notation. When it is known that $\vdash^{*\sim} = \vdash^{\sim*}$ we can write $\vdash$ rather than $\vdash^{\sim}$ and $\vdash^{*}$ rather than $\vdash^{\sim*}$ for inferences in the quotient system.

Example 4.4.
The hierarchy of equivalence relations that is implied by Corollary 4.3 is strict. We will give examples of deduction systems that satisfy one property but do not satisfy the next stronger property.

- Let $\mathbb{D} = \langle X, H, D \rangle$ be a deduction system with $X = \{a_1, a_2, b\}, H = \{h\}$, and

$$D \ = \ \{\{h\} \vdash a_1, \ \{a_2\} \vdash b\}.$$

---

[2] It is essential that the definitions of item contraction and item refinement are based on deduction sequence conservation, rather than validity conservation, in order to guarantee that refinement, as defined in Section 5.2, is a transitive relation. In Section 5.1 we will see that quotients over congruence relations are item contractions. We can make this follow as a corollary if we establish here that congruence relations are deduction sequence conserving.

Moreover, let $\sim$ be the equivalence relation on $\mathbb{D}$ defined by $a_1 \sim a_2$ and $x \sim x$ for any $x \in X$. Then it holds that $b \in \mathcal{V}(\mathbb{D}/\sim)$, but also $b \notin \mathcal{V}(\mathbb{D})/\sim$. Hence $\sim$ is an equivalence relation that is not validity conserving.

- Let $\mathbb{D} = \langle X, H, D \rangle$ be a deduction system with $X = \{a, b_1, b_2, c\}$, $H = \{h\}$, and

$$D = \{\{h\} \vdash a, \{a\} \vdash b_1, \{h\} \vdash b_2, \{b_2\} \vdash c\}.$$

Moreover, let $\sim$ be an equivalence relation on $\mathbb{D}$ defined by $b_1 \sim b_2$ and $x \sim x$ for any $x \in X$. Then, clearly, $\mathcal{V}(\mathbb{D}/\sim) = \mathcal{V}(\mathbb{D})/\sim$. But for the inference

$$[a] \vdash^{\sim*} [c]$$

in $\mathbb{D}/\sim$ there is no corresponding inference in $\mathbb{D}$. Hence $\sim$ is a validity conserving equivalence relation that is not inference conserving.

- Let $\mathbb{D} = \langle X, H, D \rangle$ be a deduction system with $X = \{a_1, a_2, b, c\}$, $H = \{h\}$, and

$$D = \{ \{h\} \vdash a_1, \{h\} \vdash b, \{a_2\} \vdash c, \{b\} \vdash c\}.$$

Moreover, let $\sim$ be an equivalence relation on $\mathbb{D}$ defined by $a_1 \sim a_2$ and $x \sim x$ for any $x \in X$. Then it is easily verified that $\vdash^{*\sim} = \vdash^{\sim*}$. But for the deduction sequence

$$\{[h]\} \vdash^{\sim} [a_i] \vdash^{\sim} [c]$$

in $\mathbb{D}/\sim$ there is no corresponding deduction sequence in $\mathbb{D}$. Hence $\sim$ is an inference conserving equivalence relation that is not deduction sequence conserving. $\qquad\Box$

Next, we turn to the notion of *congruence*. Congruence is defined with respect to *functions* over a domain. An equivalence relation $\simeq$ is a congruence relation with respect to a function $f : X^k \to X$ if for arbitrary $x_1 \simeq x'_1, \ldots, x_k \simeq x'_k$ it holds that $f(x_1, \ldots, x_k) \simeq f(x'_1, \ldots, x'_k)$. Standard handbooks on algebra (as, e.g., [Grätzer, 1979]), do not extend congruence to relations over a domain. So we will do that first.

Let us, for the sake of simplicity, look at a binary relation R. We call $\simeq$ a *congruence relation* with respect to a relation R if the following condition is satisfied:

if $x' \simeq x$ and xRy then there is some $y' \simeq y$ such that $x'Ry'$.   (4.4)

If we apply this to a function, which is a particular kind of relation, then (4.4) reads

if $x' \simeq x$ and $y = f(x)$ then there is some $y' \simeq y$ such that $y' = f(x')$

which corresponds to the standard notion of congruence. We can see R as a *nondeterministic function*. The same idea can be applied to set of deduction steps, where $\vdash$ can be seen as a nondeterministic function with a variable number of arguments. (we will swap x and y, however, as we have mostly used y to denote arguments and x to denote consequents in deduction steps). If we see $\vdash$ as an *action*, then the notion of congruence on deduction systems corresponds to the notion of *simulation* in process algebra.

Definition 4.5. (*congruence relation on a deduction system*)
Let $\mathbb{D} = \langle X, H, D \rangle$ be a deduction system. An equivalence relation $\simeq$ is called a *congruence relation on* $\mathbb{D}$ if, for any $y_1, \ldots, y_k, y_1', \ldots, y_k' \in \wp_{fin}(H \cup X)$ and $x \in X$ the following condition holds:

if $\{y_1, \ldots, y_k\} \vdash x$ and $y_1 \simeq y_1', \ldots, y_k \simeq y_k'$
then there is some $x' \in X$ such that $x' \simeq x$ and $\{y_1', \ldots, y_k'\} \vdash x'$. $\square$

Theorem 4.6. (*congruence relations are deduction sequence conserving*)
Let $\simeq$ be a congruence relation on a deduction system $\mathbb{D}$ then

$$\Delta(\mathbb{D})/\simeq = \Delta(\mathbb{D}/\simeq).$$

Proof. We only have to prove $\Delta(\mathbb{D}/\simeq) \subseteq \Delta(\mathbb{D})/\simeq$.
Without loss of generality, we only consider deductions with a finite set of antecedents. Hence it suffices to prove the following claim.
Claim: Let

$$\{[y_1], \ldots, [y_k]\} \vdash^{\simeq} [x_1] \vdash^{\simeq} \ldots \vdash^{\simeq} [x_j] \tag{4.5}$$

for some $y_1, \ldots, y_k \in H \cup X$ and $x_1, \ldots, x_j \in X$.
Then there are $y_1' \in [y_1]$, $\ldots$, $y_k' \in [y_k]$, $x_1' \in [x_1]$, $\ldots$, $x_j' \in [x_j]$ such that

$$\{y_1', \ldots, y_k'\} \vdash x_1' \vdash \ldots \vdash x_j'. \tag{4.6}$$

We prove this claim with induction on j.
The basic step $j = 1$ follows straight from the definition of $\vdash^{\simeq}$.
Next, assume that the claim holds for for $1, \ldots, j-1$, and assume (4.5) for some $y_1, \ldots, y_k, x_1, \ldots, x_j$. From (4.5) it follows that

$$\{[y_1], \ldots, [y_k], [x_1], \ldots, [x_{j-1}]\} \vdash^{\simeq} [x_j],$$

hence, by the definition of $\vdash^{\simeq}$, there are $y_1'' \in [y_1]$, $\ldots$, $y_k'' \in [y_k]$, $x_1'' \in [x_1]$, $\ldots$, $x_j'' \in [x_j]$ such that

$$\{y_1'', \ldots, y_k'', x_1'', \ldots, x_{j-1}''\} \vdash x_j''. \tag{4.7}$$

Furthermore, according the induction hypothesis, there are $y_1' \in [y_1]$, $\ldots$, $y_k' \in [y_k]$, $x_1' \in [x_1]$, $\ldots$, $x_{j-1}' \in [x_{j-1}]$ such that

$$\{y_1', \ldots, y_k'\} \vdash x_1' \vdash \ldots \vdash x_{j-1}'. \tag{4.8}$$

From (4.7) and $y_1' \simeq y_1''$, $\ldots$, $y_k' \simeq y_k''$, $x_1' \simeq x_1''$, $\ldots$, $x_{j-1}' \simeq x_{j-1}''$, the congruence property yields $x_j' \in [x_j]$ such that

$$\{y_1', \ldots, y_k', x_1', \ldots, x_{j-1}'\} \vdash x_j', \tag{4.9}$$

and (4.6) is obtained as a combination of (4.8) and (4.9). $\square$

4.2 Quotients of enhanced deduction systems

In Section 4.2 we have defined enhanced deduction systems so as to introduce a notion of syntactic correctness. Assume that an enhanced deduction system $\mathbb{E}$ is correct, and $\simeq$ is a congruence relation on $\mathbb{E}$. Does this imply that $\mathbb{E}/\simeq$ is also correct? We will show that this is not generally the case and establish a sufficient condition.

First, we extend Definition 4.1 to enhanced deduction systems in the obvious way.

Definition 4.7. (*enhanced quotient deduction system*)
Let $\mathbb{E} = \langle X, H, F, C, D \rangle$ be an enhanced deduction system, $\sim$ an equivalence relation on X. Then we define the quotient system $\mathbb{E}/\sim = \langle X/\sim, H/\sim, F/\sim, C/\sim, D/\sim \rangle$ by $X/\sim$, $H/\sim$, $D/\sim$ as in Definition 4.1 and

$$F/\sim = \{[x] \mid x \in F\},$$

$$C/\sim = \{[x] \mid x \in C\},$$

It is left to the reader to verify that $\mathbb{E}/\sim$ is indeed an enhanced deduction system. □

Definition 4.8. (*correctness preservation of equivalence relations*)
Let $\mathbb{E} = \langle X, H, F, C, D \rangle$ be an enhanced deduction system and $\sim$ an equivalence relation on $\mathbb{E}$.
$\sim$ is called *soundness preserving* if

for each $[x] \in \mathcal{V}(\mathbb{E}/\sim) \cap F/\sim$ there is some $x' \in [x] \cap F$ such that $x' \in \mathcal{V}(\mathbb{E})$.

$\sim$ is called *completeness preserving* if

for each $x \in \mathcal{V}(\mathbb{E}) \cap F$ it holds that $[x] \in \mathcal{V}(\mathbb{E}/\sim)$.

$\sim$ is called correctness preserving if it is both soundness and completeness preserving. □

Note that every equivalence relation is completeness preserving by definition.

Corollary 4.9.
If $\mathbb{E}$ is a correct enhanced deduction system, and $\sim$ is a soundness preserving equivalence relation on $\mathbb{E}$, then $\mathbb{E}/\sim$ is also a correct enhanced deduction system.

Example 4.10. (*congruence does not preserve soundness*)
We define an enhanced deduction system $\mathbb{E}$ by

$$X = \{a_1, a_2, b_1, b_2, c\},$$

$$H = \{h\},$$

$$F = \{b_2, c\},$$

$$C = \{c\},$$

$$D = \{\{h\} \vdash a_1, \{a_1\} \vdash b_1, \{a_1\} \vdash c, \{a_2\} \vdash b_2, \{a_2\} \vdash c, \}.$$

Note that $\mathbb{E}$ is correct, because $c \in \mathcal{V}(\mathbb{E})$ and $b_2 \notin \mathcal{V}(\mathbb{E})$. Furthermore we define a relation $\simeq$ on $\mathbb{E}$ by $a_1 \simeq a_2$, $b_1 \simeq b_2$ and $x \simeq x$ for any $x \in X$. It is easy to verify that $\simeq$ is a congruence relation.

Now we find $[b_2] \in F/\simeq$ and $[b_2] \notin C/\simeq$, but nevertheless $[b_2] \in \mathcal{V}(\mathbb{E}/\simeq)$. Hence $\mathbb{E}/\simeq$ is not sound.   □

In enhanced deduction systems we make a distinction between final entities in F and "intermediate" entities in $X \backslash F$. The anomaly in the above example is caused by the fact that the congruence class $[b_i]$ contains entities of both types. If congruence classes are subclasses either of $X \backslash F$ or of F, the problem cannot occur.

Definition 4.11. (*regular equivalence relation*)
Let $\mathbb{E} = \langle X, H, F, C, D \rangle$ be an enhanced deduction system. An equivalence relation $\sim$ on $\mathbb{E}$ is called *regular* if, for all $x \in F$ and $x \sim x'$ it holds that $x' \in F$.   □

We will in fact only be concerned with regular congruence relations, rather than arbitrary regular equivalence relations. We write $\cong$, rather than $\simeq$, as a standard notation for regular congruence relations.

Theorem 4.12.
A regular congruence relation on an enhanced deduction system is correctness preserving.

Proof. Let $\mathbb{E} = \langle X, H, F, C, D \rangle$ be an enhanced deduction system and $\cong$ a regular congruence relation. Assume that $\cong$ does not preserve soundness. Then there is some $[x] \in \mathcal{V}(\mathbb{E}/\cong) \cap F/\cong$ such that all $x' \in [x] \cup F$ are not valid in $\mathbb{E}$. Then either $[x]$ contains some valid x' outside F, in which case $\cong$ is not regular, or $[x] \in \mathcal{V}(\mathbb{E}/\cong) \backslash (\mathcal{V}(\mathbb{E})/\cong)$, in which case $\cong$ is not a congruence relation.   □

4.3 Quotient parsing schemata

After all the algebraic preparation we can now apply the results to parsing systems and parsing schemata.

Definition 4.13. ((*un*)*instantiated quotient parsing system*)
An (un)instantiated quotient parsing system is a deduction system $\mathbb{Q} = \mathbb{T}/\cong$ with $\mathbb{T}$ an (un)instantiated tree-based parsing system and $\cong$ a regular congruence relation on $\mathbb{T}$.

$\mathbb{T}$ is called the *underlying tree-based parsing system* of $\mathbb{Q}$.   □

Definition 4.14. (*quotient parsing schema*)
A a quotient parsing schema **Q** for a class of grammars $\mathcal{CG}$ is a function that
assigns an uninstantiated quotient parsing system to every grammar $G \in \mathcal{CG}$.
□

In Definition 3.8 we have introduced a practical notation for trees. This
can be extended to a practical notation for congruence classes of trees, as
follows.
When we referred to a tree $\langle A \rightsquigarrow \alpha \rangle$, we meant some particular tree. Note,
however, that the tree is underspecified. There could be many trees with root
A and yield α. Typically, a congruence class comprises *all* trees that suit this
partial specification. In the sequel, we write $[A \rightsquigarrow \alpha]$ for the congruence class
$[\langle A \rightsquigarrow \alpha \rangle]$ denoting all trees with root A and yield α. Or, more generally, for
any tree specification according to Definition 3.8, we denote the set of trees
satisfying the partial specification, rather than some arbitrary tree within
that set, by replacing the outermost angle brackets by square brackets. Hence

$$[A \rightsquigarrow \alpha \langle B \rightsquigarrow \beta \rangle \gamma]$$

denotes the set of all trees that conform to the picture in Figure 3.1(c), and

$$[A \rightsquigarrow \alpha \langle B_1 \cdots B_n \rightsquigarrow \beta_1 \cdots \beta_n \rangle \gamma]$$

the set of all trees that conform to the picture in Figure 3.1(d) on page 43.
In Section 3.5 we have defined a function $\mathcal{K}$ that assigns hypotheses to
any input string (cf. Definition 3.30). As hypotheses are not contracted in
a quotient system – or, to be very precise, each hypothesis is replaced by a
singleton set – we find that

$$\mathcal{K}(a_1 \ldots a_n)/\cong \ = \ \{[a \to \underline{a_i}] \mid a = a_i\} \cup \{[\# \to \underline{\#}_0], [\$ \to \underline{\$}_{n+1}]\} \qquad (4.10)$$

for any regular congruence relation $\cong$.
Hence a parsing schema **Q** is fully specified by a triple $\langle \mathcal{T}(G), D(G), \cong_G \rangle$
for an arbitrary grammar $G \in \mathcal{CG}$. For each grammar $G \in \mathcal{CG}$ and string
$a_1 \ldots a_n \in \Sigma^*$ the schema materializes to a deduction system

$$\mathbf{Q}(G)(a_1 \ldots a_n) \ = \ \langle \mathcal{T}(G), \mathcal{K}(a_1 \ldots a_n), D(G) \rangle \ / \cong_G$$

The tree-based parsing system **T** specified by $\mathcal{T}(G)$ and $D(G)$ is called the
underlying tree-based parsing schema of **Q**.

Corollary 4.15. A quotient parsing system $\mathbb{Q}$ is sound/complete/correct if
and only if the underlying parsing system $\mathbb{T}$ is sound/complete/correct.
A quotient parsing schema **Q** is sound/complete/correct if and only if the
underlying parsing schema **T** is sound/complete/correct.
□

Example 4.16. (*QCYK, a quotient parsing schema for CYK*)
A quotient parsing schema **QCYK** can be given for $\mathcal{CNF}$, the class of gram-
mars in Chomsky Normal Form.
For any grammar $G \in \mathcal{CNF}$ we define the relation $\cong$ on $\mathbb{T}_{CYK}$ by

$$\langle A \rightsquigarrow \underline{a}_{i+1} \cdots \underline{a}_j \rangle \cong \langle B \rightsquigarrow \underline{b}_{k+1} \cdots \underline{b}_l \rangle \text{ if } A = B, i = k, \text{ and } j = l.$$

The fact that $\cong$ is a congruence relation can be established straightforwardly (and we will not take the trouble to write it out in a formal manner). Let $\tau = \langle A \rightsquigarrow \underline{a}_{i+1} \cdots \underline{a}_j \rangle$ and $\sigma \cong \tau$. If τ is used in a deduction step, then the internal structure of the tree is irrelevant. The tree σ has the same root A and positions i and j can be used in exactly the same manner to deduce large trees that are congruent to trees deduced by τ.

For an arbitrary grammar $G \in \mathcal{CNF}$ we define $\mathbb{Q}_{CYK} = \langle \mathcal{I}, \mathcal{K}(a_1 \ldots a_n), D \rangle$ by

$$\mathcal{I} \quad = \quad \{ [A \rightsquigarrow \underline{a}_{i+1} \cdots \underline{a}_j] \mid A \in N \wedge \underline{a}_{i+1} \cdots \underline{a}_j \in \underline{\Sigma}^* \};$$

$$D^{(1)} \quad = \quad \{ [a \rightarrow \underline{a}_i] \vdash [A \rightarrow \langle a \rightarrow \underline{a}_i \rangle] \mid A \rightarrow a \in P \},$$

$$D^{(2)} \quad = \quad \{ [B \rightsquigarrow \underline{a}_{i+1} \cdots \underline{a}_j], [C \rightsquigarrow \underline{a}_{j+1} \cdots \underline{a}_k]$$
$$\vdash [A \rightsquigarrow \underline{a}_{i+1} \cdots \underline{a}_k] \mid A \rightarrow BC \in P \},$$

$$D \quad = \quad D^{(1)} \cup D^{(2)};$$

and $\mathcal{K}(a_1 \ldots a_n)$ as in (4.10).

When we apply the usual denotation $[A, i, j]$ for an item $[A \rightsquigarrow \underline{a}_{i+1} \cdots \underline{a}_j]$ we get the the following simplified description of $\mathbb{Q}_{CYK}$:

$$\mathcal{I}' \quad = \quad \{ [A, i, j] \mid A \in N \wedge 0 \le i \le j \wedge \exists \tau \in \mathit{Trees}(G) :$$
$$\mathit{root}(\tau) = A \wedge \mathit{yield}(\tau) \in \underline{\Sigma}^* \wedge |\mathit{yield}(\tau)| = j - i \};$$

$$D^{(1')} \quad = \quad \{ [a \rightarrow \underline{a}_i] \vdash [A, i-1, i] \mid A \rightarrow a \in P \},$$

$$D^{(2')} \quad = \quad \{ [B, i, j], [C, j, k] \vdash [A, i, k] \mid A \rightarrow BC \in P \},$$

$$D' \quad = \quad D^{(1')} \cup D^{(2')}.$$

There is but one difference with the conventional description of the CYK schema: only those items $[A, i, j]$ are in the domain for which there is at least one tree $\tau \in [A, i, j]$. It could happen, for example, that A only produces strings of even length. In that case, items $[A, i, j]$ with odd values of $j - i$ must be excluded from the domain. An *empty congruence class* is a contradiction in terms and violates the underlying mathematical theory. In Section 4.5 we will see how to deal with this problem from a practical point of view. $\square$

We have now clarified the ontological status of an item: a congruence class of trees in a deduction system. This is not unimportant. One of the advantages of the formalism developed here is that *any* item-based parser can be described in it. Different algorithms use different items; it is impossible to predict which particular type of item is going to be used in a parsing algorithm that will be discovered next week. For that reason we need such an ontological understanding. Whatever new type of parsing items somebody is going to introduce someday, it will capture those partial specifications of trees that matter for the deduction relation. That is, trees satisfying the same partial specification are congruent.

When it comes to the *use* of items in the description of practical parsing schemata, we can simplify matters a lot. In the next section we will specify the domain of a parsing schema directly as a set of items, rather than a quotient of a domain of trees.

4.4 Item-based parsing schemata

Having stated that – in principle – item-based parsing schemata can be described as quotients of tree-based parsing schemata, we will now take a much more practical approach. We may interpret an item as a *partial specification* of a tree. If there is a set of trees that conforms to this partial specification, then this set comprises an equivalence class (or indeed a congruence class) in the domain of trees for the grammar. An anomaly that may occur, however, is that such a partial specification is *inconsistent*: there is not a single tree that satisfies the specification. Hence, such an item must be associated with an empty set of trees. A parsing system will be called regular if it is (equivalent to) a quotient system. The theory of Section 4.3 is only defined on regular subsystems. For practical applications the difference is a minor one: for all parsing schemata that we will deal with, one can argue that the introduction of inconsistent items does not affect the correctness of the schema. We will treat this problem at length in 4.5.

We will now proceed to define item-based parsing schemata (in the sequel simply called *parsing schemata*) in much the same way as tree-based parsing schemata were introduced in Section 3.5. For the domain of a system we do not take a subset of $\mathcal{T}rees(G)$ but a subset of a *partition* of $\mathcal{T}rees(G)$

A partition $\Pi(X) \subset \wp(X)$ is a collection of pairwise disjunctive nonempty subsets of X such that every $x \in X$ is contained in some $\pi \in \Pi(X)$. Every partition Π defines an equivalence relation $\sim_\Pi$ by

$$x \sim_\Pi y \text{ if there is a } \pi \in \Pi(X) \text{ such that } \{x, y\} \subseteq \pi.$$

And reversed, if $\sim$ is an equivalence relation on X then $X/\sim$ is a partition of X.

Definition 4.17. (*item set*)
Let $\mathcal{T}rees(G)$ be the set of trees for some context-free grammar G. A set $\mathcal{I} \in \wp(\mathcal{T}rees(G))$ is called an *item set* if there is a partition Π of $\mathcal{T}rees(G)$ such that

$$\mathcal{I} \subseteq \Pi(\mathcal{T}rees(G)) \cup \{\emptyset\}. \qquad \square$$

Definition 4.18. (*types of items*)
Let $\mathcal{I}$ be an item set.

- An item $\iota \in \mathcal{I}$ is called *empty* if $\iota = \emptyset$.
- A non-empty item $\iota \in \mathcal{I}$ is called *completed* if, for each $\tau \in \iota$, τ is a marked parse tree for some sentence.
- A non-empty item $\iota \in \mathcal{I}$ is called *intermediate* if, for each $\tau \in \iota$, τ is a not a marked parse tree for any sentence.
- An item $\iota \in \mathcal{I}$ is called *mixed* if there are $\sigma, \tau \in \iota$ such that σ is a marked parse tree and τ is not a marked parse tree.   □

Definition 4.19. (*regular and semiregular item set*)
An item set $\mathcal{I}$ is called *regular* if it contains neither mixed items nor the empty item.
An item set $\mathcal{I}$ is called *semiregular* if it does not contain mixed items.   □

Definition 4.20. (*final items*)
Let Π be a partition of $\mathit{Trees}(G)$ for some context-free grammar G, $a_1 \ldots a_n \in \Sigma^*$ a string. The set of *final items* $\mathcal{F}_{G,\Pi}^{(n)}$ for a string of length n is defined by[3]

$$\mathcal{F}_{G,\Pi}^{(n)} = \{\iota \in \Pi(\mathit{Trees}(G)) \mid \exists \tau \in \iota : \tau \in \mathcal{P}_G^{(n)}\}.$$

The set of *correct final items* $\mathcal{C}_{G,\Pi}$ for a string $a_1 \ldots a_n$ is defined by

$$\mathcal{C}_{G,\Pi}(a_1 \ldots a_n) = \{\iota \in \Pi(\mathit{Trees}(G)) \mid \exists \tau \in \iota : \tau \in \mathcal{P}_G(a_1 \ldots a_n)\}. \quad □$$

The intention of Definition 4.20 should be clear. An item-based parser will be correct if all correct final items can be deduced from H and no other final items.

After these preliminaries, the following definitions will not come as a surprise.

Definition 4.21. ((*instantiated*) *parsing system*)
Let G be a context-free grammar and $a_1 \ldots a_n \in \Sigma^*$ an arbitrary string. A deduction system $\langle \mathcal{I}, H, D \rangle$ is called an *instantiated parsing system* for G and $a_1 \ldots a_n$ when the following conditions are satisfied:

(i) $\mathcal{I} = \mathcal{I}(G, \Pi)$ is an item set,
(ii) $\mathcal{F}_{G,\Pi}^{(n)} \subset \mathcal{I}$,
(iii) $[a \rightarrow \underline{a_i}] \in H$ for each a_i, $1 \le i \le n$.   □

Definition 4.22. (*correct parsing system*)
An instantiated parsing system $\langle \mathcal{I}, H, D \rangle$ for a grammar G and a string $a_1 \ldots a_n$ is *correct* if the enhanced deduction system

$$\langle \mathcal{I}, H, \mathcal{F}_{G,\Pi}^{(n)}, \mathcal{C}_{G,\Pi}(a_1 \ldots a_n), D \rangle$$

is correct.   □

---

[3] See Definition 3.11 for $\mathcal{P}_G^{(n)}$ and $\mathcal{P}_G(a_1 \ldots a_n)$.

Definition 4.23. (*uninstantiated parsing system*)
Let G be a context-free grammar. An *uninstantiated parsing system* for G is
a triple $\langle \mathcal{I}, \mathcal{K}, D \rangle$ where $\mathcal{K} : \Sigma^* \to \wp(\wp(\mathit{Trees}(G)))$ is a function such that $\langle \mathcal{I},$
$\mathcal{K}(a_1 \ldots a_n), D \rangle$ is a parsing system for each $a_1 \ldots a_n \in \Sigma^*$.
An uninstantiated parsing system $\langle \mathcal{I}, \mathcal{K}, D \rangle$ is *correct* if $\langle \mathcal{I}, \mathcal{K}(a_1 \ldots a_n), D \rangle$
is correct for each $a_1 \ldots a_n \in \Sigma^*$.   □

We will not make a clear distinction between instantiated and uninstantiated
parsing systems and write $\mathbb{P}(a_1 \ldots a_n)$ or simply $\mathbb{P}$ to denote both.

Definition 4.24. (*parsing schema*)
A a parsing schema $\mathbf{P}$ for a class of grammars $\mathcal{CG}$ is a function that assigns
an uninstantiated parsing system to every grammar $G \in \mathcal{CG}$.
$\mathbf{P}$ is *correct* if, for each $G \in \mathcal{CG}$, the uninstantiated parsing system $\mathbf{P}(G)$ is
correct.   □

Definition 4.25. (*regular parsing schemata*)
A parsing system $\langle \mathcal{I}, H, D \rangle$ is *regular* if $\mathcal{I}$ is a regular item set.
A parsing schema $\mathbf{P}$ for a class of grammars $\mathcal{CG}$ is *regular* if, for each $G \in \mathcal{CG}$
and each $a_1 \ldots a_n \in \Sigma^*$, the parsing system $\mathbf{P}(G)(a_1 \ldots a_n)$ is regular.   □

Definition 4.26. (*the function* $\mathcal{K}$)
In all examples of parsing systems and schemata we will use the the same
function $\mathcal{K}$, defined by

$$\mathcal{K}(a_1 \ldots a_n) = \{[a \to \underline{a}_i] \mid a = a_i\} \cup \{[\# \to \underline{\#}_0], [\$ \to \underline{\$}_{n+1}]\}.$$

As a more conventional notation for hypothesis items we will write $[a, i-1, i]$
rather than $[a \to \underline{a}_i]$. The end-of-sentence marker is denoted by $[\$, n, n+1]$,
the beginning-of-sentence marker by $[\#, -1, 0]$.   □

As we have fixed the function $\mathcal{K}$, as usual, one only needs to specify $\mathcal{I}(G, \Pi)$
and $D(G)$ for an arbitrary grammar G and a partition $\Pi(G)$ of $\mathit{Trees}(G)$
in order to give a full specification of a parsing schema. For each grammar
$G \in \mathcal{CG}$ and string $a_1 \ldots a_n \in \Sigma^*$ the schema materializes to a deduction
system

$$\mathbf{P}(G)(a_1 \ldots a_n) = \langle \mathcal{I}(G, \Pi), \mathcal{K}(a_1 \ldots a_n), D(G) \rangle.$$

For the reader who really wants to know what kind of object a recognition
schema is, in terms of set theory, it is remarked that the universal class of
parsing schemata can be characterized as a sub-class of

$$(\mathcal{CG} \to (\wp(\wp(\mathcal{U})) \times (\mathit{Sym}^* \to \wp(\wp(\mathcal{U}))) \times \wp(\wp_{fin}(\wp(\mathcal{U}) \times \wp(\mathcal{U})))))$$

Again, the fact that the universal class of parsing schemata can be formally
defined is rather more important than the particular structure of this type.

Example 4.27. (*the* **CYK** *parsing schema*)
At last, we define an item-based parsing schema **CYK** by giving an item-based parsing system $\mathbb{P}_{CYK}$ for arbitrary grammars $G \in \mathcal{CNF}$.
Let $[A, i, j]$ be an abbreviated notation for an item $[A \rightsquigarrow \underline{a}_{i+1} \ldots \underline{a}_j]$. Then $\mathbb{P}_{CYK}$ is defined by

$$\mathcal{I} \;\; = \;\; \{[A, i, j] \mid A \in N \wedge 0 \leq i < j\};$$

$$D^{(1)} \;\; = \;\; \{[a, i-1, i] \vdash [A, i-1, i] \mid A \rightarrow a \in P\},$$

$$D^{(2)} \;\; = \;\; \{[B, i, j], [C, j, k] \vdash [A, i, k] \mid A \rightarrow BC \in P\},$$

$$D \;\; = \;\; D^{(1)} \cup D^{(2)}.$$

Note the difference with Example 4.16, where the domain contained only those items such that there is a tree that fits the item. Here we do allow items for which such a tree does not exist, hence **CYK** is not a regular parsing schema. But in the sequel we will show that **CYK** is *semi*regular, which is good enough for all practical purposes.

Thus we have obtained a CYK schema within the setting of a formal theory of parsing schemata that conforms to the intuitive CYK deduction system presented in Example 3.20. □

4.5 The relation between Sections 4.3 and 4.4

A pain in the neck in the development of our theory so far is the problem of the empty item. We will now address this problem in some more detail and argue that it can be ignored for all practical purposes.

Let A be a nonterminal that produces strings of even length. Then the item $[A, 0, 3]$ – the set of trees $\langle A \rightsquigarrow \underline{a}_1 \underline{a}_2 \underline{a}_3 \rangle$ for arbitrary $a_1 a_2 a_3$ – is empty. Many items can be empty, clearly. If, for example, B does not produce trees with a yield shorter than 4, the item $[B, 0, 3]$ is empty as well. By definition, there is only one empty set. Hence, as items are sets, empty items must be identical. This seems counter-intuitive, to say the least, because the reasons for which $[B, 0, 3]$ is invalid are quite different from the reasons for which $[A, 0, 3]$ can't be deduced. This problem can be handled in several ways.

- The fundamental solution is to make a distinction between *items* and *item descriptions*. Such an approach is chosen in the formalization of feature structures (cf. [Kasper and Rounds, 1986], [Rounds and Kasper, 1986]), where a distinction is made between feature structures and feature descriptions.

  In this context this is not an attractive option, however, because it carries the obligation to formally define a rather more complicated item description language, based on a notion of *constraints on trees* rather than sets of trees. Moreover, using sets of trees as the fundamental notion is more general, because *whatever* constraint language is used to denote such constraints, these implicitly define sets of trees.

- The easy way out is not to allow the empty item in the domain. This is mathematically the most elegant option. To any definition of an item set $\mathcal{I}$ one could add that the parsing systems operates only on $\mathcal{I}\setminus\{\emptyset\}$. Moreover, if the empty item is not part of the domain, it can be shown that every item-based parsing schema is in fact a quotient of a tree-based parsing schema, and the theories of Sections 4.3 and 4.4 are equivalent.

  From a practical point of view, however, this option has the disadvantage that it is not clear a priori which items are empty. Moreover, a parsing schema for, e.g., the CYK algorithm would *not* be fully compatible with the canonical algorithm as found in the literature, where empty items are not excluded from the domain.

- The last option, finally, is simply to live with the fact that there are different denotations of a single empty item. This does not do any real harm, as long as it is guaranteed that the empty item is invalid, which seems a reasonable demand. When a parsing system is constructed by defining a regular congruence relation on a tree-based parsing system, it is logically impossible to arrive at a system that contains the empty item as an entity in the domain. Hence it surely can't be deduced.

  This option is the most attractive, because it allows the most simple definition of parsing systems in a way that does not strain the compatibility with algorithm descriptions found in the literature.

  To our framework it adds the burden that we always have to show that the empty item is invalid. This is hardly a burden, however, as for any sensible parsing system this property comes about naturally.[4]

Thus we allow a liberal form of parsing system specification, which may contain different denotations of the empty item. Every deduction step in a parsing system that is actually going to be used for the construction of a parse will be contained in the *regular subsystem*.

A more positive way of phrasing this design choice for our theory is the following. We acknowledge that there *is* a difference between items and item descriptions, but we do not prescribe a specific item description language. *Any* item description language that allows to define parsing schemata is acceptable, because the theorems are based on the items themselves, rather than on item descriptions.

---

[4] If it is ensured that the empty item (in all its denotations) is invalid, then, obviously, introduction of the empty item does not affect the correctness of a system. This will be the case in all parsing schemata that are introduced in the sequel. It is not a necessary condition, however. One could envisage parsing systems in which some denotations of the empty item can be deduced under more specific conditions.

Definition 4.28. (*semiregular parsing systems and schemata*)
A parsing system $\langle \mathcal{I}, H, D \rangle$ is *semiregular* if

(*i*) $\mathcal{I}$ is a semiregular item set
(*ii*) $\emptyset \notin \mathcal{V}(\mathbb{P})$.

A parsing schema $\mathbf{P}$ for a class of grammars $\mathcal{CG}$ is *semiregular* if, for each $G \in \mathcal{CG}$ and each $a_1 \ldots a_n \in \Sigma^*$, the parsing system $\mathbf{P}(G)(a_1 \ldots a_n)$ is semiregular. $\Box$

Definition 4.29. (*regular subsystems and schemata*)
Let $\mathbb{P} = \langle \mathcal{I}, H, D \rangle$ be a semiregular parsing system.
We define a *regular subsystem* $\mathbb{P}^r = \langle \mathcal{I}^r, H, D^r \rangle$ by

$$\mathcal{I}^r \;=\; \mathcal{I} \backslash \emptyset,$$

$$D^r \;=\; \{(Y, x) \in D \mid Y \subseteq \mathcal{I}^r \wedge x \in \mathcal{I}^r\}.$$

For a semiregular parsing schema $\mathbf{P}$ for a class of grammar $\mathcal{CG}$ we define a regular subschema $\mathbf{P}^r$ by

$$\mathbf{P}^r(G)(a_1 \ldots a_n) = (\mathbf{P}(G)(a_1 \ldots a_n))^r \qquad\qquad \Box$$

Corollary 4.30.
A semiregular parsing system $\mathbb{P}$ is sound / complete / correct if and only if its regular subsystem $\mathbb{P}^r$ is sound / complete / correct.
A semiregular parsing schema $\mathbf{P}$ is sound / complete / correct if and only if its regular subschema $\mathbf{P}^r$ is sound / complete / correct. $\Box$

In Section 6.1 we will see that restricting a semi-regular parsing system to a fully regular parsing system is a special case of a more general operation called *step deletion*.

Although it is obvious how to regularize a semi-regular system in theory, this might not be so obvious in practice. When one is confronted with a specification of an item set by means of constraints, it might be rather hard to establish whether a tree exists that satisfies those constraints. Hence, as we have extensively argued above, we settle for semi-regular parsing schemata. As long as the semi-regularity constraint is obeyed – which is typically a trivial property – we may safely ignore the empty item and its different denotations.

We can now formally clarify the relation between the quotient parsing schemata of Section 4.3 and item-based parsing schemata of Section 4.4. We cannot describe, in general, semiregular parsing schemata as quotients, but we can do so with their regular subschemata. Everything outside a semiregular subschema has been added for convenience of description but is of no importance to the correctness of a schema.

Theorem 4.31. (*regular parsing systems are quotient systems*)
Let $\mathbb{P} = \langle \mathcal{I}, H, D \rangle$ be a regular parsing system. Then there is a tree-based parsing system $\mathbb{T} = \langle \mathcal{T}_P, H', D_P \rangle$ and a regular congruence relation $\cong_P$ on $\mathbb{T}$ such that[5]

$$\langle \mathcal{T}_P, H', D_P \rangle \, / \cong_P \ \equiv \ \langle \mathcal{I}, H, D \rangle.$$

Moreover, $\mathbb{P}$ is correct if and only if $\langle \mathcal{T}_P, H', D_P \rangle \, / \cong_P$ is correct.

Proof. We define

$$\mathcal{T}_P \ = \ \{ \tau \in \mathit{Trees}(G) \mid \exists \iota \in \mathcal{I} : \ \tau \in \iota \},$$

$$H' \ = \ \{ \langle a {\rightarrow} a_i \rangle \mid [a {\rightarrow} a_i] \in H \},$$

$$\cong_P \ = \ \{ (\sigma, \tau) \in \mathcal{T} \times \mathcal{T} \mid \exists \iota \in \mathcal{I} : \ \sigma, \tau \in \iota \},$$

$$D_P \ = \ \{ \sigma_1, \dots, \sigma_k \vdash \tau \in \wp_{\mathit{fin}}(\mathcal{T}_P \cup H') \times \mathcal{T}_P \mid [\sigma_1], \dots, [\sigma_k] \vdash [\tau] \in D \}.$$

It follows straightforwardly that $\cong$ is a regular congruence relation and that $\langle \mathcal{T}_P, H', D_P \rangle / \cong_P \ \equiv \ \langle \mathcal{I}, H, D \rangle$.
It is left to the reader to verify that correctness of $\mathbb{P}$, (according to Definitions 4.22–4.24) and correctness of $\langle \mathcal{T}_P, H, D_P \rangle / \cong_P$ (according to Definitions 3.27–3.29 and Corollary 4.15) are equivalent. $\qquad\square$

4.6 Examples of parsing schemata

After all the theory in the previous sections, we will now present a few examples of nontrivial parsing schemata. We define schemata for the Earley parser (both the conventional one with top-down prediction and the bottom-up Earley parser introduced without prediction) and the Left-Corner parser.

The reader is reminded that all parsing schemata have the same function $\mathcal{K}$ that assigns hypotheses to parsing systems (cf. Definition 4.26). We will slightly simplify the notation of the hypotheses. For an arbitrary string $a_1 \dots a_n$ we define a set of hypotheses

$$\mathcal{K}(a_1 \dots a_n) \ = \ \{ [a, i-1, i] \mid a = a_i \} \cup \{ [\$, n, n+1], [\#, -1, 0] \}.$$

The beginning-of-sentence marker and end-of-sentence marker are in fact not needed here. In Chapter 6 some examples are given where these hypotheses are essential.

Before we start describing the parsing schemata, a few more notational conventions are useful. Note that, by definition, $D \subset \wp_{\mathit{fin}}(H \cup X) \times X$. Thus, if we write (parts of) D in the format

---

[5]   We anticipate the formal definition of *isomorphism* ($\equiv$) that will be given in Definition 5.4. It should be obvious what is meant.

$$\{y_1 \dots y_k \vdash x\}$$

without any further conditions, this is to be interpreted as

$$\{y_1 \dots y_k \vdash x \mid \{y_1, \dots y_k\} \subseteq H \cup X \wedge x \in X\}.$$

Furthermore, the sets $\mathcal{I}$ and D in a parsing system will be *subscripted* with the name of the schema of which this system is an instantiation. A parsing system $\mathbf{Earley}(G)(a_1 \dots a_n)$, for example, will be denoted as a triple $\langle \mathcal{I}_{Earley}, H, D_{Earley} \rangle$. The subscripts can always be deleted if the name of the parsing schema is clear from the context.

Often, $\mathcal{I}$ and D are defined as a union of different subsets. These subsets are always indicated with *superscripts*. Superscripts may also be deleted if it is not relevant in some context which particular subset of $\mathcal{I}$ or D is being referred to.

Example 4.32. (*the* **Earley** *parsing schema*)
We will define a parsing schema **Earley** on $\mathcal{CFG}$ by giving a parsing system for an arbitrary grammar $G \in \mathcal{CFG}$.

We will first define a parsing schema using the conventional Earley items, and afterwards show that the set of Earley items for a particular grammar is a semiregular item set according to Definition 4.19.

The parsing schema **Earley** is defined by specifying a parsing system $\mathbb{P}_{Earley}$ for an arbitrary grammar G as follows:

$$\mathcal{I}_{Earley} = \{[A \rightarrow \alpha \bullet \beta, i, j] \mid A \rightarrow \alpha\beta \in P \wedge 0 \le i \le j\};$$

$$D^{Init} = \{\vdash [S \rightarrow \bullet\gamma, 0, 0]\},$$

$$D^{Scan} = \{[A \rightarrow \alpha \bullet a\beta, i, j], [a, j, j+1] \vdash [A \rightarrow \alpha a \bullet \beta, i, j+1]\},$$

$$D^{Compl} = \{[A \rightarrow \alpha \bullet B\beta, i, j], [B \rightarrow \gamma \bullet, j, k] \vdash [A \rightarrow \alpha B \bullet \beta, i, k]\},$$

$$D^{Pred} = \{[A \rightarrow \alpha \bullet B\beta, i, j] \vdash [B \rightarrow \bullet\gamma, j, j]\},$$

$$D_{Earley} = D^{Init} \cup D^{Scan} \cup D^{Compl} \cup D^{Pred}.$$

D^{Scan}, D^{Compl}, and D^{Pred} conform to the *scan*, *complete*, and *predict* steps, respectively, of the Earley algorithm.

A schematic illustration of the *complete* step is given in Figure 4.1.

Deduction steps D^{Init} add the axioms that are needed to start the parser, in addition to the hypotheses derived from the sentence.

The set of final items of $\mathbb{P}_{Earley}$ (cf. Definition 4.20) and the subset of correct final items are:

$$\mathcal{F} = \{[S \rightarrow \gamma \bullet, 0, n]\},$$

$$\mathcal{C} = \{[S \rightarrow \gamma \bullet, 0, n] \mid \gamma \Rightarrow^* a_1 \dots a_n\}.$$

The set of valid items that is computed by the system is:

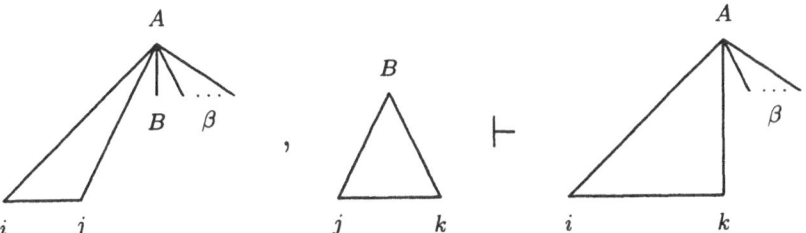

Fig. 4.1. The *complete* step

$$\mathcal{V}(\mathbb{P}_{Earley}) = \{[A\rightarrow\alpha\bullet\beta, i, j] \mid \alpha\Rightarrow^* a_{i+1}\ldots a_j \wedge$$
$$S\Rightarrow^* a_1 \ldots a_i A\gamma \text{ for some } \gamma\},$$

conforming to the Earley parser as it is known from the literature.

It is clear that a final item in $\mathcal{F}$ is valid if and only if it is a correct final item from $\mathcal{C}$. Therefore, $\mathbb{P}_{Earley}$ is correct for arbitrary G and $a_1 \ldots a_n$ and **Earley** is a correct parsing schema (for a formal proof, see [Sikkel, 1995, forthcoming]).

An Earley item $[A\rightarrow\alpha\bullet\beta, i, j]$ is, in fact, a shorthand notation for the set of trees defined by

$$[A\rightarrow \langle \alpha \rightsquigarrow \underline{a}_{i+1} \ldots \underline{a}_j \rangle \beta].$$

Special attention has to be paid to the case $\alpha = \varepsilon$. Such items have no marked leaf but can only be applied at a specific position in the sentence. Hence these are *left-marked items*, i.e., items containing left-marked trees (cf. Definition 3.12):

$$[j : \langle A\rightarrow\beta \rangle].$$

Having introduced the concept of left-marked items we could also denote them in the format of arbitrary Earley items

$$[A\rightarrow \langle \varepsilon \rightsquigarrow \underline{a}_{j+1} \ldots \underline{a}_j \rangle \beta]$$

which gives us a uniform notation for all Earley items. Thus the formal definition of the item set for a particular grammar G is

$$\mathcal{I}_{Earley}(G) = \{[A\rightarrow \langle \alpha \rightsquigarrow \underline{a}_{i+1} \ldots \underline{a}_j \rangle \beta] \mid A\rightarrow\alpha\beta \in P \wedge 0 \leq i \leq j\};$$

the operations can be defined accordingly. In order to establish the semiregularity of this set, we have to check that items are pairwise disjunct and that mixed items do not occur. All these properties follow straightforwardly from the definition. $\square$

The parsing schema **Earley** is an abstraction not only of Earley's algorithm. In Chapter 12 we will show that it is also the underlying parsing schema of an LR(0) parser.

Before we continue with the examples, one more point of friction between theory and practice has to be cleared up. As a persistent design choice, we have formulated parsing systems $\langle \mathcal{I}, H, D \rangle$ in such a way that $\mathcal{I}$ and D depend on the grammar G but not on the string and H depends on the string $a_1 \ldots a_n$ but not on the grammar. A consequence of this design choice is that some parsing systems contain a (countably infinite) number of items with position markers beyond the length of the string that is to be parsed. In the bottom-up version of Earley, for example, any item $[A \rightarrow \bullet \alpha, j, j]$ is valid. The existence of this item is a consequence of the grammar, not a consequence of the sentence. Hence it can be derived by a deduction step without antecedents $\vdash [A \rightarrow \bullet \alpha, j, j]$.

Practically speaking, this is no problem at all. It is obvious that any sensible implementation would only consider recognizing those valid items that fall within the positions spanned by the sentence. But from a theoretical perspective, however, this design is not elegant. Several solutions can be considered.

The first option is to consider items of the form $[A \rightarrow \bullet \alpha, j, j]$ as hypotheses, rather than consequents of antecedentless deduction steps. Then H contains such items only with $j \leq n$, and the problem has been solved. A minor disadvantage of this approach is that definitions of parsing schemata would have to be based on instantiated, rather than uninstantiated parsing systems. Hypotheses now depend on G as well as $a_1 \ldots a_n$. A more substantial nuisance would be that we introduce a degree of freedom in the specification of parsing systems, allowing some kind of information to be coded either in H or in D. This leads to syntactically different, equivalent denotations of a single schema. As a consequence, we would have to define a normal form for the equivalence relation in order to compare (normal forms of) different parsing schemata.

A second option is to replace antecedentless deduction steps $\vdash [A \rightarrow \bullet \alpha, j, j]$ by deduction steps $[\$, n, n+1] \vdash [A \rightarrow \bullet \alpha, j, j]$ only for $j \leq n$. While this would be adequate for the examples here, the *ad hoc* character of such a definition causes problems in Chapter 6 where we discuss filtering. It would prohibit an elegant description of the Earley schema as a top-down filtered variant of the bottom-up Earley schema.

As in previous cases we will choose a pragmatic solution, simply by arguing that the problem is not relevant for really existing parsers. Rather than the set of valid items $\mathcal{V}(\mathbb{P})$ we restrict our attention to the subset of *relevant* valid items $\mathcal{V}^{\leq n}(\mathbb{P})$ for a sentence of length n.

Definition 4.33. (*relevant valid items*)
Let $\mathbb{P} = \langle \mathcal{I}, H, D \rangle$ be a parsing system. An item $\iota \in \mathcal{I}$ is *irrelevant* for (a string of length) n if every tree $\tau \in \iota$ contains some marked terminal a_j with $j > n$ or is a left- or right-marked tree (cf. Definition 3.12) marked with some $j > n$. We write $\mathcal{I}^{>n}$ for the irrelevant items of $\mathcal{I}$.
The set of *relevant items* $\mathcal{I}^{\leq n}$ is defined by $\mathcal{I}^{\leq n} = \mathcal{I} \backslash \mathcal{I}^{>n}$.
The set of *relevant valid items* $\mathcal{V}^{\leq n}$ is given by $\mathcal{V}^{\leq n} = \mathcal{V} \cap \mathcal{I}^{\leq n}$.   □

In the following examples of parsing schemata we will only be concerned with relevant valid items.

Example 4.34. (*the* **buE** *parsing schema*)
An Earley parser proceeds through a sentence from left to right. A bottom-up parallel Earley can start at each word in the sentence in parallel. To that end, a larger set of initial deduction steps is added and the *predict* steps are discarded.
As usual, we define the parsing schema **buE** by specifying a parsing system $\mathbb{P}_{buE}$ for an arbitrary grammar G:

$$\mathcal{I}_{buE} = \{[A{\to}\alpha{\bullet}\beta, i, j] \mid A{\to}\alpha\beta \in P \wedge 0 \le i \le j\} = \mathcal{I}_{Earley},$$

$$D^{Init} = \{\vdash [A{\to}{\bullet}\alpha, j, j]\},$$

$$D^{Scan} = \{[A{\to}\alpha{\bullet}a\beta, i, j], [a, j, j+1] \vdash [A{\to}\alpha a{\bullet}\beta, i, j+1]\} = D^{Scan}_{Earley},$$

$$D^{Compl} = \{[A{\to}\alpha{\bullet}B\beta, i, j], [B{\to}\gamma{\bullet}, j, k] \vdash [A{\to}\alpha B{\bullet}\beta, i, k]\} = D^{Compl}_{Earley},$$

$$D_{buE} = D^{Init} \cup D^{Scan} \cup D^{Compl}.$$

It is left to the reader to verify that the set of relevant valid items is given by

$$\mathcal{V}^{\le n}(\mathbb{P}_{buE}) = \{[A{\to}\alpha{\bullet}\beta, i, j] \in \mathcal{I}^{\le n}_{buE} \mid \alpha {\Rightarrow}^* a_{i+1} \ldots a_j\}.$$

It is obvious, again, that from final items $[S{\to}\gamma{\bullet}, 0, n]$ for a string $a_1 \ldots a_n$, only those are valid for which $\gamma {\Rightarrow}^* a_1 \ldots a_n$. Irrelevant items surely do not contain parse trees, hence we conclude that the parsing schema is correct. $\square$

Example 4.35. (*the* **buLC** *parsing schema*)
The parsing schema **buE** is correct but it contains some slight redundancies.[6]
Suppose that we have a valid item $[A{\to}B{\bullet}\beta, i, j]$. How is such an item deduced? The only way to establish the validity of this item, is by using a valid item $[B{\to}\gamma{\bullet}, i, j]$ as an antecedent in the *complete* step

$$[A{\to}{\bullet}B\beta, i, i], [B{\to}\gamma{\bullet}, i, j] \vdash [A{\to}B{\bullet}\beta, i, j].$$

The item $[A{\to}{\bullet}B\beta, i, i]$ does not play any significant role in the bottom-up variant of Earley's algorithm; it is valid by definition. No harm is done if we delete it as an antecedent and replace the *complete* step by an – in this case – equivalent deduction step

$$[B{\to}\gamma{\bullet}, i, j] \vdash [A{\to}B{\bullet}\beta, i, j],$$

as illustrated in Figure 4.2.
A similar argument applies to items of the form $[A{\to}a{\bullet}\beta, i, j]$ and the appropriate *scan* step. Hence, most items with a dot in leftmost position serve no purpose, other than satisfying the **buE** specification for historic reasons.

---

[6] This optimization was proposed by Kilbury [1984], cf. [Leiss, 1990].

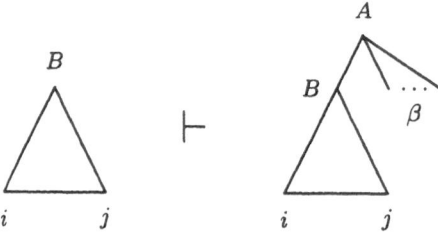

Fig. 4.2. The (bottom-up) *left-corner* step

(It should be noted, though, that items with a dot in leftmost postion are indispensible if the right-hand side of the production is empty. The above argument does not relate to items of the form $[A\rightarrow\bullet, j, j]$.)

Based on these considerations, we define a parsing schema that very similar to **buE** but slightly more economic. This schema is called **buLC**, which is an abbreviation of a *bottom-up Left Corner* schema. As usual, we specify a parsing system for an arbitrary grammar $G \in \mathcal{CFG}$, as follows:

$$\mathcal{I}^{(1)} = \{[A\rightarrow X\alpha\bullet\beta, i, j] \mid A\rightarrow X\alpha\beta \in P \wedge 0 \leq i \leq j\},$$

$$\mathcal{I}^{(2)} = \{[A\rightarrow\bullet, j, j] \mid A\rightarrow\varepsilon \in P \wedge j \geq 0\},$$

$$\mathcal{I}_{buLC} = \mathcal{I}^{(1)} \cup \mathcal{I}^{(2)};$$

$$D^{\varepsilon} = \{\vdash [A\rightarrow\bullet, j, j]\},$$

$$D^{LC(a)} = \{[a, j-1, j] \vdash [B\rightarrow a\bullet\beta, j-1, j]\},$$

$$D^{LC(A)} = \{[A\rightarrow\alpha\bullet, i, j] \vdash [B\rightarrow A\bullet\beta, i, j]\},$$

$$D^{Scan} = \{[A\rightarrow\alpha\bullet a\beta, i, j], [a, j, j+1] \vdash [A\rightarrow\alpha a\bullet\beta, i, j+1]\},$$

$$D^{Compl} = \{[A\rightarrow\alpha\bullet B\beta, i, j], [B\rightarrow\gamma\bullet, j, k] \vdash [A\rightarrow\alpha B\bullet\beta, i, k]\},$$

$$D_{buLC} = D^{\varepsilon} \cup D^{LC(a)} \cup D^{LC(A)} \cup D^{Scan} \cup D^{Compl}.$$

From the above discussion it follows that

$$\mathcal{V}^{\leq n}(\mathbb{P}_{buLC}) = \mathcal{V}^{\leq n}(\mathbb{P}_{buE}) \cap \mathcal{I}_{buLC}$$
$$= \{[A\rightarrow\alpha\bullet\beta, i, j] \in \mathcal{I}^{\leq n}_{buLC} \mid \alpha \Rightarrow^{*} a_{i+1} \ldots a_j$$
$$\wedge (\alpha \neq \varepsilon \vee \beta = \varepsilon)\}$$

and that the **buLC** schema is correct.   □

Example 4.36. (*the LC parsing schema*)
In the above example we defined **buLC** as a slightly more economic version of **buE**. If a constituent has been recognized completely, i.e., we found an item $[B\rightarrow\gamma\bullet, i, j]$, we use a *left-corner* step and recognize an item $[A\rightarrow B\bullet\beta, i, j]$. This could be done, because, in the **buE** schema, the item $[A\rightarrow\bullet B\beta, i, i]$ is

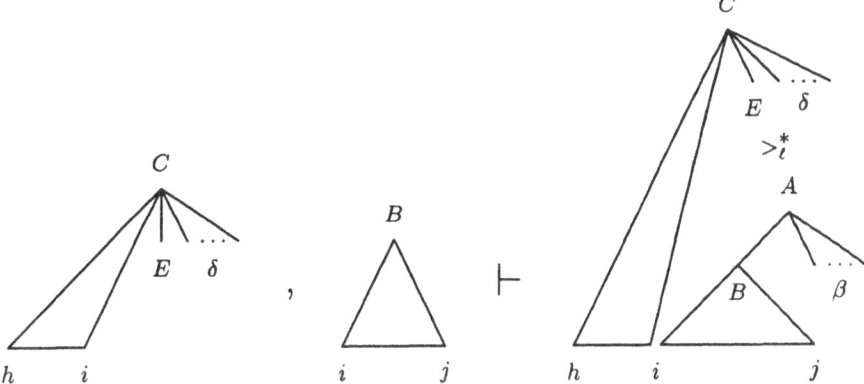

Fig. 4.3. The (*predictive*) *left-corner* step

always valid. If we try the same transformation on the (left-to-right) **Earley** schema, things get slightly more complicated. It is *not* the case that $[A{\to}{\bullet}B\beta, i, i]$ is always valid. Hence, the replacement of a deduction

$$[A{\to}{\bullet}B\beta, i, i], [B{\to}\gamma{\bullet}, i, j] \vdash [A{\to}B{\bullet}\beta, i, j]$$

by a deduction $[B{\to}\gamma{\bullet}, i, j] \vdash [A{\to}B{\bullet}\beta, i, j]$ should be allowed *only in those cases* where $[A{\to}{\bullet}B\beta, i, i]$ is actually valid. Under which conditions is this the case? The item $[A{\to}{\bullet}B\beta, i, i]$ is predicted by **Earley** only if there is some item of the form

$$[C{\to}\alpha{\bullet}A\delta, h, i]$$

It could be the case, however, that $\alpha = \varepsilon$. Then this is one of the items that is not contained in the domain of the **buLC** schema and we continue the search for an item that licences the validity of $[C{\to}{\bullet}A\delta, i, i]$. This search can end in two ways: either we find some item with the dot not in leftmost position, or (only in case $i = 0$) we may move all the way up to $[S{\to}{\bullet}\gamma, 0, 0]$. This can be formalized as follows.

The *left corner* is the leftmost symbol in the right-hand side of a production. $A{\to}X\alpha$ has left corner X; an empty production $A{\to}\varepsilon$ has left corner ε. The relation $>_\ell$ on $N \times (V \cup \{\varepsilon\})$ is defined by

$$A >_\ell U \text{ if there is a production } A{\to}\alpha \in P \text{ which has left corner } U.$$

The transitive and reflexive closure of $>_\ell$ is denoted $>_\ell^*$.
It is clear that $[A{\to}{\bullet}B\beta, i, i]$ will be recognized by the Earley algorithm if there is some valid item $[C{\to}\alpha{\bullet}E\delta, h, i]$ with $E >_\ell^* A$. Moreover, there is such an item with $\alpha \neq \varepsilon$, unless, perhaps, $i = 0$ and $E = S$. In order to deal with this exceptional case, we must make sure that items of the form $[S{\to}{\bullet}\gamma, 0, 0]$ are in the domain, all other items of the from $[A{\to}{\bullet}\alpha, i, i]$ with

$\alpha \neq \varepsilon$ are dispensable. To replace the missing *complete* steps, we introduce *left-corner* steps as follows:

$$[C \to \alpha \bullet E\delta, h, i], [B \to \gamma \bullet, i, j] \vdash [A \to B \bullet \beta, i, j] \text{ only if } E >_\ell^* A.$$

A schematic illustration is shown in Figure 4.3.

A similar argument holds for items of the form $[A \to a \bullet \beta, j - 1, j]$.

Thus we obtain a full formal description of the **LC** schema, as usual by defining a parsing system for arbitrary $G \in \mathcal{CFG}$:

$$\mathcal{I}^{(1)} = \{[A \to X\alpha \bullet \beta, i, j] \mid A \to X\alpha\beta \in P \wedge 0 \leq i \leq j\},$$

$$\mathcal{I}^{(2)} = \{[A \to \bullet, j, j] \mid A \to \varepsilon \in P \wedge j \geq 0\},$$

$$\mathcal{I}^{(3)} = \{[S \to \bullet\gamma, 0, 0] \mid S \to \gamma \in P\},$$

$$\mathcal{I}_{LC} = \mathcal{I}^{(1)} \cup \mathcal{I}^{(2)} \cup \mathcal{I}^{(3)};$$

$$D^{Init} = \{\vdash [S \to \bullet\gamma, 0, 0]\},$$

$$D^{LC(A)} = \{[C \to \gamma \bullet E\delta, h, i], [A \to \alpha \bullet, i, j] \vdash [B \to A \bullet \beta, i, j] \mid E >_\ell^* B\},$$

$$D^{LC(a)} = \{[C \to \gamma \bullet E\delta, h, i], [a, i, i+1] \vdash [B \to a \bullet \beta, i, i+1] \mid E >_\ell^* B\},$$

$$D^{LC(\varepsilon)} = \{[C \to \gamma \bullet E\delta, h, i], \vdash [B \to \bullet, i, i] \mid E >_\ell^* B\},$$

$$D^{Scan} = \{[A \to \alpha \bullet a\beta, i, j], [a, j, j+1] \vdash [A \to \alpha a \bullet \beta, i, j+1]\},$$

$$D^{Compl} = \{[A \to \alpha \bullet B\beta, i, j], [B \to \gamma \bullet, j, k] \vdash [A \to \alpha B \bullet \beta, i, k]\},$$

$$D_{LC} = D^{Init} \cup D^{LC(a)} \cup D^{LC(A)} \cup D^{LC(\varepsilon)} \cup D^{Scan} \cup D^{Compl}.$$

From the above discussion it follows that

$$\begin{aligned} \mathcal{V}^{\leq n}(\mathbb{P}_{LC}) &= \mathcal{V}^{\leq n}(\mathbb{P}_{Earley}) \cap \mathcal{I}_{LC} \\ &= \{[A \to \alpha \bullet \beta, i, j] \in \mathcal{I}_{LC}^{\leq n} \mid \alpha \Rightarrow^* a_{i+1} \ldots a_j \wedge \\ &\qquad\qquad S \Rightarrow^* a_1 \ldots a_i A\gamma \text{ for some } \gamma\}. \end{aligned}$$

It should be mentioned that this schema reflects the (generalized) Left-Corner algorithm as it has been described in the literature. *Deterministic* LC parsing has been defined by Rosenkrantz and Lewis [1970]. See also [op den Akker, 1988]. Generalized LC parsers have been described by Matsumoto [1983], Nederhof [1993], and Sikkel and op den Akker [1992, 1993]

When it comes down to implementing this schema, the efficiency can be increased by adding additional *predict* items of the form $[D, i]$, denoting the fact that *some* item of the form $[C \to \alpha \bullet D\delta, h, i]$ has been found, abstracting from items in $\mathcal{I}$ similar to the way in which items abstract from trees in $\mathcal{T}$. A more detailed treatment will be given in Chapter 10.   □

There are some obvious relations between the parsing schemata **buE**, **Earley**, **buLC** and **LC**. The definitions of these parsing schemata are not "stand-alone" definitions, in a way. We have defined **buLC** and **LC**, informally, by applying *transformations* to the parsing schemata **buE** and **Earley**. Subsequently we have given formal definitions that satisfy the intuitive understanding. In Chapters 5 and 6 we will formalize such transformations and discuss under which conditions the correctness of a schema is invariant under a transformation.

4.7 Conclusion

We have generalized the theory of tree-based parsing schemata of Chapter 3 to (item-based) parsing schemata. Tree based parsing schemata can be seen as a special case in which every item comprises a single tree.

In this chapter we have seen that there is a tension between theoretical elegance and pragmatic convenience. In order to cover schemata for parsing algorithms that appear in the literature we have gone so far as to allow items that are inconsistent with the (most elegant) underlying theory. Subsequently we have argued that the difference is not relevant for practical parsers. Semiregularity is a rather natural property of parsing schemata. A minor problem, but nevertheless another sore point, is the distinction between relevant and irrelevant valid items. Here we have settled for a minor practical inconvenience in order to avoid a major theoretical inelegance. In both cases we have extensively motivated our design choices and we have argued that different choices, looking like plausible alternatives, have more serious drawbacks.

These frictions in the theory are caused by the sometimes incompatible interests of theory and practice. If we would look at it from a purely theoretical perspective, it is very simple to come up with a smaller and rather more elegant theory, in which only regular parsing schemata are considered. Our major concern, however, is that the theory can be *applied* for the description of practical parsers; the theory is not a purpose in itself. That the parsing schemata framework can be applied to describe a variety of parsers will be shown in Chapter 6, where half a dozen parsing algorithms known from the literature are fitted into a single taxonomy of Earley-related parsing schemata. More involved applications will follow in Part III.

5. Refinement and generalization

In Chapters 3 and 4 we have formally established the notion of a parsing schema, and presented some examples. In this chapter and the next one we will discuss relations between parsing schemata.

The main notion that we are concerned with here is *refinement*. A parsing schema is a refinement of another schema when it allows more deductions or when it performs the same deductions in smaller steps. This notion has a twofold application. Firstly, we can identify some chains of refinements, describing schemata for parsers that exist in the literature. Secondly, if a parser is known to be correct, the refinement relation can be used to prove the correctness of another parser.

In Section 5.1, we go back to the more abstract setting of enhanced deduction systems and establish some general notions like homomorphism and isomorphism. Next, in 5.2, we formally introduce the notion of refinement for parsing systems and schemata. Some examples of refinements are presented in 5.3. In 5.4 we introduce *generalization*, i.e., applying a parsing schema to a larger class of grammars. Generalization usually includes refinement as well.

In Chapter 6, subsequently, we will study the notion of a *filter*. Filters are, in a general sense, the inverse of refinement: a filtered system makes less deductions or contracts sequences of deductions to single deduction steps. Using refinements and filters, a large variety of parsers can be described within a single taxonomy. In Section 6.6 an overview is given that summarizes the relation between the different kinds of relations introduced in Chapters 5 and 6.

5.1 Mappings between deduction systems

In Section 5.1 we are concerned with mappings between arbitrary enhanced deduction systems, say $\mathbb{E}_1$ and $\mathbb{E}_2$. In each case we will assume that $\mathbb{E}_1 = \langle X_1, H_1, F_1, C_1, D_1 \rangle$ and $\mathbb{E}_2 = \langle X_2, H_2, F_2, C_2, D_2 \rangle$. Furthermore, we write Δ_1 for $\Delta(\mathbb{E}_1)$ Δ_2 for $\Delta(\mathbb{E}_2)$, $\mathcal{V}_1$ for $\mathcal{V}(\mathbb{E}_1)$ and $\mathcal{V}_2$ for $\mathcal{V}(\mathbb{E}_2)$. Similar definitions apply to deduction systems $\mathbb{D}_1$ and $\mathbb{D}_2$; the only thing that has to be changed is deleting all conditions on F_i and C_i. But we are primarily interested in enhanced systems, here, because an interesting aspect of mappings between deduction systems is whether correctness is preserved.

Definition 5.1. (*pointwise extensions of a function*)
Let $\mathbb{E}_1$ and $\mathbb{E}_2$ be deduction systems, and $f : H_1 \cup X_1 \to H_2 \cup X_2$ a function. We can define a function $\hat{f} : \wp(H_1 \cup X_1) \to \wp(H_2 \cup X_2)$ that maps sets of entities into sets of entities by pointwise application, i.e.,

$$\hat{f}(Y) = \{x_2 \in X_2 \mid \exists x_1 \subseteq Y : f(x_1) = x_2\}.$$

A function f that maps $H_1 \cup X_1$ to $H_2 \cup X_2$ can also be extended to a function

$$f' : \wp_{fin}(H_1 \cup X_1) \times X_1 \to \wp_{fin}(H_2 \cup X_2) \times X_2$$

that maps deduction steps to deduction steps by pointwise application:

$$f'(Y, x) = (\hat{f}(Y), f(x)).$$

f' can be extended to $\hat{f}'$, similarly, mapping sets of deduction steps into sets of deduction steps, by analogy to the extension of f into $\hat{f}$.

In a similar vein, we can extend f into a function f'' that maps deduction sequences in $\mathbb{E}_1$ to deduction sequences in $\mathbb{E}_2$. (Note, however, that there is a consistency issue here, because it is not generally guaranteed that $f''(Y \vdash x_1 \vdash \ldots \vdash x_j)$ is a valid deduction sequence in $\mathbb{E}_2$!) And, finally, we can maps sets of deduction sequences into sets of deduction sequences by a function $\hat{f}''$. When no confusion can arise about the domain of a function, we simply write f for f', f'', $\hat{f}$, $\hat{f}'$ and $\hat{f}''$ as well.   □

The purpose of the functions $\hat{f}'$ and $\hat{f}''$ as defined above is that we can use them to state conditions on functions in a concise, well-defined and intuitively clear manner. If we state, for example, that

$$f(D_1) = D_2$$

this means

$(Y_2, x_2) \in D_2$ if and only if there are $Y_1 \in \wp_{fin}(H_1 \cup X_1)$ and $x_1 \in X_1$ such that $\hat{f}(Y_1) = Y_2$ and $f(x_1) = x_2$ and $(Y_1, x_1) \in D_1$.

Similarly,

$$f(\Delta_1) = \Delta_2$$

is a clear and concise notation for

$Y_2 \vdash_2 x_1 \vdash_2 \ldots \vdash_2 x_j$ if and only if there are $Y_1 \in \wp_{fin}(H_1 \cup X_1)$ with $\hat{f}(Y_1) = Y_2$ and $x'_1, \ldots, x'_j \in X_1$ with $f(x_i) = x'_i$ for $1 \leq i \leq j$ such that $Y_1 \vdash_1 x'_1 \vdash_1 \ldots \vdash_1 x'_j$.

Mappings – and other relations – between deduction systems can have several interesting properties. First of all, the usual properties on relations may apply. Relations like refinement, extension, generalization and various types of filters all are transitive and reflexive. Reflexivity is always trivial, transitivity sometimes. In Section 5.2 we will see that transitivity of refinement is not straightforward. Other properties that relations may have is preservation of soundness / completeness / correctness. We discuss relations *between* deduction systems here, as opposed to relations *on* (the domain of) a single deduction system.

Definition 5.2. (*preservation properties of relations*)
Let $\mathbb{E}_1$ and $\mathbb{E}_2$ be arbitrary enhanced deduction systems. A relation R between deduction systems is called *soundness / completeness / correctness preserving* if $\mathbb{E}_1 R \mathbb{E}_2$ and the soundness / completeness / correctness of $\mathbb{E}_1$ are sufficient conditions for the soundness / completeness / correctness of $\mathbb{E}_2$. Let $\mathbf{P}_1$ and $\mathbf{P}_2$ be arbitrary semiregular parsing schemata for some class of grammars $\mathcal{CG}$. A relation R between parsing schemata is called *soundness / completeness / correctness preserving*, if $\mathbf{P}_1 R \mathbf{P}_2$ and the soundness / completeness / correctness of $\mathbf{P}_1$ are sufficient conditions for the soundness / completeness / correctness of $\mathbf{P}_2$. □

Definition 5.3. (*homomorphism*)
A function $f : H_1 \cup X_1 \rightarrow H_2 \cup X_2$ is called a *homomorphism from* $\mathbb{E}_1$ *to* $\mathbb{E}_2$ if:

(i) $f(H_1) \subseteq H_2$,
(ii) $f(X_1 \backslash F_1) \subseteq X_2 \backslash F_2$,
(iii) $f(F_1) \subseteq F_2$,
(iv) $f(C_1) \subseteq C_2$,
(v) $f(D_1) \subseteq D_2$.   □

Definition 5.4. (*isomorphism*)
A homomorphism $f : X_1 \cup H_1 \rightarrow X_2 \cup H_2$ is called an *isomorphism from* $\mathbb{E}_1$ *to* $\mathbb{E}_2$ if an inverse function $f^{-1} : X_2 \rightarrow X_1$ exists and f^{-1} is a homomorphism from $\mathbb{E}_2$ to $\mathbb{E}_1$.
As a practical notation we write $X_1 \equiv_f X_2$ if f is a bijective function from X_1 to X_2. We write $\mathbb{E}_1 \equiv_f \mathbb{E}_2$ if f is an isomorphism from $\mathbb{E}_1$ to $\mathbb{E}_2$. We write $\mathbb{E}_1 \equiv \mathbb{E}_2$ if there is a function f such that $\mathbb{E}_1 \equiv_f \mathbb{E}_2$.
Two parsing schemata $\mathbf{P}_1$ and $\mathbf{P}_2$ are *isomorphic* on a class of grammars $\mathcal{CG}$ if for each $G \in \mathcal{CG}$ and for each $a_1 \ldots a_n \in \Sigma^*$ it holds that

$$\mathbf{P}_1(G)(a_1 \ldots a_n) \equiv \mathbf{P}_2(G)(a_1 \ldots a_n).$$

We write $\mathbf{P}_1 \equiv \mathbf{P}_2$ if $\mathbf{P}_1$ and $\mathbf{P}_2$ are isomorphic.   □

The inverse of an isomorphism is also an isomorphism. Furthermore, an isomorphism is correctness preserving. A homomorphism, in general, is not correctness preserving. The soundness can be violated by adding deduction steps to $\mathbb{E}_2$ that validate entities in $F_2 \backslash C_2$. The completeness can be violated by adding new, invalid entities to C_2.

Preservation of completeness can be guaranteed by demanding that the homomorphism be *surjective*, i.e., $f(H_1) = H_2$, $f(X_1 \backslash F_1) = X_2 \backslash F_2$, $f(F_1) = F_2$, $f(C_1) = C_2$, $f(D_1) = D_2$. As soundness is always the trivial part of a proof, completeness preservation is almost as useful as correctness preservation. But in the sequel we will make much use of a slightly more restricted kind of homomorphism that does preserve correctness as well.

Definition 5.5. (*item contraction function*)
A function $f : X_1 \cup H_1 \rightarrow X_2 \cup H_2$ is called an *item contraction from* $\mathbb{E}_1$ *to* $\mathbb{E}_2$ if

(i) $H_1 \equiv_f H_2$
(ii) $f(X_1 \backslash F_1) = X_2 \backslash F_2$
(iii) $f(F_1) = F_2$
(iv) $f(C_1) = C_2$
(v) $f(\Delta_1) = \Delta_2$ □

The reason that we demand that deduction *sequences* are mapped onto deduction sequences, i.e., $f(\Delta_1) = \Delta_2$, rather than $f(D_1) = D_2$, will become clear in Section 5.2 where item refinement, the inverse of item contraction, is defined. The mapping of deduction sequences, rather than deduction steps, is needed to establish transitivity of a more general notion of refinement that also includes step refinement.

Corollary 5.6.
Let $\mathbb{E}_1$ be an enhanced deduction system, $\cong$ a regular congruence relation on $\mathbb{E}$. Let $f_\cong : \mathbb{E} \rightarrow \mathbb{E}/\cong$ be the canonical function that maps x onto $[x]$. Then $f_\cong$ is an item contraction function.   □

We can apply item contraction directly to parsing schemata, but it only makes sense to do so on *regular* schemata. We can extend the idea to semiregular parsing schemata by only considering the regular subschemata.

Definition 5.7. (*the relations* $\xrightarrow{ic}$ *and* $\xRightarrow{ic}$)
Let $\mathbb{P}_1$ and $\mathbb{P}_2$ be semiregular parsing systems. The relation $\mathbb{P}_1 \xrightarrow{ic} \mathbb{P}_2$ holds if there is an item contraction function $f : \mathbb{P}_1^r \rightarrow \mathbb{P}_2^r$ between the regular subsystems of $\mathbb{P}_1$ and $\mathbb{P}_2$.
Let $\mathbf{P}_1$ and $\mathbf{P}_2$ be semiregular parsing schemata for some class of grammars $\mathcal{CG}$. The relation $\mathbf{P}_1 \xRightarrow{ic} \mathbf{P}_2$ holds if, for each $G \in \mathcal{CG}$ and $a_1 \ldots a_n \in \Sigma^*$ it holds that

$$\mathbf{P}_1(G)(a_1 \ldots a_n) \xrightarrow{ic} \mathbf{P}_2(G)(a_1 \ldots a_n).$$ □

Corollary 5.8.
The relation $\xrightarrow{ic}$ is transitive, reflexive, and correctness preserving;
The relation $\xRightarrow{ic}$ is transitive, reflexive, and correctness preserving.   □

Corollary 5.9.
The following statements hold:

- Let $\mathbb{T}$ be a tree-based parsing system, $\cong$ a regular congruence relation on $\mathbb{T}$. Then $\mathbb{T} \xrightarrow{\text{ic}} \mathbb{T}/\cong$.
- Let $\mathbb{T}$ be a tree-based parsing system, $\cong_1$ an $\cong_2$ regular congruence relations on $\mathbb{T}$ and $\cong_1 \subseteq \cong_2$ (i.e., $x \cong_1 x'$ implies $x \cong_2 x'$). Then $\mathbb{T}/\cong_1 \xrightarrow{\text{ic}} \mathbb{T}/\cong_2$.
- Let $\mathbb{P}_1$, $\mathbb{P}_2$ be semiregular parsing schemata, $\cong$ a regular congruence relation on $\mathbb{P}_1^r$, and $\mathbb{P}_1^r/\cong \equiv \mathbb{P}_2^r$. Then $\mathbb{P}_1 \xrightarrow{\text{ic}} \mathbb{P}_2$. $\qquad\qquad\square$

5.2 Refinement: a formal approach

We can see Earley-type algorithms as a refinement of CYK-type algorithms. The latter recognize constituents, whereas the former also deal with partial constituents. A single step in a CYK parser corresponds to several steps in an Earley parser.

More generally, but still informally, refinement of parsing systems (and hence parsing schemata) can be seen as consisting of two steps:

- *item refinement*: Some items are split up into smaller items; the set of deduction steps is adapted accordingly.
- *step refinement*: Single deduction steps are refined into series of deduction steps. To this end, new items can be added as well.

We will define item refinement and step refinement separately and afterwards define refinement in such a way that it is the simultaneous transitive closure of both kinds of refinement.

Definition 5.10. (*item refinement*)
Let $\mathbb{P}_1 = \langle \mathcal{I}_1, H, D_1 \rangle$ and $\mathbb{P}_2 = \langle \mathcal{I}_2, H, D_2 \rangle$ be semiregular parsing systems. The relation $\mathbb{P}_1 \xrightarrow{\text{ir}} \mathbb{P}_2$ holds if $\mathbb{P}_2 \xrightarrow{\text{ic}} \mathbb{P}_1$.
Let $\mathbf{P}_1$, $\mathbf{P}_2$ be semiregular parsing schemata for a class of grammar $\mathcal{CG}$. The relation $\mathbf{P}_1 \xRightarrow{\text{ir}} \mathbf{P}_2$ holds if $\mathbf{P}_2 \xRightarrow{\text{ic}} \mathbf{P}_1$. $\qquad\qquad\square$

Item refinement, in general, is the reverse of item contraction. But in the remainder of Chapter 5 we are specifically concerned with parsing systems and schemata, not deduction systems in general. In this more specific setting, the conditions for item contraction and refinement can be simplified. Firstly, we notice that the hypotheses will always be the same, hence the condition $H_1 \equiv_f H_2$ can be deleted. Secondly, we will introduce a simple regularity constraint on functions, that allows us to discard a few condition from Definition 5.5.

Definition 5.11. (*regular item mapping*)
Let $\mathbb{P}_1$, $\mathbb{P}_2$ be semiregular parsing systems. A function $f : \mathcal{I}_1^r \to \mathcal{I}_2^r$ is called a
regular item mapping if for all $\iota \in \mathcal{I}_1^r$ and all $\tau \in \iota$ it holds that $\tau \in f(\iota)$. $\square$

Lemma 5.12.
Let $\mathbb{P}_1$, $\mathbb{P}_2$ be semiregular parsing systems. If there is a regular item mapping
$f : \mathcal{I}_2^r \to \mathcal{I}_1^r$ such that

(*i*) $\mathcal{I}_1^r = f(\mathcal{I}_2^r)$,
(*ii*) $\Delta_1^r = f(\Delta_2^r)$,

then $\mathbb{P}_1 \xrightarrow{\text{ir}} \mathbb{P}_2$.

Proof. It suffices to show that the following inequalities hold:

(*iii*) $f(\mathcal{I}_2 \backslash \mathcal{F}_2^{(n)}) \subseteq \mathcal{I}_1 \backslash \mathcal{F}_1^{(n)}$,
(*iv*) $\mathcal{I}_1 \backslash \mathcal{F}_1^{(n)} \subseteq f(\mathcal{I}_2 \backslash \mathcal{F}_2^{(n)})$,
(*v*) $f(\mathcal{F}_2^{(n)}) \subseteq \mathcal{F}_1^{(n)}$,
(*vi*) $\mathcal{F}_1^{(n)} \subseteq f(\mathcal{F}_2^{(n)})$,
(*vii*) $f(\mathcal{C}_2) \subseteq \mathcal{C}_1$,
(*viii*) $\mathcal{C}_1 \subseteq f(\mathcal{C}_2)$.

Inequalities (*iii*), (*v*), and (*vii*) follow straight from the definition.
Inequalities (*iv*) and (*vi*) follow from (*iii*) and (*v*) in combination with (*i*)
and the fact that $\mathcal{I}_1^r$ is regular.
For (*viii*) we have to realize that $\cup \mathcal{C}_1 = \cup \mathcal{C}_2$ (both are equal to $\mathcal{P}_G(a_1 \ldots a_n)$)
by definition). Take an arbitrary $\iota_i \in \mathcal{C}_1$ and let $\tau \in \iota_1$. Then there must be
some $\iota_2 \in \mathcal{C}_2$ with $\tau \in \iota_2$. Because f is a regular item mapping, it must hold
that $f(\iota_2) = \iota_1$. $\square$

Example 5.13.
Item refinement is usually combined with step refinement. Therefore an example of item refinement in isolation may seem somewhat artificial.
Consider the parsing schema **CYK** for grammars in $\mathcal{CNF}$, cf. Example 4.27.
We can replace items of the form $[A, i, j]$ by items of the form $[A \to \alpha, i, j]$,
for each production $A \to \alpha$. If there are different productions with the same
left-hand side, the CYK item is split up accordingly. Thus we get a parsing
schema **CYK'** by defining a system $\mathbb{P}_{CYK'}$ for arbitrary $G \in \mathcal{CNF}$:

$$\mathcal{I}_{CYK'} = \{[A \to \alpha, i, j] \mid A \to \alpha \in P \wedge 0 \leq i \leq j\};$$

$$D^{(1)} = \{[a, j - 1, j] \vdash [A \to a, j - 1, j]\},$$

$$D^{(2)} = \{[B \to \beta, i, j], [C \to \gamma, j, k] \vdash [A \to BC, i, k]\},$$

$$D_{CYK'} = D^{(1)} \cup D^{(2)}.$$

It is left to the reader to verify that **CYK'** is a correct parsing schema. $\square$

If $\mathbb{P}_1 \xrightarrow{ir} \mathbb{P}_2$ then the correctness of $\mathbb{P}_2$ implies the correctness of $\mathbb{P}_1$ (Corollary 5.8). The reverse, however is *not* true. Most item refinements that are defined in a sensible manner will preserve correctness as well. But if one really wants to refine a correct system into an incorrect one, that can be done. An example of what can go wrong (only if mischief is intended) is the following.

Let us refine CYK items $[A, i, j]$ into items $[A \to \alpha, i, j]$, where $[A \to \alpha, i, j]$ denotes a set of trees $[A \to \langle \alpha \rightsquigarrow \underline{a}_{i+1} \ldots \underline{a}_j \rangle]$. Suppose, now, that we have a grammar

$$S \to AB \mid BB$$
$$A \to a,$$
$$B \to b.$$

In the CYK system for this grammar we have a deduction step

$$[A, 0, 1], [B, 1, 2] \vdash [S, 0, 2].$$

It is possible to refine this into a deduction step

$$[A \to a, 0, 1], [B \to b, 1, 2] \vdash [S \to BB, 0, 2],$$

and refine the other deduction steps as in Example 5.13. The resulting system is neither sound nor complete. For a string ab, the item $[S \to AB, 0, 2]$ that contains the (only) parse tree will not be recognized, whereas the final item $[S \to BB, 0, 2]$ that does *not* contain a parse tree is valid in this system.

A general method to make sure that item refinement is correctness preserving is the following. Let $\mathbb{P}_1$ be a correct parsing system, and $\mathbb{T}$ the underlying tree-based system of $\mathbb{P}_1^r$, i.e., there is some regular congruence relation $\cong$ such that $\mathbb{P}_1^r = \mathbb{T}/\cong_1$. if $\mathbb{P}_1$ is correct, it is usually not difficult to establish that $\mathbb{T}$ is correct as well. One has to redo the correctness proof based on trees, rather than items. If one defines a refinement $\mathbb{P}_2$ of $\mathbb{P}_1$ such that $\mathbb{P}_2^r = \mathbb{T}/\cong_2$, then $\mathbb{P}_2$ must be correct as well. This is clearly the case in Example 5.13, **CYK** and **CYK'** both have **TCYK** as underlying tree-based parsing schema.

We will now turn to step refinement, which is rather more easy to define than item refinement. Step refinement is completeness preserving. For practical applications this is almost as good as correctness preservation, because soundness is always the easy part and completeness the hard part of a correctness proof.

Definition 5.14. (*step refinement*)

Let $\mathbb{P}_1$, $\mathbb{P}_2$ be semiregular parsing systems. The relation $\mathbb{P}_1 \xrightarrow{sr} \mathbb{P}_2$ holds if

(i) $\mathcal{I}_1 \subseteq \mathcal{I}_2$,
(ii) $\vdash_1^* \subseteq \vdash_2^*$,

We call $\mathbb{P}_2$ a *step refinement* of $\mathbb{P}_1$.

Let $\mathbb{P}_1$ and $\mathbb{P}_2$ be semiregular parsing schemata for some class of grammars $\mathcal{CG}$. The relation $\mathbb{P}_1 \overset{\mathbf{sr}}{\Longrightarrow} \mathbb{P}_2$ holds if, for each $G \in \mathcal{CG}$ and for each $a_1 \ldots a_n \in \Sigma^*$,

$$\mathbb{P}_1(G)(a_1 \ldots a_n) \overset{\mathbf{sr}}{\longrightarrow} \mathbb{P}_2(G)(a_1 \ldots a_n). \qquad \square$$

Note that a sufficient condition for (ii) is $\vdash_1 \subseteq \vdash_2^*$, or even $D_1 \subseteq \vdash_2^*$. We have written $\vdash_1^*$ in the definition only because of the symmetry. The motivation for this desire for symmetry will become clear in Chapter 6; we define a series of relations, all with a similar symmetry.

Corollary 5.15. The relation $\overset{\mathbf{sr}}{\longrightarrow}$ is reflexive, transitive and completeness preserving.

The relation $\overset{\mathbf{sr}}{\Longrightarrow}$ is reflexive, transitive and completeness preserving. $\qquad \square$

Example 5.16.

We define a parsing schema **ECYK**, that is a (bottom-up) Earley-like refinement of **CYK**. Or, to be more precise, a step refinement of **CYK'**. The schema **ECYK** is defined only for grammars in $\mathcal{CNF}$. It is in fact identical to **buE** restricted to $\mathcal{CNF}$. For a grammar G in Chomsky Normal Form we define a parsing system $\mathbb{P}_{ECYK}$ by

$$\mathcal{I}_{ECYK} = \{[A \to \alpha \bullet \beta, i, j] \mid A \to \alpha\beta \in P, 0 \le i \le j\};$$

$$D^{Init} = \{\vdash [A \to \bullet\alpha, j, j]\},$$

$$D^{Scan} = \{[A \to \alpha \bullet a\beta, i, j], [a, j, j+1] \vdash [A \to \alpha a \bullet \beta, i, j+1]\},$$

$$D^{Compl} = \{[A \to \alpha \bullet B\beta, i, j], [B \to \gamma \bullet, j, k] \vdash [A \to \alpha B \bullet \beta, i, k]\},$$

$$D_{ECYK} = D^{Init} \cup D^{Scan} \cup D^{Compl}.$$

In order to prove that **CYK'** $\overset{\mathbf{sr}}{\Longrightarrow}$ **ECYK** it suffices to show, for an arbitrary grammar $G \in \mathcal{CNF}$, that

(i) $\mathcal{I}_{CYK'} \subseteq \mathcal{I}_{ECYK}$

(ii) for each $y_1, \ldots, y_k \vdash x \in D_{CYK'}$ it holds that $y_1, \ldots, y_k \vdash_{ECYK}^* x$.

We identify an item $[A \to \alpha, i, j] \in \mathcal{I}_{CYK'}$ with an item $[A \to \alpha \bullet, i, j] \in \mathcal{I}_{ECYK}$. Then, obviously, $\mathcal{I}_{CYK'} \subseteq \mathcal{I}_{ECYK}$.

As to the second condition, let $[a, j-1, j] \vdash [A \to a, j-1, j] \in D_{CYK'}$. Then, in $\mathbb{P}_{ECYK}$, we have

$$\vdash [A \to \bullet a, j-1, j-1]$$

$$[A \to \bullet a, j-1, j-1], [a, j-1, j] \vdash [A \to a\bullet, j-1, j]$$

hence $[a, j-1, j] \vdash_{ECYK}^* [A \to a\bullet, j-1, j]$.

For a deduction step $[B{\to}\beta, i, j], [C{\to}\gamma, j, k] \vdash [A{\to}BC, i, k] \in D_{CYK'}$ we have

$$\vdash [A{\to}\bullet BC, i, i],$$
$$[A{\to}\bullet BC, i, i], [B{\to}\beta\bullet, i, j] \vdash [A{\to}B\bullet C, i, j],$$
$$[A{\to}B\bullet C, i, j], [C{\to}\gamma\bullet, j, k] \vdash [A{\to}BC\bullet, i, k],$$

hence we have shown that $[B{\to}\beta\bullet, i, j], [C{\to}\gamma\bullet, j, k] \vdash^*_{ECYK} [A{\to}BC\bullet, i, k]$. $\Box$

We can now define refinement as a combination of item refinement and step refinement. Refinement is a transitive relation, but this time transitivity is not obvious from the definitions.

Definition 5.17. (*refinement*)
Let $\mathbb{P}_1$ and $\mathbb{P}_2$ be semiregular parsing systems. The relation $\mathbb{P}_1 \xrightarrow{\text{ref}} \mathbb{P}_2$ holds if there is a parsing system $\mathbb{P}_3$ such that $\mathbb{P}_1 \xrightarrow{\text{ir}} \mathbb{P}_3 \xrightarrow{\text{sr}} \mathbb{P}_2$.
Let $\mathbf{P}_1$ and $\mathbf{P}_2$ be semiregular parsing schemata. The relation $\mathbf{P}_1 \overset{\text{ref}}{\Longrightarrow} \mathbf{P}_2$ holds if there is a parsing schema $\mathbf{P}_3$ such that $\mathbf{P}_1 \overset{\text{ir}}{\Longrightarrow} \mathbf{P}_3 \overset{\text{sr}}{\Longrightarrow} \mathbf{P}_2$. $\Box$

Lemma 5.18. (*refinement lemma*)
Let $\mathbb{P}_1, \mathbb{P}_2, \mathbb{P}_3$ be semiregular parsing systems such that $\mathbb{P}_1 \xrightarrow{\text{sr}} \mathbb{P}_2 \xrightarrow{\text{ir}} \mathbb{P}_3$. Then there is a system $\mathbb{P}_4$ such that $\mathbb{P}_1 \xrightarrow{\text{ir}} \mathbb{P}_4 \xrightarrow{\text{sr}} \mathbb{P}_3$.
Let $\mathbf{P}_1, \mathbf{P}_2, \mathbf{P}_3$ be semiregular parsing schemata for some class of grammars $\mathcal{CG}$. Let $\mathbf{P}_1 \overset{\text{sr}}{\Longrightarrow} \mathbf{P}_2 \overset{\text{ir}}{\Longrightarrow} \mathbf{P}_3$. Then there is a schema $\mathbf{P}_4$ such that $\mathbf{P}_1 \overset{\text{ir}}{\Longrightarrow} \mathbf{P}_4 \overset{\text{sr}}{\Longrightarrow} \mathbf{P}_3$.

Proof. We only prove the lemma for parsing systems. Generalization to parsing schemata is as usual.
Let $f : \mathcal{I}_3^r{\to}\mathcal{I}_2^r$ be the item contraction function from $\mathbb{P}_3^r$ to $\mathbb{P}_2^r$. Then we define $\mathbb{P}_4$ by

$$\mathcal{I}_4 = \{x \in \mathcal{I}_3 \mid f(x) \in \mathcal{I}_1\},$$

$$D_4 = \{(Y, x) \in \wp_{fin}(H \cup \mathcal{I}_4) \times \mathcal{I}_4 \mid f((Y, x)) \in D_1^r \wedge Y \vdash_3^* x\}.$$

Although item contractions are usually specified by regular item mappings, this is not a requirement. So, in order to prove that $\mathbb{P}_1 \xrightarrow{\text{ir}} \mathbb{P}_4$ we have to show that the conditions for item contraction in Definition 5.5, applied to the notion of a semiregular parsing schema, are satisfied. That is, we must establish

(*i*) $\mathcal{I}_1^r{\backslash}\mathcal{F}_1^{(n)} \subseteq f(\mathcal{I}_4^r{\backslash}\mathcal{F}_4^{(n)})$,
(*ii*) $f(\mathcal{I}_4^r{\backslash}\mathcal{F}_4^{(n)}) \subseteq \mathcal{I}_1^r{\backslash}\mathcal{F}_1^{(n)}$,
(*iii*) $\mathcal{F}_1^{(n)} \subseteq f(\mathcal{F}_4^{(n)})$,
(*iv*) $f(\mathcal{F}_4^{(n)}) \subseteq \mathcal{F}_1^{(n)}$,

(v) $f(\mathcal{C}_4) \subseteq \mathcal{C}_1$,
(vi) $\mathcal{C}_1 \subseteq f(\mathcal{C}_4)$,
(vii) $\Delta_1^r \subseteq f(\Delta_4^r)$,
(viii) $f(\Delta_4^r) \subseteq \Delta_1^r$.

Moreover, in order to prove that $\mathbb{P}_4 \xrightarrow{\mathbf{sr}} \mathbb{P}_3$ we have to show that

(ix) $\mathcal{I}_4 \subseteq \mathcal{I}_3$,
(x) $\vdash_4^* \subseteq \vdash_3^*$.

The inequalities (ii), (iv), (ix), and (x) follow directly from the definition of $\mathbb{P}_4$, (viii) is a straightforward extension.
The inequalities (v) and (vi) follow from the fact that $\mathcal{C}_4 = \mathcal{C}_3$ and $\mathcal{C}_1 = \mathcal{C}_2$.
In order to prove (i) and (iii) we will first establish and auxiliary result:

(xi) $\mathcal{I}_1^r \subseteq f(\mathcal{I}_4^r)$.

A proof of (xi) is straightforward:

> Let $x \in \mathcal{I}_1^r$. Then also $x \in \mathcal{I}_2^r$, hence there is an $x' \in \mathcal{I}_3^r$ with $f(x') = x$. Then $x' \in \mathcal{I}_4^r$.
> Hence it follows that $x \in f(\mathcal{I}_4^r)$.

The inequalities (i) and (iii) follow from (ii) and (iv) combined with (xi) and the regularity of $\mathcal{I}_1^r$.
So we are left with (vii), the only case for which a proof requires some effort.

> We will use an ad-hoc notation $Y \vdash^* x_1 \vdash^* \ldots \vdash^* x_j \in \Delta$ which means that there are (possibly empty) sequences $z_{i,1}, \ldots, z_{i,m_i}$ for $1 \leq i \leq j$ such that
>
> $$Y \vdash z_{1,1} \vdash \ldots \vdash z_{1,m_1} \vdash x_1 \vdash \ldots \vdash z_{j,1} \vdash \ldots \vdash z_{j,m_j} \vdash x_j \in \Delta.$$
>
> Now we prove (vii) as follows. Let $Y \vdash_1 x_1 \vdash_1 \ldots \vdash_1 x_j \in \Delta_1^r$. Then it holds that
>
> $$Y \vdash_2^* x_1 \vdash_2^* \ldots \vdash_2^* x_j \in \Delta_2^r.$$
>
> Moreover, there are $Y' \in \wp_{fin}(H \cup \mathcal{I}_3) \times \mathcal{I}_3$ with $f(Y') = Y$ and $x_1', \ldots, x_j'$ with $f(x_1') = x_1, \ldots, f(x_j') = x_j$, such that
>
> $$Y' \vdash_3^* x_1' \vdash_3^* \ldots \vdash_3^* x_j' \in \Delta_3^r.$$
>
> Then, clearly, it follows that $Y' \vdash_4 x_1' \vdash_4 \ldots \vdash_4 x_j' \in \Delta_4^r$, hence we have shown that
>
> $$Y \vdash_1 x_1 \vdash_1 \ldots \vdash_1 x_j \in f(\Delta_3^r).$$

We conclude from (i)–(viii) that $\mathbb{P}_1 \xrightarrow{\mathbf{ir}} \mathbb{P}_4$ and from (ix)–(x) that $\mathbb{P}_4 \xrightarrow{\mathbf{sr}} \mathbb{P}_3$. $\qquad\square$

Theorem 5.19.
The relations $\xrightarrow{\mathbf{ref}}$ and $\xRightarrow{\mathbf{ref}}$ are transitive and reflexive.

Proof: directly from Lemma 5.18. $\qquad\square$

5.3 Some examples of refinement

We will informally discuss a few simple examples of refinement and in one case give a proper proof. Every refinement can be split up into two separate steps: item refinement and step refinement. Each of those steps can simply be the identity relation.

Example 5.20. (GCYK $\stackrel{\text{ref}}{\Longrightarrow}$ buE)
Generalized CYK is a variant of CYK that can handle arbitrary context-free grammars. The parsing schema **GCYK** is specified by a parsing system $\mathbb{P}_{GCYK}$ for arbitrary $G \in \mathcal{CFG}$, as follows.

$$\mathcal{I}_{GCYK} = \{[A,i,j] \mid A \in N, 0 \le i \le j\};$$

$$D^{(1,2)} = \{[X_1,i_0,i_1],\ldots,[X_k,i_{k-1},i_k] \vdash [A,i_0,i_k] \mid \\ A \to X_1 \ldots X_k \in P \wedge k \ge 1\},$$

$$D^\varepsilon = \{\vdash [A,j,j] \mid A \to \varepsilon \in P\},$$

$$D_{GCYK} = D^{(1,2)} \cup D^\varepsilon.$$

Note that for grammars $G \in \mathcal{CNF}$ it holds that $\mathbb{P}_{GCYK} = \mathbb{P}_{CYK}$ (cf. Example 4.27). The deduction steps in $D^{(1,2)}$ cover productions of the form $A \to BC$ and productions of the form $A \to a$. For grammars in Chomsky Normal Form, D^ε is empty.

Now we claim that a parsing system $\mathbb{P}_{buE}$ (cf. Example 4.34) is a refinement of $\mathbb{P}_{GCYK}$. As a first step, we refine CYK items $[A,i,j]$ into Earley items of the form $[A \to \alpha\bullet, i, j]$ for every production $A \to \alpha$ for a given left-hand side A. If there is more than one production for A this means a proper item refinement, otherwise it is just a different notation for the same partial specification of a tree with root A and yield $\underline{a}_{i+1} \ldots \underline{a}_j$. The terminal items representing the string are denoted $[a, i-1, i]$ as ever. Thus we obtain an item-refined system $\mathbb{P}_{GCYK'}$:

$$\mathcal{I}_{GCYK'} = \{[A \to \alpha\bullet, i, j] \mid A \to \alpha \in P, 0 \le i \le j\};$$

$$D^{(1,2)} = \{[X_1,i_0,i_1],\ldots,[X_k,i_{k-1},i_k] \vdash [A \to \alpha\bullet, i_0, i_k] \mid \\ A \to X_1 \ldots X_k \in P \wedge k \ge 1\}$$
$$\text{where } [X_m, i_{m-1}, i_m] \text{ denotes } [a, i_{m-1}, i_m] \text{ if } X_m = a$$
$$\text{and } [X_m, i_{m-1}, i_m] \text{ denotes } [B \to \beta\bullet, i_{m-1}, i_m] \text{ if } X_m = B,$$

$$D^\varepsilon = \{\vdash [A \to \bullet, j, j]\},$$

$$D_{GCYK'} = D^{(1,2)} \cup D^\varepsilon.$$

Next, we can straightforwardly refine $\mathbb{P}_{GCYK'}$ into $\mathbb{P}_{buE}$. Take, for example, an item of the form $[A \to bBC\bullet, i, k]$. This is valid in $\mathbb{P}_{GCYK'}$ iff there are valid items $[b, i, i+1]$, $[B \to \beta\bullet, i+1, j]$ and $[C \to \gamma\bullet, j, k]$. In $\mathbb{P}_{buE}$ an item $[A \to \bullet bBC, i, i]$ is always valid. Using the antecedents of the GCYK deduction step one by one, we deduce a sequence of items $[A \to b\bullet BC, i, i+1]$, $[A \to bB\bullet C, i, j]$, $[A \to bBC\bullet, i, k]$. $\qquad\square$

Example 5.21. (GCYK $\overset{\text{ref}}{\Longrightarrow}$ buLC $\overset{\text{ref}}{\Longrightarrow}$ buE)
In Example 4.35 we have introduced a parsing system $\mathbb{P}_{buLC}$ from a system $\mathbb{P}_{buE}$ by discarding most of the items with a dot in leftmost position. The set of deduction steps was adapted accordingly. Reversely, one could derive $\mathbb{P}_{buE}$ from $\mathbb{P}_{buLC}$ by inserting the missing items with a dot in leftmost position and adapting the set of deduction steps. It is left to the reader to verify that $\mathbb{P}_{buLC} \overset{\text{sr}}{\longrightarrow} \mathbb{P}_{buE}$ and thus $\mathbb{P}_{buLC} \overset{\text{ref}}{\longrightarrow} \mathbb{P}_{buE}$. Hence, in general, **buLC** $\overset{\text{ref}}{\longrightarrow}$ **buE**.
Similar to Example 5.20, it can also be shown that **GCYK** $\overset{\text{ref}}{\longrightarrow}$ **buLC**. □

Example 5.22. (LC $\overset{\text{ref}}{\Longrightarrow}$ Earley)
Similar to Example 5.21, one can show that **Earley** (cf. Example 4.32) is in fact a refinement of **LC** (cf. Example 4.36). The **LC** schema is more complicated than **buLC**, and we will use the occasion to give a somewhat more formal proof.

Proof. We will prove that $\mathbb{P}_{LC} \overset{\text{sr}}{\longrightarrow} \mathbb{P}_{Earley}$. for an arbitrary grammar $G \in \mathcal{CFG}$.
We abbreviate $\mathbb{P}_{Earley}$ to $\mathbb{P}_E$. We have to prove

(i) $\mathcal{I}_{LC} \subseteq \mathcal{I}_E$,
(ii) $\vdash_{LC}^* \subseteq \vdash_E^*$.

Inequality (i) follows immediately from the definitions. Rather than (ii) we will prove

(iii) if $(Y, x) \in D_{LC}$ then $Y \vdash_E^* x$,

from which (ii) follows. For the sets of deduction steps D_{LC}^{Init}, D_{LC}^{Scan} and D_{LC}^{Compl}, this is a direct consequence of (i). It remains to be shown that (iii) holds for $D_{LC}^{LC(A)}$, $D_{LC}^{LC(a)}$ and $D_{LC}^{LC(\varepsilon)}$. We will work out the $D_{LC}^{LC(A)}$ case in detail, the other cases are similar.
Let

$$[C' \to \gamma \bullet C\delta, h, i], \ [A \to \alpha \bullet, i, j] \ \vdash \ [B \to A \bullet \beta, i, j] \ \in D_{LC}^{LC(A)}.$$

Then, by the definition of $D_{LC}^{LC(A)}$, it holds that $C >_l^* B$. Assume $C >_l^k B$. Then, by the Earley *predict* we find

$$[C' \to \gamma \bullet C\delta, h, i] \ \vdash_E^k \ [B \to \bullet A\beta, i, i]$$

and, with a *complete* step,

$$[B \to \bullet A\beta, i, i], \ [A \to \alpha \bullet, i, j] \ \vdash_E \ [B \to A \bullet \beta, i, j].$$

Hence we have shown that $[C' \to \gamma \bullet C\delta, h, i], \ [A \to \alpha \bullet, i, j] \ \vdash_E^{k+1} \ [B \to A \bullet \beta, i, j]$.
□

All the above examples involve parsing schemata that are defined on $\mathcal{CFG}$. We will now look at a few parsing schemata that are defined only on $\mathcal{CNF}$. In Section 5.4, subsequently, we will extend $\mathcal{CNF}$ schemata to $\mathcal{CFG}$ schemata.

In Section 2.2 we have seen an informal example of Rytter's algorithm [Rytter, 1985], [Gibbons and Rytter, 1988]. An almost identical algorithm was described earlier by Brent and Goldschlager [1984], but received little attention because it was published in a less widely circulated journal. Both algorithms are described by a single parsing schema that we will call **Rytter**, as this is the more familiar algorithm. We will come back to Rytter's algorithm in Chapter 14.

Example 5.23. (CYK $\overset{\text{ref}}{\Longrightarrow}$ Rytter)

Apart from the terminal items in H, a Rytter parsing schema uses two types of items. Firstly there are the ordinary CYK items $[A, i, j]$, which comprise completed trees of the form $\langle A \leadsto \underline{a}_{i+1} \ldots \underline{a}_j \rangle$. We also call them *complete items* in this context. Secondly, we use *almost-complete* items for trees of the form

$$\langle A \leadsto \underline{a}_{h+1} \ldots \underline{a}_i B \underline{a}_{j+1} \ldots \underline{a}_k \rangle.$$

Such items are denoted $[A, h, k; B, i, j]$. An almost-complete item can be seen as a CYK item with a *gap*. If $[A, h, k; B, i, j]$ is valid, and another valid item $[B, i, j]$ can be deduced, then the gap can be filled and $[A, h, k]$ is also valid. The gap can also be filled with another almost-complete item; The result is an almost-complete item, again, but with a smaller gap. A complete item, finally, can be extended to an almost-complete item by combining it with a production. If there is a production $A \rightarrow BC \in P$ then a complete item $[B, i, j]$ can be extended to an almost-complete item $[A, i, k; C, j, k]$ for arbitrary k (and similarly, an almost-complete item with a leftmost gap can be created if a valid item is the rightmost right-hand side symbol of a production). As usual, we do not worry about the fact that k can be extended beyond the sentence length n. For any given sentence one could restrict the set of items to the set of relevant items for the appropriate sentence length.

For a grammar $G \in \mathcal{CNF}$ we define a parsing schema $\mathbb{P}_{Rytter}$ as follows.

$$\mathcal{I}^{(1)} \quad = \quad \{[A, i, j] \mid A \in N \wedge 0 < i < j\},$$

$$\mathcal{I}^{(2)} \quad = \quad \{[A, h, k; B, i, j] \mid A, B \in N \wedge 0 < h < i < j < k\},$$

$$\mathcal{I}_{Rytter} \quad = \quad \mathcal{I}^{(1)} \cup \mathcal{I}^{(2)};$$

$$D^{(0)} \quad = \quad \{[a, j - 1, j] \vdash [A, j - 1, j] \mid A \rightarrow a \in P\},$$

$$D^{(1a)} \quad = \quad \{[B, i, j] \vdash [A, i, k; C, j, k] \mid A \rightarrow BC \in P\},$$

$$D^{(1b)} \quad = \quad \{[C, j, k] \vdash [A, i, k; B, i, j] \mid A \rightarrow BC \in P\},$$

$$D^{(2)} \quad = \quad \{[A, h, k; B, i, j], [B, i, j] \vdash [A, h, k]\}$$

$$D^{(3)} \quad = \quad \{[A,h,m;B,i,l],[B,i,l;C,j,k] \vdash [A,h,m;C,j,k]\}$$

$$D_{Rytter} = D^{(0)} \cup D^{(1a)} \cup D^{(1b)} \cup D^{(2)} \cup D^{(3)}.$$

The operations associated with the sets of deduction steps $D^{(1)}$, $D^{(2)}$, and $D^{(3)}$, are originally called *activate*, *pebble*, and *square*, respectively. These terms stem from a "pebble" problem, where a pebble has to be laid on every node in a tree. In this context these original names do not make sense and we rather use numbers.

It is a trivial that $\mathbb{P}_{CYK} \xrightarrow{\mathbf{sr}} \mathbb{P}_{Rytter}$. □

In the above example, an intermediate parsing system between $\mathbb{P}_{CYK}$ and $\mathbb{P}_{Rytter}$ can be defined simply by discarding $D^{(3)}$ from $\mathbb{P}_{Rytter}$. Let's call this $\mathbb{P}_{R2}$ for short. The system $\mathbb{P}_{R2}$ is a step refinement of $\mathbb{P}_{CYK}$ in the most literal sense; a CYK deduction step is split up in two steps. It is also clear that $\mathbb{P}_{R2} \xrightarrow{\mathbf{sr}} \mathbb{P}_{Rytter}$, in a more degenerate way; D_{Rytter} simply contains D_{R2} as a subset.

The problem of such a conceivable parsing system **R2**, however, is that it combines *dis*advantages of both schemata. **CYK** on the one hand, finishes in linear time (in a parallel implementation) with relatively few resources. **Rytter**, on the other hand, needs much more resources in order to guarantee that all valid items are deduced in logarithmic time. The **R2** schema has the same formal complexity bounds as **CYK**, but when constant factors are taken into account it simply needs more resources – in time, space and number of processing units – than **CYK**.

A more useful intermediate algorithm located between CYK and Rytter's algorithm is described in [Sikkel, 1993a]: a parallel algorithm for *online* parsing that uses $O(n^2)$ processors to parse the next word in constant time. The classical CYK algorithm can be implemented in $O(n)$ time using $O(n^2)$ processors, as was shown by Kosaraju [1969, 1975], but only if the entire sentence is known when parsing begins. The online parallel CYK algorithm – assuming that the parser is fast enough to do all processing before the next word arrives – finishes in constant time after the last word. The parsing schema for this algorithm, called **OCYK**, extends CYK with almost-complete items that have the gap in rightmost position. Unlike almost-complete Rytter items, there is no need to specify a position to which this rightmost gap extends.

Example 5.24. (CYK $\xRightarrow{\mathbf{ref}}$ OCYK $\xRightarrow{\mathbf{ref}}$ Rytter)

In addition to $[A,i,j]$ as an abbreviation for $[A \rightsquigarrow \underline{a}_{i+1}\ldots\underline{a}_j]$, we write $[A,i,j;B]$ to denote an item

$$[A \rightsquigarrow \underline{a}_{i+1}\ldots\underline{a}_j B].$$

We specify a parsing schema **OCYK**, as usual, by defining a parsing system $\mathbb{P}_{OCYK}$ for an arbitrary grammar $G \in \mathcal{CNF}$, as follows.

$$\mathcal{I}^{(1)} \quad = \quad \{[A,i,j] \mid A \in N \wedge 0 \leq i < j\},$$

$$\mathcal{I}^{(2)} \quad = \{[A, i, j; B] \mid A, B \in N \wedge 0 \le i < j\},$$

$$\mathcal{I}_{OCYK} = \mathcal{I}^{(1)} \cup \mathcal{I}^{(2)};$$

$$D^{(0)} \quad = \{[a, j-1, j] \vdash [A, j-1, j] \mid A \rightarrow a \in P\},$$

$$D^{(1)} \quad = \{[B, i, j] \vdash [A, i, j; C] \mid A \rightarrow BC \in P\},$$

$$D^{(2)} \quad = \{[A, i, j; B], [B, j, k] \vdash [A, i, k]\}$$

$$D^{(3)} \quad = \{[A, i, j; B], [B, j, k; C] \vdash [A, i, k; C]\}$$

$$D_{OCYK} = D^{(0)} \cup D^{(1)} \cup D^{(2)} \cup D^{(3)}.$$

Clearly, $\mathbb{P}_{CYK} \xrightarrow{\text{sr}} \mathbb{P}_{OCYK}$.

Refining $\mathbb{P}_{OCYK}$ into $\mathbb{P}_{R2}$ (and subsequently to $\mathbb{P}_{Rytter}$) is not limited to step refinement, this time. Items $[A, i, j; B]$ have to be refined into items $[A, i, j; B, j, k]$ first. $\qquad\square$

5.4 Generalization

Generalization comprises two notions that may be used in combination. Firstly, a refinement, as discussed in 5.2 is a generalization; the refined system is a richer deduction system. Secondly, and more importantly, a parsing schema for a narrow class of grammars can be extended to a larger class of grammars. Often this can't be done straightforwardly (otherwise the parsing schema would simply have been defined on a larger class of grammars) but involves refinement as well. As a canonical example, we will see that the bottom-up Earley schema is a generalization of the CYK schema.

Definition 5.25. (*extension*)
Let $\mathbf{P}_1$ be a parsing schema for a class of grammars $\mathcal{CG}_1$, $\mathbf{P}_2$ a parsing schema for a class of grammars $\mathcal{CG}_2$ and $\mathcal{CG}_1 \subseteq \mathcal{CG}_2$.
Then the relation $\mathbf{P}_1 \xrightarrow{\text{ext}} \mathbf{P}_2$ holds if, for each grammar in $\mathcal{CG}_1$ and each $a_1 \ldots a_n \in \Sigma^*$,

$$\mathbf{P}_1(G)(a_1 \ldots a_n) \equiv \mathbf{P}_2(G)(a_1 \ldots a_n) \qquad\qquad\square$$

Definition 5.26. (*generalization*)
Let $\mathbf{P}_1$, $\mathbf{P}_2$ be semiregular parsing schemata.
Then the relation $\mathbf{P}_1 \xrightarrow{\text{gen}} \mathbf{P}_2$ holds if there is a semiregular parsing schema $\mathbf{P}_3$ such that $\mathbf{P}_1 \xrightarrow{\text{ref}} \mathbf{P}_3 \xrightarrow{\text{ext}} \mathbf{P}_2$. $\qquad\square$

Unlike the refinement lemma, it is obvious that if $\mathbf{P}_1 \xrightarrow{\text{ext}} \mathbf{P}_2 \xrightarrow{\text{ref}} \mathbf{P}_3$ there is a $\mathbf{P}_4$ such that $\mathbf{P}_1 \xrightarrow{\text{ref}} \mathbf{P}_4 \xrightarrow{\text{ext}} \mathbf{P}_3$. The schema $\mathbf{P}_4$ is obtained simply by restricting $\mathbf{P}_3$ to the smaller class of grammars for which $\mathbf{P}_1$ is defined.

Corollary 5.27.
The relation $\overset{\mathbf{gen}}{\Longrightarrow}$ is transitive and reflexive. $\square$

Example 5.28. (CYK $\overset{\mathbf{gen}}{\Longrightarrow}$ buE)
In Example 5.20 the Generalized CYK schema **GCYK** has been defined. It has in fact been shown that

$$\text{CYK} \overset{\mathbf{ext}}{\Longrightarrow} \text{GCYK} \overset{\mathbf{ref}}{\Longrightarrow} \text{buE.} \qquad\qquad \square$$

Above we have argued that $\overset{\mathbf{ext}}{\Longrightarrow} \overset{\mathbf{ref}}{\Longrightarrow}$ can always be replaced by $\overset{\mathbf{ref}}{\Longrightarrow} \overset{\mathbf{ext}}{\Longrightarrow}$. Swapping the relations in Example 5.28 yields the intermediate system **ECYK** that has been defined in Example 5.16:

$$\text{CYK} \overset{\mathbf{ref}}{\Longrightarrow} \text{ECYK} \overset{\mathbf{ext}}{\Longrightarrow} \text{buE.}$$

5.5 Conclusion

We have introduced refinement and extension as relations that can be used to describe a parsing schema as a generalization of another schema. Refinement is the more involved notion; extension simply means applying a schema to a larger class of grammars. Generalization is a combination of refinement and extension.

By means of some practical examples, involving algorithms known from the computer science literature, we have shown that refinement is a useful notion for relating parsing schemata to one another. It should be noted, however, that refinements are described between *existing* schemata. There is no recipe that allows to derive a better schema from a given schema by applying some kind of refinement.

Refinement means more items, more deduction steps, and more things to compute. If a refinement produces a "better" schema, then the improvement will be *qualitative*. Refining Generalized CYK to Earley is such an improvement, because the complexity of the algorithm can be reduced by considering partially recognized productions, rather than only completely recognized productions. If a refinement does not obtain such a qualitative improvement, it is likely to make a parser less efficient because more work has to be carried out.

In the next chapter we will be concerned with filtering, i.e., improving the efficiency by discarding parts of a parsing system. Filtering is in some ways the inverse of refinement. It is used for *quantitative* improvements in the efficiency: diminishing the number of valid items and deductions that have to be applied.

6. Filtering

Sometimes it is possible to argue that some deduction steps in a parsing system cannot contribute to the recognition of a parse. If such deduction steps exist, no harm is done when these are deleted from the parsing system. Such optimizations usually do not lead to a decrease in complexity bounds (otherwise the algorithm was inefficient indeed), but it is always worthwhile when a (sometimes large) percentage of computation time can be saved by cutting out redundancies. Optimization in this sense is called *filtering*.[1] In this Chapter we will define various types of filtering and see that several filters known from the literature are special cases of the general approach that is presented here.

The optimization obtained by a filter does not always come for free. The cost, usually, is a more complicated description of the parsing schema. The filtered schema may state explicitly that from a clearly defined set of deduction steps only a rather more complicatedly defined subset remains.

Another side effect of filtering is that it is often at odds with parallel implementation. The time efficiency of a parallel parser may crucially depend on a certain redundancy with respect to other resources: space and number of computing units. A typical example is the Earley parser. In its standard form, the string is necessarily processed from left to right. If the top-down filter is deleted (i.e., the *predict* operator is discarded and any item that could be predicted is added in advance) one can start parsing at every position in the sentence in parallel. In that case it is not hard to define a parser that uses $O(n)$ time on $O(n^2)$ processors. This speed-up can only be obtained at the cost of redundancy in predicted items.

---

[1] In addition to syntactic filtering one can also apply semantic filtering, i.e., discarding (parts of) parse trees that are syntactically correct but known to be irrelevant on the basis of extra-syntactical knowledge. In natural language processing, because of the ambiguity of human language, semantic disambiguation is a major issue that has generated a vast body of literature. In programming languages it is sometime convenient to specify an ambiguous grammer with additional disambiguation rules (e.g. operator precedence in arithmetic expressions). Klint and Visser [1994] and Visser [1995] discuss how semantic filtering can be integrated in the Parsing schemata framework. Here we only consider syntactic filtering.

A more dramatic example where redundancy is essential to speed up a parallel algorithm is Rytter's algorithm (cf. Examples 2.3, 5.23), It does a vast amount of redundant work, increasing the number of processors from $O(n^3)$ to $O(n^6)$, in order to finish in logarithmic time. For each binary branching parse tree there is *some* way in which it can be constructed in parallel in a logarithmic number of steps. But as it can't be foretold which way is successful, one has to try all the ways.

Cutting out redundancy may eliminate possibilities for parallel processing, but it is all the more useful in sequential implementations.

We will make a general distinction between *static* and *dynamic* filtering. At a practical level, in computer implementations of parsing algorithms, static filtering can be done *compile-time*, while dynamic filtering is done *run-time*. This is what is suggested by the terms "static" and "dynamic". On our more abstract level of parsing schemata, the characteristic difference is that static filtering is independent of the particular string that has to be parsed, whereas the effect of dynamic filtering does depend on the string. A static filter can be applied when an uninstantiated parsing schema contains items and/or derivation steps that are redundant for every input string. These can simply be discarded. Dynamic filtering, on top of that, allows certain derivation steps to be applied *only if* it follows from an already explored context in the string that such steps are meaningful in that context. That is, additional antecedents are required to derive a consequent.

As a running example in Chapter 6 we will use (a schema for) the algorithm of de Vreught and Honig [1989, 1991] and define several filters on it.

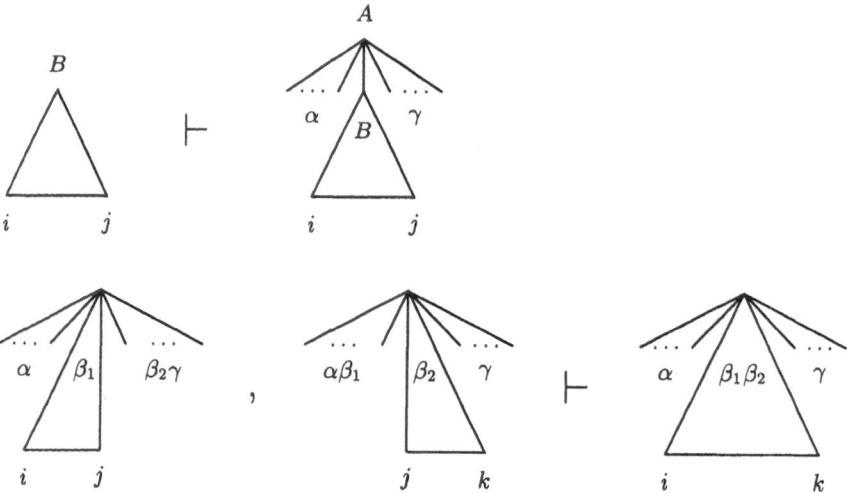

Fig. 6.1. The *include* and *concatenate* operations of **dVH**

As we will see along the way, the algorithm is related to Earley's algorithm and the LC algorithm. The main difference is that constituents need not be recognized in a left-to-right manner. The items used by de Vreught and Honig are *double dotted items* of the form $[A\rightarrow\alpha\bullet\beta\bullet\gamma, i, j]$, with the part β of the right-hand-side already expanded and α and γ still to be recognized. Such an item denotes the set of trees $[A\rightarrow\alpha \langle\beta \rightsquigarrow \underline{a}_{i+1}\ldots\underline{a}\rangle \gamma]$ (cf. Section 4.3). The algorithm of de Vreught and Honig has two basic steps, called *include* and *concatenate*. The idea of both steps is illustrated in Figure 6.1. The formal definition should be clear.

Example 6.1. (**dVH1**, *the algorithm of de Vreught and Honig*)
For an arbitrary grammar $G \in \mathcal{CFG}$ and string $a_1 \ldots a_n$ a derivation system $\mathbb{P}_{dVH1}$ is defined by

$$\mathcal{I}_{dVH1} = \{[A\rightarrow\alpha\bullet\beta\bullet\gamma, i, j] \mid A\rightarrow\alpha\beta\gamma \in P \wedge 0 \le i \le j\};$$

$$D^{Init} = \{[a, j-1, j] \vdash [A\rightarrow\alpha\bullet a\bullet\gamma, j-1, j]\},$$

$$D^{\varepsilon} = \{\vdash [B\rightarrow\bullet\bullet, j, j]\},$$

$$D^{Incl} = \{[B\rightarrow\bullet\beta\bullet, i, j] \vdash [A\rightarrow\alpha\bullet B\bullet\gamma, i, j]\},$$

$$D^{Concat} = \{[A\rightarrow\alpha\bullet\beta_1\bullet\beta_2\gamma, i, j], [A\rightarrow\alpha\beta_1\bullet\beta_2\bullet\gamma, j, k]$$
$$\vdash [A\rightarrow\alpha\bullet\beta_1\beta_2\bullet\gamma, i, k]\},$$

$$D_{dVH1} = D^{Init} \cup D^{\varepsilon} \cup D^{Incl} \cup D^{Concat}.$$

If follows easily (cf. de Vreught and Honig [1989]) that

$$\mathcal{V}^{\le n}(\mathbb{P}_{dVH1}) = \{[A\rightarrow\alpha\bullet\beta\bullet\gamma, i, j] \in \mathcal{I} \mid \beta\Rightarrow^* a_{i+1}\ldots a_j \wedge$$
$$(\beta \neq \varepsilon \vee \alpha\gamma = \varepsilon) \}.$$

Note that D^{ε} allows deduction of $[B\rightarrow\bullet\bullet, j, j]$ also for $j > n$, because D is independent of the sentence length. Hence we are only interested in the set $\mathcal{V}^{\le n}$ of valid items with position markers not exceeding n. (cf. Definition 4.33). □

Throughout Section 6 we write $\mathbb{P}_i$ to denote a parsing system $\mathbb{P}_i = \langle\mathcal{I}_i, H_i, D_i\rangle$. We will define the refinement relations on parsing systems $\mathbb{P}$, rather than on general deduction system $\mathbb{D}$, because the definitions are motivated by applications in parsing. It should be clear, however, that all these relations have obvious generalizations to arbitrary deduction systems $\mathbb{D}$ and enhanced deduction systems $\mathbb{E}$.

As a first, almost trivial example of static filtering we will look at *redundancy elimination* in Section 6.1. Static and dynamic filtering are illustrated and formally defined in Sections 6.2 and 6.3, respectively. In 6.4 we will look at an even stronger form of filtering called *step contraction*, in which sets of deduction steps can be contracted to single deduction steps.

Step contraction is the inverse of step refinement that has been introduced in Section 5.2. A typical example of step contraction has been given already in Section 4.6, where a Left-Corner parsing schema was obtained as an optimization of an Earley parsing schema. In 6.5 a taxonomy of Earley-related parsers is drawn up, making use of the filters defined in 6.2–6.4. Section 6.6, finally gives a schematic summary of all types of relations defined in Chapters 5 and 6.

6.1 Redundancy elimination

A very simple kind of static filtering is *redundancy elimination*. If a parsing system (or any other deduction system) contains steps that can be deleted without affecting the validity of any item, these steps must be redundant. The same holds for nonvalid items. As a typical example, an inconsistent item can be deleted.

Definition 6.2. (*redundancy elimination*)
Let $\mathbb{P}_1$ and $\mathbb{P}_2$ be semiregular parsing systems. The relation $\mathbb{P}_1 \xrightarrow{\text{re}} \mathbb{P}_2$ holds if

(*i*) $\mathcal{I}_1 \supseteq \mathcal{I}_2$
(*ii*) $D_1 \supseteq D_2$,
(*iii*) $\mathcal{V}(\mathbb{P}_1) = \mathcal{V}(\mathbb{P}_2)$.

Let $\mathbf{P}_1$ and $\mathbf{P}_2$ be semiregular parsing schemata for a class of grammars $\mathcal{CG}$. The relation $\mathbf{P}_1 \xRightarrow{\text{re}} \mathbf{P}_2$ holds if, for each $G \in \mathcal{CG}$ and each $a_1 \dots a_n \in \Sigma^*$,

$$\mathbf{P}_1(G)(a_1 \dots a_n) \xrightarrow{\text{re}} \mathbf{P}_2(G)(a_1 \dots a_n).\qquad \square$$

By definition, redundancy elimination is correctness preserving.

Corollary 6.3.
For any semiregular parsing system $\mathbb{P}$ it holds that $\mathbb{P} \xrightarrow{\text{re}} \mathbb{P}^r$.
For any semiregular parsing schema $\mathbf{P}$ it holds that $\mathbf{P} \xRightarrow{\text{re}} \mathbf{P}^r$. $\square$

Example 6.4. (**dVH2**, redundancy elimination)
We observe that D_{dVH1} is redundant, in the following way.
An item $[A{\rightarrow}\alpha{\bullet}XYZ{\bullet}\gamma, i, j]$ can be concatenated in two different ways:

$$[A{\rightarrow}\alpha{\bullet}X{\bullet}YZ\gamma, i, k], [A{\rightarrow}\alpha X{\bullet}YZ{\bullet}\gamma, k, j] \vdash [A{\rightarrow}\alpha{\bullet}XYZ{\bullet}\gamma, i, j];$$

$$[A{\rightarrow}\alpha{\bullet}XY{\bullet}Z\gamma, i, l], [A{\rightarrow}\alpha XY{\bullet}Z{\bullet}\gamma, l, j] \vdash [A{\rightarrow}\alpha{\bullet}XYZ{\bullet}\gamma, i, j].$$

Moreover, if $[A{\rightarrow}\alpha{\bullet}XYZ{\bullet}\gamma, i, j]$ is valid, then each of the four antecedents is also valid for some value of k and l. Hence, if we delete the former deduction step from D, the set of valid items is not affected.
In general, $[A{\rightarrow}\alpha{\bullet}\beta{\bullet}\gamma, i, j]$ with β a string of k symbols, $k \geq 2$, can be deduced in $k-1$ ways. All but one can be discarded. For an arbitrary grammar $G \in \mathcal{CFG}$ a parsing system $\mathbb{P}_{dVH2}$ is defined by

$$\mathcal{I}_{dVH2} = \{[A \rightarrow \alpha\bullet\beta\bullet\gamma, i, j] \mid A \rightarrow \alpha\beta\gamma \in P \wedge 0 \le i \le j\};$$

$$D^{Init} = \{[a, j-1, j] \vdash [A \rightarrow \alpha\bullet a\bullet\gamma, j-1, j]\},$$

$$D^{\varepsilon} = \{\vdash [B \rightarrow \bullet\bullet, j, j]\},$$

$$D^{Incl} = \{[B \rightarrow \bullet\beta\bullet, i, j] \vdash [A \rightarrow \alpha\bullet B\bullet\gamma, i, j]\},$$

$$D^{Concat} = \{[A \rightarrow \alpha\bullet\beta\bullet X\gamma, i, j], [A \rightarrow \alpha\beta\bullet X\bullet\gamma, j, k] \vdash [A \rightarrow \alpha\bullet\beta X\bullet\gamma, i, k]\},$$

$$D_{dVH2} = D^{Init} \cup D^{\varepsilon} \cup D^{Incl} \cup D^{Concat}.$$

It trivially holds that $\mathcal{I}_{dVH1} = \mathcal{I}_{dVH2}$ and $D_{dVH2} \subseteq D_{dVH1}$ Moreover from the above argumentation we know that $\mathcal{V}(\mathbb{P}_{dVH2}) = \mathcal{V}(\mathbb{P}_{dVH1})$. As this holds for arbitrary grammars, we conclude $\mathbf{dVH1} \overset{re}{\Longrightarrow} \mathbf{dVH2}$.   □

6.2 Static filtering

Static filtering means no more and no less than discarding parts of a parsing system (or, in general, a deduction system). This idea – and the following formal definition – may seem gratuitous; correctness is preserved only if one can argue that the deleted parts are indeed not relevant to the correctness of the system. But this is precisely why it fits into a general hierarchy of filtering. *Any* filter will do, as long as one is able to argue that the remaining system is still complete.

Definition 6.5. (*static filtering*)
Let $\mathbb{P}_1$ and $\mathbb{P}_2$ be semiregular parsing systems. The relation $\mathbb{P}_1 \overset{sf}{\longrightarrow} \mathbb{P}_2$ holds if

(*i*) $\mathcal{I}_1 \supseteq \mathcal{I}_2$
(*ii*) $D_1 \supseteq D_2$.

Let $\mathbf{P}_1$ and $\mathbf{P}_2$ be arbitrary parsing schemata for a class of grammars $\mathcal{CG}$. The relation $\mathbf{P}_1 \overset{sf}{\Longrightarrow} \mathbf{P}_2$ holds if, for each $G \in \mathcal{CG}$ and each $a_1 \ldots a_n \in \Sigma^*$, $\mathbf{P}_1(G)(a_1 \ldots a_n) \overset{sf}{\longrightarrow} \mathbf{P}_2(G)(a_1 \ldots a_n)$.   □

It is obvious that the relations $\overset{sf}{\longrightarrow}$ and $\overset{sf}{\Longrightarrow}$ are transitive and soundness preserving. Unlike redundancy elimination, the completeness is not automatically preserved by a static filter. In order to prove that a specific static filter preserves correctness one should argue that the deleted valid items are indeed redundant.

Example 6.6. (**dVH3**, *static filtering*)

We will further optimize the parsing system $\mathbb{P}_{dVH2}$ for some arbitrary grammar G. We observe that items of the form $[A{\rightarrow}\alpha{\bullet}\beta{\bullet}, i, j]$ with $|\alpha| \geq 1$ and $|\beta| \geq 2$ are useless in $\mathbb{P}_{dVH2}$, in the sense that they do not occur as an antecedent in any derivation step. Hence, these items can be discarded. This does effect the set of valid items; some of the discarded items were valid. But, more importantly, none of the discarded items is a final item (i.e., an item that indicates that a parse exists, cf. Definition 4.20).

Similarly, any item of the form $[A{\rightarrow}\alpha{\bullet}\beta{\bullet}\gamma, i, j]$ with $|\alpha| \geq 1$, $|\beta| \geq 2$ and $|\gamma| \geq 1$ can concatenate to the right, but cannot contribute to the recognition of a final item. The whole set

$$\{[A{\rightarrow}\alpha{\bullet}\beta{\bullet}\gamma, i, j] \mid |\alpha| \geq 1 \wedge |\beta| \geq 2\}$$

can be considered useless; it does not contain any final item and items in this set are used as antecedents only to deduce other items in this set. Hence we delete this set, and discard all deduction steps that have one of these items as antecedent or as consequent. The deduction system $\mathbb{P}_{dVH3}$ for an arbitrary grammar G is defined by

$$\mathcal{I}^{(1)} = \{[A{\rightarrow}\alpha{\bullet}X{\bullet}\gamma, i, j] \mid A{\rightarrow}\alpha X\gamma \in P \wedge 0 \leq i \leq j\}$$

$$\mathcal{I}^{(2)} = \{[A{\rightarrow}{\bullet}X\beta{\bullet}\gamma, i, j] \mid A{\rightarrow}X\beta\gamma \in P \wedge 0 \leq i \leq j\}$$

$$\mathcal{I}^{(3)} = \{[A{\rightarrow}{\bullet}{\bullet}, j, j] \mid A{\rightarrow}\varepsilon \in P \wedge j \geq 0\}$$

$$\mathcal{I}_{dVH3} = \mathcal{I}^{(1)} \cup \mathcal{I}^{(2)} \cup \mathcal{I}^{(3)}$$

$$D^{Init} = \{[a, j-1, j] \vdash [A{\rightarrow}\alpha{\bullet}a{\bullet}\gamma, j-1, j]\},$$

$$D^{\varepsilon} = \{\vdash [B{\rightarrow}{\bullet}{\bullet}, j, j]\},$$

$$D^{Incl} = \{[B{\rightarrow}{\bullet}\beta{\bullet}, i, j] \vdash [A{\rightarrow}\alpha{\bullet}B{\bullet}\gamma, i, j]\},$$

$$D^{Concat} = \{[A{\rightarrow}{\bullet}\alpha{\bullet}X\gamma, i, j], [A{\rightarrow}\alpha{\bullet}X{\bullet}\gamma, j, k] \vdash [A{\rightarrow}{\bullet}\alpha X{\bullet}\gamma, i, k]\},$$

$$D_{dVH3} = D^{Init} \cup D^{\varepsilon} \cup D^{Incl} \cup D^{Concat}.$$

From the above discussion it follows that

$$\mathcal{V}^{\leq n}(\mathbb{D}_{dVH3}) = \{[A{\rightarrow}{\bullet}X\beta{\bullet}\gamma, i, j] \in \mathcal{I} \mid X\beta \Rightarrow^{*} a_{i+1} \ldots a_j\}$$

$$\cup \{[A{\rightarrow}\alpha{\bullet}X{\bullet}\gamma, i, j] \in \mathcal{I} \mid X \Rightarrow^{*} a_{i+1} \ldots a_j\}.$$

Moreover, clearly, **dVH2** $\overset{\text{sf}}{\Longrightarrow}$ **dVH3**.   □

6.3 Dynamic filtering

The purpose of filtering is to reduce the work that needs to be done to derive all valid entities. In static filtering we did so by discarding "redundant" parts of the derivation system. It is called static, because the redundancy is independent of the particular string that is to be parsed. In a real parser this means that the filter can be applied compile-time. Dynamic filtering is more powerful. The recognition of items can be made dependent on the existence of other items. In this way context can be taken into account. If we have, for example, an item $[B \rightarrow \bullet \beta \bullet, i, j]$ and a production $A \rightarrow BC$ then we could restrict the deduction step

$$[B \rightarrow \bullet \beta \bullet, i, j] \vdash [A \rightarrow \bullet B \bullet C, i, j]$$

to those cases where a_{j+1} could be the first word of a string produced by C. That is, we could replace the deduction by a set of deductions

$$[B \rightarrow \bullet \beta \bullet, i, j], [a, j+1, j] \vdash [A \rightarrow \bullet B \bullet C, i, j]$$

only for those a such that $a \in \text{FIRST}(C)$ (cf. Definition 6.10). Hence, dynamic filtering, on a theoretical level, is simply adding antecedents to existing deductions.

In the following definition, static filtering is a special subcase of dynamic filtering. This fits the interpretation that static filtering materializes to to compile-time optimization and dynamic filtering materializes to run-time optimization; an optimization that can be done compile-time could also be done run-time instead of compile-time.

Definition 6.7. (*dynamic filtering*)

Let $\mathbb{P}_1$ and $\mathbb{P}_2$ be semiregular parsing systems. The relation $\mathbb{P}_1 \xrightarrow{\text{df}} \mathbb{P}_2$ holds if

(*i*) $\mathcal{I}_1 \supseteq \mathcal{I}_2$
(*ii*) $\vdash_1 \supseteq \vdash_2$.

Let $\mathbf{P}_1$ and $\mathbf{P}_2$ be semiregular parsing schemata for a class of grammars $\mathcal{CG}$. The relation $\mathbf{P}_1 \xRightarrow{\text{df}} \mathbf{P}_2$ holds if, for each $G \in \mathcal{CG}$ and each $a_1 \ldots a_n \in \Sigma^*$,

$$\mathbf{P}_1(G)(a_1 \ldots a_n) \xrightarrow{\text{df}} \mathbf{P}_2(G)(a_1 \ldots a_n). \qquad \square$$

Like with static filtering, it is obvious that $\xrightarrow{\text{df}}$ and $\xRightarrow{\text{df}}$ are transitive and soundness preserving.

Example 6.8. (**buE** $\xRightarrow{\text{df}}$ **Earley**)
The parsing schemata **buE** and **Earley** have been defined in Examples 4.34 and 4.32, respectively. In order to verify that **buE** $\xRightarrow{\text{df}}$ **Earley** holds, we compare the sets D_{Earley} and D_{buE} for an arbitrary grammar. The item sets are identical.

The *scan* and *complete* steps are identical in both schemata. For the *predict* and *init* steps, it suffices to verify that

$$[A \rightarrow \alpha \bullet \beta, i, j] \vdash_E [B \rightarrow \bullet \gamma, j, j]$$

in $\mathbb{P}_{Earley}$ holds only if

$$\vdash_{buE} [B \rightarrow \bullet \gamma, j, j]$$

in $\mathbb{P}_{buE}$. This is evidently the case. □

Example 6.9. (buLC $\overset{df}{\Longrightarrow}$ LC)
See Examples 4.35, 4.36 for the definitions of **buLC** and **LC**.
Similar to the previous example. □

As another example of dynamic filtering, we will look at the algorithm of de Vreught and Honig again. The more sophisticated version of the algorithm uses *bottom-up filtering*, making use of a (one-position) left and right context. An item $[A \rightarrow \alpha \bullet \beta \bullet \gamma, i, j]$ is recognized only when it can possibly contribute to a parse, given the left context a_i and the right context a_{j+1}. We define the set of *context-dependent items* $CI \subset I$ by

$$CI(G, a_1 \ldots a_n) = \{[A \rightarrow \alpha \bullet \beta \bullet \gamma, i, j] \mid$$
$$\exists \delta_1, \delta_2, \delta_3, \delta_4 : \#S\$ \Rightarrow^* \delta_1 A \delta_2 \wedge \delta_1 \alpha \Rightarrow^* \delta_3 a_i \wedge$$
$$\beta \Rightarrow^* a_{i+1} \ldots a_j \wedge \gamma \delta_2 \Rightarrow^* a_{j+1} \delta_4\}.$$

Here we use, for the first time, the beginning-of-sentence and end-of-sentence marker. These guarantee that every word, also the first and the last word, have a left and right neighbour. The beginning-of-sentence marker could be deleted, at the expense of formulating special constraints for $i = 0$. The use of the end-of-sentence marker is essential, because it is the only way to define the *nonexistence* of the $(n + 1)$-st word.

We are to design the system $\mathbb{P}_{dVH3}$ now, in such a way that $\mathcal{V}^{\leq n}(\mathbb{P}_{dVH3}) \subseteq CI$. But we cannot simply restrict the domain from $\mathcal{I}$ to CI, because CI does depend on the string to be parsed and the domain must be independent of the sentence. Hence we take a different line and operationalize the test for membership of CI within the parsing schema. We can simply follow de Vreught and Honig [1989] using the functions FIRST and FOLLOW [Aho and Ullman, 1977], and their right-to-left counterparts LAST and PRECEDE.

Definition 6.10. (*Context*, FIRST, FOLLOW, LAST, PRECEDE)
We will use FIRST(α) and LAST(α) only for strings α such that $\alpha \not\Rightarrow^* \varepsilon$.[2]

---

[2] We take advantage of the fact that FIRST(α) is used only for α that do not rewrite to (or are) the empty string. In the more general, case were FIRST is used in any context, one needs a more complicated function

$$\text{FIRST}(\alpha) = \{a \mid \exists \beta, \gamma, \delta : \#S\$ \Rightarrow^* \beta \alpha \gamma \wedge \alpha \gamma \Rightarrow^* a\delta\}.$$

Similarly for LAST.

$$\text{FIRST}(\alpha) \quad = \{a \mid \exists \beta : \alpha \Rightarrow^* a\beta\},$$

$$\text{LAST}(\alpha) \quad = \{a \mid \exists \beta : \alpha \Rightarrow^* \beta a\},$$

$$\text{FOLLOW}(X) \quad = \{a \mid \exists \alpha, \beta : \#S\$ \Rightarrow^* \alpha X a\beta\},$$

$$\text{PRECEDE}(X) \quad = \{a \mid \exists \alpha, \beta : \#S\$ \Rightarrow^* \alpha a X\beta\}.$$

The predicates $LContext$, $RContext$ and $Context$ are defined by

$$LContext(A, \alpha, a) \quad = \exists b \in \text{PRECEDE}(A) : a \in \text{LAST}(b\alpha),$$

$$RContext(A, \gamma, c) \quad = \exists b \in \text{FOLLOW}(A) : c \in \text{FIRST}(\gamma b),$$

$$Context(A, \alpha, \gamma, a, c) = LContext(A, \alpha, a) \wedge RContext(A, \gamma, c). \qquad \square$$

Corollary 6.11.
$[A \to \alpha \bullet \beta \bullet \gamma, i, j] \in \mathcal{CI}$ iff $\beta \Rightarrow^* a_{i+1} \dots a_j$ and $Context(A, \alpha, \gamma, a_i, a_{j+1})$. $\qquad \square$

The notion $Context$ is not dependent on a particular input string $a_1 \dots a_n$. We can now proceed with the definition of a parsing schema for the dVH algorithm that takes context into account. We will actually give two such schemata, **dVH4** and **dVH5**, being dynamically filtered versions of **dVH1** and **dVH3** respectively.

Example 6.12. (dVH4, *dynamic filtering***)**
For arbitrary $G \in \mathcal{CFG}$ a parsing system $\mathbb{P}_{dVH4}$ is defined by

$$\mathcal{I}_{dVH4} \quad = \{[A \to \alpha \bullet \beta \bullet \gamma, i, j] \mid A \to \alpha\beta\gamma \in P \wedge 0 \le i \le j\};$$

$$D^{Init} \quad = \{[a, j-2, j-1], [b, j-1, j], [c, j, j+1]$$
$$\vdash [A \to \alpha \bullet b \bullet \gamma, j-1, j] \mid Context(A, \alpha, \gamma, a, c)\},$$

$$D^\varepsilon \quad = \{\vdash [B \to \bullet \bullet, j, j]\},$$

$$D^{Incl} \quad = \{[a, i-1, i], [B \to \bullet \beta \bullet, i, j], [b, j, j+1]$$
$$\vdash [A \to \alpha \bullet B \bullet \gamma, i, j] \mid Context(A, \alpha, \gamma, a, b)\},$$

$$D^{Concat} = \{[A \to \alpha \bullet \beta_1 \bullet \beta_2 \gamma, i, j], [A \to \alpha \beta_1 \bullet \beta_2 \bullet \gamma, j, k]$$
$$\vdash [A \to \alpha \bullet \beta_1 \beta_2 \bullet \gamma, i, k]\},$$

$$D_{dVH4} \quad = D^{Init} \cup D^\varepsilon \cup D^{Incl} \cup D^{Concat}.$$

Note that $D^{Concat}_{dVH4} = D^{Concat}_{dVH1}$. There is no need to demand $Context(A, \alpha, \gamma, a_i, a_{k+1})$, because this follows from $Context(A, \alpha, \beta_2, a_i, a_{j+1})$ and $Context(A, \beta_1, \gamma, a_j, a_{k+1})$.

The set of relevant valid items is limited to those relevant valid items of $\mathbb{P}_{dVH1}$ that are member of $\mathcal{CI}$.

$$\mathcal{V}^{\leq n}(\mathbb{P}_{dVH4}) = \mathcal{V}^{\leq n}(\mathbb{P}_{dVH1}) \cap \mathcal{CI}$$
$$= \{[A\to\alpha\bullet\beta\bullet\gamma, i, j] \in \mathcal{I} \mid$$
$$\beta\Rightarrow^* a_{i+1}\ldots a_j$$
$$\wedge\, (\beta \neq \varepsilon \vee \alpha\gamma = \varepsilon)$$
$$\wedge\, \exists\delta_1, \delta_2 : \#S\$\Rightarrow^* \delta_1 a_i A a_{j+1}\delta_2\}.$$

We have defined operators of $\mathbb{P}_{dVH4}$ by adding antecedents to operators of $\mathbb{P}_{dVH1}$. Hence, if $Y \vdash_{dVH4} x$ it follows a fortiori that $Y \vdash_{dVH1} x$ and we conclude

dVH1 $\overset{\text{df}}{\Longrightarrow}$ dVH4. □

We have applied two filters at the parsing schema **dVH1**. On the one hand, statically, we have discarded items that cannot contribute to the recognition of a valid item. On the other hand, dynamically, we have taken context into account in the definition of the deduction steps. These optimizations are orthogonal, in the sense that they don't interfere with each other. The final version of **dVH** is obtained simply by merging the two filters.

Example 6.13. (**dVH5**, *final version*)
For an arbitrary context-free grammar the parsing system $\mathbb{P}_{dVH5}$ is defined by

$$\mathcal{I}^{(1)} = \{[A\to\alpha\bullet X\bullet\gamma, i, j] \mid A\to\alpha X\gamma \in P \wedge 0 \leq i \leq j\},$$

$$\mathcal{I}^{(2)} = \{[A\to\bullet X\beta\bullet\gamma, i, j] \mid A\to X\beta\gamma \in P \wedge 0 \leq i \leq j\},$$

$$\mathcal{I}^{(3)} = \{[A\to\bullet\bullet, j, j] \mid A\to\varepsilon \in P \wedge j \geq 0\},$$

$$\mathcal{I}_{dVH5} = \mathcal{I}^{(1)} \cup \mathcal{I}^{(2)} \cup \mathcal{I}^{(3)};$$

$$D^{Init} = \{[a, j-2, j-1], [b, j-1, j], [c, j, j+1]$$
$$\vdash [A\to\alpha\bullet b\bullet\gamma, j-1, j] \mid Context(A, \alpha, \gamma, a, c)\},$$

$$D^{\varepsilon} = \{\vdash [B\to\bullet\bullet, j, j]\},$$

$$D^{Incl} = \{[a, i-1, i], [B\to\bullet\beta\bullet, i, j], [b, j, j+1]$$
$$\vdash [A\to\alpha\bullet B\bullet\gamma, i, j] \mid Context(A, \alpha, \gamma, a, b)\},$$

$$D^{Concat} = \{[A\to\bullet\alpha\bullet X\gamma, i, j], [A\to\alpha\bullet X\bullet\gamma, j, k] \vdash [A\to\bullet\alpha X\bullet\gamma, i, k]\},$$

$$D_{dVH5} = D^{Init} \cup D^{\varepsilon} \cup D^{Incl} \cup D^{Concat}.$$

The set of relevant valid items is limited to those relevant valid items in $\mathbb{P}_{dVH3}$ that are member of $\mathcal{CI}$.

$$\mathcal{V}^{\leq n}(\mathbb{P}_{dVH5}) = \{[A\to\alpha\bullet X\beta\bullet\gamma, i, j] \in \mathcal{I} \mid$$
$$X\beta\Rightarrow^* a_{i+1}\ldots a_j$$
$$\wedge\, (\alpha = \varepsilon \vee \beta = \varepsilon)$$
$$\wedge\, \exists\delta_1, \delta_2 : \#S\$\Rightarrow^* \delta_1 a_i A a_{j+1}\delta_2\}.$$

It is left to the reader to verify

$$\text{dVH4} \overset{\text{sf}}{\Longrightarrow} \text{dVH5},$$
$$\text{dVH3} \overset{\text{df}}{\Longrightarrow} \text{dVH5}. \hspace{4cm} \square$$

In an algorithm derived from these parsing schemata one can efficiently implement the left and right context predicates by storing the allowed preceding/following terminals for every production and dot position in a table. If this implementation technique is used, it is clear that **dVH5** yields the most efficient parser of all dVH schemata, because the least number of items is recognized at negligible extra cost per reduction.

6.4 Step contraction

The final and most powerful kind of filtering is step contraction. As the name suggests, it is indeed the reverse of the step refinement relation of Section 5.2. The general idea is the following. When an algorithm takes small and easy steps, it can sometimes be speeded up by taking somewhat larger and perhaps more complicated steps. Such an optimization will typically improve an algorithm with a (small) constant factor.

It is paradoxical, perhaps, that *both* step refinement and step contraction are useful for improving the practical performance of a parser. The difference, with respect to practical implementations, is that step refinement is used for qualitative changes whereas step contraction is merely used for increasing the efficiency without making changes to the underlying principles of an algorithm. As a typical example of the former, consider **GCYK** $\overset{\text{sr}}{\Longrightarrow}$ **buE**, which decreases the complexity of a parser from $O(n^{\varrho+1})$ to $O(n^3)$, where ϱ is the length of the longest right-hand side. An example of the latter is **Earley** $\overset{\text{sc}}{\Longrightarrow}$ **GHR**, the schema for the improved Earley parser that was described by Graham, Harrison and Ruzzo [1980].

A consequence of this paradox is that step refinement and step contraction *per se* are not necessarily useful. Too much refinement yields unproductive intermediate results, while too much contraction may lead to a more complex algorithm. But the purpose of our formalism of parsing schemata is not primarily that it can be used to improve parsers; the main objective is to describe at the right level of abstraction how parsers are related to one another and what precisely is improved by introducing certain variants.

Definition 6.14. (*step contraction*)
Let $\mathbb{P}_1$, $\mathbb{P}_2$ be semiregular parsing systems. The relation $\mathbb{P}_1 \overset{\text{sc}}{\longrightarrow} \mathbb{P}_2$ holds if

(*i*) $\mathcal{I}_1 \supseteq \mathcal{I}_2$,
(*ii*) $\vdash_1^* \supseteq \vdash_2^*$.

Let $\mathbf{P}_1$ and $\mathbf{P}_2$ be semiregular parsing schemata for some class of grammars $\mathcal{CG}$. The relation $\mathbf{P}_1 \overset{sc}{\Longrightarrow} \mathbf{P}_2$ holds if, for each $G \in \mathcal{CG}$ and for each $a_1 \ldots a_n \in \Sigma^*$,

$$\mathbf{P}_1(G)(a_1 \ldots a_n) \overset{sc}{\longrightarrow} \mathbf{P}_2(G)(a_1 \ldots a_n).$$ □

Corollary 6.15.

For any two parsing systems $\mathbb{P}_1$, $\mathbb{P}_2$ or parsing schemata $\mathbf{P}_1$, $\mathbf{P}_2$ it holds that
$\mathbb{P}_1 \overset{sc}{\longrightarrow} \mathbb{P}_2$ if and only if $\mathbb{P}_2 \overset{sr}{\longrightarrow} \mathbb{P}_1$;
$\mathbf{P}_1 \overset{sc}{\Longrightarrow} \mathbf{P}_2$ if and only if $\mathbf{P}_2 \overset{sr}{\Longrightarrow} \mathbf{P}_1$. □

Any dynamic filter, as a consequence, is also a step contraction – although of a somewhat degenerate form: no real contraction of sequences of deduction steps takes place. As for proper step contractions, we could in principle make a difference between static step contractions (multiple steps in D_1 are contracted to single steps in D_2) and dynamic step contractions (also including addition of antecedents). This is of little use and only leads to more complicated definitions. All the following examples belong to the static kind.

Example 6.16. (Earley vs. Left-Corner)

In Example 5.22 we have shown that **Earley** is a step refinement of **LC**. It makes more sense to define it the other way round, because we have constructed the **LC** schema (cf. Example 4.36) as a slightly more efficient variant of Earley.

The same holds for the bottom-up variants of both algorithms. Hence,

Earley $\overset{sc}{\Longrightarrow}$ LC;
buE $\overset{sc}{\Longrightarrow}$ buLC.

In fact we have already proven this in Examples 4.36 and 4.35 where the Left-Corner schemata were introduced by stripping some redundancies from the Earley schemata. □

Example 6.17. (dVH3 $\overset{sc}{\Longrightarrow}$ buLC)

See Examples 6.6 and 4.35 for definitions of **dVH3** and **buLC**. As usual, we consider parsing systems $\mathbb{P}_{dVH3}$ and $\mathbb{P}_{buLC}$ for an arbitrary grammar G and string $a_1 \ldots a_n$.

First, we show that $\mathcal{I}_{buLC} \subseteq \mathcal{I}_{dVH3}$. There is a notational difference, because $\mathbb{P}_{dVH3}$ uses double-dotted and $\mathbb{P}_{buLC}$ single-dotted items. But it is clear that items $[A \to \alpha \bullet\bullet \beta, i, j]$ and $[A \to \bullet \alpha \bullet \beta, i, j]$ are just different denotations for a single item

$$[A \to \langle \alpha \rightsquigarrow \underline{a}_{i+1} \ldots \underline{a}_j \rangle \beta].$$

So we observe that $\mathcal{I}^{(1)}_{buLC} = \mathcal{I}^{(2)}_{dVH3}$ and $\mathcal{I}^{(2)}_{buLC} = \mathcal{I}^{(3)}_{dVH3}$, hence $\mathcal{I}_{buLC} \subset \mathcal{I}_{dVH3}$.

Next, we have to show that $\vdash^*_{buLC} \subseteq \vdash^*_{dVH3}$. To this end it suffices to show that for every deduction step $\eta_1 \ldots, \eta_k \vdash \xi \in D_{buLC}$ it holds that $\eta_1 \ldots, \eta_k \vdash^*_{dVH3} \xi$. We check each type of deduction step in $\mathbb{P}_{buLC}$:

- $D^\epsilon_{buLC} \subseteq D^\epsilon_{dVH3}$ by definition.
- $D^{LC(a)}_{buLC} \subseteq D^{Init}_{dVH3}$ by definition.
- $D^{LC(A)}_{buLC} \subseteq D^{Incl}_{dVH3}$ by definition.
- D^{Scan}_{buLC}: An arbitrary deduction step

$$[A\to\bullet\alpha\bullet a\beta, i, j], [a, j, j+1] \vdash [A\to\bullet\alpha a\bullet\beta, i, j+1]$$

  is emulated in $\mathbb{P}_{dVH3}$ by

$$[a, j, j+1] \vdash [A\to\alpha\bullet a\bullet\beta, j, j+1],$$
$$[A\to\bullet\alpha\bullet a\beta, i, j], [A\to\alpha\bullet a\bullet\beta, j, j+1] \vdash [A\to\bullet\alpha a\bullet\beta, i, j+1].$$

- D^{Compl}_{buLC}: an arbitrary deduction step

$$[A\to\bullet\alpha\bullet B\beta, i, j], [B\to\bullet\gamma\bullet, j, k] \vdash [A\to\bullet\alpha B\bullet\beta, i, k]$$

  is emulated in $\mathbb{P}_{dVH3}$ by

$$[B\to\bullet\gamma\bullet, j, k] \vdash [A\to\alpha\bullet B\bullet\beta, j, k],$$
$$[A\to\bullet\alpha\bullet B\beta, i, j], [A\to\alpha\bullet B\bullet\beta, j, k] \vdash [A\to\bullet\alpha B\bullet\beta, i, k].$$

Hence we conclude that $D_{buLC} \subseteq \vdash^*_{dVH3}$. $\qquad\qquad\qquad\square$

Next, we will introduce the improvement of the Earley algorithm by Graham Harrison and Ruzzo [1980], also known as the *GHR algorithm*. It has been designed as a step contraction of the Earley algorithm. A bottom-up variant of GHR also exists.

Another step contraction on bottom-up GHR, that will be treated subsequently, has been defined by Chiang and Fu [1984]. This last variant allows parallel implementations where it takes *exactly* n steps to parse a sentence of length n (rather than $O(n)$ steps involving a constant that is dependent on the grammar, as in bottom-up Earley, or maximally $2n$ steps as in the GHR algorithm).

Example 6.18. (GHR)
The algorithm of Graham, Harrison and Ruzzo makes two improvements upon the original definition of Earley:

- *nullable symbols* (i.e. symbols that can be rewritten to the empty string) can be skipped when the dot is worked rightwards through a production;
- *chain derivations* (i.e. derivations of the form $A\Rightarrow^+ B$) are reduced to single steps.

For an arbitrary grammar G and string $a_1 \ldots a_n$ we define a parsing system $\mathbb{P}_{GHR}$ as follows.

$$\mathcal{I}_{GHR} = \{[A\to\alpha\bullet\beta, i, j] \mid A\to\alpha\beta \in P \wedge 0 \leq i \leq j\};$$
$$D^{Init} = \{\vdash [S\to\beta\bullet\gamma, 0, 0] \mid \beta\Rightarrow^*\varepsilon\},$$

$$D^{Scan} = \{[A\rightarrow\alpha\bullet a\beta\gamma, i, j], [a, j, j+1] \vdash [A\rightarrow\alpha a\beta\bullet\gamma, i, j+1]$$
$$| \ \beta\Rightarrow^*\varepsilon\},$$

$$D^{C1} = \{[A\rightarrow\alpha\bullet B\beta\gamma, i, j], [B\rightarrow\delta\bullet, j, k] \vdash [A\rightarrow\alpha B\beta\bullet\gamma, i, k]$$
$$| \ i < j < k \wedge \beta\Rightarrow^*\varepsilon\},$$

$$D^{C2} = \{[A\rightarrow\alpha\bullet B\beta\gamma, i, i], [C\rightarrow\delta\bullet, i, j] \vdash [A\rightarrow\alpha B\beta\bullet\gamma, i, j]$$
$$| \ i < j \wedge B\Rightarrow^*C \wedge \beta\Rightarrow^*\varepsilon\},$$

$$D^{Pred} = \{[A\rightarrow\alpha\bullet B\beta, i, j] \vdash [C\rightarrow\alpha'\bullet\beta', j, j] \ | \ B\Rightarrow^*C\gamma \wedge \alpha'\Rightarrow^*\varepsilon\},$$

$$D_{GHR} = D^{Init} \cup D^{Scan} \cup D^{C1} \cup D^{C2} \cup D^{Pred}.$$

In order to verify the correctness of **GHR** – at the same time showing that **Earley** $\stackrel{sc}{\Longrightarrow}$ **GHR** – we will split the step contraction into two separate filters. As an intermediate schema we define **GHR'**. For an arbitrary G and $a_1 \ldots a_n$ we define $\mathbb{P}_{GHR'}$ by

$$\mathcal{I}_{GHR'} = \mathcal{I}_{GHR};$$

$$D^{C1}_{GHR'} = \{[A\rightarrow\alpha\bullet B\beta\gamma, i, j], [B\rightarrow\delta\bullet, j, k] \vdash [A\rightarrow\alpha B\beta\bullet\gamma, i, k] \ | \ \beta\Rightarrow^*\varepsilon\},$$

$$D^{C2}_{GHR'} = \{[A\rightarrow\alpha\bullet B\beta\gamma, i, i], [C\rightarrow\delta\bullet, i, j] \vdash [A\rightarrow\alpha B\beta\bullet\gamma, i, j] \ |$$
$$B\Rightarrow^*C \wedge \beta\Rightarrow^*\varepsilon\},$$

$$D_{GHR'} = D^{Init}_{GHR} \cup D^{Scan}_{GHR} \cup D^{C1}_{GHR'} \cup D^{C2}_{GHR'} \cup D^{Pred}_{GHR}.$$

In the first step, **Earley** $\stackrel{sc}{\Longrightarrow}$ **GHR'**, only new deduction steps are added. These extra deduction steps are contractions of steps that existed already. Hence we have only introduced redundancy and it holds that **Earley** $\stackrel{re}{\Longleftarrow}$ **GHR'**.

Secondly, from **GHR'** to **GHR** we will delete some redundancies, but different ones from those that have just been introduced. It has to be shown that steps in D^{C1} are redundant for $i = j$ or $j = k$ and steps in D^{C2} are redundant for $i = j$. Take, for example, the case that $j = k$. If one has

$$[A\rightarrow\alpha\bullet B\beta\gamma, i, j], [B\rightarrow\bullet\delta\bullet, j, j] \vdash [A\rightarrow\alpha B\beta\bullet\gamma, i, j] \in D^{C1}_{GHR'},$$

then B is nullable. Hence, for any deduction step with consequent $[A\rightarrow\alpha\bullet B\beta\gamma, i, j]$, there is a similar deduction step that skips the nullable string $B\beta$ and produces $[A\rightarrow\alpha B\beta\bullet\gamma, i, j]$ directly.

The other case are similar. Thus we conclude that **GHR'** $\stackrel{re}{\Longrightarrow}$ **GHR** and hence

Earley $\stackrel{sr}{\Longrightarrow}$ **GHR**.

The correctness of **GHR** follows from the observation that

Earley $\stackrel{re}{\Longleftarrow}$ **GHR'** $\stackrel{re}{\Longrightarrow}$ **GHR**

and the fact that $\mathcal{V}^{\leq n}$ is not affected by redundancy elimination. $\square$

Example 6.19. (buGHR)
A bottom-up variant of **GHR** is straightforward from the definitions of **buE** and **GHR**. For an arbitrary grammar G and string $a_1 \ldots a_n$ we define a parsing system $\mathbb{P}_{buGHR}$ as follows.

$$\mathcal{I}_{buGHR} = \{[A \to \alpha \bullet \beta, i, j] \mid A \to \alpha\beta \in P \land 0 \leq i \leq j\};$$

$$D^{Init} = \{\vdash [A \to \alpha \bullet \beta, j, j] \mid \alpha \Rightarrow^* \varepsilon\},$$

$$D^{Scan} = \{[A \to \alpha \bullet a\beta\gamma, i, j], [a, j, j+1] \vdash [A \to \alpha a\beta \bullet \gamma, i, j+1] \\ \mid \beta \Rightarrow^* \varepsilon\},$$

$$D^{C1} = \{[A \to \alpha \bullet B\beta\gamma, i, j], [B \to \delta \bullet, j, k] \vdash [A \to \alpha B\beta \bullet \gamma, i, k] \\ \mid i < j < k \land \beta \Rightarrow^* \varepsilon\},$$

$$D^{C2} = \{[A \to \alpha \bullet B\beta\gamma, i, i], [C \to \delta \bullet, i, j] \vdash [A \to \alpha B\beta \bullet \gamma, i, j] \\ \mid i < j \land B \Rightarrow^* C \land \beta \Rightarrow^* \varepsilon\},$$

$$D_{buGHR} = D^{Init} \cup D^{Scan} \cup D^{C1} \cup D^{C2}.$$

The fact that **buE** $\overset{sc}{\Longrightarrow}$ **buGHR** and the correctness of **buGHR** can be established as in Example 6.18 □

Example 6.20. (ChF)
A small improvement upon the bottom-up variant of the algorithm of Graham, Harrison and Ruzzo has been defined by Chiang and Fu [1984]. It is step contraction in the most literal sense of the word. The deduction steps are somewhat more complicated, but the basic idea is perfectly clear:

- If an item can be deduced by two *complete* deduction steps from D^{C1} and D^{C2} in $\mathbb{P}_{buGHR}$, where the consequent of the former is an antecedent of the latter, then contract these two steps into a single deduction step;
- Similar for D^{Scan} and D^{C2} in $\mathbb{P}_{buGHR}$.

The deduction steps in D^{Scan} and D^{C1} remain as they are. The definition of D^{C2} is adapted and a second set of *scan* steps is introduced. This results in the following parsing system.

$$\mathcal{I}_{ChF} = \{[A \to \alpha \bullet \beta, i, j] \mid A \to \alpha\beta \in P \land 0 \leq i \leq j\};$$

$$D^{Init} = \{\vdash [A \to \alpha \bullet \beta, j, j] \mid \alpha \Rightarrow^* \varepsilon\},$$

$$D^{S1} = \{[A \to \alpha \bullet a\beta\gamma, i, j], [a, j, j+1] \vdash [A \to \alpha a\beta \bullet \gamma, i, j+1] \\ \mid \beta \Rightarrow^* \varepsilon\},$$

$$D^{S2} = \{[C \to \gamma \bullet a\beta', i, j], [a, j, j+1] \vdash [A \to \alpha B\beta \bullet \gamma, i, j+1] \\ \mid B \Rightarrow^* C \land \alpha\beta\beta' \Rightarrow^* \varepsilon\},$$

$$D^{C1} = \{[A{\to}\alpha{\bullet}B\beta\gamma, i, j], [B{\to}\delta{\bullet}, j, k] \vdash [A{\to}\alpha B\beta{\bullet}\gamma, i, k]$$
$$| \ i < j < k \wedge \beta{\Rightarrow}^*\varepsilon\},$$

$$D^{C2} = \{[C{\to}\gamma{\bullet}E\beta', i, j], [E{\to}\delta{\bullet}, j, k] \vdash [A{\to}\alpha B\beta{\bullet}\gamma, i, k]$$
$$| \ i < j \wedge B{\Rightarrow}^*C \wedge \alpha\beta\beta'{\Rightarrow}^*\varepsilon\},$$

$$D_{ChF} = D^{Init} \cup D^{S1} \cup D^{S2} \cup D^{C1} \cup D^{C2}.$$

It is left to the reader to verify that **buGHR** $\overset{\mathbf{sc}}{\Longrightarrow}$ **ChF**. $\qquad\qquad\square$

In **ChF**, D^{Init} deduces more items than necessary. Only items of the form $[A{\to}\alpha{\bullet}a\beta, j, j]$ are used in subsequent steps. There is no longer a need for items of the form $[A{\to}\alpha{\bullet}B\beta, j, j]$; their use has disappeared in the step contraction $\mathbb{P}_{buGHR} \overset{\mathbf{sc}}{\longrightarrow} \mathbb{P}_{ChF}$. Hence we can apply another redundancy elimination step. Such minor optimizations have little impact, however, and we will not pursue them further.

6.5 The family of Earley-like parsing schemata

We have encountered 4 types of filters, so far: redundancy elimination, static filtering, dynamic filtering and step contraction. From the definitions it is obvious that for any class of parsing schemata

$$\overset{\mathbf{re}}{\Longrightarrow} \subseteq \overset{\mathbf{sf}}{\Longrightarrow} \subseteq \overset{\mathbf{df}}{\Longrightarrow} \subseteq \overset{\mathbf{sc}}{\Longrightarrow}.$$

We don't need to introduce a general filtering operation, because every filter is a step contraction. In Figure 6.2, an overview is given of most filtering relations between parsing schemata discussed in Chapter 6. The arrows are labelled with the most restricted type of filter that applies in each case. **dVH2** has been left out because it is only an intermediate step in the static filter from **dVH1** to **dVH3**. Each arrow is also labelled with the number of the example in which it is discussed.

Theorem 6.21.
A filtering relation holds between any two parsing schemata displayed in Figure 6.2 if and only if they are connected by a sequence of arrows.

Proof. For the individual arrows, see the examples referred to. Transitivity (and reflexivity, for empty sequences) is obvious from the definitions.
As for the *non*existence of filtering relations, this has to be verified for every not-connected pair of schemata, but it is always obvious. $\qquad\square$

The filtering relations in Figure 6.2 constitute a directed acyclic graph with several sources and several sinks. Is there a more general schema from which both **buE** and **dVH1** can be derived by applying a filter? And can the filters that produced **ChF**, **GHR**, **LC** and **dVH5** be combined, producing a

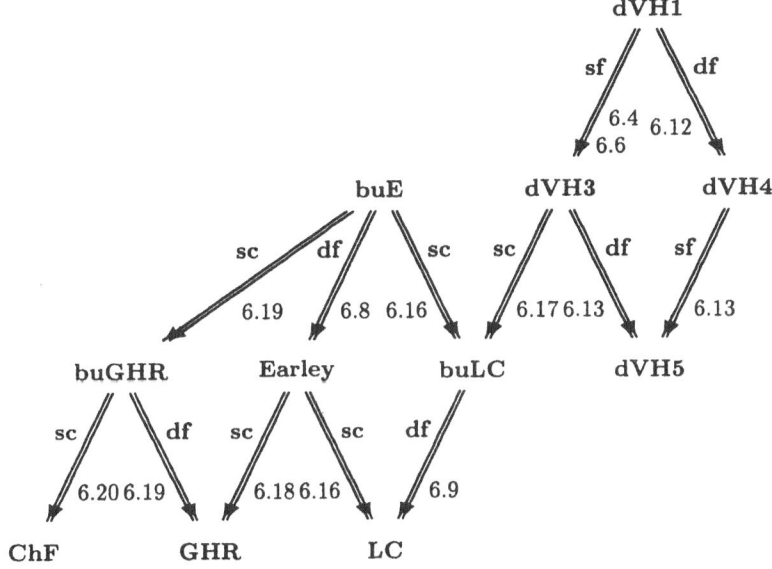

Fig. 6.2. Filtering relations between schemata discussed in Chapter 6

single, optimally filtered schema? Such schemata can indeed be derived, but their practical value is doubtful.

We have seen several examples of composite filters that are composed of "orthogonal" components. We have dealt with $\mathbf{dVH1} \overset{\mathbf{df}}{\Longrightarrow} \mathbf{dVH5}$ extensively; $\mathbf{buE} \overset{\mathbf{sc}}{\Longrightarrow} \mathbf{LC}$ is another case. In Figure 6.3 the taxonomy of Earley-like parsing schemata is extended with cross-breedings between the sinks of the graph in Figure 6.2. Not all of these schemata are equally useful, however.

The optimization of Chiang and Fu leads to a maximum *parallel* speed-up of 50 %, but does not speed up a sequential implementation. Hence a left-to-right version of **ChF** on a single processor is not faster than **GHR** – unless this is taken a starting point for another static filter, where intermediate results are discarded that have become redundant by the Chiang and Fu step contraction.

An LC parser with GHR optimizations, similarly, can be seen as a starting point for further static filtering.

A parsing schema for an algorithm that does exist in the literature is obtained by combining $\mathbf{dVH3} \overset{\mathbf{sc}}{\Longrightarrow} \mathbf{LC}$ and $\mathbf{dVH3} \overset{\mathbf{df}}{\Longrightarrow} \mathbf{dVH5}$: a left-corner parser with one symbol look-ahead. Our **LC** schema is the schema for an LC(0) parser. A one-word look-ahead can be added to **LC** like to a **dVH** schema without look-ahead. On the other hand, the **dVH5** parsing schema could be classified as $\mathbf{dVH(1,1)}$, i.e., a schema for the dVH algorithm with one-word look-back and look-ahead. The optimization to a $\mathbf{buLC(1,1)}$ schema is straightforward. **LC(1)** is obtained by adding a top-down filter as usual. The look-back has become obsolete by the top-down filter. One could also see it in a different way: a top-down filter constitutes a look-back of unlimited size. A top-down filtered parser takes everything to the left of a constituent as context for bottom-up filtering.

The parsing schemata contained in a box in Figure 6.3 are schemata for parsers that have been seriously proposed in the literature. The other ones have been added only to illustrate filtering and to complete the picture. The algorithm of de Vreught and Honig [1989] has in fact a schema that is located between **dVH4** and **dVH5**. The authors have overlooked the possibility of statically filtering **dVH2** into **dVH3** and applied the dynamic filter to **dVH2**.

A "mother" schema from which both **dVH1** and **buE** can be derived by step contraction is shown at the top of the graph, To call it **dVH0** is actually unfair to de Vreught and Honig: the schema is rather awkward as is has to combine the *inefficiencies* of dVH and bottom-up Earley.

Example 6.22. (dVH0)
For arbitrary $G \in \mathcal{CFG}$ and $a_1 \ldots a_n$ a parsing system $\mathbb{P}_{dVH0}$ is defined as follows.

$$
\begin{aligned}
\mathcal{I}_{dVH0} &= \{[A{\to}\alpha{\bullet}\beta{\bullet}\gamma, i, j] \mid A{\to}\alpha\beta\gamma \in P \wedge 0 \leq i \leq j\}; \\
D^{Init} &= \{\vdash [A{\to}\alpha{\bullet\bullet}\gamma, j, j]\}, \\
D^{Scan} &= \{[A{\to}\alpha{\bullet\bullet}a\gamma, i, i], [a, i, i+1] \vdash [A{\to}\alpha{\bullet}a{\bullet}\gamma, i, i+1]\}, \\
D^{Compl} &= \{[A{\to}\alpha{\bullet\bullet}B\gamma, i, i], [B{\to}{\bullet}\beta{\bullet}, i, j] \vdash [A{\to}\alpha{\bullet}B{\bullet}\gamma, i, j]\}, \\
D^{Concat} &= \{[A{\to}\alpha{\bullet}\beta_1{\bullet}\beta_2\gamma, i, j], [A{\to}\alpha\beta_1{\bullet}\beta_2{\bullet}\gamma, j, k] \\
&\qquad\qquad\qquad\qquad\qquad \vdash [A{\to}\alpha{\bullet}\beta_1\beta_2{\bullet}\gamma, i, k]\}, \\
D_{dVH0} &= D^{Init} \cup D^{Scan} \cup D^{Compl} \cup D^{Concat}.
\end{aligned}
$$

It is left to the reader to verify that

$$
\begin{aligned}
\mathbf{dVH0} &\overset{sc}{\Longrightarrow} \mathbf{dVH1}, \\
\mathbf{dVH0} &\overset{sc}{\Longrightarrow} \mathbf{buE}.
\end{aligned}
$$

$\square$

Figure 6.3 is far from complete; a variety of related schemata could be added. In Section 4.6 we have remarked that the **Earley** schema is also the parsing schema of a (generalized) LR(0) parser. One can define filtered versions that specify LR(k), SLR(k) and LALR(k) parsers. But we have seen enough examples here. Parsing schemata for LR-parsers will be discussed in Chapter 12. In chapter 10 we have a closer look at LC parsers.

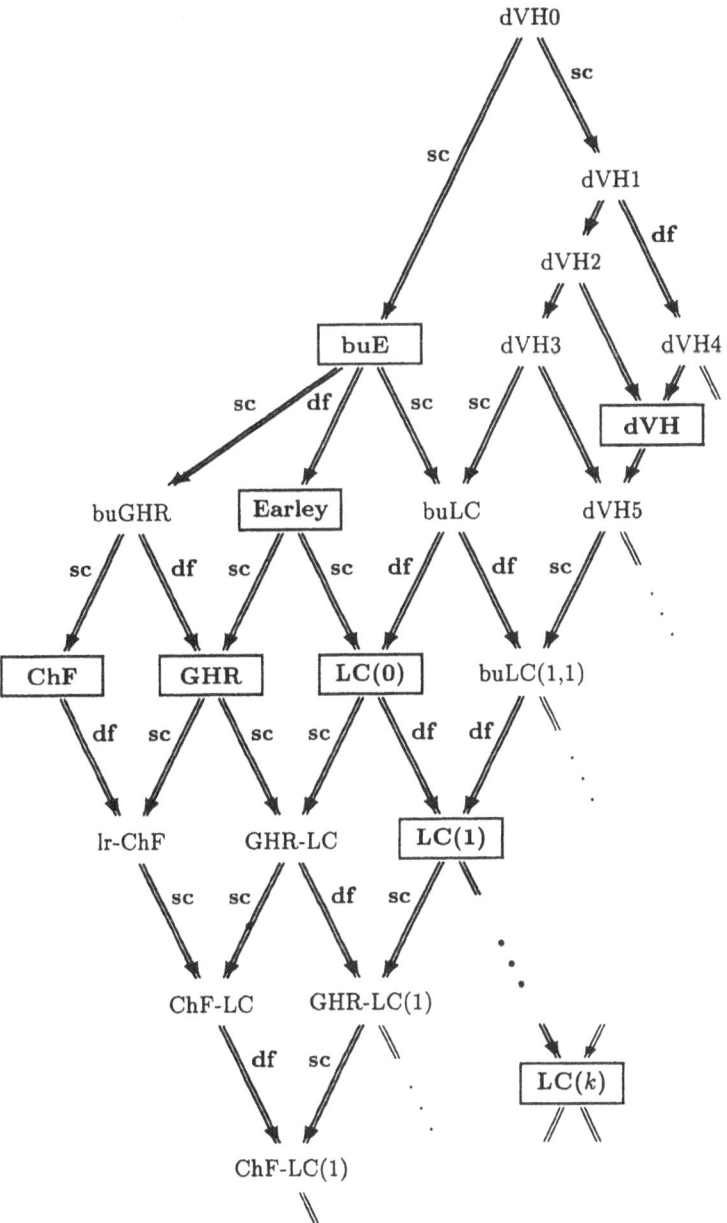

Fig. 6.3. A taxonomy of Earley-like parsing schemata

6.6 A summary of relations between parsing schemata

All relations on parsing systems that have been introduced in Chapters 5 and 6 are summarized in Figure 6.4. The same relations apply to deduction systems in general (in which case the item set $\mathcal{I}$ should be replaced by a general domain X, to be consistent with the notation used in Chapter 4). Relations that have been defined between parsing schemata are summarized in Figure 6.5.

A more refined taxonomy of relations is possible. One could define *static step contraction*, which is a superclass of static filtering and a subclass of step contraction. Step contraction, then, is a combination of static step contraction and dynamic filtering. Static step contractions can be described by a specific kind of *redundancy introduction* followed by redundancy elimination. This has been illustrated in fact in Example 6.18, where we discussed the static step contraction **Earley** $\overset{\text{sc}}{\Longrightarrow}$ **GHR**.

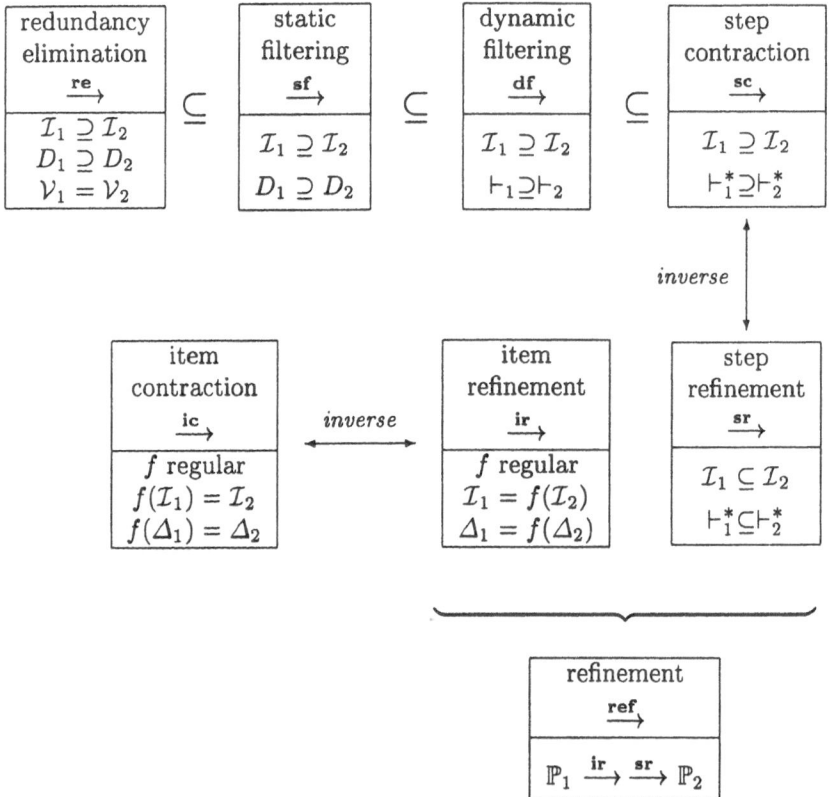

Fig. 6.4. A summary of relations between parsing systems

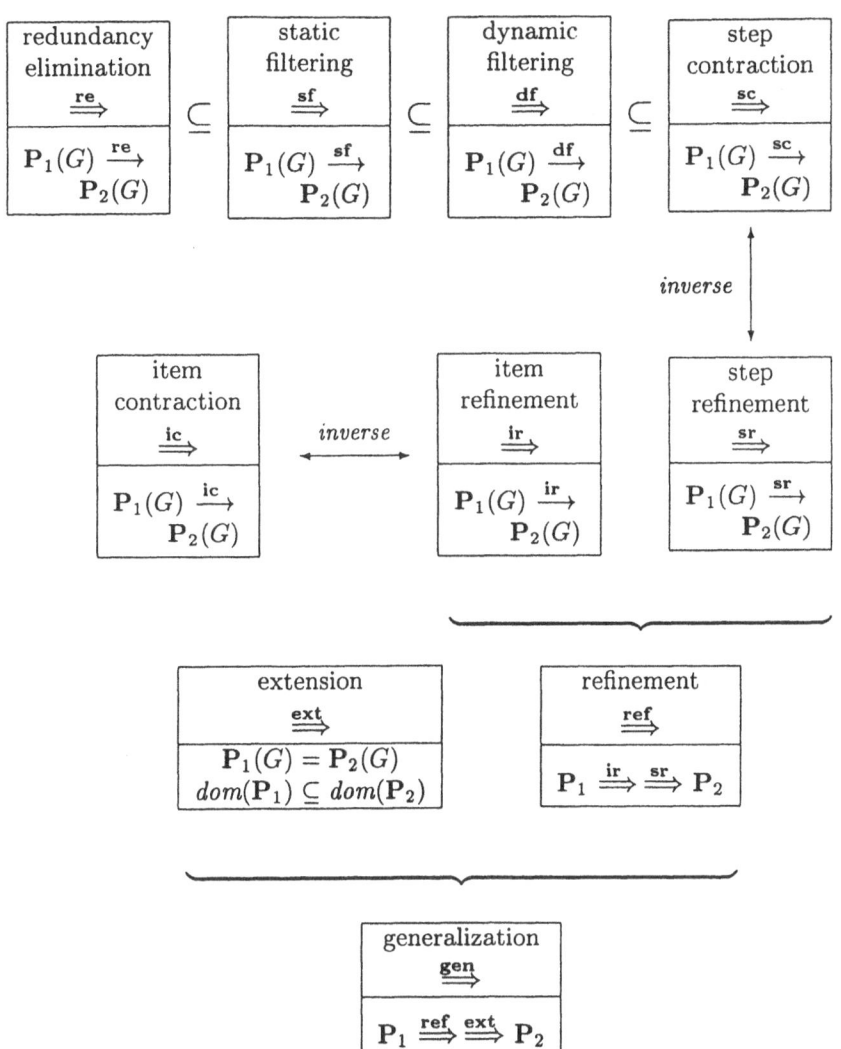

Fig. 6.5. A summary of relations between parsing schemata

6.7 Conclusion

In this chapter we have been concerned with optimization of parsing schemata. We have defined a series of filtering operations that can be used to strip spurious items and deduction steps from parsing systems. A variety of parsing schemata, describing parsing algorithms known from the computer science literature, have been captured in a single taxonomy of Earley-related parsers.

It is surprising, perhaps, that we can make a clear distinction between static filtering and dynamic filtering. The former is usually understood as "compile-time" optimization, the latter as "run-time" optimization. The distinction can be made at the abstract level of parsing schemata, because static filters are independent of the string (represented by the hypotheses) and dynamic filters may depend on the string. Static filtering means discarding irrelevant parts of a system; dynamic filtering can take context into account by adding antecedents to deduction steps.

The strongest form of filtering, step contraction, is the reverse of step refinement that was introduced in Chapter 5. Both operations are used to increase the efficiency of parsers: step contraction is used to diminish the work to be done, whereas step refinement is useful in transformations that provide a qualitative improvement in the parser. It will be clear that step refinement or step contraction *per se* is not a useful operation. Over-refinement will lead to too much work; over-contraction will lead to steps that require additional sophistication in a parser that implements such a schema.

The calculus of parsing schemata that has been developed in Chapters 5–6 is not a tool that guides a parser designer towards a schema for an optimally efficient parser. The question whether the individual deduction steps (including search techniques to retrieve the relevant antecedents) can be implemented efficiently is not discussed at this level of abstraction. Parsing schemata are a useful tool, however, to describe the relations between various parsing algorithms and to explain precisely the nature of certain optimizations.

We have now finished the formal theory of parsing schemata for context-free grammars. In Part III we will use parsing schemata as a tool for various applications (hence Part III can be seen as consisting of several, unrelated subparts). As a first undertaking, in Chapters 7–9, we will discuss how feature structures can be incorporated into parsing schemata, yielding a practical parsing schema notation for unification grammars.

Part III

APPLICATION

7. An introduction to unification grammars

In Part II we have developed a formal theory of parsing schemata for context-free grammars. In Part III we will apply this theory in several different directions. In Chapters 7–9, we discuss parsing schemata for unification grammars. In Chapters 10 and 11 we use parsing schemata to define Left-Corner and Head-Corner chart parsers. We will prove these to be correct as well. In Chapters 12 and 13, subsequently, we derive a parsing schema for Tomita's algorithm as an example of an algorithm that is not item-based. As a result, we can cross-fertilize the Tomita parser with a *parallel* bottom-up Earley parser, yielding a parallel bottom-up Tomita parser. In Chapter 14, finally, we discuss hard-wired implementations of parsing schemata, in the form of boolean circuits.

We will extend parsing schemata with feature structures, so that schemata for parsing unification grammars can be defined. In addition to items that describe how a parser deals with the context-free backbone of a grammar, we will extend the schema with a notation in which one can specify how features are transferred from one item to the other. Thus a formalism is obtained in which *feature percolation* in unification grammar parsing can be controlled explicitly. Chapter 7 is a brief, informal introduction. In Chapter 8 we give a lengthy, formal treatment of the formalism; some more practical aspects of unification grammar parsing are discussed in Chapter 9.

Unification grammars – also called unification-based grammars, constraint-based grammars, or feature structure grammars – are of central importance to current computational linguistics. As these formalisms are not widely known among computer scientists, it seems appropriate to give an introduction that should provide some intuition about what we are going to formalize.

In 7.1 a preview is given of what parsing schemata with feature structures look like. While keeping the notion of feature structures deliberately abstract and vague, the general idea of such a parsing schema stands out rather clear. In 7.2, subsequently, feature structures and unification grammars are informally introduced by means of an example. We use the PATR formalism of Shieber [1986], with a tiny change in the notation. Anyone who is familiar with PATR can skip 7.2.

7.1 Unification-based parsing schemata: a preview

A thorough, formal treatment of unification grammars and parsing schemata
for these grammars will be given in Chapter 8. As we will see, it requires quite
some space and effort to do things properly. Parsing algorithms for unification
grammars constitute a complex problem domain. A wealth of concepts is to
be introduced, properly defined and – not the least problem – provided with
clear and precise notations. We will jump ahead now and look at a glimpse
of what we are heading for. An intuitive understanding of what we are trying
to formalize may help the reader to get through the formal parts.

We address the following question: *"How can parsing schemata be enhanced with any kind of information that is added to the context-free backbone
of a grammar?"* One may think of attribute grammars, unification grammars,
affix grammars or any other formalism in which such information can be specified. We will be unspecific, for good reason. By refusing (for the moment) to
use a particular formalism we cannot get sidetracked by all its sophisticated
details.

In this section we recapitulate a simple context-free parsing schema, give
an example of the use of other grammatical information, introduce (fragments
of) a notation for it, and add this to the parsing schema.

As an example of a context-free parsing schema we recall the **Earley**
schema of Example 4.32. For an arbitrary grammar $G \in \mathcal{CFG}$ we define a
parsing system $\mathbb{P}_{Earley} = \langle \mathcal{I}, H, D \rangle$, where $\mathcal{I}$ denotes the domain of Earley
items; H (the hypotheses) encodes the string to be parsed; D comprises the
deduction steps that can be used to recognize items. Most deduction steps
are of the form $\eta, \zeta \vdash \xi$. When the *antecedents* η and ζ have been recognized,
then the *consequent* ξ can also be recognized. Some deduction steps have only
a single antecedent. Moreover, in order to start parsing, an initial deduction
step with no antecedents is included. $\mathbb{P}_{Earley}$ is defined by

$$\mathcal{I}_{Earley} = \{[A \to \alpha \bullet \beta, i, j] \mid A \to \alpha\beta \in P, 0 \le i \le j\};$$

$$H = \{[a_1, 0, 1], \ldots, [a_n, n-1, n]\};$$

$$D^{Init} = \{\vdash [S \to \bullet \gamma, 0, 0]\},$$

$$D^{Scan} = \{[A \to \alpha \bullet a\beta, i, j], [a, j, j+1] \vdash [A \to \alpha a \bullet \beta, i, j+1]\},$$

$$D^{Compl} = \{[A \to \alpha \bullet B\beta, i, j], [B \to \gamma \bullet, j, k] \vdash [A \to \alpha B \bullet \beta, i, k]\},$$

$$D^{Pred} = \{[A \to \alpha \bullet B\beta, i, j] \vdash [B \to \bullet \gamma, j, j]\},$$

$$D_{Earley} = D^{Init} \cup D^{Scan} \cup D^{Compl} \cup D^{Pred};$$

where H varies according to the string $a_1 \dots a_n$ that should be parsed. The second part of the usual set notation $\{\dots \mid \dots\}$ has been deleted in most cases; by definition, deduction steps may only use items from $\mathcal{I}$ and H.

We assume that the context-free backbone of a grammar is enhanced with additional syntactic, semantic or other linguistic information. Constituents, productions, and items can have certain *features*[1] that express information not present in the context-free part of the grammar. This information can be of different kinds. A typical use of features is the transfer of information through a parse tree. As an example, consider

> *In the production $S \to NP\ VP$, the semantics of S can be derived from the semantics of NP and VP by ...*

If each word in the lexicon has some semantics associated with it, and for each production it is known how the semantics of the left-hand side is to be derived from the right-hand side, the semantics of the sentence can be obtained compositionally from its constituents.

Another typical, more syntactic way in which features are used is to constrain the set of sentences that is acceptable to the parser. A canonical example is

> *In the production $S \to NP\ VP$, there must be (some form of) agreement between NP and VP.*

The precise nature of the agreement is irrelevant here. Either constituent will have some features that could play a role in agreement, e.g.

> *the noun phrase "the boy" is masculine, third person singular,*

but the fact that agreement is required between NP and VP is a feature of the production, not a feature of each of the constituents individually.

Let us now enhance the Earley parser with such features. If we parse a sentence "The boy ...", at some point we will recognize an item $[S \to NP \bullet VP, 0, 2]$. We could attach the previously stated information to the item, as follows

> *The NP in $[S \to NP \bullet VP, 0, 2]$ is masculine, third person singular. Hence the VP that is to follow must be masculine, third person singular.*

Next we apply the *predict* step

$$[S \to NP \bullet VP, 0, 2] \vdash [VP \to \bullet\, {}^{*}v\ NP, 2, 2],$$

in combination with a feature of the production $VP \to {}^{*}v\ NP$:

---

[1] At this level of abstraction, the word "feature" can be replaced by "attribute", "affix", etc. All of these stand for roughly the same concept, but refer to different kinds of formalisms.

> *In the production VP→·*v NP, the agreement of VP is fully deter-*
> *mined by the agreement of *v.*

Combining all this information, we obtain the following item annotated with features:

[VP→·*$v\,NP$, 2, 2]
VP must be masculine, third person singular;
hence *v must be masculine, third person singular.

Gender plays no role in verb forms in English. Demanding that the verb form be masculine is irrelevant, but harmless. If the grammar doesn't specify gender for verb forms, it follows that every form of every verb can be used in combination with a masculine subject.

An important concept that must be introduced here is *consistency*. The features of an object are called *inconsistent* if they contain conflicting information. As an example, consider the sentence "The boy scout ...", where "scout" is known to be both a noun and a verb form. If we continue from the previous item and scan a *v, we would obtain

[VP→*v·NP, 2, 3]
VP must be masculine, third person singular;
hence *v must be masculine, third person singular.
*v is either plural or first or second person singular.

This is inconsistent and therefore not acceptable as a valid item.

We need to introduce a tiny bit of notation in order to enhance the **Earley** parsing schema with features. The notation will be explained, but not defined in a mathematical sense. We write

- $\varphi_0(A$→$\alpha)$ for the features of a production A→α;
- $\varphi(X)$ for the features of a constituent X;
- $\varphi([A$→α·$\beta, i, j])$ for the features of an item $[A$→α·$\beta, i, j]$.

The index 0 for features of productions is to indicate that these are taken straight from the grammar. In both other cases, features may have accumulated by transfer from previously recognized constituents and/or items.

The features of an item comprise the features of the production and those of its constituents (as far as these are known yet). From an item, the features of each constituent mentioned in that item can be retrieved.

We will not (yet) define a domain of expressions in which features can be formulated. This is left to the imagination of the reader. We need some notation, however, to relate sets of features to one another. *Combining* the features of objects ξ and η is denoted by $\varphi(\xi) \sqcup \varphi(\eta)$. The square union ($\sqcup$) may be interpreted as conventional set union ($\cup$) if it is understood that we accumulate sets of features. Similarly, we write $\varphi(\xi) \sqsubseteq \varphi(\eta)$ (which may be interpreted as $\varphi(\xi) \subseteq \varphi(\eta)$) to denote that an object η has at least all features and values of an object ξ but may have other features and values as well.

We will now extend the **Earley** parsing schema with the possibility to include features of constituents, productions and items. The parsing schema is defined by a parsing system $\mathbb{P}_{Earley} = \langle \mathcal{I}_{Earley}, H, D_{Earley} \rangle$ for an arbitrary context-free grammar G, where the set H is determined by the string to be parsed. The domain is defined by

$$\mathcal{I}_{Earley} = \{[A \rightarrow \alpha \bullet \beta, i, j]_\xi \mid A \rightarrow \alpha\beta \in P \wedge 0 \leq i \leq j \wedge$$
$$\varphi_0(A \rightarrow \alpha\beta) \sqsubseteq \varphi(\xi) \wedge consistent(\varphi(\xi))\};$$

The ξ symbol is used only for easy reference. Subscripting $[A \rightarrow \alpha \bullet \beta, i, j]$ with ξ means that we may refer to the item as ξ in the remainder of the formula. The unabbreviated, somewhat more cumbersome notation for the same definition is

$$\mathcal{I}_{Earley} = \{[A \rightarrow \alpha \bullet \beta, i, j] \mid A \rightarrow \alpha\beta \in P \wedge 0 \leq i \leq j \wedge$$
$$\varphi_0(A \rightarrow \alpha\beta) \sqsubseteq \varphi([A \rightarrow \alpha \bullet \beta, i, j]) \wedge$$
$$consistent(\varphi([A \rightarrow \alpha \bullet \beta, i, j])) \qquad \}.$$

In words: it is mandatory that all features of a production be contained in an item that is based on that production. The item may have other features as well, as long as this does not lead to an inconsistency.

The deduction steps are the usual context-free deduction steps, annotated with how the features of the consequent are determined by the features of the antecedents:

$$D^{Init} = \{ \vdash [S \rightarrow \bullet \gamma, 0, 0]_\xi \mid \varphi(\xi) = \varphi_0(S \rightarrow \gamma)\},$$

$$D^{Scan} = \{[A \rightarrow \alpha \bullet a\beta, i, j]_\eta, [a, j, j+1]_\zeta \vdash [A \rightarrow \alpha a \bullet \beta, i, j+1]_\xi$$
$$\mid \varphi(\xi) = \varphi(\eta) \sqcup \varphi(a_\zeta)\},$$

$$D^{Compl} = \{[A \rightarrow \alpha \bullet B\beta, i, j]_\eta, [B \rightarrow \gamma \bullet, j, k]_\zeta \vdash [A \rightarrow \alpha B \bullet \beta, i, k]_\xi$$
$$\mid \varphi(\xi) = \varphi(\eta) \sqcup \varphi(B_\zeta)\},$$

$$D^{Pred} = \{[A \rightarrow \alpha \bullet B\beta, i, j]_\eta \vdash [B \rightarrow \bullet \gamma, j, j]_\xi$$
$$\mid \varphi(\xi) = \varphi(B_\eta) \sqcup \varphi_0(B \rightarrow \gamma)\},$$

$$D_{Earley} = D^{Init} \cup D^{Scan} \cup D^{Compl} \cup D^{Pred}.$$

The items have been subscripted with identifiers ξ, η, ζ for easy reference. The notation $\varphi(X_\eta)$ is used for those features of the item η that relate to constituent X.

7.2 The example grammar UG_1

We will look at a very simple example of a unification grammar. Our example grammar does not pretend to have any linguistic relevance. Moreover, the example deviates slightly from the usual examples as given by, e.g., Shieber [1986]. It is not our purpose to advocate the felicity of unification grammars to encode linguistic phenomena, but to show how context-free backbones of natural language grammars can be enhanced with features. Hence, we take the context-free example grammar that has been used in chapter 2 and simply add features to that grammar.

The **Earley** schema of the previous section is too advanced, for the time being, and we will parse strictly bottom-up in CYK fashion. If constituents B and C are known for a production $A{\rightarrow}BC$, then A can be recognized and an appropriate feature structure for it will be constructed.

Different features of a constituent can be stored in a *feature structure*. For each word in the language, the lexicon contains a feature structure[2]. The lexicon entry for the word "catches", for example, might look as follows

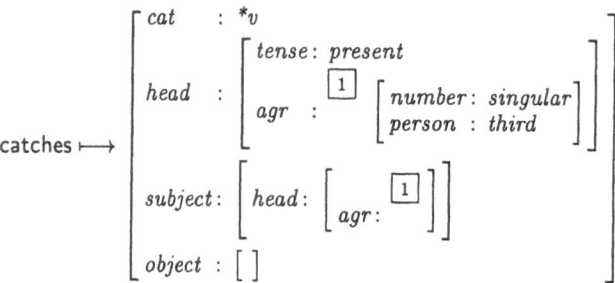

Features are listed in an *attribute-value matrix* (AVM). Every word has a feature *cat* describing the syntactic category. "Catches" has a feature *head* that contains some relevant information about the verb form. Furthermore, there are features *subject* and *object*, describing properties of the subject and direct object of the verb. The value of a feature can be some atomic symbol (as for *cat*); an AVM (as for *head* and *subject*), or unspecified (as for *object*). Unspecified features are denoted by an empty AVM, also called a *variable*. The intended meaning, in this case, is that the verb *catches* does have a direct object, but its features do not matter.

An important notion in AVMs is *coreference* (indicated by numbers contained in boxes). In the above example, the *head agr* feature is coreferenced with *subject head agr*, meaning that the agreement features of "catches" must be shared with the agreement features of its subject. Note, furthermore, that an entry within a nested structure of AVMs can be addressed by means of a *feature path*.

---

[2] If several different feature structures coexist for the same word, we will simply treat these as belonging to separate (homonym) words. Disjunction within feature structures is discussed in Section 9.4. While (a limited form of) disjunction is very useful for practical purposes, one can always interpret feature structures with disjunction as a compact representation of a set of non-disjunctive feature structures. Hence, from a theoretical point of view, disallowing disjunction is no limitation to the power of the formalism.

A first, very simple lexicon for the remainder of our canonical example sentence "the cat catches a mouse" is as follows:

the, a $\longmapsto$ $\begin{bmatrix} cat: *det \end{bmatrix}$

cat, mouse $\longmapsto$ $\begin{bmatrix} cat & : & *n \\ head: & \begin{bmatrix} agr: & \begin{bmatrix} number: & singular \\ person & : & third \end{bmatrix} \end{bmatrix} \end{bmatrix}$.

In order to parse the sentence, we need productions that tell us what to do with the features when we construct constituents. The syntactic categories of constituents are expressed by means of features, just like all other characteristic information. A formal, but somewhat austere way to express the construction of an NP from $*det$ and $*n$ is the following:

$X_0 \to X_1 \, X_2$
  $\langle X_0 \ cat \rangle \doteq NP$
  $\langle X_1 \ cat \rangle \doteq *det$ (7.1)
  $\langle X_2 \ cat \rangle \doteq *n$
  $\langle X_0 \ head \rangle \doteq \langle X_2 \ head \rangle.$

That is, if we have constituents X_1, X_2 with cat features $*det$ and $*n$, respectively, we may create a new constituent with cat feature NP. Moreover, the $head$ of X_0 is shared with the $head$ of X_2.[3]

In most, if not all grammars it will be the case that all constituents have a cat feature. Hence we can simplify the notation of production (7.1) to

$NP \to *det \; *n$
  $\langle NP \ head \rangle \doteq \langle *n \ head \rangle.$ (7.2)

The meaning of (7.1) and (7.2) is identical; the expression $\langle X_i \ cat \rangle \doteq A$ can be deleted when we substitute an A for X_i in the production. Thus we obtain context-free productions as usual, enhanced with so-called *constraints* that describe how the feature structures of the different constituents are related to one another. Hence, for the noun phrase "the cat" we may construct a feature structure with category NP and the $head$ feature taken from the noun "cat:"

the cat $\longmapsto$ $\begin{bmatrix} cat & : & NP \\ head: & \begin{bmatrix} agr: & \begin{bmatrix} number: & singular \\ person & : & third \end{bmatrix} \end{bmatrix} \end{bmatrix}$;

similarly for "a mouse." For the construction of a VP, in the same vein, we employ the following production annotated with constraints:

---

[3] In Chapter 8 we will make a distinction between *type identity* (denoted =) and *token identity* (denoted $\doteq$). As the distinction is not very relevant here, its introduction is postponed until Section 8.2, where we have developed the convenient terminology.

$VP \rightarrow {}^{*}v\ NP$
  $\langle VP\ head \rangle \doteq \langle {}^{*}v\ head \rangle$
  $\langle VP\ subject \rangle \doteq \langle {}^{*}v\ subject \rangle$
  $\langle {}^{*}v\ object \rangle \doteq \langle NP \rangle$

The verb phrase "catches a mouse" shares its *head* and *subject* features with
the verb, while the entire (feature structure of the) *NP* is taken to be the
direct object:

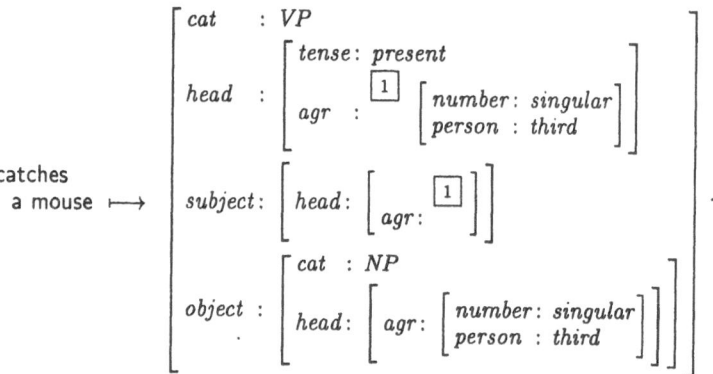

A sentence, finally, can be constructed from an *NP* and *VP* as follows:

$S \rightarrow NP\ VP$
  $\langle S\ head \rangle \doteq \langle VP\ head \rangle$
  $\langle VP\ subject \rangle \doteq \langle NP \rangle$

The sentence shares its head with the *VP*. The *subject* feature of the *VP* is
shared with all features of the *NP*. Note that (by coreference) the subject
of the verb phrase has ⟨*head*⟩ *agreement* third person singular. An *NP* can
be substituted for the subject only if it has the same agreement. If the *NP*
were to have a feature ⟨*head agr number*⟩ with value *plural*, then the *S* would
obtain both *singular* and *plural* as values for its ⟨*head agr number*⟩ feature
(because it is shared with the ⟨*subject head agr number*⟩ feature of the *VP*,
which is shared with the ⟨*head agr number*⟩ feature of the *VP*). Such a clash
of values would constitute an inconsistency, as discussed in Section 7.1. As a
feature structure for *S* we obtain

the cat catches a mouse $\longmapsto$ $\begin{bmatrix} cat & : S \\ head : & \begin{bmatrix} tense: present \\ agr\ :\ \begin{bmatrix} number: singular \\ person\ :\ third \end{bmatrix} \end{bmatrix} \end{bmatrix}$.

The entire sentence appears to have less features than its constituing parts
NP and *VP*. That is because some features were present only to guarantee
agreement between subject and verb. As the sentence has been produced,

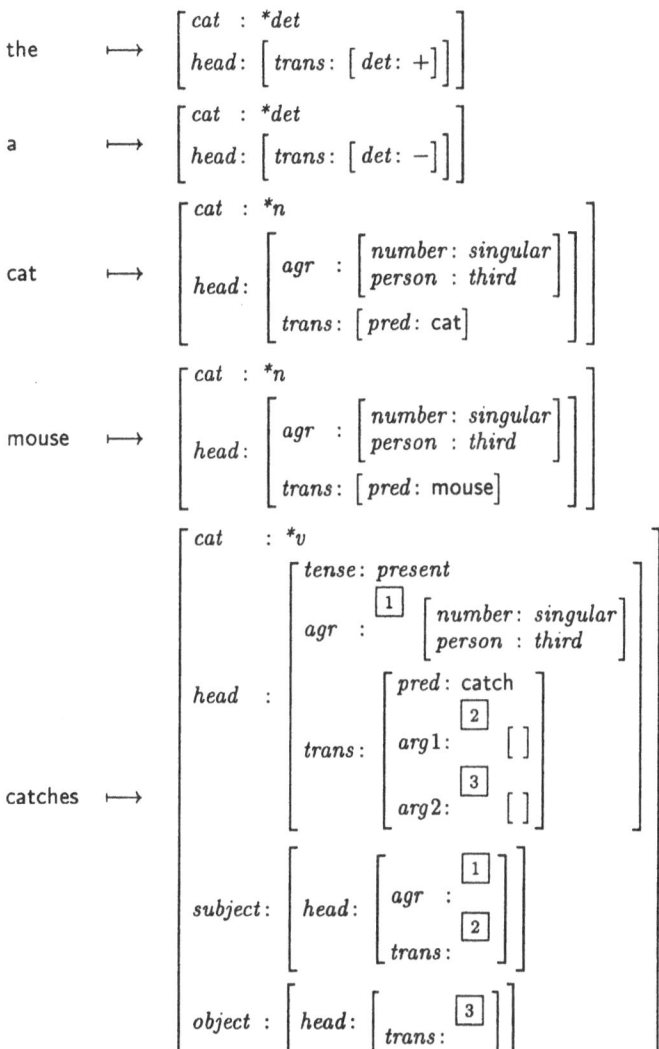

the $\longmapsto$ $\begin{bmatrix} cat & : & *det \\ head: & \begin{bmatrix} trans: & \begin{bmatrix} det: +\end{bmatrix}\end{bmatrix}\end{bmatrix}$

a $\longmapsto$ $\begin{bmatrix} cat & : & *det \\ head: & \begin{bmatrix} trans: & \begin{bmatrix} det: -\end{bmatrix}\end{bmatrix}\end{bmatrix}$

cat $\longmapsto$ $\begin{bmatrix} cat & : & *n \\ head: & \begin{bmatrix} agr & : & \begin{bmatrix} number: singular \\ person : third\end{bmatrix} \\ trans: & \begin{bmatrix} pred: cat\end{bmatrix}\end{bmatrix}\end{bmatrix}$

mouse $\longmapsto$ $\begin{bmatrix} cat & : & *n \\ head: & \begin{bmatrix} agr & : & \begin{bmatrix} number: singular \\ person : third\end{bmatrix} \\ trans: & \begin{bmatrix} pred: mouse\end{bmatrix}\end{bmatrix}\end{bmatrix}$

catches $\longmapsto$

Fig. 7.1. Part of the lexicon for UG_1

$S \rightarrow NP\ VP$
$\quad \langle S\ head \rangle \doteq \langle VP\ head \rangle$
$\quad \langle VP\ subject \rangle \doteq \langle NP \rangle$

$VP \rightarrow {}^{*}v\ NP$
$\quad \langle VP\ head \rangle \doteq \langle {}^{*}v\ head \rangle$
$\quad \langle VP\ subject \rangle \doteq \langle {}^{*}v\ subject \rangle$
$\quad \langle {}^{*}v\ object \rangle \doteq \langle NP \rangle$

$NP \rightarrow {}^{*}det\ {}^{*}n$
$\quad \langle NP\ head \rangle \doteq \langle {}^{*}n\ head \rangle$
$\quad \langle {}^{*}n\ head\ trans \rangle \doteq \langle {}^{*}det\ head\ trans \rangle$

Fig. 7.2. Some productions of UG_1

the agreement must have been okay, hence there is no need to retain this information explicitly in the feature structure for an S.

Above we have shown how syntactic constraints can be incorporated into the features of a grammar. We will also give an example of how semantic information can be collected from the lexicon and transferred upwards to contribute to the semantics of the sentence. We will use a very simple unification grammar UG_1. A relevant part of the lexicon for UG_1 is shown in Figure 7.1, the productions annotated with constraints are shown in Figure 7.2 The head of each feature structure is extended with a feature *trans(lation)*, which is only a first, easy step towards translation of the constituent to its corresponding semantics. The translation of a verb is a predicate with the (translation of the) subject as first argument and the (translation of the) object as second argument.

The production $NP \rightarrow {}^{*}det\ {}^{*}n$ has been extended with another clause, stating that the *head trans* features of **det* and **n* are to be shared. Thus we obtain, for example

$$
\text{a mouse} \longmapsto
\begin{bmatrix}
cat & : & NP \\
head: &
\begin{bmatrix}
agr & : &
\begin{bmatrix}
number: & singular \\
person & : & third
\end{bmatrix} \\
trans: &
\begin{bmatrix}
pred: & mouse \\
det & : & -
\end{bmatrix}
\end{bmatrix}
\end{bmatrix}.
$$

Because the translation of the subject and object are used as arguments for the translation of the verb, the relevant properties of subject and object are moved upward to a feature structure for the entire sentence. The reader may verify that, following the same steps as before, we obtain

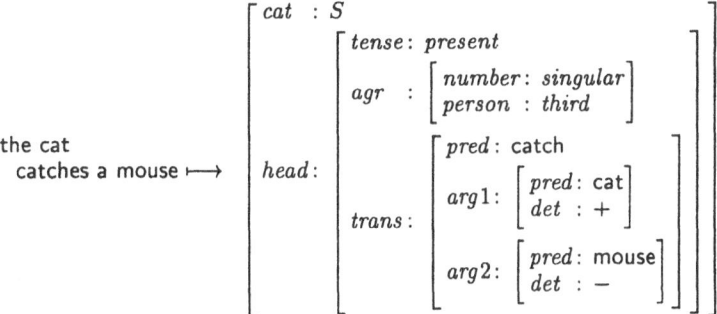

the cat
catches a mouse $\longmapsto$

Other features can be added likewise. We can add a *modifier* feature to the translation, in which modifiers like adjectives, adverbs and prepositional phrases can be stored. For a noun phrase "the very big, blue cat" we could envisage a feature structure as in Figure 7.3.

A noun phrase can include any number of modifiers, hence these are stored by means of a *list*. More sophisticated feature structure formalisms as, e.g., HPSG [Pollard and Sag, 1988], have special constructs for lists. Such constructs are convenient for notation, but not necessary. As shown in Figure 7.3, lists can be expressed in the basic formalism as well. In Section 9.5 a more complicated example is shown where lists are used for *subcategorization* of verbs.

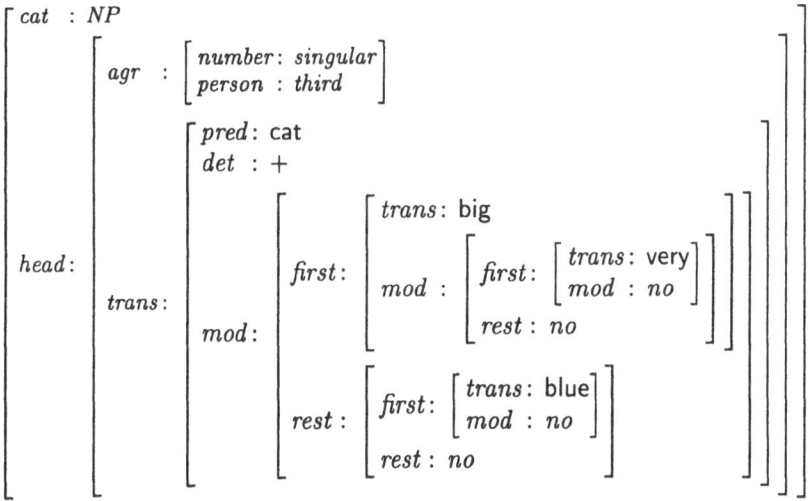

Fig. 7.3. Feature structure of "the very big, blue cat"

8. Parsing schemata for unification grammars

The last one and a half decade has witnessed an overwhelming number of different, but related unification grammar formalisms. Our informal introduction in Chapter 7 was based on PATR [Shieber, 1986], which is the smallest and simplest of these formalisms. Unlike formalisms as LFG [Kaplan and Bresnan, 1982], GPSG [Gazdar et al., 1985] or HPSG [Pollard and Sag, 1987, 1994], PATR was not primarily designed to capture some universal linguistic structure, but merely as a small, clean formalism that covers the essential properties found in most other unification grammars.

The logical foundations of constraint-based formalisms have been discussed by Kaspar and Rounds [1986], Smolka [1989, 1992] and Johnson [1991], who give various axiomatizations of feature structures in predicate logic. In such a logical approach, one describes a *constraint language* in which constraints can be expressed. Such constraints are formulae in first-order logic with equality. Constraints state that certain features must have certain values or be equal to certain other features. The semantic interpretation of such a formula (following Smolka) is a *feature graph*. The most interesting property is *satisfiability*. For a given formula it has to be decided whether a feature graph exists that is a model of the constraint.

A more fundamental treatment is given by Shieber [1992], who starts with the logical requirements for unification-based grammars and then sets out to investigate which models would be appropriate.

Our purpose, in this chapter and the next, is a rather different one. We will investigate how, for a given class of unification grammars, efficient parsers can be developed, by means of parsing schemata. Just like in the context-free case, we will be concerned with the question which items one likes to derive and which rules should be used for that. In addition, we extend the formalism with a notation that allows explicit specification of transfer of features between items.

Parsing of unification grammars is a combination of two problem areas, both of which are complex in itself. Parsing is our primary interest, and the linguistic and logical properties of unification grammars secondary. Hence we do not worry about how to specify suitable unification grammars for natural languages, nor are we particularly concerned with the logical properties of various unification grammar formalisms, but we assume a simple kind of unification grammar and address the question how efficient parsers can be defined.

In order to be precise we will give a detailed, formal account of our simple formalism, that establishes thoroughly what we have presented informally in Chapter 7. The results are virtually equal to those of Smolka and others, but we employ a rather more computational view and do not pretend to give a general treatise on unification grammars.

We do not make a distinction between syntax (constraints) and semantics (feature graphs); we see both domains as syntactic domains. The notion of satisfiability is replaced by *consistency*. There is a simple isomorphism between consistent constraints[1] and well-formed feature graphs. Thus we obtain an abstract notion of a feature structure that may materialize in two different avatars: either as a graph or as a constraint. We switch representation opportunistically to the domain that is most convenient at any given moment. For the purpose of (statically) describing a grammar, the constraint representation is the most useful. But the dynamics of a grammar, describing how a parse is to be obtained by *unification* of feature structures, are easiest understood in the feature graph domain.

Feature structures, both as graphs and constraint sets, are introduced in 8.1. For both representations we define a lattice and prove these to be isomorphic in 8.2. For a proper formalization of how features of different objects may relate to one another, we introduce *composite* feature structures in 8.3 and define lattices in 8.4. This formalism is used to define unification grammars in 8.5. Tree composition in Primordial Soup fashion is discussed in 8.6 and parsing schemata, finally, are defined in 8.7.

In 8.8, at last, we give another example. The canonical example sentence is parsed with grammar UG_1 (cf. Section 7.2) using an Earley-type parsing schema (cf. Section 7.1). An overview of other grammar formalisms is presented in 8.9, related approaches are briefly discussed in 8.10, and conclusions are summarized in 8.11.

8.1 Feature structures

We will give two different formalizations of feature structures, as *constraint sets* and *feature graphs*, and prove these to be isomorphic. The attribute-value matrix (AVM) notation will be used as a convenient, informal notation to

---

[1] From Section 8.1 onwards, we will call these *constraint sets*. A constraint as a formula in first order logic with equality can be seen as a conjunction of a series of atomic constraints. For our purposes it will be more convenient to describe this as a set of atomic constraints, rather than a conjunction.

denote feature structures. The correspondence between AVMs, feature graphs and constraint sets is straightforward. In Figure 8.1 an AVM is shown with corresponding constraint set and feature graph.

In Figure 8.1(a)–(c) it is exemplified how the information contained in an AVM can be encoded in a graph. The features are represented by edges; the atomic values are represented by labels of terminal vertices. Internal vertices carry no label; their value is the feature structure represented by the outgoing edges. The root vertex can be labelled with an identifier for the object whose features are represented here.

In order to give a formal definition of the domain of feature graphs, we first introduce some auxiliary domains from which features and values can be drawn.

Definition 8.1. (*features, constants*)
$\mathcal{F}ea$ denotes a finite set of features. We write $f, g, h, \ldots$ for elements of $\mathcal{F}ea$. *Const* denotes a finite set of constants. We write $c, d, e, \ldots$ for elements of *Const*.
It is assumed that $\mathcal{F}ea$ and *Const* are disjoint sets. Furthermore, we assume that a linear order has been defined on both sets $\mathcal{F}ea$ and *Const*.
In the sequel we will also need *sequences of features*. We write π, ϱ for elements of $\mathcal{F}ea^*$. A linear order on $\mathcal{F}ea^*$ is defined by the "lexicographic order" based on the linear order of $\mathcal{F}ea$:

(*i*) $\pi < \pi\varrho$ for non-empty feature sequences ϱ;
(*ii*) $\pi f\varrho < \pi g\varrho'$ if $f < g$.

This linear order on feature sequences will be used to define a suitable normal form for constraint sets.   □

We recall some useful notions from graph theory and introduce appropriate notations.

Definition 8.2. (DAGs)
A directed graph is a pair $\Gamma = (U, E)$, with U a set of vertices[2] and E a set of edges. An edge is a directed pair (u, v) with $u, v \in U$. Usually we write $u{\to}v$ for $(u, v) \in E$.
A (possibly empty), finite sequence of edges $u_0{\to}u_1, u_1{\to}u_2, \ldots, u_{k-1}{\to}u_k$ is called a *path*. We write $u \longrightarrow v$ for a path from u to v.
A directed graph is called *cyclic* if there is a non-empty path $u \longrightarrow u$ for some vertex $u \in U$. A graph is *acyclic* if it is not cyclic. We write DAG as abbreviation for a directed acyclic graph.
A *root* of a graph is a vertex u such that for all $v \in U$ there is a path from u to v.
A DAG is called *rooted* if it has exactly one root.

---

[2] We write U rather than V for the set of vertices, because V denotes the grammar variables $N \cup \Sigma$.

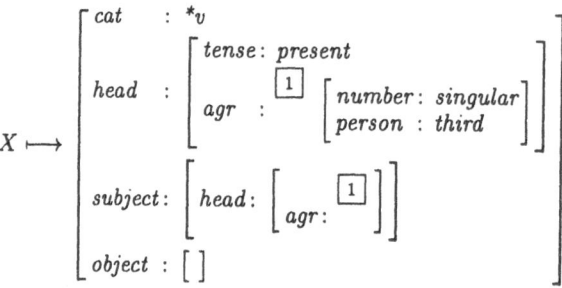

(a) an attribute value matrix

$$\{ \quad \langle X \ cat \rangle \doteq {}^*v,$$
$$\langle X \ head \ tense \rangle \doteq present,$$
$$\langle X \ head \ agr \ number \rangle \doteq singular,$$
$$\langle X \ head \ agr \ person \rangle \doteq third,$$
$$\langle X \ subject \ head \ agr \ \rangle \doteq \langle X \ head \ agr \rangle,$$
$$\langle X \ object \rangle \doteq [\ ] \qquad \}$$

(b) a constraint set

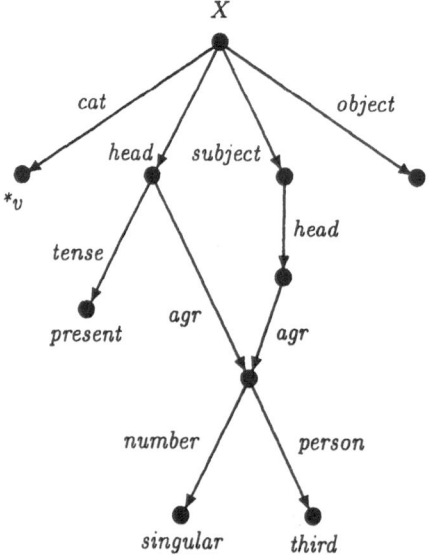

(c) a feature graph

Fig. 8.1. Three different representations of the same feature structure

An edge $u \rightarrow v$ is an *outgoing edge* of u and and *incoming edge* of v.
A *leaf* is a vertex with no outgoing edges.   □

Definition 8.3. (*feature graphs*)
$\mathcal{FG}$ is the class of finite, rooted DAGs with the following properties:

(i)   every edge is labelled with a feature;
(ii)   if f and g are labels of edges originating from the same vertex, then
         $f \neq g$;
(iii) leaves may be (but need not be) labelled with a constant;
         non-leaf vertices do not carry a label.

We write $u \xrightarrow{f} v$ if $u \rightarrow v$ is labelled f; we write $u \xrightarrow{\pi} v$ if the sequence of steps
from u to v is labelled with a sequence of features π. We write $label(u) = c$
if u is labelled with constant c and $label(u) = \varepsilon$ if u carries no label.
We write $\Gamma(X)$ for a feature graph that denotes the features of some (here
unspecified) object X.   □

An example of a constraint set was shown in Figure 8.1(b). In the definition of a constraint set, we have included a parameter X that can be used to
identify an object for which constraints are to be specified. We will not use
this parameter for a while, but include it here in anticipation of composite
constraint sets that will be defined in Section 8.3.

Definition 8.4. (*constraint set*)
Let X be a (not further specified) object. Constraints on X can be drawn
from different domains:

- The domain of *value constraints* VC is defined by

$$VC = \{\langle X\pi \rangle \doteq c \mid \pi \in \mathcal{Fea}^* \wedge c \in Const\};$$

- The domain of *coreference constraints* CC is defined by

$$CC = \{\langle X\pi \rangle \doteq \langle X\varrho \rangle \mid \pi, \varrho \in \mathcal{Fea}^*\}.$$

A *constraint set* $\chi(X)$ is a finite subset of $VC \cup CC$.
As a convenient notation[3] we write $\langle X\pi \rangle \doteq [\,]$ for contraints of the form
$\langle X\pi \rangle \doteq \langle X\pi \rangle$.
As an ad-hoc general notation we write $\langle X\pi \rangle \doteq \mu$ for a constraint, where μ
can be of the form c, $[\,]$, or $\langle X\varrho \rangle$.   □

---

[3] Alternatively we could introduce a separate domain of *existential constraints* of
the form $\langle X\pi \rangle \doteq [\,]$, with $[\,]$ a symbol not in $\mathcal{Fea}$ and $Const$ and omit constraints
of the form $\langle X\pi \rangle \doteq \langle X\pi \rangle$ from the coreference constraints. To state that "X has
an object" is more to the point than to state that "the object of X is coincident
with the object of X," but the logical implications are the same. By seeing the
former as a notational variant for the latter, we can combine the more intuitive
notation with the simpler formal model.

Next we define the closure of a constraint set. It is closed in the sense that every single piece of information that can be drawn from the given constraints is added explicitly as a separate constraint.[4]

Definition 8.5. (*closure of a constraint set*)
Let $\chi(X) \subset VC \cup CC$ be a constraint set. The *closure* of $\chi(X)$, denoted $closure(\chi(X))$, is the smallest set satisfying[5]

(*i*) $\langle X \rangle \doteq [\,] \in closure(\chi(X))$;
(*ii*)   if $\langle X\pi \rangle \doteq \mu \in \chi(X)$ then $\langle X\pi \rangle \doteq \mu \in closure(\chi(X))$;
(*iii*) if $\langle X\pi \rangle \doteq \langle X\pi' \rangle \in closure(\chi(X))$ and $\langle X\pi\varrho \rangle \doteq \mu \in closure(\chi(X))$
         then $\langle X\pi'\varrho \rangle \doteq \mu \in closure(\chi(X))$;
(*iv*)   if $\langle X\pi \rangle \doteq \langle X\varrho \rangle \in closure(\chi(X))$ then $\langle X\varrho \rangle \doteq \langle X\pi \rangle \in closure(\chi(X))$;
(*v*)   if $\langle X\pi\varrho \rangle \doteq \mu \in closure(\chi(X))$ then $\langle X\pi \rangle \doteq [\,] \in closure(\chi(X))$.

A constraint set $\chi(X)$ is called *closed* if $closure(\chi(X)) = \chi(X)$.   □

Note that $closure(\chi(X))$ need not be a constraint set according to Definition 8.4: it could be an infinite set. If, for example, $\langle X\pi \rangle \doteq \langle X\pi\varrho \rangle \in \chi(X)$ then, by (*ii*) we obtain $\langle X\pi\varrho \rangle \doteq \langle X\pi\varrho\varrho \rangle \in \chi(X)$, $\langle X\pi\varrho\varrho \rangle \doteq \langle X\pi\varrho\varrho\varrho \rangle \in \chi(X)$, and so forth.

The closure of the constraint set in Figure 8.1(b) is shown in Figure 8.2. The purpose of the "existential" constraints added in (*iv*) is to identify the existence of all substructures. We will use them for the transformation of a constraint set into a graph.

Definition 8.6. (*consistency*)
A closed constraint set $\chi(X)$ is called *consistent* if it satisfies the following properties:

(*i*)   if $\langle X\pi \rangle \doteq c \in \chi(X)$ and $\langle X\pi \rangle \doteq d \in \chi(X)$ then $c = d$;
(*ii*)   if $\langle X\pi \rangle \doteq c \in \chi(X)$ and $\langle X\pi\varrho \rangle \doteq \mu \in \chi(X)$ then $\varrho = \varepsilon$;
(*iii*) $\langle X\pi\varrho \rangle \doteq \langle X\pi \rangle$ is not in $\chi(X)$ for any π and non-empty ϱ.

An arbitrary constraint set $\chi(X)$ is called consistent if $closure(\chi(X))$ is consistent.
We write CCS for the set of consistent constraint sets.   □

Corollary 8.7.
If $\chi(X) \in CCS$ then $closure(\chi(X)) \in CCS$.   □

---

[4] Hence closure defines an equivalence relation on constraint sets: if $closure\chi_1(X)) = closure\chi_2(X))$ then χ_1 and χ_2 contain the same information. A particular representative of an equivalence class, a constraint set in *normal form* will be introduced in Definition 8.12.

[5] For non-empty constraint sets, (*i*) is implied by (*v*). The empty set is closed by adding the *empty constraint*. $\langle X \rangle \doteq [\,]$ does not convey any information about X. This is usually taken as the bottom of a feature lattice, cf. Definition 8.14. Note that transitivity (i.e., if $\langle X\pi \rangle \doteq \langle X\pi' \rangle$, $\langle X\pi' \rangle \doteq \langle X\pi'' \rangle$ in $closure(\chi(X))$ then also $\langle X\pi \rangle \doteq \langle X\pi'' \rangle$) is a consequence of (*iii*) and (*iv*).

$$\{ \quad \langle X \rangle \doteq [\,],$$
$$\langle X \ cat \rangle \doteq [\,],$$
$$\langle X \ head \rangle \doteq [\,],$$
$$\langle X \ head \ tense \rangle \doteq [\,],$$
$$\langle X \ head \ agr \rangle \doteq [\,],$$
$$\langle X \ head \ agr \ number \rangle \doteq [\,],$$
$$\langle X \ head \ agr \ person \rangle \doteq [\,],$$
$$\langle X \ subject \rangle \doteq [\,],$$
$$\langle X \ subject \ head \rangle \doteq [\,],$$
$$\langle X \ subject \ head \ agr \rangle \doteq [\,],$$
$$\langle X \ subject \ head \ agr \ number \rangle \doteq [\,],$$
$$\langle X \ subject \ head \ agr \ person \rangle \doteq [\,],$$
$$\langle X \ object \rangle \doteq [\,],$$
$$\langle X \ cat \rangle \doteq {}^*v,$$
$$\langle X \ head \ tense \rangle \doteq present,$$
$$\langle X \ head \ agr \ number \rangle \doteq singular,$$
$$\langle X \ head \ agr \ person \rangle \doteq third,$$
$$\langle X \ subject \ head \ agr \ number \rangle \doteq singular,$$
$$\langle X \ subject \ head \ agr \ person \rangle \doteq third,$$
$$\langle X \ head \ agr \ \rangle \doteq \langle X \ subject \ head \ agr \rangle,$$
$$\langle X \ subject \ head \ agr \ \rangle \doteq \langle X \ head \ agr \rangle \quad \}$$

Fig. 8.2. Closure of the constraint set in Figure 8.1(b)

Definition 8.8. (*mapping constraint sets to feature graphs*)
For each consistent constraint set $\chi(X) \in \mathcal{CCS}$ we define a graph, as follows. Vertices correspond to sets of left-hand sides of constraints. These sets, denoted $[\langle X\pi \rangle]$, are defined by

$$[\langle X\pi \rangle] = \{\langle X\pi \rangle\} \cup \{\langle X\varrho \rangle \mid \langle X\pi \rangle \doteq \langle X\varrho \rangle \in closure(\chi(X))\}.$$

The graph $\Gamma(X) = graph(\chi(X))$ is defined by

$$U = \{[\langle X\pi \rangle] \mid \langle X\pi \rangle \doteq [\,] \in closure(\chi(X))\},$$

$$E = \{[\langle X\pi \rangle] \xrightarrow{f} [\langle X\pi f \rangle] \mid \langle X\pi f \rangle \doteq [\,] \in closure(\chi(X))\}.$$

The label of a vertex $[\langle X\pi \rangle]$ is defined by

$$label([\langle X\pi \rangle]) = \begin{cases} c & \text{if } \langle X\pi \rangle \doteq c \in closure(\chi(X)) \\ \varepsilon & \text{otherwise} \end{cases}. \qquad \square$$

Lemma 8.9.
For each $\chi(X) \in \mathcal{CCS}$ it holds that $graph(\chi(X)) \in \mathcal{FG}$.

Proof. Direct from the following observations:

- if $[\langle X\pi f \rangle] \doteq [\,] \in closure(\chi(X))$ then also $[\langle X\pi \rangle] \doteq [\,] \in closure(\chi(X))$, hence E is properly defined with respect to U;
- if $[\langle X\pi \rangle] \xrightarrow{f} u$ and $[\langle X\pi \rangle] \xrightarrow{f} v$ then $u = v$;
- the graph has a root $[\langle X \rangle]$;
- there are no $\langle X\pi \rangle \doteq c$ and $\langle X\pi \rangle \doteq d$ with $c \neq d$, hence each label is uniquely defined;

- moreover, if $\langle X\pi\varrho\rangle \doteq \mu \in closure(\chi(X))$ for non-empty ϱ then the consistency of $\chi(X))$ guarantees that there is no $\langle X\pi\rangle \doteq c \in closure(\chi(X))$, hence $label([\langle X\pi\rangle]) = \varepsilon$.   □

Definition 8.10. (*mapping features graphs to constraint sets*)
For each feature graph $\Gamma(X) \in \mathcal{FG}$ we define a constraint set. To that end, we label each vertex with an auxiliary *path label*. If there are several paths to a vertex, we take the lowest one in lexicographical order. Formally: let r be the root of $\Gamma(X)$, then

$$path\_label(u) = \min\{\varrho \mid r \xrightarrow{\varrho} u\}.$$

A constraint set $constraints(\Gamma(X))$ is (uniquely) defined by

$$\chi_V(X) = \{\langle X path\_label(u)\rangle \doteq c \mid label(u) = c\},$$

$$\chi_E(X) = \{\langle X path\_label(u)\rangle \doteq [\,] \mid u \text{ is a leaf} \wedge label(u) \doteq \varepsilon\},$$

$$\chi_C(X) = \{\langle X path\_label(u)\rangle \doteq \langle X\varrho\rangle \mid r \xrightarrow{\varrho} u \wedge \varrho \neq path\_label(u)\},$$

$$\chi(X) = \chi_V(X) \cup \chi_E(X) \cup \chi_C(X).$$ □

Lemma 8.11.
For each graph $\Gamma(X) \in \mathcal{FG}$ it holds that $constraints(\Gamma(X)) \in \mathcal{CCS}$.

Proof. Let $\Gamma(X) \in \mathcal{FG}$. We verify the constraints for consistency of Definition 8.6. (*i*) follows from the definition of $\chi_V(X)$; (*ii*) because in $\Gamma(X)$ only leaves are labelled; (*iii*) because the graph is acyclic.   □

Definition 8.12. (*normal form*)
The function $nf : \mathcal{CCS} \longrightarrow \mathcal{CCS}$ is defined by

$$nf(\chi(X)) = constraints(graph(\chi(X))).$$

$nf(\chi(X))$ can be thought of as the *normal form* of a constraint set. It is, roughly speaking, a constraint set with constraints that are minimal in lexicographical order. We write $nf\mathcal{CCS}$ for the set of constraint sets that satisfy $nf(\chi(X)) = \chi(X)$.   □

In order to compute a normal form, it is not necessary to construct a graph and then afterward deconstruct it. An algorithm to obtain the normal form of a constraint set is shown in Figure 8.3. It is left to the reader to verify the correctness of this algorithm; our main concern right now is the existence of the normal form, rather than its computation.

Lemma 8.13.
When we restrict *graph* to constraints set in normal form, the functions

$$\begin{aligned} graph &: nf\mathcal{CCS} \longrightarrow \mathcal{FG} \\ constraints &: \mathcal{FG} \longrightarrow nf\mathcal{CCS} \end{aligned}$$

are bijections. Moreover, they are each other's inverse.

Proof: straightforward.   □

```
procedure normalize χ(X)
begin
        repeat each of the following steps

                replace ⟨Xπ⟩ ≐ ⟨Xϱ⟩ by ⟨Xϱ⟩ ≐ ⟨Xπ⟩
                if ϱ < π;

                replace ⟨Xπϱ⟩ ≐ μ by ⟨Xπ'ϱ⟩ ≐ μ
                if π' < π and ⟨Xπ⟩ ≐ ⟨Xπ'⟩ ∈ χ(X);

                delete ⟨Xπϱ⟩ ≐ ⟨Xπ'ϱ⟩ from χ(X)
                if ⟨Xπ⟩ ≐ ⟨Xπ'⟩ ∈ χ(X) and ϱ ≠ ε;

                delete ⟨Xπ⟩ ≐ [ ] from χ(X)
                if ⟨Xπϱ⟩ ≐ μ ∈ χ(X) for some ϱ ≠ ε
                or if ⟨Xπ⟩ = c

        until no more of these steps can be applied
end;
```

Fig. 8.3. A simple normalization procedure for constraint sets

8.2 Feature lattices

We will now define a lattice structure for constraint sets and feature graphs. First, we recall the definition of a lattice.

Definition 8.14. (*lattice*)
Let $\mathcal{X}$ be an arbitrary set (with elements $x, y, \ldots$) and $\sqsubseteq$ a partial order on $\mathcal{X}$. The pair $(\mathcal{X}, \sqsubseteq)$ is called a *lattice* if

(i)   There is a top element $T \in \mathcal{X}$ and a bottom element $B \in \mathcal{X}$ such that $B \sqsubseteq x \sqsubseteq T$ for each $x \in \mathcal{X}$.

(ii) For each pair of elements $x, y \in \mathcal{X}$ there is a *lowest upper bound* (*lub*), denoted $x \sqcup y$, that satisfies
   (a) $x \sqsubseteq x \sqcup y$ and $y \sqsubseteq x \sqcup y$;
   (b) for each z such that $x \sqsubseteq z$ and $y \sqsubseteq z$ it holds that $x \sqcup y \sqsubseteq z$.

(iii) For each pair of elements $x, y \in \mathcal{X}$ there is a *greatest lower bound* (*glb*), denoted $x \sqcap y$, that satisfies
   (a) $x \sqcap y \sqsubseteq x$ and $x \sqcap y \sqsubseteq y$;
   (b) for each z such that $z \sqsubseteq x$ and $z \sqsubseteq y$ it holds that $z \sqsubseteq x \sqcap y$.   □

Definition 8.15. ($nf\mathcal{CCS}^L$, $\mathcal{FG}^L$)
We define a set $\bot_{CCS}$ by

$$\bot_{CCS} = VC \cup CC.$$

(This is not a constraint set according to Definition 8.4, as $\bot_{CCS}$ is not finite)
We define a graph $\bot_{FG} = (U_\bot, E_\bot)$ by

$$U_\perp = r,$$

$$E_\perp = \{r \xrightarrow{f} r \mid f \in \mathcal{F}ea\}.$$

(This is not a feature graph according to Definition 8.4, as $\perp_{FG}$ is not a DAG. The vertex r can be thought of as labelled with all constants at once.) Furthermore, we extend *graph* and *constraints* by

$$graph(\perp_{CCS}) = \perp_{FG},$$

$$constraints(\perp_{FG}) = \perp_{CCS}.$$

We extend the domains of constraint sets and feature graphs by

$$nf\mathcal{CCS}^L = nf\mathcal{CCS} \cup \{\perp_{CCS}\},$$

$$\mathcal{FG}^L = \mathcal{FG} \cup \{\perp_{FG}\}.$$

When it is clear from the context which domain is meant, we drop the index and simply write $\perp$ for inconsistent.   □

Definition 8.16. (*subsumption*)[6]
A *subsumption relation* $\sqsubseteq$ is defined on $nf\mathcal{CCS}^L$ by

$$\chi_1(X) \sqsubseteq \chi_2(X) \quad \text{if} \quad closure(\chi_1(X)) \subseteq closure(\chi_2(X)).$$

A *subsumption relation* $\sqsubseteq$ is defined on $\mathcal{FG}^L$ by

$$\Gamma_1(X) \sqsubseteq \Gamma_2(X) \quad \text{if} \quad constraints(\Gamma_1(X)) \sqsubseteq constraints(\Gamma_2(X)). \qquad \square$$

Note that $\chi(X) \sqsubseteq \perp$ for any $\chi(X)$. It happens to be the case that $\perp$ is the top element of the lattice structure over constraint sets. This is somewhat unfortunate, because in lattice theory $\perp$ usually denotes the *bottom* element. On the other hand, it is not uncommon to interpret $\perp$ as "inconsistent". This notational problem can be solved, simply by reversing the lattice structure. If we write $\sqsupseteq$ and $\sqcap$, rather than $\sqsubseteq$ and $\sqcup$, we have $\perp$ as the bottom of the lattice. This is equally problematic, however, as it is not intuitively appealing to write $\sqcap$ for a symbol that is to be interpreted as a *union* of constraints. Hence we stick to the notation as introduced in Definition 8.16.

Theorem 8.17. (*lattice structure*)
(a) $(nf\mathcal{CCS}^L, \sqsubseteq)$ is a lattice with bottom $\{\langle X \rangle \doteq [\,]\}$ and top $\perp_{CCS}$.
(b) $(\mathcal{FG}^L, \sqsubseteq)$ is a lattice with bottom $graph(\{\langle X \rangle \doteq [\,]\})$ and top $\perp_{FG}$.
(c) $graph : nf\mathcal{CCS}^L \longrightarrow \mathcal{FG}^L$ is an isomorphism with respect to $\sqsubseteq$;
    $constraints : \mathcal{FG}^L \longrightarrow nf\mathcal{CCS}^L$ is the inverse isomorphism.

---

[6] There are many different ways in which subsumption is defined in the literature (e.g. $\varphi_1 \sqsubseteq \varphi_2$ if there is a homomorphism from φ_1 to φ_2). The general idea is that $\varphi_1 \sqsubseteq \varphi_2$ if the information (in whatever form) contained in φ_1 is a subset of the information contained in φ_2. We have defined the closure as an auxiliary construct to gather *all* information implied by a constraint set as separate facts. Hence, for closed sets, subsuption equals set inclusion.

Proof.

(a) The top and bottom properties are trivial.

The existence of a *lub* for any two constraint sets $\chi_1(X), \chi_2(X) \in nfCCS^L$ is shown as follows. We write χ' for $closure(\chi_1(X) \cup \chi_2(X))$. If χ' is inconsistent, then $\bot$ is obviously the *lub*.

Otherwise, assume $\chi'' \in CCS$ with $\chi_1(X) \sqsubseteq \chi''$ and $\chi_2(X) \sqsubseteq \chi''$. Then $closure(\chi_1(X)) \subseteq closure(\chi'')$, and $closure(\chi_2(X)) \subseteq closure(\chi'')$. Hence $\chi' \subseteq closure(\chi'')$, and $nf(\chi')$ is the least upper bound in $nfCCS^L$. The existence of a *glb* follows in similar fashion.

(c) Straight from Lemma 8.13 and Definition 8.16.

(b) Direct from (a) and (c). $\qquad\qquad\qquad\qquad\qquad\qquad\qquad$ $\Box$

Corollary 8.18.
For any pair of consistent constraint sets in normal form $\chi_1(X), \chi_2(X) \in nfCCS$ it holds that

$$\chi_1(X) \sqcup \chi_2(X) \;=\; nf(\chi_1(X) \cup \chi_2(X)) \qquad\qquad\qquad \Box$$

We have defined $\sqcup$ as a least upper bound, derived from the subsumption relation $\sqsubseteq$. In practical applications, we see $\sqcup$ as an *operator* that allows to construct new feature structures by merging the features of existing feature structures. How such a merge is carried out in an efficient manner is not a direct concern here. We will come back to that issue in Chapter 9.

Having proven that normal forms of consistent constraint sets and feature graphs are isomorphic, we can abstract from the particular representation and simply call it a *feature structure*. We write $\varphi(X)$ to denote a feature structure, or simply φ if it is not relevant which object X is characterized by the features in φ. A feature structure will be interpreted in an opportunistic manner either as feature graph or as constraint set, whatever is most convenient.

We write $\varphi(X).\pi$ to denote the *substructure* of $\varphi(X)$ that is (in the graph representation!) the largest subgraph of which $[\langle X\pi \rangle]$ is the root. We write $\varphi(X).\pi = c$ if (in constraint set representation!) $\langle X\pi \rangle \doteq c \in closure(\varphi(X))$.

As an informal notation for feature structures we write AVMs, feature graphs or constraint sets. It is not required that a constraint set be in normal form. Normal forms were important because the lattice structure is defined on normal forms, but for any practical application any equivalent specification of a constraint set will do as well.

At last we can now explain the difference between type identity and token identity. Consider the following feature structures:

$$\varphi_1 = \begin{bmatrix} f: \begin{bmatrix} f: c \\ g: d \end{bmatrix} \\[2ex] g: \begin{bmatrix} f: c \\ g: d \end{bmatrix} \end{bmatrix}, \quad \varphi_2 = \begin{bmatrix} f: \boxed{1} \begin{bmatrix} f: c \\ g: d \end{bmatrix} \\[2ex] g: \boxed{1} \end{bmatrix}.$$

Then the substructures $\varphi_1.f$ and $\varphi_1.g$ are called *type identical*: they have the same value, but they are different structures. The substructures $\varphi_2.f$ and $\varphi_2.g$ are called *token identical*: they refer to a single structure (and have the same value a fortiori). Note that $\varphi_1 \sqsubseteq \varphi_2$, because the constraint set of φ_2 can be obtained from the constraint set of φ_1 by *adding a constraint* (viz. $\langle Xf \rangle \doteq \langle Xg \rangle$). The difference between these structures comes to light when either structure is unified with $\varphi' = \Big[g\colon \big[h\colon e \big] \Big]$, yielding

$$
\varphi_1 \sqcup \varphi' = \left[\begin{array}{l} f\colon \left[\begin{array}{l} f\colon c \\ g\colon d \end{array} \right] \\ g\colon \left[\begin{array}{l} f\colon c \\ g\colon d \\ h\colon e \end{array} \right] \end{array} \right]
\quad \sqsubseteq \quad
\varphi_2 \sqcup \varphi' = \left[\begin{array}{l} f\colon \boxed{1} \left[\begin{array}{l} f\colon c \\ g\colon d \\ h\colon e \end{array} \right] \\ g\colon \boxed{1} \end{array} \right].
$$

In the sequel, we write the usual equality symbol ($=$) for type identity and a dotted equality symbol ($\doteq$) to denote token identity. So we have $\varphi_1.f = \varphi_1.g$, $\varphi_2.f = \varphi_2.g$, $\varphi_2.f \doteq \varphi_2.g$, but $\varphi_1.f \not\doteq \varphi_1.g$.

The difference between type identity and token identity is only relevant for substructures. For *constants* it doesn't make any difference whether a value is token identical to or a copy of some given other constant.

8.3 Composite feature structures

So far we have defined feature structures, that capture the characteristic properties of some object. It is essential, however, to add the conceptual machinery that allows us to relate the features of different objects to one another. To this end we introduce feature structures that describe the features of a (finite) *set* of objects. Features can be shared between objects by means of token identity.

Composite constraint sets for sets of objects are only a minimal extension of the constraint sets of Section 8.1: coreferencing is allowed between (features of) different objects. In the domain of feature graphs, we get a set of graphs that may share subgraphs. Or, to put it differently, we get a single graph with multiple roots.

Definition 8.19. (*multi-rooted feature graphs*)
A *multi-rooted feature graph* is a structure $\Gamma(X_1, \ldots, X_k) = (U, E, R)$ with (U, E) a finite DAG and $R = \{r_1, \ldots, r_k\} \subseteq U$, with the following properties:

(i)   every edge is labelled with a feature;
(ii)   if f and g are labels of edges originating from the same vertex, then
$f \neq g$;

(*iii*) leaves may be (but need not be) labelled with a constant, non-leaf vertices do not carry a constant label;

(*iv*) For every $u \in U$ there is some $r \in R$ such that $r \longrightarrow u$.

We call R the *root set* of the graph. The size of the root set must correspond to the number of formal parameters $X_1, \ldots, X_k$; the roots can be labelled with identifiers referring to the objects whose features are represented.[7] We write $\mathcal{MFG}$ for the class of multi-rooted feature graphs. □

Definition 8.20. (*composite constraint sets, closure*)
Let $X_1, \ldots, X_k$ denote a finite set of objects. A (composite) constraint set $\chi(X_1, \ldots, X_k)$ is a finite set of constraints from the domains of value constraints, existential constraints and *composite* coreference constraints, defined as follows:

$$VC = \{\langle X_i \pi \rangle \doteq c \mid 1 \leq i \leq k \wedge \pi \in \mathcal{F}ea^* \wedge c \in \mathcal{C}onst\},$$

$$CCC = \{\langle X_i \pi \rangle \doteq \langle X_j \varrho \rangle \mid 1 \leq i \leq k \wedge 1 \leq j \leq k \wedge \pi, \varrho \in \mathcal{F}ea^*\}.$$

Again (see Footnote 3) we write $\langle X_i \pi \rangle \doteq [\,]$ as a more convenient notation for $\langle X_i \pi \rangle \doteq \langle X_i \pi \rangle$. □

Definition 8.21. (*closure of a composite constraint set*)
Let $\chi(X) \subset VC \cup CC$ be a constraint set. The *closure* of $\chi(X)$, denoted $closure(\chi(X))$, is the smallest set satisfying

(*i*) $\langle X_i \rangle \doteq [\,] \in closure(\chi(X_1, \ldots, X_k))$ for $1 \leq i \leq k$;

(*ii*) if $\langle X_i \pi \rangle \doteq \mu \in \chi(X_1, \ldots, X_k)$
        then $\langle X_i \pi \rangle \doteq \mu \in closure(\chi(X_1, \ldots, X_k))$;

(*iii*) if $\langle X_i \pi \rangle \doteq \langle X_j \pi' \rangle$, $\langle X_i \pi \varrho \rangle \doteq \mu \in closure(\chi(X_1, \ldots, X_k))$
        then $\langle X_j \pi' \varrho \rangle \doteq \mu \in closure(\chi(X_1, \ldots, X_k))$;

(*iv*) if $\langle X_i \pi \rangle \doteq \langle X_j \varrho \rangle \in closure(\chi(X_1, \ldots, X_k))$
        then $\langle X_j \varrho \rangle \doteq \langle X_i \pi \rangle \in closure(\chi(X_1, \ldots, X_k))$;

(*v*)   if $\langle X_i \pi \varrho \rangle \doteq \mu \in closure(\chi(X_1, \ldots, X_k))$
        then $\langle X_i \pi \rangle \doteq [\,] \in closure(\chi(X_1, \ldots, X_k))$.

A constraint set $\chi(X_1, \ldots, X_k)$ is called *closed* if $closure(\chi(X_1, \ldots, X_k)) = \chi(X_1, \ldots, X_k)$. □

---

[7] Note that is it *not* required that a root r_i has no incoming edges. It is conceivable that one root is the descendant of another root (and also that several roots coincide). In that case, the features of one object are token identical with a substructure of the features of another object.

Definition 8.22. (*consistency*)

A *closed* composite constraint set $\chi(X_1, \ldots, X_k)$ is called *consistent* if it satisfies the following properties:

(*i*)   if $\langle X_i \pi \rangle \doteq c \in \chi(X_1, \ldots, X_k)$ and $\langle X_i \pi \rangle \doteq d \in \chi(X_1, \ldots, X_k)$
    then $c = d$;

(*ii*) if $\langle X_i \pi \rangle \doteq c \in \chi(X_1, \ldots, X_k)$ and $\langle X_i \pi \varrho \rangle \doteq \mu \in \chi(X_1, \ldots, X_k)$
    then $\varrho = \varepsilon$;

(*iii*) $\langle X_i \pi \varrho \rangle \doteq \langle X_i \pi \rangle$ and $\langle X_i \pi \rangle \doteq \langle X_i \pi \varrho \rangle$ are not in $\chi(X_1, \ldots, X_k)$
    for any i π, and non-empty ϱ.

An arbitrary composite constraint set $\chi(X_1, \ldots, X_k)$ is consistent if $closure(\chi(X_1, \ldots, X_k))$ is consistent.

We write $CCCS$ for the set of consistent composite constraint sets. □

Definition 8.23. (*mappings, normal form*)

The mappings *graph* and *constraints* can be extended to composite constraint sets and multi-rooted feature graphs in the obvious way (and it can be verified straightforwardly that these functions are well-defined).

The function $nf : CCCS \longrightarrow CCCS$ is defined by

$$nf(\chi(X_1, \ldots, X_k)) = constraints(graph(\chi(X_1, \ldots, X_k)));$$

We write $nfCCCS$ for the set of constraint sets that satisfy

$$nf(\chi(X_1, \ldots, X_k)) = \chi(X_1, \ldots, X_k).$$
□

Definition 8.24. (*substructures*)

Let $\Gamma(X_1, \ldots, X_k) = (U, E, \{r_1, \ldots, r_k\}) \in \mathcal{MFG}$ describe the features of a set of k objects. The feature graphs of a *subset* of this set of objects are described by a subgraph, as follows.

Let $\{X_{i_1}, \ldots, X_{i_m}\} \subset \{X_1, \ldots, X_k\}$.

Then $\Gamma(X_{i_1}, \ldots, X_{i_m}) = (U', E', \{r_{i_1}, \ldots, r_{i_m}\})$ is defined by

$$U' = \{u \in U \mid r_{i_j} \longrightarrow u \text{ for some } j \ (1 \leq j \leq m)\},$$

$$E' = \{u \rightarrow v \in E \mid u, v \in U'\}.$$

Similarly, a substructure is defined for *closed* constraint sets[8].

Let $\chi(X_1, \ldots, X_k)$ be a closed constraint set. A (closed) substructure $\chi(X_{i_1}, \ldots, X_{i_m})$ for $\{X_{i_1}, \ldots, X_{i_m}\} \subset \{X_1, \ldots, X_k\}$ is defined by

---

[8] We cannot simply apply the same definition to arbitrary constraint sets: if a feature of some X_{i_j} is token identical with an object that is no longer represented in the substructure, all constraints relating to that part of the deleted substructure must be taken into account as well. Only in closed constraint sets it is guaranteed that every feature of an object is completely described by constraints for that object.

$$\chi(X_{i_1}, \ldots, X_{i_m}) = \{\langle X_{i,\pi}\rangle \doteq c \in \chi(X_1, \ldots, X_k) \mid 1 \le j \le m\} \cup$$
$$\{\langle X_{i,\pi}\rangle \doteq [\,] \in \chi(X_1, \ldots, X_k) \mid 1 \le j \le m\} \cup$$
$$\{\langle X_{i,\pi}\rangle \doteq \langle X_{i_l}\varrho\rangle \in \chi(X_1, \ldots, X_k)$$
$$\mid 1 \le j \le m \wedge 1 \le l \le m\}.$$

For $\chi(X_1, \ldots, X_k) \in nfCCCS$ and $\{X_{i_1}, \ldots, X_{i_m}\} \subset \{X_1, \ldots, X_k\}$ we define a substructure $\chi(X_{i_1}, \ldots, X_{i_m})$ as follows.

Let $\chi'(X_1, \ldots, X_k) = closure(\chi(X_1, \ldots, X_k))$;
then $\chi(X_{i_1}, \ldots, X_{i_m}) = nf(\chi'(X_{i_1}, \ldots, X_{i_m}))$. $\qquad\square$

Definition 8.25. (*composite feature lattices*)
We define a set $\perp_{CCCS}$ by

$$\perp_{CCCS} = VC \cup CCC.$$

As inconsistent $\mathcal{MFG}$ we define a multi-rooted graph $\perp_{MFG} = (U_\perp, E_\perp, R_\perp)$ with an infinite root set:

$$U_\perp = R_\perp = \{r_1, \ldots\},$$

$$E_\perp = \{r_i \xrightarrow{f} r_j \mid r_i, r_j \in R_\perp \wedge f \in \mathcal{F}ea\}.$$

Each vertex r_i can be thought of as being labelled with all constants at once. The functions *graph* and *constraints* are extended to map $\perp_{CCCS}$ and $\perp_{MFG}$ onto each other.
We define the domains

$$nfCCCS^L = nfCCCS \cup \{\perp_{CCCS}\},$$
$$\mathcal{MFG}^L = \mathcal{MFG} \cup \{\perp_{MFG}\}. \qquad\square$$

8.4 Composite feature lattices

Before we define subsumption on composite feature structures, we must clarify the distinction between objects and formal parameters. It is our purpose to derive a binary operator $\sqcup$ that can be used to unify feature structures. A feature structure $\varphi(X_1, \ldots, X_k) \sqcup \varphi(Y_1, \ldots, Y_l)$ combines the features of both structures. It is important to know, however, which X's and which Y's refer to identical objects. Let, for example, $X_3 = Y_2$ and all other X_i and Y_j be different. Then in the unified feature structure $\varphi(X_1, \ldots, X_k) \sqcup \varphi(Y_1, \ldots, Y_l)$ there is (a parameter for) an object that will contain both the features of $\varphi(X_3)$ and $\varphi(Y_2)$. (Note, however, that $\varphi(X_3)$ and $\varphi(Y_2)$ are separate feature structures. Features can be shared across objects (or parameters) *within a single composite feature structure*, but features can *not* be shared across different composite feature structures.) Hence it is essential to know which parameters denote which objects, so that the right pairs of features are unified when we unify two composite feature structures. Therefore we assume the existence of a (possibly infinite but countable) domain of objects and postulate that each parameter refers to an object.

In a practical notation, we could annotate the unification with which parameters should be considered to refer to the same object. The above case can be denoted as

$$\varphi(X_1, \ldots, X_k) \sqcup_{X_3 = Y_2} \varphi(Y_1, \ldots, Y_l).$$

As indices to the unification we write (sequences) of equalities that denote correspondence between formal parameters of either argument. In the unlikely case that all formal parameters are different we could write $\sqcup_\emptyset$ (but this operation will not be used in the sequel). Hence, when we write an unqualified *lub* symbol $\sqcup$ it should be clear from the context which parameters of both arguments refer to the same object. This will usually be the case.

In practical use, we see $\sqcup$ as an operator that can be used to construct new feature structures from existing feature structures. But before we start using it, we have to define $\sqcup$ formally as a least upper bound in a lattice.

Definition 8.26. (*subsumption*)
A *subsumption relation* $\sqsubseteq$ is defined on $nfCCCS^L$ as follows:[9]

$\chi_1(X_1, \ldots, X_k) \sqsubseteq \chi_2(Y_1, \ldots, Y_l)$ holds if
(i) $\{X_1, \ldots, X_k\} \subseteq \{Y_1, \ldots, Y_l\}$, and
(ii) $closure(\chi_1(X_1, \ldots, X_k)) \subseteq closure(\chi_2(X_1, \ldots, X_k))$.

A subsumption relation $\sqsubseteq$ is defined on $\mathcal{MFG}^L$ by

$\Gamma_1(X_1, \ldots, X_k) \sqsubseteq \Gamma_2(Y_1, \ldots, Y_l)$ holds if
    $constraints(\Gamma_1(X_1, \ldots, X_k)) \sqsubseteq constraints(\Gamma_2(Y_1, \ldots, Y_l))$. $\square$

Theorem 8.27. (*lattice structure*)
The following statement hold:

(a) $(nfCCCS^L, \sqsubseteq)$ is a lattice with the empty set[10] as bottom and top $\perp_{CCCS}$.
(b) $(\mathcal{MFG}^L, \sqsubseteq)$ is a lattice with the empty graph as bottom and top $\perp_{MFG}$.
(c) $graph : nfCCCS^L \longrightarrow \mathcal{MFG}^L$ is an isomorphism with respect to $\sqsubseteq$;
    $constraints : \mathcal{MFG}^L \longrightarrow nfCCCS^L$ is the inverse isomorphism.

Proof: straightforward extension of the proof of Theorem 8.17 and preceding lemmata. $\square$

---

[9] In general, it will be clear how the formal parameters of the left operand of $\sqsubseteq$ correspond to formal parameters of the right operand (typically, $k = l$ and X_i corresponds to Y_i). In cases where it is not obvious (but those will not appear in this book) one could annotate $\sqsubseteq$ with correspondences, similar to $\sqcup$ discussed above.

[10] The bottom element is to be interpreted as a constraint set for *no* objects (as opposed to the empty constraint for a given object in Theorem 8.17).

Corollary 8.28.
For consistent composite constraint sets in normal form
$\chi_1(X_1,\ldots,X_k), \chi_2(Y_1,\ldots,Y_l) \in nf\mathcal{CCCS}$ it holds that

$$\chi_1(X_1,\ldots,X_k) \;\sqcup_{X_{i_1}=Y_{j_1},\ldots,X_{i_m}=Y_{j_m}}\; \chi_2(Y_1,\ldots,Y_l) =$$
$$nf(\chi_1(X_1,\ldots,X_k) \cup \chi_2(Y_1,\ldots,Y_l)$$
$$\cup \{\langle X_{i_1}\rangle \doteq \langle Y_{j_1}\rangle,\ldots,\langle X_{i_m}\rangle \doteq \langle Y_{j_m}\rangle\}). \qquad \square$$

As with constraint sets and feature graphs, we will blur the distinction between composite constraint sets and multi-rooted feature graphs. We simply write $\varphi(X_1,\ldots,X_k)$ to denote a *composite feature structure* for k objects. As in 8.1 we write Φ to denote *both* lattices $(nf\mathcal{CCCS}^L, \sqsubseteq)$ and $(\mathcal{MFG}^L, \sqsubseteq)$. If we need one particular representation we will pick the one that is easiest to work with, depending on the circumstances.

From a composite feature structure $\varphi(X_1,\ldots,X_k)$ one can derive a feature structure $\varphi(X_i)$ for any object, by taking the appropriate substructure. As a convenient notation we write

$$\varphi(X_i) \;=\; \varphi(X_1,\ldots,X_k)|_{X_i}$$

to denote that a feature structure for an object X_i is obtained by retrieving it from some composite structure.

Up to now we have only attributed features to *sets* of objects. It is possible that the objects themselves are contained in a structure of some kind. We call these *object structures* so as avoid confusion with feature structures. Typical object structures that we will use in the remainder of this chapter are

- A production $A{\rightarrow}\alpha$ from a context-free grammar. We write $\varphi(A{\rightarrow}\alpha)$ as a convenient notation for a composite feature structure $\varphi(A, X_1,\ldots,X_k)$ that describes features of left-hand and right-hand side symbols, where $\alpha = X_1,\ldots,X_k$.
- A tree $\langle A \rightsquigarrow \alpha\rangle$. We write $\varphi(\langle A \rightsquigarrow \alpha\rangle)$ as a convenient notation for a composite feature structure $\varphi(A, \ldots, X_1,\ldots,X_k)$, where $\alpha = X_1,\ldots,X_k$.
- An item $[A \rightsquigarrow \alpha]$. Items were introduced in Chapter 4 as *sets of* trees. Here we should see them as *abstractions* of trees: We only know the root and the yield of the item; we do not know (or do not want to know) the internal nodes. Consequently, features can be retrieved only from the nodes that are explicitly mentioned in the denotation of the item. Hence, a composite feature structure of an item $[A \rightsquigarrow \alpha]$ can be seen as a substructure of a composite feature structure of a tree $\langle A \rightsquigarrow \alpha\rangle$, from which the features of internal nodes have been deleted.
  We write $\varphi([A \rightsquigarrow \alpha])$ as a convenient notation for a composite feature structure $\varphi(A, X_1,\ldots,X_k)$ where $\alpha = X_1,\ldots,X_k$.
  A similar interpretation will be given to various kinds of items that give various kinds of partial specifications of trees. As an example, consider the

item $[S \rightarrow NP \bullet VP, 0, 2]$, specifying the fact than an NP has been found by scanning the first two words (but we don't care to remember what those words were). A feature structure $\varphi([S \rightarrow NP \bullet VP, 0, 2])$ will be a composite feature structure $\varphi(S, NP, VP)$ that denotes the appropriate substructure of $\varphi(\langle S \rightarrow \langle NP \rightsquigarrow \underline{a}_1 \underline{a}_2 \rangle VP \rangle)$.

8.5 Unification grammars

With the lattice of (composite) feature structures, developed in in 8.1 and 8.3, we can now formally define a unification grammar as it has been informally presented in Chapter 7.

The definition of unification grammars that we present here is not the most compact one that is possible. One could eliminate the context-free backbone and let syntactic category be a feature as any other. If one abstracts from the syntactic category as a special feature, the definitions and notations become more terse, but somewhat more obscure. For the sake of clarity and compatibility with the other chapters, we will not do so.

We take it for granted that syntactic category is such a fundamental notion that every feature structure for every constituent constraints at least a *cat* feature. Hence, in order to obtain a legible notation, we continue to call nodes in a tree by their syntactic category, like we did with context-free grammars.

Definition 8.29. (*unification grammar*)
A unification grammar is a structure

$$\mathcal{G} = (G, \Phi, \varphi_0, W, \mathcal{L}ex).$$

The different parts of this structure are defined as follows:

- $G = (N, \Sigma, P, S)$ is a context-free grammar. We write V for $N \cup \Sigma$; it is not required that $N \cap \Sigma = \emptyset$, a syntactic category is allowed to be both terminal and nonterminal.
  Furthermore, P is a *multiset* of productions, i.e., it is allowed that a single context-free production occurs more than one time.
- $\Phi = \Phi(\mathcal{F}ea, \mathcal{C}onst)$ is the lattice of feature structures based on a set of features $\mathcal{F}ea$ and a set of constants $\mathcal{C}onst$. It is assumed (but not necessary) that $\mathcal{F}ea \cap \mathcal{C}onst = \emptyset$. We assume $cat \in \mathcal{F}ea$ and $V \subseteq \mathcal{C}onst$, allowing for syntactic categories to be represented in a feature structure.
- $\varphi_0 : P \rightarrow \Phi$ is a function that a assigns a composite feature structure to each production in the context-free grammar. Let $p = A \rightarrow X_1 \ldots X_k$ for some $p \in P$ and $\varphi_0(p)$ be a feature structure $\varphi(Y_0, Y_1, \ldots, Y_k)$. Then, obviously, it is required that $\varphi(Y_0).cat = A$ and, for $1 \leq i \leq k$, $\varphi(Y_i).cat = X_i$.

Different feature structures can be attributed to a single context-free production by including the production more than once in P.[11]

- W is a set of lexicon entries, i.e., "real" word forms, as opposed to lexical categories in Σ. It is assumed (but not necessary) that $V \cap W = \emptyset$. We write $\underline{a}, \ldots$ for words in W.

- $\mathcal{L}ex$ is a function that assigns a set of feature structures to each word in W (a word may have different readings). Each $\varphi(\underline{a}) \in \mathcal{L}ex(\underline{a})$ for each $\underline{a} \in W$ must have a feature cat. Moreover, it is required that $\varphi(\underline{a}).cat \in \Sigma$.

We write $\mathcal{UG}$ for the class of unification grammars $\mathcal{G}$ that satisfy the above properties.   □

One could argue whether the lexicon is part of the grammar or a separate structure. The size of the grammar is reduced tremendously when the lexicon is not contained in the grammar. It is somewhat artificial, however, to assume a grammar with production features φ_0 existing independently of a lexicon $(W, \mathcal{L}ex)$. The trend in unification grammars is that more and more information is stored in the lexicon, and the productions merely serve to prescribe concatenation and feature unification.

The reason for introducing an alphabet W, consisting of words with lexicon entries, is the following. In context-free parsing of natural languages it is standard use to consider the *word categories*, rather than the words from the lexicon, as terminal symbols. In Chapters 2 and 3 we have introduced the notational convention that leaves $a, b, \ldots$ in a parse tree indicate a terminal symbol, while leaves $\underline{a}, \underline{b}, \ldots$ indicate that these leaves correspond to words from the actual sentence that has to be parsed. In Chapter 2 the underlined terminal symbols were added to the grammar in the following way:

- for the i-th word of the sentence, extra productions $a \rightarrow \underline{a}_i$ are added for each possible lexical category of that word.

Verification that a word occurs in the sentence, therefore, could be expressed in terms of tree operations. For each auxiliary production we can supply a feature structure structure (in constraint set notation)

$$\varphi_0(a \rightarrow \underline{a}_i) \ = \ \{\langle a \rangle \doteq \langle \underline{a}_i \rangle\}.$$

These auxiliary productions are *not* part of the grammar, but an implementation technique that is used to construct the parse of a given sentence. We will stick to this notation, for the moment, because it allows us to express the difference between terminals that have been matched with the sentence and those that haven't been matched yet.

---

[11] Alternatively, one could have P as a proper set and attribute a *set of* composite feature structures to each production. There is no need to use multisets, then, but in the remainder of the chapter the expression "$\varphi_0(A \rightarrow \alpha)$" has to be replaced by "some φ in $\varphi_0(A \rightarrow \alpha)$".

When we abstract from trees to items, in Section 8.7, we will simply have initial items of the form $[a, j - 1, j]$ with a feature structure $\varphi(a) \in \mathcal{L}ex(\underline{a}_j)$. The careful distinction between matched leaves and non-matched leaves will no longer be relevant then.

Grammars may include ε-productions. In Section 3.1 we defined trees in such a way that an ε-production generates a leaf labelled ε. Throughout the remainder of this chapter we will simply assume that such leaves labelled ε are not decorated with any features. With this restriction, an arbitrary production $A{\to}\alpha$ in all the following definitions also applies to $A{\to}\varepsilon$.

Definition 8.30. (*decorated trees*)
Let $\tau \in \mathcal{T}rees(G)$ be a tree (cf. Definition 3.10.(*iii*)) and $\varphi(\tau)$ a composite feature structure for the nodes in τ. In order to simplify notation we write $\varphi(X)$ for the feature structure of a node with label X.[12]
A *decorated tree* is a pair $(\tau, (\varphi(\tau))$ with $\tau \in \mathcal{T}rees(G)$ satisfying the following conditions:

(*i*)   for each node labelled A with children labelled $X_1, \ldots, X_k$ there is a production $A{\to}X_1 \ldots X_k \in P$ such that
$\varphi_0(A{\to}X_1 \ldots X_k) \sqsubseteq \varphi(A, X_1, \ldots, X_k)$;

(*ii*)   for each node labelled a with child labelled $\underline{a}_i$ it holds that $\varphi(a) \doteq \varphi(\underline{a}_i)$;

(*iii*) for each node labelled $\underline{a}_i$ there is some $\varphi'(\underline{a}_i) \in \mathcal{L}ex(\underline{a}_i)$ such that $\varphi'(\underline{a}_i) \sqsubseteq \varphi(\underline{a}_i)$.

We write $\mathcal{DT}rees(\mathcal{G})$ for the set of decorated trees for some unification grammar $\mathcal{G}$.   □

In 8.6, like in Chapter 2, we will construct parse trees by means of composition of smaller trees. Any tree can be composed from atomic trees. When a new tree is created that is a composition of two existing trees, its features will be merged. In this way, context-free parse trees can be obtained that are decorated with feature structures. We should make sure, however, that the feature structure of a parse tree contains only "adequate" features (in a sense to be made precise shortly) which are derived from the productions and lexicon. One can always extend the decoration of a tree by adding new features out of the blue. For a decorated parse tree, it should be required that no unnecessary features have sneaked in. The following definition rules out "over-decorated" trees.

Definition 8.31. (*adequately decorated trees*)
We define adequate decoration of trees by induction on the tree structure.[13]

---

[12] Note that different nodes of a tree may carry the same label, so we only use this notation when there can be no confusion about which node with this label is meant.

[13] The reader might wonder why we do not give a direct definition of a *minimally decorated* tree. One could call $(\tau, \varphi(\tau))$ minimally decorated if there is no decoration $\varphi'(\tau) \neq \varphi(\tau)$ such that $\varphi'(\tau) \sqsubseteq \varphi(\tau)$. The problem is, however, that

Let $G \in \mathcal{UG}$ be a unification grammar and $(\tau, \varphi(\tau))$ a decorated tree. The adequacy of the decoration $\varphi(\tau)$ is defined as follows, depending on the form of τ:[14]

- $\tau = \langle a \rightarrow \underline{a}_i \rangle$ (i.e. τ matches a terminal with a word in the sentence).
  Then the decoration is adequate if $\varphi(a) \doteq \varphi(\underline{a}_i) \in \mathcal{L}ex(\underline{a}_i)$.
- $\tau = \langle A \rightarrow \alpha \rangle$ (i.e. τ covers a single production).
  Then the decoration is adequate if $\varphi(\tau) = \varphi_0(A \rightarrow \alpha)$.
- $\tau = \langle A \rightarrow \langle \alpha \rightsquigarrow \beta \rangle \rangle$ (i.e., a production $\langle A \rightarrow \alpha \rangle$ constitutes the top of the tree).
  Let $\alpha = X_1 \ldots X_k$, $\beta = \beta_1 \ldots \beta_k$, such that $\langle X_i \rightsquigarrow \beta_i \rangle$ is a subtree of τ for $1 \leq i \leq k$.
  We distinguish between *degenerate* subtrees, having a single node $X_i = \beta_i$ and no edges and nondegenerate subtrees having more than one node and at least one edge. The (only) adequate decoration for a degenerate subtree is the empty feature structure.
  Then $\varphi(\tau)$ is an adequate decoration if there are adequately decorated trees

$$(\langle A \rightarrow \alpha \rangle, \varphi'(\langle A \rightarrow \alpha \rangle)),$$

$$(\langle X_1 \rightsquigarrow \beta_1 \rangle, \varphi'(\langle X_1 \rightsquigarrow \beta_1 \rangle)), \ \ldots, \ (\langle X_k \rightsquigarrow \beta_k \rangle, \varphi'(\langle X_k \rightsquigarrow \beta_k \rangle))$$

such that
$$\varphi(\langle A \rightarrow \langle \alpha \rightsquigarrow \beta \rangle \rangle) = \varphi'(\langle A \rightarrow \alpha \rangle) \sqcup \varphi'(\langle X_1 \rightsquigarrow \beta_1 \rangle) \sqcup \ldots$$
$$\sqcup \varphi'(\langle X_k \rightsquigarrow \beta_k \rangle). \ \square$$

Definition 8.32. (*parse tree*)
Let $\mathcal{G}$ be a unification grammar, $\underline{a}_1 \ldots \underline{a}_n$ a string in W^*. A *parse tree* for $\underline{a}_1 \ldots \underline{a}_n$ is an adequately decorated tree of the form

$$(\langle S \rightsquigarrow \underline{a}_1 \ldots \underline{a}_n \rangle, \ \varphi(\langle S \rightsquigarrow \underline{a}_1 \ldots \underline{a}_n \rangle))$$

with $\varphi(\langle S \rightsquigarrow \underline{a}_1 \ldots \underline{a}_n \rangle) \neq \bot$. $\qquad\qquad\qquad\qquad\qquad\qquad\qquad\square$

---

adequately decorated trees need not be minimal.
As an example, consider a grammar with the following productions:

(1) $A \rightarrow B$, $\ \varphi(B) = [f : a]$,
(2) $A \rightarrow B$, $\ \varphi(B) = [g : b]$,
(3) $B \rightarrow C$, $\ \varphi(B) = [g : b]$.

A tree $\langle A \rightsquigarrow C \rangle$ composed from the elementary trees of productions (1) and (3) is decorated adequately, but not minimal.
In a practical grammar, it is likely that every adequately decorated tree is also minimally decorated. One could rule out grammars that allow non-minimal adequate decoration by additional constraints on the features of the productions and lexicon. This is not very relevant for the current discussion, therefore we bypass the issue with a definition of adequacy that is based on what ought to be proper composition of decorated trees.

[14] See Definition 3.8 on page 42 for various forms of linear tree notation.

Definition 8.33. (*result*)

Let $(\langle S \rightsquigarrow \underline{a}_1 \ldots \underline{a}_n \rangle, \varphi(\langle S \rightsquigarrow \underline{a}_1 \ldots \underline{a}_n \rangle))$ be a parse for the sentence $\underline{a}_1 \ldots \underline{a}_n$. The feature structure

$$\varphi(S) = \varphi(\langle S \rightsquigarrow \underline{a}_1 \ldots \underline{a}_n \rangle)|_S$$

is called a *result* of the sentence.   □

In context-free parsing, parse trees are delivered as results. For unification grammars, it is assumed that the feature structure of the sentence symbol S contains all relevant information. The parse tree is not an interesting object as such, it serves only to compute $\varphi(S)$. Hence we can rephrase the parsing problem as follows.

> The *parsing problem*, given sentence $\underline{a}_1 \ldots \underline{a}_n \in W^*$ and a grammar $\mathcal{G}$, is to find all results $\varphi(S)$.

Unlike the context-free case, we can also define a reversed problem.[15]

> The *generation problem*, given a grammar $\mathcal{G}$ and a feature structure $\varphi(S)$, is to find a sentence $\underline{a}_1 \ldots \underline{a}_n \in W^*$ for which $\varphi(S)$ is a result.

In principle it should be possible to use a single unification grammar both for parsing and generation. If a grammar is to be used in both directions, it must be guaranteed that both the parsing algorithm and the generation algorithm halt. A unification grammar that is designed for use in a parser typically will not halt when used for generation. *Reversible* unification grammars, that can be used in either direction, are studied in by Appelt [1987], Shieber [1988], Shieber et al. [1990], Gerdemann [1991], van Noord [1993], and Strzalkowski [1994]. Minnen et al. [1995] take a single (HPSG) unification grammar and optimize it differently for parsing and generation.

8.6 Composition of decorated trees

In 8.5 we have defined what a valid parse tree is, but not yet how such a tree can be computed. We will now define an operator for tree composition. Using this operator, one can create ever larger and larger trees from the initial trees based on grammar productions and lexicon. Thus, in the framework of Chapter 2, we have a primordial soup populated with adequately decorated trees.

The primordial soup is sound if all parse trees for the sentence that may appear are adequately decorated and complete if all adequately decorated parse trees can be constructed.

---

[15] Wedekind [1988] has given such a definition for the generation problem in Lexical-Functional Grammar.

We define a decorated tree composition operator $\lhd_i$ and extend that to a nondeterministic operator by dropping the index i. For technical reasons, the context-free tree composition operator is defined slightly differently from the way it was done in Chapter 2. (The difference is merely notational, the trees that can be composed are the same).

Definition 8.34. (*context-free tree composition*)
For a context-free grammar G and any $i \in \mathbb{N}$ a partial function

$$\lhd_i \colon \mathcal{T}rees(G) \times \mathcal{T}rees(G) \longrightarrow \mathcal{T}rees(G)$$

is defined as follows. Let $\tau = \langle X_0 \rightsquigarrow X_1 \ldots X_k \rangle$ and $\sigma = \langle Y_0 \rightsquigarrow Y_1 \ldots Y_l \rangle$ be context-free trees in $\mathcal{T}rees(G)$. Then

$$\tau \lhd_i \sigma = \begin{cases} \langle X_0 \rightsquigarrow X_1 \ldots X_{i-1} \langle X_i \rightsquigarrow Y_1 \ldots Y_l \rangle X_{i+1} \ldots X_k \rangle & \text{if } X_i = Y_0, \\ \text{undefined otherwise.} \end{cases}$$

In a more practical interpretation, we interpret $\lhd_i$ as an operator to create new trees from existing trees, rather than as a function. We drop the index i and obtain a nondeterministic operator $\lhd$. $\qquad\square$

Definition 8.35. (*decorated tree composition*)
For a feature grammar $\mathcal{G}$ and any $i \in \mathbb{N}$ a partial function

$$\lhd_i \colon \mathcal{D}\mathcal{T}rees(\mathcal{G}) \times \mathcal{D}\mathcal{T}rees(\mathcal{G}) \longrightarrow \mathcal{D}\mathcal{T}rees(\mathcal{G})$$

is defined as follows. Let $(\tau, \varphi(\tau))$ and $(\sigma, \varphi(\sigma))$ be decorated trees with $\tau = \langle X_0 \rightsquigarrow X_1 \ldots X_k \rangle$ and $\sigma = \langle Y_0 \rightsquigarrow Y_1 \ldots Y_l \rangle$. Then

$$(\tau, \varphi(\tau)) \lhd_i (\sigma, \varphi(\sigma)) = \begin{cases} \text{undefined} \quad \text{if } \tau \lhd_i \sigma \text{ is undefined} \\ \qquad\qquad \text{or } \varphi(\tau) \sqcup_{X_i = Y_0} \varphi(\sigma) = \bot, \\[2mm] (\tau \lhd_i \sigma, \ \ \varphi(\tau) \sqcup_{X_i = Y_0} \varphi(\sigma)) \quad \text{otherwise.} \end{cases}$$

As in Definition 8.34 we may drop the index i and interpret $\lhd$ as a nondeterministic operator.
We write $(\tau, \varphi(\tau)) \lhd (\sigma, \varphi(\sigma)) = \bot$ if the composition is not defined for any i. $\qquad\square$

The next lemma states that composition of adequately decorated trees yields an adequately decorated tree. This result will not come as a surprise. But to be formally correct it is necessary to state it as a separate result. Adequate decoration was defined inductively by expanding a *production* tree with adequately decorated trees. It follows easily (but not by definition) that arbitrary tree composition of adequately decorated trees yields an adequately decorated tree.

Lemma 8.36.

Let $(\tau, \varphi(\tau)) \in \mathcal{DT}rees(\mathcal{G})$ and $(\sigma, \varphi(\sigma)) \in \mathcal{DT}rees(\mathcal{G})$ be adequately decorated trees. If $(\tau, \varphi(\tau)) \lhd (\sigma, \varphi(\sigma)) \in \mathcal{DT}rees(\mathcal{G})$ then $(\tau, \varphi(\tau)) \lhd (\sigma, \varphi(\sigma))$ is also adequately decorated.

Proof: by induction on the size of $(\tau, \varphi(\tau)) \lhd (\sigma, \varphi(\sigma))$.

Let $\tau = \langle A \rightarrow \langle \alpha \rightsquigarrow \beta \rangle \rangle$, $\alpha = X_1 \dots X_k$, $\beta = \beta_1 \dots \beta_k$ as in Definition 8.31. In the composed tree $\tau \lhd \sigma$, some leaf in some β_i is unified with the root of σ. Let $\varphi'(\langle X_i \rightsquigarrow \beta_i \rangle)$ be the adequate decoration of $\langle X_i \rightsquigarrow \beta_i \rangle$ from which the adequacy of $\varphi(\tau)$ is derived. Then, using the induction hypothesis, we find that

$$(\langle X_i \rightsquigarrow \beta_i \rangle \lhd \sigma, \; \varphi'(\langle X_i \rightsquigarrow \beta_i \rangle) \sqcup \varphi(\sigma))$$
$$= \; (\langle X_i \rightsquigarrow \beta_i \rangle, \varphi'(\langle X_i \rightsquigarrow \beta_i \rangle)) \; \lhd \; (\sigma, \varphi(\sigma))$$

is adequate. It is easily verified that $(\tau, \varphi(\tau)) \lhd (\sigma, \varphi(\sigma))$ is obtained by composition of $(\langle A \rightarrow \alpha \rangle, \varphi'(\langle A \rightarrow \alpha \rangle))$ with $(\langle X_1 \rightsquigarrow \beta_1 \rangle, \varphi'(\langle X_1 \rightsquigarrow \beta_1 \rangle))$, ..., $(\langle X_{i-1} \rightsquigarrow \beta_{i-1} \rangle, \varphi'(\langle X_{i-1} \rightsquigarrow \beta_{i-1} \rangle))$, $(\langle X_i \rightsquigarrow \beta_i \rangle \lhd \sigma, \; \varphi'(\langle X_i \rightsquigarrow \beta_i \rangle) \sqcup \varphi(\sigma))$, $(\langle X_{i+1} \rightsquigarrow \beta_{i+1} \rangle, \varphi'(\langle X_{i+1} \rightsquigarrow \beta_{i+1} \rangle))$, ..., $(\langle X_k \rightsquigarrow \beta_k \rangle, \varphi'(\langle X_k \rightsquigarrow \beta_k \rangle))$, as in Definition 8.31. □

Theorem 8.37. *(correctness of primordial soup for decorated trees)*

A decorated tree $(\tau, \varphi(\tau))$ with $\tau = \langle S \rightsquigarrow \underline{a}_1 \dots \underline{a}_n \rangle$ that is obtained by tree composition $\lhd$ from decorated trees of the forms

$$(\langle A \rightarrow \alpha \rangle, \varphi_0(A \rightarrow \alpha))) \quad \text{and}$$

$$(\langle a \rightarrow \underline{a}_i \rangle, \varphi(a \rightarrow \underline{a}_i))) \quad \text{with } \varphi(\underline{a}_i) \in \mathcal{L}ex(\underline{a}_i) \text{ and } \varphi(a) \doteq \varphi(\underline{a}_i)$$

is adequate. Moreover, each adequately decorated parse can be constructed from such trees.

Proof. The soundness (context-free parse trees are adequately decorated) is a direct consequence of Lemma 8.36. It is trivial to prove (with induction on the size of the tree) that *all* adequately decorated trees can be composed, hence completeness follows a fortiori. □

8.7 Parsing schemata for unification grammars

In 8.5 we have introduced unification grammars and 8.6 we have proven that the Primordial Soup framework for decorated trees is sound and complete. Integrating all this into context-free parsing schemata is mainly a matter of notation.

There is, however, a single important difference between parsing schemata for context-free grammars and unification grammars, with far-reaching consequences. In the context-free case any item needs to be recognized only once. When an already recognized item is recognized again, it should be ignored.

For unification grammars, in contrast, a single context-free item can be recognized multiple times, each time with a different decoration. These are to be regarded as different objects. Hence we may face the situation that a parsing schema with only a finite set of valid context-free items may yield infinitely many decorations to these items.

At this very abstract level we will not worry about infinitely many decorations for a single context-free item. There are various ways to construct parsing algorithms that recognize only a relevant finite subset of valid decorated items. This will be discussed at more length in Chapter 9.

We will first formulate a parsing schema **UG** that formalized what we did in Section 7.2: Constituents are recognized purely bottom-up. This can be regarded as the canonical parsing schema for unification grammars.

A domain of items can be defined by adding feature structures to the usual CYK items. We could write

$$\mathcal{I}_{UG} = \{[(X, \varphi(X)), i, j] \mid X \in V \wedge 0 \leq i \leq j \wedge \varphi(X) \neq \perp\}$$

where $\varphi(X)$ is obtained by restricting the composite feature structure of the tree $\langle X \rightsquigarrow \underline{a}_{i+1} \ldots \underline{a}_j \rangle$ to the features of the top node. Throughout the remainder of this chapter items are decorated with feature structures, therefore we do not need to mention $\varphi(X)$ explicitly in the notation of an item. Hence we write $[X, i, j]$ as usual, rather than $[(X, \varphi(X)), i, j]$.

The hypotheses represent all feature structures offered by the lexicon for all words in the sentence:

$$H = \{[a, j-1, j] \mid \varphi(a) \in \mathcal{L}ex(\underline{a}_j)\}. \tag{8.1}$$

Schema 8.38. (UG)
It is obvious, however, that deduction steps for productions with larger right-hand sides can be added in similar fashion.
For an arbitrary unification grammar $\mathcal{G} \in \mathcal{UG}$ we define a parsing system $\mathbb{P}_{UG} = \langle \mathcal{I}_{UG}, H, D_{UG} \rangle$ by

$$\mathcal{I}_{UG} = \{[X, i, j] \mid X \in V \wedge 0 \leq i \leq j \wedge \varphi(X) \neq \perp\};$$

$$\mathcal{D}^{\geq 1} = \{[X_1, i_0, i_1], \ldots, [X_k, i_{k-1}, i_k] \vdash [A, i_0, i_k]$$
$$\mid A \rightarrow X_1 \ldots X_k \in P \wedge k \geq 1 \wedge$$
$$\varphi(A) = (\varphi_0(A \rightarrow X_1 \ldots X_k) \sqcup \varphi(X_1) \sqcup \ldots \sqcup \varphi(X_k))|_A\},$$

$$\mathcal{D}^\varepsilon = \{\vdash [A, j, j] \mid A \rightarrow \varepsilon \in P \wedge \varphi(A) = \varphi_0(A \rightarrow \varepsilon)\},$$

$$D_{UG} = \mathcal{D}^{\geq 1} \cup \mathcal{D}^\varepsilon;$$

and H as in (8.1).

Many unification grammars that have been written to cover (parts of) natural languages have only productions that are unary or binary branching. In that case, the definition of D can be simplified to:

$$D^{(1)} = \{[X,i,j] \vdash [A,i,j]$$
$$| \ A{\rightarrow}X \in P \ \wedge \ \varphi(A) = (\varphi_0(A{\rightarrow}X) \sqcup \varphi(X))|_A \},$$

$$D^{(2)} = \{[X,i,j],[Yj,k] \vdash [A,i,k] \ | \ A{\rightarrow}XY \in P \ \wedge$$
$$\varphi(A) = (\varphi_0(A{\rightarrow}XY) \sqcup \varphi(X) \sqcup \varphi(Y))|_A\},$$

$$D_{UG} = D^{(1)} \cup D^{(2)}.$$

Sets of deduction steps $D^{(k)}$ for other values of k can be added likewise. □

It is not necessarily the case that the parsing schema **UG** yields a finite set of decorated items for an arbitrary grammar and sentence; even worse, the parsing problem for an arbitrary unification grammar is undecidable. Several sufficient conditions that guarantee finiteness of the **UG** schema are known from the literature,[16] but no general necessary and sufficient condition is known. Hence we simply *assume* that a grammar G has been defined in such a way that the parsing schema **UG** will halt. For unification grammars designed for parsing natural languages this does not seem to be problem. The underlying idea is that the *meaning* of a sentence, that will be captured somewhere in the result, is derived compositionally from the meaning words, via intermediate constituents; there is little reason to write a grammar such that ever more meaning is added to the same constituent.

In the sequel, we will assume that a unification grammar G has the property that for any string only a finite number of valid decorated items exists. How the grammar writer guarantees that this is the case (for example by making sure that one of the sufficient conditions is kept) is of no concern to us here. When we discuss other parsing schemata, the finiteness issue will come up again. Adding other fancy kinds of deduction steps – notably top-down prediction of features – may jeopardize the finiteness. In such a case we will show for a newly defined schema **P** that *if* a parsing system **UG**(G) halts, then **P**(G) will also halt. In other words, the finiteness in bottom-up direction is the responsibility of the grammar writer, whereas the finiteness in top-down direction is the responsibility of the parser constructor.

Earley-type parsers for unification grammars that incorporate top-down prediction are discussed, among others, by Shieber [1985a], Haas [1989], and Shieber [1992]. In Chapter 11 a *head-driven* parsing schema will be defined that starts parsing those words that can be expected to yield features that are most restrictive for top-down prediction.

---

[16] The *off-line parsability constraint* [Bresnan and Kaplan, 1982] and the stronger notion of *depth-boundedness* [Haas, 1989] guarantee a finiteness.

We will now look at an Earley parser, formalizing what has been informally explained in Section 7.1. A domain of items for the Earley schema is properly described by

$$
\mathcal{I}_{Earley(UG)} = \{[(A\rightarrow\alpha\bullet\beta, \varphi(A\rightarrow\alpha\bullet\beta)), i, j] \mid \quad (8.2)
$$
$$
A\rightarrow\alpha\beta \in P \ \wedge\ 0 \leq i \leq j \ \wedge
$$
$$
\varphi_0(A\rightarrow\alpha\beta) \sqsubseteq \varphi(A\rightarrow\alpha\bullet\beta) \ \wedge
$$
$$
\varphi(A\rightarrow\alpha\bullet\beta) \neq \bot \quad \};
$$

In order to simplify the notation, we attach identifiers to items. When an item is subscripted with a symbol $\xi, \eta, \zeta, \ldots$, this symbol can be used in the remainder of the expression to identify the item. Moreover, we write $\varphi(\xi)$ for the feature structure $\varphi(A\rightarrow\alpha\bullet\beta)$ of an item $[(A\rightarrow\alpha\bullet\beta, \varphi(A\rightarrow\alpha\bullet\beta)), i, j]_\xi$. Furthermore, as with the CYK items, we do not mention the feature structure explicitly in the item. Thus we simplify (8.2) to

$$
\mathcal{I}_{Earley(UG)} = \{[A\rightarrow\alpha\bullet\beta, i, j]_\xi \mid \quad (8.3)
$$
$$
A\rightarrow\alpha\beta \in P \ \wedge\ 0 \leq i \leq j \ \wedge
$$
$$
\varphi_0(A\rightarrow\alpha\beta) \sqsubseteq \varphi(\xi) \ \wedge\ \varphi(\xi) \neq \bot \quad \};
$$

Another useful notational convention is the following. Rather than writing $\varphi(\xi)|_X$ for the feature structure of X derived from some composite feature structure within an item ξ, we write $\varphi(X_\xi)$.

Schema 8.39. (Earley(UG))
For an arbitrary unification grammar $\mathcal{G} \in \mathcal{UG}$ a parsing system $\mathbb{P}_{Earley(UG)} = \langle \mathcal{I}_{Earley(UG)}, H, D_{Earley(UG)} \rangle$ is defined by $\mathcal{I}_{Earley(UG)}$ as in (8.3);

$$
D^{Init} = \{ \vdash [S\rightarrow\bullet\gamma, 0, 0]_\xi \mid \varphi(\xi) = \varphi_0(S\rightarrow\gamma) \},
$$

$$
D^{Scan} = \{ [A\rightarrow\alpha\bullet a\beta, i, j]_\eta, [a, j, j+1]_\zeta \vdash [A\rightarrow\alpha a\bullet\beta, i, j+1]_\xi
$$
$$
\mid \varphi(\xi) = \varphi(\eta) \sqcup \varphi(a_\zeta) \},
$$

$$
D^{Compl} = \{ [A\rightarrow\alpha\bullet B\beta, i, j]_\eta, [B\rightarrow\gamma\bullet, j, k]_\zeta \vdash [A\rightarrow\alpha B\bullet\beta, i, k]_\xi
$$
$$
\mid \varphi(\xi) = \varphi(\eta) \sqcup \varphi(B_\zeta) \},
$$

$$
D^{Pred} = \{ [A\rightarrow\alpha\bullet B\beta, i, j]_\eta \vdash [B\rightarrow\bullet\gamma, j, j]_\xi
$$
$$
\mid \varphi(\xi) = \varphi(B_\eta) \sqcup \varphi_0(B\rightarrow\gamma) \},
$$

$$
D_{Earley(UG)} = D^{Init} \cup D^{Scan} \cup D^{Compl} \cup D^{Pred};
$$

and H as in (8.1). $\qquad\qquad\square$

A unification grammar $\mathcal{G}$ for which $\mathbf{UG}(\mathcal{G})$ is finite, may cause an infinite number of top-down predictions. A simple way to solve this (and the standard way to parse a unification grammar with a conventional active chart parser) is to limit the top-down prediction to the context-free backbone and replace D^{Pred} by

$$
D^{Pred'} = \{ [A\rightarrow\alpha\bullet B\beta, i, j]_\eta \vdash [B\rightarrow\bullet\gamma, j, j]_\xi \mid \varphi(\xi) = \varphi_0(B\rightarrow\gamma) \}.
$$

It is not difficult to show that the modified Earley schema yields only finitely many different decorated items if the **UG** schema is known to do so. In Chapter 9 we will investigate more sophisticated techniques to prevent infinitely many decorations for a single context-free item.

We have given two examples of parsing schemata for unification grammars. It is clear that other context-free parsing schemata can be extended with feature structures in similar fashion.

8.8 The example revisited

We return to the example of Section 7.2 and show how the schema **Earley-UG** can be used to parse our example sentence. The lexicon and productions for the cat catches a mouse were shown in figures 7.1 and 7.2 on pages 133 and 134. In a PATR-style grammar, the composite feature structures φ_0 are typically denoted by a constraint set. Here we will represent all feature structures, single and composite, by AVMs.

In an Earley item of the form $[A \rightarrow \alpha \cdot \beta, i, j]$, we are interested only in the features of A and β. Features of A will be used to transfer information upwards through a parse tree (when an item $[A \rightarrow \alpha \beta \cdot, i, k]$ is used at some later stage as the right operand of a *predict* step). Features of β that are known already are used as a filter to guarantee that β will be of "the right kind" in whatever sense imposed by those features. The features of α need not be remembered. Features of α that are of interest for the remainder of the parsing process will have been shared with A or β, other features are irrelevant. Our purpose, here, is to construct a resulting feature for S, rather than a context-free parse.

We start with an item $[S \rightarrow \cdot NP\ VP, 0, 0]$, supplied with the features from $\varphi_0(S \rightarrow NP\ VP)$. The decorated item is shown in Figure 8.4.
No features are predicted for the subject (other than that its category should be NP). Hence, an item $[NP \rightarrow \cdot {}^*det\ {}^*n, 0, 0]$ is predicted that is decorated with $\varphi_0(NP \rightarrow {}^*det\ {}^*n)$. For the sake of brevity we skip the deduction steps

$$[NP \rightarrow \cdot {}^*det\ {}^*n, 0, 0],\ [{}^*det, 0, 1]\ \vdash\ [NP \rightarrow {}^*det \cdot {}^*n, 0, 1],$$

$$[NP \rightarrow {}^*det \cdot {}^*n, 0, 1],\ [{}^*n, 1, 2]\ \vdash\ [NP \rightarrow {}^*det\ {}^*n \cdot, 0, 2];$$

the reader may verify that the decorated item $[NP \rightarrow {}^*det\ {}^*n \cdot, 0, 2]$ as displayed in Figure 8.5 is obtained. A *complete* step combines the items of Figures 8.4 and 8.5 into a decorated item $[S \rightarrow NP \cdot VP, 0, 2]$ as shown in Figure 8.6. The features of the NP have been included in the VP through coreferencing.

From Figure 8.6 we predict an item $[VP \rightarrow \cdot {}^*v\ NP, 2, 2]$, as shown in Figure 8.7. The *subject* feature that is shared between VP and ${}^*v$ causes the subject information to be passed down to the verb. Consequently, a verb can be

$[S \rightarrow \bullet NP\ VP, 0, 0]$

$$S \longmapsto \begin{bmatrix} cat & : S \\ head: & \boxed{1} \end{bmatrix}$$

$$NP \longmapsto \boxed{2}\ \begin{bmatrix} cat: NP \end{bmatrix}$$

$$VP \longmapsto \begin{bmatrix} cat & : VP \\ head & : \boxed{1}\ [\ ] \\ subject: & \boxed{2} \end{bmatrix}$$

Fig. 8.4. The initial item

$[NP \rightarrow {}^*det\ {}^*n\bullet, 0, 2]$

$$NP \longmapsto \begin{bmatrix} cat & : NP \\ head: & \begin{bmatrix} agr & : \begin{bmatrix} number: singular \\ person\ : third \end{bmatrix} \\ trans: & \begin{bmatrix} pred: cat \\ det\ : + \end{bmatrix} \end{bmatrix} \end{bmatrix}$$

Fig. 8.5. A completed NP

$[S \rightarrow NP \bullet VP, 0, 2]$

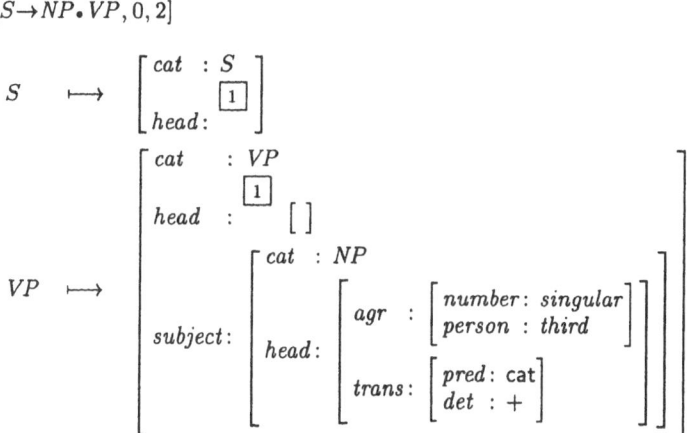

$$S \longmapsto \begin{bmatrix} cat & : S \\ head: & \boxed{1} \end{bmatrix}$$

$$VP \longmapsto \begin{bmatrix} cat & : VP \\ head & : \boxed{1}\ [\ ] \\ subject: & \begin{bmatrix} cat & : NP \\ head: & \begin{bmatrix} agr & : \begin{bmatrix} number: singular \\ person\ : third \end{bmatrix} \\ trans: & \begin{bmatrix} pred: cat \\ det\ : + \end{bmatrix} \end{bmatrix} \end{bmatrix} \end{bmatrix}$$

Fig. 8.6. *Complete* applied to Figures 8.4 and 8.5

$[VP \rightarrow \bullet *v\ NP, 2, 2]$

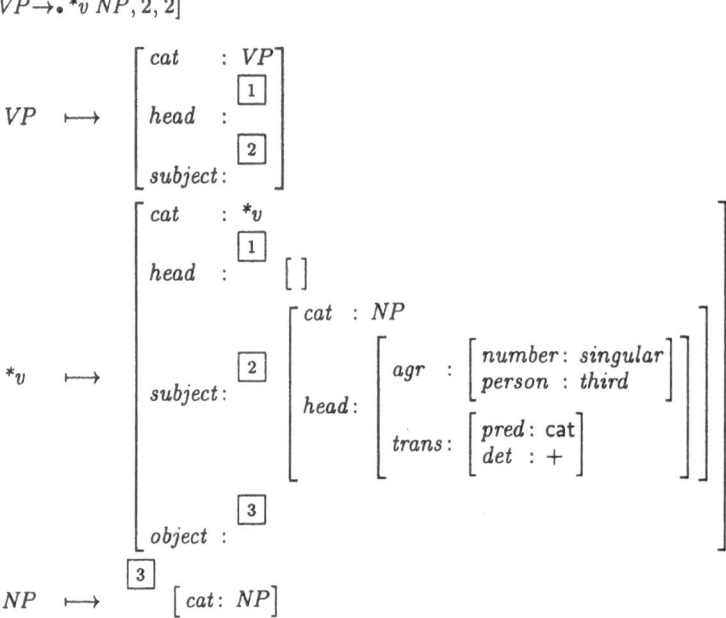

Fig. 8.7. *Predict* applied to Figure 8.6

accepted only if it allows a subject in third person singular. This is indeed the case for the initial item $[*v, 2, 3]$, decorated with the lexicon entry for catches on page 133. Hence we obtain the item $[VP \rightarrow *v \bullet NP, 2, 3]$ with a decoration as shown in Figure 8.8. The $*v$ entry has been deleted, as its salient features are also contained in the VP feature structure. Note that $\langle NP\ head\ trans \rangle$ is now coreferenced with $\langle VP\ head\ trans\ arg2 \rangle$, through the coreference in the (no longer visible) feature structure of the verb.

We can continue to deduce decorated items in similar fashion. It is left to the reader to verify that application of the deduction steps

$$[VP \rightarrow *v \bullet NP, 2, 3] \vdash [NP \rightarrow \bullet *det\ *n, 3, 3],$$

$$[NP \rightarrow \bullet *det\ *n, 3, 3],\ [*det, 3, 4] \vdash [NP \rightarrow *det \bullet *n, 3, 4],$$

$$[NP \rightarrow *det \bullet *n, 3, 4],\ [*n, 4, 5] \vdash [NP \rightarrow *det\ *n \bullet, 3, 5],$$

$$[VP \rightarrow *v \bullet NP, 2, 3],\ [NP \rightarrow *det\ *n \bullet, 3, 5],\ \vdash [VP \rightarrow *v\ NP \bullet, 2, 5],$$

$$[S \rightarrow NP \bullet VP, 0, 2],\ [VP \rightarrow *v\ NP \bullet, 2, 5] \vdash [S \rightarrow NP\ VP \bullet, 0, 5]$$

results in a decorated final item as shown in Figure 8.9.

$[VP \rightarrow *v \bullet NP, 2, 3]$

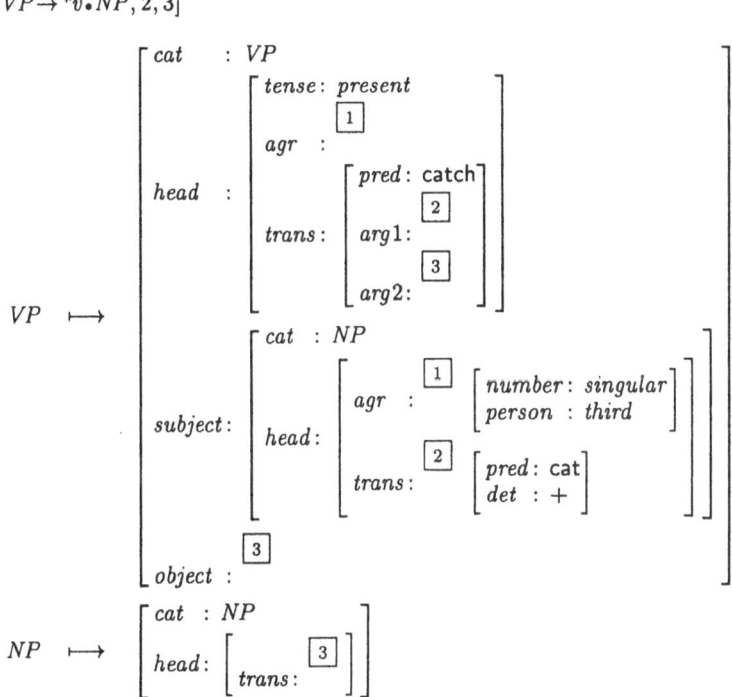

Fig. 8.8. *Scan* applied to Figure 8.7 and "catches" on page 133

$[S \rightarrow NP \, VP \bullet, 0, 5]$

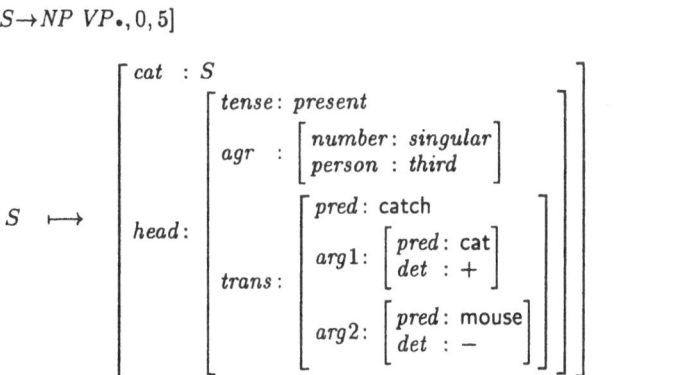

Fig. 8.9. A final item

8.9 Other grammar formalisms

We will briefly mention some different kinds of unification grammars and then discuss the related formalisms of attribute grammars and affix grammars.

The earliest type of unification grammar is Definite Clause Grammar (DCG), defined by Pereira and Warren [1980]. DCG is based on *terms* rather than feature structures. It is inextricably linked with the programming language Prolog [Clocksin and Mellish, 1981]. DCG, basically, offers some additional syntactic sugar for encoding grammars directly into Prolog.

In the last decade, a variety of grammar formalisms based on feature structure unification has emerged. The Computational Linguistics community has been enriched with Lexical-Functional Grammar (LFG) [Kaplan and Bresnan, 1982], Functional Unification Grammar (FUG) [Kay, 1979, 1985], Generalized Phrase Structure Grammar (GPSG) [Gazdar et al., 1985], PATR[17] [Shieber 1986], Categorial Unification grammar (CUG) [Uszkoreit 1986], Unification Categorial grammar (UCG) [Zeevat et al., 1987], Head-Driven Phrase Structure Grammar (HPSG) [Pollard and Sag, 1987, 1994], Unification-based Tree Adjoining Grammars (UTAG) [Vijaj-Shanker et al., 1991]. This list is not exhaustive.

The word "grammar" that appears in all these formalisms, has subtly different meanings in different cases. On the one hand, one can see grammar as a formalism that has no meaning *per se*, but can be used to encode grammars for whatever purpose. Typical examples of this class are DCG, FUG and PATR. On the other hand, one can interpret grammar as a description of phenomena that occur in natural language. Such a grammar does not only offer a formalism but, more importantly, also a linguistic *theory* that is expressed by means of that formalism. Typical examples of this class are LFG, GPSG and HPSG.

The feature structure formalism that we have used here is taken from the 1986 version of PATR (with exception of the extension to composite feature structures). It was designed by Shieber to be the most simple feature structure formalism, containing only the bare essentials. A lot of bells and whistles can be added, of course. The use of *lists*, which is admittedly cumbersome in PATR notation, can be simplified by introducing a special list notation. A useful extension to increase the efficiency of unification grammar parsing is coverage of *disjunctive feature structures*. We will come back to this in Chapter 9.

We have used untyped feature structures: any feature can have any value. In a *typed* feature structure formalism, the value of a feature is restricted to

---

[17] The formalism is called PATR-II, to be precise, and quite different from a first version of PATR that has fallen into oblivion (and hence the letters "PATR" in PATR-II no longer form an acronym).

particular types specifically defined for that feature [Emele and Zajac, 1990]. See [Carpenter, 1992] for a textbook on typed feature structures.

We have stipulated – as in PATR – that feature graphs contain no cycles. The practical reason is that it simplifies the unification algorithms, and cyclic feature structures seem to have little linguistic relevance. In HPSG, the feature formalism does not explicitly ban cycles, but in the first version [Pollard and Sag, 1987] they simply did not occur in any of the types prescribed for HPSG grammars. The 1993 version of HPSG [Pollard and Sag, 1994], however, has somewhat different types and found an application for cyclic structures. Some linguists argue that the head of a noun phrase is the determiner, rather than the noun (the so-called *DP hypothesis*). In the latest version of HPSG, this matter is solved by letting both the determiner and the noun regard themselves as head of the *NP* and each other as a subordinate constituent. Hence either constituent is subordinate to a subordinate structure of itself.

Unification grammars are related to *attribute grammars*, introduced by Knuth [1968, 1971], that have been used in compiler construction for 25 years. There are some basic differences between attribute grammars and unification grammars, but from a formal point of view there is little objection to call both constraint-based formalisms. The difference between both formalisms is to a large extent a difference in culture: attribute grammars are typically used by computer scientists to denote the semantics of programming languages, while unification grammars are typically used by computational linguists to capture syntactic and semantic properties of natural languages.

Attribute grammars stem from the age that higher programming languages all were *imperative* languages. The basic statement is the assignment: a value, obtained from evaluating an expression, is assigned to an identifier. Expressions can be functions (i.e. sub-programs computing a value) of arbitrary sophistication. Within the imperative programming paradigm, therefore, it is the most natural approach to define attributes of a constituent as functions of other attributes of other constituents. The constraints in an attribute grammar can be thought of assignments:[18]

$\langle attribute \rangle := \langle expression \rangle$

where $\langle expression \rangle$ is a function of attributes of other symbols in the same production.

Unification grammars, in comparison draw heavily upon the *declarative* programming style as incorporated in Prolog. A Prolog clause foo(X,Y) specifies the relation between X and Y. If X is instantiated then foo can be used

---

[18] One could use attribute grammars also within the functional programming paradigm. Lazy evaluation can be used to solve some dependency problems easier and more elegantly than in the imperative paradigm, but the central notion of functional dependency remains.

to assign a value to a variable Y, and reversed, if Y is instantiated then a variable X can get a value by calling foo[19]. Similarly, in unification grammars we specify (commutative) equations that have to be true. In which order the features have to be computed is irrelevant, it is not even possible to express such considerations within the formalism.

Research on attribute grammars, therefore, tends to focus on other issues than research on unification grammars. A classical issue is that of *noncircularity*: if there is a circle of attributes in a parse tree that are all functionally dependent on each other, then it is impossible to compute a decoration for the tree. An often used sufficient (but not necessary) condition is that of *L-attributedness*. An attribute grammar is L-attributed, informally speaking, if all attributes can be computed in a single pass in a top-down left-to-right walk through a context-free parse tree. A subclass that is particularly useful in compiler construction is the class of *LR-attributed* grammars. These, roughly speaking, allow the attributed to be computed on the fly by an LR parser. The literature contains a host of different parsing algorithms for LR-attributed grammars. See, e.g., Jones and Madsen [1980], Pohlmann [1983], Nakata and Sassa [1986], Sassa et al. [1987], and Tarhio [1988]). Each one defines a particular class of grammars on which it is guaranteed to work correctly. All these classes are subtly different, however, because they depend on the guts of the proposed algorithm. A taxonomy is presented by op den Akker, Melichar and Tarhio [1980]. A fundamental treatment of attribute evaluation during *generalized* LR parsing (cf. Chapter 12) is given by Oude Luttighuis and Sikkel [1992, 1993].

"There are no fundamental differences between affix grammars [...] and attribute grammars [...]", Koster [1991a] remarks in an article on affix grammars for programming languages. "The two formalisms differ in origin and notation, but they are both formalizations of the same intuition: the extension of parsers with parameters".

Affix grammars are a particular kind of *two-level* or *van Wijngaarden* grammars [van Wijngaarden, 1965], and were formalized by Koster [1971]. One can see the context-free productions of an affix grammar as *production schemata*, defining sets of productions for different combinations of affix values that can be attributed to the symbols involved in the production. Hence, even though grammars written as an affix grammar can be automatically translated to attribute grammars, and reversed, the basic formalism of affix grammars is more general, because its lacks the predominant concern with functional dependency.

---

[19] In the actual practice of Prolog programming, however, few clauses do really allow this. There is a difference between specification and computation: it is very well possible that the Prolog gets stuck in an infinite loop of the "wrong" argument is uninstantiated. This is similar to the fact that a unification grammar designed for parsing typically can't be used for generation, although the general formalism is bidirectional.

Unification grammars with a *finite* feature lattice can be formulated directly as affix grammars (so-called Affix Grammars over a Finite Lattice (AGFL), see Koster [1991b] for a simple introduction). Typically linguistic phenomena that can be modelled with finite feature lattices, or a finite domain of typed feature structures, are conjugation (i.e. the different forms of a verb) and declination (forms of nouns, adjectives, etc.,)

The main difference between affix grammars and both attribute grammars and unification grammars is again a cultural one. The school of affix grammars has its own followers and its own formalism, but the work done in that area can be formulated in terms of attribute grammars or unification grammars as well.

8.10 Related approaches

Some explicit parsing algorithms for unification grammars have been given in the literature. Haas [1989] gives a GHR algorithm (i.e. Graham, Harrison, and Ruzzo's optimization of Earley's algorithm, cf. Example 6.18) for grammars based on *terms*. A parsing schema for ID/LP grammars has been presented by Morawietz [1995].

Shieber [1992] gives an Earley parser for a general class of unification grammars, rather than just the PATR-formalism. The notation of Shieber [1992] – as opposed to the PATR variant of [Shieber, 1986], on which our treatment of unification grammars is based – allows for explicit control of feature percolation within *productions*; a production $A \rightarrow X_1 \ldots X_k$ is a structure with features $0, \ldots, k$ that address the separate constituents. Our concept of multi-rooted feature structures for describing feature sharing between different objects is more general, because it can deal with arbitrary object structures.

The subject discussed here has some clear links with Shieber [1992], but we have taken a rather different perspective. Whereas Shieber gives a most general account of unification grammars and discusses only a single parsing algorithm, we have used just a simple unification grammar but given a formalism that allows to specify arbitrary parsing algorithms in a precise but conceptually clear manner.

8.11 Conclusion

The main contribution of this chapter is the combination of parsing schemata and unification grammars in a single framework. Using the proper notation, parsing schemata for unification grammars are a straightforward extension of context-free parsing schemata. The hardest task was in fact to come up with a proper notation. Both parsing algorithms and unification grammars are complex problem domains on their own. In order to combine them into a single framework, a large conceptual machinery and a rich notation is needed. It is for good reason that most articles in the literature are specific in one domain, and informal in the other.

Context-free parsing is a *computational* problem area. A parse tree can be defined as an object that satisfies certain properties, but the only way to find these properties for a given sentence is to actually *construct* the parse tree. From this point of view, attribute grammars are the more natural way to extend context-free parsing with constraints and semantic functions. Decorating a tree with attributes (whether simultaneously or in a second pass) is indeed application of functions.

The literature on unification grammars, on the other hand, has a strong focus on the *declarative* character of such a grammar. One describes the constraints that are implied by the grammar, and the properties of individual words in the lexicon. The theory leans heavily on logic, hence the prime operational concern is that constraints can be expressed in a subset of first-order logic that allows automatic constraint resolution. This being proven, one can leave the act of *satisfying* the constraints to an appropriate machine. From this point of view it makes sense to concentrate on the static aspects of the grammar, rather than on the dynamic aspects of how to construct a parse.

The dynamics of unification and resolution *sec* have been studied extensively in the literature. It constitutes an auxiliary domain that is used as a tool in the construction of parsers for unification grammars, often in the form of the Prolog programming language. We have added a simple formalism that allows explicit specification of the dynamics of feature structure propagation in parsing algorithms.

9. Topics in unification grammar parsing

Context-free parsing schemata can be translated straightforwardly into parsing algorithms. Such naive implementations might not be the most efficient parsers, and one can improve the efficiency a lot by adding various kinds of sophistication to the algorithm, but it is obvious how a first, simple implementation can be derived from a parsing schema. For unification grammars, however, it is not self-evident how a parsing schema can be translated to even a prototype parsing algorithm. In this chapter we will discuss various issues that have to be addressed in order to obtain practical parsers for unification grammars.

This chapter mostly surveys other research, rather than presenting our own, but, for the above reason, we felt it useful to include it in this book.

An important issue that we have ignored so far is *unification*: how to compute the *lub* of two feature structures. We know that *lub*s exist, because of the lattice structure, so we can write them down in parsing schemata. But when parsing schemata are to be turned into parsing algorithms we must know how to unify. Section 9.1 gives an overview of feature structure unification and presents a simple unification algorithm in detail. More sophisticated versions are discussed in 9.2 and 9.3.

Another issue that enhances the practical value of unification grammars is disjunction within feature structures. Theoretically, a disjunctive feature structure can be seen as a short notation for a set of non-disjunctive feature structures. From a practical point of view, however, it won't do to have to rewrite everything into disjunctive normal form before feature structures can be unified. How to handle disjunction is discussed in 9.4.

In Chapter 8 we have noted that a single context-free item may, in principle, have an infinite number of different decorations. In Sections 9.5 and 9.6 we discuss *restrictors* that discard irrelevant features from a feature structure. This solves the problem of potentially infinite chains of predictions.

A more general – and more important – use of restrictors is discussed in 9.7. There are, in principle, two fundamentally different ways to construct a parse for a sentence. In a *one-pass* parser, each item is attributed with features when it is recognized. An alternative strategy is employed by a *two-*

pass parser, which constructs a set[1] of context-free parse trees first and adds suitable decorations in a second pass. Using restrictors, one can construct intermediate kinds of parsers, that take only *some* features into account in the first pass, while other features are added in a second pass.

9.1 Feature graph unification

In Chapter 8 we have dodged the issue of how to compute a *lub* $\varphi_1(X) \sqcup \varphi_2(X)$ of two arbitrary feature structures $\varphi_1(X)$ and $\varphi_2(X)$. The lattice structure guarantees its existence, and examples were simple enough to do unification "by hand".

There is a wealth of literature on the subject, one could even speak of unification theory as a field of its own. As this topic is of such central importance to unification grammars, we make a digression from the main theme and discuss the algorithmic aspects of feature structure unification in some detail.

A good introduction to unification theory is given by Siekmann [1989], a survey of algorithms and applications is provided by Knight [1989]. It is important to note, however, that unification theory is concerned with *term unification*, which is not exactly the same as feature structure unification. Feature structures can be seen as an extension of terms. The most salient difference is that feature structures allow coreferencing of *arbitrary substructures* whereas terms only allow coreferencing of *leaves*[2]. Hence it is not self-evident that a term unification algorithm can be extended to a feature structure unification algorithm. In many cases, however, the extension to feature structure unification is straightforward. In the sequel we will give such an adaptation of the algorithm of Huet [1976] as an easy and efficient algorithm for feature structure unification.

We give a formal definition of term graphs similar to Definition 8.3 for feature graphs. This is only meant to formally write down the difference between both concepts; we will make no further use of term graphs.

Definition 9.1. (*term graphs*)
We assume a domain of functions $f, g, \ldots$ where each function has a fixed *arity* (i.e. number of arguments taken by the function). Functions with 0

---

[1] Or a shared forest, cf. Section 12.4.

[2] Some term unification algorithms make use of subgraph sharing for the sake of efficiency. Consider, for example, a term $f(g(a, h(x)), h(g(a, h(x))), y)$ in which, using graph representation, the term $g(a, h(x))$ can be represented by a single subgraph. It should be stressed, though, that sharing of subgraphs in term graphs can always be done *because* it doesn't change the interpretation of the term! Token identity (other than variables carrying the same names) is a concept that simply does not apply to terms.

arguments are also called *constants*, denoted $a, b, \ldots$. Furthermore, we have a set of *variables* $x, y, \ldots$.
A term graph is a (finite) tree with the following properties

(i) Every non-leaf vertex v is labelled with a function. Let n be the arity of the function, then there are n (ordered) outgoing edges from v.
(ii) Every leaf is labelled with a constant or a variable.

The edges are not labelled.   □

A term can be extended by instantiating a variable with another term. But it is essential that the same variable (if it occurs more than once in the term) is instantiated to the same term. Hence we can see a term tree as a directed acyclic graph (DAG) that allows subgraph sharing *only* for leaves labelled with variables, not for other kinds of substructures.

We will not be concerned with terms and discuss how feature structures can be unified. This is easiest to carry out in graph representation. We will present a feature graph unification algorithm that is a straightforward adaptation of the algorithm of Huet [1976] for term unification. The task is to create a new feature graph which is the *lub* of two given feature graphs. We call the new graph the *unifact* and the given graphs the *operands*[3]. For the sake of clarity we assume that the operands are single feature graphs. Extension to composite feature graphs is trivial.

The general principle of the algorithm is quite simple. Input are two feature graphs as operands (represented by their root vertex). The algorithm computes an equivalence relation on the vertices of both operands, such that each equivalence class corresponds to a single vertex in the unifact. Initially, all equivalence classes are singletons, except the roots of the two operands, which form a single class. When two equivalent vertices have a feature in common, then the children corresponding to these features must be equivalent as well. That means, their equivalence classes have to be merged. In this way a "transitive closure" can be computed, either recursively or by keeping a list of pairs of vertices that still have to be dealt with. Unification fails (and ⊥ is delivered as unifact) if an equivalence class contains a pair of *incompatible* vertices. Two vertices are incompatible if

• one is a leaf labelled with a constant and the other is a non-leaf vertex, or
• both are leaves but labelled with different constants.

When no more equivalence classes need to be merged, and no incompatibility has appeared, the unifact can be computed by contracting the classes to single

[3] It is tempting to call a graph that is to be unified a *"unificand"*, by analogy to "operand". The proper form, however, following the Latin etymology, should be the gerundive *"unifacend"*. This does not have an equally persuasive connotation for the mathematical reader, hence we stick to "operand".

vertices. This has the consequence, however, that the operands are destroyed. Therefore, this method is called *destructive* unification. In 9.2 we will discuss a nondestructive unification algorithm.

Manipulation of the equivalence classes is done by the UNION and FIND operations as given by Aho, Hopcroft and Ullman [1974]. Vertices have an additional *class* pointer that is used for maintaining the classes. The vertices that comprise a class are linked in a tree structure (not to be confused with the DAG structure of the operands!). Each class has a unique representative: the root of its class tree.

The UNION operation merges two classes, simply by making the representative of one class a child of the representative of the other class. The latter vertex henceforth represents the merged class. As a general policy, the representative of the larger class becomes the joint class representative.

The class representative of any vertex can be found by traversing a path along the *class* pointers. The FIND operation searches for the root of a class tree in a slightly more subtle way: whenever a path to the root is accessed, all vertices on that path are made direct descendants of the root. Thus a deep class tree is flattened by access. This makes the complexity of the FIND operator (almost) independent of the size of a class.

This general scheme for merging equivalence classes is called the UNION-FIND algorithm. The complexity of a sequence of n UNION and FIND operations on a graph of arbitrary size is *almost linear*: $O(n \, \alpha(n))$, with α a very slowly increasing function. α is the inverse of a function F, characterized by $F(1) = 1$, $F(n) = 2^{F(n-1)}$. Hence we find $\alpha(2^{16}) = 4$, $\alpha(2^{65536}) = 5$. When the UNION-FIND algorithm is used for feature graph unification in the context of natural language parsing, it is pretty hard to come up with a realistic example where a class comprises as much as half a dozen vertices. Hence the non-linear factor in the complexity of the algorithm is purely theoretical and has no practical relevance at all.

In order to write down the algorithm in a more tangible form, we assume that vertices in a feature graph carry the following attributes:

- *features*: a list of pairs (f, p) with f is a feature and p a pointer to another vertex. We assume the set of possible features to be ordered, hence the list of pairs can be ordered on features.
- *kind*: indicates the kind of vertex, i.e., *constant*, *variable*, or *complex*.
- *label*: denotes the label of a vertex (only applicable to leaves), i.e., a constant.
- *class*: pointer to a vertex in the same equivalence class. If $u.class = u$ then u is the representative of the class.

There are three kinds of vertices: *complex vertices* have a non-empty list of features and no label; *constant vertices* are labelled with a constant but have no features; *variable vertices* have neither features nor label.

```
function compute_equivalence_classes(fg1, fg2: vertex): boolean;
begin
        pairs_to_unify := {(fg1, fg2)};
        while pairs_to_unify is not empty
        do      take some pair (x, y) from pairs_to_unify;
                u := FIND(x); v := FIND(y);
                if u ≠ v
                then  if compatible(u, v)
                        then   merge(u, v)
                        else   return(false)
                fi      fi
        od;
        return(true)
end;

procedure merge(u, v: vertex);
        (precondition: u, v are class representatives)
begin
        x := UNION(u, v);  (* i.e.: either x = u or x = v *)
        if x = u then y := v else y := u fi;
        if x.kind = variable and y.kind ≠ variable
        then x.kind := y.kind; x.label := y.label fi;
        for each feature-pointer-pair (f, p) ∈ y.features
        do      if there is some (f, q) ∈ x.features
                then   add (p, q) to pairs_to_unify
                else   add (f, p) to x.features
                fi
        od
end;
```

Fig. 9.1. Computation of equivalence classes

For the proper functioning of the algorithm it is essential that the representative of an equivalence class has the characteristic properties (i.e. *kind* and either *label* or *features*) of the entire class. Hence proper care has to be taken when two classes are merged. One of both representatives will become the representative of the merged class, and has to take over the relevant properties of the other representative, if not already present.

A straightforward algorithm for the computation of the equivalence classes is given in Figure 9.1. If the algorithm is run on composite feature structures, then *pairs_to_unify* should be initialized with all pairs of roots that have to be unified.

As a simple example, consider the feature graphs in Figure 9.2 as operands. Initially, *pairs_to_unify* = {(1,6)}. A call to UNION(1,6) yields 1 as representative of the combined class. (To be deterministic, we assume that the representative of the first argument is chosen if both classes are equally large). Merging the feature lists

$$1.features = [(f, 2), (g, 4)] \text{ and } 6.features = [(f, 7), (g, 7), (h, 9)]$$

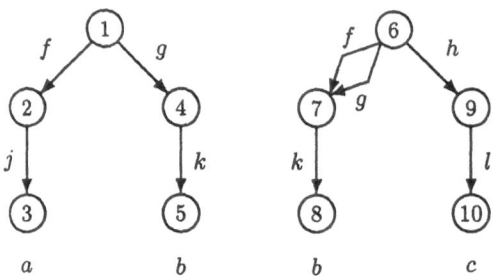

Fig. 9.2. The operands

we get

$$1.features := [(f, 2), (g, 4), (h, 9)]$$

with *pairs_to_unify* = $\{(2, 7), (4, 7)\}$. We continue taking the UNION of $\{2\}$ and $\{7\}$, yielding an equivalence class $\{2, 7\}$ represented by 2. Taking over the feature k from 7, we get

$$2.features := [(j, 3), (k, 8)].$$

A call UNION(4,7) merges the classes $\{2, 7\}$ and $\{4\}$, choosing 2 as their joint representative. Merging the features of 4 into those of 2 yields a last pair to be unified: (5,8). When this is done, we have reduced 10 vertices to 6 equivalence classes

$$\{1, 6\}, \{2, 4, 7\}, \{3\}, \{5, 8\}, \{9\}, \{10\}$$

as shown in Figure 9.3. Vertices within one class are linked with ===, the representative is indicated by a double circle. The actual tree structure of the equivalence class is irrelevant.

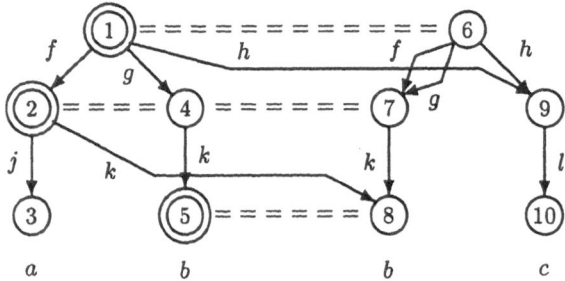

Fig. 9.3. The equivalence classes

As a final step, we have to contract the classes to single vertices. To that end, pointers to a non-representative vertex must be changed to pointers to their representatives. I.e., if (f, p) is a feature and FIND$(p) \neq p$ then it has to be replaced by $(f, \text{FIND}(p))$. In our example, the features $(g, 4)$ becomes

$(g, 2)$ in 1.*features* and $(k, 8)$ is changed to $(k, 5)$ in 2.*features*. The non-representative vertices are deleted and every class is a singleton again. The final situation is shown in Figure 9.4.

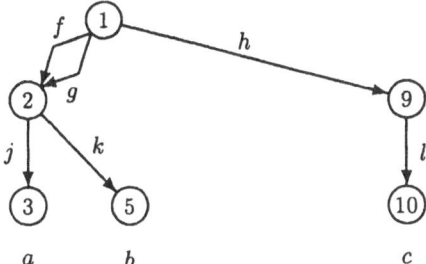

a   b   c   **Fig. 9.4.** The unifact

A point that should be noted is that we do not allow cycles in feature graphs. It is conceivable, however, that non-cyclic operands unify to a cyclic (and hence inconsistent) graph. Hence the resulting graph has to be checked for cycles before it is delivered as a unifact. In Section 9.2 we will discuss in more detail how redirecting of pointers and checking for cycles can be done in a single sweep through the graph.

The complexity of our version of Huet's algorithm for feature graph unification can be computed as follows. Let k be the maximum number of features (i.e., the maximum outdegree) of a given vertex, and n the number of vertices in feature graph. Then the algorithm has complexity $O(kn\,\alpha(kn))$. This can be seen as follows.

Pairs of vertices taken from *pairs_to_unify* come in two categories: the pair can either be already equivalent or not yet equivalent. Every pair generates two calls to FIND. Only not-yet-equivalent pairs generate a call to *merge*, which calls UNION and merges lists of up to k feature-pointer-pairs. Furthermore, up to k new pairs of vertices can be added to *pairs_to_unify*. The number of not-yet-equivalent pairs is limited to n (after which all vertices are equivalent), hence the total number of vertices, counting duplicates, that can be added to *pairs_to_unify* is kn. The $O(kn)$ already equivalent pairs generate $O(kn)$ UNION/FIND calls, the $O(n)$ not yet equivalent pairs generate $O(n)$ UNION/FIND calls and $O(kn)$ other work; two lists of feature-pointer-pairs can be merged in $O(k)$ steps when sorted on feature. Thus computing the equivalence classes takes $O(kn\,\alpha(kn))$ steps.

Subsequently, pointers to non-representative vertices have to be replaced by pointers to their representatives. This takes $O(kn)$ steps. Absence of cycles can be detected in $O(kn)$ steps using a depth-first search. In summary, $O(kn\,\alpha(kn))$ steps suffice.

Practically speaking, the factor $O(\alpha(kn))$ is constant and we obtain a complexity of $O(kn)$. Moreover, for any particular unification grammar, the number of features emerging from a particular vertex will be bound by a *constant* number k, in which case the complexity is reduced to $O(n)$. Thus the algorithm is linear for all practical purposes.

A much cited unification algorithm for feature structures is the *congruence closure* algorithm of Nelson and Oppen [1977, 1980]. A more general version is given by Gallier [1986]. The congruence closure algorithm is also based on the UNION-FIND algorithm of Aho, Hopcroft, and Ullman [1974] and can be regarded as a generalization of Huet's algorithm. It computes equivalence classes of a set of vertices of a graph consisting of an arbitrary number of components, starting from an arbitrary initial partition into classes. Nelson and Oppen give a worst-case complexity of $O(m^2)$, with m the number of edges in the graph. An implementation with a theoretically lower complexity bound $O(m \log^2 m)$ is given by Downey, Sethi, and Tarjan [1980], but it appears not to be faster in practice [Nelson and Oppen, 1980]. When restricted to c.q. reformulated specifically for feature graph unification, the congruence closure algorithm is very similar to the extension of Huet's algorithm discussed above. A recent survey of UNION-FIND and related algorithms is given by Galil and Italiano [1991].

Different unification algorithms with the same complexity as Huet's have been given by Baxter [1973] for term unification and Aït-Kaci [1984, 1986] for feature structures. Truly linear term unification algorithms also exist, but the improvement is only theoretically relevant. Linear algorithms are given by Paterson and Wegman [1987], de Champeaux [1986] and Martelli and Montanari [1977, 1982]. A quadratic ($O(n^2)$) implementation of the (originally exponential) algorithm of Robinson [1965] is given by Corbin and Bidoit [1983]. They claim their algorithm to be simpler than the algorithm of Martelli and Montanari, and faster in practical applications.

9.2 Nondestructive graph unification

The graph unification algorithm presented above destroys the operands in the process of constructing a unifact. As operands typically must be used more than once, each operand has to be copied before unification takes place. Moreover, if the unification fails, the copies are wasted entirely. It turns out that copying accounts for more than half the time spent by a parser using a destructive unification algorithm [Karttunen and Kay, 1985], [Godden, 1990]. It is not too difficult, however, to change the unification algorithm in such a way that unification is *nondestructive*, i.e., the operands are not affected by the computation of the unifact. Rather than a final situation as displayed in Figure 9.4, we would like to obtain a final situation as shown in Figure 9.5. To that end, we make the following changes to the algorithm:

- each equivalence class is represented by a *new* vertex, rather than a vertex from one of the operands.
- when the unifact has been constructed, the class pointers of the operands are reset.

An algorithm in this vein was first presented by Wroblewksi [1987]. When two singleton classes are merged, a third vertex is created as their joint representative. Only if two non-singleton classes are merged, a spurious vertex has been made, apparently, because one of both new vertices suffices to represent the merged class. Subgraphs that occur in only one of the operands have to be copied for the unifact.

Wroblewski's algorithm has some practical problem *when* to decide that a subgraph needs to be copied, which causes the algorithm to make double copies in some weird cases. See [Wroblewski, 1987] for details. For resetting the class pointers, Wroblewski suggests a simple implementation trick. Each class pointer is annotated with a *generation number*. Any pointer with an obsolete generation number should be regarded as a self-pointer (i.e. points to the vertex it originates from). Thus, after the unifact has been completed, incrementing the global generation counter suffices to reset all pointers in one stroke.

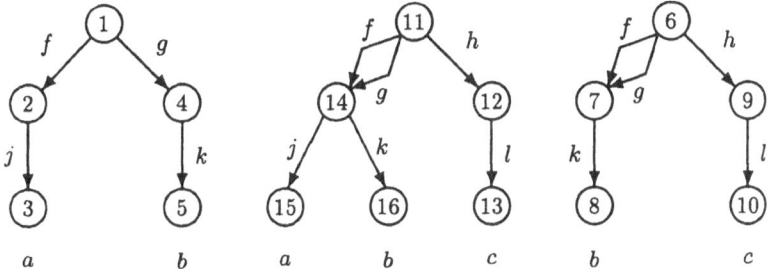

Fig. 9.5. An example of nondestructive unification

The algorithm of 9.1 can be adapted with only a few changes. In the nondestructive algorithm a vertex has the following attributes:

- *features, kind, label, class*: as in 9.1.
- *status*: takes values *old*, *new*, and *intermediate*.

All vertices of the operands are *old*, newly created vertices are *new*. The *intermediate* state is a technical aid for the construction of the unifact from the final set of equivalence classes.

We add a function *n_union* for nondestructive union. It creates a new vertex when the representatives of both classes are old. When classes represented by a new and an old vertex have to be merged, we can simply take the existing new vertex as a representative of the merged class. This is supported

```
function n_union(u, v: vertex) : vertex;
        (precondition: u, v are class representatives)
begin
        if (u.status = new or v.status = new)
        then  w := UNION(u, v)
        else   create a new vertex w;
                u.class := w; v.class := w; w.class := w;
                w.kind := variable; w.label := none;
                w.features := nil; w.status := new
        fi;
        return(w)
end;
```

Fig. 9.6. Nondestructive UNION

by the UNION implementation in [Aho et al., 1974], which takes the root of the larger class tree as the root of the merged class trees. The function n_union is defined in Figure 9.6.

Figure 9.7 shows how the equivalence classes can be computed nondestructively. It is guaranteed that the operands are not changed by the unfication algorithm, as no attribute of a vertex of an operand ever gets changed (with the exception of the *class* pointer).

The complete unification algorithm is sketched in Figure 9.8. Retrieving the unifact from the final partition into equivalence classes is somewhat different from the destructive case. In a single walk through the new graph, the applicable feature pointers are redirected, the new vertices are converted to old ones and the graph is checked for cycles.

As feature graphs are acyclic by definition, the unification should fail after all if a cycle is detected. Cycle detection can be trivially incorporated in the walk through the new graph. While going down, the status of new vertices is changed into *intermediate*; while going up, the status of vertices is changed into *new*. Clearly, the graph contains a cycle iff at some stage a new vertex is found with an intermediate daughter.

The class pointers can be reset later by walking through the operands. A more efficient implementation, as suggested above, is to keep a global generation counter; all class pointers can be invalidated by increasing the generation counter.

We will run through the example again, taking the graphs in Figure 9.2 as operands.

Computing the equivalence classes proceeds as follows. Initially there is only one pair to unify: (1,6), the pair of roots. Hence the equivalence classes {1} and {6} are merged into {1, 6, 11} with the new vertex 11 representing the class. The features of 11 are computed by merging $1.features = [(f, 2), (g, 4)]$ with $6.features = [(f, 7), (g, 7), (h, 9)]$, yielding

$$11.features = [(f, 2), (g, 4), (h, 9)]$$

```
function compute_equivalence_classes(fg1, fg2: vertex): boolean;
begin pairs_to_unify := {(fg1, fg2)};
       while pairs_to_unify is not empty
       do    take some pair (x, y) from pairs_to_unify;
             u := FIND(x); v := FIND(y);
             if u ≠ v then
                     if compatible(u, v)
                     then  merge(u, v)
                     else  return(false)
             fi     fi
       od;
       return(true)
end;

procedure merge(u, v);
begin x := n_union(u, v);
       for y := u, v
       do    if y ≠ x then
                     if x.kind = variable and y.kind ≠ variable
                     then x.kind := y.kind; x.label := y.label fi;
                     for each feature-pointer-pair (f, p) ∈ y.features
                     do    if there is some (f, q) ∈ x.features
                           then  add (p, q) to pairs_to_unify
                           else  add (f, p) to x.features;
                                 if FIND(p).status = old
                                 then copy_subgraph(FIND(p))
                           fi    fi
       od     fi    od
end;

procedure copy_subgraph(x);
       (precondition: x.class = x, x.status = old)
begin create a new vertex y; x.class := y; y.class := y;
       y.kind := x.kind; y.label := x.label; y.status := new;
       y.features := copy_list(x.features);
       for each pair (f, q) ∈ y.features
       do if q.status = old then copy_subgraph(q) fi od
end;
```

Fig. 9.7. Nondestructive computation of equivalence classes

With (2,7) and (4,7) as new pairs to be merged and the subgraph rooted by
9 to be copied. *Copy_subgraph*(9) creates a new vertex 12 as a representative
of the equivalence class {9, 12}. As 12.*features* := [(l, 10)], a new copy 13 of
vertex 10 is created, also labelled with the constant c.

Next, we merge 2 and 7 into {2, 7, 14}, with features j and k of vertex
14 pointing to 3 and 8, respectively. Using *copy_subgraph*, these vertices are
extended to equivalence classes {3, 15} and {8, 16}. One pair is left to unify:
(4,7). Hence equivalence classes {4} and {2,7,14} are merged into {2, 4, 7, 14}.
Following the definition of *merge* in Figure 9.7, we have to merge the features
of 4 and 7 into the features of 14. Both 4 and 7 have only feature k which

```
function unify(u, v: vertex): vertex
begin
        if compute_equivalence_classes(u, v)
        then   w := FIND(u);
               if not wind_up(w) then w := ⊥ fi
        else   w := ⊥
        fi;
        reset the class pointers;
        return(w)
end;

function wind_up(v: vertex): boolean;
        (redirects feature pointers as appropriate;
                makes new vertices old; checks for cycles)
begin
        if v.kind = intermediate then return(false) fi;
        if v.kind = new
        then   v.kind := intermediate;
               for each pair (f, w) ∈ v.features
               do     y := FIND(w);
                      if y ≠ w then replace (f, w) by (f, y) fi;
                      if not wind_up(y) then return(false) fi;
               od;
               v.kind := old;
        fi;
        return(true)
end;
```

Fig. 9.8. The unification algorithm

is already present in the feature list of vertex 14 (pointing to 8). Hence we add (5,8) and (8,8) to the pairs to unify. As 8 and 8 are member of the same class, no work needs to be done[4]. Unifying 5 and 8 means merging $\{5\}$ and $\{8, 16\}$ into the equivalence class $\{5, 8, 16\}$.

The list of pairs is empty now. The situation is sketched in figure 9.9. Equivalent vertices are linked by $===$, the representative is indicated with a double circle.

From the graph in figure 9.9 we can construct the unifact straightforwardly. The features of 11, $[(f, 2), (g, 4), (h, 9)]$, are replaced by

$$[(f, \text{FIND}(2)), (g, \text{FIND}(4)), (h, \text{FIND}(9))] = [(f, 14), (g, 14), (h, 12)].$$

Similarly, to $14.features$ the list

$$[(j, \text{FIND}(3)), (k, \text{FIND}(5))] = [(j, 15), (k, 16)]$$

is assigned, and so on. Thus we construct the final graph, which was displayed in figure 9.5 on page 181.

---

[4] One could also add a check in *merge* so as to prevent equivalent pairs to be put on the list of pairs to be unified.

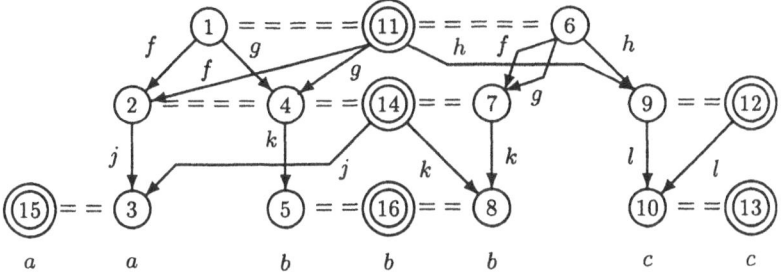

Fig. 9.9. The equivalence classes in nondestructive unification

The complexity of the nondestructive algorithm, like the destructive algorithm, is theoretically $O(kn\,\alpha(kn))$, with k the maximum outdegree of a vertex, and practically $O(kn)$. If k is considered constant (as it will be for any particular grammar) the algorithm is linear in the size of the operands.

9.3 Further improvements

In unification grammar applications, the nondestructive algorithm is more efficient than the destructive algorithm, because the operands need not be copied before unification. The algorithm presented in 9.2 is by no means optimal, however. The number of vertices to be copied can be further reduced by *subgraph sharing*. If a feature exists in only one of the operands, it is *usually* not necessary to copy the entire subgraph pointed to by that feature. The unifact could share a subgraph with one of its operands. A unification algorithm that exploits subgraph sharing could create a unifact as shown in figure 9.10. In our example, only 3 new vertices need be created, rather than 6 as in figure 9.5.

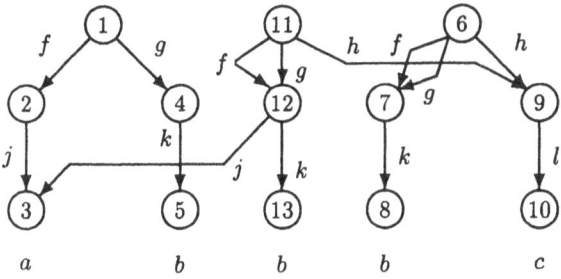

Fig. 9.10. Subgraph sharing

A unification algorithm that exploits subgraph-sharing is rather more involved; it must keep track of the conditions under which subgraph sharing is safe. Subgraph sharing and coreferencing can interfere with each other, leading to incorrect results. A more detailed treatment is given by Kogure [1990], who describes a nondestructive unification algorithm with subgraph sharing. This algorithm uses a form of lazy copying. Subgraphs are shared between the unifact and an operand as long there is no evidence that making a copy is necessary. When it is detected that a descendant of a shared vertex will be affected by unfication at some later moment, the shared subgraph needs to be copied after all.

Kogure extends his "lazy incremental copy graph unification algorithm" with a strategy that first unifies those features that are most likely to cause failure. Such a strategy could be added to Huet-type algorithms as well, as no order is prescribed in which pairs are to be taken from the list of pairs to be unified.

Karttunen and Kay [1985] use a destructive unification algorithm in combination with lazy copying: subgraphs are shared until one of the shared copies is updated. Furthermore, feature graphs are represented in [Karttunen and Kay, 1985] by means of binary trees; a parent-child relation (i.e., an edge of the feature graph) is represented by a *search path* in the binary tree. The method is not worked out in great detail in the cited article.

Pereira [1985] does not copy feature graphs, but keeps *updates* to a feature graph separately. The original feature graph is not changed, additions are kept in a separate structure. Thus the cost of making copies is traded against the cost of applying the update. This technique dates back to the theorem prover of Boyer and Moore [1972].

Karttunen's "reversible unification algorithm" [Karttunen, 1986] is in fact also a nondestructive algorithm. Only temporary changes are made to the operands. If the unification succeeds, a separate unifact is constructed.

Tomabechi [1991] merges Karttunen's approach with the nondestructive algorithm Wroblewski. He claims his algorithm to be twice as fast as Wroblewski's. Like in [Karttunen, 1986], not a single new vertex is created until the unification is known to be successful. From Wroblewski [1987] he takes the technique to undo all temporary changes to the operands in one stroke by using a global generation counter.

Emele [1991] in a very readable paper comes up with an algorithm that merges the approaches of Pereira [1985] and Wroblewski [1987] in an elegant fashion. Vertices carry generation numbers. In addition, each feature graph is associated with some specific generation. When a vertex is changed in a later generation, a forwarding pointer to a new vertex is made. Thus a vertex has a history over time, represented by a chain of vertices with non-decreasing generation numbers. When a feature graph of a particular generation has to be retrieved, each vertex in this graph is found by following the path of forwarding pointers up to the last vertex that has a generation number not exceeding the generation asked for. In Emele's algorithm the unifact is in fact the next generation of one of its operands. From a single root, the unifact can be retrieved using a higher generation number, while the operand can be retrieved using a lower generation number.

A disadvantage of Emele's approach is that the paths of forwarding pointers cannot be shortened. Hence the complexity of searching a graph (and, consequently, the complexity of unification) is dependent on the length of its history as well as its size. This makes the theoretical complexity essentially non-linear. It seems likely, however, that Emele's algorithm might be superior in practice.

Finally, a somewhat different approach is taken by Godden [1990] who introduces "lazy unification", i.e., unification (rather than copying) of substructures is delayed. This is in principle an interesting idea, but it needs substantial additional overhead. While obtaining a speedup of 50 % compared to naive, destructive unification, his algorithm is substantially slower than the ones from Tomabechi and Emele.

It has been remarked by several of the authors cited above that it depends on the particular application which approach to reduce copying will perform best.

9.4 Disjunctive feature structures

By far the most interesting extension to the unification grammar formalism is the use of *disjunctive* feature structures. For a verb form "catch", for example, we would like to write

$$\langle \text{catch } head \ agr \rangle \ = \ \begin{bmatrix} number\colon plural \end{bmatrix} \ \lor \ \begin{bmatrix} number\colon singular \\ person \ \colon 1st \lor 2nd \end{bmatrix}$$

One could also add negation, and simply write down that the agreement of "catch" is *not* third person singular.

It is always possible to avoid disjunction *within* feature structures by rewriting them into disjunctive normal form. For the verb form "catch" we would then obtain three lexicon entries with agreement features *plural, first person singular* and *second person singular*, respectively[5]. But for the sake of efficiency it is not desirable to use disjunctive normal form.

---

[5] The lexicon may also contain other entries for "catch" as, e.g., a verb in infinitival form. But that entry does not specify any agreement.

In order to obtain a graph representation for disjunctive feature structures, we can modify the graph representation of standard feature structures as follows. Every vertex is split into two vertices: a "top half" called a *feature vertex* and a "bottom half" called a *value vertex*. All incoming edges go to the feature vertex; all outgoing edges start from the value vertex. In the standard case, without disjunction, every feature has exactly one value, i.e., every feature vertex has a single outgoing edge to its corresponding value vertex.

In a disjunctive feature graph it is possible that a feature vertex is linked to different value vertices. If a feature vertex is linked to *no* value vertex, this represents an inconsistency. A disjunctive feature graph is shown in figure 9.11. Feature vertices are represented by △, value vertices by ▽. In figure 9.11(a) the bipartite graph is shown. In a rather more practical notation, as shown in figure 9.11(b), feature vertices that have exactly one value are combined with their value vertices.

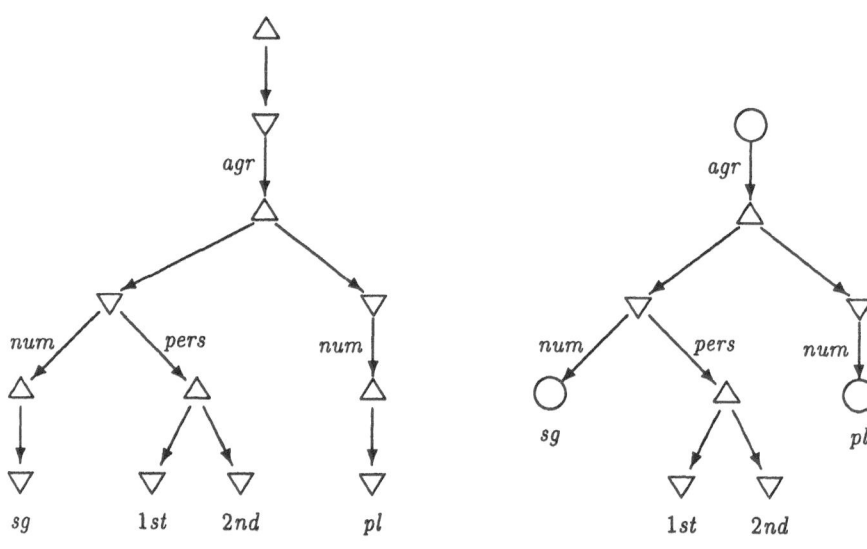

Fig. 9.11. A disjunctive feature graph

The same information can be represented by different feature graphs. It is always possible to push the disjunction upwards to the top level. In that way we only have to deal with standard feature graphs, but the number of different alternatives may grow rather large. For the simple example in figure 9.11, two alternatives are shown in figure 9.12. In figure 9.12(b) we have moved all disjunctions to the root and we have obtained a disjunction over three nondisjunctive feature structures.

A graph representation for disjunctive feature structures is formally defined as follows.

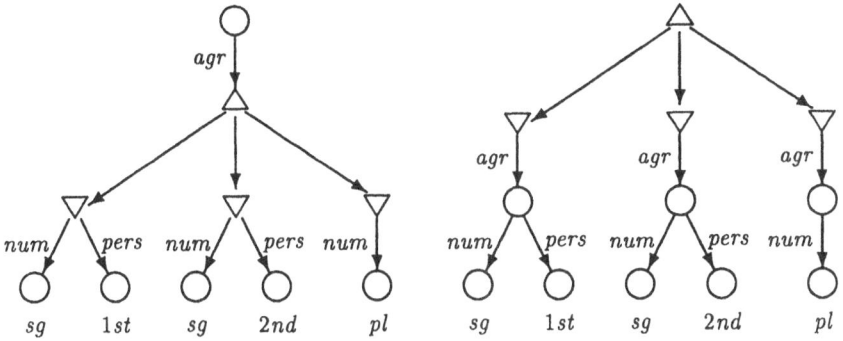

Fig. 9.12. Other graphs that carry the same information

Definition 9.2. (*disjunctive feature graphs*)
A *bipartite directed graph* $G = \langle V_1, V_2, E_{1 \to 2} E_{2 \to 1} \rangle$ has two sets of vertices V_1, V_2. Edges in $E_{1 \to 2}$ go from a vertex in V_1 to a vertex in V_2, edges in $E_{2 \to 1}$ go from a vertex in V_2 to a vertex in V_1. There are no edges connecting any pair of vertices within V_1 or V_2.
The class of disjunctive feature graphs, $\mathcal{DFG}$, is the class of finite, rooted, bipartite DAGs $\langle V_f, V_v, E_{f \to v}, E_{v \to f} \rangle$ with the following properties:

(*i*)   the root is an element of V_f, all leaves are in V_v;
(*ii*)   every edge in $E_{v \to f}$ is labelled with a feature;
(*iii*) if f and g are labels of edges originating from the same vertex in V_v, then $f \neq g$;
(*iv*)   all vertices in V_f have at least one outgoing edge;
(*v*)   leaves are labelled with atomic values, non-leaf vertices have no label.
□

When we restrict the formalism to disjunctive feature *trees*, i.e., coreferencing is not allowed, the unification algorithms can be adapted straightforwardly. Let x and y be two feature vertices, $\{u_1, \ldots, u_m\}$ the value vertices that are successors of x and $\{v_1, \ldots, v_m\}$ the value vertices that are successors of y. When x and y have to be unified, a new set of $m \times n$ value vertices $\{w_{11}, \ldots, w_{mn}\}$ is created, where w_{ij} merges the features of u_i and v_j. If u_i and v_j appear to be inconsistent, then w_{ij} can be discarded. Only if *all* w are inconsistent, the unification of x and y is inconsistent.

Extension of disjunctive feature graphs to a domain of *multi-rooted* disjunctive feature graphs $\mathcal{MDFG}$ is straightforward.

When coreferencing is allowed, one has to take care that disjunction and coreferencing do not interfere with each other. This can always be avoided by pushing all disjunctions outwards, until we have a disjunction over nondisjunctive feature structures. In a more subtle approach we could allow coreferencing and disjunction within a feature structure as long as certain restrictions are fulfilled.

Definition 9.3. (*safe disjunction*)

A vertex v in a disjunctive feature graph is called *circumventible* if it has an ancestor and a descendant such that there is a path from the ancestor to the descendant that does not pass through v.

A disjunctive feature graph is called *safe* when every circumventible feature vertex has exactly one successor.   □

A unification algorithm for disjunctive feature graphs is safe if it makes sure that no unsafe feature graphs are created. A variety of unification algorithms for disjunctive feature graphs has been published, and we will not further pursue this matter here.

Kasper [1987a] has proven that unification of disjunctive feature structures is $\mathcal{NP}$-complete. But worst cases do not apply in ordinary grammars. Kasper [1987a,b], Eisele and Dörre [1988], and Dörre and Eisele [1990] have come up with algorithms that perform well in the average case. Some recent studies devoted to various kinds of disjunctive feature structure unification are given by Maxwell and Kaplan [1989], Carter [1990], Hegner [1991], Nakano [1991]. A book with several other articles on this subject is edited by Trost [1993].

Véronis [1992] has presented a mathematical framework for disjunctive feature structures based on hypergraphs, rather than bipartite graphs.

9.5 Restriction

In general, many different decorations can be recognized for a single context-free item. There are two general methods to reduce the number of decorations in a chart parser for unification grammars.

Firstly, we can apply the notion of subsumption. When different decorations $\varphi_1(\iota)$ and $\varphi_2(\iota)$ are recognized for some item ι, and it holds that $\varphi_1 \sqsubseteq \varphi_2$, then we only need to retain $(\iota, \varphi_1(\iota))$ on the chart and we can delete $(\iota, \varphi_2(\iota))$. We have assumed that only such unification grammars $\mathcal{G}$ are used for which the parsing system $\mathbf{UG}(\mathcal{G})$ is guaranteed to be finite. Hence, by applying this subsumption criterion, a finite set of recognized decorated items can be replace by a smaller set.

A more fundamental problem, is the possibly infinite set of decorations that can be produced by adding top-down passing of features in a parsing schema. We will discuss this problem in detail and present *restrictors* as introduced by Shieber [1985a],[6] to guarantee finiteness of the Earley schema for unification grammars.

---

[6] It is important to note that we use the terminology and notation of [Shieber, 1985a], not that of [Shieber, 1992]. Restriction, denoted ↾, is replaced in the latter source by the a restriction function ϱ. Moreover, the restriction symbol ↾ is used there for a different purpose, viz., restriction of top-level features (and dependent substructures) by narrowing the domain from which these are drawn.

A restrictor is a kind of filter that can be used to remove irrelevant features from a feature structure. It is not necessary to define restrictors for a particular grammar "by hand"; in 9.6 it is shown how default restrictors can be defined as a function of the grammar. A different use of restrictors is discussed in 9.7, where only a restricted set of features is taken into account in the first pass of a parser and secondary features are added in a second pass. But before we introduce restrictors we will motivate their need by means of an example.

We will look at an example of a grammar for which the Earley schema produces an infinite number of items. *Subcategorization* of verbs can be encoded in feature structures by giving a list of complements that a verb should have. The verb "catches" has two complements (subject and direct object), which can be expressed in a lexicon entry as in Figure 9.13. A verb that takes also an indirect object will have a complement list of three *NP*s. Other verbs could take a *PP* as complement.

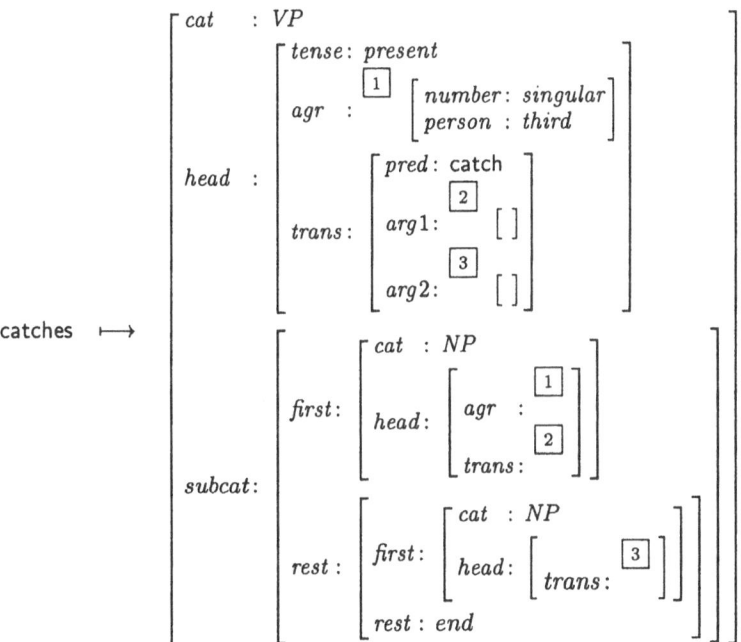

Fig. 9.13. Lexical entry for "catches" with subcategorisation list

When subcategorization is deferred to the lexicon, the grammar could have a production like

$VP_1 \rightarrow VP_2\ NP$
$\quad \langle VP_1\ head \rangle \doteq \langle VP_2\ head \rangle$
$\quad \langle VP_1\ subcat\ first \rangle \doteq \langle VP_2\ subcat\ first \rangle$
$\quad \langle VP_1\ subcat\ rest \rangle \doteq \langle VP_2\ subcat\ rest\ rest \rangle$
$\quad \langle NP \rangle \doteq \langle VP_2\ subcat\ rest\ first \rangle$

The *VPs* are indexed to distinguish them from each other. The complement list in the *subcat* feature of VP_1 is one shorter than the corresponding list of VP_2. That means (when applied to the verb "catches") that a transitive verb combined with a direct object yields a structure that has the subcategory of an intransitive verb. The first complement slot, which is reserved for the subject of the verb, is not affected. But all post-complements of the verb can be swallowed in this way, until a *VP* is left with only one (subject) complement.

$[S \rightarrow NP \bullet VP, 0, 2]$

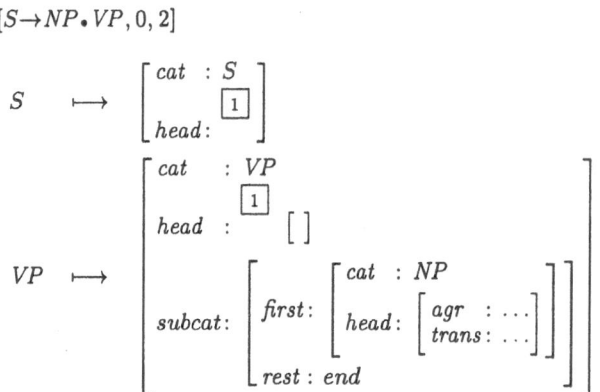

Fig. 9.14. The subject has been recognized

In the **Earley** schema for unification grammars, a problem occurs when we are to predict a *VP*. Suppose that we have a recognized item $[S \rightarrow NP \bullet VP, 0, 2]$ as in Figure 9.14. We can predict an item $[VP \rightarrow \bullet VP\ NP, 2, 2]$, shown in Figure 9.15. Now we can predict *another* item $[VP \rightarrow \bullet VP\ NP, 2, 2]$ with a different feature structure, shown in Figure 9.16. We can continue along this line, predicting new *VPs* with ever more complements.

There is no theoretical reason why such problems should occur in top-down prediction and *not* in bottom-up parsing. One can construct unification grammars that cause a parser to loop infinitely in either direction. But, from a practical point of view, it is reasonable to expect that a unification grammar, using the schema **UG**, will yield only a finite number of different constituents for any sentence. It less reasonable to expect the grammar writer to take into account sophisticated parsing techniques, such as top-down prediction in order to reduce the amount of recognized constituents that do not contribute to a parse of the sentence. Therefore it makes sense to state

$[VP_1 \rightarrow \bullet VP_2\, NP, 2, 2]$

$$VP_1 \longmapsto \begin{bmatrix} cat & : VP \\ & \boxed{1} \\ head & : \\ subcat: & \begin{bmatrix} first: & \boxed{2} \\ rest: & \boxed{3} \end{bmatrix} \end{bmatrix}$$

$$VP_2 \longmapsto \begin{bmatrix} cat & : VP \\ & \boxed{1} \\ head & : \quad [\,] \\ subcat: & \begin{bmatrix} first: & \boxed{2} \begin{bmatrix} cat & : NP \\ head: & \begin{bmatrix} agr & : \dots \\ trans: & \dots \end{bmatrix} \end{bmatrix} \\ rest : & \begin{bmatrix} first: & \boxed{4} \\ rest : & \boxed{3} \quad end \end{bmatrix} \end{bmatrix} \end{bmatrix}$$

$$NP \longmapsto \boxed{4} \; [\, cat: NP\,]$$

Fig. 9.15. A VP predicted from Figure 9.14

that preventing infinite loops in bottom-up parsing is the responsibility of the grammar, whereas preventing infinite loops in top-down prediction is the responsibility of the parser.

A general solution to the above problem, due to Shieber [1985a], is called *restriction*. The basic idea is quite simple. When an item is predicted, only a *relevant subset* of the features is used. Irrelevant features, or sub-features beyond a certain depth are simply deleted. In the case of the subcategorization list, for example, we could decide that $\langle VP\ subcat\ first \rangle$ and $\langle VP\ subcat\ rest\ first \rangle$ are relevant features, while $\langle VP\ subcat\ rest\ rest \rangle$ is not relevant. When the irrelevant tail of the subcategorization list is stripped off, the items in Figures 9.15 and 9.16 become identical, and no more different items $[VP \rightarrow \bullet VP\, NP, 2, 2]$ can be predicted.

Restriction of features in predicted items might, in general, lead to recognition of "useless" items that are incompatible with the features that have been deleted. But, much more importantly, it will prevent an infinite sequence of predictions. When the features in predicted items are restricted to a finite domain, it follows immediately that only a finite number of items can be predicted.

$[VP_1 \rightarrow \bullet\, VP_2\, NP, 2, 2]$

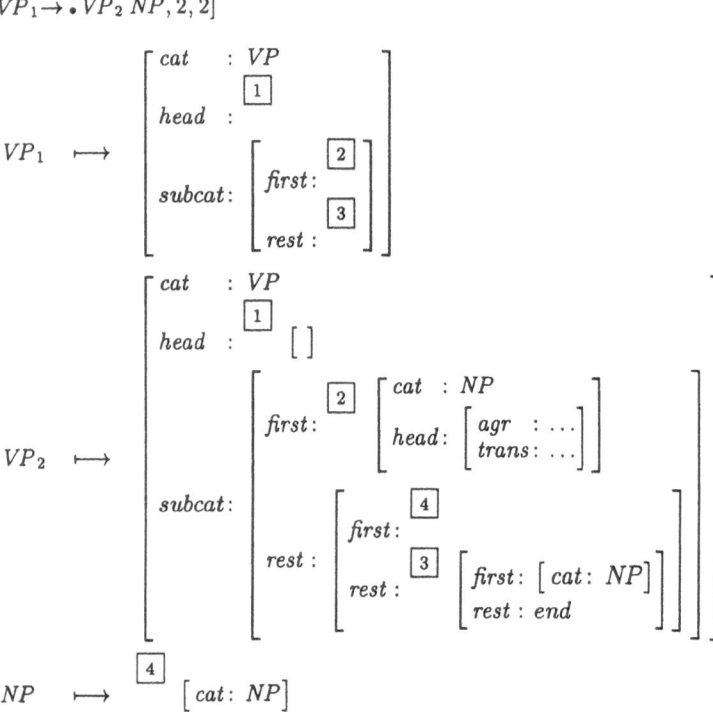

$NP \longmapsto \boxed{4} \left[\, cat:\ NP\,\right]$

Fig. 9.16. A *VP* predicted from Figure 9.15

Further elaborations of the use of restriction are given by Gerdeman [1989], Bouma [1991], Nakazawa [1991] and Harrison and Ellison [1992]. Haas [1989] presents a general Earley-like parsing algorithm for *depth-bounded* unification grammars. A grammar is depth-bounded if all parse trees for all sentences have a finite depth. A simple unification grammar with subcategorization as in the above example is depth-bounded, because every verb has a finite number of complements. The user is referred to the cited papers for further details. We will only incorporate Shieber's general solution into our parsing schema.

A *restrictor* is a feature structure that contains no constants and no coreferences. One could see it – in graph notation – as feature *tree* where the leaves carry no labels, or – in constraint notation – as a set of feature paths. We will use the AVM notation also for restrictors. The only difference in notation is that we may delete the [ ] symbols to indicate that a feature has no value; any feature without sub-features has no value by definition.

The idea, then, is the following. When a feature structure is restricted by some restrictor, only those features remain that are explicitly mentioned in the restrictor. The *constant values* of the features allowed by the restrictor are not prescribed and can vary according to the circumstances. In figure 9.17 a suitable restrictor is shown for a *VP* for a grammar with subcategorization by means of a complement list.

$$
\Psi(VP) \; = \;
\begin{bmatrix}
cat & : \\
head & : \\
subcat: &
\begin{bmatrix}
first: & \begin{bmatrix} head: & \begin{bmatrix} agr: & \begin{bmatrix} number: \\ person \; : \end{bmatrix} \end{bmatrix} \end{bmatrix} \\[4ex]
rest \; : & \begin{bmatrix} first: & \begin{bmatrix} cat: \end{bmatrix} \end{bmatrix}
\end{bmatrix}
\end{bmatrix}
$$

Fig. 9.17. A suitable *VP* restrictor

The agreement of the subject is retained by the restrictor, because this is precisely what prediction is being used for. The *trans* feature of the subject can be disposed of, as it has no relevance to the recognition of a verb phrase. When subject and *VP* are combined using a production $S \rightarrow NP\ VP$ the translations of the *NP* and *VP* will be combined into a *trans* feature for S.

We will now give a formal definition of restrictors and restriction.

Definition 9.4. (*restrictor*)
A restrictor is a constraint set that contains only existential constraints, i.e., constraints of the form $\langle X\pi \rangle \doteq [\ ]$. □

In a more practical notation, one could describe a restrictor as a set of paths, rather than a set of constraints. But by defining a restrictor as a (special kind of) constraint set, closure, normal form and constraint graphs follow automatically from Section 8.1. *Composite* restrictors can be defined in similar fashion. We will only use restrictors with a single parameter, however. We write $\Psi(X)$ for a restrictor[7], whether it is a constraint set, a feature graph or a feature structure in general.

Next we define *restriction*, i.e., the application of a restrictor to a feature structure. We will define it in the constraint set domain, but it extends to the feature graph domain as usual. Informally, applying a restrictor means that those features that occur in the restrictor remain, *with their constant values*. Formally, this is defined as follows.

Definition 9.5. (*restriction*)
Let $\chi(X)$ be a constraint set and $\Psi(X)$ a restrictor. The *restriction of* $\chi(X)$ *by* $\Psi(X)$ is the set $\chi'(X) \subseteq \chi(X)$ that satisfies the following conditions:

---

[7] Shieber [1985a] used Φ to denote a restrictor, but we must use another symbol because Φ, in this chapter, denotes the domain of feature structures.

(i) if $\langle X\pi \rangle \doteq \mu \in closure(\chi'(X))$ then $\langle X\pi \rangle \doteq [\,] \in closure(\Psi(X))$;
(ii) if $\chi''(X) \subseteq \chi(X)$ satisfies (i) then $\chi''(X) \sqsubseteq \chi'(X)$.

It is easy to verify that $\chi'(X)$ is uniquely determined.
We write $\chi(X) \upharpoonright \Psi(X)$ for the restriction of $\chi(X)$ by $\Psi(X)$.   □

It is important to note the difference between the restriction operator $\upharpoonright$ and the *glb* operator $\sqcap$. If we have, for example,

$$\varphi(X) \;=\; \begin{bmatrix} number: singular \\ person \;: third \end{bmatrix},$$

$$\Psi(X) \;=\; \begin{bmatrix} number: \end{bmatrix} \;=\; \begin{bmatrix} number: [\,] \end{bmatrix}$$

Then we obtain

$$\varphi(X) \upharpoonright \Psi(X) \;=\; \begin{bmatrix} number: singular \end{bmatrix},$$

$$\varphi(X) \sqcap \Psi(X) \;=\; \begin{bmatrix} number: [\,] \end{bmatrix}.$$

9.6 Default restrictors

If we define a restrictor for each nonterminal $B \in N$, we can change the *predict* rule of the Earley parsing schema to

$$D^{Pred} \;=\; \{[A \rightarrow \alpha \bullet B\beta, i, j]_{\eta} \;\vdash\; [B \rightarrow \bullet \gamma, j, j]_{\xi}$$
$$\mid \varphi(\xi) = \varphi(B_{\eta}) \upharpoonright \Psi(B) \;\sqcup\; \varphi_0(B \rightarrow \gamma)\}$$

(where we assume that $\upharpoonright$ has operator precedence over $\sqcup$). Hence we could extend a unification grammar to a structure

$$\mathcal{G} = (G, \Phi, \Psi, \varphi_0, W, \mathcal{L}ex)$$

with Ψ a function that assigns a restrictor to every nonterminal. But this is not a satisfactory solution. One should not change the definition of a grammar only to allow certain efficient parsing techniques if this can also be obtained with grammars as in Definition 8.29. Hence we introduce the notion of a *default restrictor* that is uniquely determined by G and φ_0.

The default restrictor for a nonterminal B can be defined informally as the set of features for B that is obtained by collecting all features for B from all productions in which it occurs as a right-hand side symbol. One can take all feature structures for B from productions $A \rightarrow \alpha B\beta$, throw away coreference and constant values and then unify the remaining structures. (Note that this cannot lead to inconsistency; because of the absence of atomic values there can be neither value/value clashes nor feature/value clashes.)

Formally, a default restrictor is defined as follows.

Definition 9.6. (*default restrictor*)

Let $\mathcal{G} = (G, \Phi, \varphi_0, W, \mathcal{L}ex)$ be a unification grammar. For each $B \in N$ a default restrictor $\Psi_0(B)$ is defined as the (unique) restrictor that satisfies the following conditions:

(i) for any production $A{\rightarrow}\alpha B\beta \in P$ it holds that

$$\varphi_0(A{\rightarrow}\alpha B\beta)|_B \;=\; \varphi_0(A{\rightarrow}\alpha B\beta)|_B \upharpoonright \Psi_0(B),$$

(ii) for any $\Psi(B)$ that satisfies (i) it holds that $\Psi_0(B) \sqsubseteq \Psi(B)$.

It is left to the reader to verify that Ψ_0 is finite and uniquely defined. The default restrictor, hence, can be seen as a function $\Psi_0 : N \times \varphi_0 {\rightarrow} \Phi$. $\square$

Thus, finally, we can write down a restrictive version of the Earley parsing schema.

Schema 9.7. (Earley(R))

For an arbitrary unification grammar $\mathcal{G} = (G, \Phi, \varphi_0, W, \mathcal{L}ex) \in \mathcal{UG}$ a parsing system $\mathbb{P}(\mathcal{I}_{Earley(R)}, H, D_{Earley(R)})$ is defined by

$$\mathcal{I}_{Earley(R)} = \{[A{\rightarrow}\alpha{\bullet}\beta, i, j]_\xi \mid A{\rightarrow}\alpha\beta \in P \wedge 0 \leq i \leq j \wedge$$
$$\varphi_0(A{\rightarrow}\alpha\beta) \sqsubseteq \varphi(\xi) \wedge \varphi(\xi) \neq \bot\};$$

$$D^{Init} = \{\vdash [S{\rightarrow}{\bullet}\gamma, 0, 0]_\xi \mid \varphi(\xi) = \varphi_0(S{\rightarrow}\gamma)\},$$

$$D^{Scan} = \{[A{\rightarrow}\alpha{\bullet}a\beta, i, j]_\eta, [a, j, j+1]_\zeta \vdash [A{\rightarrow}\alpha a{\bullet}\beta, i, j+1]_\xi$$
$$\mid \varphi(\xi) = \varphi(\eta) \sqcup \varphi(a_\zeta)\},$$

$$D^{Compl} = \{[A{\rightarrow}\alpha{\bullet}B\beta, i, j]_\eta, [B{\rightarrow}\gamma{\bullet}, j, k]_\zeta \vdash [A{\rightarrow}\alpha B{\bullet}\beta, i, k]_\xi$$
$$\mid \varphi(\xi) = \varphi(\eta) \sqcup \varphi(B_\zeta)\},$$

$$D^{Pred} = \{[A{\rightarrow}\alpha{\bullet}B\beta, i, j]_\eta \vdash [B{\rightarrow}{\bullet}\gamma, j, j]_\xi$$
$$\mid \varphi(\xi) = \varphi(B_\eta) \upharpoonright \Psi_0(B) \sqcup \varphi_0(B{\rightarrow}\gamma)\},$$

$$D_{Earley(R)} = D^{Init} \cup D^{Scan} \cup D^{Compl} \cup D^{Pred},$$

and H as in (8.1). $\square$

Theorem 9.8. (*halting of* **Earley(R)**)

For any unification grammar $\mathcal{G} \in \mathcal{UG}$ and any string $\underline{a}_1 \ldots \underline{a}_n \in W$ it holds that

if $\mathcal{V}(\mathbf{UG}(\mathcal{G})(\underline{a}_1 \ldots \underline{a}_n))$ is finite,
then also $\mathcal{V}(\mathbf{Earley(R)}(\mathcal{G})(\underline{a}_1 \ldots \underline{a}_n))$ is finite.

Proof: straightforward. $\square$

9.7 Two-pass parsing

So far we have assumed that a parse for a unification grammar is constructed by a parsing schema that employs decorated items. This can be called *one-pass* parsing, because the parse trees and their decorations (of which only relevant parts are represented) are constructed simultaneously. As an alternative, one could apply *two-pass* parsing to unfication grammars, as follows:

- in the first pass a forest of context-free parse trees is constructed;
- in the second pass these parse trees are decorated;
  trees with an inconsistent decoration are discarded.

One could refine the two-pass scheme into an arbitrary number of passes, where each one adds some more detail to the end-product of the previous pass. One finds parsers for programming languages that have four or more passes. Details of such implementations are of no importance here, but the distinction between one-pass and two-pass is a fundamental one in our general framework.

In a two-pass parser, the first pass actually contains two phases. In the first phase a set of items is recognized (based on some context-free parsing schema) as usual. In the second phase of pass one, the recognized items that do not contribute to a parse are located and discarded. How much items remain depends on the grammar, the parsing schema and the sentence, but typically only a small percentage remains.

While it is true that some valid context-free items are not recognized by a one-pass parser (due to inconsistent decorations), two pass-parsing seems to be rather more efficient than one-pass parsing. Unification is a rather expensive operation, and by two-pass parsing a number of irrelevant unification can be avoided.

The above considerations are as vague as they are general, because much depends on the nature of the unification grammar. We have assumed, for the sake of simplicity, that there is some context-free backbone to the grammar. It is within the limits of the formalism, however, to construct a grammar with a context-free backbone

$$N = \{X\}, \quad \Sigma = \{X\}, \quad P = \{X{\to}X,\ X{\to}XX\}, \quad S = X$$

and leave the traditional lexical category to some particular categorization feature. This is in fact the way in which a unification grammar *without* a context-free backbone is to be emulated in our framework. It is clear that two-pass parsing does not make sense for such a grammar.

In a more subtle approach we do not need to make a binary choice between one-pass parsing and two-pass parsing. An intermediate form can, in general terms, be described as follows:

- in the first pass, only some primary features are used, the remaining secondary features are disregarded;
- in a second pass, the full decoration of the remaining items is obtained.

A formalism in which such an intermediate parser can be described has been introduced already in 9.5. We can describe the primary features of each nonterminal A by a restrictor $\Psi(A)$. All feature structures in the first pass are trimmed by a restrictor, both in bottom-up and top-down direction. It is important to remark that restricted features constitute a finite domain. That is, a context-free backbone enhanced with primary features is a context-free grammar[8] and thus constitutes a *larger* context-free backbone for (essentially) the same grammar.

After the first pass, all recognized items that do not contribute to a parse can be discarded. The secondary features, subsequently, are added only to the remaining items.

A specification of an intermediate parser can be given by means of a parsing schema and an additional restrictor function $\Psi : N \rightarrow \Phi$ that defines the primary features. For the *implementation* of such a parser it might be advantageous to compile the context-free backbone with primary features into a larger context-free grammar. This can be done mechanically.

Nagata [1992] reports on an experiment with a parser for Japanese, where the original "course-grained" unification grammar (i.e., a grammar with few context-free productions) was turned into a medium-grained grammar by writing out the verb subcategorizations in the context-free backbone. He obtained the following results for a representative set of Japanese sentences.

rule granularity	course	medium	medium
number of passes	one	one	two
average runtime	30.2 sec	17.8 sec	8.7 sec
relative speed	1.0	1.7	3.5

Maxwell and Kaplan [1993] did similar experiments with a (LFG) grammar for English and come up with similar results.

While it is only natural that enlarging the context-free backbone is done by hand for first experiments, this technique can be described at a very high level in parsing schemata with the use of restrictors. An implementation that compiles a mixed parser for a given unification grammar and restriction function would be a very useful tool for investigating which features should be primary in order to obtain an efficient parser.

---

[8] One can obtain a context-free grammar from a unification grammar with a *finite* feature domain by treating each possible feature structure as a separate grammar symbol and writing out the productions for all (finite) cases accordingly

9.8 Conclusion

This chapter did not present new results (with exception of the notion of a default restrictor in Section 9.6) but reviewed several issues of importance for the procedural aspects of unification grammar parsers.

Most important for the over-all subject of this book, viz., parsing of context-free backbones of grammars, is Section 9.7. Some experiments with restricted one-pass parsers have been carried out independently for a Japanese and an English unification grammar. Both were equally encouraging. These experiments were conducted by rewriting (by hand) the unification grammar such that some important features were taken into the context-free backbone. The framework that is described here allows to specify which features are primary and which features are secondary at the level of a parsing schema.

The trend in unification grammars has been to encode more and more information into the lexicon and less and less in the context-free rewrite rules. With context-free backbones dwindling away, context-free parsing techniques seemed to be less and less relevant for unification grammars. The experiments of Nagata and Maxwell and Kaplan have indicated that, while highly lexicalized grammars with only a few productions are useful for specification purposes, an efficient *implementation* of a parser for such a grammar makes use of a larger context-free backbone defined by primary features. The impact of this conclusion is threefold:

- an interesting research issue is how to determine an optimal set of primary features;
- there is a need for unification grammar parser generators that take a parsing schema, grammar, and a restriction function as input and generate a two-pass parser for the augmented context-free backbone;
- context-free parsing, which seemed to lose much of its relevance for natural language parsing, is fully back on stage.

10. Left-Corner chart parsing

In Chapters 10 and 11 we apply the notion of parsing schemata to define Left-Corner and Head-Corner chart parsers. These two chapters can be read as a separate paper. From the theory that has been developed in Part II, we will use the notation, and the general idea of what a parsing schema is, but not much of the underlying theory.

Chart parsers can be seen as rather straightforward implementations of parsing schemata.[1] In Chapters 12–14 we will see other, more involved implementations of some simple parsing schemata; here we will develop rather complicated parsing schemata and do not worry a lot about implementation. We will briefly recapitulate the general notion of a chart parser and then present schemata, rather than parsing algorithms – leaving it to the reader to work out the appropriate details necessary to construct a full-fledged parser.

Chapters 10 and 11 are based on joint work with Rieks op den Akker. Parts of it have been published in [Sikkel and op den Akker, 1993, 1996], some more details can be found in the technical report [Sikkel and op den Akker, 1992]. New in these chapters is the embedding in the general framework of parsing schemata. The most substantial extensions to the cited material are the definition of a Head-Corner parser for unification grammars in 11.8 and a detailed complexity analysis of the simplified context-free Head-Corner parser in 11.6.

In Chapter 11 we will discuss Head-Corner parsing. The idea is to do the most important words first, and fill in the gaps later. The parser is rather complicated, due to the non-sequential way in which a string is processed. The easiest way to understand and formally define a Head-Corner parser is to see it as a generalization of a Left-Corner parser. This chapter, therefore, can be seen as an introduction to Chapter 11. It should be remarked, however, that Left-Corner parsers are interesting in their own right, not just as a preliminary to the more complicated Head-Corner parsers. In Chapters 4 and 6 we have given an LC parsing schema and shown that it is in fact a filtered (i.e., more efficient) version of the Earley schema. A disadvantage was that the description of the LC schema was rather more complicated, there

---

[1] Historically one should see this the other way round, of course. Parsing schemata were invented as a rather straightforward abstraction of chart parsers.

is more variety in the types of deduction steps. The LC schemata that will be defined here are in fact easier to read; we will make a somewhat more liberal use of items and introduce auxiliary items that do not fit exactly in the theory of Part II (but the theory could be expanded straightforwardly).

The reader who thumbs through this chapter might easily be put off by the seemingly overwhelming amount of formulae. We would like to stress, however, that most of these can be skipped without losing track of the discussion. The emphasis is on the intuition behind the schemata. From the informal discussion and examples, one should be able to get fairly good idea of what is going on. The formal details, then, only serve to lay down precisely what has been stated already informally. Most of the mathematics is covered in separate sections (10.3 and 10.5) that can be skipped entirely by the less mathematically inclined reader.

A brief, informal introduction to chart parsing is given in Section 10.1. We define a Left-Corner parser in 10.2 and prove it to be correct in 10.3. The items that are used by the Left-Corner parser can be simplified, at the cost of slightly more complicated deduction steps. This is dealt with in 10.4. In Section 10.5, the relation between the two parsing schemata given here and the LC schema of Chapter 4 is studied, making use of the parsing schemata transformations defined in Chapters 5 and 6. Conclusions are summarized in 10.6.

10.1 Chart parsers

The notion of a chart parser was introduced by Martin Kay [1980]. The presentation of chart parsers that is given here is somewhat unconventional, because we start from the notion of a parsing schema. For a conventional description of chart parsing, see, e.g., Winograd [1983]. We will first recapitulate some important concepts of part II and then introduce the Earley chart parser. As a running example, we use the same sentence and grammar G_1, again, that has been used for illustration in previous chapters as well.

The notational conventions for context-free grammars that were introduced in Section 3.1 apply throughout this chapter and the next one. We write $A, B, \ldots$ for nonterminal symbols; $a, b, \ldots$ for terminal symbols; $X, Y, \ldots$ for arbitrary symbols; $\alpha, \beta \ldots$ for arbitrary strings of symbols. Positions in the string $a_1 \ldots a_n$ are denoted by $, i, j, k, \ldots$ and l, r.

A *parsing system* for some grammar G and string $a_1 \ldots a_n$ is a triple $\mathbb{P} = \langle \mathcal{I}, H, D \rangle$ with $\mathcal{I}$ a set of items, H an initial set of items (also called *hypotheses*) and D a set of *deduction steps* that allow to derive new items from already known items. The hypotheses in H encode the sentence that is to be parsed. For a sentence $a_1 \ldots a_n$ we take

$$H = \{[a_1, 0, 1], \ldots, [a_n, n-1, n]\}. \tag{10.1}$$

It is not relevant whether H is contained in item set $\mathcal{I}$ or not; for the sake of brevity we may omit the hypotheses when we specify an item set $\mathcal{I}$. Deduction steps in D are of the form

$$\eta_1, \ldots, \eta_k \vdash \xi.$$

The items $\eta_1, \ldots, \eta_k \in H \cup \mathcal{I}$ are called the *antecedents* and the item $\xi \in \mathcal{I}$ is called the *consequent* of a deduction step. If all antecedents of a deduction step are recognized by a parser, then the consequent should also be recognized. The set of *valid items* $\mathcal{V}(\mathbb{P})$ is the smallest subset of $\mathcal{I}$ that contains the consequents of those deduction steps that have only hypotheses and valid items as antecedents.

A parsing system $\mathbb{P}$ is called *instantiated* if hypotheses for a particular sentence are included. An *uninstantiated parsing system* only defines $\mathcal{I}$ and D for a particular grammar G; H is a formal parameter that can be instantiated to a set of hypotheses (10.1) for any given input string. A *parsing schema* is defined for a class of grammars. For any particular given grammar a schema instantiates to an uninstantiated parsing system.

In order to define a parsing schema, one defines a parsing system for an arbitrary grammar G. As a typical example, consider the parsing schema **Earley** (that was discussed more thoroughly in Example 4.32). For an arbitrary context-free grammar G we have a system $\mathbb{P}_{Earley} = \langle \mathcal{I}_{Earley}, H, D_{Earley} \rangle$ with

$$\mathcal{I}_{Earley} = \{[A \to \alpha \bullet \beta, i, j] \mid A \to \alpha\beta \in P, 0 \le i \le j\}$$

$$D^{Init} = \{\vdash [S \to \bullet \gamma, 0, 0]\},$$

$$D^{Scan} = \{[A \to \alpha \bullet a\beta, i, j], [a, j, j+1] \vdash [A \to \alpha a \bullet \beta, i, j+1]\},$$

$$D^{Compl} = \{[A \to \alpha \bullet B\beta, i, j], [B \to \gamma \bullet, j, k] \vdash [A \to \alpha B \bullet \beta, i, k]\},$$

$$D^{Pred} = \{[A \to \alpha \bullet B\beta, i, j] \vdash [B \to \bullet \gamma, j, j]\},$$

$$D_{Earley} = D^{Init} \cup D^{Scan} \cup D^{Compl} \cup D^{Pred};$$

and H to be instantiated for any input string by (10.1). Note that the *initial* deduction steps have no antecedent; these are valid for every sentence. The set of valid items for a string $a_1 \ldots a_n$ is

$$\mathcal{V}(\mathbb{P}_{Earley}) = \{[A \to \alpha \bullet \beta, i, j] \mid \alpha \Rightarrow^* a_{i+1} \ldots a_j \wedge$$
$$S \Rightarrow^* a_1 \ldots a_i A\gamma \text{ for some } \gamma\},$$

A *parser* is obtained from a parsing schema by adding data structures and control structures. A chart parser, in its general form, is a most rudimentary kind of parser.

A chart parser is equipped with two data structures, called *chart* and *agenda*. Both data structures contain items that have been recognized by the parser. The control structure, in its elementary form, is very simple. At each step an item – the *current* item – is taken from the agenda and moved to the chart. For each deduction step that has the current item as one of its antecedents, the chart is searched for the other antecedents. If all antecedents of a deduction step are on the chart, then the consequent of that step is added to the agenda (unless it is already contained in the chart or agenda). The initial chart contains the hypotheses, representing (the lexical categories of) the words of the sentence. The initial agenda contains all items that can be deduced by an *antecedentless* deduction step as the *initialize* above. The most general specification of a chart parser is presented in Figure 10.1.

```
program chart parser
begin
      create initial chart and agenda;
      while agenda is not empty
      do    delete (arbitrarily chosen) current item from agenda;
            for each item that can be recognized by current
                              in combination with other items in chart
            do    if item is neither in chart nor in agenda
                  then add item to agenda fi
      od    od
end.
```

Fig. 10.1. General schema for a chart parser

In this general set-up, every deduction step can be successfully applied only once. The antecedent that is the last one to be added to the chart will trigger recognition of the consequent. It is evident that all valid items – and only those – are added to the chart in due course. If there is a finite number of valid items[2] then the agenda must become empty sometime and the chart parser finishes.

The basic chart parser is nondeterministic, in the sense that a current item is selected randomly from the agenda. A deterministic chart parser is obtained by specifying how the next current item is to be selected. The agenda can be structured as a stack (last in, first out), a queue (first in, first out), or a priority queue (priority by a linear order on $\mathcal{I}$). Sophistication in searching

---

[2] We only consider *relevant* items. There are parsing schemata for which antecedentless deduction steps deduce items for every possible sentence position. As the set of deduction steps – by definition – is independent of the sentence, such a schema yields an infinite number of valid initial items, in order to cope with sentences of arbitrary length. An item is relevant for a given sentence if positions markers contained in the item refer to positions that do not extend beyond the length of the sentence. Cf. Definition 4.33.

can be added by providing additional structure to the chart. See, e.g., Nijholt [1994] for various standard ways to structure a chart.

As an example, consider the Earley chart parser. The initial chart contains H as in (10.1), the initial agenda is the set $\{[S\rightarrow\bullet\gamma,0,0] \mid S\rightarrow\gamma \in P\}$. For each item that is taken from the agenda it must be checked whether a *predict*, *scan* or *complete* step can be applied.

The canonical Earley chart parser, also called *active chart parser*, imposes some ordering on the agenda (but the parser is still nondeterministic; different items may have equal priority). An item $[A\rightarrow\alpha\bullet\beta,i,j]$ has priority over an item $[A'\rightarrow\alpha'\bullet\beta',i',j']$ if $j < j'$. The sentence is processed in left-to-right fashion: An item $[A\rightarrow\alpha a\bullet\beta,i,j+1]$ that has successfully scanned word $j+1$ will remain on the agenda until all valid items with right position marker $\leq j$ have been recognized and moved to the chart. Because of this ordering, some of the searches for fellow antecedents can be eliminated. If the current item is of the form $[A\rightarrow\alpha\bullet B\beta,i,j]$, one must predict items of the form $[B\rightarrow\bullet\gamma,j,j]$. A *complete* needs to be attempted *only if* there is an empty production $B\rightarrow\varepsilon$. There is no need to look for items $[B\rightarrow\gamma\bullet,j,k]$ with $j < k$ because these cannot be in the chart yet. Items of the form $[A\rightarrow\alpha\bullet a\beta,i,j]$ and $[A\rightarrow\alpha\bullet B\beta,i,j]$ are called *active items* and look forward (to the right) for a match; items of the form $[a,j-1,j]$ and $[A\rightarrow\alpha\bullet,i,j]$ are called *passive items* and look backward (to the left) for a match.

Grammar G_1 is defined by the productions

$S\rightarrow NP\ VP$,
$NP\rightarrow {}^*det\ {}^*n$,
$VP\rightarrow {}^*v\ NP$.

This grammar produces only one sentence: the lexical categories of our canonical example sentence "the cat catches a mouse." It is on purpose that we choose a grammar that allows only a single parse tree. The intuition behind the various chart parsers that will be introduced here can be explained by visualizing how each parser steps through this single parse tree.

Any reasonable grammar will allow different sentences and parse trees. A chart parser, then, will walk through all parse trees for the sentence and all partial parse trees for valid prefixes of that sentence. But all these tree walks are interlaced; from their general behaviour it is not at all obvious that the Earley, LC and HC chart parsers actually perform tree walks. If some specific tree is singled out, however, the items that relate only to that particular tree will follow some pattern that is characteristic for the chart parser under discussion. Hence we take an example in which only a single parse tree exists; in this way the salient features of our different chart parsers will stand out.

It is *not* a general feature of chart parsers that they recognize all items for a given tree by making some walk through that tree. A CYK chart parser clearly does not do that. That the Earley and LC parsers do perform a left-to-right walk through a parse tree is a consequence of the underlying design decision that the entire left context is taken into account for item recognition. In this way the work for a sequential parser is minimized, but possibilities for parallel processing greatly reduced.

The final chart of the Earley chart parser for grammar G and the example sentence is shown in Figure 10.2. For each item it is indicated how it was added to the chart. In Figure 10.3 a top-down left-to-right walk through the parse tree is shown. We distinguish *steps down* from a nonterminal to a nonterminal, *steps up* from a nonterminal to a nonterminal, and *terminal steps* from a nonterminal down to a terminal and up again.

	item	motivation
(i)	[*det, 0, 1]	initial chart
(ii)	[*n, 1, 2]	initial chart
(iii)	[*v, 2, 3]	initial chart
(iv)	[*det, 3, 4]	initial chart
(v)	[*n, 4, 5]	initial chart
(0)	[S→•NP VP, 0, 0]	initial agenda
(1)	[NP→•*det *n, 0, 0]	predict(0)
(2)	[NP→*det•*n, 0, 1]	scan(1,i)
(3)	[NP→*det *n•, 0, 2]	scan(2,ii)
(4)	[S→NP•VP, 0, 2]	compl(0,3)
(5)	[VP→•*verb NP, 2, 2]	predict(4)
(6)	[VP→*verb•NP, 2, 3]	scan(5,iii)
(7)	[NP→•*det *n, 3, 3]	predict(6)
(8)	[NP→*det•*n, 3, 4]	scan(7,iv)
(9)	[NP→*det *n•, 3, 5]	scan(8,v)
(10)	[VP→*verb NP•, 2, 5]	complete(6,9)
(11)	[S→NP VP•, 0, 5]	complete(4,10)

Fig. 10.2. The final Earley chart

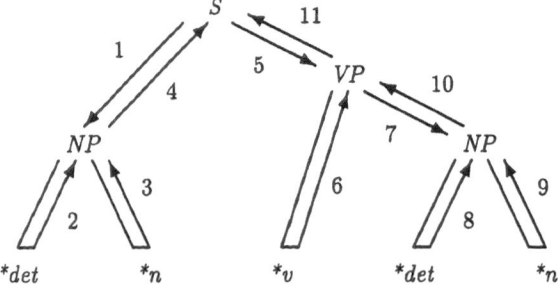

Fig. 10.3. The Earley tree walk

A terminal step comprises two steps, in fact. It is counted as a single step so as to create a one-to-one correspondence between non-initial items on the chart and steps in the tree walk. A terminal step from A down to a and back to A corresponds to *scanning* an a in a production with left-hand side A; a step up from B to A corresponds to a *complete* in which the dot is moved over a B in a production with left-hand side A; a step down from A to B corresponds to *predict*ing a production with left-hand side B.

10.2 Left-Corner chart parsing

We will define a chart parser that is based on a generalization of the Left-Corner (LC) algorithm known from the literature.

Deterministic Left-Corner parsing[3] has been introduced by Rosenkrantz and Lewis [1970]. An extensive treatise on LC parsing is given by op den Akker [1988]. First ideas of a generalized LC parser,[4] although not under that name, can be traced back to Pratt [1975]. A left-corner style parser in Prolog was presented by Matsumoto et al. [1983]. Their BUP parser overcomes the general problem in Definite Clause Grammars that left-recursion cannot be handled. BUP is limited to acyclic, ε-free grammars. As usual in Prolog implementations, ambiguities are handled by backtracking. A different way to handle ambiguities is by means of a graph-structured stack.[5] A left-corner parser based on such a data structure is described by Nederhof [1993]. Our approach to LC parsing is chart-based. It is in fact quite similar to the directed bottom-up parser of Kay [1980].

We describe a (generalized) Left-Corner parsing algorithm in the form of a chart parser. The line of presentation is somewhat different from Chapter 4, where a parsing schema **LC** was derived from the *Earley* schema. We will first concentrate on the intuition and describe the parser from a "left-corner" perspective. A derivation of this parser from the schemata in Part II is postponed to 10.5.

---

[3] In a deterministic parser, not more than a single action can be undertaken in any circumstances. One could think of a chart parser where there is never more than a single item on the agenda. A deterministic parser can parse a sentence in linear time, but in order to obtain determinism, the class of grammars that can be used has to be severely restricted. This is, in general, acceptable for programming languages but impossible for natural languages. A necessary (but not sufficient) condition for determinism is that the grammar be unambiguous.

[4] The term "Generalized LC" has been introduced by Demers [1977] for a rather different concept. He generalized the notion of Left Corner, deriving a framework that describes a class of parsers and associated grammars ranging from $LL(k)$ via $LC(k)$ to $LR(k)$. In the context of Natural Language parsing, the more obvious meaning of generalized LC parsing is that the grammar need not be $LC(k)$ for any k. Hence, the parser is nondeterministic; for a chart parser this does not cause problems.

The semantic ambiguity of the noun phrase "Generalized LC parsing" duly reflects the syntactic ambiguity: we are concerned with [Generalized [Left-Corner Parsing]], whereas Demers discussed [[Generalized Left-Corner] parsing].

[5] Cf. Chapter 12 where a graph-structured stack for a generalized LR parser is discussed.

A Left-Corner parser, like an Earley parser, proceeds through the sentence from left to right. The type of items and the motivation behind the steps is different, however. An important difference is in the way in which top-down predictions are used to guide the bottom-up recognition. *Predict* steps in Earley's algorithm are replaced by *goals* that the LC parser tries to satisfy in a purely bottom-up manner. Bottom-up recognition is guided towards the right goal by means of the *left-corner relation*.

Definition 10.1. (*transitive and reflexive left-corner relation*)
The *left corner* is the leftmost symbol in the right-hand side of a production. $A \rightarrow X\alpha$ has left corner X; an empty production $A \rightarrow \varepsilon$ has left corner ε. The relation $>_\ell$ on $N \times (V \cup \{\varepsilon\})$ is defined by

$A >_\ell U$ if there is a production $A \rightarrow \alpha \in P$ which has left corner U.

The transitive and reflexive closure of $>_\ell$ is denoted $>_\ell^*$.   □

For our trivial example grammar the transitive left-corner relation $>_\ell^*$ comprises

$$S >_\ell^* S, \ S >_\ell^* NP, \ S >_\ell^* {}^*det,$$

$$NP >_\ell^* NP, \ NP >_\ell^* {}^*det, \ VP >_\ell^* VP, \ VP >_\ell^* {}^*v.$$

The LC chart parser uses the following kinds of items:

$[i, A]$: *predict items* or *goals*,
$[A; B \rightarrow \alpha \bullet \beta, i, j]$: *left-corner* (*LC*) *items*,
$[a, j - 1, j]$: terminal items as in the Earley chart parser.

Recognition of items should be interpreted as follows.

- A predict item $[i, A]$ will be recognized if preceding items indicate that a constituent A should be looked for, starting at position i.
- An LC item $[A; B \rightarrow \alpha \bullet \beta, i, j]$ will be recognized if $[i, A]$ is set as a goal, A could start with a B (i.e. $A >_\ell^* B$) and $\alpha \Rightarrow^* a_{i+1} \ldots a_j$ has been established. In other words, an LC item incorporates a prefix for a given goal.

Parsing our sentence starts with a goal $[0, S]$. The first word is $[{}^*det, 0, 1]$. It is known by the parser that $^*det$ is a transitive left-corner of S. We can "move up" one step from $^*det$ in the tree walk if we find a symbol A such that $S >_\ell^* A$ and $A >_\ell {}^*det$. In our case, this symbol is NP and the deduction step that applies here is

$$[0, S], \ [{}^*det, 0, 1] \ \vdash \ [S; NP \rightarrow {}^*det \bullet {}^*n, 0, 1].$$

The *scan* that includes the noun in the recognized part of the NP is similar to Earley's:

$$[S; NP \rightarrow {}^*det \bullet {}^*n, 0, 1], \ [n, 1, 2] \ \vdash \ [S; NP \rightarrow {}^*det \ {}^*n \bullet, 0, 2].$$

Having recognized a complete NP, we can move up again to a left-hand side symbol that is nearer to S.

$$[S; NP{\rightarrow}{}^*det\ {}^*n{\bullet}, 0, 2] \ \vdash\ [S; S{\rightarrow}NP{\bullet}VP, 0, 2].$$

In general it is not necessary that both S symbols refer to the same node in the parse tree. If the grammar would have a production $S{\rightarrow}S\ PP$, we might step up later from the left-hand side S to a mother node also labelled S.

We have now deduced an item with the dot preceding a nonterminal symbol. We carry out a *predict* step that is not so much different from Earley's:

$$[S; S{\rightarrow}NP{\bullet}VP, 0, 2] \ \vdash\ [2,\ VP].$$

The LC parser continues in similar fashion. The final chart is shown in figure 10.4 (the initial chart has been deleted for the sake of brevity). In the *motivation* column the names and antecedents of the deduction steps are listed. For left-corner steps we distinguish between terminal and nonterminal left corners (generically denoted by letters a and A).

	item	*motivation*
(0)	$[0, S]$	initial agenda
(1)	$[S; NP{\rightarrow}{}^*det{\bullet}{}^*n, 0, 1]$	*left-corner(a)* (0,*i*)
(2)	$[S; NP{\rightarrow}{}^*det\ {}^*n{\bullet}, 0, 2]$	*scan*(1,*ii*)
(3)	$[S; S{\rightarrow}NP{\bullet}VP, 0, 2]$	*left-corner(A)* (2)
(4)	$[2, VP]$	*predict*(3)
(5)	$[VP; VP{\rightarrow}{}^*v{\bullet}NP, 2, 3]$	*left-corner(a)* (4,*iii*)
(6)	$[3, NP]$	*predict*(5)
(7)	$[NP; NP{\rightarrow}{}^*det{\bullet}{}^*n, 3, 4]$	*left-corner(a)* (6,*iv*)
(8)	$[NP; NP{\rightarrow}{}^*det\ {}^*n{\bullet}, 3, 5]$	*scan*(7,*v*)
(9)	$[VP; VP{\rightarrow}{}^*v\ NP{\bullet}, 2, 5]$	*complete*(5,8)
(10)	$[S; S{\rightarrow}NP\ VP{\bullet}, 0, 5]$	*complete*(3,9)

Fig. 10.4. A completed LC chart (excluding terminal items)

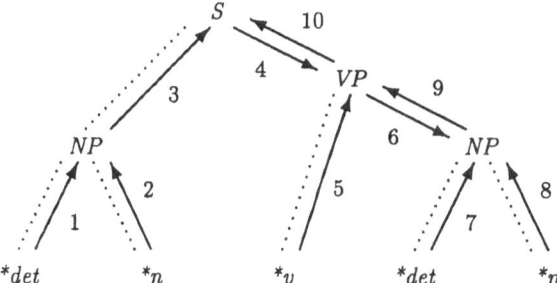

Fig. 10.5. The left-corner tree walk

The corresponding left-corner tree walk is shown in Figure 10.5. Like the Earley tree walk, the parse tree is visited in top-down left-to-right order. The main difference is that steps down to left corners do not cause the recognition of an item; these steps are encoded in the $>_\ell^*$ relation and do not need to be taken explicitly. Steps down to nonterminal daughters that are not a left corner correspond to setting a new goal. Terminal daughters are *scanned* in a single step. These steps are in fact identical to the terminal steps in the Earley tree walk. The layout in figure 10.5 has been adapted, however, to underline the bottom-up direction of item recognition. The idea is that

- top-down arrows correspond to setting new goals,
- bottom-up arrows correspond to recognizing LC items.

We will define a parsing schema[6] that underlies the LC chart parser. The parsing schema is called **pLC** for *predictive* LC, because the identifier **LC** was already used in Chapter 4 for Example 4.36.

Schema 10.2. (pLC)
We define a parsing system $\mathbb{P}_{pLC}$ for an arbitrary context-free grammar $G \in \mathcal{CFG}$. The domain $\mathcal{I}_{pLC}$ is given by

$$\mathcal{I}^{Pred} = \{[i, A] \mid A \in N \wedge i \geq 0\},$$

$$\mathcal{I}^{LC(i)} = \{[A; B \rightarrow X\alpha.\beta, i, j] \mid A \in N \wedge A >_\ell^* B \\ \wedge B \rightarrow X\alpha\beta \in P \wedge 0 \leq i \leq j\},$$

$$\mathcal{I}^{LC(ii)} = \{[A; B \rightarrow., j, j] \mid A \in N \wedge A >_\ell^* B \wedge B \rightarrow \varepsilon \in P \wedge j \geq 0\},$$

$$\mathcal{I}_{pLC} = \mathcal{I}^{Pred} \cup \mathcal{I}^{LC(i)} \cup \mathcal{I}^{LC(ii)}.$$

It is important to remark that LC items $[A; B \rightarrow \alpha.\beta, i, j]$ exist *only* for A and B such that $A >_\ell^* B$. Deduction steps, by definition, can only deduce items in $\mathcal{I}$. Hence, when we specify the various kinds of deduction steps, we need not state explicitly that items $[A; B \rightarrow \alpha.\beta, i, j]$ may occur as a consequent only if $A >_\ell^* B$. This is enforced implicitly by the definition of the domain of items.

For the set of deduction steps, we define subsets for *initialize*, *scan* and *complete* steps similar to the Earley schema. *Predict* steps set new goals as explained above. The *left-corner* steps come in three varieties, for terminal, nonterminal and empty left corners, generically denoted by a, A and ε. The set D is defined by

$$D^{Init} = \{\vdash [0, S]\},$$

$$D^{LC(a)} = \{[i, C], [a, i, i+1] \vdash [C; B \rightarrow a.\beta, i, i+1]\},$$

---

[6] Parsing schemata is this chapter are more liberal than the parsing schemata defined in 4. Here we define types of items *ad hoc*, such that these suit our purposes, while in Chapter 4 items were defined as a subset of a partition of the set of trees for a given grammar In 10.5 we will argue that our liberal approach here is in fact an extension of the formal theory of Part II.

$$D^{LC(A)} = \{[C; A \rightarrow \gamma\bullet, i, j] \vdash [C; B \rightarrow A\bullet\beta, i, j]\},$$

$$D^{LC(\epsilon)} = \{[i, C] \vdash [C; B \rightarrow \bullet, i, i]\},$$

$$D^{Pred} = \{[C; B \rightarrow \alpha\bullet A\beta, i, j] \vdash [j, A]\},$$

$$D^{Scan} = \{[C; B \rightarrow \alpha\bullet a\beta, i, j], [a, j, j+1] \vdash [C; B \rightarrow \alpha a\bullet\beta, i, j+1]\},$$

$$D^{Compl} = \{[C; B \rightarrow \alpha\bullet A\beta, i, j], [A; A \rightarrow \gamma\bullet, j, k] \vdash [C; B \rightarrow \alpha A\bullet\beta, i, k]\},$$

$$D_{pLC} = D^{Init} \cup D^{LC(a)} \cup D^{LC(A)} \cup D^{LC(\epsilon)} \cup D^{Pred} \cup D^{Scan} \cup D^{Compl}.$$

With the set of hypotheses H as a formal parameter for the string to be parsed, we have fully specified the parsing system $\mathbb{P}_{pLC} = \langle \mathcal{I}_{pLC}, H, D_{pLC} \rangle$.
□

A chart parser is obtained from **pLC** as follows.

- The initial chart comprises the hypotheses for the given sentence;
- the initial agenda contains the consequent of the (only) *initialize* deduction step.

10.3 Correctness of the LC chart parser

The chart parser based on **pLC** is correct if, for an arbitrary grammar G and any string $a_1 \ldots a_n$, it holds that

$$[S; S \rightarrow \gamma\bullet, 0, n] \in \mathcal{V}(\mathbb{P}_{pLC}) \text{ if and only if } S \Rightarrow \gamma \Rightarrow^* a_1 \ldots a_n.$$

(cf. Definition 4.22).

Unlike for the Earley chart parser, however, it not trivial to determine the set of valid items $\mathcal{V}(\mathbb{P}_{pLC})$. We will proceed as follows. First a set of *viable* items is postulated, i.e., items that ought to be recognized by the parser. Subsequently, we will prove that $\mathcal{V}(\mathbb{P}_{pLC})$ contains all viable items and no other items.

Definition 10.3. (*(pLC-)viable items*)
We define *pLC-viability* (or shortly *viability*) for each type of item.

- Let Ω denote the set of viable predict items. Ω is the smallest set satisfying the following conditions:
  ○ $[0, S] \in \Omega$;
  ○ if there are $A, B, C, X, \alpha, \beta, i, j$ such that
    (*i*) $[i, A] \in \Omega$,
    (*ii*) $A >_l^* B$,
    (*iii*) $B \Rightarrow X\alpha C\beta$,
    (*iv*) $X\alpha \Rightarrow^* a_{i+1} \ldots a_j$
    then $[j, C] \in \Omega$.

- A left-corner item $[A; B \rightarrow \alpha \bullet \beta, i, j]$ is viable if
  - (i) $[i, A]$ is viable,
  - (ii) $A >_\ell^* B$,
  - (iii) $B \Rightarrow \alpha\beta$, and
  - (iv) $\alpha \Rightarrow^* a_{i+1} \dots a_j$.
- A terminal item $[a, j-1, j]$ is viable if $a = a_j$. $\square$

Note that, by definition, items $[A; B \rightarrow \alpha \bullet \beta, i, j]$ come in two variants: either $\alpha \neq \varepsilon$ or $\alpha = \beta = \varepsilon$. Both cases are covered in the above definition; it should be clear that $\mathcal{I}$ does not contain items $[A; B \rightarrow \bullet \beta, i, j]$ with $\beta \neq \varepsilon$.

It is possible to give a direct characterization of viable predict items that is equivalent to the inductive specification in the above definition.

Lemma 10.4.
Let Ω be as in Definition 10.3 and Ω' defined by

$$\Omega' \;=\; \{[0, S]\} \cup \{[i, A] \mid \exists k, B, X, \alpha, \beta, \gamma : \; S \Rightarrow^* a_1 \dots a_k B \gamma \wedge$$
$$B \Rightarrow X \alpha A \beta \wedge$$
$$X \alpha \Rightarrow^* a_{k+1} \dots a_i \; \}.$$

Then $\Omega' = \Omega$.

Proof. The proof makes use of the "walk length function" w that will be defined in the proof of Lemma 10.7. Therefore it is postponed to page 215. $\square$

From Definition 10.3 it follows immediately how the grammatical correctness of a string can be expressed by means of viable LC items.

Corollary 10.5.
An item $[S; S \rightarrow \gamma \bullet, 0, n]$ is pLC-viable for a string $a_1 \dots a_n$ if and only if $S \Rightarrow \gamma \Rightarrow^* a_1 \dots a_n$. $\square$

In order to establish the correctness of the LC parser it remains to be proven that viability and validity are equivalent properties in **pLC**.

Lemma 10.6. Any item contained in $\mathcal{V}(\mathbb{P}_{pLC})$ is is pLC-viable (i.e., the LC chart parser is sound).

Proof. This follows straightforwardly from the following observations:

- all initial items are viable;
- for each deduction step in D it holds that viability of the consequent is implied by the viability of the antecedents. $\square$

Lemma 10.7.
All pLC-viable items are contained in $\mathcal{V}(\mathbb{P}_{pLC})$ (i.e., the LC chart parser is complete).

Proof. We will first explain the general idea, which is quite simple, before we spell out the somewhat cumbersome details.

A generic method to prove the completeness of a parsing schema (and hence a chart parser) is the following. To each viable item ξ a number $f(\xi)$ is assigned, that has some relation to the minimum number of steps needed for recognizing ξ. If we are able to establish for each viable item ξ

there is a deduction step $\eta_1, \ldots, \eta_k \vdash \xi$ such that $\eta_1, \ldots \eta_k$ are viable and, moreover,

$$f(\xi) > f(\eta_i) \text{ for } 1 \leq i \leq k, \tag{10.2}$$

then it follows by induction on the value of f that all viable items are valid. The key problem is to pick the right function f.

For our LC chart parser we define a function w that corresponds to the (length of the top-down left-to-right) *walk* through a (partial) parse tree that is needed to derive the item. For the tree walk we count all edge traversals; the dotted lines in Figure 10.5 as well as the arrows. The definition of w makes use of the following parameters:

- π: the size of the tree walk for the relevant predict item;
- λ: the number of edges traversed in top-down direction by the $>_\ell^*$ relation;
- μ: length of a derivation $X\alpha \Rightarrow^\mu a_{i+1} \ldots a_j$ for items $[A; B \rightarrow X\alpha \cdot \beta, i, j]$.

Furthermore, we have to take into account that in general different (partial) parse trees may exist that account for the same item. Hence we have to take the minimum number of steps in such a walk in an arbitrary tree.

The partial function $w : \mathcal{I}_{pLC} \twoheadrightarrow \mathbb{N}$ is defined by

- $w([0, S]) = 0$,
- $w([j, C]) = \min\{\pi + (\lambda+1) + 2\mu \mid \exists A, B, X, \alpha, \beta, i, j :$
  $[A; B \rightarrow X\alpha \cdot C\beta, i, j]$ is viable $\wedge$
  $\pi = w([i, A]) \wedge$
  $A >_\ell^\lambda B \wedge$
  $X\alpha \Rightarrow^\mu a_{i+1} \ldots a_j \}$
- $w([A; B \rightarrow \alpha \cdot \beta, i, j]) = \min\{\pi + \lambda + 2\mu \mid \pi = w([i, A]) \wedge$
  $A >_\ell^\lambda B \wedge$
  $\alpha \Rightarrow^\mu a_{i+1} \ldots a_j \}$
- $w([j, C])$ and $w([A; B \rightarrow \alpha \cdot \beta, i, j])$ are undefined if the conditions in the preceding two cases cannot be satisfied (i.e., the minimum is taken over an empty set).

We count 2μ, as each edge of the derivation tree is traversed twice. For predict items $[j, C]$ we count $\lambda + 1$ because λ edges are skipped by $A >_\ell^* B$ and an additional edge is moved down from B to C.

In order to finish the proof we have to establish

(i) $w(\xi)$ is defined for every viable item ξ;
(ii) condition (10.2) holds for each viable ξ.

As to the first point, it is easy to verify that for each viable item there are at least one π, λ, μ for which the conditions are fulfilled, hence, (by induction on the definition of viability) w is defined for all viable items.

Thus it remains to be shown for each viable item ξ that there is a deduction step $\eta_1, \ldots, \eta_k \vdash \xi$ such that all η_i are viable and have a lower w-value than ξ. We will spell it out as an exemplary case; in subsequent proofs this part will be omitted. We distinguish between

- predict-items (a);
- different types of LC items:
  - LC items with the dot in leftmost position (b);
  - LC with a single symbol preceding the dot:
    - a terminal symbol preceding the dot (c),
    - a nonterminal symbol preceding the dot (d);
  - LC items with two or more symbols preceding the dot:
    - a terminal symbol immediately preceding the dot (e),
    - a nonterminal symbol immediately preceding the dot (f).

For viable items of each type we will give a deduction step with viable antecedents and show that the condition on w-values is satisfied.

(a) Let $\xi = [j, C]$.

From the viability of ξ we obtain that there are $A, B, X, \alpha, \beta, i, \pi, \lambda, \mu$ such that

(i) $[i, A]$ is viable,

(ii) $s([i, A]) = \pi$,

(iii) $A >_\ell^\lambda B$,

(iv) $B \Rightarrow X\alpha C\beta$,

(v) $X\alpha \Rightarrow^\mu a_{i+1} \ldots a_j$,

(vi) $w(\xi) = \pi + (\lambda + 1) + 2\mu$.

From (i)–(v) it follows that $\eta = [A; B \rightarrow X\alpha \cdot C\beta]$ is viable and $\eta \vdash \xi$.

Moreover, $w(\eta) = \pi + \lambda + 2\mu = w(\xi) - 1$.

(b) Let $\xi = [A; B \rightarrow \cdot, i, i]$ be viable.

ξ can only be recognized by $[i, A] \vdash \xi$, where $A >_\ell^* B$.

Moreover, $w(\xi) = w([i, A]) + \lambda + 2$ with minimal λ such that $A >_\ell^\lambda B$.

(c) Let $\xi = [A; B \rightarrow a \cdot \beta, i, i+1]$ be viable.

ξ can only be recognized by $[i, A] \vdash \xi$, where $A >_\ell^* a$.

Moreover, $w(\xi) = w([i, A]) + \lambda + 2$ with minimal λ such that $A >_\ell^\lambda a$.

(d) Let $\xi = [A; B \rightarrow C \cdot \beta, i, j]$ be viable.

There must be some viable $\eta = [A; C \rightarrow \gamma \cdot, i, j]$ such that $[i, A], \eta \vdash \xi$.

Let $A >_\ell^\lambda B$ and $C \Rightarrow^\mu a_{i+1} \ldots a_j$ for minimal λ and μ,

then $A >_\ell^{\lambda+1} C$ and $\gamma \Rightarrow^{\mu-1} a_{i+1} \ldots a_j$.

Hence, $w(\xi) = w([i, A]) + \lambda + 2\mu) > w([i, A])$.

Moreover, $w(\eta) = w[i, A] + (\lambda + 1) + 2(\mu - 1) = w(\xi) - 1$.

(e) Let $\xi = [A; B{\to}X\alpha a.\beta, i, j]$ be viable.
   Then $\eta = [A; B{\to}X\alpha.a\beta, i, j-1]$ is viable and $\eta, [j-1, a, j] \vdash \xi$.
   Clearly, $w(\eta) = w(\xi) - 2$.

(f) Let $\xi = [A; B{\to}X\alpha C.\beta, i, k]$ be viable.
   Then it must hold that
   (i) $[i, A]$ is viable.
   Furthermore, there are j, λ, p, q such that
   (ii) $A >_\ell^\lambda B$,
   (iii) $X\alpha{\Rightarrow}^p a_{i+1} \ldots a_j$,
   (iv) $C{\Rightarrow}\gamma{\Rightarrow}^{q-1} a_{j+1} \ldots a_k$,
   (v) $w(\xi) = w([i, A]) + \lambda + 2(p + q)$.
   From (i)–(iii) it follows that $\eta = [A; B{\to}X\alpha.C\beta, i, j]$ is viable and $[j, C]$
   is viable.
   With (iv) we obtain that $\zeta = [C; C{\to}\gamma., j, k]$ is viable.
   Furthermore, $\eta, \zeta \vdash \xi \in D$ and if follows that $w(\eta) = w(\xi) - q < w(\xi)$;
   $w(\zeta) = w([j, C]) + 2(q-1) \le w([i, A]) + (\lambda+1) + 2(p+q-1) = w(\xi) - 1$.

Hence we may conclude, by simultaneous induction on the w-value for all
types of items, that pLC-viable items are contained in $\mathcal{V}(\mathbb{P}_{pLC})$. □

Theorem 10.8. (*correctness of the* **pLC** *chart parser*)
For any grammar $G \in \mathcal{CFG}$ and string $a_1 \ldots a_n$ it holds that

$$[S; S{\to}\gamma., 0, n] \in \mathcal{V}(\mathbb{P}_{pLC}) \text{ if and only if } S{\Rightarrow}\gamma{\Rightarrow}^* a_1 \ldots a_n.$$

Proof: directly from Lemmata 10.6 and 10.7 and Corollary 10.5 □

It has been left to prove that the equality $\Omega = \Omega'$ holds for Ω, Ω' as defined
in Definition 10.3 and Lemma 10.4. In that proof we make use of the tree
walk function that has been defined in the proof of Lemma 10.7 (but, in order
to avoid circularity, none of the results established after Lemma 10.4 should
be used).

Proof of Lemma 10.4.

(i) $\Omega \subset \Omega'$ is proven by induction on on $w([i, A])$.
   Let $[j, C] \in \Omega$ be viable and predicted by $[A; B{\to}X\alpha.C\beta, i, j]$. Then from
   $w([i, A]) < w([j, C])$ we may assume $[i, A] \in \Omega'$ and it follows trivially
   that $[j, C] \in \Omega'$.

(ii) $\Omega \supset \Omega'$ is obtained as follows.
   Let $[i, A] \in \Omega'$, $S{\Rightarrow}^* a_1 \ldots a_h B\gamma$, $B{\Rightarrow}X\alpha A\beta$, $X\alpha{\Rightarrow}^* a_{k+1} \ldots a_i$.
   In the derivation $S{\Rightarrow}^* a_1 \ldots a_h B\gamma$, we must identify the *most direct an-*
   cestor of B (or possibly B itself) which is *not* a left corner. Let's call
   this D. If B is not a left corner, then D is B. Otherwise, B has been
   produced by some $E{\to}\alpha' B\beta'$. If $\alpha' \ne \varepsilon$, then $D = E$, otherwise E will
   have been produced by some $F{\to}\alpha'' E\beta''$, and so on.
   D has been produced by some $C{\to}Y\delta D\gamma'$, hence there is a derivation

$$S \Rightarrow^* \delta'C\gamma'' \Rightarrow \delta'Y\delta D\gamma'\gamma'' \Rightarrow^* a_1 \ldots a_h D\gamma'\gamma'' \Rightarrow^* a_1 \ldots a_h B\gamma.$$

Clearly, $[h, D] \in \Omega$, $D >_{\ell}^* B$, $B \Rightarrow X\alpha A\beta$, $X\alpha \Rightarrow^* a_{h+1} \ldots a_i$, hence $[i, A] \in \Omega$. $\qquad\qquad\square$

10.4 An LC chart parser with simplified items

An LC item $[A; B \rightarrow \alpha \bullet \beta, i, j]$ can be seen as consisting of a *predicted part* $[A, i]$ and a *recognized part* $[B \rightarrow \alpha \bullet \beta, i, j]$. The LC chart parser can be simplified somewhat by disconnecting these two parts. The predict parts correspond to predict items that are contained on the chart already; the recognized parts are in fact conventional Earley items.

The reason for *not* introducing this simplification straight away is the relation between the LC chart parser and the HC chart parser that will be discussed in the next chapter. In the HC case there are good reasons for keeping the predicted and recognized parts within a single item, when unification grammars rather than context-free grammars are used.

A simplified parsing schema for the LC chart parser, **sLC**, is derived from the **pLC** schema as follows.

- LC items are replaced by Earley items,
- The deduction steps are extended, where necessary, with extra antecedents and conditions.

Schema 10.9. (sLC)
We define a parsing system $\mathbb{P}_{sLC}$ for an arbitrary context-free grammar $G \in \mathcal{CFG}$. The domain $\mathcal{I}_{sLC}$ en deduction steps $\mathcal{D}_{sLC}$ are given by

$$\mathcal{I}^{Pred} = \{[i, A] \mid A \in N \land i \geq 0\},$$

$$\mathcal{I}^{LC(i)} = \{[B \rightarrow X\alpha \bullet \beta, i, j] \mid B \rightarrow X\alpha\beta \in P \land 0 \leq i \leq j\},$$

$$\mathcal{I}^{LC(ii)} = \{[B \rightarrow \bullet, j, j] \mid B \rightarrow \varepsilon \in P \land j \geq 0\},$$

$$\mathcal{I}_{sLC} = \mathcal{I}^{Pred} \cup \mathcal{I}^{LC(i)} \cup \mathcal{I}^{LC(ii)};$$

$$D^{Init} = \{\vdash [0, S]\},$$

$$D^{LC(a)} = \{[i, C], [a, i, i+1] \vdash [B \rightarrow a \bullet \beta, i, i+1] \mid C >_{\ell}^* B\},$$

$$D^{LC(A)} = \{[i, C], [A \rightarrow \gamma \bullet, i, j] \vdash [B \rightarrow A \bullet \beta, i, j] \mid C >_{\ell}^* B\},$$

$$D^{LC(\varepsilon)} = \{[i, C] \vdash [B \rightarrow \bullet, i, i] \mid C >_{\ell}^* B\},$$

$$D^{Pred} = \{[B \rightarrow \alpha \bullet C\beta, i, j] \vdash [j, C]\},$$

$$D^{Scan} = \{[B \rightarrow \alpha \bullet a\beta, i, j], [a, j, j+1] \vdash [B \rightarrow \alpha a \bullet \beta, i, j+1]\},$$

$$D^{Compl} = \{[B{\rightarrow}\alpha{\bullet}A\beta, i, j], [A{\rightarrow}\gamma{\bullet}, j, k] \vdash [B{\rightarrow}\alpha A{\bullet}\beta, i, k]\},$$

$$D_{sLC} = D^{Init} \cup D^{LC(a)} \cup D^{LC(A)} \cup D^{LC(\varepsilon)} \cup D^{Pred} \cup D^{Scan} \cup D^{Compl}.$$

With the set of hypotheses H to be instantiated by (10.1) for any string, we have fully specified a parsing system $\mathbb{P}_{sLC} = \langle \mathcal{I}_{sLC}, H, D_{sLC} \rangle$ for an arbitrary grammar $G \in \mathcal{CFG}$. □

The set of valid items $\mathcal{V}(\mathbb{P}_{sLC})$ for any sentence $a_1 \ldots a_n$ is given by

- $[a, j-1, j]$ is valid iff $a = a_j$
- $[i, A]$ is valid if
  - $[i, A] = [0, S]$, or
  - if there are $k, B, X, \alpha, \beta, \gamma$ such that
    $S{\Rightarrow}^* a_1 \ldots a_k B\gamma$, $B{\Rightarrow}X\alpha A\beta$, and $X\alpha{\Rightarrow}^* a_{k+1} \ldots a_i$.
    (cf. Lemma 10.4).
- An Earley item $[A{\rightarrow}\alpha{\bullet}\beta, i, j]$ is valid if there is a γ such that
    $S{\Rightarrow}^* a_1 \ldots a_i A\gamma$ and $X\alpha{\Rightarrow}^* a_{i+1} \ldots a_j$.
  Note, again, that this applies only to items in $\mathcal{I}_{sLC}$, i.e., $\alpha \neq \varepsilon$ or $\alpha = \beta = \varepsilon$.

The correctness of the above characterization of $\mathcal{V}(\mathbb{P}_{sLC})$ follows straightforwardly from Theorem 10.8 and the relation between sLC and pLC that will be established in the next section.

10.5 The relation between pLC, sLC, and LC

We will now compare the parsing schemata pLC and sLC with LC as defined in Example 4.36 and establish relations between these schemata as defined in Chapters 5 and 6.

We have to differentiate between the schemata defined in Chapter 4, called *basic schemata* henceforth, and the more liberal parsing schemata that we introduced in this chapter. Items in the domain of a basic parsing schema, by definition, are the equivalence classes of a particular relation on the set of trees. Hence, the domain of a basic parsing schema is a subset of a partition of the set of trees.[7] This is not the case for the domains $\mathcal{I}_{pLC}$ and $\mathcal{I}_{sLC}$.

Let us look at sLC first. The Earley items in sLC are identical to the items of LC as defined in Example 4.36 (with one exception: the special items $[S{\rightarrow}{\bullet}\gamma, 0, 0]$ are not used in sLC). The predict items, on the other hand should be regarded as *equivalence classes of LC items*. The meaning of recognizing a predict item $[i, A]$ is to denote that *some* Earley item $[D{\rightarrow}\gamma{\bullet}A\delta, h, i]$ has been recognized. By making the item set more sophisticated we have decreased the number of deduction steps, notwithstanding the fact that we have *increased* the number of valid items.

---

[7] Note, however, that a schema may also contain items that denote the empty set; cf. Section 4.5

One could argue that the **sLC** chart parser is an implementation of the underlying basic parsing schema **LC**. By adding predict items to the chart parser we have created a data structure that stores the relevant properties of items to be used as possible antecedents. Hence, the **sLC** chart parser is an optimization of a chart parser directly based on **LC**, without this extra data structure. The tree walk of a chart parser based on **LC** is shown in Figure 10.6. Less items are recognized, but the higher search costs are not displayed in the figure.

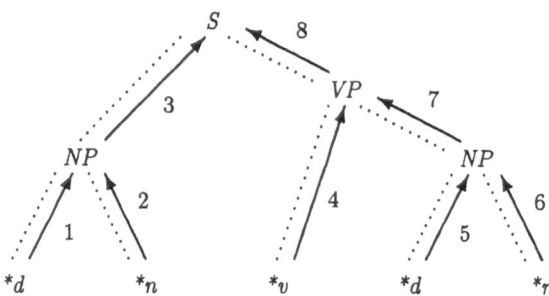

Fig. 10.6. A tree walk according to the schema **LC**

In a similar way, the **pLC** chart parser can be seen as an extension of the **sLC** chart parser. LC items are annotated with the predict item that cause their recognition. This is a useful feature when the predicted symbol carries attributes that might rule out certain applications of *left-corner* deduction steps. For context-free parsing it only increases the number of items. Hence this is not an optimization. We have introduced **pLC** primarily as a step towards the definition of the schema **pHC** in Chapter 11.

We can apply the relations between parsing schemata that were defined in Part II. The definitions of parsing schemata in this chapter are based on intuition and not formally derived from the theory in Part II. As a result, it *roughly* holds that **sLC** is a step refinement of **LC** and it *roughly* holds that **pLC** is a step refinement of **sLC**. "Roughly" means, here, that a few inessential details have to be swept under the rug. In order to get things fit exactly, we will define two auxiliary parsing schemata **LC'** and **pLC'** that differ from **LC** and **pLC** only in minute (and for practical purposes irrelevant) details.

The schema **LC'** differs from **LC** in the following respect:

- All items of the form $[S \to \cdot\gamma, 0, 0]$ in $\mathcal{I}_{LC}$ are collapsed into a single item $[0, S]$ in $\mathcal{I}_{LC'}$; antecedents in deduction steps are adapted accordingly.

Then the (rather trivial) item contraction relation **LC** $\overset{\text{ic}}{\Longrightarrow}$ **LC'** holds.

The schema **pLC'** differs from **pLC** in the following respect:

- *left-corner*(A) deduction steps $[C; A{\rightarrow}\gamma{\bullet}, i, j] \vdash [C; B{\rightarrow}A{\bullet}\beta, i, j]$ in D_{LC} are replaced in $D_{LC'}$ by *left-corner*(A) deduction steps

$$[i, C], [C; A{\rightarrow}\gamma{\bullet}, i, j] \vdash [C; B{\rightarrow}A{\bullet}\beta, i, j].$$

Then the relation **pLC** $\overset{\text{df}}{\Longrightarrow}$ **pLC'** holds, as a *dynamic filter* may add antecedents to deduction steps. This is a particularly degenerate case of dynamic filter (and not worth to coin a special name for) as the added antecedents don't filter anything. An item $[C; A{\rightarrow}\gamma{\bullet}, i, j]$ cannot be recognized without having recognized $[i, C]$ before.

Having settled these details, we can now state the desired result.

Theorem 10.10. (*relations between* **LC**, **sLC** *and* **pLC**)
The following step refinement and item refinement relations hold:

$$\textbf{LC'} \overset{\text{sr}}{\Longrightarrow} \textbf{sLC} \overset{\text{ir}}{\Longrightarrow} \textbf{pLC'}.$$

Proof. It is clear from the definitions that $\mathcal{I}_{LC'} \subset \mathcal{I}_{sLC}$ and it follows straightforwardly that $\vdash^*_{LC'} \subset \vdash^*_{sLC}$, hence **LC'** $\overset{\text{sr}}{\longrightarrow}$ **sLC**.
The item contraction function $f : \mathcal{I}_{pLC'} \rightarrow \mathcal{I}_{sLC}$ is defined by

$$f([A; B{\rightarrow}\alpha{\bullet}\beta, i, j]) = [B{\rightarrow}\alpha{\bullet}\beta, i, j].$$

It follows immediately that $\mathcal{I}_{sLC} = f(\mathcal{I}_{pLC'})$ and $\Delta_{sLC} = f(\Delta_{pLC'})$,

hence **sLC** $\overset{\text{ir}}{\Longrightarrow}$ **pLC'**.   □

We recall from Corollary 5.8 that item contraction (the inverse of item refinement) is correctness preserving.[8] Hence, as we have proven **pLC** correct, the correctness of **sLC** follows.

Informally we write $\approx$ for the trivial relations that denote irrelevant syntactic differences between parsing schemata. Hence, informally, the results of this section can be summarized as

$$\textbf{LC} \approx \textbf{LC'} \overset{\text{sr}}{\Longrightarrow} \textbf{sLC} \overset{\text{ir}}{\Longrightarrow} \textbf{pLC'} \approx \textbf{pLC} .$$

10.6 Conclusion

The LC parsing is well-known, both in the Computer Science and Computational Linguistics literature (cf. Rosenkrantz and Lewis [1970], Pratt [1975], Matsumoto [1983], op den Akker [1988], Resnik [1992], and Nederhof [1993])

---

[8] Note, however, that because of the more sophisticated items **sLC** and **pLC** do not belong to the class of semiregular parsing schemata to which Corollary 5.8 applies. The extension with predict items and LC items is inessential, however, and a similar result for these parsing schemata can be derived from Definition 5.5.

but it is not very common to describe an LC parser as a chart parser. By doing so, the very close relations between LC parsing and Earley chart parsing have been made explicit in a simple way (informally in Section 4.6 and more formally in Example 5.22). In this chapter we have given a somewhat more convenient description of an LC chart parser, making use of additional *predict* items.

A chart parser is not necessarily the most efficient implementation of the LC algorithm, Nederhof [1993, 1994a, 1994b] has defined a generalized LC parser based on a graph-structured stack and discusses further optimizations. The advantage of describing the LC parser as a chart parser – other than a nice application of the framework developed in part II – is that it is a more general description. In the next chapter we will introduce parsing schemata **pHC** and **sHC** for Head-Corner parsers that are straightforward extensions of the schemata **pLC** and **sLC**.

11. Head-Corner chart parsing

"Our Latin teachers were apparently right", Martin Kay [1989] remarks, "You should start [parsing] with the main verb. This will tell you what kinds of subjects and objects to look for and what cases they will be in. When you come to look for these, you should also start by trying to find the main word, because this will tell you most about what else to look for."

In this chapter we introduce and analyse a few parsing schemata for Head-Corner (HC) parsers, that implement the general idea of head-driven parsing as sketched by Kay in his usual lucid style. When it comes down to defining the details with mathematical rigor, it is indeed a lot of detail we get involved with. Looking at the important words first means jumping up and down the sentence. Keeping track of where you have been and where the next interesting word might be located requires a more sophisticated administration than simply working through the sentence from left to right. In order to understand what is going on, it is of great help to have grasped the ideas behind the LC parsers presented in Chapter 10. HC parsing can be seen as a generalization of LC parsing – it is just a different corner we start with, all the rest is similar (but involves more bookkeeping). As in the previous chapter, the mathematical details of correctness proofs and complexity analysis are put into separate sections. These can be skipped without losing the thread of the discussion.

Before we start to define Head-Corner parsers, we need to have some notion of a head. For this purpose we introduce context-free head grammars in Section 11.1. In 11.2 we introduce a predictive HC chart parsing schema **pHC** as a generalization of **pLC**. The correctness of **pHC** is proven in 11.3. This schema is the basis for two further developments.

For Head-Corner parsing of context-free grammars, we develop a simplified schema **sHC** in 11.4 (and prove this to be correct in 11.5). A detailed complexity analysis in 11.6 will show that, despite the increased sophistication in administrative details, the schema can be implemented with a worst-case complexity that is as good as that of Graham, Harrison, and Ruzzo's variant of the Earley parser – the optimal worst-case complexity for practical context-free parsers known today. The relation between **pHC**, **sHC** and the parsing schemata of Part II is established in 11.7.

In Section 11.8 we extend the schema **pHC** to parsing of unification grammars, using the notation that was developed (and motivated) in Chapter 8. Related approaches are briefly discussed in 11.9, conclusions follow in 11.10.

Like Chapter 10, this chapter is based on cooperative work with Rieks op den Akker ([Sikkel and op den Akker, 1992, 1993, 1996]). Section 11.8 is based on a Head-Corner parser for unification grammars that has been defined and implemented by Margriet Verlinden [1993]. The detailed complexity analysis in 11.6, the embedding of the HC parsers in the parsing schemata framework in 11.7, and the schema for a HC parser for unification grammars in 11.8 have not been published before.

11.1 Context-free Head Grammars

In order to start parsing a constituent from its head, we have to formally introduce the notion of a head. For context-free grammars this is done as follows.

Definition 11.1. (*heads in context-free grammars*)
A *context-free head grammar* is a 5-tuple $G = (N, \Sigma, P, S, h)$, with h a function that assigns a natural number to each production in P.
Let $|p|$ denote the length of the right-hand side of p. Then h is constrained to the following values:

- $h(p) = 0$ for $|p| = 0$,
- $1 \leq h(p) \leq |p|$ for $|p| > 0$.

The *head* of a production p is the $h(p)$-th symbol of the right-hand side; empty productions have head ε. □

In a much more practical notation for head grammars, we do not define the function h explicitly, but simply underline the head of each production. The head grammar G for our running example is given by

$$S \rightarrow NP\ \underline{VP},$$
$$VP \rightarrow \underline{{}^*v}\ NP,$$
$$NP \rightarrow {}^*det\ \underline{{}^*n}.$$

While there is a linguistic motivation for the notion of a head in natural language grammars (we come back to this in Section 11.8), this is not the case for arbitrary context-free grammars. One could argue that heads are not part of the grammar but a function that is attributed to the grammar *by the designer of the parser*. Given a context-free grammar, one could ask the question which allocation of heads is optimal for the (worst-case or average-case) efficiency of a parser. We will not address such questions here, and take the allocation of heads as given. A special case that must be mentioned, however, is the following:

$r(p) = 1$ for all nonempty productions p,

i.e., the head of each production is the left corner. In that case the HC and LC chart parser will be identical.[1]

11.2 A predictive Head-Corner chart parser

A Left-Corner parser proceeds through sentence from left to right; a Head-Corner (HC) parser starts with the more important words, leaving the less important words to be processed later. How this works in detail is the subject of this section.

For the LC chart parser that was introduced in 10.2 there is no need to state that it is predictive. LC parser have that property by definition. The bottom-up parsing schema **buLC** as defined in Chapter 4 is in fact a notational variant of bottom-up Earley and has been introduced only as an auxiliary construct for the derivation of the schema **LC**. For head-corner parsers the inclusion of top-down prediction is not self-evident; it is the combination of HC chart parsing and top-down prediction that is the innovative aspect of the parser presented here. At the same conference where Kay made his general statement on head-driven parsing that was quoted in the introduction to this chapter, Satta and Stock [1989] presented a head-driven chart parser that works purely bottom-up. The Head-Corner parser to be presented here can roughly be classified as an extension of the Satta and Stock parser with top-down prediction as proposed by Kay.

We introduce the HC chart parser in the same way as the LC chart parser in Section 10.2.

Definition 11.2. (*transitive and reflexive head-corner relation*)
The relation $>_h$ on $N \times (V \cup \{\varepsilon\})$ is defined by

$A >_h U$ if there is a production $p = A \rightarrow \alpha \in P$ with U the head of p.

The transitive and reflexive closure of $>_h$ is denoted $>_h^*$.   □

For our trivial example grammar, the relation $>_h^*$ comprises

$S >_h^* S, \quad S >_h^* VP, \quad S >_h^* {}^* v,$

$VP >_h^* VP, \quad VP >_h^* {}^* v, \quad NP >_h^* NP, \quad NP >_h^* {}^* n.$

---

[1] There are some notational differences, of course, caused by the more general nature of the HC parser. Furthermore, there is a tiny difference in implementation (pointed out to me by Margriet Verlinden): the HC parsing schemata allow the parser to leave gaps in carrying out head-corner steps (even though this does not make sense when all heads are leftmost), whereas the LC parsing schemata do not allow such gaps.

If the relation $A>_h^* a$ holds between a nonterminal A and a terminal a, we call a a *lexical head* of A. For grammar G, lexical heads of a sentence must be of the category $*v$.

The HC chart parser uses the following kinds of items:

$[l, r, A]$: *predict items* or *goals*,

$[l, r, A; B{\rightarrow}\alpha{\bullet}\beta{\bullet}\gamma, i, j]$: *head-corner (HC) items*,

$[a, j - 1, j]$: terminal items as in the Earley chart parser.

The items of the HC chart parser are more complex than the items of the LC chart parser, due to the fact that constituents no longer are recognized from left to right. Recognition of items should be interpreted as follows.

- A predict item $[l, r, A]$ is recognized if a constituent A must be looked for, located somewhere between l and r. Such a constituent should either stretch from l up to some j (if we are working to the right from the head of some production) or from r down to some j (if we are working to the left from the head of some production), with $l \leq j \leq r$. But, as we start parsing A from a lexical head that might be located anywhere between l and r, the distinction between these two cases is irrelevant.
- An HC item $[l, r, A; B{\rightarrow}\alpha{\bullet}\beta{\bullet}\gamma, i, j]$ is recognized if $[l, r, A]$ has been set as a goal, $A>_h^* B$ holds, and $\beta {\Rightarrow}^* a_{i+1} \ldots a_j$ has been established. Such an item will only be recognized if the head of $B{\rightarrow}\alpha\beta\gamma$ is contained in β.

In order to get an intuitive idea of what is going on, we will first look at the walk through our single parse tree that is performed by the HC chart parser. A formal definition is given afterwards. The *head-corner tree walk* for our example is shown in Figure 11.1. It is similar to the left-corner tree walk in Figure 10.5. There is only one difference: from a nonterminal we first visit (the subtree with as it root) the head daughter.

By analogy to the LC case, steps down to a nonterminal head are absent. No steps down need be taken by the algorithm along paths of heads, as these are encoded in the relation $>_h^*$. Steps down to *non-head* nonterminal daughters correspond to setting new goals. The final chart of the head-corner parser is shown in Figure 11.2. The numbers of the items on the chart correspond to the labels of arrows in Figure 10.5. The names of the steps that appear in the *motivation* column should be clear, by analogy to the LC chart parser. Note, however, that unlike the LC case, we sometimes proceed in rightward direction and sometimes in leftward direction. As a consequence, two different cases of *scan*, *complete* and *predict* steps exist.

Schema 11.3. (pHC)
We define a parsing system $\mathbb{P}_{pHC}$ for an arbitrary context-free head grammar G. The domain $\mathcal{I}_{pHC}$ is given by

$$\mathcal{I}^{Pred} = \{[l, r, A] \mid A \in N \ \wedge \ 0 \le l \le r\},$$

$$\mathcal{I}^{HC(i)} = \{[l, r, A; B \to \alpha \bullet \beta_1 X \beta_2 \bullet \gamma, i, j] \mid A \in N \ \wedge \ A >_h^* B \ \wedge \\ B \to \alpha \beta_1 \underline{X} \beta_2 \gamma \in P \ \wedge \ 0 \le l \le i \le j \le r\},$$

$$\mathcal{I}^{HC(ii)} = \{[l, r, A; B \to \bullet\bullet, j, j] \mid A \in N \ \wedge \ A >_h^* B \ \wedge \\ B \to \varepsilon \in P \ \wedge \ 0 \le l \le j \le r\},$$

$$\mathcal{I}_{pHC} = \mathcal{I}^{Pred} \cup \mathcal{I}^{HC(i)} \cup \mathcal{I}^{HC(ii)}.$$

It should be noted that some restrictions are enforced by the the definition of the domain. The left-hand side of the recognized part must be a transitive/reflexive head of the nonterminal in the goal part. Hence this condition need not be stated again when we define the deduction steps.

The set of hypotheses is a formal parameter that can be instantiated for any particular sentence. In this case, however, unlike the schema **pLC**, we need to be able to derive the length of the sentence from the set of hypotheses. This information is provided by a special end-of-sentence marker. Hence, for arbitrary sentences $a_1 \dots a_n$ a set of hypotheses is defined as

$$H = \{[a_1, 0, 1], \ \dots, \ [a_n, n-1, n], \ [\$, n, n+1]\} \tag{11.1}$$

The definition of D_{pHC} looks complicated because of the complexity of the items and the multitude of different cases. The best way to understand the

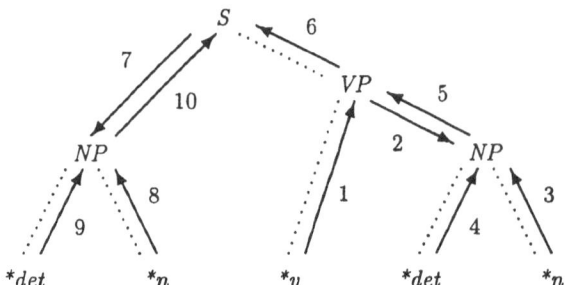

Fig. 11.1. A head-corner tree walk

Fig. 11.2. A completed HC chart (excluding terminal items)

	item	motivation
(0)	$[0, 5, S]$	initial agenda
(1)	$[0, 5, S; VP \to \bullet *v \bullet NP, 2, 3]$	head-corner(a) (0,iii)
(2)	$[3, 5, NP]$	right predict (1)
(3)	$[3, 5, NP; NP \to *det \bullet *n\bullet, 4, 5]$	head-corner(a) (2,v)
(4)	$[3, 5, NP; NP \to \bullet *det \ *n\bullet, 3, 5]$	left scan (3,iv)
(5)	$[0, 5, S; VP \to \bullet *v \ NP\bullet, 2, 5]$	right complete (1,4)
(6)	$[0, 5, S; S \to NP \bullet VP\bullet, 2, 5]$	head-corner(A) (5)
(7)	$[0, 2, NP]$	left predict (6)
(8)	$[0, 2, NP; NP \to *det \bullet *n\bullet, 1, 2]$	head-corner(a) (7,ii)
(9)	$[0, 2, NP; NP \to \bullet *det \ *n\bullet, 0, 2]$	left scan (8,i)
(10)	$[0, 5, S; S \to \bullet NP \ VP\bullet, 0, 5]$	left complete (6,9)

definition is to keep in mind that each type of deduction step is a straightforward extension of a corresponding type of LC deduction step. We distinguish subsets of D for *initialize, terminal head-corner, nonterminal head-corner, empty head-corner, left predict, right predict, left scan, right scan, left complete,* and *right complete* deduction steps. The different kinds of head-corner steps are abbreviated with the symbols a, A, and ε as usual.

$$D^{Init} \;\; = \;\; \{[\$,n,n+1] \;\vdash\; [0,n,S]\},$$

$$D^{HC(a)} \;\; = \;\; \{[l,r,A],\,[b,j-1,j] \;\vdash\; [l,r,A;B{\to}\alpha{\bullet}b{\bullet}\gamma,j-1,j]\},$$

$$D^{HC(A)} \;\; = \;\; \{[l,r,A;C{\to}{\bullet}\delta{\bullet},i,j] \;\vdash\; [l,r,A;B{\to}\alpha{\bullet}C{\bullet}\gamma,i,j]\},$$

$$D^{HC(\varepsilon)} \;\; = \;\; \{[l,r,A],\;\vdash\; [l,r,A;B{\to}{\bullet}{\bullet},j,j]\},$$

$$D^{lPred} \;\; = \;\; \{[l,r,A;B{\to}\alpha C{\bullet}\beta{\bullet}\gamma,i,j] \;\vdash\; [l,i,C]\},$$

$$D^{rPred} \;\; = \;\; \{[l,r,A;B{\to}\alpha{\bullet}\beta{\bullet}C\gamma,i,j] \;\vdash\; [j,r,C]\},$$

$$D^{lScan} \;\; = \;\; \{[a,j-1,j],\,[l,r,A;B{\to}\alpha a{\bullet}\beta{\bullet}\gamma,j,k] \\ \vdash\; [l,r,A;B{\to}\alpha{\bullet}a\beta{\bullet}\gamma,j-1,k]\},$$

$$D^{rScan} \;\; = \;\; \{[l,r,A;B{\to}\alpha{\bullet}\beta{\bullet}a\gamma,i,j],\,[a,j,j+1] \\ \vdash\; [l,r,A;B{\to}\alpha{\bullet}\beta a{\bullet}\gamma,i,j+1]\},$$

$$D^{lCompl} \;\; = \;\; \{[l,j,C;C{\to}{\bullet}\delta{\bullet},i,j],\,[l,r,A;B{\to}\alpha C{\bullet}\beta{\bullet}\gamma,j,k] \\ \vdash\; [l,r,A;B{\to}\alpha{\bullet}C\beta{\bullet}\gamma,i,k]\},$$

$$D^{rCompl} \;\; = \;\; \{[l,r,A;B{\to}\alpha{\bullet}\beta{\bullet}C\gamma,i,j],\,[j,r,C;C{\to}{\bullet}\delta{\bullet},j,k] \\ \vdash\; [l,r,A;B{\to}\alpha{\bullet}\beta C{\bullet}\gamma,i,k]\},$$

$$D_{pHC} \;\; = \;\; D^{Init} \cup D^{HC(a)} \cup D^{HC(A)} \cup D^{HC(\varepsilon)} \cup D^{lPred} \cup D^{rPred} \cup \\ D^{lScan} \cup D^{rScan} \cup D^{lCompl} \cup D^{rCompl}.$$

Thus we have fully specified a parsing system $\mathbb{P}_{pHC} = \langle \mathcal{I}_{pHC}, H, D_{pHC} \rangle$ for an arbitrary context-free head grammar G.   □

The chart parser based on **pHC** does not need the additional hypothesis $[\$,n,n+1]$. The initial chart contains $[a_1,0,1],\dots,[a_n,n-1,n]$; the initial agenda is set to $[0,n,S]$ as before. The end-of-sentence marker was included in the parsing schema only because D, by definition, is independent of (the length of) the string that is to be parsed. The chart is initialized for a particular given sentence.

Head-corner parsing of natural language reduces the ambiguity during the construction of a parse. Recognizing the head of a phrase first enables a more effective use of feature inheritance for the recognition of other parts of a phrase. A disadvantage, in the case of context-free grammars, is the increased complexity caused by the non-sequential way in which the sentence is processed. Some deduction steps involve 5 position markers, which means that a straightforward chart parser implementation needs $O(n^5)$ steps in the worst case. In Section 11.4 we introduce a simplified HC chart parser that has the usual $O(n^3)$ worst-case complexity. Like in the LC case, we split the items in a predicted part and a recognized part. In this case it is not entirely trivial, however, that the worst-case complexity is cubic.

Things are different for parsing unification grammars. The usual context-free worst-case complexity analysis is of little value. By keeping the predicted and recognized part within a single item, the features structures of both parts can share substructures. For "reasonable" unification grammars, this should be a much more important factor for the efficiency of the algorithm than the risk of a worst-case explosion of items. While it is always possible to blow up the efficiency of unification grammar parsers with carefully constructed nasty grammars, it is simply assumed that natural language grammars are not worst-case. In Section 11.8 we discuss an extension of the HC chart parser with feature structures.

11.3 Correctness of the HC chart parser

Similar to the correctness proof of the LC chart parser, we will first postulate a set of viable items and afterwards prove that all viable items and no others are valid.

Definition 11.4. (*(pHC-)viable items*)
We define *pHC-viability* (or shortly *viability*) for each of the types of items used.

- Let Ω denote the set of viable predict items. Ω is the smallest set satisfying the following conditions:
  - $[0, n, S] \in \Omega$,
  - if $[l, r, A] \in \Omega$ and there are $B, C, X, \alpha, \beta, \gamma, i, j$ such that
    (*i*) $A >_h^* B$,
    (*ii*) $B \rightarrow \alpha \underline{X} \beta C \gamma \in P$,
    (*iii*) $X\beta \Rightarrow^* a_{i+1} \ldots a_j$, and
    (*iv*) $l \le i \le j \le r$
    then $[j, r, C] \in \Omega$,
  - if $[l, r, A] \in \Omega$ and there are $B, C, X, \alpha, \beta, \gamma, i, j$ such that
    (*i*) $A >_h^* B$,
    (*ii*) $B \rightarrow \alpha C \beta \underline{X} \gamma \in P$,
    (*iii*) $\beta X \Rightarrow^* a_{i+1} \ldots a_j$, and
    (*iv*) $l \le i \le j \le r$
    then $[l, i, C] \in \Omega$.

- A head-corner item $[l, r, A; B \rightarrow \alpha \bullet \beta \bullet \gamma, i, j]$ is viable if
  - (i) $[l, r, A]$ is viable,
  - (ii) $A >_h^* B$,
  - (iii) $l \leq i \leq j \leq r$,
  - (iv) $\beta \Rightarrow^* a_{i+1} \ldots a_j$, and
  - (v) β contains the head of $B \rightarrow \alpha \beta \gamma$.
- A terminal item $[a, j-1, j]$ is viable if $a = a_j$;
  furthermore, $[\$, n, n+1]$ is viable.   □

Note that the definition of viable head-corner items covers both $\mathcal{I}^{HC(i)}$ and $\mathcal{I}^{HC(ii)}$. If $\beta = \varepsilon$ then $\alpha = \gamma = \varepsilon$, $i = j$, and ε is the head of $B \rightarrow \alpha \beta \gamma$.

Unlike the LC case, there is no straightforward direct definition of viability of predict items, due to the non-sequential nature of the HC parser.

Corollary 11.5. An item $[0, n, S; S \rightarrow \bullet \beta \bullet, 0, n]$ is pHC-viable for a string $a_1 \ldots a_n$ if and only if $S \Rightarrow \beta \Rightarrow^* a_1 \ldots a_n$.   □

Lemma 11.6.
Any item contained in $\mathcal{V}(\mathbb{P}_{pHC})$ is is pHC-viable
(i.e., the HC chart parser is sound).

Proof: straightforward, as Lemma 10.6.   □

Lemma 11.7.
All pHC-viable items are contained in $\mathcal{V}(\mathbb{P}_{pHC})$
(i.e., the LC chart parser is complete).

Proof. We follow the same line as in the proof of Lemma 10.7. We define a function w, the *tree walk* function, that assigns a rank value to all viable items. In order to prove (by induction on w) that each viable item is valid, it suffices that show that for each viable item ξ is the consequent of some deduction step $\eta_1, \ldots, \eta_k \vdash \xi$ with $w(\eta_i) < w(\xi)$ for $1 \leq i \leq k$.
We define the function w for each item such that it corresponds to the minimum length of a head-corner walk through a (partial) parse tree that is needed to derive the item. We count all edge traversals, also the dotted lines in Figure 11.1. The definition of w makes use of parameters π, λ, and μ that encode the w-value of a relevant predict item, the number of edges skipped by the $>_h^*$ relation, and the length of a derivation of the recognized part. See the proof of Lemma 10.7 for a more detailed account.
The partial function $w : \mathcal{I}_{pHC} \rightarrow \mathbb{N}$ is defined by

- $w([0, n, S]) = 0;$
- $w([i, j, C]) = \min(\quad \{\pi + (\lambda + 1) + 2\mu \mid \exists A, B, \alpha, \beta, \gamma, l, h :$
  $[l, j, A; B \rightarrow \alpha \cdot \beta \cdot C\gamma, h, i]$ is viable
  $\wedge\ \pi = w([l, j, A])$
  $\wedge\ A >^\lambda_h B$
  $\wedge\ \beta \Rightarrow^\mu a_{h+1} \ldots a_i \quad \}$

  $\cup \{\pi + (\lambda + 1) + 2\mu \mid \exists A, B, \alpha, \beta, \gamma, r, k :$
  $[i, r, A; B \rightarrow \alpha C \cdot \beta \cdot \gamma, j, k]$ is viable
  $\wedge\ \pi = w([i, r, A])$
  $\wedge\ A >^\lambda_h B$
  $\wedge\ \beta \Rightarrow^\mu a_{j+1} \ldots a_k \quad \}\ )$

- $w([l, r, A; B \rightarrow \alpha \cdot \beta \cdot \gamma, i, j]) = \min(\{\pi + \lambda + 2\mu \mid \pi = w([l, r, A]) \wedge$
  $A >^\lambda_H B\ \wedge$
  $\beta \Rightarrow^\mu a_{i+1} \ldots a_j \quad \}$

- $w([i, j, C])$ and $w([l, r, A; B \rightarrow \alpha \cdot \beta \cdot \gamma, i, j])$ are undefined if the conditions in the preceding two cases cannot be satisfied (i.e., the minimum is taken over an empty set).

It is easy to verify that for each viable item there are at least one π, λ, μ for which the conditions are fulfilled, hence, (by induction on the definition of viability) w is defined for all viable items.

For each viable item ξ, by analogy to the left-corner case, one can straightforwardly find a deduction step $\eta_1, \ldots, \eta_k \vdash \xi$ with $w(\eta_i) < w(\xi)$. We will not write out the individual cases. $\square$

Theorem 11.8. (*correctness of the* **pHC** *chart parser*)
For any context-free head grammar G and string $a_1 \ldots a_n$ it holds that

$$[0, n, S; S \rightarrow \cdot \beta \cdot, 0, n] \in \mathcal{V}(\mathbb{P}_{pHC}) \text{ if and only if } S \Rightarrow \beta \Rightarrow^* a_1 \ldots a_n.$$

Proof: directly from Lemmata 11.6 and 11.7 and Corollary 11.5 $\square$

11.4 HC chart parsing in cubic time

The purpose of this section is to derive a variant of the Head-Corner chart parser that conforms to the usual worst-case complexity bounds for context-free chart parsing. In contrast to the LC case, this is not trivial.

In two steps we change the schema **pHC** into a simple schema **sHC**. We also spend a few words on further optimizations. The correctness of **sHC** will be proven in Section 11.5, a detailed complexity analysis follows in 11.6.

Like in the left-corner case, we can split the HC items into a predicted and recognized part. We will call this schema **sHC'**. Some more modifications need to be carried through in order to obtain the desired parsing schema **sHC** that can be implemented in cubic time.

We use the following kinds of items

$[l, r, A]$: predict items,

$[B \rightarrow \alpha \bullet \beta \bullet \gamma, i, j]$: *double dotted* (DD) *items*,

$[a, j - 1, j]$: terminal items.

The double dotted items have the obvious interpretation. For each such item that is recognized it will hold that $\beta \Rightarrow^* a_{i+1} \ldots a_j$.

Schema 11.9. (sHC')
We define a parsing system $\mathbb{P}_{sHC'}$ for an arbitrary context-free head grammar G. The domain $\mathcal{I}_{sHC'}$ is given by

$$\mathcal{I}^{Pred} = \{[l, r, A] \mid A \in N \wedge 0 \leq l \leq r\},$$

$$\mathcal{I}^{HC(i)} = \{[B \rightarrow \alpha \bullet \beta_1 X \beta_2 \bullet \gamma, i, j] \mid B \rightarrow \alpha \beta_1 \underline{X} \beta_2 \gamma \in P \wedge 0 \leq i \leq j\},$$

$$\mathcal{I}^{HC(ii)} = \{[B \rightarrow \bullet \bullet, j, j] \mid B \rightarrow \varepsilon \in P \wedge j \geq 0\},$$

$$\mathcal{I}_{sHC'} = \mathcal{I}^{Pred} \cup \mathcal{I}^{HC(i)} \cup \mathcal{I}^{HC(ii)}.$$

In **pHC** only combinations of predicted and recognized parts were considered with a relevant head-corner relation; this was enforced by the definition of $\mathcal{I}_{pHC}$. In $\mathcal{I}_{sHC'}$ the predicted and recognized parts have been separated into different items, hence we must explicitly restrict the deduction steps only to the appropriate cases. Note that a predicted part is needed for the *scan* and *complete* steps; it provides a scope within which the position markers of the item can be extended by moving the dots outward. In the LC case, there is no need to monitor such a scope, because the LC schemata proceeds through the sentence in contiguous fashion.

Thus we obtain the following definition of D:

$$D^{Init} = \{[\$, n, n + 1] \vdash [0, n, S]\},$$

$$D^{HC(a)} = \{[l, r, A], [b, j - 1, j]$$
$$\vdash [B \rightarrow \alpha \bullet b \bullet \gamma, j - 1, j] \mid A >_h^* B \wedge l < j \leq r\},$$

$$D^{HC(A)} = \{[l, r, A], [C \rightarrow \bullet \beta \bullet, i, j]$$
$$\vdash [B \rightarrow \alpha \bullet C \bullet \beta, i, j] \mid A >_h^* B \wedge l \leq i \leq j \leq r\},$$

$$D^{HC(\varepsilon)} = \{[l, r, A] \vdash [B \rightarrow \bullet \bullet, j, j] \mid A >_h^* B \wedge l \leq j \leq r\},$$

$$D^{lPred} = \{[l, r, A], [B \rightarrow \alpha C \bullet \beta \bullet \gamma, i, j]$$
$$\vdash [l, i, C] \mid A >_h^* B \wedge l \leq i \leq j \leq r\},$$

$$D^{rPred} = \{[l, r, A], [B \rightarrow \alpha \bullet \beta \bullet C \gamma, i, j]$$
$$\vdash [j, r, C] \mid A >_h^* B \wedge l \leq i \leq j \leq r\},$$

$$D^{lScan} = \{[l,r,A],\ [a,j-1,j],\ [B{\rightarrow}\alpha a{\bullet}\beta{\bullet}\gamma,j,k]$$
$$\vdash [B{\rightarrow}\alpha{\bullet}a\beta{\bullet}\gamma,j-1,k]\ \mid\ A>_h^* B\ \wedge\ l<j\leq k\leq r\},$$

$$D^{rScan} = \{[l,r,A],\ [B{\rightarrow}\alpha{\bullet}\beta{\bullet}a\gamma,i,j],\ [a,j,j+1]$$
$$\vdash [B{\rightarrow}\alpha{\bullet}\beta a{\bullet}\gamma,i,j+1]\ \mid\ A>_h^* B\ \wedge\ l\leq i\leq j<r\},$$

$$D^{lCompl} = \{[l,r,A],\ [C{\rightarrow}{\bullet}\delta{\bullet},i,j],\ [B{\rightarrow}\alpha C{\bullet}\beta{\bullet}\gamma,j,k]$$
$$\vdash [B{\rightarrow}\alpha{\bullet}C\beta{\bullet}\gamma,i,k]\ \mid\ A>_h^* B\ \wedge\ l\leq i\leq k\leq r\},$$

$$D^{rCompl} = \{[l,r,A],\ [B{\rightarrow}\alpha{\bullet}\beta{\bullet}C\gamma,i,j],\ [C{\rightarrow}{\bullet}\delta{\bullet},j,k]$$
$$\vdash [B{\rightarrow}\alpha{\bullet}\beta C{\bullet}\gamma,i,k]\ \mid\ A>_h^* B\ \wedge\ l\leq i\leq k\leq r\},$$

$$D_{sHC'} = D^{Init}\cup D^{HC(a)}\cup D^{HC(A)}\cup D^{HC(\varepsilon)}\cup D^{lPred}\cup D^{rPred}\cup$$
$$D^{lScan}\cup D^{rScan}\cup D^{lCompl}\cup D^{rCompl}.$$

With H for an arbitrary sentence as defined in (11.1) we have fully specified a parsing system $\mathbb{P}_{sHC'} = \langle \mathcal{I}_{sHC'}, H, D_{sHC'}\rangle$ for an arbitrary context-free head grammar G.   □

A chart parser is obtained from the parsing schema as usual; The *init* step should be interpreted as initializing the agenda with $[0,n,S]$ for a given sentence. The end-of-sentence marker is not used by the chart parser. It was introduced only to specify the schema independent of a particular sentence length.

The number of items that can be recognized now is $O(n^2)$, but the work involved for an arbitrary current item is more than linear. Because the *complete* steps have 5 positions markers, they account for $O(n^5)$ complexity. We will define a schema **sHC** as a modification of **sHC'**, in such way that it can be implemented with $O(n^3)$ complexity. At the same time we include some changes that reduce the complexity in terms of the size of the grammar. These will be discussed at length in 11.6.

- By an appropriate change in the definition of D we will reduce the number of position markers in *complete* steps to 3 and increase the positions markers involved in a *predict* step to 5. This leaves $O(n^5)$ as the complexity of a naive, straightforward implementation of the chart parser. In 11.6, however, we will argue that all predict step can be dealt with in $O(n^3)$ time by adding suitable auxiliary data structures to the implementation.

We will change the schema, such that the following statement holds:

$$\text{if } [l,r,A]\in \mathcal{V} \text{ then } [i,j,A]\in\mathcal{V} \text{ for arbitrary } l\leq i\leq j\leq r. \qquad (11.2)$$

As a result, we can change the position markers l and r in the *complete* steps to i and j; similar for the *scan* steps.

In order to achieve (11.2), however, some more work must be done by the *init* and *predict* steps. *Init* now simply recognizes $[i,j,S]$ for all applicable i and j.

In the *left predict* we can replace

$$[l, r, A], [B{\rightarrow}\alpha C{\bullet}\beta{\bullet}\gamma, j, k] \vdash [l, j, C]$$

as defined in **sHC'** by

$$[l, k, A], [B{\rightarrow}\alpha C{\bullet}\beta{\bullet}\gamma, j, k] \vdash [A, h, i]$$

with $l \leq h \leq i \leq j$ and $A{>}_h^* B$. A similar extension of *right predict* steps is made. As a consequence, the validity of $[l, k, A]$ implies the validity of $[h, i, A]$ for intervals located between l and r.[2] Hence we may restrict the *left complete* steps

$$[l, r, A], [C{\rightarrow}{\bullet}\gamma{\bullet}, i, j], [B{\rightarrow}\alpha C{\bullet}\beta{\bullet}\gamma, j, k] \vdash [B{\rightarrow}\alpha{\bullet}C\beta{\bullet}\gamma, i, k]$$

as defined in **sHC'** to only the cases

$$[i, k, A], [C{\rightarrow}{\bullet}\gamma{\bullet}, i, j], [B{\rightarrow}\alpha C{\bullet}\beta{\bullet}\gamma, j, k] \vdash [B{\rightarrow}\alpha{\bullet}C\beta{\bullet}\gamma, i, k].$$

Right complete steps are restricted in the same fashion.

In a similar way, we can restrict the position markers in the various HC steps.

- A second change is (a slight modification of) an optimization suggested by Satta and Stock [1989]. Suppose the grammar has a production $A{\rightarrow}X\underline{Y}Z$. Furthermore, let $[A{\rightarrow}{\bullet}XYZ{\bullet}, h, k]$ be valid. Then, starting from an item $[A{\rightarrow}X{\bullet}Y{\bullet}Z, i, j]$ there are two ways to recognize the entire production. One could start either by moving the left dot leftwards or by moving the right dot rightwards. Clearly, if the two mentioned items are valid then $[A{\rightarrow}{\bullet}XY{\bullet}Z, h, j]$ and $[A{\rightarrow}X{\bullet}YZ{\bullet}, i, k]$ must be valid as well.

  We will simply discard the second option and state as a general rule that expansion to the right is allowed *only* when the left dot is in leftmost position[3].

- A third change that is merely of an administrative nature is the introduction of a new kind of items. We use *CYK items* of the form $[A, i, j]$ to

---

[2] It can be shown that the same condition holds if for a less liberal expansion of the *predict rules*, that take only 4 position markers. It suffices to add *predict* steps
$$[h, k, A], [B{\rightarrow}\alpha C{\bullet}\beta{\bullet}\gamma, j, k] \vdash [A, h, i]$$
with $h \leq i \leq j$ and $A{>}_h^* B$, because for any predicted $[l, k, A]$ it is clear that $[h, k, A]$ with $l \leq h \leq k$ can also be predicted; similarly for *right predict*. But the extra degree of freedom has no bearing on the complexity of the algorithm (as we will prove in Section 11.6) and might offer better opportunities for efficient implementation, because the whole range of *predicts* can be dealt with in a single operation, rather than having to do a series of predicts for each applicable value of i.

[3] For grammars with rather long right hand sides (and centrally located heads) one could think of more sophisticated criteria. Satta and Stock allow expansion in *arbitrary* direction and then administrate that the other direction is blocked. This is a rather academic problem, however; productions with the head neither in left nor right position are very hard to find, if at all existent.

denote that an *arbitrary* production with left-hand side A has been recognized between positions i and j. This extension has some influence on the efficiency of the parser, but is also useful to simplify the notation. We may write $[X, i, j]$ as a generic notation for a completely recognized constituent that is either a terminal ($[a, i, j]$) or a nonterminal ($[A, i, j]$). Hence, in the notation of the parsing schema, a *scan* can be seen now as a special case of a *complete*. CYK items $[A, i, j]$ are recognized by *pre-complete* steps of the form

$$[A \to \beta\bullet, i, j] \vdash [A, i, j].$$

Thus we obtain the following definition for a a parsing schema **sHC**.

Schema 11.10. (sHC)
We define a parsing system $\mathbb{P}_{sHC}$ for an arbitrary context-free head grammar G, incorporating the changes discussed above.

$$\mathcal{I}^{Pred} = \{[l, r, A] \mid A \in N \wedge 0 \leq l \leq r\},$$

$$\mathcal{I}^{HC(i)} = \{[B \to \alpha\bullet\beta X\bullet\gamma, i, j] \mid B \to \alpha\beta\underline{X}\gamma \in P \wedge 0 \leq i \leq j\},$$

$$\mathcal{I}^{HC(ii)} = \{[B \to \bullet\alpha X\beta\bullet\gamma, i, j] \mid B \to \alpha\underline{X}\beta\gamma \in P \wedge 0 \leq i \leq j\},$$

$$\mathcal{I}^{HC(iii)} = \{[B \to \bullet\bullet, j, j] \mid B \to \varepsilon \in P \wedge j \geq 0\},$$

$$\mathcal{I}^{CYK} = \{[A, i, j] \mid A \in N \wedge 0 \leq i \leq j\},$$

$$\mathcal{I}_{sHC} = \mathcal{I}^{Pred} \cup \mathcal{I}^{HC(i)} \cup \mathcal{I}^{HC(ii)} \cup \mathcal{I}^{HC(iii)} \cup \mathcal{I}^{CYK};$$

$$D^{Init} = \{[\$, n, n+1] \vdash [i, j, S] \mid 0 \leq i \leq j \leq n\},$$

$$D^{HC} = \{[i, j, A], [X, i, j] \vdash [B \to \alpha\bullet X\bullet\beta, i, j] \mid A >_h^* B\},$$

$$D^{HC(\varepsilon)} = \{[j, j, A] \vdash [B \to \bullet\bullet, j, j] \mid A >_h^* B\},$$

$$D^{lPred} = \{[l, r, A], [B \to \alpha C\bullet\beta\bullet\gamma, k, r] \\ \vdash [i, j, C] \mid A >_h^* B \wedge l \leq i \leq j \leq k\},$$

$$D^{rPred} = \{[l, r, A], [B \to \bullet\beta\bullet C\gamma, l, i] \\ \vdash [j, k, C] \mid A >_h^* B \wedge i \leq j \leq k \leq r\},$$

$$D^{preCompl} = \{[A \to \beta\bullet, i, j] \vdash [A, i, j]\},$$

$$D^{lCompl} = \{[i, k, A], [X, i, j], [B \to \alpha X\bullet\beta\bullet\gamma, j, k] \\ \vdash [B \to \alpha\bullet X\beta\bullet\gamma, i, k] \mid A >_h^* B\},$$

$$D^{rCompl} = \{[i, k, A], [B \to \bullet\beta\bullet X\gamma, i, j], [X, j, k] \\ \vdash [B \to \bullet\beta X\bullet\gamma, i, k] \mid A >_h^* B\},$$

$$D_{sHC} = D^{Init} \cup D^{HC} \cup D^{HC(\varepsilon)} \cup D^{lPred} \cup D^{rPred} \cup \\ D^{preCompl} \cup D^{lCompl} \cup D^{rCompl}.$$

Thus we have fully specified a parsing system $\mathbb{P}_{sHC} = \langle \mathcal{I}_{sHC}, H, D_{sHC} \rangle$ for an arbitrary context-free head grammar G.   □

Although we have established the optimal worst-case complexity bounds that could reasonably be obtained (cf. Section 11.6), the efficiency in practical cases can be increased a lot by adding more sophistication to the simplified chart parser, both at schema level by applying some more filters and at implementation level by introducing appropriate data structures. We will not further pursue the matter of optimizing the chart parser by application of filters, but only give some hints.

- A predicted item should fit to the left, fit to the right, or both. This can be expressed by using predict items of the form $[=l, =r, A]$, $[\geq l, =r, A]$ and $[=l, \leq r, A]$ with the obvious interpretation. When looking for an X such that $A >_h^* X$, one could distinguish (nonexclusively) between cases where
  - X must occur at the left (i.e., if $A \Rightarrow^* \alpha X \beta$ then $\alpha = \varepsilon$),
  - X need not occur at the left (i.e., $A \Rightarrow^* a\alpha X\beta$),
  and similarly for right alignment. The head-corner operator can use alignment information to discard useless valid items.
- A dynamic filter that uses one position look-ahead and one position look-back may prevent recognition of a number of useless valid items at fairly low cost.

11.5 Correctness of sHC

We describe the transformation from **pHC** to **sHC** in terms of the relations of Chapters 5 and 6. For each step, additionally, we will argue that the correctness is preserved.

As in the LC case (cf. Section 10.5), we define an auxiliary system **pHC'**, which is a trivial dynamic filter of **pHC**, adding spurious antecedents to deduction steps that do not filter anything. To each deduction step in $HC(A)$, *lpred*, *rpred*, *lcompl*, and *rcompl*, we add an antecedent $[l, r, A]$, reduplicating the recognized part of the antecedent HC item. It follows trivially that $\mathcal{V}(\mathbb{P}_{pHC}) = \mathcal{V}(\mathbb{P}_{pHC'})$.

The transformation from **sHC'** to **sHC** cannot be directly expressed in the available terminology, and we introduce an auxiliary schema **sHC''** as an intermediate step. The different transformation steps from **sHC'** to **sHC** are partly filters and partly refinements. We will define **sHC''** such that it is a refinement of **sHC'** and a filter can be applied to obtain **sHC**. The schema is defined, as usual, by a parsing system $\mathbb{P}_{sHC''}$ for an arbitrary context-free head grammar G:

$$\mathcal{I}^{Pred} \quad = \quad \{[l,r,A] \mid A \in N \land 0 \le l \le r\},$$

$$\mathcal{I}^{HC(i)} \quad = \quad \{[B \to \alpha \bullet \beta_1 X \beta_2 \bullet \gamma, i, j] \mid B \to \alpha \beta_1 \underline{X} \beta_2 \gamma \in P \land 0 \le i \le j\},$$

$$\mathcal{I}^{HC(ii)} \quad = \quad \{[B \to \bullet \bullet, j, j] \mid B \to \varepsilon \in P \land j \ge 0\},$$

$$\mathcal{I}^{CYK} \quad = \quad \{[A, i, j] \mid A \in N \land 0 \le i \le j\},$$

$$\mathcal{I}_{sHC''} \quad = \quad \mathcal{I}^{Pred} \cup \mathcal{I}^{HC(i)} \cup \mathcal{I}^{HC(ii)} \cup \mathcal{I}^{CYK};$$

$$D^{Init} \quad = \quad \{[\$, n, n+1] \vdash [i, j, S] \mid 0 \le i \le j \le n\},$$

$$D^{HC} \quad = \quad \{[l, r, A],\ [X, i, j] \\ \vdash [B \to \alpha \bullet X \bullet \beta, i, j] \mid A >_h^* B \land l \le i \le j \le r\},$$

$$D^{HC(\varepsilon)} \quad = \quad \{[l, r, A] \vdash [B \to \bullet \bullet, j, j] \mid A >_h^* B \land l \le j \le r\},$$

$$D^{lPred} \quad = \quad \{[l, r, A],\ [B \to \alpha C \bullet \beta \bullet \gamma, k, r] \\ \vdash [i, j, C] \mid A >_h^* B \land l \le i \le j \le k\},$$

$$D^{rPred} \quad = \quad \{[l, r, A],\ [B \to \alpha \bullet \beta \bullet C\gamma, l, i] \\ \vdash [j, k, C] \mid A >_h^* B \land i \le j \le k \le r\},$$

$$D^{preCompl} \quad = \quad \{[A \to \bullet \beta \bullet, i, j] \vdash [A, i, j]\},$$

$$D^{lCompl} \quad = \quad \{[l, r, A],\ [X, i, j],\ [B \to \alpha X \bullet \beta \bullet \gamma, j, k] \\ \vdash [B \to \alpha \bullet X \beta \bullet \gamma, i, k] \mid A >_h^* B \land l \le i \le k \le r\},$$

$$D^{rCompl} \quad = \quad \{[l, r, A],\ [B \to \alpha \bullet \beta \bullet X\gamma, i, j],\ [X, j, k] \\ \vdash [B \to \alpha \bullet \beta X \bullet \gamma, i, k] \mid A >_h^* B \land l \le i \le k \le r\},$$

$$D_{sHC''} \quad = \quad D^{Init} \cup D^{HC} \cup D^{HC(\varepsilon)} \cup D^{lPred} \cup D^{rPred} \cup \\ D^{preCompl} \cup D^{lCompl} \cup D^{rCompl}.$$

Theorem 11.11. (*Correctness of* sHC)
The following relations hold:

$$\text{pHC} \stackrel{df}{\Longrightarrow} \text{pHC'} \stackrel{ic}{\Longrightarrow} \text{sHC'} \stackrel{sr}{\Longrightarrow} \text{sHC''} \stackrel{sf}{\Longrightarrow} \text{sHC}.$$

Moreover, each of these parsing schemata is correct.

Proof.

- The correctness of **pHC** was established in Theorem 11.8, the correctness of **pHC'** follows from the above argument.
- The item contraction from **pHC'** to **sHC'** is similar to the LC case; item contraction preserves correctness.[4]

---

[4] That is, when Corollary 5.8 is extended to the type of parsing systems we deal with here; cf. footnote 8 in Chapter 10, page 219.

- In schema **sHC"** we have inserted CYK items and *pre-complete* steps. These constitute a straightforward step refinement. A second step refinement is the recognition of extra predict items $[i, j, A]$ with $l \leq i \leq j \leq r$ for each recognized predict item $[l, r, A]$. In **sHC"** these items are spurious, however, because we have not discarded any *complete* step. It is easy to show (by induction on the length of the derivation from the hypotheses) that if $[B \rightarrow \alpha \bullet \beta \bullet \gamma, i, j] \in \mathcal{V}(\mathbb{P}_{sHC''})$ then also $[B \rightarrow \alpha \bullet \beta \bullet \gamma, i, j] \in \mathcal{V}(\mathbb{P}_{sHC'})$. The reverse is trivial. Hence, from the correctness of **sHC'** it follows that **sHC"** is correct.

- The transformation from **sHC"** to **sHC** consists of two static filters. Firstly, trimming down the *complete* steps and *head corner* steps to the case $l = i$, $j = r$ is a mere redundancy elimination; the set of valid items is not affected. Secondly, the Satta and Stock filter removes some of the DD items of the form $[A \rightarrow X\alpha \bullet \beta \bullet \gamma, i, j]$; but, evidently, the validity of DD items of the form $[A \rightarrow \bullet \beta \bullet, i, j]$ is not affected. Hence **sHC** is correct as well.   □

11.6 Complexity analysis of sHC

We will first do a complexity analysis in terms of the sentence length only. After having shown that an implementation in $O(n^3)$ time is possible, we also pay attention to the size of the grammar as a complexity factor. We obtain the same worst-case complexity bounds as the GHR algorithm, which proves that that additional sophistication of a HC parser does not lead to an increase in formal complexity.

The space complexity is $O(n^2)$, obviously, because each type of item contains two position markers. An upper bound for the time complexity can be estimated by assuming that each of the $O(n^2)$ possible valid items will trigger each applicable type of deduction step.

All *head corner* steps contribute $O(n^2)$. A (non-empty) head-corner step can be triggered in two different ways: either by taking $[i, j, A]$ or by taking $[X, i, j]$ from the agenda.

All *complete* steps, similarly, contribute a factor $O(n^3)$. A *complete* step can be triggered in three different ways: by taking each kind of item from the agenda and searching the chart for the two other items. (It is rather unlikely, but nevertheless possible, that a predict item taken from the agenda will trigger a scan/complete step that produces a hitherto unrecognized item. We will not look for optimization in this respect; our prime concern now is cubic time complexity).

The hard case is the set of $O(n^5)$ *predict* steps. Let us have a closer look at *left predict* steps, having the form

$$[l, r, A], [B \rightarrow \alpha C {\bullet} \beta {\bullet} \gamma, k, r] \vdash [i, j, C]$$

with $l \leq i \leq j \leq k \leq r$. We define an *invocation* of a *left predict* as a situation in which one antecedent is taken from the agenda and a corresponding antecedent is found on the chart. An invocation,

$$[l, r, A], [B \rightarrow \alpha C {\bullet} \beta {\bullet} \gamma, k, r] \vdash \ldots \tag{11.3}$$

corresponds to a set of *left predict* steps for appropriate i and j values of the consequent. It is irrelevant whether $[l, r, A]$ comes from the agenda and the item $[B \rightarrow \alpha C {\bullet} \beta {\bullet} \gamma, k, r]$ is already present on the chart or reversed. Only a cubic number of different possibilities exist, hence at most $O(n^3)$ invocations occur.

At each invocation, however, there are in general $O(n^2)$ different consequents. Thus a total number of $O(n^5)$ times a consequent is computed, looked for in chart and agenda, and added if not yet present. As only $O(n^2)$ *different* consequents of *left predict* steps exist, some wastage can be avoided with a more sophisticated book-keeping technique.

We call an invocation of the form (11.3) *successful* if $[l, k, C]$ is neither present on the chart nor on the agenda and *unsuccessful* if $[l, k, C]$ is already present on the chart or pending on the agenda. In the latter case, every $[i, j, C]$ with $l \leq i \leq j \leq k$ must also be present in chart or agenda.
There are at most $O(n^3)$ unsuccessful invocations, for each combination of position markers l, k, r. For each unsuccessful invocation only a constant amount of work needs to be done (i.e. verifying that $[l, k, C]$ has indeed been recognized already).
The number of *successful* invocations, on the other hand, is limited to $O(n^2)$, because only $O(n^2)$ different predict items exist. The amount of work that is carried out by an *individual* successful invocation is possibly quadratic. The fact that matters here, however, is that the total amount of work to be done by *all* successful invocations must not be more than cubic. This is established as follows.

We will give an informal example, rather than a formal proof. The predict items are stored in a table in the form of an upper triangular matrix, indexed by the positions markers (like a CYK matrix). The item $[i, j, A]$ is represented by writing an A in table entry $T_{i,j}$. The matrix contains both the chart and the agenda (the agenda could be represented, for example, by keeping a linked list of matrix entries). Suppose we predict

$$[1, r, A], [B \rightarrow \alpha C {\bullet} \beta {\bullet} \gamma, 7, r] \vdash \ldots$$

and we have a predict table that already contains some entries for C as shown in Figure 11.3. Clearly, one only has to add C's to all table entries marked $*$.

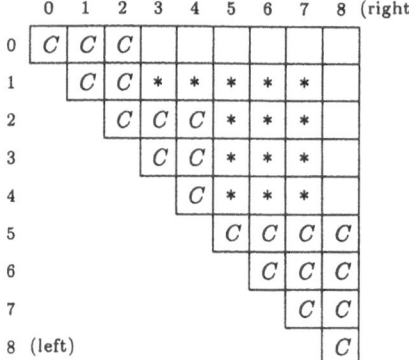

Fig. 11.3. Table entries to which a C must be added

It is obvious that the total amount of new C's added in this way is quadratic – the table is only quadratic in size. Unfortunately, however, things are slightly more complicated. On top of adding C's to the indicated positions, one also has to find out that the other positions left/down from the starting point $T_{1,7}$ do contain C's already. To that end, we check the matrix column by column. In each column we may stop when we hit a field containing a C. Moreover, if we hit upon a column that contains a C already in the first position we are interested in, no further columns need be checked.

We call an access to a matrix entry a *successful access* if no C is present yet and an *unsuccessful access* if it contains a C already. The total number of successful accesses is clearly quadratic. The total number of unsuccessful accesses is estimated as follows; For each successful invocation, a linear number of columns is checked, leading to $O(n)$ unsuccessful accesses (see Figure 11.4). Hence the total number of unsuccessful accesses is at most $O(n^3)$.

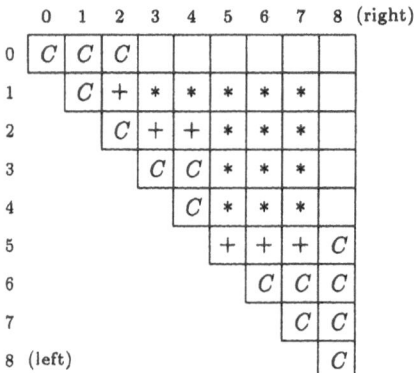

Fig. 11.4. Unsuccessful accesses ('+')

Thus, in summary, we have in the worst case

- $O(n^2)$ successful accesses by successful invocations
- $O(n^3)$ unsuccessful accesses by successful invocations
- $O(n^3)$ unsuccessful invocations; for each one a single unsuccessful access.

We will now include the size of the grammar in the complexity analysis. The size of the grammar can be captured in a single figure, denoted $|G|$, which is obtained by counting every left-hand-side symbol and every right-hand-side symbol in every production:

$$|G| \ = \ \sum_{A \to \alpha \in P} (1 + |\alpha|). \tag{11.4}$$

For a more refined analysis, we use $|N|$: the number of nonterminals, $|V|$: the number of terminals and nonterminal symbols, $|P|$: the number of productions and ϱ: the length of the longest right-hand side of any production. For some technical computations we also need another, rather ad hoc parameter h: the maximum number of productions that have an identical non-empty head.

In order to determine the space complexity, we list the various tables that are used by the parser.

- The chart and agenda are stored in tables of size $O(|G|n^2)$.
- It is assumed that the relation $>_h^*$ is available in tabular form (if not, this has repercussions on the time complexity). This table consumes $O(|N||V|)$ space.
- The predict table as discussed above takes $O(|N|n^2)$ space.
- We use a table in which we can find all productions for a given head. (Not relevant for the space complexity).
- We also use a *dotted rules table* which, for a given nonterminal A, yields all double dotted rules of the forms $B \to \alpha A \bullet \beta \bullet \gamma$ and $B \to \bullet \beta \bullet A \gamma$ that are used in DD items in **sHC**. (Not relevant for the space complexity).

Hence we obtain a total space complexity

$$O(|N||V| + |G|n^2).$$

The time complexity for each type of deduction step is determined as follows. For every type of antecedent we multiply the maximal number of antecedents of that type with the time complexity of searching for applicable fellow antecedents and the recognition of (the appropriate set of) consequents.

head corner: we distinguish three cases for head corners C, a and ε.

(*i*)   for $A >_h^* B$, $B \to \alpha \underline{a} \gamma \in P$, $0 < j \leq n$:

$$[j-1, j, A], \ [a, j-1, j] \ \vdash \ [B \to \alpha \bullet a \bullet \beta, j-1, j],$$

(*ii*) for $A >_h^* B$, $B \to \alpha \underline{C} \gamma \in P$, $0 \leq i \leq j \leq n$:

$$[i, j, A], \ [C, i, j] \ \vdash \ [B \to \alpha \bullet C \bullet \beta, i, j],$$

(*iii*) for $A >_h^* B$, $B \to \varepsilon \in P$, $0 \leq j \leq n$:

$$[j, j, A] \ \vdash \ [B \to \bullet \bullet, j, j];$$

The only case that is relevant for complexity bounds is (*ii*).
$O(|N|n^2)$ predict items each invoke a search over the $|P|$ productions; checking whether a head has been recognized needs constant time, yielding $O(|N||P|n^2)$.
The sub-case where the rule is triggered by a CYK item is somewhat more difficult. For each of the $O(|N|n^2)$ CYK items at most h productions have to be considered, for each of which an $O(|N|)$ match with predict items has to be attempted, yielding $O(|N|^2 h n^2)$.

predict: for $A >_h^* B$, $0 \leq l \leq i \leq j \leq k \leq r \leq n$:

$$[l, r, A], \ [B \to \alpha C \bullet \beta \bullet \gamma, k, r] \ \vdash \ [i, j, C],$$

$$[l, r, A], \ [B \to \bullet \beta \bullet C \gamma, l, i] \ \vdash \ [j, k, C];$$

We have dealt with the five position markers above. For computing the complexity, here, we simply assume that invocations are unsuccessful. The work caused by the $O(n^2)$ successful accesses in successful invocations is counted separately (and contributes only $O(1)$ in each case). Hence we obtain $O(|N|n^2)$ invocations triggered by predict items, causing an $O(|G|n)$ search for applicable DD items. When the predict is triggered by one of the $O(|G|n^2)$ DD items, an $O(|N|n)$ search finds the appropriate predict items. Hence the complexity is $O(|N||G|n^3)$.

pre-complete: for $0 \leq i \leq j \leq n$:

$$[A \to \bullet \alpha \bullet, i, j] \ \vdash \ [A, i, j]$$

scan: for $A >_h^* B$, $0 \leq i \leq j \leq n$:

$$[j-1, k, A], \ [a, j-1, j], \ [B \to \alpha a \bullet \beta \bullet \gamma, j, k] \ \vdash \ [B \to \alpha \bullet a \beta \bullet \gamma, j-1, k]$$

$$[i, j+1, A], \ [B \to \bullet \beta \bullet a \gamma, i, j], \ [a, j, j+1] \ \vdash \ [B \to \bullet \beta a \bullet \gamma, i, j+1]$$

Pre-complete and scan are not relevant for the time complexity bounds.

complete: for $A >_h^* B$, $0 \leq i \leq j \leq k \leq n$:

$$[i, k, A], \ [C, i, j], \ [B \to \alpha C \bullet \beta \bullet \gamma, j, k] \ \vdash \ [B \to \alpha \bullet C \beta \bullet \gamma, i, k]$$

$$[i, k, A], \ [B \to \bullet \beta \bullet C \gamma, i, j], \ [C, j, k] \ \vdash \ [B \to \bullet \beta C \bullet \gamma, i, k]$$

$O(|N|n^2)$ predict items trigger $O(|G|n)$ work;
$O(|G|n^2)$ DD items trigger $O(|N|n)$ work.
For the $O(|N|n^2)$ CYK items the accounting is slightly more complicated. If a *complete* is triggered by a CYK item, we first search for relevant DD items. The number of different DD items that can match a CYK item will differ according to the nonterminal in the CYK item. The relevant DD items can be found with the dotted rule table and checked for on the chart and agenda in constant time per DD item. Hence, if we count all *completes* triggered by CYK items, rather than individual cases, we find a total of $O(|G|n^3)$ combinations of CYK and DD items. In each case, an $O(|N|)$ search for an applicable predict item has to be carried out.
Thus we find a total time complexity of $O(|N||G|n^3)$ for the complete operation.

In summary, for the head-corner chart parser that implements **sHC** we find a total time complexity

$$O(|N|^2hn^2 + |N||G|n^3)$$

Theorem 11.12. (*complexity of* **sHC**)
Let h denote the maximum number of productions having the same head. Assuming[5] that $O(|N|h) \leq O(|G|n)$ the parsing schema **sHC** can be implemented using

$O(|N||V|) + O(|G|n^2)$ space, and
$O(|N||G|n^3)$ time

Proof. Direct from the above discussion.   □

How does this result relate to the complexity of standard parsing algorithms? The practically optimal complexity bounds[6] that have been established so far are $O(|G|n^3)$ for parsers without prediction and $O(|N||G|n^3)$ for parsers with prediction [Graham, Harrison, and Ruzzo, 1980] We will briefly explain this.
Consider the improved Earley chart parser defined by Graham, Harrison and Ruzzo [1980]. Parsing schemata **GHR** and **buGHR** were defined in Examples 6.18 and 6.19, respectively, for the predictive and bottom-up variant. The GHR parsers can be extended with a *pre-complete* similar to the

---

[5] A counterexample to this assumption are, e.g, the grammars defined by

$$P_k = \{S \rightarrow A_i \mid 1 \leq i \leq k\} \cup \{A_i \rightarrow B \mid 1 \leq i \leq k\} \cup \{B \rightarrow a\}$$

with $O(|N|h) = k^2 > k = O(|G|n)$. It is clear, though, that the assumption holds for any reasonable grammar that has not been specifically designed as a counterexample.

[6] Less than cubic time complexity bounds have been established by Valiant [1975]. This result has only theoretical value, however. The constants involved are so large that conventional cubic-time parsing algorithms perform much better than Valiant's algorithm on any realistic parsing problem.

one introduced here. Whenever an item $[A{\rightarrow}\gamma{\bullet}, i, j]$ is recognized, we store in a separate CYK table the item $[A, i, j]$. Hence the most complex set of deduction steps, the *complete* steps, are, for $0 \le i \le j \le k \le n$:

$$[A{\rightarrow}\alpha{\bullet}B\beta, i, j], \ [B, j, k] \ \vdash \ [A{\rightarrow}\alpha B{\bullet}\beta, i, k]$$

There are $O(|G|n^2)$ active items, causing $O(n)$ work each to search for the appropriate $[B, j, k]$, yielding a total of $O(|G|n^3)$ for *complete* steps triggered by active items.

There are $O(|N|n^2)$ passive (CYK) items, causing $O(|G|n)$ work each to search the appropriate $[A{\rightarrow}\alpha{\bullet}B\beta, i, j]$, yielding a total of $O(|G||N|n^3)$ for *complete* steps triggered by passive items. This last figure determines the complexity of the conventional GHR algorithm with prediction.

It is possible to reduce the complexity of GHR by a factor $|N|$, by making sure – in our terminology – that *all* complete steps are triggered by active items. If passive items do not have to look around for matching active items, one only has a complexity of $O(|G|n^3)$. In the bottom-up variant, without prediction, this is accomplished by appropriate scheduling. When an item of the form $[A{\rightarrow}\alpha{\bullet}B\beta, i, j]$ is found, searching for some particular $[B, j, k]$ is deferred to the moment that all items with positions markers j and k have been found.

In the conventional GHR parser with top-down prediction this type of scheduling is not possible. Hence it follows that top-down filtering – which will decrease the sequential computation time in ordinary cases – has a negative effect on the worst-case complexity.

Thus we have shown that the parsing schema **sHC** can be implemented with the same worst-case time complexity as the GHR algorithm, which has the optimal known worst-case complexity bounds. The GHR complexity bounds can be improved by a factor $|N|$ if the top-down prediction is discarded. The same applies to Head-Corner parsing. In 11.7 we will define a bottom-up HC parsing schema **buHC** (as an intermediate step in the derivation of **sHC** from **dVH**). It can be verified straightforwardly that **buHC** can be implemented in $O(|G|n^3)$ time. The only additional complexity factor involved in HC parsing might be the $O(|N||V|)$-sized table to store the relation $>_h^*$.

11.7 The relation between pHC, sHC, and dVH

Comparing head-corner parsing schemata with other schemata defined in previous sections and chapters meets with the formal problem that context-free head grammars are different from context-free grammars. So, in order to define relations between context-free parsing schemata and head-corner parsing schemata, one should first extend the context-free parsing schemata to (context-free) head grammars. A generic way to do this is the following:

apply the context-free schema as usual and ignore the head function.

Thus one obtains proper generalizations in the sense of Chapter 5. Yet this does not seem quite right. The problem is that head grammars are not just a generalization of context-free grammars; head grammars are a somewhat ad-hoc formalism that has been designed with the specific purpose of using linguistic head information to guide an otherwise context-free parser. The extension of a grammar G to a head grammar G makes sense only if the concept head is used in some way or other.

An equally gratuitous solution is simply to state that

Every context-free grammar is considered equivalent to a head-grammar with the head function h limited to the values 0 and 1 (i.e., all heads are left corners).

from this perspective, if follows easily that HC schemata are a generalizations of LC schemata. Yet this is not satisfying either. The notion of a head is simply nonexistent in context-free grammars and there is no a priori reason why heads should be allocated to left corners. If heads are to be used it seems more proper to allocate heads in some meaningful way. From that perspective, HC schemata are *not* generalizations of LC schemata.

The HC schemata can be embedded in the theory of Chapters 4 and 5 if we simply add a head function to a context-free grammar (and do not ask the question how the heads were allocated). As a starting point we take the parsing schema **dVH1**. In Chapter 6 we have transformed **dVH1** to **buLC** and then applied a dynamic filter to obtain **LC**. A basic parsing schema (i.e., every tree occurs only in one item) for bottom-up Head-Corner parsing can be straightforwardly derived from **dVH1**. Rather than the static filter of De Vreught and Honig, which implies that right-hand sides of productions are processed from left to right, we apply the same strategy as in **sHC**, i.e., starting from the head we work right-to-left, until a prefix of the right-hand side has been obtained. Subsequently, the remainder is done in left-to-right fashion.

Schema 11.13. (buHC)

A parsing system $\mathbb{P}_{buHC}$ for an arbitrary context-free head grammar G is defined by

$$\mathcal{I}^{HC(i)} = \{[B \rightarrow \alpha_{\bullet}\beta X_{\bullet}\gamma, i, j] \mid B \rightarrow \alpha\beta\underline{X}\gamma \in P \wedge 0 \leq i \leq j\},$$

$$\mathcal{I}^{HC(ii)} = \{[B \rightarrow_{\bullet}\alpha X\beta_{\bullet}\gamma, i, j] \mid B \rightarrow \alpha\underline{X}\beta\gamma \in P \wedge 0 \leq i \leq j\},$$

$$\mathcal{I}^{HC(iii)} = \{[B \rightarrow_{\bullet\bullet}, j, j] \mid B \rightarrow \varepsilon \in P \wedge j \geq 0\},$$

$$\mathcal{I}_{buHC} = \mathcal{I}^{HC(i)} \cup \mathcal{I}^{HC(ii)} \cup \mathcal{I}^{HC(iii)};$$

$$D^{Init} \;=\; \{[\$, n, n+1] \;\vdash\; [0, n, S]\},$$

$$D^{HC(a)} \;=\; \{[a, j-1, j] \;\vdash\; [B{\to}\alpha{\bullet}a{\bullet}\gamma, j-1, j]\},$$

$$D^{HC(A)} \;=\; \{[A{\to}{\bullet}\beta{\bullet}, i, j] \;\vdash\; [B{\to}\alpha{\bullet}A{\bullet}\gamma, i, j]\},$$

$$D^{HC(\varepsilon)} \;=\; \{\vdash\; [B{\to}{\bullet}{\bullet}, j, j]\},$$

$$D^{lScan} \;=\; \{[a, j-1, j],\, [B{\to}\alpha a{\bullet}\beta{\bullet}\gamma, j, k] \;\vdash\; [B{\to}\alpha{\bullet}a\beta{\bullet}\gamma, j-1, k]\},$$

$$D^{rScan} \;=\; \{[B{\to}{\bullet}\beta{\bullet}a\gamma, i, j],\, [a, j, j+1] \;\vdash\; [B{\to}{\bullet}\beta a{\bullet}\gamma, i, j+1]\},$$

$$D^{lCompl} \;=\; \{[A{\to}{\bullet}\delta{\bullet}, i, j],\, [B{\to}\alpha A{\bullet}\beta{\bullet}\gamma, j, k] \;\vdash\; [B{\to}\alpha{\bullet}A\beta{\bullet}\gamma, i, k]\},$$

$$D^{rCompl} \;=\; \{[B{\to}{\bullet}\beta{\bullet}A\gamma, i, j],\, [A{\to}{\bullet}\delta{\bullet}, j, k] \;\vdash\; [B{\to}{\bullet}\beta A{\bullet}\gamma, i, k]\},$$

$$D_{buHC} \;=\; D^{HC(a)} \cup D^{HC(A)} \cup D^{HC(\varepsilon)} \cup D^{lScan} \cup D^{rScan} \cup$$
$$D^{lCompl} \cup D^{rCompl}$$

with H as in (11.1) on page 225.   □

This schema has been obtained from **dVH1** by the following transformations:

- the *concatenate* has been contracted with an *init* step (yielding *left/right scan*) and with an *include* step (yielding *left/right complete*);
- a static filter restricts the *init* and *include* steps of de Vreught and Honig to heads only (yielding $HC(a)$ and $HC(A)$);
- (our version of) the Satta and Stock filter (cf. page 232) has been applied.

Hence, $\mathbf{dVH1} \overset{sc}{\Longrightarrow} \mathbf{buHC}$. It is possible to add top-down filtering to **buHC** and define a basic parsing schema **HC**. From this, similar to the LC case, **sHC** and **pHC** can be derived by introducing higher-level items. The number of different cases in **HC** is embarrassingly high, however, and we will not take the trouble to write out the complete schema. It suffices to remark that a predict item $[l, r, A]$ is in fact an abbreviation of the existence of either a pair of double dotted items

$$[D{\to}\gamma{\bullet}C\delta, h, l],\; [B{\to}\alpha A{\bullet}\beta, r, k] \;\; \text{with } C >_h^* B$$

or a pair of double dotted items

$$[D{\to}\gamma C{\bullet}\delta, r, k],\; [B{\to}\alpha{\bullet}A\beta, h, l] \;\; \text{with } C >_h^* B.$$

Special items like $[S{\to}{\bullet}{\bullet}\gamma, 0, 0]$ and $[S{\to}\gamma{\bullet}{\bullet}, 0, 0]$ can be introduced to handle initial cases.

11.8 HC parsing of unification grammars

We will describe a predictive HC chart parser for unification grammars. We give a schema in the notation of Chapter 8 of a parser that was described by Margriet Verlinden [1993].

We will first recall some bits of notation that have been formally introduced in Chapter 8. Here only an informal understanding of feature structures is needed.

A constituent X has a feature structure $\varphi(X)$ in the usual way. We do not make a distinction between *feature graphs, constraint sets* and *attribute-value matrices* (AVMs). In chapter 8 we have formalized feature graphs and constraint sets and shown that these are isomorphic. We use AVMs as an informal notation for both.

Moreover, we have introduced *composite* feature structures that cover the features of a related set of objects. Consider a production

$$S \rightarrow NP\ VP$$
$$\langle S\ head \rangle \doteq \langle VP\ head \rangle \qquad\qquad (11.5)$$
$$\langle VP\ subject \rangle \doteq \langle NP \rangle \ .$$

It does not only state that the *VP* has a subject, but also that that *VP*'s subject is *token identical* with the *NP*. We write $\doteq$ for token identity and $=$ for type identity. In Figure 11.5 the constraint set in (11.5) is replaced by a composite feature structure in AVM notation. In general we write $\varphi_0(A \rightarrow \alpha)$ for the constraints on a production $A \rightarrow \alpha$. We do not have a special notation for composite AVMs, other than listing them together. In a composite feature structure, coreferences may occur between different AVMs for different objects.

$S \rightarrow NP\ VP$

$$S \quad \longmapsto \quad \begin{bmatrix} cat & : & S \\ head : & \boxed{1} \end{bmatrix}$$

$$NP \quad \longmapsto \quad \boxed{2} \quad \begin{bmatrix} cat: NP \end{bmatrix}$$

$$VP \quad \longmapsto \quad \begin{bmatrix} cat & : & VP \\ head & : & \boxed{1} \quad [\ ] \\ subject : & \boxed{2} \end{bmatrix}$$

Fig. 11.5. Constraints (11.5) denoted by a composite feature structure

Other composite objects for which we define composite feature structures are items on a chart. In a conventional Earley parser we may obtain an item $[S \rightarrow NP\ VP\bullet, 0, n]$. The features of all three constituents in the item, and coreferences between these feature structures, are covered in a composite feature structure denoted $\varphi([S\rightarrow NP\ VP_\bullet, 0, n])$. If some NP and VP are known, the features of $[S\rightarrow NP\ VP_\bullet, 0, n]$ can be computed by means of the equation

$$\varphi([S\rightarrow NP\ VP_\bullet, 0, n]) = \varphi_0(S\rightarrow NP\ VP) \sqcup \varphi(NP) \sqcup \varphi(VP). \qquad (11.6)$$

It is important to notice that items on a chart are *immutable*. So, if features from some item are going to be used for the computation of features of another item, we use type identity (copying of features) rather than token identity (sharing of features). If we would have written $\doteq$, rather than $=$, in equation (11.6), something radically different would have been expressed, i.e., that the features of NP and VP themselves are merged into a larger feature structure for the final item, rather than *copies of* the feature structures of NP and VP. Features are never shared across different items on the chart.[7]

The initial chart contains items for the words in the sentence with feature structures taken from the lexicon. If the lexicon offers multiple feature structures for a single word, then multiple items for that word will be present on the initial chart. In a parsing schema it is specified how feature structures are to be computed for items that will be added to the chart. For each deduction step (in the context-free backbone) the feature structure of the consequent can be seen as a function of the feature structures of the antecedents.

There is an important difference in prediction by an Earley chart parser and prediction by an LC or HC chart parser. In the Earley chart parser, prediction corresponds to *stepwise* stepping down along a path in the parse tree (cf. Figure 10.3 on page 206). In the LC and HC case, a goal is set and then one starts to parse bottom-up towards that goal (cf. Figures 10.5 and 11.1 on pages 209 and 225). This leads to different approaches and problems in prediction of features. Prediction in an Earley chart parser may suffer from the defect that ever more complicated feature structures are added to the same context-free item. We have extensively discussed this in Section 9.5. This problem cannot occur in an LC/HC chart parser, because sequences of predict steps in the Earley sense do not occur.

In context-free HC prediction we use the relation $>_h^*$ to decide whether a recognized constituent can be the transitive head of a goal. If $A >_h^* B$ there is *some* chain of productions $A \Rightarrow^* \gamma B\delta$, but we don't know which one. The only thing we know is that B is a transitive head of A. It is possible to predict some features of B from features of A only under some special conditions. Suppose that some feature f is *always* shared between the left-hand side of a production and the head, for each production in the grammar. Then, through

---

[7] In an efficient implementation, however, some features can be shared under some conditions, to minimize the amount of copying that needs to be done. These conditions roughly amount to the principle that not a single feature, value, or coreference can be added to an item because of any computation with any other item. Hence, conceptually, we can see features of separate items a separate, immutable structures. See also Section 9.3.

any sequence of productions, A's feature f will be related to B's feature f if $A >_h^* B$ holds, even though A and B may never occur together within a single item. The f feature of B will percolate upwards through a chain of successive items when we move bottom-up from B towards the goal A. Such a feature is called a *transitive* feature.

A typical example of a transitive feature is the the *agr* feature that is used for agreement between *VP* and *NP*. The constraint that there must be subject-verb agreement is laid down in the production $S \to NP\ VP$, which can be found at the very top of a parse tree. The agreement features of the *NP*, however, are derived from some noun that is the *lexical head* of the *NP*. Similarly, the agreement features of the *VP* are derived from the main verb, the lexical head of the *VP*. So, if we have found a *VP* with agreement third person singular, we set as a sub-goal an *NP* with agreement third person singular. Because agreement is a transitive feature, we only need to look at third person singular nouns as possible candidates for a lexical head.

Not only top-level features can be transitive, also sub-features sub-sub-features and so on. In the following definition, therefore, we use a *feature sequence* π, that addresses an arbitrary position in a nested feature structure, rather than a feature f. For the time being we assume that a unification grammar is obtained by adding features to a context-free head grammar (but in the sequel we reverse this and obtain the context-free heads from the features in a unification grammar).

Definition 11.14. (*transitive features*)
Let $\mathcal{G}$ be a unification grammar (cf. Definition 8.29) with a head grammar G as context-free backbone.
A feature (sequence) π is called *transitive* for a grammar $\mathcal{G}$ if for each production $A \to \alpha \underline{B} \gamma$ where π occurs as a feature for A in $\varphi_0(A \to \alpha \underline{B} \beta)$ the following conditions hold:

(i)   the constraint $\langle A\pi \rangle \doteq \langle B\pi \rangle$ occurs in $\varphi_0(A \to \alpha \underline{B} \beta)$,
(ii) for each non-empty production $B \to \gamma \underline{C} \delta \in P$, The constraint $\langle B\pi \rangle \doteq \langle C\pi \rangle$ occurs in $\varphi_0(B \to \gamma \underline{C} \delta)$.

For empty productions $A \to \varepsilon$, a feature of $\langle A\pi \rangle$ may, but need not be specified.
□

In order to simplify notation, we will assume that all transitive features are sub-features of a single top-level feature called *head*. That is, we require that

every production $A \to \alpha \underline{B} \gamma \in P$ has a constraint $\langle A\ head \rangle \doteq \langle B\ head \rangle$.

This condition can always be fulfilled. If some constituents have no transitive features at all, then their *head* features will be empty. If some features are transitive, but not sub-feature of *head*, then such features will simply not be taken into account in the HC prediction.

We will now turn this around and define a *head unification grammar* as a unification grammar that obeys certain restrictions.

Definition 11.15. (*head unification grammar*)
A unification grammar[8] $\mathcal{G} \in \mathcal{UG}$ is called a head unification grammar if it satisfies the following *head property*:

> For each nonempty production $A \to X_1 \ldots X_k \in P$ there is a unique i ($1 \le i \le k$) such that
>
> $$\langle A head \rangle \doteq \langle X_i head \rangle$$
>
> is contained in $\varphi_0(A \to X_1 \ldots X_k)$.

The right-hand side symbol X_i with i according to the head property is called the *head* of the production $A \to X_1 \ldots X_k$.
For an empty production the head property does not apply and we call ε the head of the production.
We write $h\mathcal{UG}$ for the class of head unification grammars.   □

The head property is not an unreasonable demand on unfication grammars. In HPSG, for example, there is a general principle that the syntactic and semantic features of a constituent are those of its head. So the restriction from $\mathcal{UG}$ to $h\mathcal{UG}$ is not very severe. One can always turn a unification grammar into a head unification grammar by adding empty *head* features (and first renaming possibly existing *head* features that were used for other purposes).

We will now define a basic feature structure $\varphi_0([l, r, A; B \to \alpha \bullet \beta \bullet \gamma, i, j])$ for a head-corner item. Whenever an item of this form is added to the chart, it will be decorated with a feature structure that is obtained from this basic composite feature structure and features from other items that caused it to be recognized. The basic feature structure is defined by

$$\varphi_0([l, r, A; B \to \alpha \bullet \beta \bullet \gamma, i, j]) \\ = \varphi_0(B \to \alpha \beta \gamma) \sqcup \{\langle A\ head \rangle \doteq \langle B\ head \rangle\}, \tag{11.7}$$

i.e., the basic composite feature structure of an item comprises the basic feature structure of the production in the recognized part, augmented with *head* coreference of the left-hand side symbol with the constituent in the predicted part.

After this preparatory work, we can extend the parsing schema **pHC** straightforwardly to the class of grammars $h\mathcal{UG}$.

Schema 11.16. (pHC(UG))
We define a parsing system $\mathbb{P}_{pHC(UG)}$ for an arbitrary grammar $G \in h\mathcal{UG}$. A set of hypotheses is defined as in (11.1) on page 225, where (like in Chapter 8) it is assumed that the for an item $[a, j-1, j]$, the feature $\varphi(a).cat$ gives a

---

[8] See Definition 8.29 for the class of unification grammars $\mathcal{UG}$.

lexical category for the j-th word of the sentence. Multiple items $[a, j-1, j]$ may be contained in the set H of hypotheses.

We assume a single hypothesis $[\$, n, n+1]$ with $\varphi(\$) = [\,]$.

The domain $\mathcal{I}_{pHC}$ is given by

$$\mathcal{I}^{Pred} = \{[l, r, A] \mid A \in N \wedge 0 \le l \le r \wedge \varphi(A) \neq \bot\},$$

$$\mathcal{I}^{HC(i)} = \{[l, r, A; B \to \alpha \bullet \beta_1 X \beta_2 \bullet \gamma, i, j]_\xi \mid \begin{aligned}&A \in N \wedge A >_h^* B \wedge \\ &B \to \alpha \beta_1 \underline{X} \beta_2 \gamma \in P \wedge \\ &0 \le l \le i \le j \le r \wedge \\ &\varphi_0(\xi) \sqsubseteq \varphi(\xi) \wedge \varphi(\xi) \neq \bot\ \},\end{aligned}$$

$$\mathcal{I}^{HC(ii)} = \{[l, r, A; B \to \bullet \bullet, j, j]_\xi \mid \begin{aligned}&A \in N \wedge A >_h^* B \wedge \\ &B \to \varepsilon \in P \wedge 0 \le l \le j \le r \wedge \\ &\varphi_0(\xi) \sqsubseteq \varphi(\xi) \wedge \varphi(\xi) \neq \bot\qquad \},\end{aligned}$$

$$\mathcal{I}_{pHC} = \mathcal{I}^{Pred} \cup \mathcal{I}^{HC(i)} \cup \mathcal{I}^{HC(ii)};$$

with $\varphi_0(\xi)$ for an item ξ as in (11.7).

We add identifiers $\xi, \eta, \zeta, \ldots$ as subscripts to an item. By writing $[l, r, A; B \to \alpha \bullet \beta_1 X \beta_2 \bullet \gamma, i, j]_\xi$ we indicate that wherever ξ is written elsewhere in the same formula, this is an abbreviation for $[l, r, A; B \to \alpha \bullet \beta_1 X \beta_2 \bullet \gamma, i, j]$.

The set of deduction steps $D_{pHC(UG)}$ is defined by adding the specification of feature structures of consequents to the deduction steps of D_{pHC}. In most cases this is entirely straightforward.

$$D^{Init} = \{[\$, n, n+1] \vdash [0, n, S]_\xi \mid \begin{aligned}&\varphi(S_\xi).cat = S \wedge \\ &\varphi(S_\xi).head = \varphi_0(S).head \\ &(\text{where } \varphi_0(S) = \varphi_0(S \to \gamma)|_S) \text{ for some } S \to \gamma \in P)\},\end{aligned}$$

$$D^{HC(a)} = \{[l, r, A]_\eta,\ [b, j-1, j]_\zeta \vdash [l, r, A; B \to \alpha \bullet b \bullet \gamma, j-1, j]_\xi \mid \varphi(\xi) = \varphi_0(\xi) \sqcup \varphi(A_\eta) \sqcup \varphi(b_\zeta)\},$$

$$D^{HC(A)} = \{[l, r, A; C \to \bullet \delta \bullet, i, j]_\eta \vdash [l, r, A; B \to \alpha \bullet C \bullet \gamma, i, j]_\xi \mid \varphi(\xi) = \varphi_0(\xi) \sqcup \varphi(C_\eta)\},$$

$$D^{HC(\varepsilon)} = \{[l, r, A]_\eta \vdash [l, r, A; B \to \bullet \bullet, j, j]_\xi \mid \varphi(\xi) = \varphi_0(\xi) \sqcup \varphi(A_\eta)\},$$

$$D^{lPred} = \{[l, r, A; B \to \alpha C \bullet \beta \bullet \gamma, i, j]_\eta \vdash [l, i, C]_\xi \mid \begin{aligned}&\varphi(C_\xi).cat = \varphi(C_\eta).cat \wedge \\ &\varphi(C_\xi).head = \varphi(C_\eta).head\},\end{aligned}$$

$$D^{rPred} = \{[l, r, A; B \to \alpha \bullet \beta \bullet C \gamma, i, j]_\eta \vdash [j, r, C]_\xi \mid \begin{aligned}&\varphi(C_\xi).cat = \varphi(C_\eta).cat \wedge \\ &\varphi(C_\xi).head = \varphi(C_\eta).head\},\end{aligned}$$

$$D^{lScan} = \{[a,j-1,j]_\eta, [l,r,A; B\rightarrow\alpha a\bullet\beta\bullet\gamma, j, k]_\zeta$$
$$\vdash [l,r,A; B\rightarrow\alpha\bullet a\beta\bullet\gamma, j-1, k]_\xi$$
$$\mid \varphi(\xi) = \varphi(\zeta) \sqcup \varphi(a_\eta)\},$$

$$D^{rScan} = \{[l,r,A; B\rightarrow\alpha\bullet\beta\bullet a\gamma, i, j]_\eta, [a,j,j+1]_\zeta$$
$$\vdash [l,r,A; B\rightarrow\alpha\bullet\beta a\bullet\gamma, i, j+1]_\xi$$
$$\mid \varphi(\xi) = \varphi(\eta) \sqcup \varphi(a_\zeta)\},$$

$$D^{lCompl} = \{[l,j,C; C'\rightarrow\bullet\delta\bullet, i, j]_\eta, [l,r,A; B\rightarrow\alpha C\bullet\beta\bullet\gamma, j, k]_\zeta$$
$$\vdash [l,r,A; B\rightarrow\alpha\bullet C\beta\bullet\gamma, i, k]_\xi$$
$$\mid \varphi(C_\eta).cat = \varphi(C'_\eta).cat \wedge$$
$$\varphi(\xi) = \varphi(\zeta) \sqcup \varphi(C'_\eta) \qquad \},$$

$$D^{rCompl} = \{[l,r,A; B\rightarrow\alpha\bullet\beta\bullet C\gamma, i, j]_\eta, [j,r,C; C'\rightarrow\bullet\delta\bullet, j, k]_\zeta$$
$$\vdash [l,r,A; B\rightarrow\alpha\bullet\beta C\bullet\gamma, i, k]_\xi$$
$$\mid \varphi(C_\zeta).cat = \varphi(C'_\zeta).cat \wedge$$
$$\varphi(\xi) = \varphi(\eta) \sqcup \varphi(C'_\zeta) \qquad \},$$

$$D_{pHC(UG)} = D^{Init} \cup D^{HC(a)} \cup D^{HC(A)} \cup D^{HC(\varepsilon)}$$
$$\cup D^{lPred} \cup D^{rPred} \cup D^{lScan} \cup D^{rScan} \cup D^{lCompl} \cup D^{rCompl}.$$

In the *predict* steps it is to be understood that the predicted item has only two features: head (possibly with sub-features) and syntactic category. We could just have copied the entire feature structure of C into the predicted item. But the other features will not be used, so we may leave them out just as well.

In the *complete* steps we have made a distinction between C and C'. In an item $[l,j,C; C'\rightarrow\bullet\delta\bullet, i, j]$, it is possible, but not necessary to identify the predicted C with the the recognized C'. If $C >_h^+ C$, then C' could also be a descendant of C. Unlike the context-free case C and C' are not identical: it holds that $\varphi(C).cat = \varphi(C').cat$ and $\varphi(C).head \doteq \varphi(C').head$, but C' may have different features as well, which C has not.

Thus we have completed the description of a parsing system $\mathbb{P}_{pHC(UG)} = \langle \mathcal{I}_{pHC(UG)}, H, D_{pHC(UG)}\rangle$ for an arbitrary grammar $\mathcal{G} \in h\mathcal{UG}$. $\square$

Note that, in general, parsing of unification grammars is not guaranteed to halt. In chapters 8 and 9 we have *assumed* that a grammar $\mathcal{G}$ is used such that no infinite chain of deductions occurs in bottom-up direction, i.e., $\mathcal{V}(\mathbf{UG}(\mathcal{G})(a_1 \ldots a_n))$ is finite for any $a_1 \ldots a_n$. It is clear that this condition suffices to guarantee that $\mathcal{V}(\mathbf{pHC}(\mathbf{UG})(\mathcal{G})(a_1 \ldots a_n))$ is finite as well.

11.9 Related approaches

The use of head-driven prediction to enhance the efficiency was suggested by Kay [1989]. Satta and Stock [1989] described the first head-driven chart parser. Their parser is purely bottom-up and does not use prediction. The **buHC** schema as described in 11.7 is closely related to the algorithm of Satta and Stock. The main difference is they do not prescribe whether one should proceed from the head to the left or to the right. Both cases are allowed; in either case the other way is blocked by keeping the appropriate administration. The difference is marginal, however, because almost all productions in (man-made) natural language grammars are binary (or unary); in these cases there is no choice of direction.

Satta and Stock [1994] discuss Head-Corner chart parsing in a general framework for bidirectional parsing and give similar comparable worst-case complexity bounds. Further Head-Corner parsing algorithms for context-free grammars, based on variants of LR parsing, (see Chapter 12) are introduced by Nederhof and Satta [1994]

The context-free head grammars in Section 11.1 should not be confused with Head Grammars as introduced by Pollard [1984]. These can handle discontinuous constituents by means of "head wrapping". Head Grammars extend the class of recognizable languages to *mildly* context-sensitive languages [Joshi et al., 1991]. Van Noord [1991] describes a Prolog implementation of a head-corner parser for languages with discontinuous constituents. A Head-Corner parser for lexicalized Tree-Adjoining Grammars is given by van Noord [1994]. Veenstra [1995] describes a Head-Corner parser for Chomsky's [1992] Minimalist Program.

Bouma and van Noord [1993] have experimented with various parsing strategies for unification grammars and concluded that for important classes of grammars it is fruitful to apply parsing strategies that are sensitive to the linguistic notion of a head.

The concept of Head-Corner parsing is no longer restricted to theoretical discussions. Head-Corner parsing techniques have been sucessfully employed in several natural language processing systems (which employ grammars targeted to specific semantic domains): the SCHISMA theater information system [op den Akker et al., 1995], the PLINIUS knowledge base of abstracts of publications in Chemistry journals [ter Stal 1996], and the OVIS telephone information system for public transport in the Netherlands [van Noord, 1996]. Van Noord discusses the Prolog implementation of the parser in detail and shows that in this specific context the Head-Corner parser is *much* more efficient (roughly an order of magnitude) than rival bottom-up parsers that have been considered for deployment in the OVIS system.

11.10 Conclusion

Head-Corner parsing is rather tricky, because of the non-contiguous manner in which a sentence is processed. Hence it is not a coincidence that the parsing schemata presented here are the most complicated ones in this book. The summit in this respect is the Head-Corner parsing schema for unification grammars, which reaches the limits of readability. What it offers, on the other hand, is a formal specification of feature percolation in a nontrivial parsing algorithm.

This chapter shows the capabilities of the parsing schemata framework to get a formal grip on complicated parsers. The correctness proof of the HC schemata contains some bits of hand-waving (i.e., referring to the easier LC case) but within acceptable limits, even for a more theoretically inclined audience. The complexity analysis of **sHC** is useful, because it shows that the increase in administration does not need to affect the worst-case complexity.

On a more practical level, it is justified to ask whether the additional complications of Head-Corner (rather than Left-Corner) parsing are worth the trouble. In my Ph.D. Thesis [Sikkel, 1993b] I wrote

> Head-Corner parsing is a nice idea – at a sufficiently abstract level.
> [...] It is not clear whether the gain in efficiency offsets the increase
> in bothersome details. Much depends on the grammar [...]

Since then, Head-Corner parsers has been successfully used in several unrelated natural language processing systems, and proved to be rather efficient. In an environment where *robust* parsing is called for – the input could be incorrect or incomplete, in particular when it is provided by a speech recognizer – Left-Corner parsers do not perform well [van Noord, 1996], and Head-Corner techniques are clearly superior.

12. Generalized LR parsing

Generalized LR parsing has become popular in the second half of the 1980s, after the publication of Tomita's algorithm [Tomita, 1985]. The theoretical foundation of this approach is in fact much older and dates back to Lang [1974].

In the context of this book, LR[1] parsers are of interest because they are *not* chart parsers. In previous chapters we have argued that chart parsers fit into the parsing schemata framework in a trivial way. LR parsers are of quite a different nature, and it is to be expected that they fit into the framework in a nontrivial way.

In this chapter we investigate how parsing schemata for LR parsers can be defined. While chart parsers use items *run-time* to guide the parsing process, LR parsers use similar items *compile-time* to compute the parsing table in which the control functions are laid down. Therefore we will partly "uncompile" the LR parsers and visualise how a sentence is processed by adding run-time items to the LR parse stack. This allows a comparison between both types of parses at item level. It follows easily that the **LR(0)** parsing schema is almost identical to the **Earley** schema defined in Chapter 4.

In the next chapter we will used this insight and cross-fertilize a *parallel* Earley parser with Tomita's algorithm so as to obtain a parallel Tomita parser.

Chapters 12 and 13 are self-contained and can be read as a single, separate paper. In fact we will spend more than half of this chapter introducing Tomita's algorithm. Deterministic LR parsing is part of the basic education of any computer scientist, but *Generalized* LR parsing is much less known in that field. Readers who are familiar with the basic traits of LR parsing can move straight to Section 12.3 and those who are familiar with Tomita's algorithm may skip 12.3–12.5 as well.

---

[1] A note on terminology: The notion *LR* can be used in several more specific or more generic senses. *LR* denotes *deterministic* LR parsers and *GLR* generalized or *nondeterministic* LR parsers. When determinism is not at all relevant, we write LR rather than the more cumbersome *(G)LR*. Furthermore, LR parsers can be divided into SLR, LALR and (canonical) LR parsers. We use LR in the wider sense, unless explicitly stated otherwise.

After some preliminaries in Section 12.1, LR parsing is informally introduced in 12.2. The basic idea of Generalized LR parsing is stated in 12.3. Tomita's algorithm, treated in 12.4, is obtained by adding a graph-structured stack as an efficient data structure to cope with the nondeterminism of the LR parser. A formal definition is given in 12.5; this serves as a reference for the formal definition of our Parallel Bottom-up Tomita parser in the next chapter. Some pros and cons of Tomita's algorithm are discussed in 12.6.

In 12.7 we will partly uncompile the algorithm and introduce the "Annotated Tomita" variant that shows items also at run-time. Parsing schemata for LR(0)-based and SLR(1)-based Tomita parsers are given in 12.8. We will prove the correctness of the SLR(1) schema. Some conclusions follow in 12.9.

The presentation of Tomita's algorithm is based on Tomita [1985] (the formal definition in Section 12.5 is after Lankhorst [1991]). The comparison of Tomita's algorithm with Earley's algorithm is based on [Sikkel, 1991]. The presentation of this comparison has been simplified a lot, however, by making use of parsing schemata.

12.1 Preliminaries

A more extensive definition of context-free grammars has been given in Section 3.1 Here we briefly summarize the notational conventions and recall some standard notions of parsing theory that are needed for LR parsing.

Let $G = (N, \Sigma, P, S)$ be a context-free grammar. We write V for $N \cup \Sigma$. A grammar G is called *reduced* if every symbol can occur in a parse, i.e.

(i) $\forall X \in V \ \exists \alpha, \beta \in V^* : \ S \Rightarrow^* \alpha X \beta$,
(ii) $\forall X \in V \ \exists x \in \Sigma^* : \ X \Rightarrow^* x$.

The only use of non-reduced grammars is to serve as counterexamples to theorems. In this chapter we have to exclude them explicitly, to be formally correct, because constituents X that obey (ii) but not (i) will never be recognized by an LR parser.

For each grammar $G = (N, \Sigma, P, S)$ we define an *augmented grammar* $G' = (N', \Sigma', P', S')$ by

$$N' = N \cup \{S'\},$$

$$\Sigma' = \Sigma \cup \{\$\},$$

$$P' = P \cup \{S' \rightarrow S\$\},$$

with S' and \$ symbols not occurring in V. We write V' for $N' \cup \Sigma'$.
The following notational conventions will be applied consistently throughout this chapter. We write

$A, B, C, \ldots$ for variables ranging over N',
$X, Y, \ldots$ for variables ranging over V',
$a, b, \ldots$ for variables ranging over Σ',
$x, z, \ldots$ for variables ranging over Σ'^*,
$\alpha, \beta, \gamma, \ldots$ for variables ranging over V'^*.
ε for the empty string.

We write $\alpha \Rightarrow \beta$ if there are γ_1, γ_2 such that $\alpha = \gamma_1 A \gamma_2$, $\beta = \gamma_1 \delta \gamma_2$ and $A \rightarrow \delta \in P'$.

We write $\alpha \Rightarrow_{rm} \beta$ if there are γ, x such that $\alpha = \gamma A x$, $\beta = \gamma \delta x$ and $A \rightarrow \delta \in P'$.

A string γ is called a *sentential form* if $S \Rightarrow^* \gamma$.

A string γ is called a *rightmost sentential form* if $S \Rightarrow^*_{rm} \gamma$.

A derivation $S \Rightarrow_{rm} \ldots \Rightarrow_{rm} \gamma$ is called a *rightmost derivation* of γ.

The functions FIRST and FOLLOW are redefined for augmented grammars (but to the same effect as FIRST and FOLLOW Definition 6.10).

The function FOLLOW : $N \rightarrow \wp(\Sigma')$ defines the terminal symbols that can follow a given nonterminal in a sentential form, i.e.,

$$\text{FOLLOW}(A) = \{a \mid \exists \alpha, \beta : S' \Rightarrow^* \alpha A a \beta\}.$$

The function FIRST : $V^+ \rightarrow \wp(\Sigma')$ is defined as follows. If $\alpha \Rightarrow^* a\beta$ then $a \in$ FIRST(α). Furthermore, if $\alpha \Rightarrow^* \varepsilon$ then any terminal that can follow α in a sentential form is also contained in FIRST(α). Formally,

$$\text{FIRST}(\alpha) = \{a \mid \exists \beta, \gamma, \delta : S' \Rightarrow^* \beta \alpha \gamma \wedge \alpha \gamma \Rightarrow^* a \delta\}.$$

We will use FIRST also with a *set of strings* as parameter. It should be obvious that

$$\text{FIRST}(\{\alpha_1, \ldots, \alpha_k\}) = \text{FIRST}(\alpha_1) \cup \ldots \cup \text{FIRST}(\alpha_k).$$

12.2 LR parsing

A brief, informal introduction to (deterministic) LR parsing is given in this section. We refer to the abundant literature for a more comprehensive treatment.

The theory of LR parsing has been covered by many authors. LR parsing was introduced by Knuth [1965]. More efficient variants, viz. SLR and LALR parsing, were defined by DeRemer [1969, 1971]. But LR parsing became a useful technique for compiler construction only after automatic generation of parsing tables became feasible. This was first described by Lalonde et al. [1971]. A well-known LALR(1) *compiler-compiler* is YACC [Johnson 1975].

More treatments of LR parsing theory are given by Aho and Ullman [1972, 1977], Harrison [1978], Aho, Sethi and Ullman [1986], Grune and Jacobs

[1990], and Leermakers [1993]. We follow Aho and Ullman in the sense that states of a parser are introduced as *sets of LR-items*. Sippu and Soisalon-Soininen [1990] follow a more theoretical line and define states of a parser as *equivalence classes of viable prefixes*. An extensive bibliography on LR parsing is given by Nijholt [1983].

An LR parser is a deterministic push-down automaton. It uses a single data structure, a stack containing *states*. The top element of the stack is the state the parser is in. The parser proceeds through the sentence by two types of actions:

- *shift*: a word is read from the sentence and a new state is pushed onto the stack;
- *reduce*: a sequence of states is popped from the stack and a new state is pushed onto the stack.

There are two additional actions that stop the parser: an *error* will occur if the string being parsed is not a valid sentence; an *accept* action acknowledges the fact that a valid sentence has been scanned.

The next action is determined by the state and a prefix of the remainder of the input. LR parsers differ according to how many words are used to determine the next action. Usually a single word look-ahead is used.

In down-to-earth examples of LR parsers the general idea of a push-down automaton is slightly modified. For illustrative purposes, the states on the stack are interlaced with grammar symbols. These grammar symbols represent parts of the parse that have been determined so far. In the remainder of this chapter we will only use this more legible form of LR parsers.

As an example grammar in this section we use the following grammar G_3 (that is specifically designed to highlight some interesting aspects of LR parsing):

(1)	$S \rightarrow NP\ VP$		(5)	$VP \rightarrow {}^*v$
(2)	$S \rightarrow S\ PP$		(6)	$VP \rightarrow {}^*v\ NP$
(3)	$NP \rightarrow {}^*n$		(7)	$PP \rightarrow {}^*prep\ NP.$
(4)	$NP \rightarrow {}^*det\ {}^*n$			

The action function is coded into a *parsing table*. The parsing table for G_3 is shown in Figure 12.1. The *action table* is a matrix in which the next action can be found for every (top of stack) state and lexical category. The end-of-sentence marker $ is taken to be the next lexical category when the entire sentence has been scanned. The *goto table* is used to determine the next state in case of a *reduce* and will be explained by an example shortly. The table also contains a column labelled *LR(0) items* that we will ignore for the time being.

The *shift* actions are denoted by "*sh k*" with k a state number. *Reduce* actions are denoted by "*re p*" with p (the number of) a production of the grammar. Empty entries in the action table denote *errors*,

		action					goto			
	LR(0) items	*d	*n	*v	*p	$	NP	VP	PP	S
0	S'→•S$ S→•NP VP S→•S PP NP→•*n NP→•*det *n	sh1	sh2				4			8
1	NP→*det•*n		sh3							
2	NP→*n•			re3	re3	re3				
3	NP→*det *n•			re4	re4	re4				
4	S→NP•VP VP→•*v VP→•*v NP			sh5				7		
5	VP→*v• VP→*v•NP NP→•*n NP→•*det *n	sh1	sh2		re5	re5	6			
6	VP→*v NP•				re6	re6				
7	S→NP VP•				re1	re1				
8	S'→S•$ S→S•PP PP→•*prep NP				sh9	acc			11	
9	PP→*prep•NP NP→•*n NP→•*det *n	sh1	sh2				10			
10	PP→*prep NP•				re7	re7				
11	S→S PP•				re2	re2				

Fig. 12.1. A parsing table for G_3

the *accept* action is abbreviated *acc*. We will parse our canonical example sentence the cat catches a mouse represented by the lexical categories *det *n *v *det *n. We show the working of the parser by a sequence of *configurations* that represent the entire stack and the remainder of the input. The top of the stack is at the right, next to the remaining input. We start with only the initial state 0 as the stack contents.

$$0 \qquad \text{*det *n *v *det *n \$.} \qquad (12.1)$$

In the action table for state 0 and category *det we find "sh1". The *det is shifted and the next state is 1:

$$0\text{—*det—}1 \qquad \text{*n *v *det *n \$.} \qquad (12.2)$$

In the action table we find "sh3" at table entry *action*[1, *n]. Hence the next configuration is

$$0\text{—*det—}1\text{—*n—}3 \qquad \text{*v *det *n \$.} \qquad (12.3)$$

The next action (for 3 and *v) is "re4". This causes the following steps.

- The topmost two states and grammar symbols *det—1—*n—3 are deleted from the stack. These represent the right-hand side of production 4.
- The next state is determined by the top of the truncated stack and the left-hand side symbol of production 4. In the goto table we find that state 0 and nonterminal NP yield state 4.
- The left-hand side symbol and new state are pushed onto the stack.

This reduction yields the new configuration

$$0—NP—4 \qquad *v \ *det \ *n \ \$. \tag{12.4}$$

Next, we find $action[4, *v] = sh5$, yielding

$$0—NP—4—*v—5 \qquad *det \ *n \ \$. \tag{12.5}$$

Note that in state 5 it does depend on the next word which action is to be taken. If it is *prep or $, then the verb phrase comprises only a *v, which should be reduced now. If a *det or *n follows, on the other hand, the verb phrase contains an object, which should be shifted first. In this case we find $action[5, *det] = sh1$. Proceeding in similar fashion, we get a sequence of configurations

$$0—NP—4—*v—5—*det—1 \qquad *n \ \$ \ ; \tag{12.6}$$

$$0—NP—4—*v—5—*det—1—*n—3 \qquad \$ \ ; \tag{12.7}$$

$$0—NP—4—*v—5—NP—6 \qquad \$ \ ; \tag{12.8}$$

$$0—NP—4—VP—7 \qquad \$ \ ; \tag{12.9}$$

$$0—S—8 \qquad \$. \tag{12.10}$$

Finally we find $action[8, \$] = accept$, i.e., the sentence was indeed correct.

So far we have recognized the sentence but not yet constructed a parse. This is done as follows. From each configuration we can derive a rightmost sentential form (if the sentence was accepted) by concatenating the stack and the remaining input and deleting the states and the end-of-sentence marker:

$$*det \ *n \ *v \ *det \ *n, \tag{12.11}$$

$$NP \ *v \ *det \ *n, \tag{12.12}$$

$$NP \ *v \ NP, \tag{12.13}$$

$$NP \ VP, \tag{12.14}$$

$$S. \tag{12.15}$$

Shifts are ineffective to the sentential form, reductions produce a new one. The rightmost sentential forms (12.11)–(12.15) comprise a rightmost derivation in reversed order. Hence all that has to be done to uniquely encode the

```
function closure(I: set of items): set of items;
begin
        items := I;
        while there is an item A→α•Bγ ∈ items
                and a production B→β ∈ P such that B→•β ∉ items
                do items := items ∪ {B→•β} od;
        closure := items;
end;
```

Fig. 12.2. The closure of a set of LR(0) items

parse tree is to output a sequence of reductions (and output whether the parser was stopped by *accept* or *error*).

The parser is called an **LR** parser because it proceeds from **L**eft to right, constructs a **R**ightmost derivation. There are various types of LR parsers that we will not discuss here. The current one is called an *SLR(1)* parser; It is a *simple* LR parser and uses *one* symbol look-ahead.

In the example, we identified states by a number. This is only for easy reference. A state in fact constitutes a set of so-called *LR(0) items*, cf. Figure 12.1. An item is an object of the form $A→α•β$ with $A→αβ$ a production. Unlike Earley items, the LR(0) items do not contain position markers. Whenever a state s occurs on top of the stack and $A→α•β ∈ s$, the parser has recognized $α$ somewhere in the sentence. The positions delineating $α$ can be derived from the composition of the stack. In Section 12.7 we will do so explicitly.

LR(0) items $A→α•$ with a dot in rightmost position are called *final items*; those of the form $A→•β$ with a dot in leftmost position are called *initial items*.

The initial state 0 contains the item $S'→•S\$$, i.e., we have to start recognizing the entire sentence. There are two ways to recognize a sentence: by $S→NP\ VP$ or by $S→S\ PP$. For either rewrite rule we add an initial item $S→•NP\ VP$ and $S→•S\ PP$, respectively. Similarly, there are two rewrite rules for NP and we add $NP→•\ ^*n$ and $NP→•\ ^*det\ ^*n$ to state 0. In this way we have computed the *closure* of $S'→•S\$$. An algorithmic definition of closure is given in Figure 12.2.

A sentence could start with $^*det$, as in our example sentence. For that case, the action table must contain a *shift* for state 0 and $^*det$. The new state (labelled 1) is obtained by moving the dot over $^*det$. We take the closure again, but no initial items are added because the symbol following the dot is a terminal. Similarly, a *shift* and a new state is defined for the case that a sentence starts with $^*n$.

In state 1 only a single action is possible. One has just shifted a $^*det$ and this must be followed by shifting a $^*n$. This leads to state 3, $\{NP→\ ^*det\ ^*n•\}$, containing a single final item. The only feasible action is *re4*. Note that this

---

function *next_state*(*I*: *set of items*, *X*: *symbol*): *set of items*;
begin
      next_state := *closure*({$A{\rightarrow}\alpha X{\bullet}\beta \mid A{\rightarrow}\alpha{\bullet}X\beta \in I$})
end;

function *all_states*: *set of sets of items*
begin
      $C := \{closure(\{S'{\rightarrow}{\bullet}S\$\})\}$;
      while there is an item set $I \in C$ and a symbol $X \in V$
              such that *next_state*$(I, X) \neq \emptyset$ and *next_state*$(I, X) \notin C$
              do $C := C \cup \{next\_state(I, X)\}$ **od**;
      all_states := C
end;

Fig. 12.3. Computation of the set of states

is entered into the action table only for symbols in FOLLOW(*NP*). If, e.g., another *n were to follow the input is not a correct sentence and the parser could stop right away.

If *det *n is reduced to *NP*, the symbols and state numbers *det—1—*n—3 are replaced by *NP* and a new state number. This new state number should be found in the goto table. Hence, *goto*[0,*NP*] yields a new state, labelled 4:

$$closure(\{S{\rightarrow}NP{\bullet}VP\}) = \{S{\rightarrow}NP{\bullet}VP,\ VP{\rightarrow}{\bullet}\,{}^{*}v,\ VP{\rightarrow}{\bullet}\,{}^{*}v\,NP\}.$$

Shifting a *v moves us to state 5. Both rewrites of *VP* can start with a *v, hence state 5 comprises

$$closure(\{VP{\rightarrow}{}^{*}v{\bullet},\ VP{\rightarrow}{}^{*}v{\bullet}\,NP\}).$$

The remainder of the table is computed in similar fashion. Worth mentioning is state 8, which contains an item $S'{\rightarrow}S{\bullet}\$$. An entire sentence has been recognized, hence *action*[8,\$] = *accept*. It is conceivable, however, that the input string has not been processed completely. A prepositional phrase may follow, hence *action*[8,*PP*] yields a *shift*.

An algorithmic definition of the set of states and the parsing table is given in Figures 12.3 and 12.4.

12.3 Generalized vs. deterministic LR parsing

An LR parser, in order to be deterministic, may only have a single action in each table entry. If an entry contains more than one action there is a *conflict* and the parser doesn't know what to do. A grammar is called SLR(1) if the parsing table for that grammar does not contain any conflict. A language is called SLR(1) if it can be described by an SLR(1) grammar. The class of SLR(1) grammars is a severely restricted subset of the the class of context-free

```
procedure construct SLR(1) table
begin
        C := all_states;
        for each I ∈ C
        do      for each a ∈ Σ' do action[I, a] := ∅ od;
                for each item ∈ I
                do      case item of
                        A→α•aβ:
                                if A→α•aβ = S'→S•$
                                then   action[I,$] := action[I, $] ∪ {accept}
                                else   action[I, a] :=
                                        action[I, a] ∪ {shift next_state(I, a)}
                                fi
                        A→α•Bβ:
                                goto[I, B] := next_state(I, B)
                        A→α•:
                                for each a ∈ FOLLOW(A)
                                do      action[I, a] :=
                                        action[I, a] ∪ {reduce A→α}
                        od      esac   od;
                        for each a ∈ Σ' do
                                if action[I, a] = ∅ then action[I, a] := {error} fi
        od      od
end;
```

Fig. 12.4. The computation of an SLR(1) parsing table

grammars. A necessary (but not sufficient) condition is that the grammars is not ambiguous. While most programming languages can be described by LR grammars, this clearly does not hold for natural language grammars.

With some more sophistication, however, LR parsing techniques can be used for natural language grammars. The central idea is to replace the word *conflict* by *ambiguity*. Thus we obtain a *nondeterministic* pushdown automaton that is known as a *Generalized LR (GLR)* parser. If the state of the parser and the look-ahead allow for different actions, a nondeterministic choice is made. A sentence is correct if and only if there is *some* run of the nondeterministic LR parser that accepts its. More specifically, the set of parse trees of a sentence is characterized by (the rightmost derivations produced by) all successful runs of the parser.

Nondeterministic automata are useful constructs only from a theoretical perspective. If we are to find all parse trees for a given sentence, we need some practical way to determine all successful runs of the nondeterministic machine. A general approach to handle nondeterministic push-down transducers dates back to an early paper of Lang [1974]. But it has remained rather unknown until the mid-eighties, when Tomita [1985] published his Generalized LR algorithm, written for an audience of computational linguists rather than theoretical computer scientists. A similar algorithm was independently discovered by van der Steen [1987].

In Section 12.4 we will give an informal introduction to Tomita's algorithm. A formal definition is presented in 12.5.

12.4 Tomita's algorithm

For an exposition of Tomita's algorithm we use the canonical example grammar G_4 (which is obtained by adding a production $NP \rightarrow *n$ to grammar G_2 that was used in previous examples). defined by the productions

(1) $S \rightarrow NP\ VP$ (5) $NP \rightarrow NP\ PP$
(2) $S \rightarrow S\ PP$ (6) $PP \rightarrow *prep\ NP$
(3) $NP \rightarrow *n$ (7) $VP \rightarrow *v\ NP.$
(4) $NP \rightarrow *det\ *n$

The canonical example sentence is "I saw a man with a telescope", represented by the lexical categories

$$*n\ *v\ *det\ *n\ *prep\ *det\ *n. \tag{12.16}$$

Both parses are represented in Figure 12.5, in a structure that is called a *shared forest*; "forest" because it comprises a set of trees, "shared" because identical subtrees are represented only once.

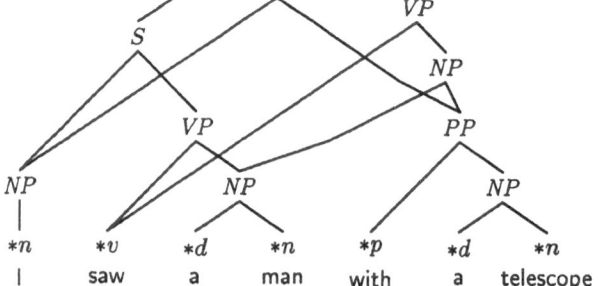

Fig. 12.5. A shared forest

The parsing table is shown in Figure 12.6. Ambiguities arise in states 11 and 12. With look-ahead *prep, both a *shift* and a *reduce* are possible, depending on where the *PP* is to be attached.

A first, naive approach to nondeterministic LR parsing is the following. Whenever an ambiguity arises, a different copy of the stack is made for each possible action. Thus we get a set of stacks that is managed in parallel. If some stack brings the parser in a state where no action is possible, this stack is discarded. Hence, the set of stacks that remains when the entire sentence has been processed yields the set of parse trees for the sentence.

	LR(0) items	action table					goto table			
		*d	*n	*v	*p	$	NP	VP	PP	S
0	S'→•S$ S→•NP VP S→•S PP NP→•*n NP→•*det *n NP→•NP PP	sh3	sh4				2			1
1	S'→S•$ S→S•PP PP→•*prep NP				sh6	acc			5	
2	S→NP•VP NP→NP•PP VP→•*v NP PP→•*prep NP			sh7	sh6			8	9	
3	NP→*det•*n		sh10							
4	NP→*n•			re3	re3	re3				
5	S→S PP•				re2	re2				
6	PP→*prep•NP NP→•*n NP→•*det *n NP→•NP PP	sh3	sh4				11			
7	VP→*v•NP NP→•*n NP→•*det *n NP→•NP PP	sh3	sh4				12			
8	S→NP VP•				re1	re1				
9	NP→NP PP•			re5	re5	re5				
10	NP→*det *n•			re4	re4	re4				
11	PP→*prep NP• NP→NP•PP PP→•*prep NP			re6	re6 sh6	re6			9	
12	VP→*v NP• NP→NP•PP PP→•*prep NP			re7	re7 sh6	re7			9	

Fig. 12.6. A parsing table for G_4

The various stacks are synchronized on *shift* actions. That is, all possible reductions are carried out until each stack is to do a *shift*. In Figure 12.7 the set of stacks is shown that is obtained after parsing a (prefix of a) string

*n *v *det *n *prep *det *n *prep *det *n *prep .

The topmost 5 stacks are identical, but correspond to the 5 different parses for a sentence ending with two *PP*s. This is clearly an inefficient way of working. If two stacks have the same top state, they will behave identical upto the moment that this state is removed by a reduction. Hence identical top parts of stacks can be merged. Thus we obtain a *tree-structured* stack, shown in Figure 12.8. In this case there is only a single top state, in general there may be several tops states.

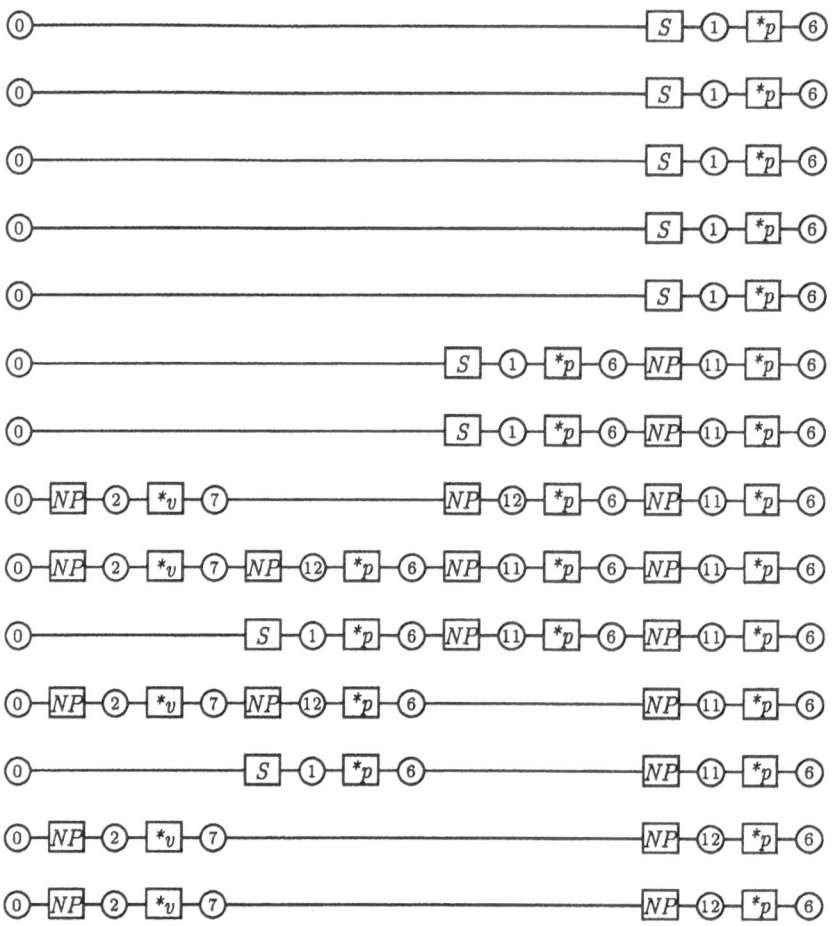

Fig. 12.7. Maintaining a set of stacks

A second optimization is possible. We could also share bottom parts of the stacks, when a copy of a stack has to be made. Thus we obtain the *graph-structured* stack as shown in Figure 12.9. Note that each single stack in Figure 12.7 corresponds to a path in the tree in Figure 12.8 and to a path in the graph in Figure 12.9. All three figures contain the same information.

In order to formally define a generalized LR parser with a graph-structured stack, one has to keep in mind that the graph is in fact a compact representation of a set of stacks defined by the paths in the graph. Each stack is operated by its own nondeterministic LR parser; all parsers synchronize on *shifts*. Hence it is is clear how to derive a definition of a GLR parser from the definition of a deterministic LR parser. The result is rather complicated, however, and we do not take the trouble to write it down. In Section 12.5 a

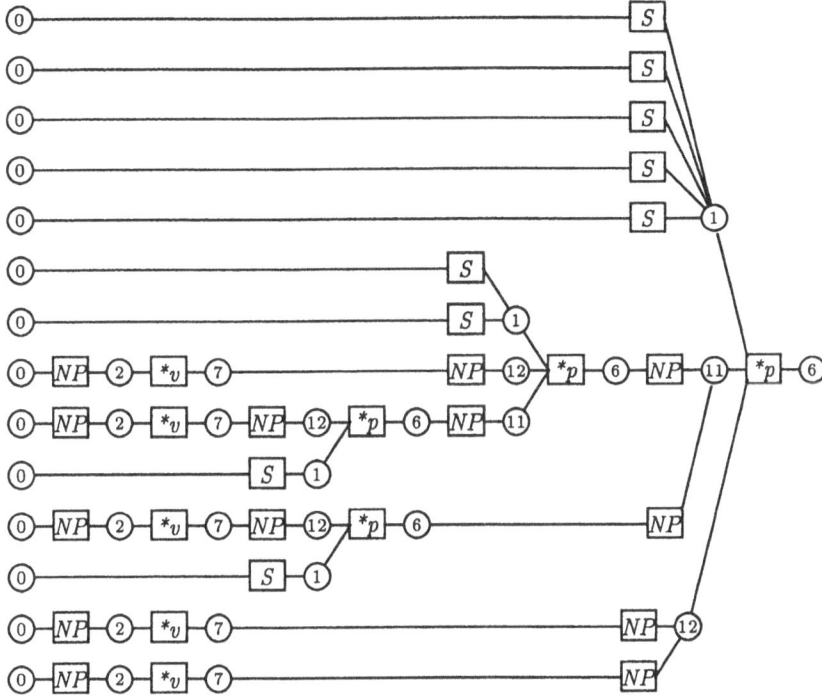

Fig. 12.8. A tree-structured stack

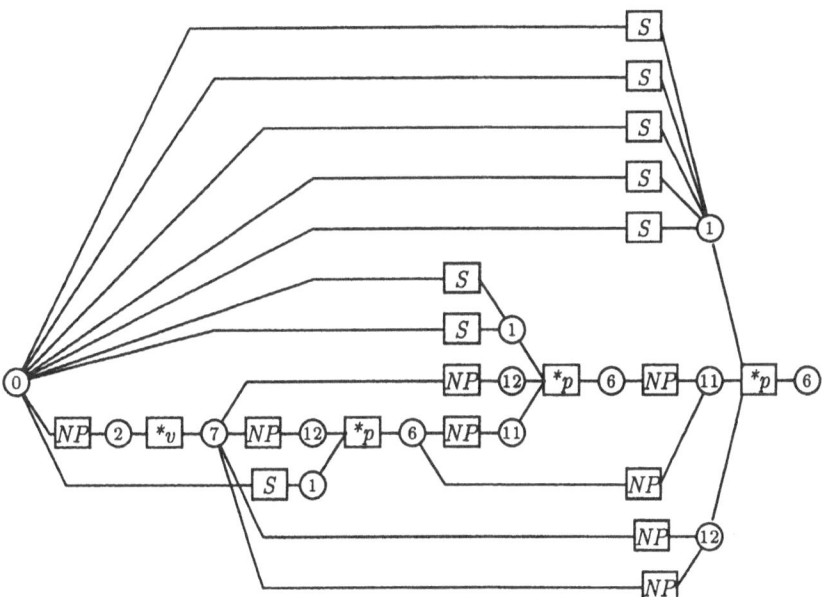

Fig. 12.9. A graph-structured stack

formal definition is given of an optimized version of the GLR parser that will be discussed next.

So far we have only considered *recognition* of a sentence by a GLR parser. In order to yield a forest of parse trees, we have to keep some additional administration. We will maintain a *parse list* of nodes that occur in a the parse forest with pointers to their daughter nodes. To that end, the algorithm is modified as follows.

- Upon a *shift*, the terminal that is shifted is added to the parse list. The symbol vertex is labelled with the index in the parse list, rather than with the symbol itself.
- Similarly, upon a *reduce*, an entry into the parse list is made for the left-hand side symbol of the reduced production. A list of pointers to its daughter nodes (the just removed indices of right-hand side symbols) is contained in the parse list entry.

Figure 12.10 shows the parse list corresponding to the shared forest of "I saw a man with a telescope".

0	$[*n$ "I"$]$			
1	$[NP$ (0)$]$	9	$[*det$ "a"$]$	
2	$[*v$ "saw"$]$	10	$[*n$ "telescope"$]$	
3	$[*det$ "a"$]$	11	$[NP$ (9 10)$]$	
4	$[*n$ "man"$]$	12	$[PP$ (8 11)$]$	
5	$[NP$ (3 4)$]$	13	$[NP$ (5 12)$]$	
6	$[VP$ (2 5)$]$	14	$[VP$ (2 13)$]$	
7	$[S$ (1 6)$]$	15	$[S$ (1 14)$]$	**Fig. 12.10.** List representa-
8	$[*prep$ "with"$]$	16	$[S$ (7 12)$]$	tion of a shared forest

When a sentence has n parse trees, then the shared forest will have n root nodes. The shared forest of the 5 parse trees of the sentence "I saw a man in the park with a telescope" is shown in Figure 12.11. But, just as we share bottom parts of parse trees, we could also share top parts of parse trees. If a nonterminal symbol rewrites to the same part of the sentence in different ways, it needs to be represented only once. The different nodes in the shared forest are grouped into a single so-called *packed node* that comprises several *sub-nodes*. This is illustrated in Figure 12.12, where packed nodes are represented by rectangles and sub-nodes by symbols contained in the rectangle. The graph structure that is obtained in this way is called a *packed shared forest*.

The shared forest (represented by a parse list) in Figure 12.10 had two root nodes. In order to obtain a packed shared forest, the two nodes

15    $[S$ (1 14)$]$
16    $[S$ (7 12)$]$

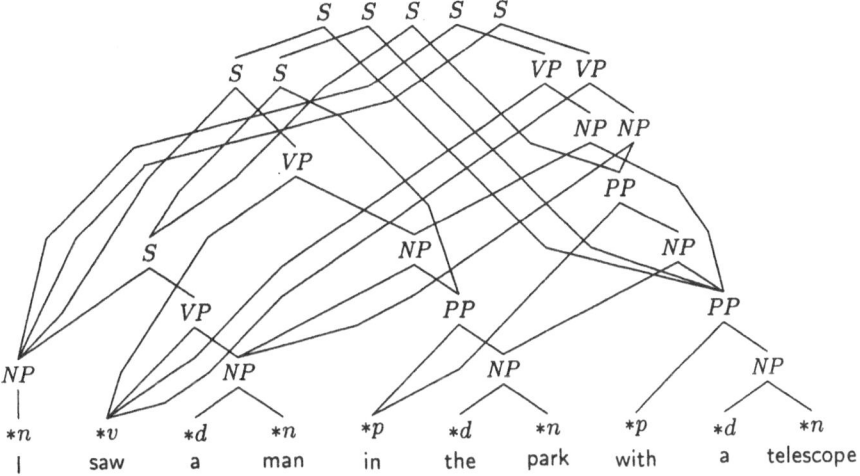

Fig. 12.11. A more complicated shared forest

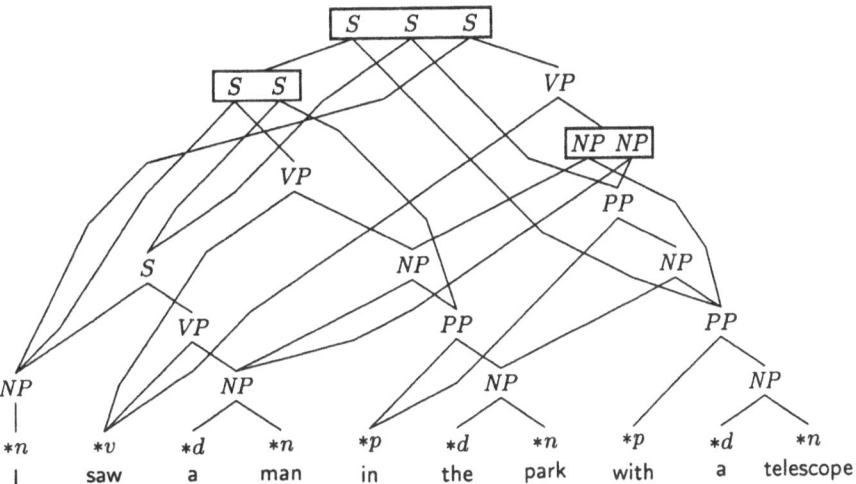

Fig. 12.12. A packed shared forest

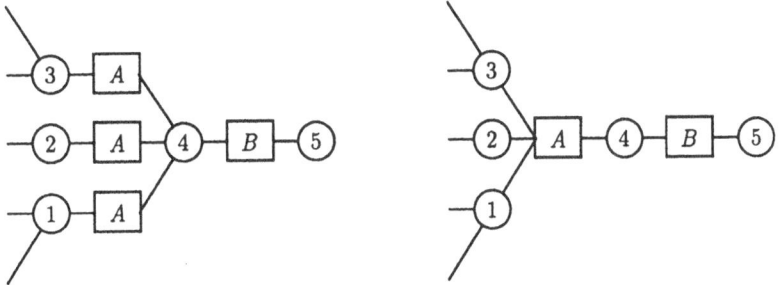

Fig. 12.13. Symbol vertices are merged into a single vertex

have to be replaced by a single node

15   $[S\ (1\ 14)\ (7\ 12)]$.

We need to adapt the algorithm, so as to make sure that the a packed node in the packed shared forest corresponds to a symbol node in the graph-structured stack.

- Whenever a state vertex is preceded by several symbol vertices that refer to (different entries of) the same grammar symbol, these symbol vertices are merged into a single vertex. The corresponding entries in the parse list are merged into a single entry, representing a packed node in the packed shared forest.

This is illustrated in Figure 12.13.

In a graph-theoretically more elegant description, a packed shared forest should be defined as a *bipartite directed graph*: a graph with two distinct types of nodes and edges only between nodes of different types. To that end, assume that every node is a packed node. "Ordinary" nodes, then, are packed nodes with only a single sub-node. Moreover, consider packed nodes and sub-nodes as separate nodes; a packed node has edges to each of its sub-nodes. A sub-node has edges to its packed successor nodes. Such an approach is taken by Rekers [1992], who uses *symbol nodes* for the packed nodes and *rule nodes*, labelled with the applicable rewrite rule, for the sub-nodes. Based on this bipartite graph structure, Rekers optimizes the packing of the forest and extends his GLR parser to the class of reduced context-free grammars (Tomita's algorithm cannot handle certain kinds of grammars, cf. Section 12.6).

For the current exposition, we will follow the informal approach of Tomita.

As an example, we will look at a few interesting situations that occur while parsing "I saw a man in the park with a telescope." Each figure contains

- the graph-structured stack;
- at each top of the stack, the next action(s) that have to be performed;
- the parse list representation of the packed shared forest.

We have labelled the parse list with letters, rather than numbers, because numbers are used in the graph structured stack to indicate states.

The first ambiguity occurs when "I saw a man" has been processed, cf. Figure 12.14. In the parsing table in Figure 12.6 we find $action[12, *prep] = \{sh6, re7\}$. Hence, while we await the shift on one branch of the stack, reductions of $VP \rightarrow *v\ NP$ and $S \rightarrow NP\ VP$ are carried out on another branch, cf. Figure 12.15.

Both tops of the stack are to shift to state 6 now, and the branches can be merged. After shifting $*prep$, $*det$, and $*n$, and reducing $NP \rightarrow *det\ *n$ the situation in Figure 12.16 is obtained.

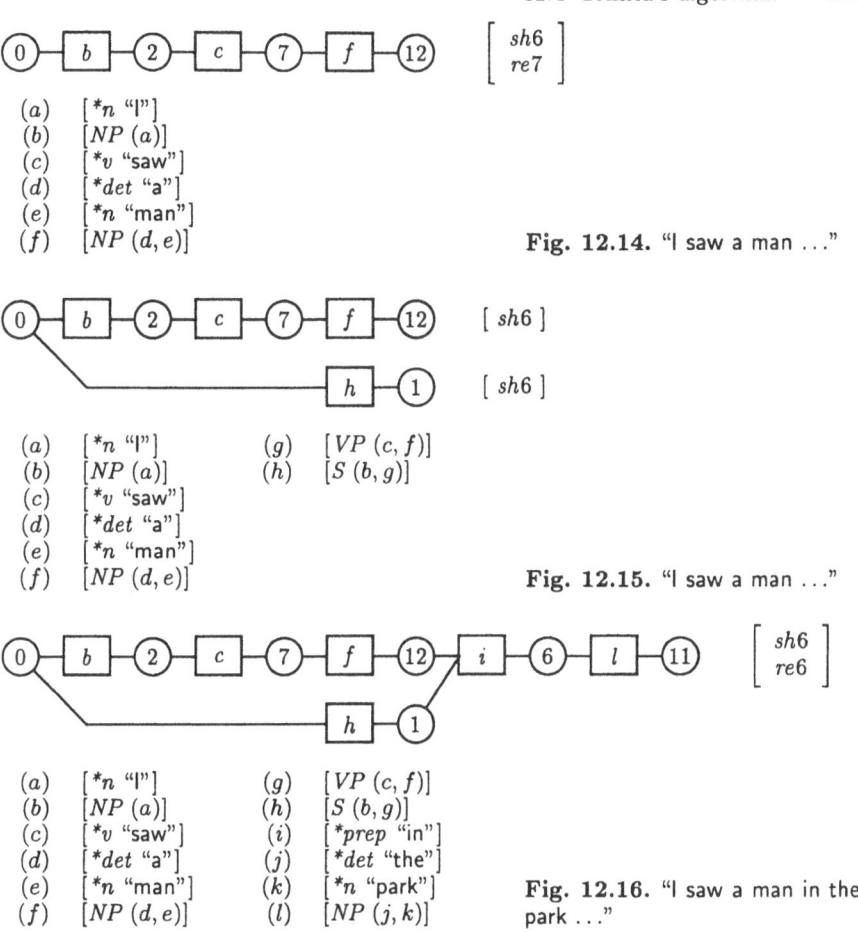

(a) $[^*n$ "I"]
(b) $[NP\,(a)]$
(c) $[^*v$ "saw"]
(d) $[^*det$ "a"]
(e) $[^*n$ "man"]
(f) $[NP\,(d,e)]$

Fig. 12.14. "I saw a man ..."

(a) $[^*n$ "I"]   (g) $[VP\,(c,f)]$
(b) $[NP\,(a)]$ (h) $[S\,(b,g)]$
(c) $[^*v$ "saw"]
(d) $[^*det$ "a"]
(e) $[^*n$ "man"]
(f) $[NP\,(d,e)]$

Fig. 12.15. "I saw a man ..."

(a) $[^*n$ "I"]   (g) $[VP\,(c,f)]$
(b) $[NP\,(a)]$ (h) $[S\,(b,g)]$
(c) $[^*v$ "saw"]   (i) $[^*prep$ "in"]
(d) $[^*det$ "a"]   (j) $[^*det$ "the"]
(e) $[^*n$ "man"]   (k) $[^*n$ "park"]
(f) $[NP\,(d,e)]$ (l) $[NP\,(j,k)]$

Fig. 12.16. "I saw a man in the park ..."

As we carry out *re*6, we have to add a *PP* to the state vertices that are 4 positions down from the top of the stack. We find two different state vertices (labelled 12 and 1), and both must be extended with a *PP* symbol vertex. The result of this reduction is shown in Figure 12.17. Note that *goto*[12,*PP*] = 9 and *goto*[1,*PP*] = 5, hence the two new branches of the stacks cannot be merged. But, as both branches contain the same *PP* "in the park", the two symbol vertices are labelled with the same entry in the parse list.

After all further reductions are carried out, and two *S* vertices covering "I saw a man in the park" are merged into a single vertex, we get the situation that is shown in Figure 12.18.

Parsing continues in similar fashion with the next *PP* "with a telescope". After the last word has been shifted, branches of the stack synchronize on *accept*, rather than *shift*. The final situation is shown in Figure 12.19.

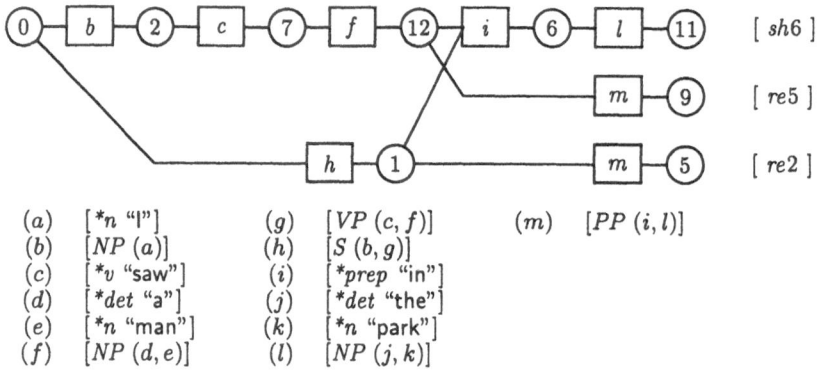

(a)	$[*n \ \text{"I"}]$	(g)	$[VP \ (c, f)]$	(m)	$[PP \ (i, l)]$
(b)	$[NP \ (a)]$	(h)	$[S \ (b, g)]$		
(c)	$[*v \ \text{"saw"}]$	(i)	$[*prep \ \text{"in"}]$		
(d)	$[*det \ \text{"a"}]$	(j)	$[*det \ \text{"the"}]$		
(e)	$[*n \ \text{"man"}]$	(k)	$[*n \ \text{"park"}]$		
(f)	$[NP \ (d, e)]$	(l)	$[NP \ (j, k)]$		

Fig. 12.17. "I saw a man in the park ..."

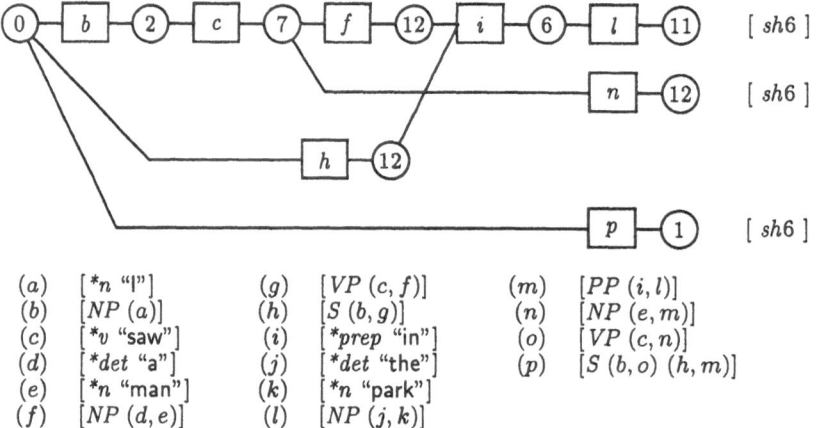

(a)	$[*n \ \text{"I"}]$	(g)	$[VP \ (c, f)]$	(m)	$[PP \ (i, l)]$
(b)	$[NP \ (a)]$	(h)	$[S \ (b, g)]$	(n)	$[NP \ (e, m)]$
(c)	$[*v \ \text{"saw"}]$	(i)	$[*prep \ \text{"in"}]$	(o)	$[VP \ (c, n)]$
(d)	$[*det \ \text{"a"}]$	(j)	$[*det \ \text{"the"}]$	(p)	$[S \ (b, o) \ (h, m)]$
(e)	$[*n \ \text{"man"}]$	(k)	$[*n \ \text{"park"}]$		
(f)	$[NP \ (d, e)]$	(l)	$[NP \ (j, k)]$		

Fig. 12.18. "I saw a man in the park ..."

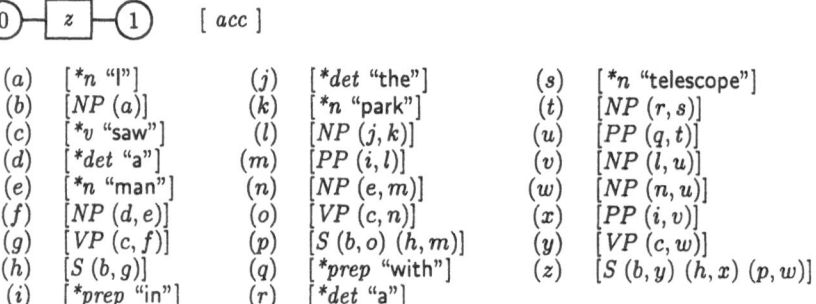

(a)	$[*n \ \text{"I"}]$	(j)	$[*det \ \text{"the"}]$	(s)	$[*n \ \text{"telescope"}]$
(b)	$[NP \ (a)]$	(k)	$[*n \ \text{"park"}]$	(t)	$[NP \ (r, s)]$
(c)	$[*v \ \text{"saw"}]$	(l)	$[NP \ (j, k)]$	(u)	$[PP \ (q, t)]$
(d)	$[*det \ \text{"a"}]$	(m)	$[PP \ (i, l)]$	(v)	$[NP \ (l, u)]$
(e)	$[*n \ \text{"man"}]$	(n)	$[NP \ (e, m)]$	(w)	$[NP \ (n, u)]$
(f)	$[NP \ (d, e)]$	(o)	$[VP \ (c, n)]$	(x)	$[PP \ (i, v)]$
(g)	$[VP \ (c, f)]$	(p)	$[S \ (b, o) \ (h, m)]$	(y)	$[VP \ (c, w)]$
(h)	$[S \ (b, g)]$	(q)	$[*prep \ \text{"with"}]$	(z)	$[S \ (b, y) \ (h, x) \ (p, w)]$
(i)	$[*prep \ \text{"in"}]$	(r)	$[*det \ \text{"a"}]$		

Fig. 12.19. "I saw a man in the park with a telescope."

12.5 A formal definition of Tomita's algorithm

We give a formal definition of Tomita's algorithm in the style of [Tomita, 1985]. The reason for writing out this definition is that it is a starting point for the formal definition of our PBT algorithm in Chapter 13.

A minor error in Tomita's algorithm has been repaired. A *set* of top nodes, rather than a single top node is returned. Different nodes for a single constituent cannot be shared when these lead to different states of the parser. This may also apply to roots of the parse tree. This enhancement is due to Lankhorst [1991], who also gives the following example. Take the following grammar

$S' \rightarrow S\$$
$S \rightarrow AA$
$A \rightarrow a$
$A \rightarrow \varepsilon$.

The resulting parse list for a string a is:

1 $[A]$	4 $[a]$	7 $[S\ (1,5)]$
2 $[A]$	5 $[A\ (4)]$	8 $[A]$
3 $[S\ (1,2)]$	6 $[A\ (4)]$	9 $[S\ (6,8)]$.

The result delivered by Tomita's original algorithm is node 9 as a root of the parse forest, being the last node found by an *accept* action. Node 7 is also a root, however, and therefore should also be delivered as result.

In the description of the algorithm the arrows are directed *from right to left* (in the illustrations in the previous section). A top of the stack is a *source* of the graph, the bottom of the stack is the *sink*. This is counterintuitive, perhaps, but has some advantages for implementation.

In the formal description we use the following functions and global variables:

Γ: graph-structured stack. This is a directed, acyclic graph with a single leaf node, v_0, labelled with state number s_0. Γ is initialized in PARSE and altered in REDUCER, E-REDUCER, and SHIFTER.

T: shared packed forest. This is a directed graph (V, E) in which each vertex $v \in V$ may have more than one successor list $\langle v, L \rangle \in E$. Initialized in PARSE and altered in REDUCER, E-REDUCER, and SHIFTER.

r: the result. This is a set of vertices of T which refer to the roots of the parse forest. Initialized in PARSE and altered in ACTOR.

$U_{i,j}$: set of vertices of Γ; $U_{i,0}$ is created created when parsing a_i, $U_{i,j}$ with $j > 0$ when parsing the j-th ε after a_i.

A: subset of "active" vertices of $U_{i,j}$ on which reductions and shift actions can be carried out. A is initialized in PARSEWORD and altered in ACTOR and E-REDUCER.

R: set of edges to be reduced. Each element is a triple $\langle v, x, p \rangle$ with $v \in U_{i,j}$, $x \in$ SUCCESSORS(v) and p a non-empty production of G. $\langle v, x, p \rangle \in R$ means that *reduce* p is to be applied on the path starting with the edge from v to x. REDUCER will take care of it. R is initialized in PARSEWORD and altered in ACTOR and REDUCER.

R_e: set of vertices on which an ε-reduction is to be carried out. Each element is a pair $\langle v, p \rangle$ with $v \in U_{i,j}$ and p and ε-production. $\langle v, p \rangle \in R_e$ means that *reduce* p is to be applied on the vertex v. E-REDUCER will carry out this reduction. R_e is initialized in PARSEWORD and altered in ACTOR and E-REDUCER.

Q: set of vertices to be shifted on. $\langle v, s \rangle \in Q$ means that *shift* s is to be carried out on v. SHIFTER will take care of this. Q is initialized in PARSEWORD and altered in ACTOR and SHIFTER.

LEFT(p):   left-hand side of production p.

$|p|$:   length of the right-hand side of production p.

STATE(v):   takes a vertex in Γ as its argument and returns the state label of this vertex.

SYMBOL(x):   takes a vertex in Γ as its argument and returns the symbol label of this vertex. This label is a link to a vertex in T.

SUCCESSORS(v):   takes a vertex in Γ as its argument and returns the set of all vertices x in Γ such that there is an edge from v to x.

GOTO(s, A):   looks up the goto table and returns a state number. s is a state number and A is a grammar symbol.

ACTION(s):   looks up the action table and returns a set of actions. s is a state number.

ADDSUBNODE(v, L):   takes a vertex v in T and a successor list L as arguments and adds $\langle v, L \rangle$ to E in $T = (V, E)$.

The parser is defined by the following set of procedures

procedure PARSE$(G, a_1 \ldots a_n)$
begin
    $a_{n+1} := \$$;
    $\Gamma := \emptyset; T := \emptyset; r := \emptyset$;
    create in Γ a vertex v_0 labelled s_0;
    $U_{0,0} := \{v_0\}$;
    for $i := 0$ **to** n **do** PARSEWORD(i) **od**;
    return r, the set of roots of the parse forest
end PARSE;

procedure PARSEWORD(i)
begin
  $j := 0$; $A := U_{i,0}$;
  $Q := \emptyset$; $R := \emptyset$; $R_e := \emptyset$;
  repeat
    if $A \neq \emptyset$ **then** ACTOR
    elseif $R \neq \emptyset$ **then** REDUCER
    elseif $R_e \neq \emptyset$ **then** E-REDUCER
    fi
  until $A = \emptyset$ **and** $R = \emptyset$ **and** $R_e = \emptyset$;
  SHIFTER
end PARSEWORD;

procedure ACTOR
begin
  remove one element v from A;
  for all $\alpha \in$ ACTION(STATE(v))
  do **if** $\alpha = accept$
    then $r := r \cup \{v\}$;
    elseif $\alpha = shift$
    then $Q := Q \cup \{\langle v, \text{GOTO}(\text{STATE}(v), a_{i+1})\rangle\}$
    elseif $\alpha = reduce\ p$ **and** p is not an ε-production
    then for all $x \in$ SUCCESSORS(v)
      do $R := R \cup \{\langle v, x, p\rangle\}$ **od**
    elseif $\alpha = reduce\ p$ **and** p is an ε-production
    then $R_e := R_e \cup \{\langle v, p\rangle\}$
    fi
  od
end ACTOR;

procedure REDUCER
begin
    remove one element $\langle v, x, p \rangle$ from R;
    $N := $ LEFT(p);
    for all y such that there is a path of length $2|p| - 2$ from x to y
    do $L := ($SYMBOL$(z_1), \ldots, $SYMBOL$(z_{|p|}))$, **where**
                      $z_1 = x_1$, $z_{|p|} = y$ and $z_2, \ldots, z_{|p|-1}$ are
                             symbol vertices on the path from x to y;
        for all s such that
                    $\exists w(w \in$ SUCCESSORS$(y) \wedge$ GOTO$($STATE$(w), N) = s)$
        do $W := \{w \mid w \in$ SUCCESSORS$(y) \wedge$
                                   GOTO$($STATE$(w), N) = s\}$;
        if $\exists u(u \in U_{i,j} \wedge$ STATE$(u) = s)$
        then **if** there is an edge from u to a vertex z
                            such that SUCCESSORS$(z) = W$
                then ADDSUBNODE$($SYMBOL$(z), L)$
                else create in T a node m labelled N;
                      ADDSUBNODE(m, L);
                      create in Γ a vertex z labelled m;
                      create in Γ an edge frome u to z;
                      for all $w \in W$
                      do create in Γ an edge from z to w **od**
                      if $u \notin A$
                      then **for all** q such that
                                  reduce $q \in$ ACTION(s)
                            and q is not an ε-production
                        do $R := R \cup \{\langle u, z, q \rangle\}$ **od**
                      fi
                fi
        else create in T a node m labelled N;
             ADDSUBNODE(m, L);
             create in Γ two vertices u and z
                      labelled s and m, respectively ;
             create in Γ an edge from u to z;
             for all $w \in W$
             do create in Γ and edge from z to w **od**;
            $U_{i,j} := U_{i,j} \cup \{w\}$;
            $A := A \cup \{w\}$
        fi
      od
    od
end REDUCER;

procedure E-REDUCER
begin
       $U_{i,j+1} := \emptyset$;
       for all s such that
                    $\exists \langle v, p \rangle \in R_e$ such that GOTO(STATE(v), LEFT(p)) $= s$
       do $N :=$ LEFT(p);
              create in T a node m labelled N;
              ADDSUBNODE(m, NIL);
              create in Γ two vertices u and z labelled s and m, respectively;
              create in Γ and edge from u to z;
              $U_{i,j+1} := U_{i,j+1} \cup \{w\}$;
              for all $\langle v, p \rangle \in R_e$ such that GOTO(STATE(v), LEFT(p)) $= s$
              do create in Γ an edge from x to v **od**;
              $R_e := \emptyset$;
              $A := U_{j+1}$;
              $j := j + 1$
       od
end E-REDUCER;

procedure SHIFTER
begin
       $U_{i+1,0} := \emptyset$;
       create in T a node m labelled a_{i+1};
       for all s such that $\exists v(\langle v, s \rangle \in Q)$
       do   create in Γ two vertices x and w labelled s and m, respectively;
              create in Γ and edge from w to x;
              $U_{i+1,0} := U_{i+1,0} \cup \{w\}$;
              for all v such that $\langle v, s \rangle \in Q$
              do create an edge from x to v **od**
       od
end SHIFTER;

12.6 Pros and cons of Tomita's algorithm

We will first review the efficiency of Tomita's algorithm, and then discuss some limitations and extensions.

Tomita claims his algorithm to be five times faster than Earley's original algorithm [Earley, 1970] and two times faster than the improved version of Graham, Harrison and Ruzzo [1980], based on experiments with context-free grammars for (parts of) the English language. A worst-case analysis is somewhat more involved. Earley's algorithm has $O(n^3)$ worst-case complexity for a sentence of length n. The worst-case complexity of Tomita's algorithm depends on the length of the right-hand side of the grammar. Let ϱ be the length of the longest right-hand side of a production. Then the worst-case complexity of Tomita's algorithm is $O(n^{\varrho+1})$. Johnson [1989] gives an argument for this complexity based on the number of edges in a packed shared forest for very ambiguous grammars. A constructive way to derive this complexity bound is the following.

We can divide the set of state vertices U in the graph-structured stack at any time into subsets $U_0, \ldots, U_k$, where k is the number of words that has been scanned. U_i contains those state vertices that have been created between scanning word i and word $i + 1$. The size of U_i is limited by a constant (the number of states). Suppose, now, that a reduction has to be carried out on a top of the stack $v \in U_k$, for a production with ϱ right-hand side symbols. Then all paths from v with length 2ϱ have to be followed, in order to determine the *ancestors*[2] (the vertices onto which the left-hand side symbol has to be shifted).

How many paths of length 2ϱ from v could exist? Because we have merged corresponding symbol vertices preceding a state vertex, there is only one edge from each state vertex to its preceding symbol vertex. Thus we ignore the symbol vertices and move directly from state vertex to state vertex. Retracing the right-hand side, we have to move the dot back over all ϱ symbols. When the grammar is sufficiently ambiguous, for a state vertex in U_j its successor state vertex can be located in any U_i with $0 \leq i \leq j$. Starting in U_k, and doing this ϱ times, we find $O(k^\varrho)$ possibilities. Hence the total cost for the reduction of a vertex in U_k are $O(k^\varrho)$.

As the size of U_k is $O(1)$, all reductions in U_k can be handled in $O(k^\varrho)$ time. As we have to do this for k ranging from 0 to n, we find a total time complexity for all $n + 1$ positions of $O(n^{\varrho+1})$.

It has been remarked by Kipps [1989] that a Tomita *recognizer* can be constructed with a worst-case complexity $O(n^3)$. Using a more sophisticated

---

[2] These are called ancestors by Kipps [1989]. Because the edges of the graphs point in reverse direction, (cf. Section 12.5, which follows Tomita [1985] in that respect), in graph theory terminology these should be called *descendants*. Ancestor is the more appropriate name, it seems, because an ancestor is older (put on the stack earlier) than the vertex of which it is an ancestor.

graph search algorithm, the $O(n)$ ancestors of a vertex that has to be reduced can be found in $O(n^2)$ time. The price for a reduction of the worst-case complexity is high, however. On any grammar that is not nearly worst-case, the computing time will only increase because of the extra administration and the unnecessary sophistication of the graph search algorithm. Also, the problem that the packed shared forest may extend beyond $O(n^3)$ is not solved. But the same problem applies to Earley's algorithm when a packed shared forest has to be constructed from the completed chart. In order to make sure that the size of the forest is $O(n^3)$ in the worst case, one can share corresponding *prefixes of right-hand sides* as well; cf. Leermakers [1991] and Billot and Lang [1989].

From the above discussion it is clear that Tomita's algorithm is superior to Earley and GHR on "easy" grammars, but inferior on "difficult" grammars. Tomita claims that all natural language grammars are easy, i.e., *almost* LR and *almost* ε-free. We do not know of an empirical study that has systematically tested Tomita's algorithm against GHR for a large variety of natural language grammars.

Not all context-free grammars can be parsed by Tomita's algorithm. There are two classes of grammars for which the algorithm doesn't finish: cyclic grammars and hidden left-recursive grammars. We will briefly discuss each case.

A grammar is *cyclic* if $A \Rightarrow^+ A$ for some nonterminal $A \in N$. The problem is clear: whenever an A is put onto the stack, no further *shift* takes place as the algorithm doesn't stop reducing ever more A's.

A more subtle class of grammars that busts the algorithm are *hidden left-recursive grammars*.[3] A grammar is hidden left-recursive if there are A, B, α, β such that

(i) $A \Rightarrow^* B\alpha A\beta$,
(ii) $B\alpha \Rightarrow^* \varepsilon$.

When $\beta \Rightarrow^* \varepsilon$ the grammar is cyclic, but in general it is not necessarily the case that β rewrites to ε. Consider the grammar, defined by the productions

$\{S \rightarrow ASb, \; S \rightarrow a, \; A \rightarrow \varepsilon\}$.

The parser sees an a as the first word. How many times should $A \rightarrow \varepsilon$ be reduced before we do the first *shift*? In order to deal with arbitrary sentences of the form ab^*, an infinite amount of shifts is needed. This is reflected by the parsing table for this grammar, which remains in the same state after reducing $A \rightarrow \varepsilon$.

---

[3] The term *hidden left-recursive* is due to Nederhof [1993]. Nozohoor-Farshi [1989] called such grammars *ill-formed*, for want of a better word. In [Lankhorst and Sikkel, 1991], [Sikkel and Lankhorst, 1992] we called them *pseudo-cyclic*.

One could wonder whether hidden left-recursive grammars are relevant to natural language parsing. Nederhof and Sarbo [1993] report to have found a grammar for Dutch, the Deltra grammar developed at the Delft University of Technology [Schoorl and Belder, 1990], that has a hidden left-recursive context-free backbone.

The problem with hidden left-recursive grammars, which was overlooked by Tomita [1985], has been solved by Nozohoor-Farshi [1989]. He introduces a cycle in the stack which can be unrolled as many times as needed. A more fundamental solution is proposed by Nederhof and Sarbo [1993]. They leave the stack acyclic and make it optional whether the stack contains nullable right-hand side symbols in a reduction. Rekers [1992] has eliminated the problem of hidden left-recursion in yet another way, by optimizing the sharing of the graph-structured stack. The infinite sequence of A's, all describe the empty string at position 0. Hence, in Rekers' optimally shared stack, an infinite sequence of state vertices that would be generated by Tomita collapses into a single state vertex. Like the algorithms of Nederhof and Sarbo [1993] and Rekers [1992], the The PBT algorithm that will be discussed in Chapter 13 can deal with arbitrary (reduced) context-free grammars.

Generalized LR parsing has been extended to context-sensitive grammars by Harkema and Tomita [1991]. Other papers on Tomita's algorithm can be found in [Tomita, 1991] and [Heemels et al., 1991].

12.7 An annotated version of Tomita's algorithm

We annotate Tomita's parse stack with Earley items. For a fair comparison with the Earley chart parser, we use a generalized LR(0) parser, without look-ahead. In Section 12.8, subsequently, we will define parsing schemata for LR(0) and SLR(1), based on the items with which the stack is annotated here.

The canonical Tomita parser is based on (generalized) SLR(1). We start with a slightly different Tomita parser, based on LR(0), because for this one it is easiest to derive a parsing schema. Moreover, the LR(0) Tomita parser is the basis for constructing the parallel Tomita parser in the next chapter.

There are a few subtle difference between LR(0) parsers on the one hand and all other LR parsers on the other hand. No look-ahead is used, hence the type of the next action is determined only by the top state of the stack. If *shift* is a possible action, the next state depends also on the particular symbol that is shifted. To that end, the *goto* table covers nonterminal and terminal symbols alike. Whenever a symbol is pushed onto the stack, the combination of state and symbol determines the next state. The *error* action no longer exists now. From the construction of the parsing table it follows that each state has some valid action. Errors occur, however, when a *shift* is done but

	LR(0) items	action	*d	*n	*v	*p	$	NP	VP	PP	S
			— goto table								
0	S'→.$S$$ S→.NP VP S→.S PP NP→.*n NP→.*det *n NP→.NP PP	sh	3	4				2			1
1	S'→S.$ S→S.PP PP→.*prep NP	sh				6	acc			5	
2	S→NP.VP NP→NP.PP VP→.*v NP PP→.*prep NP	sh			7	6			8	9	
3	NP→*det.*n	sh		10							
4	NP→*n.	re3									
5	S→S PP.	re2									
6	PP→*prep.NP NP→.*n NP→.*det *n NP→.NP PP	sh	3	4				11			
7	VP→*v.NP NP→.*n NP→.*det *n NP→.NP PP	sh	3	4				12			
8	S→NP VP.	re1									
9	NP→NP PP.	re5									
10	NP→*det *n.	re4									
11	PP→*prep NP. NP→NP.PP PP→.*prep NP	re6 sh				6				9	
12	VP→*v NP. NP→NP.PP PP→.*prep NP	re7 sh				6				9	

Fig. 12.20. An annotated LR(0) parsing table for G_4

there is no next state for the symbol that is shifted. Then the shift is cancelled and the branch of the stack on which a shift was tried can be removed. An annotated LR(0) parsing table for grammar G_4 is shown in Figure 12.20. Note that the *accept* is in fact disguised as a *shift*. If a *shift* is decided upon and the goto table yield *acc*, the parser moves to a special *accept* state that is not shown in the parsing table. Alternatively, one could explicitly include a state {S'→$S$$.} and offer *accept* as the only possible action in that state.

The class of deterministic SLR(1) grammars is strictly larger than the class of deterministic LR(0) grammars. This is exemplified by G_3 (cf. Figure 12.1 on page 257). The SLR(1) table has no ambiguities. In an LR(0) table, state 5 would offer both *sh* and *re5*. Without look-ahead one cannot deterministically decide whether the verb has a direct object.

Having introduced the annotated LR(0) parsing table, we can now give an explicit correspondence between the parse stack and LR(0) items on the one hand and Earley-type items on the other hand. The latter ones, having the general format $[A\rightarrow\alpha\bullet\beta, i, j]$ are called *marked LR(0) items* in this context. We will first introduce an *annotated LR(0) Tomita parser* that incorporates marked items into its parse stack, and then derive a parsing schema for the domain of marked items that is implemented by an LR(0) Tomita parser.

Let G be a context-free grammar and G' its augmented grammar. The set of marked items for G' is defined by

$$\mathcal{I}_{LR(0)} = \{[A\rightarrow\alpha\bullet\beta, i, j] \mid A\rightarrow\alpha\beta \in P' \wedge 0 \leq i \leq j\}. \tag{12.17}$$

The graph-structured stack can be described as a bipartite directed graph $\Gamma = (U, Y; E)$, where U is the set of state vertices, Y the set of symbol vertices, and E the set of edges connecting vertices to one another. For the sake of simplicity, we run the algorithm only as a recognizer. Hence, symbol vertices are labelled with grammar symbols and no parse list is produced. We write SYMBOL(y) for the label of a symbol vertex $y \in Y$. We write STATE(u) for the state with which a state vertex $u \in U$ is labelled. The set of state vertices U that is used for parsing a sentence $a_1 \ldots a_n$ can be partitioned into $U_0 \cup \ldots \cup U_n$. The subset U_i contains those state vertices that are put onto the stack when the words $a_{i+1} \ldots a_n\$$ remain on the input.

The Annotated LR(0) Tomita algorithm is obtained from the LR(0) Tomita algorithm by two simple changes in the way the stack is maintained. Firstly, when a reduction is carried out there is no need to delete the part of the stack that is being reduced. We can simply leave it in the graph and start a new branch from the appropriate state vertex. It is remarked by Tomita [1985] that this does not change the algorithm in any way (and in fact Tomita doesn't prune branches of the graph either), only the presentation of what a graph-structured stack looks like is different.

Secondly, we will label the state vertices with sets of marked items, denoted ITEMS(u) for any $u \in U_j \subset U$. For every LR(0) item $A\rightarrow\alpha\bullet\beta \in$ STATE(u), we add one (sometimes a few) marked item $[A\rightarrow\alpha\bullet\beta, i, j]$ to ITEMS(u). We have to determine, however, which position markers should be contained in the marked item. This is done as follows.

- The right position marker corresponds to the subset U_j of U.
  That is, if $[A\rightarrow\alpha\bullet\beta, i, j] \in$ ITEMS(u) then $u \in U_j$.
- For initial items, the left and right position marker coincide.
  That is, if $[A\rightarrow\bullet\beta, i, j] \in$ ITEMS(u) then $i = j$.
- For non-initial items, the left position marker is determined as follows.
  Let $A\rightarrow\alpha X\bullet\beta \in$ STATE(u) then u is the predecessor[4] of a symbol vertex y

---

[4] We assume here that edges are directed from right to left, i.e., from the tops of the stack towards the root. Because of the way in which the stack is constructed (and the standard way to depict a stack with the root at the left and the tops at

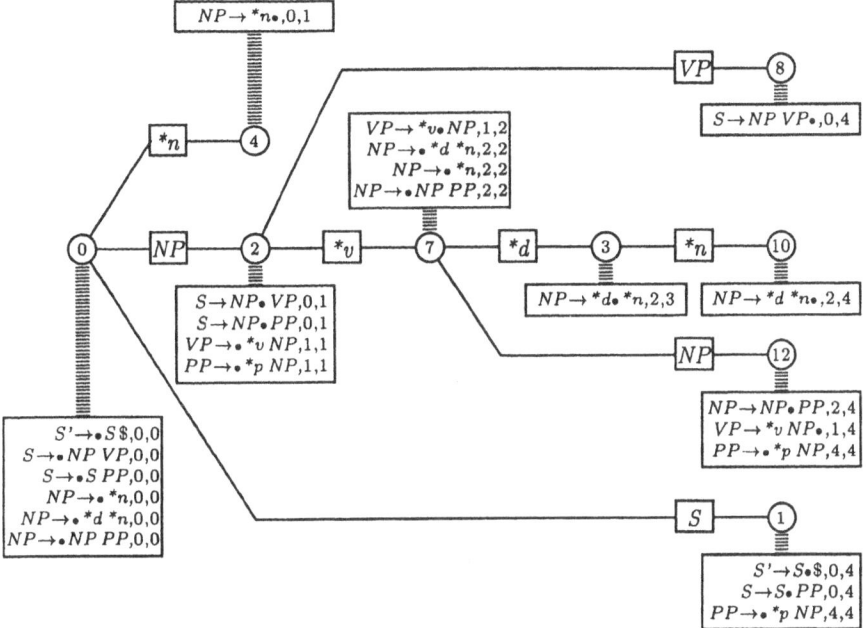

Fig. 12.21. Annotated stack for I saw a man...

with SYMBOL$(y) = X$. For each state vertex v that is a successor of y it holds that ITEMS(v) contains some Earley item $[A{\to}\alpha{\bullet}X\beta,i,k]$.
For all successors v of y and for all values of i such that $[A{\to}{\bullet}X\beta,i,k] \in$ ITEMS(v), an Earley item $[A{\to}X{\bullet}\beta,i,j]$ is added to ITEMS(u).

As output of the annotated Tomita parser we will consider the marked LR(0) items that appear in the final graph-structured stack, rather than the parse list. In Figure 12.21 and Figure 12.22 the annotated graph-structured stack is shown for "I saw a man with a telescope".

Definition 12.1. (*LR(0)-viable items*)A marked LR(0) item $[A{\to}\alpha{\bullet}\beta,i,j]$ is called *LR(0)-viable for a string* $a_1 \ldots a_n$ if, there is some $z \in \Sigma^*$ such that

(i) $S'{\Rightarrow}^*a_1 \ldots a_iAz\$,$
(ii) $\alpha{\Rightarrow}^*a_{i+1} \ldots a_j.$ □

In the sequel we will prove that a final stack of the annotated LR(0) Tomita parser contains all viable marked items and no other ones. But first we recapitulate (in a much simplified form) the essential notions of parsing schemata and parsing systems.

---

the right) this seems the wrong way around. This "reversed" direction of edges is chosen because of some implementations details that do not matter right here. We stick to this terminology here to be compatible with the formal definition of Tomita's algorithm that has been presented in 12.5.

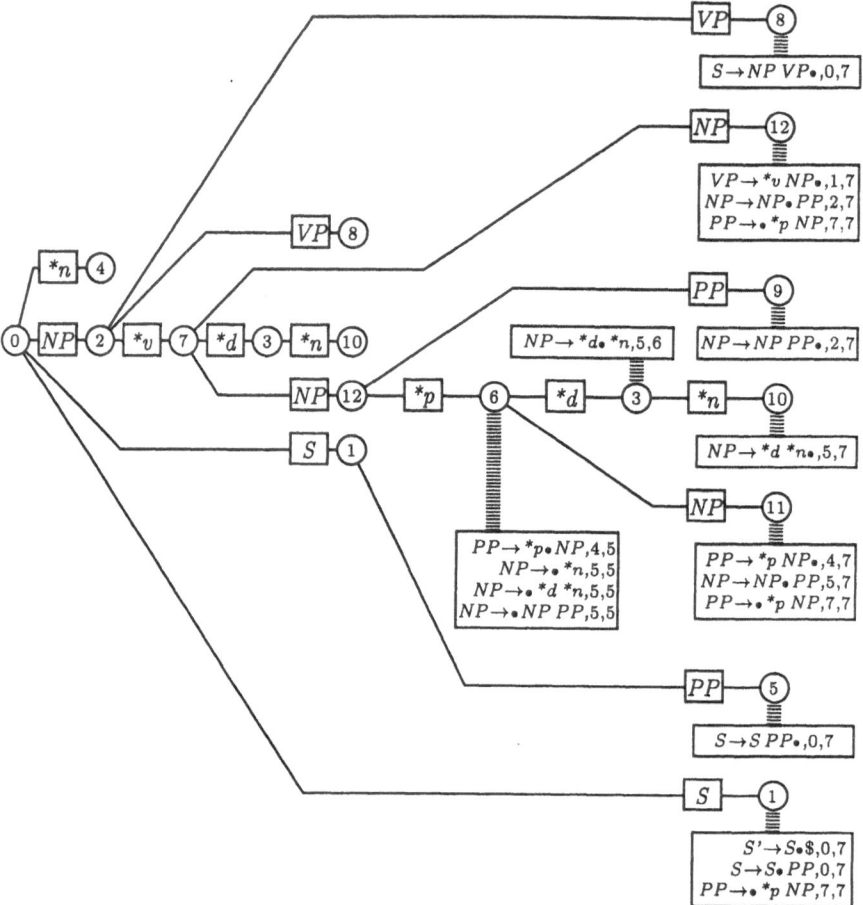

Fig. 12.22. Annotated stack for ... with a telescope ...

12.8 Parsing Schemata for LR(0) and SLR(1)

A *parsing system* for some grammar G and string $a_1 \ldots a_n$ is a triple $\mathbb{P} = \langle \mathcal{I}, H, D \rangle$ with $\mathcal{I}$ a set of items, H an initial set of items and D a set of *deduction steps* that allow to derive new items from already known items. The set of initial items H encodes the sentence that is to be parsed. For a sentence $a_1 \ldots a_n$ we take

$$H = \{[a_1, 0, 1], \ldots, [a_n, n-1, n], [\$, n, n+1]\}. \tag{12.18}$$

The item set $\mathcal{I}$ for an LR(0) parsing system has been specified in (12.17) on page 280. Deduction steps in D are of the form

$$\eta_1, \ldots, \eta_k \vdash \xi.$$

The items $\eta_1, \ldots, \eta_k$ are called the *antecedents* and the item ξ is called the *consequent* of a deduction step. If all antecedents of a deduction step are recognized by a parser, then the consequent should also be recognized. An item $[A \rightarrow \alpha \bullet \beta, i, j] \in \mathcal{I}$ is *valid* in $\mathbb{P}$ if it can be recognized from the initial set H by applying a sequence of deduction steps.

A parsing system $\mathbb{P}$ is defined for a particular grammar and string. An *uninstantiated parsing system* only defines $\mathcal{I}$ and D for a particular grammar G. Such a system can be instantiated by adding a set of hypotheses for a particular string $a_1 \ldots a_n$. A *parsing schema* is defined for a class of grammars. For each grammar in this class, it defines an uninstantiated parsing system.

Let us now define a parsing schema **LR(0)**, abstracting from all the algorithmic details of an annotated LR(0) Tomita parser. The schema is defined for reduced acyclic context-free grammars without hidden left-recursion. We specify the parsing schema by defining a parsing system $\mathbb{P}_{LR(0)} = \langle \mathcal{I}_{LR(0)}, H, D_{LR(0)} \rangle$ for an arbitrary grammar G and string $a_1 \ldots a_n$. $\mathcal{I}_{LR(0)}$ and H have already been defined above, so we only have to determine the set of deduction steps $D_{LR(0)}$ that is implemented by our annotated Tomita parser. D can be divided into distinct subsets.

Initial LR(0) items are contained in a state of the parser because they are contained in the closure of some non-initial item. Similarly, initial marked items in ITEMS(u) of some state vertex u can be computed by a closure operation on marked items. The set of deduction steps that describes all closures is specified by:[5]

$$D^{Cl} = \{[A \rightarrow \alpha \bullet B\beta, i, j] \vdash [B \rightarrow \bullet \gamma, j, j]\}. \tag{12.19}$$

If the string γ in (12.19) starts with a nonterminal, then $[B \rightarrow \bullet \gamma, j, j]$ is the antecedent of another closure step. Hence we do not need to specify explicitly that the transitive closure has to be taken, as in the algorithm in Figure 12.2.

In order to start the parser, we need an initial deduction step without antecedents:

$$D^{Init} = \{\vdash [S' \rightarrow \bullet S\$, 0, 0]\}. \tag{12.20}$$

The other marked items of the initial vertex u_0 can be deduced from $[S' \rightarrow \bullet S\$, 0, 0]$ by deduction steps in D^{Cl}.

A *shift* action is feasible in a state that contains an LR(0) item $A \rightarrow \alpha \bullet a\beta$. I.e., a shift is possible from a state vertex having a marked item $[A \rightarrow \alpha \bullet a\beta, i, j]$. The shift is successful for this particular item only if the next word of input is indeed a. Thus we obtain the set of *shift* deduction steps:

---

[5] A remark on the notation of (12.19): all items that occur in a deduction step must, by definition, be taken from $\mathcal{I}$ or H. Hence conditions like, e.g., $B \rightarrow \gamma \in P'$ need not be stated again. So, in this case, the entire right part of the usual set notation $\{\ldots \mid \ldots\}$ is absent.

$$D^{Sh} = \{[A\rightarrow\alpha.a\beta,i,j],[a,j,j+1] \vdash [A\rightarrow\alpha a.\beta,j,j+1]\}. \qquad (12.21)$$

Finally we turn to the most difficult case, the reduction. A *reduce* action is possible in a state that contains a final LR(0) item, i.e., a *reduce* is possible from a state vertex that contains a final marked item. Let $[B\rightarrow\gamma.,i,j] \in$ STATE(u) for some u, with $\gamma = X_1\ldots X_k$. Then we can retrace a path of symbol and state vertices labelled with (among others)

$$X_k, \ [B\rightarrow X_1\ldots X_{k-1}.X_k,i,j_{k-1}], \quad \ldots, \quad X_1, \ [B\rightarrow.X_1\ldots X_k,i,i].$$

Let v be the vertex such that $[B\rightarrow.\gamma,i,i] \in$ ITEMS(v). Then there must be a non-final marked item in the same item set such that $[B\rightarrow.\gamma,i,i]$ can be derived from it by *closure* steps. Assume

$$[A\rightarrow\alpha.B\beta,h,i] \in \text{ITEMS}(v)$$

Then from v we have to extend the stack with a symbol vertex labelled B that has v as its successor and a predecessor state vertex w such that $[A\rightarrow\alpha B.\beta,h,j] \in$ ITEMS(w). All the intermediate vertices that were retraced in order to find v are not essential for the reduction.[6] Hence, the essential properties of a reduction are covered by the set of deduction steps

$$D^{Re} = \{[A\rightarrow\alpha.B\beta,h,i],[B\rightarrow\gamma.,i,j] \vdash [A\rightarrow\alpha B.\beta,h,j]\}. \qquad (12.22)$$

Now we have enumerated all deduction steps that specify how marked items are added to the graph-structured stack of the annotated LR(0) Tomita parser. This is summarized in the following parsing schema.

Schema 12.2. (LR(0))
The parsing schema **LR(0)** is defined for reduced acyclic context-free grammars without hidden left-recursion. Let G be such a grammar and G' the augmented grammar. A parsing system

$$\mathbb{P}_{LR(0)} = \langle \mathcal{I}_{LR(0)}, H, D_{LR(0)}\rangle$$

is defined by

$$\mathcal{I}_{LR(0)} = \{[A\rightarrow\alpha.\beta,i,j] \mid A\rightarrow\alpha\beta \in P' \wedge 0 \le i \le j\};$$

$$D^{Init} = \{\vdash [S'\rightarrow.S\$,0,0]\},$$

$$D^{Cl} = \{[A\rightarrow\alpha.B\beta,i,j] \vdash [B\rightarrow.\gamma,j,j]\},$$

$$D^{Sh} = \{[A\rightarrow\alpha.a\beta,i,j],[a,j,j+1] \vdash [A\rightarrow\alpha a.\beta,j,j+1]\},$$

---

[6] These vertices are not essential in then sense that they provide merely a data structure that allow to retrieve vertices v satisfying $[A\rightarrow\alpha.B\beta,h,i] \in$ ITEMS(v). Data structures are abstracted from in parsing schemata, hence the steps that need to be taken to find such vertices v do not show up in the deduction step. Searching the intermediate vertices *is* essential for the (in)efficiency of Tomita's algorithm when a massively ambiguous grammar with long right-hand sides is used, cf. Section 12.6. I.e., for such grammars a graph-structured stack is an inefficient *implementation* of the schema **LR(0)**.

$$D^{Re} \;\; = \;\; \{[A\rightarrow\alpha\bullet B\beta, h, i], [B\rightarrow\gamma\bullet, i, j] \;\vdash\; [A\rightarrow\alpha B\bullet\beta, h, j]\},$$

$$D_{LR(0)} \; = \; D^{Init} \cup D^{Cl} \cup D^{Sh} \cup D^{Re};$$

The set of hypotheses H depends on the input string, cf. (12.18) on page 282.

□

It is not a coincidence that this schema is very similar to the schema **Earley** defined in Example 4.32. The *predict, scan* and *complete* deduction steps in the Earley schema correspond to the *closure, shift* and *reduce* steps here. There are only two inessential differences between the parsing schemata **Earley** and **LR(0)**:

- **Earley** is defined for all context-free grammars, whereas **LR(0)** is only defined for reduced acyclic grammars without hidden left-recursion.
- **LR(0)** augments the grammar with an extra production $S'\rightarrow S\$$.

Corollary 12.3.
A marked LR(0) item is valid in **LR(0)** for some grammar G and sentence $a_1 \ldots a_n$ if and only if the item is LR(0)-viable for G and $a_1 \ldots a_n$ (cf. Definition 12.1 on page 281). □

Next, we will define a parsing schema for (generalized) SLR(1) by examining the differences between the LR(0) and SLR(1) Tomita parser. We have not defined an algorithm for the construction of an LR(0) table, but is it clear from the examples how this should be done. The relation between the SLR(1) and LR(0) tables is characterized as follows.

- $sh\ s' \in action_{LR(0)}[s]$ if and only if $sh\ s' \in action_{SLR(1)}[s, a]$ for some $a \in \Sigma'$;
- $re\ k \in action_{LR(0)}[s]$ if and only if $re\ k \in action_{SLR(1)}[s, a]$ for some $a \in \Sigma'$;
- $s' \in goto_{LR(0)}[s, a]$ if and only if $sh\ s' \in action_{SLR(1)}[s, a]$;
- $s' \in goto_{LR(0)}[s, A]$ if and only if $s' \in goto_{SLR(1)}[s, A]$.

This leads to the following differences for the parsing schemata:

- The *closure* deduction steps are identical, as the construction of the set of states is not affected.
- The *shift* deduction steps are identical. When the LR(0) parser decides to shift, this will only lead to a new entry in the stack if the goto table yields a new state for the shifted terminal.
- There is a difference in *reduce* deduction steps. In the SLR(1) case, a reduction is carried out only if this is licensed by the look-ahead symbol. In grammar G_3, for example, as defined on page 256, the SLR(1) parser will reduce a *v by a production $VP\rightarrow{}^*v$ only if it is followed by an end-of-sentence marker. The LR(0) parser always reduces *v to VP.

These observations are laid down in the following parsing schema.

Schema 12.4. (SLR(1))

The parsing schema **SLR(1)** is defined for reduced acyclic context-free grammars without hidden left-recursion. Let G be such a grammar and G' the augmented grammar. A parsing system $\mathbb{P}_{SLR(1)} = \langle \mathcal{I}_{SLR(1)}, H, D_{SLR(1)} \rangle$ is defined by

$$\mathcal{I}_{SLR(1)} = \{[A \rightarrow \alpha \cdot \beta, i, j] \mid A \rightarrow \alpha\beta \in P' \wedge 0 \leq i \leq j\};$$

$$D^{Init} = \{ \vdash [S' \rightarrow \cdot S\$, 0, 0]\},$$

$$D^{Cl} = \{[A \rightarrow \alpha \cdot B\beta, i, j] \vdash [B \rightarrow \cdot \gamma, j, j]\},$$

$$D^{Sh} = \{[A \rightarrow \alpha \cdot a\beta, i, j], [a, j, j+1] \vdash [A \rightarrow \alpha a \cdot \beta, i, j+1]\},$$

$$D^{Re} = \{[A \rightarrow \alpha \cdot B\beta, h, i], [B \rightarrow \gamma \cdot, i, j], [a, j, j+1]$$
$$\vdash [A \rightarrow \alpha B \cdot \beta, h, j] \mid a \in \text{FOLLOW}(B)\},$$

$$D_{SLR(1)} = D^{Init} \cup D^{Cl} \cup D^{Sh} \cup D^{Re};$$

The set of hypotheses H depends on the input string, cf. (12.18 on page 282.)

□

Note that is it possible to exploit the look-ahead more efficiently, for example by using $a \in \text{FIRST}(\beta\,\text{FOLLOW}(A))$, rather than $a \in \text{FOLLOW}(B)$ to filter irrelevant items. Also, one could apply a filter to the *scan* steps. But the schema has been defined such that incorporates exactly the same look-ahead that is used in the construction of an SLR(1) parsing table.

We call an item *SLR(1)-valid* for a grammar G and string $a_1 \ldots a_n$ if it is a valid item in the SLR(1) parsing system for G and $a_1 \ldots a_n$.

A characterization of the set of valid items is somewhat more involved in the SLR(1) case than in the LR(0) case. We define a set of *viable* items, the items that ought to be recognized, and then sketch a proof that this equals the set of valid items.

Definition 12.5. (*SLR(1)-viable items*)

The set of SLR(1)-viable items (or *viable* items for short) is the smallest subset of $\mathcal{I}_{SLR(1)}$ satisfying the following conditions:

- $[S' \rightarrow \cdot S\$, 0, 0]$ is viable;
- $[A \rightarrow \alpha a \cdot \beta, i, j+1]$ is viable if
  (i) $S' \Rightarrow^* a_1 \ldots a_i A z\$$ for some z,
  (ii) $\alpha \Rightarrow^* a_{i+1} \ldots a_j$;
- $[A \rightarrow \alpha B \cdot \beta, i, k]$ is viable if there are z and $j < k$ such that
  (i) $S' \Rightarrow^* a_1 \ldots a_i A z\$$,
  (ii) $\alpha \Rightarrow^* a_{i+1} \ldots a_j$,
  (iii) $B \Rightarrow^* a_{j+1} \ldots a_k$,
  (iv) $a_{k+1} \in \text{FOLLOW}(B)$;

- $[A{\rightarrow}\alpha B{\bullet}\beta, i, j]$ is viable if
  - (i) $S'{\Rightarrow}^* a_1 \ldots a_i A z\$$ for some z,
  - (ii) $\alpha{\Rightarrow}^* a_{i+1} \ldots a_j$,
  - (iii) $B{\Rightarrow}^* \varepsilon$,
  - (iv) $[A{\rightarrow}\alpha{\bullet}B\beta, i, j]$ is viable,
  - (v) $a_{j+1} \in \mathrm{FOLLOW}(B)$;
- $[C{\rightarrow}{\bullet}\gamma, t, j]$ is viable if there is a viable item $[A{\rightarrow}\alpha{\bullet}B\beta, i, j]$ such that $B{\Rightarrow}^+_{rm} C\delta$ for some δ.[7] $\square$

The recursion in this definition only relates to *nullable* symbols (i.e., B such that $B{\Rightarrow}^*\varepsilon$). These have to be taken proper care of. Consider, for example a grammar G defined by productions

$$S{\rightarrow}ABA, \quad S{\rightarrow}CBC, \quad A{\rightarrow}a, \quad B{\rightarrow}\varepsilon, \quad C{\rightarrow}c$$

and an input string ac. Then $[S{\rightarrow}AB{\bullet}A, 0, 1]$ is *not* viable, even though conditions (i), (ii), (iii) and (v) of the second last bullet are satisfied. The deduction step

$$[S{\rightarrow}A{\bullet}BA, 0, 1], [B{\rightarrow}{\bullet}, 1, 1], [c, 1, 2] \vdash [S{\rightarrow}AB{\bullet}A, 0, 1]$$

is never activated because $[S{\rightarrow}A{\bullet}BA, 0, 1]$ cannot be recognized; reduction of the first A is prevented by the look-ahead c.

Theorem 12.6. *(SLR(1)-validity)*
An item in $\mathcal{I}_{SLR(1)}$ is SLR(1)-valid if and only if it is SLR(1)-viable.

Proof (sketch).[8]

(i) *An SLR(1)-valid item is SLR(1)-viable:*
It has to be verified that every deduction step with hypotheses and/or viable items as antecedents has a viable consequent. This can be checked straightforwardly for each of the different kinds of deduction steps.

(ii) *An SLR(1)-viable item is SLR(1)-valid:*
With the same technique that was applied in Chapters 10 and 11 one can define a *walk length function* on viable items. For each viable item (except the initial item) a deduction step can be found such that the antecedents are hypotheses and/or viable items with a strictly lower walk length value. Hence, by induction on walk length, each viable item is shown to be valid. $\square$

---

[7] $\Rightarrow^+_{rm}$ denotes *rightmost* derivation.

[8] There is not much point in repeating, with different details, the somewhat lengthy argument in Section 10.3. See [Sikkel, 1995, forthcoming] for a general approach to these kind of proofs. A complete proof of Theorem 12.6 is given in [Sikkel, 1995].

12.9 Conclusion

We have derived some parsing schemata for (Generalized) LR parsers. Similar schemata for SLR(k), canonical LR(k) and LALR(k) can be added in the same fashion. In this way we have shown that parsing schemata can be used to describe parsing algorithms that are quite different from chart parsers.

The LR parsing schemata show the close relation between Generalized LR parsing – in particular Tomita's algorithm – and the conventional Earley parser. A more rigorous approach, in which the Earley parsing schema is transformed into a pushdown-automaton is given in [Sikkel, 1995, forthcoming]. Here it is insight, more than formal proof, that interested us.

In the next chapter we will exploit the relation between the parsers of Earley and Tomita for the definition of a *parallel* Tomita parser, obtained by cross-fertilizing Tomita's algorithm with a bottom-up parallelization of an Earley parser.

13. Parallel Bottom-up
Tomita parsing

In the previous chapter we have derived the parsing schema **LR(0)** and concluded that the differences with **Earley** are trivial details. Hence there is a structural correspondence between Earley chart parser and generalized LR parsers. This correspondence can be used to cross-fertilize different variants of either kind algorithm. A particularly interesting example that we will discuss here is the Parallel Bottom-up Tomita (PBT) algorithm [Lankhorst and Sikkel, 1991], [Sikkel and Lankhorst, 1992], where the conventional parallelization of Earley's algorithm is applied to the Tomita parser.

The PBT algorithm improves upon the canonical Tomita parser in several respects. Only a theoretical advantage is that it works for all (reduced) context-free grammars and obtains optimal sharing in the parse forest. An interesting practical property for large grammars is that parsing tables are small and can be computed in linear time. PBT has been implemented and empirically tested against Tomita's algorithm. It turns out that PBT is faster for long sentences and slower for short sentences; it is difficult to give a break-even point. Even though the speed-up is not overwhelming, we see this as a moderately positive result. The algorithm *works*[1] and has some theoretical advantages over the canonical Tomita parser. And, more important in the setting of this book, it shows that it is possible to design novel, useful algorithms by cross-breeding different algorithms with related underlying parsing schemata.

In 13.1 we define a parsing schema **PBT** that relates to **LR(0)** as **buE** relates to **Earley**. The basic algorithm is explained in 13.2 and a more efficient variant in 13.3, followed by the construction of the (distributed) parse list in 13.4. A formal specification of the PBT algorithm is presented in 13.5. In 13.6 the empirical test results are reported on. A brief overview of related approaches is given in 13.7, followed by conclusions in 13.8.

---

[1] It is very hard, if at all possible, to predict theoretically how communication bottlenecks and uneven load distribution will degrade the performance of an algorithm that looks nice on paper. See Thompson [1989], for example, for a parallel parser that gets *slower* the more processors are used for the job.

This chapter is based on cooperative work with Marc Lankhorst. A full account of the PBT parser is given in [Lankhorst and Sikkel, 1991], and overview has been published as [Sikkel and Lankhorst, 1992].

13.1 The PBT parsing schema

The obvious way to make a parallel implementation of a Tomita parser is to allocate each stack to a different process. Two such implementations, in a parallel logic programming language, have been presented by Tanaka and Numazaki. Maintaining a graph-structured stack would require too much synchronisation, therefore they work in parallel on separate copies of linear stacks [Tanaka and Numazaki, 1989], or with tree-structured stacks [Numazaki and Tanaka, 1990]. A similar line of parallelization is followed by Thompson, Dixon, and Lamping [1991]. They modify a nondeterministic shift/reduce parser in such a way that $O(n)$ time complexity is obtained if there are enough resources to fork off a separate process for each ambiguity. We look at the problem of Generalized LR parsing from quite a different angle. One could say that our view is perpendicular to the above approaches.

A straightforward parallel version of Earley's algorithm is obtained by discarding the top-down filter. This eliminates the need to parse the sentence in left-to-right fashion, one can start parsing at each word of the sentence in parallel; cf. Section 4.6 where the bottom-up Earley schema **buE** has been defined. In a similar vein, we will delete the top-down prediction from Generalized LR parsing, and define a Tomita-like parser with an underlying parsing schema that is almost identical to **buE**. Our *Parallel Bottom-up Tomita* (*PBT*) parser will not use look-ahead; it can be seen as a parallelization of the LR(0)-based Tomita parser.

Schema 13.1. (PBT)
The parsing schema **PBT** is defined for all reduced context-free grammars (cf. page 254). Let G' be the the augmented grammar of some reduce grammar G. A parsing system $\mathbb{P}_{PBT} = \langle \mathcal{I}_{PBT}, H, D_{PBT} \rangle$ is defined by

$$\mathcal{I}_{PBT} = \{[A \to \alpha \bullet \beta, i, j] \mid A \to \alpha\beta \in P' \land 0 \le i \le j\};$$

$$D^{Init} = \{\vdash [A \to \bullet \alpha, j, j]\},$$

$$D^{Sh} = \{[A \to \alpha \bullet a\beta, i, j], [a, j, j+1] \vdash [A \to \alpha a \bullet \beta, i, j+1]\},$$

$$D^{Re} = \{[A \to \alpha \bullet B\beta, h, i], [B \to \gamma \bullet, i, j] \vdash [A \to \alpha B \bullet \beta, h, j]\},$$

$$D_{PBT} = D^{Init} \cup D^{Sh} \cup D^{Re}.$$

The main difference between **PBT** and **buE** is the use of the extra production $S' \to S\$$ with which the grammar has been augmented. Furthermore, **buE** is also defined for non-reduced context-free grammars. $\qquad\square$

13.2 A PBT parser

We will define a Tomita-like parallel parsing algorithm that implements the **PBT** schema. In fact we only define a recognizer here, similarly to the annotated version of Tomita's algorithm. The architecture of the PBT parser comprises a sequence of of processes $P_0, \ldots, P_n$, communicating in a pipeline. See Figure 13.1. Each process computes its own part of the (distributed) parse list. But we will defer construction of the parse list until Section 13.4. If less than n processors are available for parsing a sentence $a_1 \ldots a_n$, then several processes can be shared by a single processor. The task of a process P_i is to recognize all constituents that start at position i in the sentence.

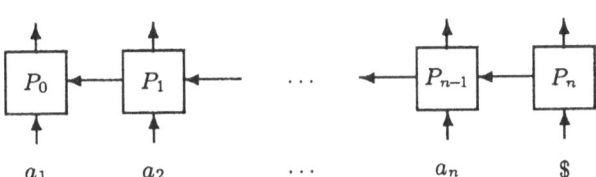

Fig. 13.1. A pipeline of processes

For technical reasons, recognized constituents will always be tagged with position markers. We write $\langle i, X, j \rangle$ for a constituent X that spans the substring $a_{i+1} \ldots a_j$ of the sentence. We use angular brackets rather than square brackets so as to underline the difference with marked LR(0) items. It is more convenient to start a marked symbol with the left position marker for reasons that will become clear in Section 13.4.

Marked items are used only in the annotated versions of Tomita-like parsers and can be disposed of. Marked symbols, on the other hand, are essential for the algorithmic details of the PBT parser. Whenever a constituent is recognized by some process P_i it is passed down the pipeline in leftward direction. If, for example, P_i has recognized a prepositional phrase $\langle i, PP, j \rangle$, then some other process P_h, having recognized a noun phrase $\langle h, NP, i \rangle$ might pick it up and construct a composite noun phrase $\langle h, NP, j \rangle$ using the production $NP \rightarrow NP\ PP$.

Each process runs and adapted version of a Tomita parser and creates its private graph-structured stack. Process P_i starts with recognizing its "own" word a_i and delivers a constituent $\langle i, a, i+1 \rangle$ down the pipeline. Subsequently, it reads a stream of symbols from its right neighbour, takes appropriate actions, and sends the stream of symbols to its left neighbour. For each constituent that is passed down the pipeline, P_i tries whether it fits somewhere onto its graph-structured stack. If so, the stack is expanded with a symbol vertex and a state vertex. If the new state vertex allows a reduction, the reduced symbol is added to the stack and inserted into the stream of symbols. The last symbol in the stream is $\langle n, \$, n+1 \rangle$. Process P_i terminates after the end-of-sentence marker has been read and passed on.

	LR(0) items	action	goto *d	*n	*p	*v	S	NP	PP	VP	$
0	$S'\to{\bullet}S\$$ $S\to{\bullet}NP\ VP$ $NP\to{\bullet}{*}det\ {*}n$ $NP\to{\bullet}{*}n$ $NP\to{\bullet}NP\ PP$ $PP\to{\bullet}{*}prep\ NP$ $VP\to{\bullet}{*}v\ NP$ $VP\to{\bullet}VP\ PP$	sh	4	5	6	7	1	2		3	
1	$S'\to S{\bullet}\$$	sh									acc
2	$S\to NP{\bullet}VP$ $NP\to NP{\bullet}PP$	sh							9	8	
3	$VP\to VP{\bullet}PP$	sh							10		
4	$NP\to{*}det{\bullet}{*}n$	sh		11							
5	$NP\to{*}n{\bullet}$	re3									
6	$PP\to{*}prep{\bullet}NP$	sh						12			
7	$VP\to{*}v{\bullet}NP$	sh						13			
8	$S\to NP\ VP{\bullet}$	re1									
9	$NP\to NP\ PP{\bullet}$	re4									
10	$VP\to VP\ PP{\bullet}$	re7									
11	$NP\to{*}det\ {*}n{\bullet}$	re2									
12	$PP\to{*}prep\ NP{\bullet}$	re5									
13	$VP\to{*}v\ NP{\bullet}$	re6									

Fig. 13.2. An annotated PBT parsing table for G_5

We will first look at an example and give a specification of the differences between the LR(0) algorithm and PBT afterwards. The example makes use of a slightly different grammar G_5:

(1) $S\to NP\ VP$
(2) $NP\to{*}det\ {*}n$
(3) $NP\to{*}n$
(4) $NP\to NP\ PP$
(5) $PP\to{*}prep\ NP$
(6) $VP\to{*}v\ NP$
(7) $VP\to VP\ PP$.

The difference between G_4 and G_5 is that a PP on sentence level is attached to the VP rather than to the S symbol. There is no linguistic motivation (as for all the example grammars), the purpose of this change is simply to allow for a better example.

In order to show the distributed nature of the PBT algorithm, we single out one specific process and trace its behaviour on the example sentence "I saw a man with a telescope." We will focus on proces P_1 that is to recognize all constituents starting with the second word "saw." The adapted parsing table is shown in Figure 13.2. We will first follow the example and discuss the construction of the parsing table afterwards.

The stream of symbols that is read from P_2 in due course[2] is

$\langle 2, NP, 4 \rangle$, $\langle 4, PP, 7 \rangle$, $\langle 2, NP, 7 \rangle$, $\langle 7, \$, 8 \rangle$.

We start with an empty stack, represented by a single state vertex labelled 0. First, P_1's terminal symbol $\langle 1, {}^*v, 2 \rangle$ is shifted. A symbol vertex and state vertex are added to the stack as usual. No reduction can be made, so we read $\langle 2, NP, 4 \rangle$ from the pipe. In state 7 this can be shifted. The new state is 13, requiring action $re\ VP \to {}^*v\ NP$. So we create a symbol vertex labelled $\langle 1, VP, 4 \rangle$ and start a new branch of the stack from the state vertex preceding $\langle 1, {}^*v, 2 \rangle$. The new state is 3. The stack that has been created so far is depicted in Figure 13.3. For the sake of clarity the state vertices are grouped into subsets U_j with j the right position marker of the preceding symbol. In the PBT algorithm it is essential that branches of the stack are not pruned. As we will see in the sequel, the vertex in state 7 in U_2 will be used to shift another NP onto.

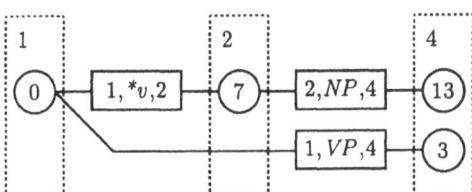

Fig. 13.3. The stack after reducing $\langle 1, VP, 4 \rangle$

The next symbol that appears in the stream is $\langle 4, PP, 7 \rangle$. This shifted in state 3 (at position 4) and $\langle 1, VP, 4 \rangle \langle 4, PP, 7 \rangle$ is reduced to $\langle 1, VP, 7 \rangle$. Note that $\langle 4, PP, 7 \rangle$ could not be shifted from state 13 – there is no entry in the goto table – although $\langle 2, NP, 4 \rangle \langle 4, PP, 7 \rangle$ is reducible to a compound NP. This is because P_1 only creates new symbols that start at position 1. As we read the next symbol, it turns out that $\langle 2, NP, 7 \rangle$ has indeed been created by P_2. It is shifted at position 2. Subsequently we can reduce a verb phrase $\langle 1, VP, 7 \rangle$. This symbol is already present in the stack and need not be added again. The last symbol, $\langle 7, \$, 8 \rangle$, cannot be shifted anywhere. It also signals the end of the stream, hence P_1 has finished its task. The final parse stack of P_1 is shown in Figure 13.4.

Symbols are sent on to the left neighbour as soon as they are read or created, in order to minimize waiting time. Some ordering requirements must be made, however, so as to guarantee the correctness of the algorithm. When a process has to decide whether the next symbol $\langle i, X, j \rangle$ fits anywhere onto

---

[2] This is in fact an optimized version of the algorithm. In a more simple version, *all* symbols recognized by all processes $P_2, \ldots, P_7$ pass through P_1. In the optimized version, a symbol is discarded by some process P_i if it can be argued that none of the processes $P_0, \ldots P_{i-1}$ can use it, irrespective of the categories of their words $a_1, \ldots, a_i$. This will be discussed in more detail in 13.3.

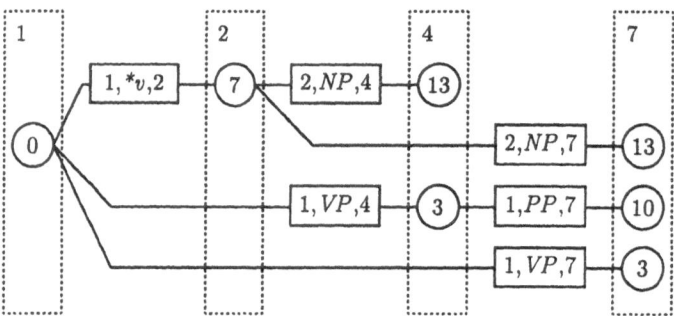

Fig. 13.4. The final stack of P_1

the stack, it is essential that all symbols $\langle k, Y, l \rangle$ with $k \leq l \leq i$ must have been received and, if necessary, added to the stack. For symbols with $i < j$ this is no problem. Whenever a symbol $\langle i, X, j \rangle$ causes a reduction at process P_h with $h \leq i$, then the reduced symbol $\langle h, Y, j \rangle$ is inserted into the stream directly after $\langle i, X, j \rangle$ and the ordering constraint is kept automatically. Some care must be taken in case of ε-productions, however. In order to guarantee that all state vertices onto which a symbol can be shifted are created before the symbol arrives, we have to ensure the following conditions:

- A symbol of the form $\langle j, X, j \rangle$ must precede all symbols $\langle j, Y, k \rangle$ with $j < k$.
- All symbols of the form $\langle i, Y, j \rangle$ with $i < j$ must precede a symbol $\langle j, X, j \rangle$.
- Symbols of the form $\langle j, X, j \rangle$ and $\langle j, Y, j \rangle$ must *precede each other*.

The first two conditions are easy to satisfy. Above we have given a slightly oversimplified description of the algorithm. Before the "own" terminal symbol is processed, P_j carries out all reductions of nullable constituents at position j. The third condition is rather more awkward. A nullable symbol has to be re-tried for a shift after other nullable symbols at the same position have been received.

For grammars where large subtrees can be rewritten to ε, one could pre-compute all nullable symbols, start each process with this pre-computed stack, and also pre-compute an order in which (possibly multiple copies of) nullable symbols have to be sent down the pipe. In that case the third condition can be dropped and some work of each process is done compile-time rather than run-time. We have not added such sophistication to our implementation, however. For natural language grammars this is hardly an issue. We did implement a simplification of the *reduce* action. Rather than carrying out a proper reduction, a recognized symbol is pushed back onto the input and subsequently *shift*ed just like any other symbol.

The construction of the PBT parsing table is in fact much simpler than the construction of any LR table. It is easy to prove that the number of states

```
function next_state(I: set of items, X: symbol): set of items;
begin
        if I = S'→S•$ and X = $
        then    next_state := accept
        else    next_state := {A→αX•β | A→α•Xβ ∈ I}
        fi
end;

function all_states: set of sets of items
begin
        s₀ := {A→•α | A→α ∈ P'};
        C := {s₀};
        while there is a state I ∈ C and a symbol X ∈ V'
                such that next_state(I, X) ≠ ∅ and next_state(I, X) ∉ C
                do C := C ∪ {next_state(I, X)} od;
        all_states := C
end;

procedure construct PBT table
begin
        C := all_states;
        for each I ∈ C
        do      action[I] := ∅;
                for each X ∈ V' do goto[I, X] := error od;
                for each item ∈ I
                do      case item of
                        A→α•aβ:
                                action[I] := action[I] ∪ {shift};
                                goto[I, a] := next_state(I, a)
                        A→α•Bβ:
                                goto[I, B] := next_state(I, B)
                        A→α•:
                                action[I] := action[I] ∪ {reduce A→α}
                        esac
        od      od
end;
```

Fig. 13.5. computation of the PBT states and parsing table

is $O(|G|)$, i.e., linear in the size of the grammar.[3] If only non-empty entries in the *goto* table are represented, the size of the parsing table is $O(|G|)$. And, more importantly, computing the table take $O(|G|)$ time.

The cause of this simplicity is the absence of the notion of a *closure*. This is because P_i only has to recognize constituents starting at position i. If (in the annotated version) an item $[A→α•Bβ, i, j]$ has been computed, with $i < j$, there is no need to start parsing B. This is the task of process I_j. If such a B exists, it will simply arrive through the pipeline. An algorithm for computation of the PBT parsing table is presented in Figure 13.5.

---

[3] See (11.4) on page 239 for a definition of $|G|$.

The differences between PBT and the LR(0) Tomita parser can be summarized as follows.

- Every process P_i runs an adapted parsing table without look-ahead defined by the algorithm in Figure 13.5.
- The algorithm that is run by each process does not synchronise on *shifts*; therefore the ordering requirements as stated on page 294 must be obeyed.
- Two position markers are tagged onto each recognized symbol, in order to keep track of the substring that is spanned by the symbol.
- On a *reduce* it is not allowed to prune the reduced branch of the stack.

A complete specification of the PBT algorithm, compatible in style with the specification of Tomita's algorithm, is given in Section 13.5. For acyclic grammars without hidden left-recursion, it is straightforward to verify that a state vertex u can be annotated with a set of marked LR(0) items ITEMS(u) and that the annotated PBT algorithm duely implements the **PBT** parsing schema.

Surprisingly, perhaps, the PBT algorithm also works for cyclic and hidden left-recursive grammars. We will come back to this in Section 13.4, where we discuss the construction of a parse list.

13.3 A more efficient PBT parser

The PBT algorithm as discussed above suffers from some inefficiency. Most recognized symbols can be used only locally and it may easily lead to a communication bottleneck if every symbol is passed down the entire pipeline. In the example on page 293, only four symbols were received by P_1: two *NP*s, a *PP* and an end-of-sentence marker. Filtering of useless symbols had been applied there already. Without such a communication filter, P_1 would receive the following stream of symbols:

$$\langle 2, *det, 3 \rangle, \ \langle 3, *n, 4 \rangle, \ \langle 3, NP, 4 \rangle, \ \langle 2, NP, 4 \rangle, \ \langle 4, *prep, 5 \rangle,$$
$$\langle 5, *det, 6 \rangle, \ \langle 6, *n, 7 \rangle, \ \langle 6, NP, 7 \rangle, \ \langle 5, NP, 7 \rangle, \ \langle 4, PP, 7 \rangle,$$
$$\langle 3, NP, 7 \rangle, \ \langle 2, NP, 7 \rangle, \ \langle 7, \$, 8 \rangle.$$

The majority of these symbols can be discarded higher up in the pipeline. We will define two criteria to detect that a symbol is useless for the remainder of the pipeline and should be discarded.

The first case is simple. Consider a symbol $X \in V$ that appears only as the *first* symbol in left-hand sides of productions. In such a case, a symbol $\langle i, X, j \rangle$ can only be used by process P_i and by no other process. As an example, consider *det, which only appears in the production $NP \rightarrow *det \ *n$. When P_5 finds a determiner $\langle 5, *det, 6 \rangle$ it can only contribute to the recognition of *NP*s starting at position 5. Hence, it need not be sent on to P_4 and further down.

Formally,

- **communication savings rule I**:
  P_i writes a symbol $\langle i, X, j \rangle$ to P_{i-1} only if there are A, Y, α, β such that $A \rightarrow Y \alpha X \beta \in P$.

A communication savings table for grammar G_5 is shown in figure 13.6.

*det	*n	*v	*prep	NP	PP	VP	S
−	+	−	−	+	+	+	−

(+ in entry X means: P_i passes symbols $\langle i, X, j \rangle$ to P_{i-1})

Fig. 13.6. Communication savings table I for G_5

A second, somewhat more involved communication savings scheme is the following. Each process P_i has its "own" terminal a_{i+1}. Is it possible, knowing the marked terminal $\langle i, a_{i+1}, i+1 \rangle$, to discard symbols $\langle i+1, X, j \rangle$ that arrive from P_{i+1}? Evidently, $\langle i+1, X, j \rangle$ can only contribute to a parse if $X \in \text{FOLLOW}(a_{i+1})$. If X cannot logically follow a_{i+1} then the marked symbol can be discarded. An example of this is $\langle 3, NP, 4 \rangle$. An NP cannot follow *det, but P_3 has no way of knowing that this is indeed the case. So the NP is sent on to P_2, which is able to determine that $\langle 3, NP, 4 \rangle$ is indeed useless.

A more subtle filtering scheme is possible, however. As an example, consider the marked symbol $\langle 6, {}^*n, 7 \rangle$ that is received by P_5. This is clearly a useful symbol; ${}^*n \in \text{FOLLOW}({}^*det)$ and it is used to construct $\langle 5, NP, 7 \rangle$. But we will argue that it can *not* be used by $P_0, \ldots, P_4$ and hence need not be sent on. A close inspection of the parsing table in Figure 13.2 shows that some ${}^*n$ can be used only if a process has an *immediately preceding* *det on its stack. As $\langle 5, {}^*det, 6 \rangle$ is not sent on to P_1, by communication savings rule I, there is no way in which any process down the pipeline could do anything useful with $\langle 6, {}^*n, 7 \rangle$. In general, if P_i owns terminal $\langle i, a, i+1 \rangle$, a symbol $\langle i+1, X, j \rangle$ needs to be passed on if the combination aX appears somewhere but *not* at the beginning a left-hand side, or else if a combination AX appears in the right-hand side of a production and A produces a string ending with a. More formally:

- **communication savings rule II**:
  P_i, having recognized a terminal symbol $\langle i, a, i+1 \rangle$, writes a marked symbol $\langle i+1, X, j \rangle$ to P_{i-1} only if one of the following cases applies:
  (i)   there are B, Y, α, β such that $B \rightarrow Y \alpha a X \beta \in P$;
  (ii) there are B, A, X, α, β such that $B \rightarrow \alpha A X \beta \in P$ and $a \in \text{LAST}(A)$.[4]

Communication savings table II for grammar G_5 is shown in Figure 13.7. See Lankhorst and Sikkel [1991] for an algorithm that computes communication savings table II for an arbitrary grammar.

---

[4] LAST is the mirror image of FIRST, cf. Section 12.1.

$a \setminus X$	$^*det$	$^*n$	$^*v$	$^*prep$	NP	PP	VP	S
$^*det$	−	−	−	−	−	−	−	−
$^*n$	−	−	−	−	−	+	+	−
$^*v$	−	−	−	−	−	−	−	−
$^*prep$	−	−	−	−	−	−	−	−

(+ in entry $[a, X]$ means: if $a_{i+1} = a$ then P_i passes $\langle i + 1, X, j \rangle$ to P_{i-1})

Fig. 13.7. Communication savings table II for G_5

It is possible to define grammars in which some junk will slip through the mazes of our two filters and more sophisticated filtering mechanisms would provide smaller optimizations. Consider, for example, a grammar

$$\{S \to abD, \quad S \to ccD, \quad D \to d, \quad D \to cd\}$$

and an input string $abcd$. Then P_2, owning a terminal $\langle 2, c, 3 \rangle$, will pass $\langle 3, D, 4 \rangle$ that satisfies communication rules I and II(i). In this case P_1 could detect, when it is supplied with enough sophistication, that $\langle 3, D, 4 \rangle$ is no longer useful. We conjecture, however, that adding such sophistication will only be detrimental to the average-case efficiency of the algorithm; weird constructions like this are unlikely to appear in natural language grammars.

13.4 The construction of a distributed parse list

The PBT parser can be easily extended with the computation of a packed shared forest, represented by a parse list. Each process computes its own part of the parse list. That is, the output of P_i contains all entries in the parse list with left position marker i. We need to make a single technical adjustment, however. Entries in the parse list of P_i may contain pointers to entries in other parts of the distributed parse list. To that end we tag such pointers onto the symbols that are passed down the pipeline. The left position marker i of a symbol is annotated with its local label in the parse list. Marked symbols now have the format $\langle i.k, X, j \rangle$, where k indicates the k-th entry in the parse list of P_i. The combination of left place marker and local label provides a unique reference across the different partial parse lists. In Figure 13.8 a parse list for the example sentence is shown.

The parse forest is not identical to the one produced by Tomita's algorithm. The nodes in our parse forest satisfy the following specification:

- a node $\langle i, X, j \rangle$ is contained in the forest if and only iff $X \Rightarrow^* a_{i+1} \ldots a_j$.

The PBT forest contains more nodes that are not reachable from the root, because the top-down filtering has been discarded. On the other hand, if $X \Rightarrow^* a_{i+1} \ldots a_j$, then it is guaranteed that the PBT forest contains a *unique* node $\langle i, X, j \rangle$ (possibly containing multiple sub-nodes). In Tomita's algorithm, a symbol that spans some specific part of the sentence is *usually* represented by a single node. Sharing may fail, however, when identical symbol

symbol	children
$\langle 6.1, {}^*n, 7\rangle$	
$\langle 6.2, NP, 7\rangle$	(6.1)
$\langle 5.1, {}^*det, 6\rangle$	
$\langle 5.2, NP, 7\rangle$	(5.1, 6.1)
$\langle 4.1, {}^*prep, 5\rangle$	
$\langle 4.2, PP, 5\rangle$	(4.1, 5.2)
$\langle 3.1, {}^*n, 4\rangle$	
$\langle 3.2, NP, 4\rangle$	(3.1)
$\langle 3.3, NP, 7\rangle$	(3.2, 4.2)
$\langle 2.1, {}^*det, 3\rangle$	
$\langle 2.2, NP, 4\rangle$	(2.1, 3.1)
$\langle 2.3, NP, 7\rangle$	(2.2, 4.2)
$\langle 1.1, {}^*v, 2\rangle$	
$\langle 1.2, VP, 4\rangle$	(1.1, 2.2)
$\langle 1.3, VP, 7\rangle$	(1.1, 2.3) (1.2, 4.2)
$\langle 0.1, {}^*n, 1\rangle$	
$\langle 0.2, NP, 1\rangle$	(0.1)
$\langle 0.3, S, 4\rangle$	(0.2, 1.2)
$\langle 0.4, S, 7\rangle$	(0.2, 1.3)

Fig. 13.8. The parse list, root node is 0.4

vertices on the stack are followed by different state vertices. Hence an exact specification of Tomita's parse forest is very complicated (in fact Tomita doesn't give one), as it depends on the idiosyncrasies of the particular LR parsing table.

A more substantial improvement upon Tomita's algorithm, from a theoretical perspective, is that PBT runs on arbitrary context-free grammars. Consider, again, the hidden left-recursive grammar

$$\{S \to A\,S\,b, \quad S \to a, \quad A \to \varepsilon\},$$

that was used as a counterexample in Section 12.6. Tomita's algorithm, anticipating an arbitrary number of b's, creates infinitely many A's for a start. The infinite series of reductions is driven by

$$closure(\{S \to A \bullet Sb\}) \;=\; \{S \to A \bullet Sb, \; S \to \bullet ASb\}.$$

When the parser gets into this state, with look-ahead a, it will ε-reduce an A and move on to *the same* state. PBT, in contrast, will only reduce a single $\langle 0, A, 0\rangle$. There is no cycle in the parsing table because the closure function was not used in its construction. In Figure 13.9 the graph-structured PBT stack of P_0 is shown for the sentence ab. The parse list is given in shown in Figure 13.10.

Cyclic grammars are also parsed in a natural way, without the need for extra sophistication. Consider the grammar $\{S \to S, \; S \to a\}$, and the sentence a. When $\langle 0, S, 1\rangle$ is recognized, it is reduced to $\langle 0, S, 1\rangle$, which is already present, and need not be added again. Thus the parser will add the corresponding node as a sub-node to *itself*. The complete parse list is shown in Figure 13.12. The parse forest is drawn as a graph in Figure 13.11.

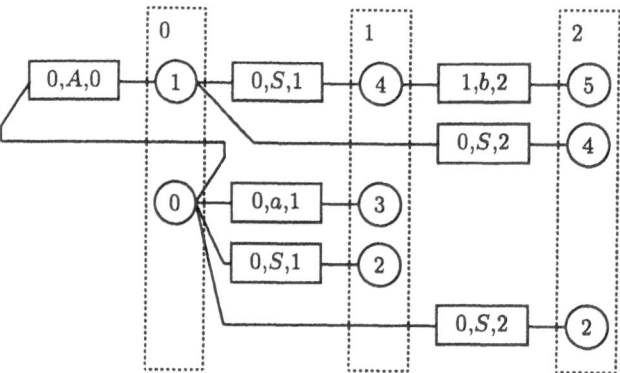

Fig. 13.9. Parse stack of P_0 for the sentence ab

symbol	children
$\langle 2.1, A, 2\rangle$	()
$\langle 1.1, A, 1\rangle$	()
$\langle 1.2, b, 2\rangle$	
$\langle 0.1, A, 0\rangle$	()
$\langle 0.2, a, 1\rangle$	
$\langle 0.3, S, 1\rangle$	(0.2)
$\langle 0.4, S, 2\rangle$	(0.1, 0.3, 1.2)

Fig. 13.10. Parse list of P_0 for the sentence ab

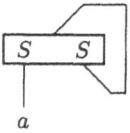

Fig. 13.11. Parse forest for a,
$G = \{S \rightarrow S,\ S \rightarrow a\}$

symbol	children
$\langle 0.1, a, 1\rangle$	
$\langle 0.2, S, 1\rangle$	(0.2), (0.1)

Fig. 13.12. The parse list for a,
$G = \{S \rightarrow S,\ S \rightarrow a\}$

Rekers, in Chapter 1 of his Ph.D Thesis [1991], discusses how optimal node sharing and parsing of arbitrary context-free grammars can be obtained. In PBT these features come about naturally.

13.5 A formal definition of the PBT algorithm

The following formal description of PBT is based on Lankhorst [1991]. It is in a style similar to the formal description of Tomita's algorithm in Section 12.5.

It is useful, perhaps, to remind the reader that the direction of the edges is from the top of the stack to the bottom (i.e., in all figures, from right to left).

In the formal description we use the following functions and global variables:

Γ_i: graph-structured stack in processor P_i. This is a directed, acyclic graph with a single leaf node, v_0, labelled with state number s_0. Γ is initialized in PARSE and altered in SHIFTER.

T_i: shared packed forest in processor P_i. This is a directed graph (V_i, E_i) in which each vertex $v \in V_i$ may have more than one successor list $\langle v, L \rangle \in E_i$. Initialized in PARSE and altered in REDUCER, E-REDUCER, and SHIFTER.

r_i: the result returned by processor P_i. This is a set of vertices of T_i which form the roots of the parse forest in P_i. r_0 contains the global result. Initialized in PARSE and altered in SHIFTER.

$U_{i,k}$: set of vertices of Γ_i, for which the following property holds:

$u \in U_{i,k} \Rightarrow$ some partial parse of the substring $a_{i+1} \ldots a_k$ of the input string (produced by P_i) is contained in the portion of the stack following u.

Initialized in PARSEWORD and altered in SHIFTER.

A: subset of "active" vertices of $U_{i,k}$ on which reductions and shift actions can be carried out. A is initialized in PARSEWORD and altered in ACTOR and SHIFTER.

R: set of edges to be reduced. Each element is a triple $\langle v, x, p \rangle$ with $v \in U_{i,k}$, $x \in$ SUCCESSORS(v) and p a non-empty production of G. $\langle v, x, p \rangle \in R$ means that $reduce$ p is to be applied on the path starting with the edge from v to x. REDUCER will take care of it. R is initialized in PARSEWORD and altered in ACTOR, REDUCER, and SHIFTER.

R_e: set of vertices on which an ε-reduction is to be carried out. Each element is a pair $\langle v, p \rangle$ with $v \in U_{i,k}$ and p and ε-production. $\langle v, p \rangle \in R_e$ means that $reduce$ p is to be applied on the vertex v. E-REDUCER will carry out this reduction. R_e is initialized in PARSEWORD and altered in ACTOR and E-REDUCER.

Q: set of vertices to be shifted on. If $\langle j, X, k \rangle$ is to be shifted, Q is defined as follows:

$$Q = \{\langle v, s \rangle \mid v \in V \wedge s = \text{GOTO}(\text{STATE}(v), sym) \notin \{error, accept\}\}.$$

In this definition, $V \subseteq U_{i,j}$ is a set of vertices on which a shift action may be carried out. $\langle v, s \rangle \in Q$ means that $shift$ s is to be carried out on v. SHIFTER will take care of this. Q is local to SHIFTER.

S: contains the symbols $\langle j, X, j \rangle$ which have so far been read by processor P_i. When a symbol $\langle k, X, l \rangle$ $(l > j)$ is read from the pipeline, the elements of S are written to the pipeline and S is emptied. S is initialized and altered in PARSEWORD and used in SHIFTER.

LEFT(p): left-hand side of production p.

$|p|$:   length of the right-hand side of production p.

STATE(v): takes a vertex in Γ_i as its argument and returns the state label of this vertex.

SYMBOL(x): takes a vertex in Γ_i as its argument and returns the symbol label of this vertex. This label is a link to a vertex in T_i.

SUCCESSORS(v): takes a vertex in Γ_i as its argument and returns the set of all vertices x in Γ_i such that there is an edge from v to x.

GOTO(s, A): looks up the goto table and returns a state number. s is a state number and A is a grammar symbol.

ACTION(s): looks up the action table and returns a set of actions. s is a state number.

ADDSUBNODE(v, L): takes a vertex v in T_i and a successor list L as arguments and adds $\langle v, L \rangle$ to E_i in $T_i = (V_i, E_i)$.

BUFFER($\langle i.m, A, j \rangle$): buffers a symbol $\langle i.m, A, j \rangle$ in a first-in first-out buffer. When a READ action is executed, this buffer is read, and only if it is empty a symbol is read directly from the incoming pipe.

READ($\langle i.m, A, j \rangle$): reads a symbol $\langle i.m, A, j \rangle$ from the buffer or incoming pipe.

WRITE($\langle i.m, A, j \rangle$): writes a symbol $\langle i.m, A, j \rangle$ into the outgoing pipe.

PUSH($\langle i.m, A, j \rangle$): pushes a symbol $\langle i.m, A, j \rangle$ back into the incoming pipe.

s_i: state i of the parsing table, consisting of a set of dotted rules.

$g_{i,X}$: state to go to from state s_i on symbol X, defined as
$$\{A \rightarrow \alpha X \bullet \beta \mid A \rightarrow \alpha \bullet X \beta \in s_i\}.$$

The parser is defined by the following set of procedures

procedure PARSE($G, a_1 \ldots a_n$)
begin
     $a_{n+1} := \$$;
     for $i := 0$ **to** n **in parallel**
     do $\Gamma_i := \emptyset$; $T_i := \emptyset$; $r_i := \emptyset$;
           create in Γ_i a vertex v_0 labelled s_0;
           PARSEWORD(i)
     od;
     return r_0, the set of roots of the parse forest
end PARSE;

procedure PARSEWORD(i)
begin
  $k := i;\ \ U_{i,k} := \{v_0\};\ \ A := U_{i,k};$
  $R := \emptyset;\ \ R_e := \emptyset;\ \ S := \emptyset;$
  $previous := 0;$
  INPUT($\langle i, a_{i+1}, i+1\rangle$);
  create in T_i a node m labelled a_{i+1};
  PUSH($\langle i.m, a_{i+1}, i+1\rangle$);
  repeat
    while $A \neq \emptyset$ **do** ACTOR **od**;
    while $R \neq \emptyset$ **do** REDUCER **od**;
    if $R_e \neq \emptyset$ **then** E-REDUCER **fi**;
    READ($\langle first.label, sym, last\rangle$);
    if $last \neq previous$
    then for all $\langle j.l, X, j\rangle \in S$ **do** WRITE($\langle j.l, X, j\rangle$) **od fi**;
    $S := \emptyset;$
    $previous := last;$
    if $first = last$
    then $S := S \cup \{\langle first.label, sym, last\rangle\}$
    else WRITE($\langle first.label, sym, last\rangle$)
    fi;
    SHIFTER($\langle first.label, sym, last\rangle, U_{i,first}$);
    $k := last;$
  until $sym = \$$
end PARSEWORD;

procedure ACTOR
begin
  remove one element v from A;
  for all $\alpha \in$ ACTION(STATE(v))
  do **if** $\alpha = reduce\ p$ **and** p is not an ε-production
    then **for all** $x \in$ SUCCESSORS(v)
      do $R := R \cup \{\langle v, x, p\rangle\}$ **od**
    elseif $\alpha = reduce\ p$ **and** p is an ε-production
    then $R_e := R_e \cup \{\langle v, p\rangle\}$
    fi
  od
end ACTOR;

procedure REDUCER
begin
      remove one element $\langle v, x, p \rangle$ from R;
      $N := \text{LEFT}(p)$;
      for all y such that there exists a path of length $2|p| - 2$ from x to y
      do $L := (\text{SYMBOL}(z_1), \ldots, \text{SYMBOL}(z_{|p|}))$, where
                        $z_1 = x_1$, $z_{|p|} = y$ and $z_2, \ldots, z_{|p|-1}$ are
                        symbol vertices in the path from x to y;
           for all s such that
                        $\exists w (w \in \text{SUCCESSORS}(y) \wedge \text{GOTO}(\text{STATE}(w), N) = s)$
           do $W := \{ w \mid w \in \text{SUCCESSORS}(y)$
                                $\wedge \ \text{GOTO}(\text{STATE}(w), N) = s \}$;
              if $\exists u (u \in U_{i,k} \wedge \text{STATE}(u) = s)$
              then if there is an edge from u to a vertex z
                              such that $\text{SUCCESSORS}(z) = W$
                  then ADDSUBNODE($\text{SYMBOL}(z), L$)
                  else if T_i does not contain
                                      a node m labelled N
                      then create in T_i a node m labelled N **fi**;
                      ADDSUBNODE(m, L);
                      BUFFER($\langle i.m, N, k \rangle$)
              else if T_i does not contain a node m labelled N
              then create in T a node m labelled N **fi**;
              ADDSUBNODE(m, L);
              BUFFER($\langle i.m, N, k \rangle$);
           fi
           od
      od
end REDUCER;

procedure E-REDUCER (* will only be called if $k = i$ *)
begin
      for all $\langle v, p \rangle \in R_e$
      do $N := \text{LEFT}(p)$;
           create in T_i a node m labelled N;
           ADDSUBNODE(m, NIL);
           BUFFER($\langle i.m, N, k \rangle$)
      od;
      $R_e := \emptyset$;
end E-REDUCER;

procedure SHIFTER($\langle first.label, sym, last \rangle, V$)
begin

    $r_i := r_i \cup \{\text{SYMBOL}(m) \mid m \in \text{SUCCESSORS}(v) \wedge v \in V \wedge$
                                   $\text{GOTO}(\text{STATE}(v), sym) = accept\}$;

    $Q := \{\langle v, s \rangle \mid v \in V \wedge s = \text{GOTO}(\text{STATE}(v), sym) \notin \{error, accept\}\}$;

    $W := 0$;

    for all s such that $\exists v(\langle v, s \rangle \in Q)$

    do   **if** $\exists w \in U_{i,last} \wedge \text{STATE}(w) = s)$

           then create in Γ_i a vertex x labelled $first.label$;

                   create in Γ_i and edge from w to x;

                   for all v such that $\langle v, s \rangle \in Q$

                   do create in Γ_i and edge from x to v **od**;

                   if $w \notin A$

                   then for all q such that $reduce\ q \in \text{ACTION}(s)$

                                            and q is not an ε-production

                       do $R := R \cup \{\langle w, x, q \rangle\}$ **od**

                   fi

           else create in Γ_i two vertices w and x labelled

                                      s and $first.label$, respectively;

                   create in Γ_i an edge from w to x;

                   for all v such that $\langle v, s \rangle \in Q$

                   do create in Γ_i an edge from x to v **od**;

                   $U_{i,last} := U_{i,last} \cup \{w\}$;

                   $A := A \cup \{w\}$;

                   $W := W \cup \{w\}$;

        fi

    od;

    if $W \neq \emptyset$

    then for all $\langle last.m, X, last \rangle \in \mathcal{S}$

           do SHIFTER($\langle last.m, X, last \rangle, W$) **od**

    fi

end SHIFTER;

13.6 Empirical results

The PBT algorithm has been tested in a series of experiments in which parallel execution was simulated on a single workstation, In this way we could experiment with an arbitrary number of (simulated) processors.

The simulation set-up is as follows. Each (virtual) process is run consecutively. The stream of symbols is stored internally, rather than written to a pipe. When the next virtual process is started, the clock is reset. For every (simulated) read and write an extra processing time of 1 ms is counted. Each symbol that is sent from one virtual process to another is timestamped. When a process receives a symbol with a time stamp later than its own time, the clock is updated and the waiting time accounted for.

We[5] implemented PBT in the language C and re-implemented Tomita's algorithm so as to ensure compatibility. We have not attempted to optimize run-time efficiency at the expense of straightforwardness. The timing experiments have been conducted on a Commodore Amiga because of its accurate timing capabilities.

The grammars and example sentences are the ones given by Tomita [1985]. Grammar I is the example grammar G_5. Grammars II, III and IV have 42, 223 and 386 rules, respectively. Sentence set A contains 40 sentences, taken from actual publications, as listed in the appendix of [Tomita, 1985]. Set B is constructed as $*n *v *det *n(*prep *det *n)^{k-1}$ with k ranging from 1 to 13. In Figures 13.13 and 13.14 the timing results for set B and grammars III and IV are plotted on a double logarithmic scale. These figures show that gain in speed due to parallelization outweighs the additional communication overhead only if a sentence is sufficiently long. An exact break-even point cannot be given, as it depends on the grammar, the sentence, the characteristics of the parallel architecture and the implementation.

Similarly, Figure 13.14 shows that the extra overhead for filtering pays off only if the sentence is not too small. We could tip the balance somewhat more in favour of PBT by improving the filter. In the program that was used to produce these plots, the filter has a computational complexity linear in the size of the grammar. In retrospect, this could have been handled rather more efficiently. Adding sophistication to handling the graph structured stack and parsing table look-up could improve the performance in absolute terms; relatively it would make less difference, however, as all programs would benefit from it.

Testing sentence set A produces plots of a more varied nature, as sentences of comparable length may differ a lot in complexity. Using linear regression analysis, we found the overall trend to be similar to the results for set B. A series of other plots can be found in [Lankhorst and Sikkel, 1991].

---

[5] This work was done by Marc Lankhorst.

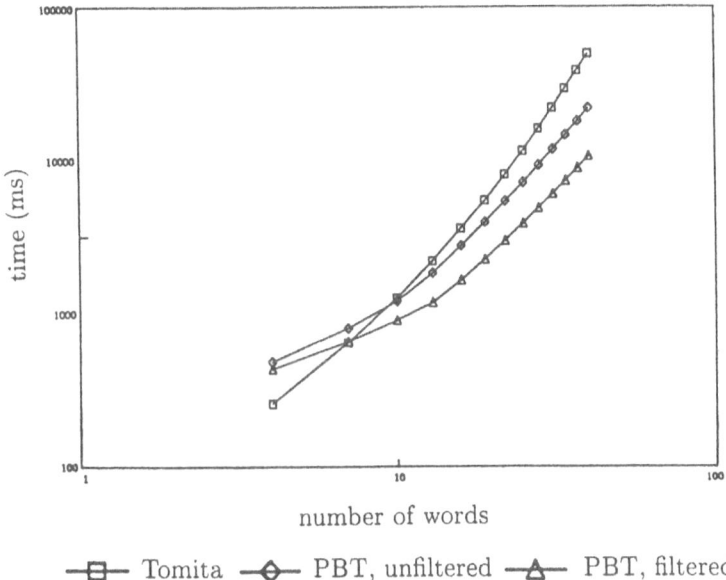

Fig. 13.13. Sentence set B and grammar III

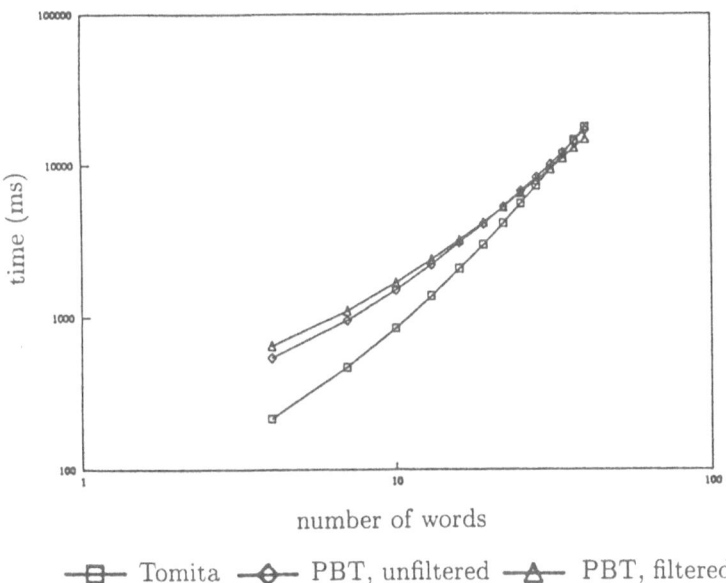

Fig. 13.14. Sentence set B and grammar IV

| algorithm | grammar | |
	III	IV
Tomita	$O(n^{2.21})$	$O(n^{2.61})$
PBT, unfiltered	$O(n^{1.62})$	$O(n^{2.19})$
PBT, with filtering	$O(n^{1.50})$	$O(n^{1.86})$

Fig. 13.15. Estimated asymptotic complexity for set B

The complexity of a parsing algorithm can be measured as a function of the length of the input sentence. For formal languages this makes sense, as strings (i.e., computer programs) can be very long indeed. For natural languages this is a rather doubtful measure. The size of the grammar, usually *much* larger than the average sentence, is constant and therefore considered irrelevant. Moreover, constant factors as discussed above are abstracted from. Nevertheless, sentence set B shows the complexity of the algorithms rather nicely, because of the combinatorial explosion of *PP* attachment ambiguities. For set B and grammars III and IV we estimated the asymptotic complexity. These figures, for what they are worth, are shown in Figure 13.15. Similar computations for sentence set A confirm the trend that the complexity of PBT, using n parallel processes, is roughly $O(\sqrt{n})$ better than Tomita's algorithm. Hence, waiting time and uneven load balancing accounts for a factor $O(\sqrt{n})$ as well. See [Lankhorst and Sikkel, 1991], again, for all the details.

Finally, we have estimated the speed of the PBT algorithm as a function of the number of processors. The 37 processes for the sentence 13 of set B have been allocated to any number of processors ranging from 1 to 37, with the processes evenly distributed over the processors. Let p be the number of processors, then there is natural number k such that $k \leq 37/p < k + 1$. The higher ranked processes are grouped into clusters of $k + 1$, the lower ranked ones in clusters of k per processor. The results are shown in Figure 13.16. The decline is sharpest when incrementing p causes a decrease of k, in which case the processor handling $P_0, \ldots, P_{k-1}$ is relieved of one of its processes.

13.7 Related approaches

A Parallel LR parser that also uses a "bottom-up" approach to parallelization has been defined by Fischer [1975]. But the similarity to PBT is merely superficial. Fischer runs Synchronous Parsing Machines (SPM's) on various parts of the sentence in parallel. An SPM tries to parse its part of the input until it hits upon the starting point of its successor and then its merges with its successor. The fundamental difference with PBT is that Fischer's algorithm really merges parse stacks. PBT has separate parse stacks, but each processor may use nonterminals reduced by other processors as if they were terminal symbols. Moreover, Fischer's approach is only defined for LR grammars and cannot easily be extended to GLR.

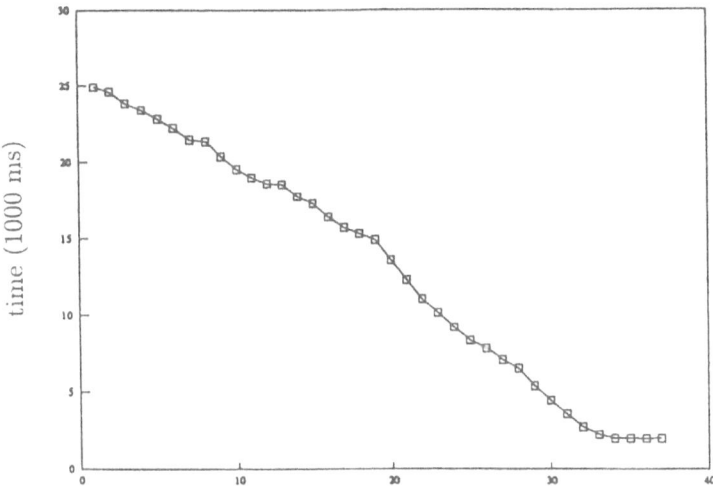

Fig. 13.16. Performance vs. number of processors

Parallelization by allocating different branches of the stack, cf. [Tanaka and Numazaki, 1989], [Numazaki and Tanaka, 1990], [Thompson et al., 1991], was already discussed in Section 13.1.

Thompson [1989, 1994] obtains several parallel chart parsers by distributing the chart. A parallel parser based on systolic matrix multiplication is also given in [Thompson, 1994].

13.8 Conclusion

The Parallel Bottom-up Tomita parser has been developed as a cross-fertilization of Tomita's algorithm with the bottom-up parallelization of Earley's algorithm. This could be accomplished rather straightforwardly because, in Chapter 12, we have shown that the algorithms of Tomita and Earley have underlying parsing schemata that are almost identical.

The parallelization does not offer a tremendous speed-up, but we nevertheless we see it as a moderate success. Experimental results show a reduction of the complexity in terms of the length of the sentence (for a few example grammars, *not* in the worst case) of a factor $O(\sqrt{n})$ by using n processors. The remaining $O(\sqrt{n})$ is spent on the slightly more complicated structure of the parser, communication, and uneven load balancing. We have shown that parallel parsing is feasible.

A spin-off effect of PBT is that the parsing table is constructed in linear time. Construction of LR parsing tables for large grammars is very costly. Hence, a PBT parser, also in a sequential implementation, is an useful tool for development and debugging of grammars. Whenever the grammar is changed, a new parsing table can be constructed on the fly.

14. Boolean circuit parsing

In the previous chapters we have discussed how parsing schemata can be instantiated to parsing algorithms of various kinds. Such algorithms can be coded into programming languages and then executed on a computer system.

As a last application of the theory of parsing schemata we will look at the possibilities of coding schemata (or, to be precise, uninstantiated parsing systems) directly into hardware. Several *connectionist* approaches to parsing have been proposed, cf. Fanty, [1986], Selman and Hirst, [1987], Howells, [1988], Nakagawa and Mori, [1988], and Nijholt, [1990], in which a large number of simple processing units are linked into a highly interconnected network. For an arbitrary parsing system we can define a *boolean circuit*, which is a particularly simple kind of connectionist network.

Because of the massive parallelism involved, connectionist implementations of parsers can be really fast. This might be of interest for *real-time* systems. Furthermore, it has been argued that it is possible to integrate such a connectionist syntactic parser with semantic and pragmatic analysis (cf., e.g., [Waltz and Pollack, 1988], [Cottrell, 1989]). We will not further go into these aspects, and concentrate on syntactic analysis.

In order to investigate how fast parsing can be done in principle, we push parallelism to the limit and investigate logarithmic-time boolean circuits. We obtain complexity bounds that conform to those known for fast parallel algorithms on parallel random access machines. This result is of theoretical, rather than practical value, however, because the number of processing units and the connectivity is unrealistically high.

This chapter is almost self-contained. Some basic understanding of parsing systems and schemata is needed and there are some references to examples in Chapters 4–6. The general idea of logarithmic-time parsing, for the sake of simplicity exemplified by binary branching grammars, is explained in detail.

A short recapitulation and some additional concepts specific to this chapter are given in Section 14.1. We will make a tiny change in the notation of parsing systems. Unlike the previous chapters, the focus is now on *uninstantiated* parsing systems: a network is constructed that can parse arbitrary sentences according to some specific grammar.

In 14.2 we present a recognizing network for binary branching grammars. In 14.3 this is extended to a parsing network that encodes a shared forest for a given sentence. In 14.4 we filter irrelevant parts from the network and briefly discuss how this network construction can be applied to arbitrary context-free grammars.

A logarithmic-time parallel parsing algorithm, which is a slight modification of Rytter's algorithm, is presented in Section 14.5. The fact that the algorithm is indeed logarithmic-time is proven in 14.6. A boolean circuit implementation is given in 14.7. In 14.8 we look at this problem from a more general perspective; Rytter's algorithm can be seen as a specific instance of a more general notion of *conditional* parsing systems that can be used to flatten trees of deduction steps.

Related approaches are briefly discussed in 14.9, conclusions follow in 14.10.   ·

This chapter is based on a technical report [Sikkel, 1990], parts of which have been published in [Sikkel and Nijholt, 1991]. The presentation has been improved, however, by making use of parsing schemata. In particular the generalization to logarithmic-time boolean circuits for arbitrary grammars follows straightforwardly as a combination of different results.

14.1 Preliminary concepts

In this chapter, the emphasis is more on *un*instantiated parsing systems than instantiated parsing systems and parsing schemata. We will give a definition of uninstantiated parsing systems that is slightly different (from Definition 4.23), so as to allow these systems to be implemented in boolean circuits.

The notational conventions for context-free grammars that were introduced in Section 3.1 apply throughout this chapter. We write $G = (N, \Sigma, P, S)$ for a context-free grammar with terminals N, nonterminals Σ, productions P and start symbol S. We write $L(G)$ for the language generated by G, i.e., $a_1 \ldots a_n \in L(G)$ iff $S \Rightarrow^* a_1 \ldots a_n$. We write $A, B, \ldots$ for nonterminal symbols; $a, b, \ldots$ for terminal symbols; $X, Y, \ldots$ for arbitrary symbols; $\alpha, \beta \ldots$ for arbitrary strings of symbols. Positions in the string $a_1 \ldots a_n$ are denoted by h, i, j, k, l, m.

An *instantiated parsing system* for some grammar G and an arbitrary string $a_1 \ldots a_n$ is a triple $\mathbb{P}(a_1 \ldots a_n) = \langle \mathcal{I}, H, D \rangle$ with $\mathcal{I}$ a set of items, H an initial set of items (also called *hypotheses*) and D a set of *deduction steps* that allow to derive new items from already known items. The hypotheses in H encode the sentence that is to be parsed. For a sentence $a_1 \ldots a_n$ we take

$$H = \{[a_1, 0, 1], \ldots, [a_n, n-1, n], [\$, n, n+1]\}; \qquad (14.1)$$

at the $(n+1)$-st position we always add an end-of-sentence marker $\$. Note that different hypotheses $[a, i-1, i]$ and $[b, i-1, i]$ may occur if the i-th word falls into different lexical categories. The hypotheses are always defined by (14.1). Deduction steps in D are of the form

$$\eta_1, \ldots, \eta_k \vdash \xi.$$

The items $\eta_1, \ldots, \eta_k \in H \cup \mathcal{I}$ are called the *antecedents* and the item $\xi \in \mathcal{I}$ is called the *consequent* of a deduction step. If all antecedents of a deduction step are recognized by a parser, then the consequent should also be recognized. The set of *valid items* $\mathcal{V}(\mathbb{P}(a_1 \ldots a_n))$ is the smallest subset of $\mathcal{I}$ that contains the consequents of those deduction steps that have only hypotheses and valid items as antecedents.

Whether the hypotheses H are part of the item set $\mathcal{I}$ or outside $\mathcal{I}$ does not really matter. In previous chapters we have treated hypotheses as separate entities (i.e., $H \cap \mathcal{I} = \emptyset$), simply because that was more convenient for specifying parsing systems. In this chapter we have strong reasons for changing this convention. We will consider the items of the form $[a, i-1, i]$ to be included in $\mathcal{I}$.[1] So we find, for any given string $a_1 \ldots a_n$ that $[\$, n, n+1]$ is the only hypothesis that is not included in $\mathcal{I}$.

An *uninstantiatated* parsing system specifies all objects and deduction steps that can be used to parse sentences according to some grammar G. We are interested in constructing parsers by means of boolean circuits. The construction of a parser cannot be dependent on any particular string, so we have to include all *potential* hypotheses for all strings.

Definition 14.1. (*(uninstantiated) parsing system*)
An uninstantiated parsing system for some grammar G is a triple $\langle \mathcal{I}, \mathcal{H}, D \rangle$ with the set of *potential* hypotheses $\mathcal{H}$ defined by

$$\mathcal{H} = \{[a, i-1, i] \mid a \in \Sigma \cup \{\$\} \wedge i \geq 1\} \tag{14.2}$$

An (uninstantiated) parsing system can be instantiated for a particular string $a_1 \ldots a_n$ by selecting a set of *actual* hypotheses $H \subseteq \mathcal{H}$ according to (14.1). □

In boolean circuits the remaining potential hypotheses $\mathcal{H} \backslash H$ will still be included in the system, but simply remain invalid.

We write $\mathbb{P}$ for an uninstantiated parsing system, and $\mathbb{P}(a_1 \ldots a_n)$ for an instantiated parsing system. A *parsing schema* $\mathbf{P}$ defines a parsing system $\mathbb{P} = \mathbf{P}(G)$ for all G in some class of context-free grammars.

---

[1] The reason for this is that we want items of the form $[a, i-i, i]$ to be included in the set of valid items and the set of *parsable* items that will be introduced in in Section 14.3. When we present a set of valid items, e.g., in the form of a CYK recognition table, we usually do not include the end-of-sentence marker. Thus the Figures 14.1 and 14.3 cover exactly the set of valid resp. parsable items.

Definition 14.2. (*binary branching grammar*)
A context-free grammar G is *binary branching* if all productions in P have the form

$$A \to XY.$$

We write $\mathcal{BB}$ for the set of binary branching context-free grammars.   □

Binary branching grammars are strongly related to, but formally different from grammars in Chomsky Normal Form. The former have the advantage that CYK parsers are strictly binary as well. This will be of help when we convert linear-time parsing networks to logarithmic-time parsing networks; such networks are easiest to define on binary systems.[2]

Definition 14.3. (*binary parsing system*)
An (uninstantiated) parsing system $\mathbb{P} = \langle \mathcal{I}, \mathcal{H}, D \rangle$ is called *binary* if

$$D \subseteq (\mathcal{H} \cup \mathcal{I})^2 \times \mathcal{I},$$

that is, every deduction step has exactly 2 antecedents.   □

Example 14.4. (**CYKbb**)
As an example, we will define a slightly modified CYK parsing schema for binary branching grammars. For an arbitrary grammar $G \in \mathcal{BB}$ we define a parsing system $\mathbb{P} = \langle \mathcal{I}_{CYKbb}, \mathcal{H}, D_{CYKbb} \rangle$ by

$$\mathcal{I}_{CYKbb} = \{[A, i, j] \mid A \in N \wedge 0 \leq i \wedge i + 1 < j\},$$
$$\cup \{[a, i-1, i] \mid a \in \Sigma \wedge i \geq 1\},$$

$$D_{CYKbb} = \{[X, i, j], [Y, j, k] \vdash [A, i, k] \mid A \to XY \in P\},$$

and $\mathcal{H}$ according to (14.2).
The system can be instantiated by choosing a set of hypothesis $H \subseteq \mathcal{H}$ for a string $a_1 \ldots a_n$ according to (14.1).   □

Example 14.5.
As a more concrete example, we will look at the instantiated parsing system

CYKbb(G_2)(the flies like the marmelade).

The grammar G_2 was defined (in Chapter 2) by the productions

$$
\begin{array}{lll}
S & \to & NP\ VP \mid S\ PP \\
NP & \to & *det\ *n \mid NP\ PP, \\
VP & \to & *v\ NP, \\
PP & \to & *prep\ NP.
\end{array}
$$

---

[2] Generalization to parsing systems of arbitrary arity will follow later. So this is *not* an essential restriction on the types of grammars and languages that can be handled (binary branching grammars do not generate sentences of length 1 and 0) but a temporary restriction to simplify the presentation.

Lexical categories of the relevant words are defined by

$$
\begin{aligned}
\text{*}n &\rightarrow \quad \text{flies} \mid \text{marmelade,} \\
\text{*}det &\rightarrow \quad \text{the,} \\
\text{*}v &\rightarrow \quad \text{flies} \mid \text{like,} \\
\text{*}prep &\rightarrow \quad \text{like;}
\end{aligned}
$$

but in our binary approach these are not considered to be part of the grammar. So we find a set of hypotheses

$$
[\text{*}det, 0, 1], \ [\text{*}n, 1, 2], \ [\text{*}v, 1, 2], \ [\text{*}v, 2, 3], \ [\text{*}prep, 2, 3],
$$
$$
[\text{*}det, 3, 4], \ [\text{*}n, 4, 5], \ [\$, 5, 6].
$$

The set of valid items can be represented in the usual upper triangular CYK recognition table. A symbol X is written into table entry $T_{i,j}$ if $[X, i, j]$ is valid. The table representing the valid items for the given grammar and sentence is shown in Figure 14.1.   □

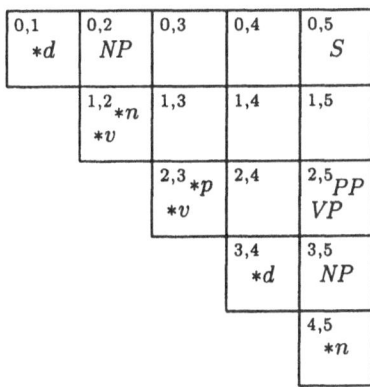

Fig. 14.1. CYK recognition table for Example 14.5.

In Chapters 3 and 4 we have enhanced parsing systems with a notion of correctness. For each sentence length n there is a set of *final items* $\mathcal{F}^{(n)} \subseteq \mathcal{I}$. An item can be seen as the set of trees that conform to the properties specified by the item. A final item, then, can be seen as a set of parse trees. In a correct parsing system, a final item is valid if and only if it contains a parse tree for the given sentence. In the CYK case there is only a single final item for each n: we find $\mathcal{F}^{(n)} = \{[S, 0, n]\}$. In general, there can be several final items. In an Earley-type parsing system (cf. Section 4.6), we have final items of the form $[S \rightarrow \gamma \bullet, 0, n]$, as many as there are productions with left-hand side S.

14.2 Recognizing networks

Before we define boolean circuits, we will first augment parsing systems with a special item *accept*, that is valid if and only if $a_1 \ldots a_n \in L(G)$. In a recognizing network, the well-formedness of the string that is being parsed ran be read off by inspecting the status of a special *accept* node.

Definition 14.6. (*augmented parsing system*)
For each (uninstantiated) parsing system $\langle \mathcal{I}, \mathcal{H}, D \rangle$ with $\mathcal{H}$ as in (14.2), an *augmented* parsing system $\hat{\mathbb{P}} = \langle \hat{\mathcal{I}}, \mathcal{H}, \hat{D} \rangle$ is defined by

$$\hat{\mathcal{I}} = \mathcal{I} \cup \{accept\},$$

$$\hat{D} = D \cup \{\xi, [\$, i, i+1] \vdash accept \mid i \geq 0 \wedge \xi \in \mathcal{F}^{(i)}\}.$$

with $\mathcal{F}^{(i)}$ the set of final items for a string of length i.
An instantiated parsing system $\langle \mathcal{I}, H, D \rangle$, likewise, can be extended to an augmented instantiated parsing system $\langle \hat{\mathcal{I}}, H, \hat{D} \rangle$. In that case, the extension to $\hat{D}$ will be ineffective for any $i \neq n$.   □

Corollary 14.7.
Let $\mathbb{P}$ by a correct parsing system (cf. Definitions 4.20 and 4.22) and $\hat{\mathbb{P}}$ the augmented system of $\mathbb{P}$. Then it holds for any $a_1 \ldots a_n \in \Sigma^*$ that

$$accept \in \mathcal{V}(\hat{\mathbb{P}}(a_1 \ldots a_n)) \text{ if and only if } a_1 \ldots a_n \in L(G).$$ □

We will now define a boolean circuit for an arbitrary parsing system and strings up to some maximum string length ℓ, based on the connectionist network of Fanty [1985, 1986]. A boolean circuit can be seen as a directed graph, where the nodes are processing units and the edges are connections between these processing units. A node has a set of *inputs* (incoming connections from other nodes) and a set of *outputs* (outgoing connections to other nodes). Each node can be in two states: activated ("on") or not activated ("off"). If a node is "on", it sends an "on" signal on all of its outputs; If a node is "off", it sends an "off" signal on all of its outputs. The activation of a node is a function of the signals that it receives on its inputs. We will only use two different kinds of nodes.

- An OR-node is "on" if it receives at least one "on" signal (and an arbitrary number of "off" signals).
  We will indicate OR-nodes by double parentheses (( )).
- An AND-node is "on" if it does not receive any "off" signal (and an arbitrary number of "on" signals).
  We will indicate AND-nodes by double acute angular brackets ≪ ≫.

A parsing system has an infinite number of items and deduction steps. For implementation in a boolean circuit, however, it is required that the system be finite. We will obtain this by assuming a maximum string length ℓ and building a network that can handle all strings $a_1 \ldots a_n$ with $0 \leq n \leq \ell$. For any given ℓ we can define a *restricted* augmented system $\hat{\mathbb{P}}_\ell = \langle \hat{\mathcal{I}}_\ell, \mathcal{H}_\ell, \hat{D}_\ell \rangle$, that comprises the part of $\hat{\mathbb{P}}$ that is relevant for strings up to a length ℓ. We will not take the trouble to give a formal definition of $\hat{\mathbb{P}}_\ell$, for any particular system it will always be clear which items are in $\hat{\mathcal{I}}_\ell$ and which are in $\hat{\mathcal{I}} \backslash \hat{\mathcal{I}}_\ell$; similarly for $\mathcal{H}_\ell$ and $\hat{D}_\ell$.

It is not necessarily true that restricting a system to a maximum sentence length makes it finite. Let G be a cyclic grammar, and $\mathbb{T}$ a *tree-based* parsing system for G. That is, every single tree is a separate item. Strings of finite length generate an infinite number of trees for cyclic grammars, hence a system that is restricted to some maximum string length will still be infinite. In an *item-based* system it is possible (but not necessarily the case) that this infinite number of trees is represented by a finite number of items. E.g. the Earley schemata in Examples 4.32 and 4.34, when applied to cyclic grammars, will yield finite restricted parsing systems.

Example 14.8.
Let G be a binary branching grammar. The parsing system $\mathbb{P}$ in the Example 14.4 can be augmented to $\hat{\mathbb{P}}$ and restricted to $\hat{\mathbb{P}}_\ell$ as follows. The system $\hat{\mathbb{P}}_\ell = \langle \hat{\mathcal{I}}_\ell, \mathcal{H}_\ell, \hat{D}_\ell \rangle$ is defined by

$$\hat{\mathcal{I}}_\ell \;=\; \{[X,i,j] \in \mathcal{I} \mid j \leq \ell\} \cup \{accept\};$$

$$\mathcal{H}_\ell \;=\; \{[a,i-1,i] \mid a \in \Sigma \wedge 1 \leq i \leq \ell\} \cup \{[\$,i,i+1] \mid 0 \leq i \leq \ell\};$$

$$\hat{D}_\ell^{(1)} \;=\; \{[X,i,j],[Y,j,k] \vdash [A,i,k] \mid A{\rightarrow}XY \in P\},$$

$$\hat{D}_\ell^{(2)} \;=\; \{[S,0,i],[\$,i,i+1] \vdash accept\},$$

$$\hat{D}_\ell \;=\; \hat{D}_\ell^{(1)} \cup \hat{D}_\ell^{(2)}.$$

Note that it is not necessary to define bounds on the position markers in $\hat{D}_\ell$. All items in a deduction step, by definition, must be drawn from the item set of the hypotheses. That is, it holds by definition that $\hat{D}_\ell \subseteq \wp_{fin}(\hat{\mathcal{I}}_\ell \cup \mathcal{H}_\ell) \times \hat{\mathcal{I}}_\ell$.
□

Definition 14.9. (*recognizing network*)
Let $\mathbb{P} = \langle \mathcal{I}, \mathcal{H}, D \rangle$ be an arbitrary parsing system, and $\hat{\mathbb{P}}_\ell$ the augmented system restricted to some maximum sentence length ℓ. A recognizing network for $\hat{\mathbb{P}}_\ell$ is a boolean circuit that has the following nodes:

- an OR-node $((\eta))$ for each $\eta \in \hat{\mathcal{I}}_\ell \cup \mathcal{H}_\ell$;
- an AND-node $\ll\eta_1,\ldots,\eta_k;\xi\gg$ for each $\eta_1,\ldots,\eta_k \vdash \xi \in \hat{D}_\ell$;

and the following connections:

- an edge $((\eta_i)) \longrightarrow \ll\eta_1,\ldots,\eta_k;\xi\gg$ for each $\eta_1,\ldots,\eta_k \vdash \xi \in \hat{D}_\ell$
and $1 \leq i \leq k$;

- an edge $\ll\eta_1,\ldots,\eta_k;\xi\gg \longrightarrow ((\xi))$ for each $\eta_1,\ldots,\eta_k \vdash \xi \in \hat{D}_\ell$.   □

Initially, all nodes are "off". It is assumed that the valid hypotheses are activated (and will remain to be activated) by external stimuli, derived from the "real" sentence. When this happens, a wave of activation will spread through the network.

It is easiest to think of time as divided into discrete *clock ticks*. At $t = 0$, only the valid hypotheses are "on". At $t = i$, for $i > 0$, the outputs of a node are determined as a function of the inputs at $t = i - 1$. From the set-up of the recognizing network it is clear that some "off" nodes will be turned "on" at some moment in time, but no "on" node will be turned "off" again. If the network is finite, it must become stable after a finite amount of time.

An example of a tiny part of a network (after Fanty [1986]) is shown in Figure 14.2. Suppose that there is a production $A{\rightarrow}BC$, then there are three AND-nodes for deduction steps that may activate a node $(([A, 2, 8]))$ from valid pairs of nodes $(([B, 2, j]))$, $(([C, j, 8]))$ for $j = 4, 5, 6$. Hence $(([A, 2, 8]))$ will be activated if there is (at least) one pair of applicable B and C nodes where both nodes are "on".

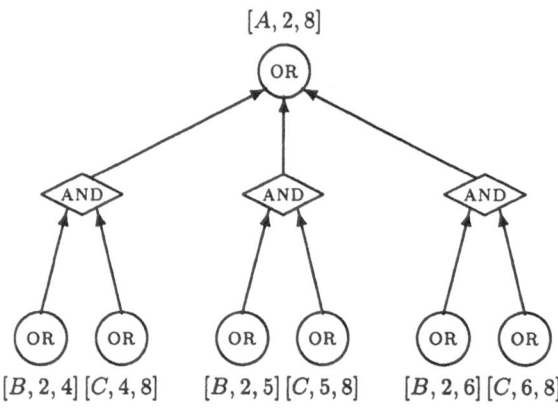

$[A, 2, 8]$

$[B, 2, 4]\ [C, 4, 8]$ $[B, 2, 5]\ [C, 5, 8]$ $[B, 2, 6]\ [C, 6, 8]$

Fig. 14.2. A fraction of a recognizing network

Theorem 14.10. (*validity in a finite recognizing network*)
Let $\mathbb{P}$ be a parsing system and $\hat{\mathbb{P}}_\ell$ for some maximum string length ℓ be finite. Let $a_1 \ldots a_n$ with $n \le \ell$ be the input to the recognizing network according to Definition 14.9. Then the network will stabilize after a finite number of clock ticks. Moreover, A node $((\xi))$ for $\xi \in \hat{\mathcal{I}}_\ell$ will be "on" in the stable network if and only if $\xi \in \mathcal{V}(\hat{\mathbb{P}}(a_1 \ldots a_n))$.
Proof: trivial.   □

Consequently, the *accept* node will be activated if and only if $a_1 \ldots a_n \in L(G)$.

14.3 Parsing networks

A recognizing network computes the correctness of a string. The *accept* node will be activated if and only if the presented string constitutes a valid sentence. Furthermore, each node that represents an item will be activated if and only if the item is valid.

It is not possible to yield a set of parses as output of a boolean circuit (unless we add nodes that could represent all possible parse trees). But we can do better than offer only a set of valid items. We can make a distinction between

- valid items that represent a partial parse tree for the given string,
- valid items that do not represent any tree that is part of a parse tree for the given string.

The former type of valid items will be called *parsable* items.

The parsable items for Example 14.5 are shown in Figure 14.3. The item $[PP, 2, 5]$ in Figure 14.1 has been deleted; it is valid, but not used in the context of the entire sentence. Similarly, the hypotheses that "flies" is a verb and "like" is a preposition are valid but not parsable for this sentence.

0,1	0,2	0,3	0,4	0,5
$*d$	NP			S
	1,2	1,3	1,4	1,5
	$*n$			
		2,3	2,4	2,5
		$*v$		VP
			3,4	3,5
			$*d$	NP
				4,5
				$*n$

Fig. 14.3. CYK table with parsable items for Example 14.5

In the sequel we will extend recognizing networks to parsing networks, that compute all parsable items for a given sentence. But first, we give a formal definition of parsability.

Definition 14.11. (*parsable items*)
Let $\hat{\mathbb{P}} = \langle \hat{\mathcal{I}}, \mathcal{H}, \hat{D} \rangle$ be an augmented parsing system, $\mathcal{V} = \mathcal{V}(\hat{\mathbb{P}}(a_1 \dots a_n))$ the set of valid items for some string $a_1 \dots a_n$. The set of *parsable items* $\mathcal{W} = \mathcal{W}(\hat{\mathbb{P}}(a_1 \dots a_n))$ is defined as the smallest set satisfying

(i) if $accept \in \mathcal{V}$ then $accept \in \mathcal{W}$;
(ii) if $\xi \in \mathcal{W}$ and there are $\eta_1, \dots, \eta_k \in \mathcal{V}$ such that $\eta_1, \dots, \eta_k \vdash \xi \in \hat{D}$ then $\eta_1, \dots, \eta_k \in \mathcal{W}$.

For an unaugmented parsing system $\mathbb{P} = \langle \mathcal{I}, \mathcal{H}, D \rangle$ and a string $a_1 \ldots a_n$, an item $\xi \in \mathcal{I}$ is called *parsable* if it is parsable in $\hat{\mathbb{P}}$ for $a_1 \ldots a_n$.   □

The following corollary can be employed for the local design of the network:

Corollary 14.12.
Let $\hat{\mathbb{P}} = \langle \hat{\mathcal{I}}, \mathcal{H}, \hat{D} \rangle$ be an augmented parsing system. An item $\xi \neq accept$ in $\mathcal{I}$ is parsable for some string $a_1 \ldots a_n$ if and only if there are $\zeta_1, \ldots, \zeta_k, \eta \in \hat{\mathcal{I}}$ such that

(*i*) $\xi, \zeta_1, \ldots, \zeta_k$ are valid,
(*ii*) $\xi, \zeta_1, \ldots, \zeta_k \vdash \eta \in \hat{D}$,
(*iii*) η is parsable.   □

Armed with Definition 14.11 and Corollary 14.12 we can now extend the recognizing network to a parsing network. A node that represents an item in the recognizing network will be activated iff the item is valid. A supplementary node in the parsing network will be activated iff the item is parsable. After *accept* has been turned "on", a wave of activation spreads through the supplementary part of the network in reverse direction.

Definition 14.13. (*parsing network*)
Let $\mathbb{P} = \langle \mathcal{I}, \mathcal{H}, D \rangle$ be an arbitrary parsing system, and $\hat{\mathbb{P}}_\ell$ the augmented system restricted to some maximum sentence length ℓ. A parsing network for $\hat{\mathbb{P}}_\ell$ is a boolean circuit that consists of the following nodes:

- OR-nodes $((\eta))$ and $((\mathcal{P}\eta))$ for each $\eta \in \hat{\mathcal{I}}_\ell \cup \mathcal{H}_\ell$;
- AND-nodes $\ll\eta_1, \ldots, \eta_k; \xi\gg$ and $\ll\mathcal{P}\,\eta_1, \ldots, \eta_k; \xi\gg$
  for each $\eta_1, \ldots, \eta_k \vdash \xi \in \hat{D}_\ell$;

and the following connections:

- $((accept)) \longrightarrow ((\mathcal{P}\,accept))$,
- $((\eta_i)) \longrightarrow \ll\eta_1, \ldots, \eta_k; \xi\gg$ for $\eta_1, \ldots, \eta_k \vdash \xi \in \hat{D}_\ell$
  and $1 \leq i \leq k$,
- $\ll\eta_1, \ldots, \eta_k; \xi\gg \longrightarrow ((\xi))$ for $\eta_1, \ldots, \eta_k \vdash \xi \in \hat{D}_\ell$,
- $\ll\eta_1, \ldots, \eta_k; \xi\gg \longrightarrow \ll\mathcal{P}\,\eta_1, \ldots, \eta_k; \xi\gg$ for $\eta_1, \ldots, \eta_k \vdash \xi \in \hat{D}_\ell$,
- $((\mathcal{P}\xi)) \longrightarrow \ll\mathcal{P}\,\eta_1, \ldots, \eta_k; \xi\gg$ for $\eta_1, \ldots, \eta_k \vdash \xi \in \hat{D}_\ell$,
- $\ll\mathcal{P}\,\eta_1, \ldots, \eta_k; \xi\gg \longrightarrow ((\mathcal{P}\eta_i))$ for $\eta_1, \ldots, \eta_k \vdash \xi \in \hat{D}_\ell$
  and $1 \leq i \leq k$.   □

The supplementary $\mathcal{P}$ nodes are used to distinguish the parsable items from the valid nonparsable items. When these (and the connected edges) are deleted, the recognizing network of Definition 14.9 remains. An example of a fraction of a parsing network in shown in Figure 14.4. This is a simplification of the recognizing network of Fanty [1986].[3]

---

[3]   In Fanty's network, there is (in our notation) also an edge $((\xi)) \longrightarrow ((\mathcal{P}\xi))$ for every $\xi \in \hat{\mathcal{I}}_\ell$. Moreover, a node $((\mathcal{P}\xi))$ is a special kind of "AND-OR-node" that

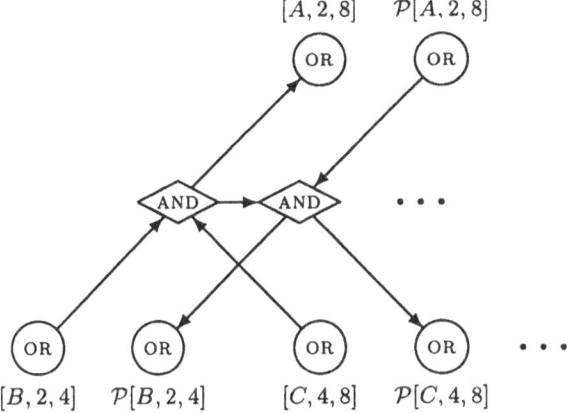

Fig. 14.4. A fraction of a parsing network

Theorem 14.14. (*validity in a finite parsing network*)
Let $\mathbb{P}$ be a parsing system and $\hat{\mathbb{P}}_\ell$ for some maximum string length ℓ be finite. Let $a_1 \ldots a_n$ with $n \leq \ell$ be the input to the parsing network according to Definition 14.13. Then the network will stabilize after a finite number of clock ticks.
A node $((\mathcal{P}\xi))$ for $\xi \in \hat{\mathcal{I}}_\ell$ will be "on" in the stable network if and only if $\xi \in \mathcal{W}(\hat{\mathbb{P}}(a_1 \ldots a_n))$.
Furthermore, a node $\ll\mathcal{P}\,\eta_1, \ldots, \eta_k; \xi\gg$ will be "on" in the stable network if and only if $\{\eta_1, \ldots, \eta_k, \xi\} \subseteq \mathcal{W}(\mathbb{P}(a_1 \ldots a_n))$.

Proof: straightforward from the above discussion.   □

   In a CYK-like network (and in many other networks that are derived from sensible parsing schemata) we can see the activated $\mathcal{P}$ nodes a a representation of a *shared parse forest* (in Chapters 12 and 13 also called *packed shared parse forest*). A parse node $((\mathcal{P}[X, i, j]))$ will be activated if and only if X occurs in a parse of $a_1 \ldots a_n$ as a constituent that spans the substring $a_{i+1} \ldots a_j$. Moreover, any pair of constituents Y, Z into which X can be decomposed can be found by inspecting the activity of the nodes $\ll\mathcal{P}\,[Y, i, k], [Z, k, j]; [X, i, j]\gg$.

ORs all signals coming from above and ANDs the result this with the signal from $((\xi))$. This extra edge can be deleted because any node $\ll\mathcal{P}\,\xi, \zeta_1, \ldots, \zeta_k; \eta\gg$ that provides input "from above" to $((\mathcal{P}\xi))$ can be activated only if $((\xi))$ has been activated. More importantly, the special type of node introduced by Fanty reduces to a conventional OR-node. Fanty's original design – which was duly copied by Nijholt [1990] and Sikkel [1990] – is correct but unnecessarily complicated.

14.4 Some further issues

In the previous sections we have defined the basics of boolean circuit implementations of parsing schemata. There are some further issues, treated at length in [Sikkel, 1990], that can be dealt with rather tersely here. Most of it follows directly from results that have been covered elsewhere in this book.

To start with, one can apply *meta-parsing*, as it has been called by Nijholt [1990]. The parsing network according to Definition 14.13 may contain spurious nodes. If an item $[A, i, j]$ is not parsable for any well-formed sentence, then it can just as well be deleted from the network. The network need only contain nodes for *potentially* parsable items. The necessarily unparsable items can be separated from the potentially parsable ones as follows. Let $\langle \mathcal{I}, \mathcal{H}, D \rangle$ be an uninstantiated parsing system, and $\langle \hat{\mathcal{I}}_\ell, \mathcal{H}_\ell, \hat{D}_\ell \rangle$ the augmented system for some maximum string length ℓ. We can instantiate the system by choosing $H = \mathcal{H}_\ell$, that is, validating *all* hypotheses. If we run the (simulated) network, then a parse node $((\mathcal{P}\xi))$ will be activated if and only if there is *some* string $a_1 \ldots a_n$ with $n \le \ell$ such that $\xi \in \mathcal{W}(\hat{\mathbb{P}}_\ell(a_1 \ldots a_n))$.

If $((\mathcal{P}\xi))$ is not activated by meta-parsing, then the item ξ can be deleted from the parsing system, and the nodes $((\xi))$ and $((\mathcal{P}\xi))$ can be deleted from the network. The same applies to any deduction step in which a necessarily unparsable item appears, either as antecedent or as consequent.

The above meta-parsing algorithm takes for granted that we are are only interested in valid sentences. If a string is offered that is not contained in the language, we might be interested in finding at least those parts that can be recognized. To that end, we can employ a weaker meta-parsing algorithm that discards those items ξ for which $\xi \notin \mathcal{V}(\mathbb{P}(a_1 \ldots a_n))$ for any string. The weak meta-parsing algorithm yields the *regular subsystem* that has been discussed in Section 4.5.

The *complexity* of a boolean circuit parser is measured as follows. The *size* of the network is determined by the number of nodes. The total number of connections between nodes is linear in the size of the network, if the number of antecedents for any individual deduction step is limited by some small constant. This will be the case for all parsing systems that we discuss here.[4] As the *time complexity* of a network we count the number of clock ticks that is needed to obtain the final, stabilized situation.

Note that any individual network is finite. The size of the network is measured as a function of the maximum string length ℓ and the size $|G|$ of

---

[4] A counterexample to this assumption is, for example, the **GCYK** parsing schema (cf. Example 5.20) applied to grammars with arbitrarily large right-hand sides of productions. This may yield systems where the number of connections is quadratic, rather than linear, in the number of nodes.
So, to be formally correct, we should add *connectivity* as a complexity factor and in all applicable cases argue that the connectivity is of the same order as the size of the network.

the grammar (cf. equation (11.4) on page 239). Let $\mathbb{P}_\ell = \langle \mathcal{I}_\ell, \mathcal{H}_\ell, D_\ell \rangle$ be a network, restricted to some maximum string length ℓ. The size of the network, then, is simply $O(|\mathcal{I}_\ell| + |\mathcal{H}_\ell| + |D_\ell|)$.

For a CYK network we find a time complexity of $O(n)$ and a network size of $O(|G|\ell^3)$: the largest factor is the number of deduction steps $[X, i, j], [Y, j, k] \;\vdash\; [A, i, k]$ for each production $A \to XY$ and arbitrary $0 \leq i < j < k \leq \ell$.

Fanty's network is defined only for binary branching grammars. The same technique can be applied to define a boolean circuit parser for arbitrary context-free grammars. In Section 3 of [Sikkel, 1990], Fanty's technique is applied to construct a boolean circuit parser based on the algorithm of Chiang and Fu [1984] (cf. Example 6.20). A similar network (in fact a simpler one, see footnote 3 on page 320) is obtained by applying the network construction of Definition 14.13 to a parsing system $\mathbf{ChF}(G)$ for an arbitrary grammar $G \in \mathcal{CFG}$.

Most parsing systems have a few *initial* deduction steps that have no antecedents. In a parsing network, these are mapped onto AND-nodes with no inputs. In the definition of AND-nodes we have anticipated this: an AND-node will be activated if none of its inputs is off. This is clearly the case for AND-nodes without input, hence all nodes of this type will be active at time $t = 1$.

14.5 Rytter's algorithm

Further on in this chapter, in Section 14.7, we will define a boolean circuit implementation of Rytter's algorithm. The recognition part of such a network follows directly from the validity of the Rytter parsing schema and the network construction of Definition 14.9. Extending the recognizing network to a parsing network can – in this particular case – be done rather more simple than with the construction of Definition 14.13.

The more difficult issue is to prove that the network will stabilize in logarithmic time. A formal proof that Rytter's algorithm works in logarithmic time is given in Section 14.6. In this section we will introduce Rytter's algorithm and provide the intuition on which the proof in 14.6 is based.

As before, we only consider binary branching grammars. This restriction is not essential, but of great help to simplify the notation. In Section 14.8 we will briefly discuss how the approach can be generalized to parsing systems for arbitrary context-free grammars.

The easiest way to explain Rytter's algorithm is to start with the items that are used. CYK uses items of the form $[X, i, j]$. Such an item is valid if

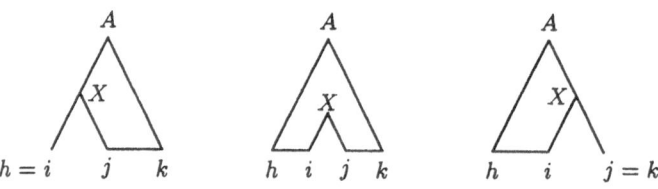

Fig. 14.5. Different kinds of Rytter items

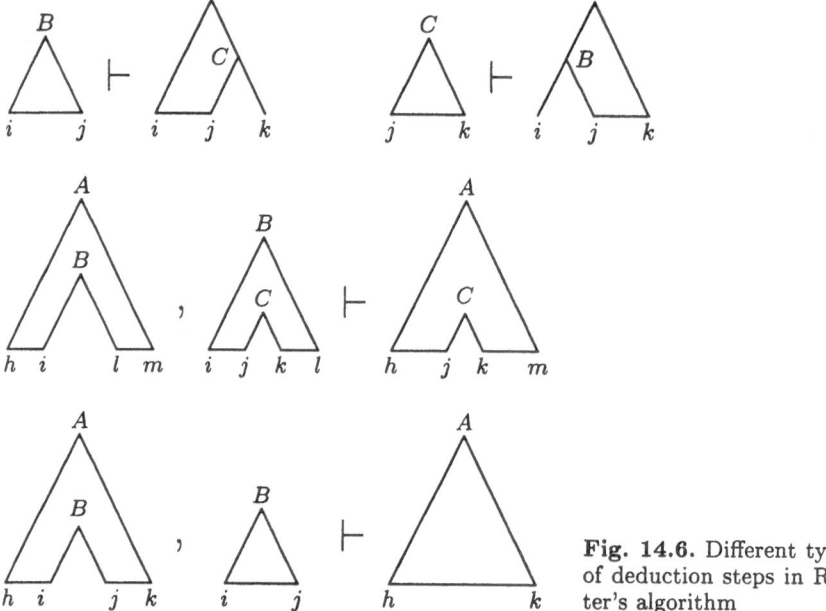

Fig. 14.6. Different types of deduction steps in Rytter's algorithm

$X \Rightarrow^* a_{i+1} \dots a_j$. Rytter's algorithm, in addition, uses items $[A, h, k; X, i, j]$. Such an item is valid if

$$A \Rightarrow^* a_{h+1} \dots a_i X a_{j+1} \dots a_k.$$

This can be seen as a CYK item with a *gap*; the missing part $[X, i, j]$ still has to be filled, in order to obtain the validity of $[A, h, k]$. See Figure 14.5. We could also see such an item as a *conditional* CYK item: validity of $[A, h, k; X, i, j]$ can be interpreted as

if $[X, i, j]$ is valid then $[A, h, k]$ is also valid.

Let $A \rightarrow XY$ be a production in P. A CYK deduction step $[X, i, j], [Y, j, k] \vdash [A, i, k]$ can be refined into two steps:

$$[X, i, j] \quad \vdash \quad [A, i, k; Y, j, k],$$

$$[A, i, k; Y, j, k], \ [Y, j, k] \quad \vdash \quad [A, i, k].$$

The gap in the intermediate item is *rightmost*. Another possibility to deduce $[A, i, j]$ is by means of an item with a *leftmost* gap $[A, i, k; X, i, j]$.

Specific for Rytter's algorithm is the addition of a simple combination rule: two conditional items can be combined into a single one if the "outside" of one item matches the "inside" of another item. A graphical impression of the different types of deduction steps in Rytter's algorithm is shown in Figure 14.6.

A parsing schema for Rytter's algorithm for binary branching grammars is defined as follows. This is a minor modification of the schema that was presented in Example 5.23.

Schema 14.15. (Rbb)
For an arbitrary binary branching grammar $G \in \mathcal{BB}$ we define a parsing system $\mathbb{P}_{Rbb} = \langle \mathcal{I}_{Rbb}, \mathcal{H}, D_{Rbb} \rangle$ by

$$\mathcal{I}^{(1)} = \{[A, i, j] \mid A \in N \wedge 0 < i \wedge i + 1 < j\}$$
$$\cup \{[a, i - 1, i] \mid a \in \Sigma \wedge i \geq 1\},$$

$$\mathcal{I}^{(2)} = \{[A, h, k; X, i, j] \mid [A, h, k] \in \mathcal{I} \wedge [X, i, j] \in \mathcal{I}$$
$$\wedge\ h \leq i \leq j \leq k \wedge (h \neq i \text{ or } j \neq k)\}$$

$$\mathcal{I}_{Rbb} = \mathcal{I}^{(1)} \cup \mathcal{I}^{(2)};$$

$$\mathcal{H} = \{[a, i - 1, i] \mid a \in \Sigma \wedge i \geq 1\};\ \cup\ \{[\$, i, i + 1] \mid i \geq 0\};$$

$$D^{(1a)} = \{[X, i, j] \vdash [A, i, k; Y, j, k] \mid A \rightarrow XY \in P\},$$

$$D^{(1b)} = \{[Y, j, k] \vdash [A, i, k; X, i, j] \mid A \rightarrow XY \in P\},$$

$$D^{(2)} = \{[A, h, k; X, i, j], [X, i, j] \vdash [A, h, k]\}$$

$$D^{(3)} = \{[A, h, m; B, i, l], [B, i, l; X, j, k] \vdash [A, h, m; X, j, k]\}$$

$$D_{Rbb} = D^{(1a)} \cup D^{(1b)} \cup D^{(2)} \cup D^{(3)}.$$

The system $\mathbb{P}_{Rbb}$ can be augmented to $\hat{\mathbb{P}}_{Rbb}$ in the usual way, and restricted to a maximum sentence length ℓ by considering only items $[X, i, j]$ with $j \leq \ell$ and $[A, h, k; X, i, j]$ with $k \leq \ell$.   □

Combining pairs of conditional items by $D^{(3)}$ is the key to logarithmic-time parsing. This will be shown by the following example.

Example 14.16.
Consider a grammar defined by

$$S \rightarrow aS \mid ab$$

and the string $aaab$. A parse tree for this string is shown in Figure 14.7. The CYK algorithm will need n steps to parse a string of length n, no matter how much parallelism is employed. A parallel Rytter parser will process a

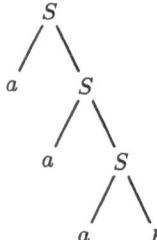

Fig. 14.7. A parse tree for $aaab$

string $aaab$ as follows. From each of the hypotheses $[a, i-1, i]$ we can obtain conditional items

$[a, 0, 1] \vdash [S, 0, 4; S, 1, 4],$

$[a, 1, 2] \vdash [S, 1, 4; S, 2, 4],$

$[a, 2, 3] \vdash [S, 2, 4; b, 3, 4].$

The antecedents of these three deduction steps, in combination with the hypothesis $[b, 3, 4]$, can be combined into a final item by pairwise combination. We have

$[S, 0, 4; S, 1, 4], [S, 1, 4; S, 2, 4] \vdash [S, 0, 4; S, 2, 4],$

$[S, 2, 4; b, 3, 4], [b, 3, 4] \vdash [S, 2, 4],$

and, subsequently,

$[S, 0, 4; S, 2, 4], [S, 2, 4] \vdash [S, 0, 4].$

It is clear that (for this grammar) a parallel Rytter parser will parse any sentence in logarithmic time. That this also holds for arbitrary grammars, remains to be proven.   □

In order to deepen our understanding of what is going on here, we will look at an implementation of the above Rytter system for an arbitrary grammar on a *parallel random access machine* (PRAM). This is an often used abstract machine model for the definition of parallel algorithms. A PRAM consists of an (in principle unbounded) number of different processors that have access to a central shared memory. There are in fact various PRAM models, that differ according the possibilities for concurrent memory access. We will make use of a so-called *WRAM*: different processors may read the same memory location at the same time; concurrent writing into the same memory location is allowed *only if* these processors write the same value.

Algorithm 14.17. (*logarithmic-time recognizer for binary branching grammars*)
For the sake of simplicity we will only consider the recognition algorithm, and do not (yet) bother to determine a parse forest. We consider an instantiated

parsing system for some string $a_1 \ldots a_n$, so we can restrict the system to the actual string length n, rather than some arbitrary maximum string length ℓ.

We write ξ as a generic notation for CYK items in $\mathcal{I}_n^{(1)}$ and $\langle \xi \leftarrow \eta \rangle$ as a generic notation for items in $\mathcal{I}_n^{(2)}$. If $\xi = [A, h, k]$ and $\eta = [X, i, j]$ then $\langle \xi \leftarrow \eta \rangle = [A, h, k; X, i, j]$.

For each item $\xi \in \mathcal{I}_n^{(1)}$ we introduce a boolean predicate $recognized(\xi)$; for each item $\langle \xi \leftarrow \eta \rangle \in \mathcal{I}_n^{(2)}$ we introduce a boolean predicate $proposed(\langle \xi \leftarrow \eta \rangle)$. At the end of the algorithm, $recognized(\xi)$ will be $true$ iff $\xi \in \mathcal{V}(\mathbb{P}(a_1 \ldots a_n))$ and $proposed(\langle \xi \leftarrow \eta \rangle)$ will be $true$ iff $\langle \xi \leftarrow \eta \rangle \in \mathcal{V}(\mathbb{P}(a_1 \ldots a_n))$. We define procedures $initialize$, $propose$, $combine$, and $recognize$ as follows.

> **procedure** $initialize$
> **begin**
> > **for all** $\xi \in \mathcal{I}_n^{(1)}$ **do** $recognized(\xi) := false$ **od**;
> > **for all** $\langle \xi \leftarrow \eta \rangle \in \mathcal{I}_n^{(2)}$ **do** $proposed(\langle \xi \leftarrow \eta \rangle) := false$ **od**;
> > **for all** $\xi \in H$ **do** $recognized(\xi) := true$ **od**
>
> **end**;
> **procedure** $propose$
> **begin**
> > **for all** $A \rightarrow XY \in P$ and appropriate $0 \le i \le j \le k \le n$
> > **do**   **if** $recognized([X, i, j])$
> > > **then** $proposed([A, i, k; Y, j, k]) := true$ **fi**;
> > > **if** $recognized([Y, j, k])$
> > > **then** $proposed([A, i, k; X, i, j]) := true$ **fi**
> >
> > **od**
>
> **end**;
> **procedure** $combine$
> **begin**
> > **for all** $\langle \xi \leftarrow \eta \rangle, \langle \eta \leftarrow \zeta \rangle \in \mathcal{I}_n^{(2)}$
> > **do**   **if** $proposed(\langle \xi \leftarrow \eta \rangle)$ **and** $proposed(\langle \eta \leftarrow \zeta \rangle)$
> > > **then** $proposed(\langle \xi \leftarrow \zeta \rangle) := true$ **fi**
> >
> > **od**
>
> **end**;
> **procedure** $recognize$
> **begin**
> > **for all** $\langle \xi \leftarrow \eta \rangle \in \mathcal{I}_n^{(2)}$
> > **do**   **if** $proposed(\langle \xi \leftarrow \eta \rangle)$ **and** $recognized(\eta)$
> > > **then** $recognized(\xi) := true$ **fi**
> >
> > **od**
>
> **end**;

It is clear that each of the above procedures can be executed in constant time on a WRAM, given $O(n^6)$ processors and $O(n^4)$ shared memory. With some more care the space complexity can be reduced to $O(n^2)$ (cf. Gibbons and Rytter, [1988]), but at the expense of some clarity. For our boolean circuit implementation this is irrelevant; it does not use memory. A variant of Rytter's algorithm can now be defined as follows.[5]

> **procedure** *Rytter's algorithm (modified)*
> **begin**
>   *initialize*;
>   *propose*;
>   **repeat** $\lceil {}^2\log n\rceil$ **times**
>   **begin**
>   *recognize*;
>   *propose*;
>   *combine*;
>   *combine*
>   **end**;
>   **if** *recognized*$([S, 0, n])$ **then** *accept* **else** *reject* **fi**
> **end**;

where $\lceil {}^2\log n\rceil$ is the smallest natural number $\geq {}^2\log n$. Hence, for example, 5 steps suffice for any sentence of up to 32 words. For a sentence of 1000 words only 10 steps are needed (but at the cost of some 10^{18} processors, which is not very realistic). $\qquad\qquad\qquad\qquad\qquad\qquad\qquad\qquad\qquad\qquad\square$

For the CYK algorithm we used an upper triangular recognition matrix T_{CYK}. For Rytter's algorithm we can use a similar recognition structure T_R, which is not a matrix but a pyramid. Table entries have three indices: the leftmost and rightmost position marker (as with CYK) and, thirdly, the *size* of an item. The size is the number of words in the string that is covered by an item. Formally:

$$size([X, i, j]) = j - i \text{ for any } [X, i, j] \in \mathcal{I}^{(1)}, \tag{14.3}$$

$$\begin{aligned} size([A, h, k; X, i, j]) &= size([A, h, k]) - size([X, i, j]) \\ &= h - k - i + j \end{aligned} \tag{14.4}$$
$$\text{for any } [A, h, k; X, i, j] \in \mathcal{I}^{(2)}.$$

A recognized item of the form $[X, i, j]$ will be stored in table entry $T_{i,j,j-i}$; a proposed item of the form $[A, h, k; X, i, j]$ will be stored in table entry $T_{h,k,h-k-j+i}$. All items of size 1 will be stored in the bottom layer of the

---

[5] In the original version of Rytter's algorithm the initialization consists of *initialize* only, a step comprises a call to *propose*, *combine*, *combine*, *recognize* in that order. The reason to change this is that it allows introduction of loop invariants (14.5) and (14.6). Gibbons and Rytter employ a rather more complicated loop invariant, for which reason their proof is rather more cumbersome.

The *propose*, *combine*, and *recognize* steps were called *activate*, *square* and *pebble*, originally. As the term *activate* had to be changed, so as to avoid confusion with activation of a node, we have also replace the other terms with words that seem more appropriate in this context.

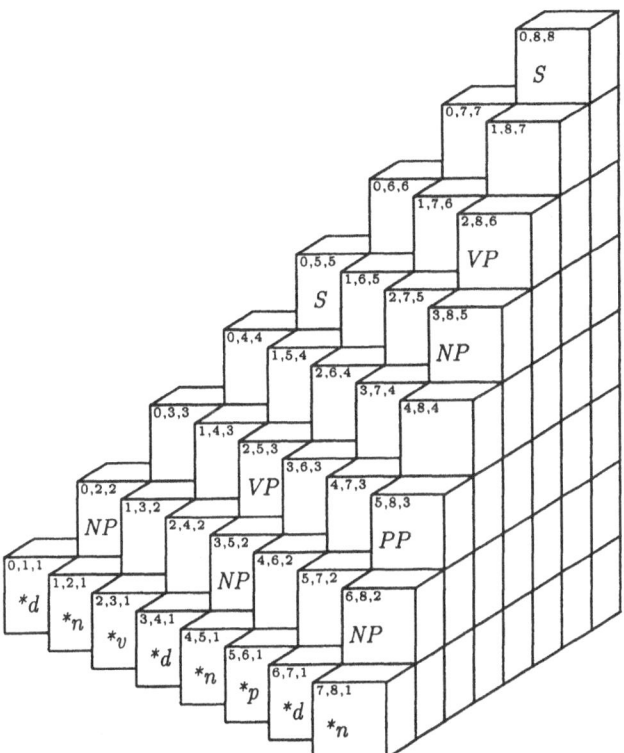

Fig. 14.8. An example of a Rytter recognition table

table; all items of size k in the k-th (horizontal) layer. Note, furthermore, that all cubes $T_{i,j,k}$ on the surface satisfy $k = j - i$. Hence, all proper CYK items will be stored in these surface cubes. Items $[A, h, k; X, i, j]$ will be in a cube inside the table, that is located exactly $j - i$ positions down from $T_{h,k,k-h}$. Hence, in Figure 14.8 only the proper CYK items are visible; proposed items with a gap are hidden under the surface. If the hidden cubes are deleted, the conventional CYK table remains.

The reason for constructing the pyramid-shaped table in Figure 14.8 is that it can be employed to visualize the logarithmic nature of Rytter's algorithm. We can cut the table into slices, such that each slice will be filled by a single step of the algorithm. This is shown in Figure 14.9. In the above definition of Rytter's algorithm it is in fact allowed that in step i items are recognized in some slice $j > i$. The algorithm can be improved by regarding in step i only those items that should go into slice i. But the important thing to notice, whether or not such a filter is applied, is that every valid item in slice i must have been recognized after i steps.

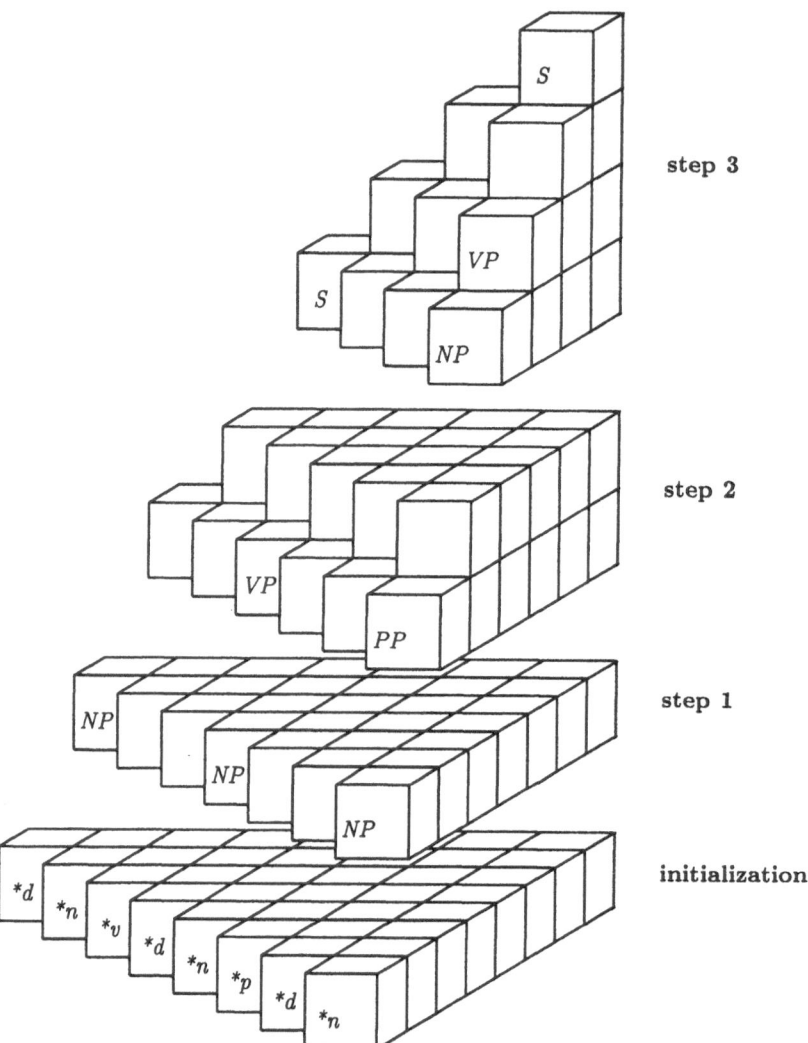

Fig. 14.9. Visualization of steps in Rytter's algorithm

That is, the algorithm satisfies the following *loop invariant* statements:

if $\xi \in \mathcal{V}(\mathbb{P}(a_1 \dots a_n))$ and $size(\xi) \leq 2^k$
then *recognized*(ξ) after k steps;

$$(14.5)$$

if $\langle \xi \leftarrow \eta \rangle \in \mathcal{V}(\mathbb{P}(a_1 \dots a_n))$ and $size(\langle \xi \leftarrow \eta \rangle) \leq 2^k$
then *proposed*$(\langle \xi \leftarrow \eta \rangle)$ after k steps.

$$(14.6)$$

A proof will be given in the next section.

One may wonder why it is necessary to include two calls to *combine* within a single step. For the grammar in Example 14.16, a single *combine* per step will clearly be sufficient. That the second *combine* is necessary to guarantee the loop invariants (14.5) and (14.6) is shown by the following example.

Example 14.18.
Consider a grammar that has the productions

$$
\begin{aligned}
S &\rightarrow SA \mid aa, \\
A &\rightarrow bB, \\
B &\rightarrow SS.
\end{aligned}
$$

We can define a series of trees $\tau_1, \dots,$ by

$$
\begin{aligned}
\tau_1 &= \langle S \rightarrow aa \rangle, \\
\tau_{k+1} &= \langle S \rightsquigarrow \tau_k b \tau_k \tau_k \rangle,
\end{aligned}
$$

see Figure 14.10. It is easy to verify that, when only a single *combine* is executed per step, recognition of τ_{k+1} will take two more steps than recognition of τ_k, while $size(\tau_{k+1}) = 3.size(\tau_k) + 1$. But to stay within the desired complexity bounds, two more steps should be able to cope with a size multiplication by 4. Hence, for large enough k this must fail. The reader may verify that τ_5 yields a string of length 202. If only one *combine* operation per step were allowed, then it would take 9 steps to compute $\mathcal{V}(\mathbb{P}(a_1 \dots a_{202}))$, while $\lceil {}^2 \log 202 \rceil = 8$. □

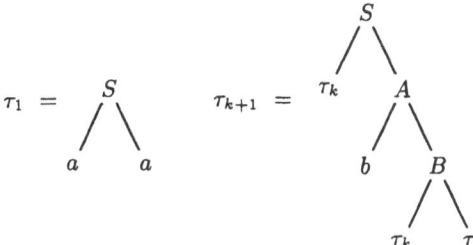

Fig. 14.10. Recursive definition of tree τ_k in Example 14.18

14.6 Correctness of Rytter's algorithm

The soundness of Rytter's algorithm, as presented in the previous section, is trivially obtained from the fact that each of the procedures *initialize*, *propose*, *combine*, and *recognize* is sound. The completeness of the algorithm follows from the loop invariants (14.5) and (14.6). The major task is to establish these loop invariants.

The correctness proof that is given here may seem far from trivial. It should be noted, however, that it is rather more simple than the original proof of the "pebble game" by Gibbons and Rytter [1988]. Space complexity on a WRAM is irrelevant for our purpose of constructing a boolean circuit implementation. At the expense of $O(n^4)$, rather than $O(n^2)$ space complexity we have been able to introduce a simple loop invariant — and to simplify the presentation of the algorithm. The sliced pyramid in Figure 14.9 only applies to our version of Rytter's algorithm, not to the original algorithm.

We will introduce a few *ad hoc* concepts that are useful to simplify the proof. Firstly, for easy reference, the operations within some step k are numbered as follows:

k.1   *recognize*
k.2   *propose*
k.3   *combine*
k.4   *combine*

Next, we assume that $\mathcal{I}^{(2)}$ contains items of the form $\langle \xi \leftarrow \xi \rangle$ for any $\xi \in \mathcal{I}^{(1)}$. Such items have zero size (the item is nothing but a large gap) but will turn out to be practical as a boundary case. It is assumed that $\langle \xi \leftarrow \xi \rangle \in \mathcal{V}(\mathbb{P}(a_1 \ldots a_n))$ for any ξ. Moreover, it is assumed that *proposed*($\langle \xi \leftarrow \xi \rangle$) has been set to *true* in the initialization phase.

Furthermore, we replace the *size* function on items by a *rank* function that corresponds to the step number after which an item must have been recognized/proposed (if it is valid). We define

$$rank(\xi) \quad = \quad k \quad \text{for } 2^{k-1} < size(\xi) \le 2^k,$$

$$rank(\langle \xi \leftarrow \eta \rangle) \quad = \quad k \quad \text{for } 2^{k-1} < size(\langle \xi \leftarrow \eta \rangle) \le 2^k,$$

$$rank(\langle \xi \leftarrow \xi \rangle) \quad = \quad -1$$

We can apply the notion of rank also to binary trees. An item $[X, i, j]$ can be seen as a collection of binary trees with $j - i$ leaves. Hence the rank of a binary tree is the (rounded) logarithm of the size of its yield. Furthermore, the rank of a *node* in a tree is the rank of the sub-tree of which that node is the root.

An important observation is that every binary tree of rank $k \ge 1$ has a node of rank k such that both children of this node have rank $< k$. We call this the *critical node*. In order to find the critical node, start searching at the top. If both children have rank $< k$, then stop. Otherwise, go to the child with largest rank (which must be k) and continue searching from there.

We will generalize this idea to items, and show the existence of a critical item.

Definition 14.19. (*critical item*)
Let $\xi \in \mathcal{I}^{(1)}$, $rank(\xi) = k$. An item $\theta \in \mathcal{I}^{(1)}$ is called *critical to* ξ if

(*i*) $\langle \xi \leftarrow \theta \rangle \in \mathcal{V}(\mathbb{P}(a_1 \ldots a_n))$,
(*ii*) $rank(\theta) = k$,
(*iii*) there are $\eta, \zeta \in \mathcal{V}(\mathbb{P}(a_1 \ldots a_n))$ such that
$\qquad rank(\eta) \leq k - 1$, $rank(\zeta) \leq k - 1$, and $\eta, \zeta \vdash_{CYK} \theta$.

(where $\eta, \zeta \vdash_{CYK} \xi$ is a convenient abbreviation for "there are A, X, Y, i, j, k such that $\eta = [X, i, j]$, $\zeta = [Y, j, k]$ and $\theta = [A, i, k]$ and, moreover, $A \rightarrow XY \in P$.") □

Lemma 14.20.
For every item $\xi \in \mathcal{V}(\mathbb{P}(a_1 \ldots a_n))$ with $rank(\xi) \geq 1$ there is an item $\theta \in \mathcal{V}(\mathbb{P}(a_1 \ldots a_n))$ such that θ is critical to ξ.

Proof. Let $\xi \in \mathcal{V}(\mathbb{P}(a_1 \ldots a_n))$ and $rank(\xi) = k \geq 1$.
Then there must be a pair of items $\phi, \psi \in \mathcal{V}(\mathbb{P}(a_1 \ldots a_n))$ such that $\phi, \psi \vdash_{CYK} \xi$. Without loss of generality, we assume $rank(\phi) \geq rank(\psi)$.
If $rank(\phi) < rank(\xi)$ then $\theta = \xi$ and (*i*)–(*iii*) in Definition 14.19 are satisfied.
If $rank(\phi) = rank(\xi) = k$ we can recursively search for a θ that is critical to ϕ. There must be a pair $\phi', \psi' \in \mathcal{V}(\mathbb{P}(a_1 \ldots a_n))$ such that $\phi', \psi' \vdash_{CYK} \phi$ and $rank(\phi') \geq rank(\psi')$. In this way we find a sequence $\phi, \phi', \phi'', \phi''', $ and so on. Note, however, that $rank(\xi) = rank(\phi) = rank(\phi') = \ldots$ but that $size(\xi) > size(\phi) > size(\phi') > \ldots$; hence the recursion must end at some critical item. It is easy to verify that if θ is critical to $\ldots, \phi'', \phi', \phi$ then it is also critical to ξ. □

Corollary 14.21.
Let $\langle \xi \leftarrow \theta \rangle \in \mathcal{V}(\mathbb{P}(a_1 \ldots a_n))$, and θ critical to ξ.
Then $rank(\langle \xi \leftarrow \theta \rangle) < rank(\xi)$. □

If $proposed(\langle \xi \leftarrow \eta \rangle)$ is *true* at some moment, then this must have been caused by a *propose* or by a *combine* operation. If it was a *combine*, then there is a θ such that $\langle \xi \leftarrow \eta \rangle$ was obtained as a combination of previously proposed $\langle \xi \leftarrow \theta \rangle$ and $\langle \theta \leftarrow \eta \rangle$. Each of these has been proposed either by a *propose* or by a *combine* operation, and so on. Ultimately, every proposed item with a gap can be broken down into a sequence of items with a gap, all fitting into each other, such that each item in this sequence has been proposed by a *propose* operation. This is formalized as follows.

Definition 14.22. (*item path*)

Let $\langle\xi{\leftarrow}\eta\rangle \in \mathcal{V}(\mathbb{P}(a_1 \ldots a_n))$. A sequence of valid items $\zeta_0, \ldots, \zeta_p$ is called an *item path* from ξ to η if

(*i*) $\zeta_0 = \xi$ and $\zeta_p = \eta$,

(*ii*)   for each i with $1 \le i \le p$ there is some $\theta_i \in \mathcal{V}(\mathbb{P}(a_1 \ldots a_n))$ such that $\theta_i, \zeta_i \vdash_{CYK} \zeta_{i-1}$,

(*iii*)   for each i and j with $0 \le i < j \le p$ it holds that $\langle\zeta_i, \zeta_j\rangle \in \mathcal{V}(\mathbb{P}(a_1 \ldots a_n))$.   □

Lemma 14.23.

for every $\langle\xi{\leftarrow}\eta\rangle \in \mathcal{V}(\mathbb{P}(a_1 \ldots a_n))$ there is an item path from ξ to η.

Proof: direct from the above discussion.   □

The reason for retrieving an item path is that, in the sequel, we will need to cut an item $\langle\xi{\leftarrow}\eta\rangle$ of rank k into pieces of rank $< k$. To that end, we need one more auxiliary concept. A *critical step* on an item path is located such that both remaining parts, above and below the critical step, are of lower rank.

Definition 14.24. (*critical step on an item path*)

Let $\langle\xi{\leftarrow}\eta\rangle \in \mathcal{V}(\mathbb{P}(a_1 \ldots a_n))$ and $rank(\langle\xi{\leftarrow}\eta\rangle) = k > 0$. Furthermore, let $\xi = \zeta_0, \ldots, \zeta_p = \eta$ be an item path from ξ to η. An item $\langle\zeta_{i-1}, \zeta_i\rangle$ is called a *critical step of* $\zeta_0, \ldots, \zeta_p$ if

(*i*) $rank(\langle\xi{\leftarrow}\zeta_{i-1}\rangle) \le k - 1$,

(*ii*) $rank(\langle\zeta_i, \eta\rangle) \le k - 1$,   □

Lemma 14.25.

For every $\langle\xi{\leftarrow}\eta\rangle \in \mathcal{V}(\mathbb{P}(a_1 \ldots a_n))$ there is a critical step on every item path from ξ to η.

Proof: trivial   □

Having introduced all the necessary technical machinery, we can now prove the loop invariants.

Lemma 14.26.

Algorithm 14.17 satisfies the following statements for any k

$(\mathbf{I})_k:$ if $\xi \in \mathcal{V}(\mathbb{P}(a_1 \ldots a_n))$ and $rank(\xi) \le k$
then $proposed(\xi)$ after k steps;

$(\mathbf{II})_k:$ if $\langle\xi{\leftarrow}\eta\rangle \in \mathcal{V}(\mathbb{P}(a_1 \ldots a_n))$ and $rank(\langle\xi{\leftarrow}\eta\rangle) \le k$
then $proposed(\langle\xi{\leftarrow}\eta\rangle)$ after k steps.

These are reformulations of the loop invariants (14.5) and (14.6); an index k has been added for easy reference.

Proof. The correctness of $(\mathbf{I})_0$, $(\mathbf{II})_0$, and $(\mathbf{I})_1$ are trivial. We will complete the proof by showing that the implication

$$(\mathbf{II})_{k-1} \wedge (\mathbf{I})_k \implies (\mathbf{II})_k \wedge (\mathbf{I})_{k+1} \tag{14.7}$$

holds for any $k \geq 1$. So we assume $(\mathbf{II})_{k-1}$ and $(\mathbf{I})_k$.

$(\mathbf{II})_k$:

> Let $\langle \xi \leftarrow \eta \rangle \in \mathcal{V}(\mathbb{P}(a_1 \ldots a_n))$ and $rank(\langle \xi \leftarrow \eta \rangle) = k \geq 1$. We will show that $\langle \xi \leftarrow \eta \rangle$ must have been proposed after step k.
> Let $\langle \phi \leftarrow \psi \rangle$ be a critical step on an item path from ξ to η.
> Then there is some $\psi' \in \mathcal{V}(\mathbb{P}(a_1 \ldots a_n))$ such that $\psi', \psi \vdash_{CYK} \phi$ (cf. Definition 14.22.(ii)).
> Furthermore, $rank(\langle \xi \leftarrow \phi \rangle) \leq k - 1$, $rank(\langle \psi \leftarrow \eta \rangle) \leq k - 1$ (cf. Lemma 14.25), and, obviously, $rank(\psi') = rank(\langle \phi \leftarrow \psi \rangle) \leq k$. See Figure 14.11.

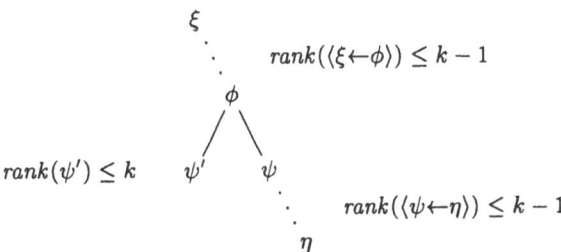

Fig. 14.11. A sketch of the proof of $(\mathbf{II})_k$

Consequently, we find:

after step $k-1$:	$proposed(\langle \xi \leftarrow \phi \rangle)$	(from $(\mathbf{II})_{k-1}$),
	$proposed(\langle \psi \leftarrow \eta \rangle)$	(from $(\mathbf{II})_{k-1}$);
after step $k.1$:	$recognized(\psi')$	(from $(\mathbf{I})_k$);
in step $k.2$:	$\psi' \vdash_R \langle \phi \leftarrow \psi \rangle$;	
in step $k.3$:	$\langle \xi \leftarrow \phi \rangle, \langle \phi \leftarrow \psi \rangle \vdash_R \langle \xi \leftarrow \psi \rangle$;	
in step $k.4$:	$\langle \xi \leftarrow \psi \rangle, \langle \psi \leftarrow \eta \rangle \vdash_R \langle \xi \leftarrow \eta \rangle$;	

> where $\vdash_R$ indicates deduction by Rytter's algorithm.

$(\mathbf{I})_{k+1}$:

> Let $\xi \in \mathcal{V}(\mathbb{P}(a_1 \ldots a_n))$ and $rank(\xi) = k + 1 \leq 2$. We will show that ξ must have been recognized after step $k + 1$. By Lemma 14.20 there is some $\theta \in \mathcal{V}(\mathbb{P}(a_1 \ldots a_n))$ critical to ξ, and there are η, ζ with rank $\leq k$ such that $\eta, \zeta \vdash_{CYK} \theta$ (cf. Definition 14.19).
> It must hold that $\langle \xi \leftarrow \theta \rangle \in \mathcal{V}(\mathbb{P}(a_1 \ldots a_n))$. Note, furthermore, that $rank(\langle \xi \leftarrow \theta \rangle) \leq k$.

We distinguish two cases: $\xi \neq \theta$ and $\xi = \theta$. First, we assume $\xi \neq \theta$.

Let $\langle\phi\!\leftarrow\!\psi\rangle$ be a critical step on an item path from ξ to θ, similar to the above case. The situation is depicted in Figure 14.12.

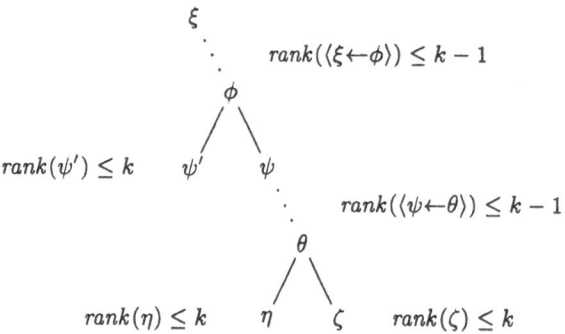

Fig. 14.12. A sketch of the proof of $(\mathbf{I})_{k+1}$

Consequently, we find:

after step $k-1$:	$proposed(\langle\xi\!\leftarrow\!\phi\rangle)$	(from $(\mathbf{II})_{k-1}$),
	$proposed(\langle\psi\!\leftarrow\!\theta\rangle)$	(from $(\mathbf{II})_{k-1}$);
after step $k.1$:	$recognized(\eta)$	(from $(\mathbf{I})_k$),
	$recognized(\zeta)$	(from $(\mathbf{I})_k$),
	$recognized(\psi')$	(from $(\mathbf{I})_k$);
in step $k.2$:	$\psi' \vdash_R \langle\phi\!\leftarrow\!\psi\rangle,$	
	$\eta \vdash_R \langle\theta\!\leftarrow\!\zeta\rangle;$	
in step $k.3$:	$\langle\xi\!\leftarrow\!\phi\rangle, \langle\phi\!\leftarrow\!\psi\rangle \vdash_R \langle\xi\!\leftarrow\!\psi\rangle,$	
	$\langle\psi\!\leftarrow\!\theta\rangle, \langle\theta\!\leftarrow\!\zeta\rangle \vdash_R \langle\psi\!\leftarrow\!\zeta\rangle;$	
in step $k.4$:	$\langle\xi\!\leftarrow\!\psi\rangle, \langle\psi\!\leftarrow\!\zeta\rangle \vdash_R \langle\xi\!\leftarrow\!\zeta\rangle;$	
in step $(k+1).1$:	$\langle\xi\!\leftarrow\!\zeta\rangle, \zeta \vdash_R \xi.$	

Otherwise, if $\xi = \theta$, it is clear that $\eta, \zeta \vdash_R \theta$ will be applied in step $(k+1).1$.

Thus we have finished the proof of implication (14.7).   □

Theorem 14.27. (*correctness Rytter's algorithm*)
Algorithm 14.17 is correct.

Proof. Soundness is straightforward from the definition of the algorithm; completeness has been proven in Lemma 14.26.   □

14.7 A parsing network for Rytter's algorithm

A parsing network for Rytter's algorithm can be obtained by applying the network construction of Definition 14.13 to a parsing system according to Schema 14.15. A more subtle approach is possible, however, if we realize that it is only items of the form $[X, i, j]$ that we are interested in. The items with a gap $[A, h, k; X, i, j]$ have only been introduced as auxiliary constructs, so as to allow recognition in logarithmic time. If we restrict the notion of *parsability* to items without a gap, we can extend the recognition algorithm to a parsing algorithm somewhat more easily.

As a direct consequence of the definition of parsability (cf. Definition 14.11), we find that an item $[X, i, j]$ is parsable, that is, $[X, i, j] \in \mathcal{W}(\mathbb{P}(a_1 \ldots a_n))$, if and only if

(*i*) $[X, i, j] \in \mathcal{V}(\mathbb{P}(a_1 \ldots a_n))$,
(*ii*) $[S, 0, n; X, i, j] \in \mathcal{V}(\mathbb{P}(a_1 \ldots a_n))$.

The loop invariant (14.6) guarantees that every valid item $[S, 0, n; X, i, j]$ will have been proposed by the recognition algorithm. So the only thing we have to do for every recognized item is to check for an appropriate proposed item with a gap.

Algorithm 14.28. (*logarithmic-time parser for binary branching grammars*)
The recognition algorithm 14.17 is extended to a parsing algorithm by adding a procedure *parse* that needs to be called only once, after the **repeat** loop has finished. We add a boolean predicate *parse* for every $\xi \in \mathcal{I}^{(1)}$. This will be set to *true* if $\xi \in \mathcal{W}(\mathbb{P}(a_1 \ldots a_n))$.

```
procedure parse
begin
        for all ξ ∈ I⁽¹⁾ do parsed(ξ) := false od;
        if recognized([S, 0, n])
        then  parsed([S, 0, n]) := true;
                for all [X, i, j] ∈ I⁽¹⁾
                do    if proposed([S, 0, n; X, i, j])
                      and recognized([X, i, j])
                      then parsed([X, i, j]) := true fi
                od
        fi
    end;                                                    □
```

A parsing network for Rytter's algorithm is defined as follows.

Definition 14.29. (*a parsing network for Rytter's algorithm*)
Let $\mathbb{P} = \langle \mathcal{I}, H, D \rangle$ by a Rytter parsing system as in Schema 14.15, $\mathbb{P}_\ell$ the system restricted to some maximum sentence length ℓ. A recognizing network for $\mathbb{P}_\ell$ is a boolean circuit that has the following nodes

(a)	an OR-node $((accept))$,	
(b)	an AND-node $\ll accept, i \gg$	for $0 \leq i \leq \ell$,
(c)	an OR-node $((\xi))$	for each $\xi \in \mathcal{I}_\ell^{(1)} \cup \mathcal{H}_\ell$,
(d)	a parse node $\ll \mathcal{P}\xi \gg$	for each $\xi \in \mathcal{I}_\ell^{(1)}$,
(e)	an auxiliary node $((\mathcal{Q}\xi))$	for each $\xi \in \mathcal{I}_\ell^{(1)}$,
(f)	an OR-node $(((\xi \leftarrow \eta)))$	for each $\langle \xi \leftarrow \eta \rangle \in \mathcal{I}_\ell^{(2)}$;
(g)	an AND-node $\ll \langle \xi \leftarrow \eta \rangle, \eta \gg$	for each $\langle \xi \leftarrow \eta \rangle \in \mathcal{I}_\ell^{(2)}$;
(h)	an AND-node $\ll \langle \xi \leftarrow \eta \rangle, \langle \eta \leftarrow \zeta \rangle \gg$	for each $\langle \xi \leftarrow \eta \rangle, \langle \eta \leftarrow \zeta \rangle \in \mathcal{I}_\ell^{(2)}$;

and the following connections:

(i)	$((\eta)) \longrightarrow (((\xi \leftarrow \zeta)))$	for $\eta, \zeta \vdash_{CYK} \xi$
		(or $\zeta, \eta \vdash_{CYK} \xi$),
(ii)	$(((\xi \leftarrow \eta))) \longrightarrow \ll \langle \xi \leftarrow \eta \rangle, \eta \gg$	for each $\langle \xi \leftarrow \eta \rangle \in \mathcal{I}_\ell^{(2)}$,
(iii)	$((\eta)) \longrightarrow \ll \langle \xi \leftarrow \eta \rangle, \eta \gg$	for each $\langle \xi \leftarrow \eta \rangle \in \mathcal{I}_\ell^{(2)}$,
(iv)	$\ll \langle \xi \leftarrow \eta \rangle, \eta \gg \longrightarrow ((\xi))$	for each $\langle \xi \leftarrow \eta \rangle \in \mathcal{I}_\ell^{(2)}$,
(v)	$(((\xi \leftarrow \eta))) \longrightarrow \ll \langle \xi \leftarrow \eta \rangle, \langle \eta \leftarrow \zeta \rangle \gg$	for each $\langle \xi \leftarrow \eta \rangle, \langle \eta \leftarrow \zeta \rangle \in \mathcal{I}_\ell^{(2)}$,
(vi)	$(((\eta \leftarrow \zeta))) \longrightarrow \ll \langle \xi \leftarrow \eta \rangle, \langle \eta \leftarrow \zeta \rangle \gg$	for each $\langle \xi \leftarrow \eta \rangle, \langle \eta \leftarrow \zeta \rangle \in \mathcal{I}_\ell^{(2)}$,
(vii)	$\ll \langle \xi \leftarrow \eta \rangle, \langle \eta \leftarrow \zeta \rangle \gg \longrightarrow (((\xi \leftarrow \zeta)))$	for each $\langle \xi \leftarrow \eta \rangle, \langle \eta \leftarrow \zeta \rangle \in \mathcal{I}_\ell^{(2)}$,
$(viii)$	$(([\$, i, i+1])) \longrightarrow \ll accept, i \gg$	for $2 \leq i \leq \ell$,
(ix)	$(([S, 0, i])) \longrightarrow \ll accept, i \gg$	for $2 \leq i \leq \ell$,
(x)	$\ll accept, i \gg \longrightarrow ((accept))$	for $2 \leq i \leq \ell$,
(xi)	$(([S, 0, k; X, i, j])) \longrightarrow ((\mathcal{Q}[X, i, j]))$	for $[S, 0, k; X, i, j] \in \mathcal{I}_\ell^{(2)}$,
(xii)	$((\mathcal{Q}\xi)) \longrightarrow \ll \mathcal{P}\xi \gg$	for each $\xi \in \mathcal{I}_\ell^{(1)} \cup \mathcal{H}_\ell$:
$(xiii)$	$((\xi)) \longrightarrow \ll \mathcal{P}\xi \gg$	for each $\xi \in \mathcal{I}_\ell^{(1)} \cup \mathcal{H}_\ell$. □

The condition $\zeta, \eta \vdash_{CYK} \xi$ in (i) is redundant, because antecedents of deduction steps are not ordered. Note, furthermore, that (i) denotes *unary* deduction steps, hence there is no need for an intermediate AND-node. As a consequence, a *propose* needs only one clock tick, while all *recognize* and *combine* need two clock ticks each.

Theorem 14.30. (*boolean circuit implementation of Rytter's algorithm*)
Let $\mathbb{P}_\ell$ be an uninstantiated Rytter system according to Schema 14.15 for some grammar $G \in \mathcal{BB}$. Let a boolean circuit for some maximum string length ℓ be given by Definition 14.29. Then the following statements hold:

- $((accept))$ will be activated if and only if $a_1 \ldots a_n \in L(G)$,
- $((\xi))$ will be activated if and only if $\xi \in \mathcal{V}(\mathbb{P}(a_1 \ldots a_n))$,
- $(((\xi \leftarrow \eta)))$ will be activated if and only if $\langle \xi \leftarrow \eta \rangle \in \mathcal{V}(\mathbb{P}(a_1 \ldots a_n))$,

- $\ll\mathcal{P}\xi\gg$ will be activated if and only if $\xi \in \mathcal{W}(\mathbb{P}(a_1\ldots a_n))$,
- The network is in a stable state after $7\lceil^2\log n\rceil + 3$ clock ticks.
- The network has $O(|V|^3\ell^6)$ nodes and edges, with $|V| = |N\cup\varSigma|$ the number of different grammar symbols.

Proof: straightforward from Theorem 14.27 and Definition 14.29.   □

The network that has been defined above contains a lot of nodes and edges that are not useful. Just like in the CYK case, useless parts can be removed by *meta-parsing*, where the network is started with all hypotheses in $\mathcal{H}_\ell$ validated. If $\ll\mathcal{P}\xi\gg$ remains inactive, then $(\!(\xi)\!)$, $(\!(\mathcal{Q}\xi)\!)$, and $\ll\mathcal{P}\xi\gg$ can be deleted. Furthermore, if $(\!(\!(\langle\xi\!\leftarrow\!\eta\rangle)\!)\!)$ remains inactive, then this can be deleted from the network as well. The AND-nodes that implement deduction steps can be trimmed accordingly. Note that we have defined parsability only for items ξ, not for items $\langle\xi\!\leftarrow\!\eta\rangle$. Hence if, say, ξ is valid but *not* parsable, a valid item $\langle\xi\!\leftarrow\!\eta\rangle$ may remain while ξ is being discarded. If we run the meta-parsing algorithm a second time on the already optimized network, some more items $\langle\xi\!\leftarrow\!\eta\rangle$ and corresponding AND-nodes and edges can be deleted. Two iterations of the meta-parsing algorithm suffice, a third iteration will not filter out any other nodes.

The same result is obtained if the first iteration of meta-parsing only considers items of the form ξ and the second iteration only considers items of the form $\langle\xi\!\leftarrow\!\eta\rangle$.

As in Section 14.4 we can employ a weaker meta-parsing algorithm if we would be interested to collect all valid items for (possibly incorrect) sentences. In that case, a single iteration of the meta-parsing algorithm suffices, in which invalidity, rather than unparsability is used as the criterion to discard nodes.

14.8 Conditional parsing systems

A Rytter system for a binary branching grammar has been obtained from a CYK system for binary branching grammars by adding conditional items and changing the deduction steps. This approach can be generalized to other parsing systems as well. In this way we can obtain logarithmic-time parallel parsing algorithms and boolean circuit implementations for arbitrary context-free grammars.

We will define conditional parsing systems for arbitrary parsing systems. For the sake of simplicity, we will first do this for binary branching parsing systems, where every deduction step has exactly two antecedents. Afterwards we generalize this to deduction steps with any number of antecedents. The generalization is not difficult, but involves some more details that distract from the simplicity of the basic idea.

Definition 14.31. (*potential ancestor*)
Let $\mathbb{P} = \langle \mathcal{I}, \mathcal{H}, D \rangle$ be a parsing system, $\xi \in \mathcal{I}$. The *potential ancestors* of ξ are inductively defined by

(*i*) if $\eta_1, \ldots, \eta_k \vdash \xi \in D$ then, for $1 \leq i \leq k$, η_i is a potential ancestor of ξ.
(*ii*) if ζ is a potential ancestor of ξ and $\eta_1, \ldots, \eta_k \vdash \zeta \in D$ then, for $1 \leq i \leq k$, η_i is a potential ancestor of ξ. □

Definition 14.32. (*conditional binary branching parsing system*)
Let $\mathbb{P} = \langle \mathcal{I}, \mathcal{H}, D \rangle$ be an (uninstantiated) binary branching parsing system, (cf. Definition 14.3).
A *conditional binary branching parsing system* $\mathbb{C} = \langle \mathcal{I} \cup \mathcal{J}, \mathcal{H}, \mathcal{D} \rangle$ is defined by

$$\mathcal{J} \quad = \quad \{ \langle \xi \leftarrow \eta \rangle \mid \xi, \eta \in \mathcal{I} \wedge \eta \text{ is a potential ancestor of } \xi \};$$

$$\mathcal{D}^{(1)} \quad = \quad \{ \zeta \vdash \langle \xi \leftarrow \eta \rangle \mid \eta, \zeta \vdash \xi \in D \},$$

$$\mathcal{D}^{(2)} \quad = \quad \{ \eta, \langle \xi \leftarrow \eta \rangle \vdash \xi \},$$

$$\mathcal{D}^{(3)} \quad = \quad \{ \langle \xi \leftarrow \eta \rangle, \langle \eta \leftarrow \zeta \rangle \vdash \langle \xi \leftarrow \zeta \rangle \}.$$

$$\mathcal{D} \quad = \quad \mathcal{D}^{(1)} \cup \mathcal{D}^{(2)} \cup \mathcal{D}^{(3)} \qquad \qquad \square$$

The reader may verify that if $\mathbb{P}$ is a CYK system for a grammar $G \in \mathcal{BB}$, (cf. Example 14.4), then $\mathbb{C}$ is a Rytter system as defined by Schema 14.15.

Next, we will consider the case that deduction steps have *at most* two antecedents. We may also have unary deduction steps of the form $\eta \vdash \xi$ or even 0-ary deduction steps $\vdash \xi$. For unary deduction steps, we can distinguish between *initial* deduction steps, where the antecedent is a hypothesis, and *non-initial* deduction steps where the antecedent is not a hypothesis. The former type is hardly relevant, because these are only used in the first step for further initialization. The non-initial unary deduction steps need some special treatment if we are to retain the recursive doubling technique that changes linear-time parallel algorithms into logarithmic-time parallel algorithms. The general idea is quite simple: if $\eta, \zeta \vdash \xi$ and $\xi \vdash^* \theta$, then we add a deduction step $\eta, \zeta \vdash \theta$. This technique has been applied by Graham, Harrison, and Ruzzo, for example, to obtain a more efficient Earley parser (cf. Example 6.18). Note that $\xi \vdash^* \theta$ does not necessarily imply that only unary deduction steps are applied. A deduction sequence $\xi \vdash \ldots \vdash \theta$ could include deduction steps of any arity.

Definition 14.33. (*binary closure of deduction steps*)
Let $\mathbb{P} = \langle \mathcal{I}, \mathcal{H}, D \rangle$ be a parsing system, where no deduction steps in D have more than 2 antecedents. The *binary closure* $\overline{D}$ of D is defined by

$$\overline{D}^{(0)} = \{ \vdash \theta \mid \vdash \xi \wedge \xi \vdash_D^* \theta \},$$

$$\overline{D}^{(1)} = \{ \eta \vdash \theta \mid \eta \in \mathcal{H} \wedge \eta \vdash_D^* \theta \},$$

$$\overline{D}^{(2)} = \{ \eta, \zeta \vdash \theta \mid \eta, \zeta \vdash_D \xi \wedge \xi \vdash_D^* \theta \},$$

$$\overline{D} = \overline{D}^{(0)} \cup \overline{D}^{(1)} \cup \overline{D}^{(2)}.$$

Where $\vdash_D$ and $\vdash_D^*$ denote (transitive closure of) deduction steps in D.
Note that all 0-ary and unary deduction steps in the binary closure are initial.
$\square$

Definition 14.34. (*conditional parsing system*)
Let $\mathbb{P} = \langle \mathcal{I}, \mathcal{H}, D \rangle$ be an (uninstantiated) parsing system, such that no deduction step in D has more than 2 antecedents.
A *conditional parsing system* $\mathbb{C} = \langle \mathcal{I} \cup \mathcal{J}, \mathcal{H}, \mathcal{D} \rangle$ is defined by

$$\mathcal{J} = \{ \langle \xi \leftarrow \eta \rangle \mid \xi, \eta \in \mathcal{I} \wedge \eta \text{ is a potential ancestor of } \xi \};$$

$$\mathcal{D}^{Init} = \overline{D}^{(0)} \cup \overline{D}^{(1)},$$

$$\mathcal{D}^{(1)} = \{ \zeta \vdash \langle \xi \leftarrow \eta \rangle \mid \eta, \zeta \vdash \xi \in \overline{D} \},$$

$$\mathcal{D}^{(2)} = \{ \eta, \langle \xi \leftarrow \eta \rangle \vdash \xi \},$$

$$\mathcal{D}^{(3)} = \{ \langle \xi \leftarrow \eta \rangle, \langle \eta \leftarrow \zeta \rangle \vdash \langle \xi \leftarrow \zeta \rangle \},$$

$$\mathcal{D} = \mathcal{D}^{Init} \cup \mathcal{D}^{(1)} \cup \mathcal{D}^{(2)} \cup \mathcal{D}^{(3)}. \qquad \square$$

Example 14.35.
The algorithm of Chiang and Fu, laid down in the parsing schema **ChF** is a further small optimization of the GHR algorithm without top-down filtering. Like the Earley-algorithm, items $[A \rightarrow \alpha \bullet \beta, i, j]$ are recognized if $\alpha \Rightarrow^* a_{i+1} \ldots a_j$. By making use of binary closure techniques, it is guaranteed that all items with position markers i, j can be computed simultaneously in one step, when all items of the form $[A \rightarrow \alpha \bullet \beta, i, k]$ and $[A \rightarrow \alpha \bullet \beta, k, j]$ with $i < k < j$ are known. See Example 6.20 on page 115 for the details. Let $\mathbb{P}_{ChF}$ be a parsing system for any context-free grammar $G \in \mathcal{CFG}$. A conditional system $\mathbb{C}_{ChF}$, according to definition 14.34, can be implemented in a boolean circuit in logarithmic time, similar to the Rytter case. A detailed treatment is given in [Sikkel, 1990]. $\square$

Another example of a logarithmic-time algorithm for arbitrary context-free grammars is the "fast" version of the algorithm of de Vreught and Honig [1990, 1991] (cf. Chapter 6).

We have not yet covered parsing systems with ternary and higher order deduction steps. For a deduction step

$$\eta_1, \ldots, \eta_k \vdash \xi$$

we can define conditional items

$$\langle \xi \leftarrow \eta_1, \ldots, \eta_j \rangle \quad \text{for } 1 < j < k$$

and deduction steps

$$\langle \xi \leftarrow \eta_1 \ldots, \eta_j \rangle, \eta_j \vdash \langle \xi \leftarrow \eta_1 \ldots, \eta_{j-1} \rangle.$$

These are of little practical use. If a deduction system has deduction steps with 3 or more antecedents, it is more usual to apply a *step refinement* (cf. Chapter 5), to reduce these to binary deduction steps. In Example 5.20 we have defined the *generalized* CYK algorithm for arbitrary context-free grammars. Because of the arbitrary number of antecedents (corresponding to the length of the right-hand side of a production), the complexity of a GCYK parser can be arbitrarily large as well. The canonical way to tackle this is to refine GCYK into a bottom-up Earley parser, that scans right-hand sides of productions one at the time. The dotted productions $A \rightarrow \alpha \bullet \beta$ that are used in Earley items constitute a *bilinear cover* of the grammar; cf. Leermakers [1989].

In some cases we have added antecedents to deduction steps to apply *dynamic filtering*; some antecedents are not used in the construction of the consequent, but encode conditions on the environment for applying deduction steps. Examples are the parsing schemata 6.12 and 6.13 for de Vreught and Honig's algorithm and the context-free head-corner schema 11.10. In all of these cases only two antecedents are used for "constructing" the consequent, hence the recursive doubling technique can be used with proper adaptation. Further details are beyond the scope of this chapter.

14.9 Related approaches

A logarithmic-time algorithm that is almost identical to Rytter's algorithm has in fact been published earlier by Brent and Goldschlager [1984].

Our version of Rytter's algorithm is slightly different from the original [Rytter, 1985], [Gibbons and Rytter, 1988]. The advantage of our presentation is twofold. On the one hand we have obtained an easy loop-invariant, that simplifies the presentation as well as the correctness proof. On the other hand, a boolean circuit implementation in $O(\log n)$ time with $O(n^6)$ processing units can be obtained. While $O(n^6)$ processing units is the minimum that is known for logarithmic-time parsing algorithms on a WRAM, it is not self-evident that the same complexity bounds apply to a boolean circuit implementation.[6]

A logarithmic-time algorithm for arbitrary context-free grammars has been defined by De Vreught and Honig [1990, 1991]. This is a conditional variant of their algorithm that has been discussed extensively in Chapter 6. A conditional variant of the algorithm of Chiang and Fu [1984] is worked out in detail in [Sikkel, 1990].

Boolean circuits can be seen as a specific kind of *neural networks*. A neural network consists of a large number of simple processing units, that compute the output as a function of the input. Neurons can be "on" and "off", as our nodes, but the function that is used to compute the state of a neuron is different. Typically, a sigmoid function over the weighted sum of the inputs determines the *probability* of activating a neuron.

The main difference, however, between our connectionist implementations by means of boolean circuits and mainstream neural networks research is that of *local* vs. *distributed* representation. Characteristic for neural networks is the holistic representation of information. Concepts are represented by *activation patterns*, rather than individual neurons [Rumelhart and McClelland, 1986], [McClelland and Rumelhart, 1986]. A typical application of neural networks is pattern recognition. When some input is offered to a network, it will stabilize in the state that represents the best fitting pattern from a set of patterns that the network has learned to recognize.

In our approach, concepts are mapped to nodes: if an item is valid or parsable, one specific node will be activated to indicate this fact. This localist approach is also used in other parsing networks that are called "connectionist" or "neural". Our linear-time parsing network is (a small improvement of) Fanty's network [1985, 1986]; a generalization to Earley's algorithm is given by Nijholt [1990]. Selman and Hirst [1987] describe a Boltzmann machine parser; Howells [1988] gives a relaxation algorithm that uses decay over time; Nakagawa and Mori [1988] present a parallel left-corner parser incorporated in a learning network. A neural network with distributed representation is used by Drossaers [1992] for recognition of regular languages.

The inherent parallelism in connectionist networks offers possibilities to integrate syntactic processing with semantic processing and disambiguation. This has been studied, among others, by Waltz and Pollack [1988], Cottrell and Small [1984] and Cottrell [1989].

---

[6] There is a general method to convert algorithms on parallel random access machines to boolean circuits, due to Stockmeyer and Viskhin [1984], but that would yield an implementation with $O(n^{13})$ units in this specific case.

14.10 Conclusion

Parsing schemata can be encoded straightforwardly into boolean circuits in such a way that valid items are represented by activated nodes. In this chapter we have added the notion *parsability*, that applies to those items that are not only valid but also have been effective in recognizing the sentence. The set of activated parse nodes in a boolean circuit gives an encoding of the shared parse forest of a sentence.

These techniques are straightforward adaptations of a network design originally described by Fanty [1985]. We have shown that this can also be applied to logarithmic-time algorithms. Along the way, we have simplified both the presentation and the correctness proof of Rytter's algorithm.

In 14.8 we have shown that Rytter's algorithm can be seen as a specific instance of a more general notion of conditional parsing systems that can be applied to other parsing schemata, so as to obtain logarithmic-time networks that parse arbitrary context-free grammars.

The results for logarithmic-time boolean circuits have theoretical, rather than practical value, because the number of processing units that is required is unrealistically high. But it is an indication that boolean circuits provide a useful abstract machine model for parallel parsing algorithms. This observation is not unimportant, because any (uninstantiated) parsing system can be trivially implemented as a boolean circuit.

15. Conclusions

Some of the material that has been presented is new, some other material has been included so as to make the book coherent and self-contained. Our specific research contributions are summarized in Section 15.2. But first we make some general remarks in 15.1, drawing together the results from the different topics that were discussed. Some ideas for future research are presented in 15.3.

15.1 Some general remarks

Many different parsing algorithms can be found in the computer science and computational linguistics literature. Algorithms differ a lot with respect to languages in which they are expressed, data structures used, degree of formality, class of grammars that can be handled, etc. Things get more complicated – and more varied – when we consider parallel, rather than sequential algorithms.

A useful, if not necessary, starting point for comparing the relative merits of different parsing algorithms is a description of those algorithms in a common formalism. In this book we propose *parsing schemata* as a framework for description and comparison of parsing algorithms. We have given numerous examples of parsing algorithms, both sequential and parallel, that can be described relatively straightforwardly within the parsing schemata framework. Moreover, we have also given some examples of *cross-fertilization* where properties of different algorithms can be mixed, once the correspondence in underlying structure has been uncovered.

A second advantage of the use of parsing schemata is that it allows us to divide the parsing problem into two smaller, less complicated problems. Parsing schemata constitute a well-defined level of abstraction between grammars and algorithms. An implicit specification of the correct syntactic analyses of a sentence is given by the grammar; a parsing algorithm gives and explicit recipe for computing these. Parsing schemata define the steps that have to be taken, but without specifying data structures, control structures and communication structures. Efficient parsers may involve a lot of such details. By using a parsing schema as a high-level specification one can separate the issues that relate to syntactic analysis from the issues that relate to the structure of efficient programs.

The absence of algorithmic detail is both an asset and a liability. There is a gain in conceptual clarity. The essential properties of an algorithm are captured more easily, simply because a lot of detail is absent. The other side of the coin, however, is that is it not a priori clear whether a schema can be implemented efficiently. We have used parsing schemata most successfully for the description, reconstruction, optimization and cross-fertilization of *existing* algorithms, that were known to be efficient. The parsing schemata framework offers only limited insights into the efficiency of possible implementations.

We have worked out a single concept, on a theoretical level in Part II and in a series of applications in Part III. It is this combination that, in our view, constitutes the main value of this book.

Theory makes abstractions, and application requires detail. At some places, most prominently in Chapter 4, we have noted that these two interests can be at odds with each other. If our only concern had been to come up with an elegant framework of how parsing works *in theory*, we could interpret an item set as quotient over a congruence relation on a set of trees, and not worry about the practical details. If, on the other hand, our only purpose had been to provide a practical notation for conceptually clear descriptions of parsing algorithms, the underlying mathematics could simply be deleted. But without such a theoretical understanding, it could have been just a coincidence that sensible parsing schemata can be drawn up for all the algorithms that we have studied. Armed with a theoretical foundation, we can claim that the framework applies to constructive parsing in general.

The theoretical foundation and practical applications reinforce each other, so that the value of the parsing schemata framework is more than the sum of both parts.

15.2 Research contributions of this book

A formalization of the notion of parsing schemata has been given in Chapters 3 and 4. Various kinds of relations between parsing schemata were defined in Chapters 5 and 6. Refinement and generalization, in Chapter 5, are used to obtain qualitative improvements in schemata. By making smaller steps and producing more intermediate results, the complexity of some schemata can be reduced and/or the applicable class of grammars enlarged. Filtering, as discussed in Chapter 6, is used for quantitative improvements: irrelevant parts of a deduction system can be discarded. A hierarchy of filters could be expressed concisely and elegantly at the abstract level of parsing schemata. As an extensive example, we have presented various variants of Earley's algorithm, de Vreught and Honig's algorithm and the (generalized) LC algorithm within a single taxonomy.

In Chapter 8 we have extended parsing schemata to unification grammars by adding feature structures to a context-free backbone. As a result, we have obtained a formalism in which feature percolation in parsing algorithms for unification grammars can be defined explicitly in a simple way.

The most interesting conclusion from Chapter 9 is that – even though context-free syntax is generally considered unimporant for unification grammars – context-free parsing techniques have a role to play in the construction of efficient unification grammar parsers. The efficiency of a parser can be enhanced by extracting a context-free backbone from a unification grammar that includes more than just a *category* feature.

The major contribution of Chapters 10 and 11 is the specification, correctness proof and complexity analysis of predictive Head-Corner parsing schemata. It was proven that despite the increase in administrative burden, the worst-case complexity of Head-Corner parsers is not worse than the complexity of conventional Earley parsers (provided that proper data structures are used).

The Head-Corner parser for unification grammars that was presented here does not provide the last and ultimate truth about Head-Corner parsing of natural languages. Interesting work in this area is going on elsewhere. Our prime objective here was to show that parsing schemata are an effective tool to get a formal grip on highly complicated algorithms.

In Chapter 12 we presented Tomita's Generalized LR parser, with the purpose of showing that the notion of a parsing schema can also be applied to parsers with an algorithmic structure that is rather different from the various types of chart parsers discussed so far. Having clarified the close relation between the algorithms of Earley and Tomita, we could cross-fertilize the bottom-up parallelization of Earley with the graph-structured stack of Tomita. The resulting parallel bottom-up Tomita parser, that was presented in Chapter 13, is a successful example of combining properties of different algorithms with related underlying parsing schemata.

In Chapter 14 we have shown that boolean circuits provide a suitable abstract machine model for (massively) parallel implementations of parsing schemata. As an exemplary non-trivial case, Rytter's logarithmic-time parsing algorithm has been treated in detail.

15.3 Ideas for future research

The central notion of parsing schemata has been discussed in sufficient detail, but there are always some side issue that raise further questions. Some of these could become topics of substantial further research.

- Efficient parsing of unification grammars is an issue that attracts a lot of attention. Unification is an expensive operation, that accounts for most of the total processing time of a unification grammar parser. Hence any increase in the efficiency of unification speeds up the parser with almost the same factor. Much effort has been spent on speeding up unification, and reasonably efficient unification algorithms are available now.

  Another way to increase the efficiency of unification grammar parsing is to limit the number of unifications that have to be carried out. To this end, one can apply the filtering techniques known from context-free parsing.

  There are indications that considerable savings can be obtained by extending the context-free backbone of a unification grammar with some key features. The optimal boundary between *phrasal* and *functional* constraints, as these are called by Maxwell and Kaplan [1993], is a subject that merits a more structured investigation.

- Head-Corner parsing has been described on a rather theoretic level. In the area of Natural Language Processing Head-Corner parsers have been successfully employed (see, e.g. [van Noord, 1996]). More is to be said about under which conditions and for which reasons Head-Corner parsers perform well in practical applications.

- This study did not shed much light on the feasibility of parallel parsing. The results of the PBT study in Chapter 13 are somewhat inconclusive, The simulation experiment was moderately encouraging, but indeed only a simulation. Real parallel parser implementations (e.g. [Thompson, 1994]) report moderate, but not really convincing successes.

  The question whether parallel parsing is practically feasible, therefore, is still open for debate.

- Boolean circuits have been introduced as an abstract parallel machine model, rather than a serious proposal for parallel implementation. Chapter 14 presents ideas and examples, rather than a systematic investigation. On a theoretic level, the boolean circuit model could serve as a basis for a more thorough treatment of the complexity of parsing schemata.

Bibliography

AHO, A.V., HOPCROFT, J.E. and ULLMAN, J.D. (1974): *The Design and Analysis of Computer Algorithms*, Addison-Wesley, Reading, Mass.

AHO, A.V., SETHI, R. and ULLMAN, J.D. (1986): *Compilers: Principles, Techniques and Tools*. Addison-Wesley, Reading, Mass.

AHO, A.V. and ULLMAN, J.D. (1972): *The Theory of Parsing, Translation and Compiling Vol. I: Parsing*. Prentice-Hall, Englewood Cliffs, N.J.

AHO, A.V.. and ULLMAN, J.D. (1977): *Principles of Compiler Design*. Addison-Wesley, Reading, Mass.

AÏT-KACI, H. (1984): A Lattice Theoretic Approach to Computation Based on a Calculus of Partially Ordered Type Structures. Ph.D. Thesis, University of Pennsylvania, Philadelphia.

AÏT-KACI, H. (1986): An Algebraic Semantics Approach to the Effective Resolution of Type Equations. *Theoretical Computer Science* **45**, pp. 293–351.

OP DEN AKKER, R. (1988): *Parsing Attribute Grammars*. Ph.D. Thesis, Department of Computer Science, University of Twente, Enschede, the Netherlands.

OP DEN AKKER, R., TER DOEST, H., MOLL, M. and NIJHOLT, A. (1995): Parsing in Dialogue Systems Using Typed Feature Structures. *4th International Workshop on Parsing Technologies*, Prague, Czech Republic, pp. 10–11.

OP DEN AKKER, R., MELICHAR, B. and TARHIO, J. (1990): The Hierarchy of LR-Attributed Grammars. *International Conference on Attribute Grammars and their Applications*, Paris. Lecture Notes on Computer Science 416, Springer-Verlag, Berlin.

ALBLAS, H., OP DEN AKKER, R., OUDE LUTTIGHUIS, P. and SIKKEL, K. (1994): A bibliography on Parallel Parsing. *ACM SIGPLAN Notices* **29**, No. 1, pp. 54–65.

APPELT, D.E. (1987): Bidirectional Grammars and the Design of Natural Language Generation Systems. *3rd Workshop on Theoretical Issues in Natural Language Processing*, New Mexico State University, pp. 206–212.

BAXTER, L. (1973): An Efficient Unification Algorithm. Technical Report CS-73-23, University of Waterloo, Ontario, Canada.

BERRY, G. and BOUDOL, G. (1990): The Chemical Abstract Machine. *17th ACM Symposium on Principles of Programming Languages*, San Francisco, pp. 81–94.

BHARATI, A., CHAITANYA, V. and SANGAL, R. (1995): *Natural Language Processing: A Paninian Perspective*. Prentice-Hall of India, New Delhi, India.

BILLOT, S. and LANG, B. (1989): The Structure of Shared Forests in Ambiguous Parsing. *27th Annual Meeting of the Association for Computational Linguistics, (ACL'89)* Vancouver, pp. 143–151.

BLOOMFIELD, L. (1927): On Recent Work in General Linguistics. *Modern Philology* **25**, pp. 211–230.

BLOOMFIELD, L. (1933): *Language*. Holt, Rinehart and Winston, New York.

BOUMA, G. (1991): Prediction in Chart Parsing Algorithms for Categorial Unification Grammar. *5th European Chapter of the Association of Computational Linguistics*, (*EACL'91*), Berlin, pp. 179–184.

BOUMA, G., and VAN NOORD, G. (1993): Head-driven Parsing for Lexicalist Grammars: Experimental Results. *6th Meeting of the European Chapter of the Association of Computational Linguistics* (*EACL'93*), Utrecht, pp. 71–80.

BRENT, R.P. and GOLDSCHLAGER, L.M. (1984): A Parallel Algorithm for Context-Free Parsing. *Australian Computer Science Communications* **6** (7), pp. 7.1 –7.10.

BOYER, R.S. and MOORE, J.S. (1972): The Sharing of Structure in Theorem-Proving Programs. *Machine Intelligence* **7**, pp. 101–116.

CARPENTER, B. (1992): *The Logic of Typed Feature Structures.* Cambridge Tracts in Theoretical Computer Science 32, Cambridge University Press, Cambridge, UK.

CARTER, D. (1990): Efficient Disjunctive Unification for Bottom-Up Parsing. *International Conference on Computational Linguistics* (*COLING'90*), Helsinki, Vol. 3, pp. 70–75.

DE CHAMPEAUX, D. (1986): About the Paterson-Wegman Linear Unification Algorithm. *Journal of Computer and System Science* **32**, pp. 79–90.

CHANDY, K.M. and MISRA, J. (1988): *Parallel Program Design: A Foundation.* Addison Wesley, Reading, Mass.

CHIANG, Y.T. and FU, K.S. (1984): Parallel Parsing Algorithms and VLSI implementations for Syntactic Pattern Recognition. *IEEE Transactions on Pattern Analysis and Machine Intelligence*, **PAMI-6** (1984) pp. 302–314.

CHOMSKY, N. (1957): *Syntactic Structures.* Mouton & Co., The Hague, the Netherlands.

CHOMSKY, N. (1965): *Aspects of Theory of Syntax.* MIT Press, Cambridge, Mass.

CHOMSKY, N. (1981): *Lectures on Government and Binding.* Foris Publications, Dordrecht, the Netherlands.

CHOMSKY, N. (1992): A minimalist program for linguistic theory. MIT Occasional Papers in Linguistics, MIT, Cambridge, Mass.

CLOCKSIN, W.F. and MELLISH, C.S. (1981): *Programming in Prolog.* Springer-Verlag, New York. 4th edition 1994.

COHEN, J. (1990): Constraint Logic Programming Languages. *Communications of the ACM* **33** (7), pp. 52–68.

CORBIN and BIDOIT, M. (1983): A Rehabilitation of Robinson's Unification Algorithm. *Information Processing* **83**, pp. 73–79.

COTTRELL, G.W. (1989): *A connectionist approach to word sense disambiguation.* Morgan Kaufmann Publishers, Los Altos, Ca.

COTTRELL, G.W. and SMALL, S.L. (1984): Viewing Parsing as Word Sense Discrimination: A Connectionist Approach. In: B.G. Bara and G. Guida (Eds.), *Computational Models of Natural Language Processing*, Elsevier Science Publishers, pp. 91–119.

DEMERS, A.J. (1977): Generalized Left Corner Parsing. *4th ACM Symposium on Principles of Programming Languages*, pp. 170–182.

DEREMER, F.L. (1969): Practical Translators for LR(k) Languages. Ph.D. Thesis, MIT, Cambridge, Mass.

DEREMER, F.L. (1971): Simple LR(k) grammars. *Communications of the ACM* **14**, pp. 94–102.

DÖRRE, J. and EISELE, A. (1990): Feature Logic with Disjunctive Unification. *International Conference on Computational Linguistics* (*COLING'90*), Helsinki, Vol. 2, pp. 100–105.

DROSSAERS, M.F.J. (1992): Hopfield Models as Nondeterministic Finite-State Machines. *14th International Conference on Computational Linguistics (COLING'92)*, Nantes, France, pp. 113–119.

DOWNEY, P.J. , SETHI, R. and TARJAN, R.E. (1980): Variations on the Common Subexpression Problem. *Journal of the ACM* **27**, pp. 758–771.

EARLEY, J. (1968): An Efficient Context-Free Parsing Algorithm. Ph.D. Thesis, Carnegie-Mellon University, Pittsburgh, Pa.

EARLEY, J. (1970): An Efficient Context-Free Parsing Algorithm. *Communications of the ACM* **13**, pp. 94–102.

EISELE, A. and DÖRRE, J. (1988): Unification of Disjunctive Feature Descriptions. *26th Annual Meeting of the Association of Computational Linguistics (ACL'88)*, Buffalo, N.Y., pp. 286–294.

EMELE, M.C. (1991): Unification with Lazy Non-Redundant Copying. *29th Annual Meeting of the Association of Computational Linguistics (ACL'91)*, Berkeley, Ca., pp. 323–330.

EMELE, M.C. and ZAJAC, R. (1990): Typed Unification Grammars. *13th International Conference on Computational Linguistics (COLING'90)* Vol. 3, Helsinki, Finland, pp. 182–198.

FANTY, M.A. (1985): Learning in Structured Connectionist Networks. Report TR 252, Computer Science Department, University of Rochester, Rochester, NY.

FANTY, M.A. (1986): Context-free Parsing in Connectionist Networks. In: J.S. Denker (Ed.), *Neural Networks for Computing*, Snowbird, Utah, AIP conference proceedings 151, American Institute of Physis, pp. 140–145.

FISCHER, C.N. (1975): Parsing Context-free Languages in Parallel Environments. Report 75-237, Department of Computer Science, Cornell University, Ithaca, N.Y.

GALIL, Z. and ITALIANO, G.F. (1991): Data Structure and Algorithms for Disjoint Set Union Problems. *ACM Computing Surveys* **23**, pp. 319–344.

GALLIER, J.H. (1986): *Logic for Computer Science, foundations of Automatic Theorem Proving*. Harper & Row, New York.

GAZDAR, G., KLEIN, E., PULLUM, G.K. and SAG, I.A. (1985): *Generalized Phrase Structure Grammar*. Harvard University Press, Cambridge, Mass.

GERDEMANN, D.D. (1989): Using Restriction to Optimize Unification. *1st International Workshop on Parsing Technologies (IWPT'89)*, Pittsburgh, Pa., 8–17.

GERDEMANN, D.D. (1991): Parsing and Generation of Unification Grammars. Ph.D. Thesis, Report CS-91-06, Beckman Institute for Advanced Science and Technology, University of Illinois at Urbana-Champaign.

GIBBONS, A. and RYTTER, W. (1988): *Efficient Parallel Algorithms*. Cambridge University Press, Cambridge, UK.

GINSBURG, S. AND RICE, H. (1962): Two families of languages related to ALGOL. *Journal of the ACM* **9**, pp. 350–371.

GODDEN, K. (1990): Lazy Unification. *28th Annual Meeting of the Association for Computational Linguistics (ACL'90)*, Pittsburgh, Pa., pp. 180–187.

GRÄTZER, G. (1979): *Universal Algebra*, 2nd Edition. Springer-Verlag, New York.

GRAHAM, S.L., HARRISON, M.A. and RUZZO, W.L. (1980): An Improved Context-Free Recognizer. *ACM Transactions on Programming Languages and Systems* **2**, pp. 415–462.

GROSZ, B.J., SPARCK JONES, K. and WEBBER, B.L. (EDS.) (1982): *Readings in Natural Language Processing*, Morgan Kaufmann, Los Altos, Ca.

GRUNE, D. and JACOBS, C.J.H. (1990): *Parsing Techniques: A Practical Guide*. Ellis Horwood, New York.

HAAS, A. (1989): A Parsing Algorithm for Unification Grammar. *Computational Linguistics* **15**, pp. 219–232.

HAHN, U. and ADRIAENS, G. (EDS.) (1994): *Parallel Natural Language Processing*. Ablex Publishing Corporation, Norwood, NJ.

HARKEMA, H. and TOMITA, M. (1991): A Parsing Algorithm for Non-Deterministic Context-Sensitive Languages. In: Heemels, R., Nijholt, A., and Sikkel, K. (Eds.), Tomita's algorithm – Extensions and Applications, *1st Twente Workshop on Language Technology*, University of Twente, Enschede, the Netherlands, pp. 21–31.

HARRISON, M.A. (1978): *Introduction to Formal Language Theory*. Addison-Wesley, Reading, Mass.

HARRISON, S.P. and ELLISON, T.M. (1992): Restriction and Termination in Parsing with Feature-Theoretic Grammars. *Computational Linguistics* **18**, pp. 519–530.

HEEMELS, R., NIJHOLT, A., and SIKKEL, K. (EDS.) (1991): Tomita's algorithm – Extensions and Applications. Proceedings *1st Twente Workshop on Language Technology*, University of Twente, Enschede, the Netherlands.

HEGNER, S.J. (1991): Horn Extended Feature Structures: Fast Unification with Negation and Limited Disjunction. *5th European Chapter of the Association for Computational Linguistics (EACL'91)*, Berlin, pp. 33–38.

HOWELLS, T. (1988): VITAL: a Connectionist Parser. *10th Conference of the Cognitive Science Society*, pp. 18–25.

HUET, G. (1976): Résolution d'equations dans les langages d'ordre $1, 2, \ldots, \omega$: Thèse de Doctorat d'Etat. Université de Paris VII.

VON HUMBOLDT, W. (1836): *Über die Verschiedenheit des menschlichen Sprachbaues*. In: *Über die Kawisprache auf der Insel Java*, 1. Teil, Abhandlungen der Akademie der Wissenschaften zu Berlin.

HUYBREGTS, M.A.C. (1984): The Weak Inadequacy of context-free Phrase Structure Grammars. In: de Haan, G., Trommelen, M., and Zonneveld, W. (Eds.), *Van Periferie naar Kern*, Foris Publications, Dordrecht, the Netherlands.

JAFFAR, J. and LASSEZ, J.-L. (1987): Constraint Logic Programming. *11th ACM Symposium on Principles of Programming Languages*, München, pp. 500–506.

JANSSEN, W., POEL, M., SIKKEL, K., and ZWIERS, J. (1991): The Primordial Soup Algorithm – A Systematic Approach to the Specification and Design of Parallel Parsers. In: J. van Leeuwen (Ed.), *Computing Science in the Netherlands, (CSN'91)*, Stichting Informatica Onderzoek in Nederland, pp. 298–314.

JANSSEN, W., POEL, M., SIKKEL, K. and ZWIERS, J. (1992): The Primordial Soup Algorithm. *14th International Conference on Computational Linguistics (COLING'92)*, Nantes, France, pp. 373–379.

JOHNSON, M. (1989): The Computational Complexity of Tomita's Algorithm. *International Workshop on Parsing Technologies (IWPT'89)*, Carnegie Mellon University, Pittsburgh, Pa., pp. 203–208.

JOHNSON, M. (1991): Features and Formulae. *Computational Linguistics* **17**, pp. 131–151.

JOHNSON, S.C. (1975): Yet Another Compiler-Compiler. Computer Science Technical Report 32, Bell Laboratories, Murray Hill, NJ.

JONES, M.D. and MADSEN, M. (1980): Attribute-influenced LR parsing. In: M.D. Jones (Ed.), *Aarhus Workshop on Semantics-Directed Compiler Generation*, Springer-Verlag, Berlin, pp. 393–407.

JOSHI, A.K., LEVY, L.S. and TAKAHASHI, M. (1975): Tree Adjunct Grammars. *Journal of Computer and System Sciences* **10**, pp. 136–163.

JOSHI, A., VIJAY-SHANKER, K. and WEIR, D. (1991): The Convergence of Mildly Context-Sensitive Grammar Formalisms. In: P. Sells et al. (Eds.), *Foundational Issues in Natural Language Processing*, MIT Press, Cambridge, Mass., pp. 31–81.

KAPLAN, R.M. and BRESNAN, J. (1982): Lexical-Functional Grammar: a formal system for grammatical representation. In: J. Bresnan (Ed.), *The Mental Representation of Grammatical Relations*, MIT Press, Cambridge, Mass., pp. 173–281.

KARTTUNEN, L. and KAY, M. (1985): Structure Sharing with Binary Trees. *23rd Annual Meeting of the Association for Computational Linguistics (ACL'85)*, Chicago, pp. 133–136A.

KARTTUNEN, L. (1986): D-PATR: A Development Environment for Unification-Based Grammars. Technical Report CSLI-86-61, Center for the Study of Language and Information, Stanford University, Stanford, Ca.

KASAMI, T. (1965): An Efficient Recognition and Syntax Analysis Algorithm for Context-Free Languages. Scientific Report AFCRL-65-758, Air Force Cambridge Research Laboratory, Bedford, Mass.

KASPER, R.T. (1987a): Feature Structures: A Logical Theory with Applications to Language Analysis. Ph.D. Thesis, University of Michigan.

KASPER, R.T. (1987b): A Unification Method for Disjunctive Feature Descriptions. *25th Annual Meeting of the Association of Computational Linguistics (ACL'87)*, Stanford, Ca., pp. 235–242.

KASPER, R.T. and ROUNDS, W.C. (1986): A Logical Semantics for Feature Structures. *24th Annual Meeting of the Association of Computational Linguistics (ACL'86)*, New York, pp. 257–266.

KAY, M. (1979): Functional Unification Grammar. *5th Annual Meeting of the Berkeley Linguistics Society*, Berkeley, Ca.

KAY, M. (1980): Algorithm Schemata and Data Structures in Syntactic Processing. Report CSL-80-12, Xerox PARC, Palo Alto, Ca. (reprinted in: [Grosz et al., 1982]):

KAY, M. (1985): Parsing in Functional Unification Grammar. In: D.R. Dowty, L. Karttunen, and A. Zwicky (Eds.), *Natural Language Parsing*, Cambridge University Press, Cambridge, UK, pp. 251–278.

KAY, M. (1989): Head Driven Parsing. *1st International Workshop on Parsing Technologies (IWPT'89)*, Pittsburgh, Pa., pp. 52–62.

KEMPEN, G. and VOSSE, T. (1990): Incremental Syntactic Tree Formation in Human Sentence Processing: an Interactive Architecture based on Activation Decay and Simulated Annealing. *Connection Science* 1, pp. 273–290.

KILBURY, J. (1984): Chart parsing and the Earley algorithm. In: U. Klenk (Ed.), *Kontextfreie Syntaxen und verwandte Systeme*, Linguistische Arbeiten 155, Max Niemeyer Verlag, Tübingen, Germany, pp. 76–89.

KIPPS, J.R. (1989): Analysis of Tomita's Algorithm for General Context-Free Parsing. *International Workshop on Parsing Technologies (IWPT'89)*, Carnegie Mellon University, Pittsburgh, Pa., pp. 182–192.

KLINT, P. and VISSER, E. (1994): Using Filters for the Disambiguation of Context-free Grammars. Proc. ASMICS Workshop on Parsing Theory, Milan, October 1994, Report 126-94, Dept. of Computer Science, University of Milan, Italy.

KNIGHT, K. (1989): Unification: A Multidisciplinary Survey. *Computing Surveys* 21, pp. 93–124.

KNUTH, D.E. (1965): On the Translation of Languages from Left to Right. *Information and Control* 8, pp. 607–639.

KNUTH, D.E. (1968): Semantics of Context-Free Languages. *Mathematical Systems Theory* 2, pp. 127–145.

KNUTH, D.E. (1971): Semantics of Context-Free Languages, Correction. *Mathematical Systems Theory* 5, pp. 95–96.

KOGURE, K. (1990): Strategic Lazy Incremental Copy Graph Unification. *International Conference on Computational Linguistics (COLING'90)*, Helsinki, Vol. 2, pp. 223–228.

KOSARAJU, S.R. (1969): Computations on Iterative Automata. Ph.D. Thesis, University of Pennsylvania, Philadelphia, Pa.

KOSARAJU, S.R. (1975): Speed of Recognition of Context-Free Languages by Array Automata. *SIAM Journal on Computing* **4**, pp. 331–340.

KOSTER, C.H.A. (1971): Affix Grammars. In: J.E.L. Peck (Ed.), *Algol 68 Implementation*, North-Holland Publishing Company, Amsterdam.

KOSTER, C.H.A. (1991a): Affix Grammars for Programming Languages. In: H. Alblas, B. Melichar (Eds.), *Attributed Grammars, Applications and Systems*, Lecture Notes in Computer Science 545, Springer-Verlag, Berlin, pp. 358–373.

KOSTER, C.H.A. (1991b): Affix Grammars for Natural Languages. In: H. Alblas, B. Melichar (Eds.), *Attributed Grammars, Applications and Systems*, Lecture Notes in Computer Science 545, Springer-Verlag, Berlin, pp. 469–484.

KUHN, T. (1970): *The Structure of Scientific Revolutions*. University of Chicago Press, Chicago.

LALONDE, W.R., LEE, E.S. and HORNING, J.J. (1972): An LALR(k) parser generator. *IFIP Congress '71*, pp. 153–157.

LANG, B. (1974): Deterministic Techniques for Efficient Non-Deterministic Parsers. *2nd Colloquium on Automata, Languages and Programming*, Lecture Notes in Computer Science 14, Springer-Verlag, Berlin, pp. 255–269.

LANG, B. (1989): A Uniform Formal Framework for Parsing. *International Workshop on Parsing Technologies (IWPT'89)*, Pittsburgh, Pa., pp. 28–42.

LANKHORST, M.M. (1991): PBT: A Parallel Bottom-up Variant of Tomita's Parsing Algorithm. M.Sc. Thesis, Department of Computer Science, University of Twente, Enschede, the Netherlands.

LANKHORST, M.M. and SIKKEL, K. (1991): PBT: A Parallel Bottom-up Tomita Parser. Memoranda Informatica 91-69, Department of Computer Science, University of Twente, Enschede, the Netherlands.

LEERMAKERS, R. (1989): How to Cover a Grammar. *27th Annual Meeting of the Association for Computational Linguistics (ACL'89)*, Vancouver, pp. 135–142.

LEERMAKERS, R. (1991): Non-deterministic Recursive Ascent Parsing. *5th Meeting of the European Chapter of the Association for Computational Linguistics (EACL'91)*, Berlin, pp. 87–91.

LEERMAKERS, R. (1993): *The Functional Treatment of Parsing*, Kluwer Academic Publishers, Dordrecht, the Netherlands.

LEISS, H. (1990): On Kilbury's modification of Earley's algorithm. *ACM Transactions on Programming Languages and Systems* **12**, 610–640.

MANASTER-RAMER, A. (1987): Dutch as a Formal Language. *Linguistics and Philosophy* **10**, pp. 221–246.

MARTELLI, A. and MONTANARI, U. (1977): Theorem Proving with Structure Sharing and Efficient Unification. *International Joint Conference on Artificial Intelligence (IJCAI'77)*, p. 543.

MARTELLI, A. and MONTANARI, U. (1982): An Efficient Unification Algorithm. *ACM Transactions on Programming Languages and Systems* **4**, pp. 258–282.

MATSUMOTO, Y. TANAKA, H., HIRAKAWA, H., MIYOSHI, H. and YASUKAWA, H. (1983): BUP: a bottom-up parser embedded in Prolog. *New Generation Computing* **1**, pp. 145–158.

MAXWELL III, J.T. and KAPLAN, R.M. (1989): An Overview of Disjunctive Constraint Satisfaction. *1st International Workshop on Parsing Technologies (IWPT'89)*, Pittsburgh, Pa., pp. 18–27.

MAXWELL III, J.T. and KAPLAN, R.M. (1993): The Interface between Phrasal and Functional Constraints. *Computational Linguistics* **19**, 571–590.

McCLELLAND, J.L. and RUMELHART, D.E. (1986): *Parallel Distributed Processing: Explorations in the Microstructure of Cognition. Vol. 2.* MIT Press, Cambridge, Mass.

MENDELSOHN, E. (1964): *Introduction to Mathematical Logic.* Van Nostrand, New York.

MINNEN, G., GERDEMANN, D., and GÖTZ, T. (1995): Off-line Optimization for Earley-Style HPSG Processing. *7th Meeting of the European Chapter of the Association of Computational Linguistics (EACL'95)*, Dublin, Ireland, pp. 173–179.

MONTAGUE, R. (1974): *Formal Philosophy: Selected Papers of Richard Montague.* R.H. Thomason (Ed.), Yale University Press.

MORAWIETZ, F. (1995): A Unification-based ID/LP Parsing Schema. *4th International Workshop on Parsing Technologies*, Prague, Czech Republic, 162–173.

NAGATA, M. (1992): An Empirical Study on Rule Granularity and Unification Interleaving Toward an Efficient Unification-Based Parsing System. *14th International Conference on Computational Linguistics (COLING'92)*, Nantes, France, pp. 177–183.

NAKAGAWA, H. and MORI, T. (1988): A Parser Based on Connectionist Model. *12th International Conference on Computational Linguistics (COLING'88)*, Budapest, pp. 454–458.

NAKANO, M. (1991): Constraint Projection: An Efficient Treatment of Disjunctive Feature Descriptions. *29th Annual Meeting of the Association of Computational Linguistics, (ACL'91)*, Berkeley, Ca., pp. 307–314.

NAKATA, I. and SASSA, M. (1986): L-attributed LL(1) grammars are LR(1)-attributed. *Information Processing Letters* **23**, pp. 325–328.

NAKAZAWA, T. (1991): An Extended LR Parsing Algorithm for Grammars Using Feature-Based Syntactic Categories. *5th European Chapter of the Association for Computational Linguistics (EACL'91)*, Berlin, pp. 69–74.

NAUR, P. (ED.) (1960): Report on the algorithmic language ALGOL 60. *Communications of the ACM* **3**, pp. 299–314.

NEDERHOF, M.J. (1993): Generalized Left-Corner Parsing. *6th Meeting of the European Chapter of the Association of Computational Linguistics, (EACL'93)*, Utrecht, pp. 305–314.

NEDERHOF, M.J. (1994a): Linguistic Parsing and Program Transformations. Ph.D. Thesis, University of Nijmegen, the Netherlands.

NEDERHOF, M.J. (1994b): An Optimal Tabular Parsing Algorithm. *32nd Annual Meeting of the Association for Computational Linguistics (ACL'94)*, Las Cruces, New Mexico, pp. 117–124.

NEDERHOF, M.J. and SARBO, J.J. (1993): Increasing the Applicability of LR Parsing. *3rd International Workshop on Parsing Technologies (IWPT'93)*, Tilburg and Durbuy, Netherlands/Belgium, pp. 187–201.

NEDERHOF, M.J. and SATTA, G. (1994): An Extended Theory of Head-Driven Parsing. *32nd Meeting of the Association of Computational Linguistics (ACL '94)*, Las Cruces, New Mexico, pp. 210–217.

NELSON, G. and OPPEN, D.C. (1977): Fast Decision Algorithms Based on Congruence Closure. *18th Annual Symposium on the Foundations of Computer Science*, Providence, Rhode Island.

NELSON, G. and OPPEN, D.C. (1980): Fast Decision Procedures Based on Congruence Closure. *Journal of the ACM* **27**, pp. 356–364.

NIJHOLT, A. (1983): Deterministic Top-Down and Bottom-Up Parsing: Historical Notes and Bibliographies. Mathematical Centre, Amsterdam.

NIJHOLT, A. (1988): *Computers and Languages - Theory and Practice*. Studies in Computer Science and Artificial Intelligence 4, North-Holland Publishing Company, Amsterdam.

NIJHOLT, A. (1990): Meta-Parsing in Neural networks. In: R. Trappl (Ed.), *10th European Meeting on Cybernetics and System Research*, Vienna, pp. 969–976.

NIJHOLT, A. (1994): Parallel Approaches to Context-Free Language Parsing. In: U. Hahn and G. Adriaens (Eds.), *Parallel Natural Language Processing*, Ablex Publishing Corporation, Norwood, NJ, pp. 135–167.

VAN NOORD, G. (1991): Head Corner Parsing for Discontinuous Constituency. *29th Annual Meeting of the Association of Computational Linguistics (ACL'91)*, Berkeley, Ca., pp. 114–121.

VAN NOORD, G.J.M. (1993): Reversibility in Natural Language Processing. Ph.D. Thesis, University of Utrecht, the Netherlands.

VAN NOORD, G. (1994): Head Corner Parsing for TAG. *Computational Intelligence* 10, pp. 525–534.

VAN NOORD, G. (1996): An Efficient Implementation of the Head-corner Parser. NWO Priority Programme Language and Speech Technology, document 25. Available from the author at Alfa-Informatica, Faculty of Arts, University of Groningen, the Netherlands.

NOZOHOOR-FARSHI, R. (1989): Handling of Ill-designed Grammars in Tomita's Parsing Algorithm. *International Workshop on Parsing Technologies (IWPT '89)*, Carnegie Mellon University, Pittsburgh, Pa., pp. 182–192.

NUMAZAKI, H. and TANAKA, H. (1990): A New Parallel Algorithm for Generalized LR Parsing, *13th International Conference on Computational Linguistics (COLING'90)*, Helsinki, Vol. 2, pp. 304–310.

OUDE LUTTIGHUIS, P. (1991): Optimal Parallel Parsing of Almost All $LL(k)$ grammars. Memoranda Informatica 91-37, Department of Computer Science, University of Twente, Enschede, the Netherlands.

OUDE LUTTIGHUIS, P. and SIKKEL, K. (1992): Attribute Evaluation during Generalized Parsing. Memoranda Informatica 92-85, Computer Science Department, University of Twente, Enschede, the Netherlands.

OUDE LUTTIGHUIS, P. and SIKKEL, K. (1993): Generalized LR Parsing and - Attribute Evaluation. *3rd International Workshop on Parsing Technologies (IWPT'93)*, Tilburg and Durbuy, Netherlands/Belgium, pp. 219–233.

PATERSON, M.S. and WEGMAN, M.N. (1978): Linear Unification. *Journal of Computer and System Science* 16, pp. 158–167.

PEREIRA, F.C.N. (1985): A Structure-Sharing Representation for Unification-Based Grammar Formalisms. *23rd Annual Meeting of the Association of Computational Linguistics (ACL'85)*, Chicago, pp. 137–144.

PEREIRA, F.C.N. and WARREN, D.H.D. (1980): Definite Clause Grammars for Language Analysis - A Survey of the Formalism and a Comparison with Augmented transition Networks. *Artificial Intelligence* 13, pp. 231–278.

PEREIRA, F.C.N. and WARREN, D.H.D. (1983): Parsing as Deduction. *21st Annual Meeting of the Association of Computational Linguistics (ACL'83)*, Cambridge, Mass., pp. 137–144.

POHLMANN, W. (1983): LR parsing of affix grammars. *Acta Informatica* 20, pp. 283–300.

POLLARD, C. (1984): Generalized Phrase Structure Grammars, Head Grammars and Natural Languages. Ph.D. Thesis, Department of Linguistics, Stanford University.

POLLARD, C. and SAG, I.A. (1987): *An Information-Based Syntax and Semantics, Vol. 1: Fundamentals*. CSLI Lecture Notes 13, Center for the Study of Language and Information, Stanford University, Stanford, Ca.

POLLARD, C. and SAG, I.A. (1994):   *Head-Driven Phrase Structure Grammar*, University of Chicago Press, Chicago.

PRATT, V.R. (1975): LINGOL – A Progress Report. *4th International Joint Conference on Artificial Intelligence (IJCAI'75)*, pp. 422–428.

PROUDIAN, D. and POLLARD, C. (1985): Parsing head-driven phrase structure grammar. *23th Annual Meeting of the Association of Computational Linguistics (ACL'85)*, Chicago, pp. 167–171.

PULLUM, G.K. and GAZDAR, G. (1982): Natural Languages and Context-Free Languages. *Linguistics and Philosophy* 4, pp. 471–504.

REKERS, J. (1992): Parser Generation for Interactive Environments. Ph.D. Thesis, University of Amsterdam.

RESNIK, P. (1992): Left-Corner Parsing and Psychological Plausibility. *International Conference on Computational Linguistics (COLING'92)*, Nantes, France, pp. 191–197.

ROBINSON, J.A. (1965): A Machine-Oriented Logic Based on the Resolution Principle. *Journal of the ACM* 12, pp. 23–41.

ROSENKRANTZ, D.J. and LEWIS, P.M. (1970): Deterministic Left Corner Parsing. *11th Annual Symposium on Switching and Automata Theory*, pp. 139–152.

ROUNDS, W.C. and KASPER, R.T. (1986): A Complete Logical Calculus for Record Structures Representing Linguistic Information. *1st IEEE Symposium on Logic in Computer Science*, Boston, Mass., pp. 38–43.

RUMELHART, D.E. and MCCLELLAND, J.L. (1986): *Parallel Distributed Processing: Explorations in the Microstructure of Cognition. Vol. 1*. MIT Press, Cambridge, Mass.

RYTTER, W. (1985): On the recognition of context-free languages. *5th Symposium on Fundamentals of Computation Theory*, Lecture Notes in Computer Science 208, Springer-Verlag, Berlin, pp. 315–322.

SAGER, N. (1981): *Natural Language Information Processing*. Addison-Wesley, Reading, Mass.

SASSA, M., ISHIZUKA, H., and NAKATA, I. (1987): ECLR-attributed grammars: a practical class of LR-attributed grammars. *Information Processing Letters* 24, pp. 31–41.

SATTA, G. and STOCK, O. (1989): Head-Driven Bidirectional Parsing: A Tabular Method. *International Workshop on Parsing Technologies (IWPT'89)*, Pittsburgh, Pa., pp. 43–51.

SATTA, G. and STOCK, O. (1994): Bidirectional context-free grammar parsing for natural language processing. *Artificial Intelligence* 69, pp. 123–164.

SCHABES, Y. and JOSHI, A.K. (1991): Tree-Adjoining Grammars and Lexicalized Grammars. In: Nivat, M. (Ed.), *Definability and Recognizability of Sets of Trees*, Elsevier, Amsterdam.

SCHABES, Y. and WATERS, R.C. (1993): Lexicalized Context-Free Grammars. *21st Annual Meeting of the Association of Computational Linguistics (ACL'93)*, Columbus, Ohio, pp. 121–129.

SCHOORL, J.J. and BELDER, S. (1990): Computational Linguistics at Delft: A Status Report. Report WTM/TT 90-09, Applied Linguistics Unit, Delft University of Technology,

SELMAN, B. and HIRST, G. (1987): Parsing as an Energy Minimation Problem. In: *Genetic Algorithms and Simulated Annealing*, Research notes in AI, Morgan Kaufmann Publishers, Los Altos, Ca., pp. 141–154.

SHIEBER, S.M. (1985a): Using Restriction to Extend Parsing Algorithms for Complex Feature-Based Formalisms. *23rd Annual Meeting of the Association of Computational Linguistics, (ACL'85)*, Chicago, pp. 145–152.

SHIEBER, S.M. (1985b): Evidence against the Context-Freeness of Natural Language. *Linguistics and Philosophy* 8, pp. 333–343.

SHIEBER, S.M. (1986): *An Introduction to Unification-Based Approaches to Grammar*. CSLI Lecture Notes 4, Center for the Study of Language and Information, Stanford University, Stanford, Ca.

SHIEBER, S.M. (1988): A Uniform Architecture for Parsing and Generation. *International Conference on Computational Linguistics (COLING'88)*, Budapest, pp. 614–619.

SHIEBER, S.M. (1992): *Constraint-Based Grammar Formalisms: Parsing and Type Inference for Natural and Computer Languages*. The MIT Press, Cambridge, Mass.

SHIEBER, S.M., PEREIRA, F.C.N., VAN NOORD, G. and MOORE, R.C. (1990): Semantic-Head-Driven Generation. *Computational Linguistics* 16, pp. 30–42.

SIEKMANN, J.H. (1989): Unification Theory. *Journal of Symbolic Computation* 7, pp. 207–274.

SIKKEL, K. (1990): Connectionist Parsing of Context-Free Grammars. Memoranda Informatica 90-30, Department of Computer Science, University of Twente, Enschede, the Netherlands.

SIKKEL, K. (1991): Cross-Fertilization of Earley and Tomita. In: Wouden, T. van der and Sijtsma, W. (Eds.), *Computational Linguistics in The Netherlands, Papers of the first CLIN meeting, Utrecht, 1990*, OTS, University of Utrecht, pp. 133–148.

SIKKEL, K. (1993a): Parallel On-Line Parsing in Constant Time per Word. *Theoretical Computer Science* 120, pp. 303–310.

SIKKEL, K. (1993b) Parsing Schemata. Ph.D. Thesis, University of Twente, Enschede, the Netherlands.

SIKKEL, K. (1995): Parsing Schemata and Correctness of Parsing Algorithms. In: Nijholt, A., Scollo, G. and Steetskamp, R. (Eds.), *AMAST Workshop on Algebraic Methods in Language Processing (AMiLP '95)*, Enschede, the Netherlands, pp. 83–97.

SIKKEL, K. (forthcoming): Parsing Schemata and Correctness of Parsing Algorithms. *Theoretical Computer Science* (Accepted for publication).

SIKKEL, K. and OP DEN AKKER, R. (1992): Left-Corner and Head-Corner Chart Parsing. Memoranda Informatica 92-55, Department of Computer Science, University of Twente, Enschede, the Netherlands.

SIKKEL, K. and OP DEN AKKER, R. (1993): Predictive Head-Corner Chart Parsing. *3rd International Workshop on Parsing Technologies (IWPT'93)*, Tilburg and Durbuy, Netherlands/Belgium, pp. 267–276.

SIKKEL, K, and OP DEN AKKER, R. (1996): Predictive Head-Corner Parsing. In H. Bunt, M. Tomita, (Eds.), *Recent Advances in Parsing Technology*, Kluwer, Boston, Mass., pp. 171–184.

SIKKEL, K. and LANKHORST, M. (1992): A Parallel Bottom-Up Tomita Parser. In: G. Görz (Ed.), *1. Konferenz Verarbeitung Natürlicher Sprache (KONVENS'92)*, Nürnberg, Germany, Informatik Aktuell, Springer-Verlag, Berlin, pp. 238–247.

SIKKEL, K. and NIJHOLT, A. (1991): An Efficient Connectionist Context-Free Parser. *2nd International Workshop on Parsing Technologies (IWPT'91)*, Cancun, Mexico, pp. 117–126.

SIPPU, S., and SOISALON-SOININEN, E. (1988): *Parsing Theory, Vol. I: Languages and Parsing*. EATCS Monographs on Theoretical Computer Science, Springer-Verlag, Berlin.

SIPPU, S. and SOISALON-SOININEN, E. (1990): *Parsing Theory, Vol. II: LR(k) and LL(k) Parsing*. EATCS Monographs on Theoretical Computer Science, Springer-Verlag, Berlin.

SMOLKA, G. (1989): Feature Constraint Logics for Unification Grammars. IWBS Report 93, Institut für Wissensbasierte Systeme, IBM Deutschland, Stuttgart, Germany.

SMOLKA, G. (1992): Feature Constraint Logics for Unification Grammars. *Journal of Logic Programming* 12, pp. 51–87.

STAAL, F. (1969): Sanskrit Philosophy of Language. *Current Trends in Linguistics* 5, pp. 499–531.

TER STAL W.G., (1996): Automated Interpretation of Nominal Compounds in a Technical Domain. Ph.D. Thesis, University of Twente, Enschede, The Netherlands.

VAN DER STEEN, G.J. (1987): A Program Generator for Recognition, Parsing and Transduction with Syntactic Patterns. Ph.D. Thesis, University of Utrecht. Also published as *CWI Tract* 55, Centre for Mathematics and Computer Science, Amsterdam (1988).

STOCKMEYER, L. and VISHKIN, U. (1984): Simulation of Parallel Random Access Machines by Circuits, *SIAM Journal of Computing* 13, pp. 409–422.

STRZALKOWSKI, T., (ED.) (1994): *Reversible Grammar in Natural Language Processing*. Kluwer Academic Publishers, Dordrecht, the Netherlands.

TANAKA, H. and NUMAZAKI, H. (1989): Parallel Generalized LR Parsing based on Logic Programming. *1st International Workshop on Parsing Technologies (IWPT'89)*, Pittsburgh, Pa., pp. 329–338.

TARHIO, J. (1988): Attributed grammars for one-pass compilation. Ph.D. Thesis, Report A-1988-11, Department of Computer Science, University of Helsinki, Finland.

THOMPSON, H.S. (1989): Chart Parsing for Loosely Coupled Parallel Systems. *1st International Workshop on Parsing Technologies, (IWPT'89)*, Pittsburgh, Pa., pp. 320–328.

THOMPSON, H.S. (1994): Parallel Parsers for Context-Free Grammars – Two Actual Implementations Compared. In: U. Hahn and G. Adriaens (Eds.), *Parallel Natural Language Processing*, Ablex Publishing Corporation, Norwood, NJ, pp. 168–187.

THOMPSON, H.S, DIXON, M. and LAMPING, J. (1991): Compose-Reduce Parsing. *29th Annual Meeting of the Association of Computational Linguistics, (ACL '91)*, Berkeley, Ca., pp. 87–97.

TOMABECHI, H. (1991): Quasi-Destructive Graph Unification. *29th Annual Meeting of the Association of Computational Linguistics, (ACL'91)*, Berkeley, Ca., pp. 315–322.

TOMITA, M. (1985): *Efficient Parsing for Natural Language*. Kluwer Academic Publishers, Boston, Mass.

TOMITA, M. (ED.) (1991): *Generalized LR Parsing*. Kluwer Academic Publishers, New York.

TROST, H. (ED.) (1993): *Feature Formalisms and Linguistic Ambiguity*. Ellis Horwood Ltd., Chichester, UK.

USZKOREIT, H. (1986): Categorial Unification Grammars. *International Conference on Computational Linguistics (COLING'90)*, pp. 187–194.

VALIANT, L.G. (1975): General Context-Free Recognition in Less than Cubic Time. *Journal of Computer and System Sciences* 10, pp. 308–315.

VEENSTRA, M. (1995): A Minimalist Head-Corner Parser. *33rd Meeting of the Association of Computational Linguistics (ACL'95)*, Cambridge, Mass., pp. 338–340.

VERLINDEN, M. (1993): Head-Corner Parsing of Unification Grammars: A Case Study. In: Sikkel, K., Nijholt, A. (Eds.), Parsing Natural Language, *6th Twente Workshop on Language Technology* (*TWLT6*), University of Twente, Enschede, the Netherlands, pp. 71–84.

VÉRONIS, J. (1992): Disjunctive Feature Structures as Hypergraphs. *International Conference on Computational Linguistics* (*COLING'92*), Nantes, France, pp. 498–504.

VIJAY-SHANKER, K. and JOSHI, A.K. (1991): Unification-Based Tree Adjoining Grammars. In Wedekind, J. (Ed.), *Unification-Based Grammars*, MIT Press, Cambridge, Mass.

VISSER, E. (1995): A Case Study in Optimizing Parsing Schemata by Disambiguation Filters. Report P9507, Dept. of Computer Science, University of Amsterdam, the Netherlands.

DE VREUGHT, J.P.M. and HONIG, H.J. (1989): A Tabular Bottom-Up recognizer, Report 89-78, Department of Applied Mathematics and Informatics, Delft University of Technology, Delft, the Netherlands.

DE VREUGHT, J.P.M. and HONIG, H.J. (1990): General Context-free Parsing. Report 90-31, Department of Applied Mathematics and Informatics, Delft University of Technology, Delft, the Netherlands.

DE VREUGHT, J.P.M. and HONIG, H.J. (1991): Slow and Fast Parallel Recognition. *2nd International Workshop on Parsing Technologies* (*IWPT'91*, Cancun, Mexico, pp. 127–135.

WALTZ, D.L. and POLLACK, J.B. (1988): Massively Parallel Parsing: A Strongly Interactive Model of Natural Language Interpretation. In: Waltz, D.L. and Feldman, J.A., *Connectionist Models and their Implications*, Readings from Cognitive Science, Ablex Publishing Corporation, Norwood, NJ, pp. 181–204.

WEDEKIND, J. (1988): Generation as Structure Driven Derivation *12th International Conference on Computational Linguistics* (*COLING'88*), Budapest, pp. 732–737.

WIJNGAARDEN, A. VAN (1965): Orthogonal Design and Description of a Formal Language. Report MR76, Mathematical Centre, Amsterdam.

WILLEMS, M. (1992): The Chemistry of Language – a graph-theoretical study of Linguistic Semantics. Ph.D. Thesis, Department of Applied Mathematics, University of Twente, Enschede, The Netherlands.

WINOGRAD, T. (1983): *Language as a Cognitive Process. Vol. I: Syntax*. Addison-Wesley, Reading, Mass.

WROBLEWSKI, D.A. (1987): Nondestructive graph unification. *6thAnnual Conference of the American Association of Artificial Intelligence* (*AAAI'87*), pp. 582–587.

YOUNGER, D.H. (1967): Recognition of context-free languages in time n^3, *Information and Control* **10**, pp. 189–208.

ZEEVAT, H., KLEIN, E. and CALDER, J. (1987): An Introduction to Unification Categorial Grammar. In: Haddock, N.J., Klein, E. and Morill, G. (Eds.), *Edinburgh Working Papers in Cognitive Science, Vol. 1: Categorial Grammar, Unification Grammar and Parsing*, Center for Cognitive Science, University of Edinburgh.

Index

Texts in Theoretical Computer Science – An EATCS Series

Monographs in Theoretical Computer Science – An EATCS Series

Former volumes appeared as
EATCS Monographs on Theoretical Computer Science